T0181808

Lecture Notes in Computer Science　　10917

Commenced Publication in 1973
Founding and Former Series Editors:
Gerhard Goos, Juris Hartmanis, and Jan van Leeuwen

More information about this series at http://www.springer.com/series/7409

Vincent G. Duffy (Ed.)

Digital Human Modeling

Applications in Health, Safety, Ergonomics, and Risk Management

9th International Conference, DHM 2018
Held as Part of HCI International 2018
Las Vegas, NV, USA, July 15–20, 2018
Proceedings

 Springer

Editor
Vincent G. Duffy
Purdue University
West Lafayette, IN
USA

ISSN 0302-9743   ISSN 1611-3349   (electronic)
Lecture Notes in Computer Science
ISBN 978-3-319-91396-4   ISBN 978-3-319-91397-1   (eBook)
https://doi.org/10.1007/978-3-319-91397-1

Library of Congress Control Number: 2018942339

LNCS Sublibrary: SL3 – Information Systems and Applications, incl. Internet/Web, and HCI

Printed on acid-free paper

This Springer imprint is published by the registered company Springer International Publishing AG part of Springer Nature
The registered company address is: Gewerbestrasse 11, 6330 Cham, Switzerland

Foreword

The 20th International Conference on Human-Computer Interaction, HCI International 2018, was held in Las Vegas, NV, USA, during July 15–20, 2018. The event incorporated the 14 conferences/thematic areas listed on the following page.

A total of 4,373 individuals from academia, research institutes, industry, and governmental agencies from 76 countries submitted contributions, and 1,170 papers and 195 posters have been included in the proceedings. These contributions address the latest research and development efforts and highlight the human aspects of design and use of computing systems. The contributions thoroughly cover the entire field of human-computer interaction, addressing major advances in knowledge and effective use of computers in a variety of application areas. The volumes constituting the full set of the conference proceedings are listed in the following pages.

I would like to thank the program board chairs and the members of the program boards of all thematic areas and affiliated conferences for their contribution to the highest scientific quality and the overall success of the HCI International 2018 conference.

This conference would not have been possible without the continuous and unwavering support and advice of the founder, Conference General Chair Emeritus and Conference Scientific Advisor Prof. Gavriel Salvendy. For his outstanding efforts, I would like to express my appreciation to the communications chair and editor of *HCI International News*, Dr. Abbas Moallem.

July 2018   Constantine Stephanidis

HCI International 2018 Thematic Areas
and Affiliated Conferences

Thematic areas:

- Human-Computer Interaction (HCI 2018)
- Human Interface and the Management of Information (HIMI 2018)

Affiliated conferences:

- 15th International Conference on Engineering Psychology and Cognitive Ergonomics (EPCE 2018)
- 12th International Conference on Universal Access in Human-Computer Interaction (UAHCI 2018)
- 10th International Conference on Virtual, Augmented, and Mixed Reality (VAMR 2018)
- 10th International Conference on Cross-Cultural Design (CCD 2018)
- 10th International Conference on Social Computing and Social Media (SCSM 2018)
- 12th International Conference on Augmented Cognition (AC 2018)
- 9th International Conference on Digital Human Modeling and Applications in Health, Safety, Ergonomics, and Risk Management (DHM 2018)
- 7th International Conference on Design, User Experience, and Usability (DUXU 2018)
- 6th International Conference on Distributed, Ambient, and Pervasive Interactions (DAPI 2018)
- 5th International Conference on HCI in Business, Government, and Organizations (HCIBGO)
- 5th International Conference on Learning and Collaboration Technologies (LCT 2018)
- 4th International Conference on Human Aspects of IT for the Aged Population (ITAP 2018)

Conference Proceedings Volumes Full List

1. LNCS 10901, Human-Computer Interaction: Theories, Methods, and Human Issues (Part I), edited by Masaaki Kurosu
2. LNCS 10902, Human-Computer Interaction: Interaction in Context (Part II), edited by Masaaki Kurosu
3. LNCS 10903, Human-Computer Interaction: Interaction Technologies (Part III), edited by Masaaki Kurosu
4. LNCS 10904, Human Interface and the Management of Information: Interaction, Visualization, and Analytics (Part I), edited by Sakae Yamamoto and Hirohiko Mori
5. LNCS 10905, Human Interface and the Management of Information: Information in Applications and Services (Part II), edited by Sakae Yamamoto and Hirohiko Mori
6. LNAI 10906, Engineering Psychology and Cognitive Ergonomics, edited by Don Harris
7. LNCS 10907, Universal Access in Human-Computer Interaction: Methods, Technologies, and Users (Part I), edited by Margherita Antona and Constantine Stephanidis
8. LNCS 10908, Universal Access in Human-Computer Interaction: Virtual, Augmented, and Intelligent Environments (Part II), edited by Margherita Antona and Constantine Stephanidis
9. LNCS 10909, Virtual, Augmented and Mixed Reality: Interaction, Navigation, Visualization, Embodiment, and Simulation (Part I), edited by Jessie Y. C. Chen and Gino Fragomeni
10. LNCS 10910, Virtual, Augmented and Mixed Reality: Applications in Health, Cultural Heritage, and Industry (Part II), edited by Jessie Y. C. Chen and Gino Fragomeni
11. LNCS 10911, Cross-Cultural Design: Methods, Tools, and Users (Part I), edited by Pei-Luen Patrick Rau
12. LNCS 10912, Cross-Cultural Design: Applications in Cultural Heritage, Creativity, and Social Development (Part II), edited by Pei-Luen Patrick Rau
13. LNCS 10913, Social Computing and Social Media: User Experience and Behavior (Part I), edited by Gabriele Meiselwitz
14. LNCS 10914, Social Computing and Social Media: Technologies and Analytics (Part II), edited by Gabriele Meiselwitz
15. LNAI 10915, Augmented Cognition: Intelligent Technologies (Part I), edited by Dylan D. Schmorrow and Cali M. Fidopiastis
16. LNAI 10916, Augmented Cognition: Users and Contexts (Part II), edited by Dylan D. Schmorrow and Cali M. Fidopiastis
17. LNCS 10917, Digital Human Modeling and Applications in Health, Safety, Ergonomics, and Risk Management, edited by Vincent G. Duffy
18. LNCS 10918, Design, User Experience, and Usability: Theory and Practice (Part I), edited by Aaron Marcus and Wentao Wang

http://2018.hci.international/proceedings

9th International Conference on Digital Human Modeling and Applications in Health, Safety, Ergonomics, and Risk Management

Program Board Chair(s): **Vincent G. Duffy,** *USA*

- André Calero Valdez, Germany
- Elsbeth De Korte, The Netherlands
- Maria De Marsico, Italy
- Onan Demirel, USA
- Afzal A. Godil, USA
- Ravindra Goonetilleke, Hong Kong, SAR China
- Akihiko Goto, Japan
- Hiroyuki Hamada, Japan
- Dan Högberg, Sweden
- Hui-min Hu, P.R. China
- Noriaki Kuwahara, Japan
- Lingxi Li, USA
- Claudio Loconsole, Italy
- Thaneswer Patel, India
- Daniele Regazzoni, Italy
- Caterina Rizzi, Italy
- Juan A. Sanchez-Margallo, Spain
- Leonor Teixeira, Portugal
- Renran Tian, USA
- Mani Venkatesh, Portugal
- Anita Woll, Norway
- Kuan Yew Wong, Malaysia
- Shuping Xiong, Korea
- James Yang, USA

The full list with the Program Board Chairs and the members of the Program Boards of all thematic areas and affiliated conferences is available online at:

http://www.hci.international/board-members-2018.php

HCI International 2019

The 21st International Conference on Human-Computer Interaction, HCI International 2019, will be held jointly with the affiliated conferences in Orlando, FL, USA, at Walt Disney World Swan and Dolphin Resort, July 26–31, 2019. It will cover a broad spectrum of themes related to Human-Computer Interaction, including theoretical issues, methods, tools, processes, and case studies in HCI design, as well as novel interaction techniques, interfaces, and applications. The proceedings will be published by Springer. More information will be available on the conference website: http://2019.hci.international/.

General Chair
Prof. Constantine Stephanidis
University of Crete and ICS-FORTH
Heraklion, Crete, Greece
E-mail: general_chair@hcii2019.org

http://2019.hci.international/

Contents

Motion Modelling and Rehabilitation

User Diversity and Well-being

Nursing and Medical Applications

Transportation Human Factors

Anthropometry, Ergonomics and Design

Assessment of Types of Prototyping in Human-Centered Product Design

Salman Ahmed[✉], Jianfu Zhang, and Onan Demirel

Oregon State University, Corvallis, OR, USA
ahmedsal@oregonstate.edu

Abstract. One of the challenges that human-centered product designers face while generating and validating a design concept is the dilemma of whether to build a full physical prototype, a full computational simulation or a combination of both. A full physical prototype can assist designers to evaluate the human-product interactions with high-fidelity, but it requires additional time and resources when compared to a computational prototype, which is a cheaper option but provides low-fidelity. Human-product interactions often require complex motions and postures, and the interaction can vary due to multiple reasons such as individual differences, routine and emergency procedures, environmental conditions etc. In this paper, reach postures of a pilot during a routine and an emergency procedure are evaluated through a full computational and a mixed prototype. It is found that pilot's reaching strategy, based on the joint angles, during the emergency procedure is different than that of the routine procedure for the same reaching posture. It is also found that the full computational prototype that utilizes the empirical whole-body posture prediction has limitations in reflecting the individual variations in reaching strategies during the emergency procedure. However, the mixed prototype can simulate the emergency procedure and can capture the difference of reaching posture that occurs during an emergency event.

Keywords: Human-centered product design · Prototyping · Emergency event

1 Introduction

In the fast-paced product development economies where the customer demands change rapidly and the market is globally competitive, new products need to be designed and manufactured in a short turnaround time with equal or improved quality. Products that do not meet customer demands rarely make it a market success. Thus, a successful product not only needs to be designed and manufactured in a quicker and cost-effective way, but must be easy and comfortable to use, create positive experiences, and hold minimum risk of injury. The product development strategy needs human-centered approach to incorporate human-factors engineering principles and guidelines. Traditionally, human-factors guidelines are usually applied in the later stage of preliminary design by employing physical prototypes because the detailed information regarding human product interactions are not readily available [1, 2]. Also, it is recommended to

© Springer International Publishing AG, part of Springer Nature 2018
V. G. Duffy (Ed.): DHM 2018, LNCS 10917, pp. 3–18, 2018.
https://doi.org/10.1007/978-3-319-91397-1_1

use prototyping early in the design stage to identify the human factors requirements [3]. However, the traditional reactive human factors approach which relies on physical prototypes or retrofitting and modifying ergonomically bad/poor products based on human factors guidelines and checklists have major shortcomings such as time-to-market and aggregated cost. Instead, a proactive approach which assesses the comfort and the risk of injury on computational models, as products are designed, has the potential to reduce time and cost associated with physical full-scale prototyping. One way of performing a proactive ergonomic analysis is by employing a full computational prototype or a mixture of computational or physical prototyping techniques during concept development stage. A full computational prototype may consist of a CAD (Computer Aided Design) model representing a product or a workspace and a DHM (Digital Human Modeling) software to evaluate ergonomics. In mixed prototyping, the product or the workspace can either be created using CAD and a human subject is immersed into the CAD environment using a VR (Virtual Reality) headset. Another alternative method is to superimpose CAD environment on a very rudimentary physical prototype using an Augmented Reality (AR).

Computational prototyping is less costly to build, more flexible, and less time consuming compared to full-scale physical prototyping [4, 5]. Though the computational prototyping with DHM is faster to build and is more flexible in comparison to full physical prototyping, it has limitations in modeling and simulating the complex interactions between the human and the product with high accuracy and precision [6]. Thus, one of the challenges that human-centered product designers face while generating and validating a design concept is the dilemma of whether to build a full-physical prototype, a full computational simulation or a combination of both.

This paper proposes a method to partially mitigate the dilemma of types of prototyping to be used in a human centered design approach via VR and a marker-less motion capture system. The study utilizes a Microsoft Kinect based motion capture system with a DHM software to predict the performance of a civilian airplane pilot during an emergency case. Specifically, the motion capture system is used with a VR headset to capture the variation in reaching strategies in an emergency situation. The different strategies of a reaching task adopted by human subject due to an emergency event or routine work can be identified using mixed prototyping where the subject uses a VR headset to interact with workspace and performs the emergency protocols. The comparison between full computational prototype and mixed prototype in the context of type of event, i.e. emergency or routine tasks, can help designers to choose what type of prototyping to be used early in design.

The organization of the paper is as follows: Sect. 2 gives a brief literature review of the types of prototypes available and the challenges that designers often confronts. Also, the research gap is discussed in this section. In Sect. 3, the design methodology and the case study are presented. Results are depicted in Sect. 4 and finally the insight and discussions are presented in Sect. 5.

2   Literature Review

Prototyping is referred as an essential part of the product development and manufacturing process required for assessing the form, fit and functionality of a design before a significant investment in tooling is made [7]. The purpose of prototyping should not be only limited to the evaluation of products but it should be also viewed as part of a design process [8]. Prototyping can help designers to reflect on the design ideas and to explore new ideas. However, one of the challenges human-centered product designers face while generating and validating a design concept is the dilemma of whether to build a full-scale physical prototype, a full computational simulation or a combination of both. Incorrect decisions taken regarding what type of prototyping to use could cause a company to waste time, money and even decrease the quality of the product. Other factors that also need to be considered before building a prototype is the level of complexity and the fidelity of the prototype to address human-product interactions. Also, the number of prototypes to be built and at what stage of the design process they should be built need careful considerations so that effective and efficient assessment of form, fit and functionality of the design can be executed.

The dilemma of using a full-scale physical prototyping, a full computational simulation or a mixed prototyping arises due to a number of reasons. Physical prototypes are often more accurate and effective for representing the shape, composition and functionality of the final product in comparison to virtual prototypes [9, 10]. However, virtual prototyping is less costly to build, more flexible, and less time consuming when compared to physical prototyping [4, 5]. Virtual prototypes used during the conceptual stage can help to reduce the use of physical prototyping, thus reducing time and money [11]. Though physical prototypes made by rapid prototyping are highly accurate, they sometime shrink or have rough surfaces which require further machining. Thus, they may be dimensionally inaccurate, whereas computational prototypes do not have this problem [12]. Also, physical prototypes are difficult or sometimes infeasible to modify or to add further modifications once they are constructed. This inflexibility also poses further problems when new design ideas need to be prototyped after receiving initial design revisions and feedbacks [13]. If the product to be designed requires high level of complex interactions with humans, where precision, accuracy, fidelity becomes a critical concern, then physical prototyping is often the preferred method. On the other hand, if the physical prototype is expensive to build or improbable to construct due its cost and environmental constraints (e.g., as zero gravity in space module) then computational prototyping is preferred. However, the literature does not provide guidelines to decide what type of prototype, i.e. full physical or full computational or a mix of both should be used when assessing the interactions between users and the products. There are also no comprehensive guidelines which categorize the scale or level of interactions between users and products.

There are various methods to create a full computational prototype. This paper focuses on the of CAD models to construct the product or environment and the use of DHM to assess human-product interactions. Digital Human Modeling (DHM) refers to the methodology of digitally representing humans within a computer or virtual environment to facilitate the prediction of performance and/or safety of a worker [1, 2]. DHM manikins consist of visualization of the human body as well as the mathematics and science in the background that enable designers to evaluate the effectiveness of a design, often, focusing on biomechanics (e.g., L4/L5 compression forces) and ergonomics (e.g., NIOSH lifting index) assessments of postures [15, 16]. DHM approach offers designers the capability to visualize and to evaluate product performance early in the design before a physical product is constructed [17, 18]. This proactive approach has the advantage of potentially reducing the need of full-scale physical prototyping and extensive human-subject data collection.

DHM also has shortcomings in taking into account of variation in posture changes (e.g., reach envelope) and fails to identify different strategies that can be used by human to perform the same routine task. This inadequacy is recognized in the literature of DHM and is considered as one of the grand challenges, including the fidelity of anthropometry, realistic visualization, accuracy of posture and motion, number of degrees of freedom (DOF), predictive capabilities, etc. In other words, fidelity concerns in DHM considers "to which extend does DHM represent/replicate the reality?" [19–22].

On the other hand, mixed prototype combines the advantages of full computational prototypes, i.e. quick evaluation of various design alternatives, flexibility, etc. and advantages of physical prototype such as sense of touch, individual differences, fidelity etc. [23]. One way of creating a mixed prototype is by immersing the human subject into the CAD environment of product or workspace through VR technology, which is defined in *Academic Press dictionary of science and technology* as 'a computer simulation of a system, either real or metaphorical, that allows a user to perform operations on a simulated system and shows the effects in real time; e.g., a system for architects might allow the user to "walk" through a proposed building design, displaying how the building would look to someone actually inside it' [24]. Although VR enables the user to interact with the product or workplace and gives the feeling of being part of the virtual scene, a standalone VR system does not provide haptic feedback [25].

Though mixed prototyping combines both computational and physical prototypes, it is neither as fast and flexible as a full computational prototype and nor as accurate as full physical prototypes. To the best knowledge of the author, there is no literature which addresses the type of prototyping that needs to be created to take into the account of reach strategies in different task conditions (e.g., during routine versus emergency protocol). Hence, in this paper, a comparison of two types of prototypes is made focusing on various reach strategies that can arise due to emergency event. Specifically, the case study of the emergency protocol involves various tasks that a pilot needs to perform in the event of a fire in cockpit, i.e. (a) reaching to the oxygen mask compartment, (b) reaching to the circuit breaker, (c) reaching to the front control panel and (d) reaching to the throttle lever are simulated using both full computational prototype and mixed prototype. More details about the case study is given in Sect. 4.

3   Methodology

Various attempts have been taken to develop a taxonomy of classification of prototypes such as cost, stage of design, level of abstraction or realism, and intended evaluation purpose [26, 27]. The shortcoming of these classifications is that they are unable to cover and distinguish the entire prototype design space [28]. It is out of the scope of this paper to refer to all the classification of prototypes and point out the effectiveness and completeness of each of them. Hence, one of the classifications of a prototype called Hierarchical Morphological Prototyping (HMP) Options Taxonomy is discussed in this paper [28].

Hierarchical Morphological Prototyping's (HMP) classification of prototyping is based on variety, complexity and fidelity because based on these three types it should be possible to distinguish any complete prototype [28–30]. The first level of classification is in the terms of variety, i.e., whether the prototype is physical or non-physical. Non- physical prototypes are made using computational tools such as Computer aided design (CAD), Finite Element Analysis (FEA), Digital Human Modeling (DHM), sketches, pictures, etc. [28]. In the second level of classification, the prototype is divided based on complexity or in other words whether the whole system, e.g. a complete car, or a sub-system, e.g. an engine, or a component, e.g. piston rod is prototyped. The last level of classification is based on fidelity where the prototypes are categorized based on the depth of true representation of the final product. Figure 1 can further help to understand this category. One of the shortcoming of this classification is that HMP has not considered mixed prototyping as one of the variety of prototype.

Complexity of human-product interaction is a concern that designers need to be wary about the amount of interactivity required between user and product during prototyping. From Fig. 1, it can be seen that if there is high interaction between user and product then the practice is to lean towards full prototype, i.e. physical prototype. On the other hand, if the interactivity level is low then full simulation, i.e. computational prototyping is preferred. It is because of the lack of fidelity in the human modeling software to accurately predict and represent human postures and tasks. There are limitations to simulate the lifelike human motion and accurate posture predictions for many complex tasks by the existing digital human modeling tools [31].

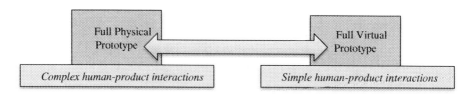

Fig. 1.   Human aspects of design in a digital enterprise are shown on a continuum [31, 32]

As stated above that incomplete classification and reasoning for the type of prototyping exist in the literature, however, there is no taxonomy and reasoning of prototyping to be employed is found for prototyping human-product or human-workspace interactions. In this research, a partial classification of prototyping human-product interactions is given in Fig. 2 based on the concept of Hierarchical Morphological Prototyping (HMP) Options Taxonomy.

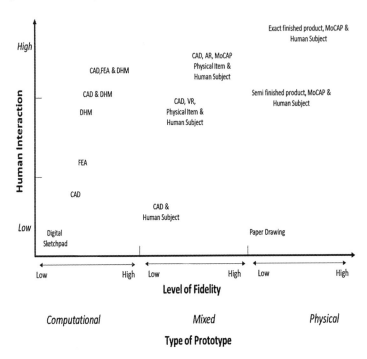

Fig. 2. Human-product/workspace prototyping classification

Figure 2 provides a classification of prototyping for products or workspaces which require human interaction. The vertical axis represents the level of human-product interaction and horizontal axis represents types of prototypes which is further categorized into level of fidelity. Figure 2 shows that the products which have low level of interactivity can be prototyped by either using digital sketchpad, CAD or simply by paper drawing. However, sophisticated and expensive prototypes need to be created to evaluate products which have high-level of human-product interaction. Full scale computational prototypes created using CAD, FEA and DHM can evaluate products which requires low to mid-level of human interaction. Products with high level of human-product interactions can be evaluated by creating physical prototypes representing the partial or finished product with Motion Capture (MoCAP) and human subject or by using mixed prototypes.

However, no comprehensive guidelines exist which states what type of prototype, i.e. full computational, physical or mixed, should be used based on the level of human-product interaction. Also, guidelines regarding what fidelity and the complexity of the prototype should be created which can take into account of the level of human-product interaction is not comprehensive. Hence, in this study two types of prototypes, i.e. full computation (CAD and DHM) and mixed reality (CAD, VR and human subjects) are studied on the pilot-cockpit case study. This study helps to understand what type of prototype to be used based on the level of human interaction. In the next section, a case study is performed to assess reach posture strategies inside a cockpit using fully computational prototype and mixed prototypes. The goal is to get a more detailed insight on the type of prototypes to be used based on human-product interaction and the level of fidelity required.

4   Case Study

Several civilian air-planes have been reported to have the issue of cockpit fire originating from a heater due to a loose screw which causes jolts of electricity around the cockpit panel, flames, smokes and shattering of inner ply of windscreen [33–36]. In this event of emergency due to fire in cockpit, pilots wear an oxygen mask and reaches the kill switch/circuit breaker located at the overhead panel and then grabs fire extinguisher to put out the fire [33, 36]. In this paper this emergency event is studied using both fully computational prototype and mixed prototype to see how pilots 'perform a sequence of task, i.e., (a) tries to reach the oxygen mask, (b) reaching circuit breaker, (c) reaching front panel and (c) reaching the throttle. Cockpit of Boeing 767 is shown in Fig. 3.

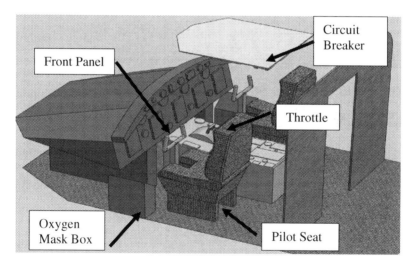

Fig. 3.   Partial Cockpit of Boeing 767

From Fig. 3, it is seen that the oxygen mask is located inside a box which is positioned at the left side of the pilot and the circuit breaker is located on the overhead panel which is 153 cm above from the cockpit floor. The cockpit CAD model represents the pilot seat, oxygen mask box, position of circuit breaker and the distance between the overhead panel and base and other instruments dimensionally accurate to the best ability of the author. Figure 4 shows the detail of the circuit board and top view of Boeing 767 cockpit. The CAD model in Figs. 3 and 4 is used in both of the prototypes to represent a generic cockpit. The full computational prototyping and mixed reality prototyping of Boeing 767 to perform a sequence of task by a pilot is discussed in the following sections.

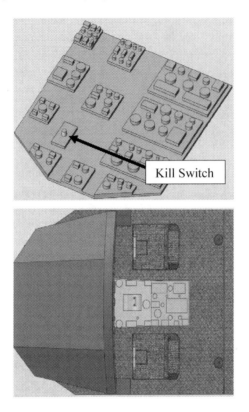

Fig. 4. Details of circuit breaker and top view of Boeing 767 Cockpit

4.1 Computational Prototype

The full computational prototype is created using SolidWorks by CAD modeling and using JACK for ergonomic analysis as can be seen in Fig. 5.

As stated earlier, the computational prototype of the cockpit is created using Solid-Works to build a CAD model of the cockpit. Then, it is imported in JACK to perform and analyze the sequence of task a pilot goes through in the event of a cockpit fire emergency. The pilot is represented in JACK using a custom created manikin of 168 cm height and 70 kg weight. JACK is used to analyze: (a) the reach strategy of the pilot while reaching the oxygen mask on his left side of the cockpit, (b) reaching the circuit breaker in the overhead panel, (c) reaching the front panel, and (d) reaching the throttle lever in the event of emergency fire. The results, i.e. reach strategies are discussed in Sect. 5. In the next subsection, the creation and usage of mixed reality is presented.

Fig. 5. Full computational prototyping using JACK.

4.2 Mixed Prototype

The mixed prototype is created using the same CAD file as seen in Fig. 4 and imported in SimLab Composer 8 and projected using HTC Vibe Virtual Reality (VR). A human subject of exact anthropometry as inserted in computational prototyping (JACK) is used in the mixed reality prototyping to mimic a pilot. The same sequence of tasks as performed in computational prototyping are performed by the human subject while seating over a physical chair which has the same height as the pilot seat shown in Fig. 5. The mixed reality setup is shown in Figs. 6 and 7.

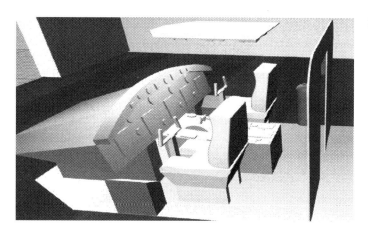

Fig. 6. Cockpit CAD viewed in SimLab

As can be seen in Figs. 6 and 7, the human subject is immersed in the virtual reality of the cockpit and placed on the exact position as the manikin is positioned on the pilot's seat in Fig. 5. The human subject is sitting on physical chair which has the similar

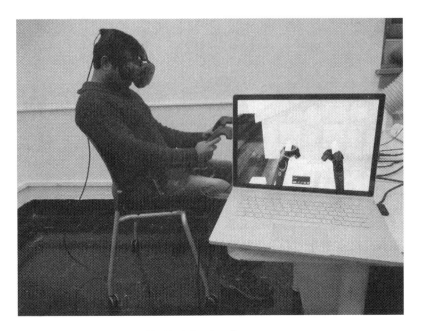

Fig. 7. Mixed reality setup.

dimensions as the pilot seat. The subject is holding wands (virtual controllers) in both hands which mimics grabbing the yoke in a cockpit as shown in the laptop screen of Fig. 7.

The human subject is instructed to do the exact sequence of task as done by the manikin in computational prototyping twice. During the first time, the human subject performs the sequence of task in a routine phase which mimics what a pilot is doing during a regular routine operation. However, during the second time, the subject is prompted to do the same of sequence of task but in an emergency case (e.g., the cockpit is in fire) so that subject's actions now mimic the actual sequence performed by a pilot in the event of cockpit fire emergency. In both cases, Kinect is used as marker less motion capturing device to capture the various hand and head angles of the human subject in real-time while performing the sequence.

The computational prototype and mixed reality prototype are evaluated by comparing the corresponding angles created by the Manikin in JACK and human subject in mixed reality which is discussed in next section.

5   Results

As mentioned in Sect. 4 that a sequence of task i.e. (a) the reach strategy of the pilot while reaching the oxygen mask on his left side, (b) reaching the circuit breaker in the overhead panel, (c) reaching the front panel and (d) reaching the throttle lever in the event of emergency fire is simulated using both full computational and mixed reality prototyping. Figure 8 shows the task completed using these two prototypes side by side.

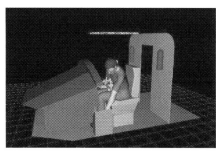

(a) The reach strategy of the pilot while reaching the oxygen mask on his left side

(b) The reach strategy of the pilot while reaching the circuit breaker

(c) The reach strategy of the pilot while reaching the front panel

(d) The reach strategy of the pilot while reaching the throttle lever

Fig. 8. Simulating a sequence of task, reaching (a) oxygen mask box (b) circuit breaker, (c) front panel and (d) throttle lever in Boeing 767cockpit using JACK (left) and mixed reality (right)

The intra-class correlation (ICC) analysis is done for mixed reality prototype to see whether the trials are consistent or not. Also, intra-class correlation between the routine and emergency event is measured to see the effect of emergency event on the reach postures. The intra-class correlation is presented in Table 1.

Table 1. Intra-class correlation between types of prototypes and between routine and emergency event

	Mixed reality (routine)	Mixed reality (emergency)	Mixed reality (routine)	Full computational (routine)	Mixed reality (routine)	Mixed reality (emergency)
ICC	0.927	0.975	0.779		0.743	

The results from these two types of prototyping is presented in Table 2. It shows the angles for Upper Arm Flexion Right/Left, for both type of prototypes and for all the steps in the sequence. Further, the mixed reality prototype has two sets of data which represents a pilot following a routine procedure and the other one is an emergence procedure. JACK does not simulate emergency procedure, so it has only one set of data.

Table 2. Descriptive statistic - comparison of reach posture strategy between full computational prototype and mixed reality prototype.

	Angles	Min	Max	Mean	SD
Full computational prototype (JACK)	Reaching oxygen mask using upper arm flexion left	36.7	36.7	36.7	0
	Reaching circuit breaker using upper arm flexion right	143.2	143.2	143.2	0
	Reaching front panel using upper arm flexion right	58.9	58.9	58.9	0
	Reaching throttle using upper arm flexion right	5.4	5.4	5.4	0
Mixed reality prototype (routine)	Reaching oxygen mask using upper arm flexion left	14.3	15.5	15.0	0.6
	Reaching circuit breaker using upper arm flexion right	12.9	18	14.9	2.7
	Reaching front panel using upper arm flexion right	13.7	19.8	16.2	3.2
	Reaching throttle using upper arm flexion right	6.6	6.9	6.8	0.2
Mixed reality prototype (emergency)	Reaching Oxygen mask using upper arm flexion left	11.5	13.8	12.7	1.3
	Reaching circuit breaker using upper arm flexion right	15.4	22	19.9	3.1
	Reaching front panel using upper arm flexion right	24	27.7	26.5	1.7
	Reaching throttle using upper arm flexion right	6.3	10.2	7.6	1.8

Table 2 shows the descriptive statistical values of reach postures angles for computation and mixed reality prototyping. Full computational prototype provides the same angle value for any particular reach posture. Also, it does not have the capability of simulating the emergency event hence the full computational prototype has only one set of data of zero standard deviation. The mixed reality prototype produces different set of data in each trial and can also account for emergency event.

6   Discussion

Table 2 shows the results obtained by comparing the two types of prototypes used to simulate the routine procedure and emergency event procedure in Boeing 767 cockpit. Table 1 shows that the intra-class correlation is 0.779 between computational prototype and mixed reality prototype for routine reach postures. It is due to the low fidelity of the Kinect to capture angles accurately. The inaccuracy is further exacerbated due to the sitting posture of the human subject. The lack of fidelity in capturing the human subject motion has caused a difference of result between the computational prototype and mixed reality prototype.

The minimum, maximum, mean and standard deviation of these trials are also presented in Table 2. The intra-class correlation within the three trails and four trails of the routine and emergency postures are 0.927 and 0.975 respectively as can be seen in Table 1. ICC results show that there is an excellent consistency within the trials of routine and emergency reach postures respectively. Also form Table 1, the intra-class correlation between the mean values of routine and emergency reach postures are 0.743, which shows a fair correlation.

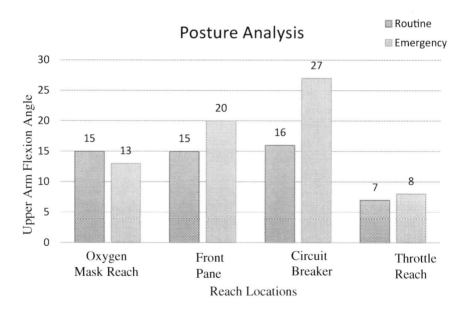

Fig. 9.   Posture analysis in routine and emergency events in mixed reality prototype

Figure 9 shows the difference of upper arm flexion angles due to routine and emergency reach postures. It shows that emergency event does affect the normal postures. It is because in an emergency event, pilot tries to perform the task quicker compared to routine work. Another possible reason of difference is that pilots may even assume an uncomfortable posture so that the task can be done immediately.

This result is also in accordance to the study of whether discomfort affects the arm reaching movement while seated [37]. In this paper performing the sequence of task in a normal routine manner is regarded as comfortable reaching strategy and performing the sequence in emergency event is considered as discomforting reaching strategy. It is because in an emergency situation pilots tend to perform the task as fast as possible without considering the comfort of postures whereas in routine procedure pilots performs the tasks by taking the time and reaching through comfortable postures.

This study compares two types of prototypes, i.e. full computational prototype and mixed reality prototype by comparing the reaching motion strategy during routine procedure and emergency procedure in case study of Boeing 767 cockpit. It is found that most of the angle values between computational prototype and mixed reality prototype has fair correlation according to intra-class correlation analysis. This difference is attributed to low fidelity of the marker less motion capture device used and also due to the seated posture of the human subject. However, it is found from intra-class correlation analysis that there is an excellent consistency on correlations results of 0.927 and 0.975 within the trials of the mixed reality prototype for capturing routine work and emergency event reaching postures. It is also found that the intra-class correlation between the routine and emergency event is fairly correlated with correlation value of 0.743. Results suggest that emergency event does have an effect on reach strategies of pilots. The small difference of upper arm flexion angle shows that the human subject performs a different reach strategy during an emergency event as compared to normal routine posture. Hence, these studies show that while simulating emergency situation, a mixed reality prototype can better capture the different human postures compared to digital human modeling approach. It is because DHM always uses the same inverse kinematic algorithm to predict a posture for a given starting and ending point and cannot take into account of different postures that arise due to emergency situation.

This study has compared two prototypes in a case study of Boeing 767 cockpit emergency fire event. However, there are some limitations in this study. The first limitation is that a low fidelity marker-less motion capture device is used to capture the motion of a human subject. The second limitation is that only one human subject is used in the study to show a proof of concept, so the statistical significance of the difference of result is not established. The third limitation is that only the end static posture of the human subject is studied and the whole dynamic postures from start finish are not evaluated. A study of the dynamic posture from start to end between the routine event and emergency event would provide a more insight on how the posture changes due to emergency event.

Future studies will be done to address the limitations mentioned above. A high fidelity motion capture system can provide a more accurate data collection. Also, a comprehensive study with a larger subject population is required to capture variation among people from different anthropometries. Finally, studying the dynamic posture can shed more insight on how the routine posture and emergency posture differs so that it can be taken into account while designing a cockpit.

Acknowledgements. This research is supported by The National Aeronautics and Space Administration (NASA) award number 80NSSC17M0019. Any opinions or findings of this work are the responsibility of the authors, and do not necessarily reflect the views of the sponsors or collaborators.

References

1. Beevis, D., Denis, G.S.: Rapid prototyping and the human factors engineering process. Appl. Ergon. **23**(3), 155–160 (1992)
2. Meister, D.: Systems design, development and testing. In: Handbook of Human Factors (1987)
3. Andriole, S.: Storyboard Prototyping: A New Approach to User Requirements Analysis. QED Information Sciences, Wellesley (1989)
4. Bi, Z.M.: Computer integrated reconfigurable experimental platform for ergonomic study of vehicle body design. Int. J. Comput. Integr. Manuf. **23**(11), 968–978 (2010)
5. Bullinger, H.-J., Dangelmaier, M.: Virtual prototyping and testing of in-vehicle interfaces. Ergonomics **46**(1–3), 41–51 (2003)
6. Colombo, G., Cugini, U.: Virtual humans and prototypes to evaluate ergonomics and safety. J. Eng. Des. **16**(2), 195–203 (2005)
7. Pham, D., Gault, R.: A comparison of rapid prototyping technologies. Int. J. Mach. Tools Manuf. **38**(10–11), 1257–1287 (1998)
8. Lim, Y.-K., Stolterman, E., Tenenberg, J.: The anatomy of prototypes: prototypes as filters, prototypes as manifestations of design ideas. ACM Trans. Comput. Interact. **15**(2), 1–27 (2008)
9. Broek, J.J., Sleijffers, W., Horváth, I., Lennings, A.F.: Using physical models in design. In: Proceedings of CAID/CD 2000 Conference, pp. 155–163 (2000)
10. Ferrise, F., Bordegoni, M., Cugini, U.: Interactive virtual prototypes for testing the interaction with new products. Comput. Aided. Des. Appl. **10**(3), 515–525 (2013)
11. Mutambara, A.G.O., Durrant-whyte, H.F.: Estimation and control for a modular wheeled mobile robot. IEEE Trans. Control Syst. Technol. **8**(1), 35–46 (2000)
12. Binnard, M.: Design by Composition for Rapid Prototyping. Stanford University, Stanford (1999)
13. Zorriassatine, F., Wykes, C., Parkin, R., Gindy, N.: A survey of virtual prototyping techniques for mechanical product development. Proc. Inst. Mech. Eng. Part B J. Eng. Manuf. **217**(4), 513–530 (2003)
14. Demirel, H.O., Duffy, V.G.: Applications of digital human modeling in industry. In: Duffy, Vincent G. (ed.) ICDHM 2007. LNCS, vol. 4561, pp. 824–832. Springer, Heidelberg (2007). https://doi.org/10.1007/978-3-540-73321-8_93
15. Demirel, H.O., Duffy, V.G.: Digital human modeling for product lifecycle management. In: Duffy, V.G. (ed.) ICDHM 2007. LNCS, vol. 4561, pp. 372–381. Springer, Heidelberg (2007). https://doi.org/10.1007/978-3-540-73321-8_43
16. Sundin, A., Ortengren, R.: Applications conclusions and the future system development. In: Handbook of Human Factors and Ergonomics, pp. 1053–1074 (2006)
17. Webber, B.L., Phillips, C.B., Badler, N.I.: Simulating Humans: Computer Graphics, Animation, and Control, p. 288. Oxford University Press, Oxford (1993)

18. Zhang, X., Chaffin, D.B.: Digital human modeling for computer-aided ergonomics. Interv. Control Appl. Occup. Ergon. (2006). (Chapter 10)

19. Desjardins, P., Plamondon, A., Gagnon, M.: Sensitivity analysis of segment models to estimate the net reaction moments at the L5/S1 joint in lifting. Med. Eng. Phys. **20**(2), 153–158 (1998)

20. Riemer, R., Lee, S.-W., Zhang, X.: Full body inverse dynamics solutions: an error analysis and a hybrid approach (2002)

21. Chaffin, D.B., Erig, M.: Three-dimensional biomechanical static strength prediction model sensitivity to postural and anthropometric inaccuracies. IIE Trans. **23**(3), 215–227 (1991)

22. Chaffin, D.B., Faraway, J.J., Zhang, X., Woolley, C.: Stature, age, and gender effects on reach motion postures. Hum. Fact. J. Hum. Fact. Ergon. Soc. **42**(3), 408–420 (2000)

23. Barbieri, L., Angilica, A., Bruno, F., Muzzupappa, M.: Mixed prototyping with configurable physical archetype for usability evaluation of product interfaces. Comput. Ind. **64**(3), 310–323 (2013)

24. Morris, C.: Academic Press Dictionary of Science and Technology. Gulf Professional Publishing, Houston (1992)

25. Grajewski, D., Górski, F., Zawadzki, P., Hamrol, A.: Application of virtual reality techniques in design of ergonomic manufacturing workplaces. Procedia Comput. Sci. **25**, 289–301 (2013)

26. Pahl, G., Beitz, W.: Engineering design: a systematic approach. In: Engineering Design: A Systematic Approach, vol. 11, p. 544 (2013)

27. Wood, K.L., Otto, K.N.: Product Design: Techniques in Reverse Engineering and New Product Development. Tsinghua University Press, Beijing (2001)

28. Stowe, D.T.: Investigating the role of prototyping in mechanical design using case study validation (2008)

29. Jönsson, A., Broman, G.: lean prototyping of multi-body and mechatronic systems. Ph.D. thesis, Department of Mechanical Engineering, p. 133 (2004)

30. Tseng, M.M.: A framework of virtual design for product customization. In: IEEE 6th International Conference on Emerging Technologies and Factory Automation Proceedings, EFTA 1997, pp. 7–14 (1997)

31. Duffy, V.G.: Modified virtual build methodology for computer-aided ergonomics and safety. Hum. Fact. Ergon. Manuf. **17**(5), 413–422 (2007)

32. Demirel, H.O.: Modular human-in-the-loop design framework based on human factors. Purdue University, 2015

33. How a faulty heater caused the windshield in the Cockpit of a passenger jet to shatter - thousands of feet above the Atlantic – Daily Mail Online. http://www.dailymail.co.uk/news/article-1290535/How-faulty-heater-caused-windshield-cockpit-passenger-jet-shatter-thousands-feet-Atlantic.html. Accessed 23 Jan 2018

34. Incidents, events involving Boeing Cockpit fires - The San Diego Union-Tribune. http://www.sandiegouniontribune.com/sdut-incidents-events-involving-boeing-cockpit-fires-2010jun29-story.html. Accessed 23 Jan 2018

35. Cockpit fire: historical examples - MH370debris. https://sites.google.com/site/mh370debris/home/alternate-explanation/cockpit-fire-historical-examples. Accessed 08 Feb 2018

36. Fire in the Cockpit - Plane & Pilot Magazine. http://www.planeandpilotmag.com/article/fire-in-the-cockpit/#.Wme_sK6nF9M. Accessed 23 Jan 2018

37. Chevalot, N., Xuguang, W.: An experimental investigation of the discomfort of arm reaching movements in a seated position. SAE Trans. **113**(1), 98–103 (2004)

The Role of Standardization for Occupational Safety and Health (OSH) and the Design of Safe and Healthy Human-Computer Interaction (HCI)

Michael Bretschneider-Hagemes[✉], Sebastian Korfmacher,
and Katharina von Rymon Lipinski

Commission for Occupational Health and Safety and Standardization (KAN),
Sankt Augustin, Germany
{bretschneider,korfmacher,vonRymonLipinski}@kan.de

Abstract. The relationship between standardization and HCI design often appears contradictory to those involved: on the one hand, standardization, presumed to be rigid and conservative; on the other, the HCI community, presumed to be trendy and innovative. However, HCI design and the resulting products benefit from the application of standards. The consideration of standards is often the essential key to smooth market access – especially in the field of safety and security. It also supports task-oriented, user-optimized and health-friendly design of HCI – ISO 9241 "Ergonomics of human-system interaction" exemplifies this connection.

The conference contribution gives insights into the field of standardization and provides an overview of the relationship between standardization, occupational safety and health (OSH) and HCI. The process of standards development and participation in standardization is presented in the context of the legal framework – exemplified by the European system. In addition, the reference to occupational health and safety and the aspects of digitalization are explained by examples.

Keywords: Digitalization of work · Safety · Healthy workplace
Standardization

1   Why Does Standardization Matter for HCI?

Standardization has the effect of making things fit. A folded sheet of paper of a standard size fits into an envelope. Nuts fit on screws. Besides governing the safety of products, standards also govern such things as services, methods and management systems. According to ISO, the International Standards Organization, an International Standard provides rules, guidelines or characteristics for activities or for their results, aimed at achieving the optimum degree of order in a given context.

Standards support economic activity, facilitate international trade, and often permit access to markets. Companies can reduce their costs by applying standards rather than reverting to solutions of their own that entail long development times.

© Springer International Publishing AG, part of Springer Nature 2018
V. G. Duffy (Ed.): DHM 2018, LNCS 10917, pp. 19–28, 2018.
https://doi.org/10.1007/978-3-319-91397-1_2

Standards also contribute to safety at work. Although they are often not immediately evident, they influence the world of work by regulating safety conditions and thereby reducing the number of accidents. They also describe how the interaction between human beings and machines, including computers, is to be shaped. Standards have long been used as a point of reference for the design of human-computer interfaces (HCIs).

2   How Can Stakeholders Get Involved in the Standardization Process?

At first glance, the process of standards development seems opaque. Numerous points exist however at which influence can be brought to bear upon the text of a standard. HCI designers and OSH experts alike thus have the opportunity to play a part in shaping the content and quality of a standard, either indirectly or directly.

Every standardization project begins with the idea for a standard. In principle, anyone – not just institutions, but even individual members of the public – may submit an application for the development of a standard to their national standards institute, and thus literally set standards.

The national standards organization reviews whether the proposal should be taken up directly at international level at ISO, the International Standards Organization. If the ISO members (i.e. the national standards institutes) signal sufficient support for the proposal and their willingness to participate, and funding of the work is assured, ISO assigns the project to a Technical Committee (TC), which in turn assigns the work to one of its Working Groups (WGs). Whether a work item is taken up depends entirely upon the voting members of ISO. For this reason, it is particularly important to enlist the support of other countries in advance. Through active observation of standardization work in progress and cooperation with OSH experts in other countries, influence can be brought to bear upon the standardization process at an early stage.

Mirror committees support the standardization process at national level. The ISO members post delegates to the TC. The delegates present their respective national opinions and have the function of liaising between the international and national standardization levels. The ISO members post experts to the WG who primarily present their personal expert opinions. Positions can therefore best be presented through active involvement in the standardization activity at international level and in the mirror committees.

The WG produces a committee draft (CD), upon which the national standards organizations are required to comment within three months. If a consensus is reached, each ISO member submits the draft international standard (DIS) to a national public enquiry, in which all stakeholders are able to submit comments upon it to their respective national standards organizations. The comments are incorporated into the DIS, and the WG produces a final draft international standard (FDIS).

The FDIS is presented to the ISO members once again for voting. At this stage, the ISO members are able only to approve or reject the FDIS, or to abstain; comments on its content are no longer possible.

The adoption of international standards in the European or national bodies of standards is not mandatory. If international standards are to be adopted in the European body of standards, they can be modified with respect to the international version. However, the Frankfurt and Vienna Agreements are intended to promote adoption of international standards unchanged in the European body of standards.

International standards are reviewed routinely every five years. New comments can be submitted at this point. In addition, a reasoned request for review of a standard can be presented at any time.

3   Standardization, OSH and HCI

Product standards serve as the framework for the design of work equipment. To a large degree, the mandatory risk assessments to be performed by employers in Germany concern the use of these products as work equipment. If they are not designed with consideration for the manner of their use and the safety and health of their users, they may give rise to hazards and impairing stress. As a result, standardization processes are highly relevant to occupational safety and health when they concern OSH aspects not merely explicitly (this, however, violates the principles of standardization agreed in Germany [1]), but implicitly.

The body of regulations of the German Social Accident Insurance refers directly to the specific standards in order for compliance to be assured with the statutory OSH arrangements in the area of HCI. For example: *"The statutory framework of the German Ordinances on workplaces and on VDU work, in conjunction with rules and standards currently in force, serve as the basis. DGUV Informative publication 215-450 concerning software ergonomics thus serves as the reference document for the German Social Accident Insurance in this area, and provides practical assistance. (…) The requirements of the standard can be applied both during assessment of interfaces of a*

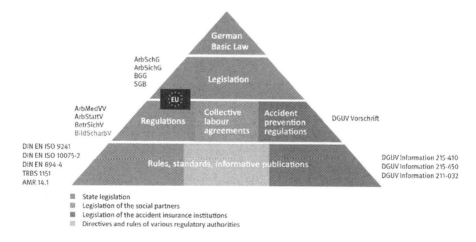

Fig. 1. Pyramid showing OSH legislation relating to software ergonomics (see [2]; with kind permission of the DGUV)

software application already in existence or under development, and during the procurement of software" [2] (unofficial translation). Figure 1 summarizes the complex relationship between HCI and German OSH legislation. The relevant standards serve to support and detail the primary legislation.

The relationship between standardization, occupational safety and health, and HCI thus constitutes a framework for design activity that is binding upon HCI designers and product developers. It provides an opportunity for products not only to meet with high acceptance among users (good usability and UX), but also to assure a high level of legal security for commercial users and customers.

This relationship is illustrated below with reference to examples. The aspect of usability with reference to ISO 9241 [3] is considered, as is the issue of safety and security as a future sphere of standardization, and HCI.

3.1   Standardization and Usability

For a good decade, ISO 9241 has been an established reference framework for the design of interfaces for human-computer interaction that are usable and fit for purpose. It has been implemented in this time as an ISO and EN ISO standard, i.e. at international, European and national level. In practical terms it is therefore regarded as supporting the statutory German Ordinance on workplaces, which was updated in 2016. This item of legislation requires interfaces for human-computer interaction at the workplace to be subject to the requirements for the humane design of work. This enables impairing mental stress caused by operation of the equipment and actual hazards caused by incorrect operation to be reduced or even prevented. The original version of ISO 9241 has been followed by numerous supplements and specifications. The core of the standard continues to be the seven principles of dialogue design, which are described in the part "Ergonomics of human-system interaction" [3]. These principles are: suitability for the task; self-descriptiveness; controllability; conformity with user expectations; error tolerance; suitability for individualisation; and suitability for learning. The principles are increasingly being made the subject of the occupational safety of workers at work in the context of risk assessments, and also of upstream occupational safety and health in the context of product design.

The human-machine interface on a printer operated by touchscreen serves as an illustrative example of this relationship with reference to three of the seven principles concerning dialogues:

Suitability for the Task
The user must be able to complete his or her work task efficiently by means of the software. This typically includes the facility for recognizing the progress of work, the provision of all required information, and where applicable the provision of IT resources. For the example of the user interface of a printer, this means that the required settings for a paper format can be made; that information is displayed on a lack of suitable paper or a low toner level; and that the progress of a running print job is shown.

Self-descriptiveness

The interface must be sufficiently self-descriptive to be used intuitively at least by the intended user group. In other words, a highly specialized machine must be self-descriptive for experts, but not necessarily for unskilled personnel. Conversely, a printer is used by a large number of people with widely differing levels of training. In this case, the interface must be self-descriptive to a much broader user base. This includes feedback to the user on errors and/or successful progress of the work process. The printer interface thus provides clear indication of the options and reports successful completion of the print job, or interruptions in its progress.

Accordingly, a standard must also contain criteria for analysing the context, the tasks and the users, as has been the case in ISO 9241-210 since 2010 [4].

Conformity with User Expectations

Conformity with user expectations is derived from cognitive models of the users and the consistency of the design. In this context, "cognitive models" refers to the existing horizon of the users' expectations. With regard to the printer's user interface, this may mean for example that the structure of menus should already be familiar to users from their use of common operating systems. If this structure is also consistent, i.e. the print menu retains its logic across all hierarchical levels, the result is greater conformity with expectations, and unnecessary stress is avoided during use.

The dialogue principles, including the examples referred to here, ensure that good practice is observed. This benefits the designers of the interface on the one hand, and purchasers, users, and OSH experts in companies on the other.

3.2   Safety and Security

The digitalization of production (termed "Industry 4.0" in Germany) means that installations, machines and human beings are to be able to communicate with each other irrespective of product brand [5]. Even should direct human-computer interaction be reduced owing to high levels of networking and automated control (machine-to-machine communication), the issue will still be relevant to the HCI community, since direct HCI will be replaced by indirect HCI in this case. This aspect was referred to by Mark Weiser when speaking of *"the computer for the 21st century* [6]: in *ubiquitous computing*, HCI refers to implicit interaction with interfaces that are absorbed into the environment within which human beings act, becoming regarded as a part of it. This aspect now also points to the fact that the HCI community must complete a transition, namely from the design of direct HCI to the design of indirect HCI in ubiquitous computing.

This presents a challenge, of which safety and security are a part. Smart manufacturing (described in more detail below) is one specific application scenario.

The accompanying increase in the level of networking results in more and more IT systems being used in production. As a result, industrial control systems (ICSs) are increasingly being targeted by the same cyberattacks as those affecting conventional office IT systems. This is where the aspects of safety and security converge.

A danger exists not only for infrastructures that are directly connected to the Internet, but also for those indirectly connected to it. Besides selective attacks, cyberattacks may also take the form of malware without a specific target [7]. Cyberattacks upon IT systems and industrial control systems can result in the safety of the machine or installation being impaired, thereby giving rise to hazards for human beings. Machines and installations must therefore address aspects not only of safety but also of security, in order for IT and industrial control systems to be protected against cyberattack and impairments to their safety. To provide a better understanding of the different aspects and the interdependencies between them, the essential strategies and objectives of safety and security will first be considered separately.

Safety and security are normally two quite distinct spheres. The safety of a system as a whole is determined by a large number of individual systems. These in turn may employ different technologies, such as mechanical, hydraulic, electrical, electronic, or programmable electronic technology. Safety is understood to be the freedom from unacceptable risk (refer for example to ISO/IEC Guide 51). The aspect of functional safety in particular is affected by issues of security. Functional safety applies to control systems of all kinds; it ensures that safety functions are executed correctly in the event of a fault. Functional safety contributes to overall safety, and also safeguards human health.

The strategy of functional safety is one of risk reduction. Following a risk assessment, the contribution to be made by each individual safety function that is performed by the control system is defined. The requirement is for a safe state to be reached in the event of a fault. This is synonymous with freedom from unacceptable risk. Safety functions are placed in "Categories" according to the probability of a dangerous failure of the safety function per hour. The greater the requirements upon the safety function, the higher the required Category.

By contrast, "security" essentially refers to the ability of an IT system to withstand attack and the associated disruptions and malfunctions. A range of strategies, such as "defence in depth" and "security by design", are intended to assure this protection.

The specific measures to be taken for security depend upon the motivation of the attacker. A distinction is therefore drawn between a coincidental maloperation and an intentional attack employing considerable resources. This distinction is categorized by "security levels", or SLs.

The greatest difference between safety and security is that security must address an attack scenario that is continually changing. By contrast, the threat to be addressed by functional safety does not change (provided the level of the accepted risk does not change, for example owing to ongoing development of the state of the art). This explains the difference between the strategies for implementing safety and security.

The increase in security-related threats gives rise to a new form of threat to safety: attacks on IT systems may have a negative effect upon their safety, irrespective of whether the attacks are targeted or not and whether machines and installations are connected directly or indirectly to the Internet.

The relationship between safety and security is currently the subject of heated discussion. Some experts consider a threat to safety and thus to human beings unlikely, since attackers, such as hackers, are pursuing business models based upon monetary gain. The business model may for example take the form of encryption that cripples the IT systems, making machinery and installations unavailable to the operator; the data are decrypted again only once a ransom has been paid. Attackers may however not be fully able to assess the consequences of manipulation; consequently, it may present a direct or indirect hazard to human beings. The general assumption that human health and safety cannot be the target of hacking attacks because this does not form part of the hackers' business model is therefore incorrect.

In standardization, functional safety is largely described by the IEC 61508 series of standards serving as a generic standard, IEC 61511 for the process industry, and ISO 13849 and IEC 62061 for machinery. IT security is described by the IEC 62443 series; the standards in this series are currently being developed or revised.

Standards governing functional safety have existed for a long time. However, they do not consider the possible threats and hazards presented by networked machines. Very diverse standardization activities are therefore currently in progress concerning safety and security. For the most part, the purpose of these activities is to present the relationship between safety and security and to offer solutions by which the requirements of these different spheres can be met. IEC/TR 63069 and IEC 63074, currently under development, are examples worthy of mention. At ISO level, ISO/TR 22100-4 is currently being developed. This standard is intended to describe the relationship between ISO 12100, governing safety, and IT security for machinery. At national level in Germany, VDE Application Rule 2802-1 also exists. Further parts of this standard are to appear in the future.

Owing to the diversity of standardization activity in the area of safety and security, it is important that it be coordinated and its content reconciled across the standards organizations, in order to prevent overlap and duplication in standards development work. This also requires close cooperation between the respective experts, in order for them to acquire an understanding of the different philosophies.

3.3   Smart Manufacturing

A vision of the future is that custom products with a batch size of one will be available for the price of mass-produced products. This is to be made possible by "smart manufacturing". One aspect of this is self-configuring production. The precise definition of "smart manufacturing" is currently being formulated in standardization work at ISO level by the "Smart Manufacturing Coordinating Committee", SMCC [8]. Its publication is anticipated in the near future.

In order for the vision of self-configuring production to become reality, communication between the items of machinery and plant employed, irrespective of product manufacturer, is essential. Interfaces and communication protocols must therefore be standardized. Only then can industrial processes be organized and controlled for this purpose. Reference architecture models are therefore currently under development throughout the world:

The "Reference architecture model Industry 4.0", or RAMI 4.0, is currently being developed in Germany. This model is focused upon manufacturing, and is being standardized by DIN SPEC 91345:2016-04. In the US, the Industrial Internet Consortium (IIC) is developing the Industrial Internet Reference Architecture, or IIRA for short.

The IIRA is broader in its scope than its German counterpart: for example it covers business processes in the public sector, energy, transport and health, in addition to manufacturing. In order for communication to be possible independently of the manufacturer, overlaps between different reference architecture models must be avoided. Activities and convergence initiatives have therefore already been launched to link RAMI 4.0 and IIRA in a suitable manner in the future [9]. These activities must be extended to include other reference architectures, in order to permit worldwide, manufacturer-independent communication.

4   Regarding the Role of the Commission for Occupational Health and Safety and Standardization (KAN)

In general KAN focuses on:

- *formulating fundamental OSH positions on important issues of the standardization process,*
- *assessing the content of standards to determine whether they meet the OSH requirements from the German point of view and comply with the protection goals specified in European directives,*
- *exerting influence on standardization programmes and mandates (mandates are issued by the European Commission to the private CEN/CENELEC standards bodies).*
- *checking whether there is a need for standardization from the point of view of OH&S,*
- *obtaining and providing or distributing information on standardization work for the OH&S experts.*

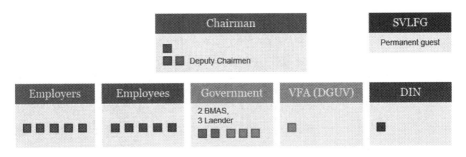

Key:
BMAS: Federal Ministry of Labour and Social Affairs; VFA: Association for the Promotion of Occupational Safety in Europe; DGUV: German Social Accident Insurance; DIN: German Standards Insitute

"KAN (17 members) brings together the institutions concerned with Occupational Health and Safety (OH&S) in Germany.

KAN is composed of five representatives each from the employers, the trade unions and the State, (…) plus one representative each from DIN German Institute for Standardization and The Association for the Promotion of Occupational Health and Safety in Europe (VFA)/German Social Accident Insurance (DGUV), which represents the committees of experts of the statutory accident insurance institutions.

With the Social Insurance for Agriculture, Forestry and Horticulture (SVLFG) as a permanent guest, all statutory accident insurance institutions are thus involved in KAN's work (…).

This essentially tripartite membership complies with the demand of the Machinery Directive 2006/42/EC (Art. 7 Par. 4) for an improvement in the involvement of the social partners in standardization. KAN has gone a step further by establishing one office each for the social partners at the Secretariat" (see KAN-Website).

In the field of digitalization numerous national and international standardization activities are currently in progress. "KAN considers it important for OSH aspects to be considered and addressed at an early stage during the standards development process. Cooperation and dialogue between the various standards organizations is also important in order for overlap to be avoided" [10].

The particular make-up of KAN includes the direct involvement of the social partners. The presenter of this paper represents the interests of the trade unions within KAN, and also on a number of advisory councils concerning digitalization at the German Federal Ministry of Labour and Social Affairs (BMAS) and in the research community (Hans Böckler foundation).

5   Conclusions

In the light of the diverse challenges facing the world of work owing to digitalization, the relationship between standardization, OSH and HCI cannot be ignored. Both usability (as discussed here with reference to the example of principles for dialogues) and the aspects of the safety and security of machinery and installations are crucial to the promotion of acceptance and safety, and also to compliance with national and international occupational safety and health regulations.

The relationship, formulated here with specific reference to HCI in the first instance, will develop at breakneck pace, irrespective of the development of technology as a whole. In the relationship described here, HCI developers and OSH experts will find a strategy for cooperation in the mutual interest.

References

1. Gemeinsamer Standpunkt (GDS) des Bundesministers für Arbeit und Sozialordnung, der obersten Arbeitsschutzbehörden der Länder, der Träger der gesetzlichen Unfallversicherungen, der Sozialpartner sowie des DIN Deutsches Institut für Normung e.V. zur Normung im Bereich der auf Artikel 118a des EWG-Vertrags gestützten Richtlinien. In: Bundesarbeitsblatt 1/1993, pp. 37–39. (Also: Bundesministerium für Arbeit und Soziales, Grundsatzpapier zur Rolle der Normung im betrieblichen Arbeitsschutz – announcement by BMAS, 24 November 2014, GMBl 2015, no. 1, p. 2)
2. DGUV: DGUV-Information 215-450, p. 7. Software Ergonomie, Berlin (2016)
3. ISO 9241-110: Ergonomics of Human-System Interaction – Part 110: Dialogue Principles (ISO 9241-110:2006), German Version EN ISO 9241-110:2006
4. ISO 9241-210: Ergonomics of Human-System Interaction – Part 210: Human-Centred Design for Interactive Systems (ISO 9241-210:2010), German Version EN ISO 9241-210:2010

5. Manzei, C., Schleupner, L., Heinze, R. (eds.): Industrie 4.0 im internationalen Kontext, p. 23 f (2017)
6. Weiser, M.: The Computer for the 21st Century. Sci. Am. (1991)
7. BSI-Veröffentlichungen zur Cyber-Sicherheit – Industrial Control System Security Top 10 Bedrohungen und Gegenmaßnahmen (2016)
8. KANBrief, April 2017
9. https://www.produktion.de/iot-by-sap/iot-by-sap/rami-und-iira-verschmelzen-jetzt-zum-welt-modell-4-0-318.html?page=1
10. KAN Website. www.kan.de

Using 3D Scan to Determine Human Body Segment Mass in OpenSim Model

Jing Chang[1(✉)], Damien Chablat[2], Fouad Bennis[1], and Liang Ma[3]

[1] Ecole Centrale de Nantes, Laboratoire des Sciences du Numérique de Nantes
(LS2N), UMR CNRS 6004, 44321 Nantes, France
{Jing.chang,Fouad.Bennis}@ls2n.fr

[2] CNRS, Laboratoire des Sciences du Numérique de Nantes (LS2N),
UMR CNRS 6004, 44321 Nantes, France
Damien.Chablat@ls2n.fr

[3] Department of Industrial Engineering, Tsinghua University,
Beijing 100084, People's Republic of China
liangma@tsinghua.edu.cn

Abstract. Biomechanical motion simulation and dynamic analysis of human joint moments will provide insights into Musculoskeletal Disorders. As one of the mainstream simulation tools, OpenSim uses proportional scaling to specify model segment masses to the simulated subject, which may bring about errors. This study aims at estimating the errors caused by the specifying method used in OpenSim as well as the influence of these errors on dynamic analysis. A 3D scan is used to construct subject's 3D geometric model, according to which segment masses are determined. The determined segment masses data is taken as the yardstick to assess the errors of OpenSim scaled model. Then influence of these errors on the dynamic calculation is evaluated in the simulation of a motion in which the subject walks in an ordinary gait. Result shows that the mass error in one segment can be as large as 5.31% of overall body weight. The mean influence on calculated joint moment varies from 0.68% to 12.68% in 18 joints.

In conclusion, a careful specification of segment masses will increase the accuracy of the dynamic simulation. As far as estimating human segment masses, the use of segment volume and density data can be an economical choice apart from referring to population mass distribution data.

Keywords: Musculoskeletal Disorders · Biomechanical analysis
Virtual human model · OpenSim · Body segment mass

1 Introduction

Musculoskeletal Disorders (MSDs) makes up the vast proposition of the occupational diseases [1]. Inappropriate physical load is viewed as a risk factor of

© Springer International Publishing AG, part of Springer Nature 2018
V. G. Duffy (Ed.): DHM 2018, LNCS 10917, pp. 29–40, 2018.
https://doi.org/10.1007/978-3-319-91397-1_3

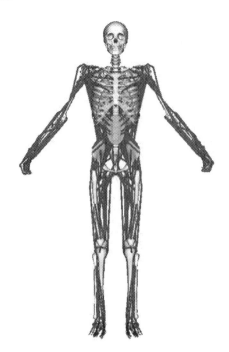

Fig. 1. A generic OpenSim model.

MSD [2]. Biomechanical analysis of joint moments and muscle loads will provide insight into MSDs.

Over the past decades, many tools have been developed for biomechanical simulation and analysis. OpenSim [3] is a virtual human modeling software that has been widely used for motion simulation and body/muscle dynamic analysis [4,5]. The simulation in OpenSim should be based on a generic virtual human that consists of bodies, muscles, joint constraints, etc., as shown in Fig. 1.

A simulation is generally started by scaling the generic model specifically to the subjects geometric and mass data. The subjects body geometric data is obtained using a motion capture system, which records the spatial positions of flash reflecting markers that attached to the specific locations of the subject; then the generic OpenSim model is adjusted geometrically with attempts to minimize the position deviations between virtual markers and corresponding real markers. This makes a subject-specific model out of the generic model.

The geometrical adjustment increases the accuracy of posture simulation and kinematic analysis that follow. For accurate dynamic analysis, the body segment inertial parameters, such as segment masses, should also be adjusted specifically to each subject. In OpenSim, this adjustment is carried out by scaling the mass of each segment of the generic model proportionately with respect to the whole body mass of the subject.

This method of determining segment mass is based on the assumption that the mass distribution among body segments is similar among humans, which is not always the case. For example, the mean mass proportion of the thigh has been reported to be 10.27% [6], 14.47% [7], 9.2% [8], and 12.72% [9], which indicates significant individual difference. Therefore, the scaling method used by OpenSim is likely to cause errors in the following dynamic analysis. There is a necessity to estimate the errors.

This paper aims at estimating the errors caused by the scaling method used in OpenSim. Firstly, subject's segment masses are determined based on the accordingly 3D geometric model constructed with the help of 3D scan. The determined data is taken as an approximation to the true value of the subject's segment mass. Secondly, this set of data, as well as the proportionately scaled segment mass data, is used to specify a generic OpenSim model. Errors caused by proportionately scaling are calculated. Finally, influence of the errors on dynamics analysis is checked on a simulation of a walking task.

The method to approximate subject's segment masses, model specification and dynamic simulation are described in Sect. 2. Results are presented in Sect. 3. These results are then discussed in Sect. 4, followed by a conclusion in Sect. 5.

2   Methodology

2.1   Approximating Segment Masses with 3D Scan

A whole-body 3D scan was conducted to a male subject (31 years old, 77.0 kg, 1.77 m) with a low-cost 3D scanner (Sense^{TM} 3D scanner). Before scanning, reflecting markers were placed on the subject to notify the location of each joint plate as shown in Fig. 2. The locations of the joint plates were set according to Drillis [10], which meant to facility the dismemberment of the 3D model. During scanning, careful caution was taken to make sure that no extra contact between limbs and the torso. The scanned 3D model was stored in a stl mesh file, as shown in Fig. 3.

Then the 3D model was dismembered into 15 parts in the way that described by Drillis [10]. Body markers and body parts lengths are referred. An example of the dismembered body part (Pelvis) is shown in Fig. 4. Then, the volume of each body part was calculated.

To analyze the results obtained, the water displacements of eight distal body parts (hands, lower arms, feet, lower legs) were also measured, as described by Drilis [10].

2.2   Specification of OpenSim Models to the Subject

In this step, a generic OpenSim model is specified to our subject in aspect of body segment mass. The model is developed by Delp et al. [11] (http:// simtk-confluence.stanford.edu:8080/display/OpenSim/Gait+2392+and+2354+ Models). It consists of 12 bodies, 23 degrees of freedom, and 52 muscles (Fig. 5).

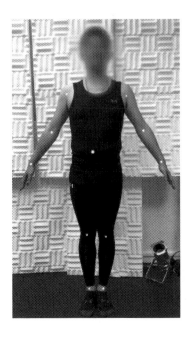

Fig. 2. Body markers that indicate the location of joint plates.

The unscaled version of the model represents a subject that is about 1.8 m tall and has a mass of 75.16 kg. The approximating body segment mass data obtained from the process in Sect. 2.1 as well as the proportionately weight-scaled body segment mass data is used to specific the generic model. The former is considered as the yardstick to estimate the error of the latter.

2.3 Dynamic Simulation in OpenSim

An simulation is conducted on the two specific models. Simulation data comes from previous researches [12]. The subject walks two steps in 1.2 s in an ordinary gait. Data of Spatial posture is collected at a frequency of 60 Hz and the and ground reaction forces at a frequency of 600 Hz. Inverse dynamic analysis is conducted on both models. Joint moments are calculated and compared between the two models.

3   Results

3.1   The Estimation of Body Segment Masses

Significant difference was found between volumes calculated from the 3D scanned geometric model and that measured by water displacement. For lower leg, the difference is as large as 27% (4.5 l vs. 3.3 l). To approximate the real segment masses, assumption is made that the volume distribution of the 3D model merged

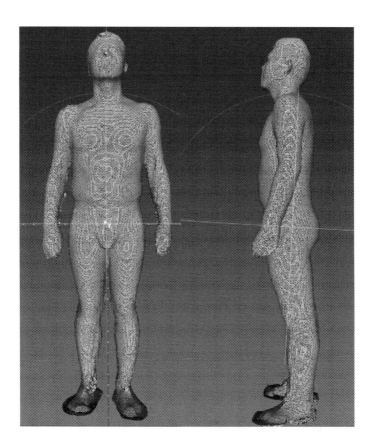

Fig. 3. The 3D geometric model of the subject generated by 3D scan.

Fig. 4. The mesh of pelvis dismembered from the whole-body 3D model.

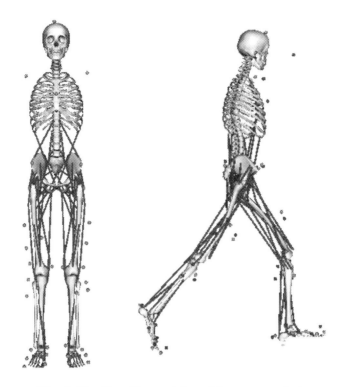

Fig. 5. The OpenSim model used for error analysis.

by 3D scan among head, torso, pelvis, and upper limbs is the same as that of the real subject. Density data of the body parts [13] were used to calculate the whole-body density of the subject, which, as well as body weight, gives estimation of whole-body volume. Then the overall volume was distributed to each segment with respect to the relative volume ratio of the 3D geometric model. In this way, segment volumes and masses are approximated.

Relative data is shown in Table 1. The whole-body volume calculated from the 3D geometric model is 7.31% larger than the estimated whole-body volume (81.81 l–76.24 l). The whole body density is estimated to be 1.01 g/ml. Mass proportion of the thigh is about 11.30%, which is between that reported by Clauser et al. (10.27%) [6], Okada (9.2%) [8] and by De Leva (14.47%) [7], Durkin and Dowling (12.72%) [9].

Table 1. Volume, density and mass of the whole body and segments.

	Overall	Pelvis	Head	Torso	Upper arm-l	Upper arm-r	Lower arm-l	Lower arm-r	Upper leg-l	Upper leg-r	Lower leg-l	Lower leg-r	Foot-l	Foot-r	Hand-l	Hand-r
Volume(l)-3D scanned model	81.81	11.29	5.65	29.90	1.63	1.72	1.38	1.34	8.74	8.65	4.42	4.53	1.06	0.89	0.49	0.58
Volume(l)-water displacement							1.01	1.12			3.25	3.35	1.00	1.00	0.46	0.46
Volume(l)-estimated	76.24	10.81	5.41	28.64	1.56	1.65	1.01	1.12	8.37	8.29	3.25	3.35	1.00	1.00	0.46	0.46
Density (kg/l)[13]	1.01	1.01	1.07	0.92	1.06	1.06	1.10	1.10	1.04	1.04	1.08	1.08	1.08	1.08	1.11	1.11
Estimated mass (kg)		10.92	5.79	26.35	1.66	1.75	1.11	1.23	8.71	8.62	3.51	3.62	1.08	1.08	0.51	0.51

Table 2. Errors of proportionally scaled segment masses with respect to the approximate masses.

	Pelvis	Torso	Upper leg-l	Upper leg-r	Lower leg-l	Lower leg-r	Talus	Calcaneus
Approximate mass (kg)	10.92	38.91	8.71	8.62	3.51	3.62	0.07	0.87
Proportionally scaled mass (kg)	11.98	34.82	9.46	9.46	3.76	3.76	0.10	1.28
Absolute error (kg)	1.06	-4.08	0.75	0.84	0.25	0.15	0.03	0.41
Percentage of absolute error in overall body weight	1.37%	-5.30%	0.98%	1.10%	0.33%	0.19%	0.04%	0.53%
Relate error	9.66%	-10.49%	8.67%	9.80%	7.26%	4.06%	47.42%	47.42%

3.2 Errors Analysis of the OpenSim Scaled Model Specific to the Subject

Segment masses generated by proportionately scale and 3D modeling are used to specify the OpenSim generic model, which bring about two specific models (noted as scaled model and approximate model). Table 2 shows the segment mass data of the two models. Errors of the scaled model segment mass are between 4.06% and 47.42%. The most significant error merges from foot data which, however, represents only a small part of the overall body mass.

3.3 Motion Simulation and Dynamic Analysis

Both the proportionately scaled segment mass data and approximate segment mass data are used to specify the OpenSim generic model, bringing about two specific models (noted as scaled model and approximate model).

Motion simulation is conducted on the two models. The simulated motion includes two steps of walking, lasting for 1.2 s. Since the two models differ in only segment mass, no difference in kinematic analysis is shown. As an example, the angles, velocity and acceleration of right hip flexion is shown in Fig. 6.

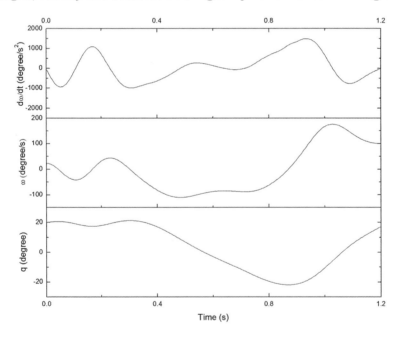

Fig. 6. Coordinate (q), velocity (ω), acceleration (dω/dt) of right hip flexion in the motion.

Inverse dynamic analysis on the two models generates different results. Figure 7 shows the right hip flexion moments calculated from the two models. With the approximate model as yardstick, the error of the calculated right hip flexion moment of the scaled model has a mean of 1.89 Nm, which is 10.11% of its mean absolute value. A total of 18 joint moments was calculated. The means of error percentage vary from 0.65% to 12.68%, with an average of 5.01%. Relative data are shown in Table 3.

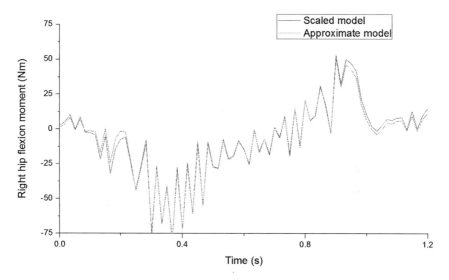

Fig. 7. Right hip flexion moments calculated from the two models.

4   Discussions

4.1   The Use of 3D Scan in the Estimation of Body Segment Masses

In previous researches, the inertial parameters of human body segment are usually determined by two means: (i) Applying predictive equations generated from database [7], (ii) Medical scanning of live subjects [14], and (ii) Segments geometric modelling [15]. The use of the first one, as stated by Durkin and Dowling [9], is limited by its sample population. Furthermore, the difference in segmentation methods makes it difficult to combine various equations [16]. The second method, medical scanning, such as dual energy X-ray absorptiometry is more accurate in obtaining body segment inertial parameters [17]. But it is more expensive and time-consuming.

In this study, body segment masses are estimated by segment density data and segment volume. 3D scan is used to estimate body segment volume. In this process, errors may merge from two aspects.

First, it is assumed that density data of each segment is constant among humans. This assumption may bring errors. Traditional body composition method defines two distinct body compartments: fat and lean body (fat-free). Fat has a density of 0.90 g/ml, while lean body has a density of 1.10 g/ml [18]. Subjects body fat rate may influence the segment density. However, the range

Table 3. Errors of the joint moments calculated from the scaled model, with respect to that from the approximate model

	Mean of error (Nm)	Mean of instant moment (Nm)	Mean of error percentage
Pelvis tilt	6.73	64.12	10.50%
Pelvis list	4.06	37.78	10.75%
Pelvis rotation	1.02	17.78	5.74%
Right hip flexion	1.89	18.73	10.11%
Right hip adduction	0.48	18.57	2.60%
Right hip rotation	0.07	3.47	2.13%
Right knee angle	0.65	19.21	3.40%
Right ankle angle	0.31	38.68	0.80%
Right subtalar angle	0.06	9.02	0.65%
Left hip flexion	2.27	17.90	12.68%
Left hip adduction	0.80	24.99	3.18%
Left hip rotation	0.10	4.28	2.23%
Left knee angle	0.83	19.37	4.28%
Left ankle angle	0.36	30.18	1.19%
Left subtalar angle	0.07	7.65	0.91%
Lumbar extension	5.47	60.85	9.00%
Lumbar bending	3.05	37.37	8.17%
Lumbar rotation	0.33	17.98	1.85%

of density variation is smaller than that of the mass distribution. Therefore, the use of density and volume may reduce the estimation error of segment mass.

For example, in the current study, the thigh, with a volume of 8.35 l, holds a mass proportion that would vary from 9.74% (all fat, density = 0.90 g/ml) to 11.90% (fat-free, density = 1.10 g/ml). This range is much narrower than that found in previous research (from 9.2% [8] to 14.47% [7]).

Second, 3D scan is used to build up 3D geometric model and calculate segment volumes. Significant difference exists between volumes calculated and volumes measured by water displacement. To approximate the real volume, assumption is made that the 3D geometric model has the same volume distribution with that of the subject, which may bring error.

In summary, as a simple and low-cost method of segment mass determination, the use of density data and 3D geometric model is more likely to reduce the estimation error. 3D scan is an easy way to construct a 3D geometric model, but attention should be payed to the model's volume errors. The method used in this study to approximate the real segment volumes with 3D scanned model needs to be examined in future researches.

4.2 The error and error significance of the proportionately scaled model

Proportional scaling is efficient to specific a generic model. In this study, relative errors of segment masses of the scaled model are between 4.06%–47.42%. The error of torso mass is 4.09 kg, which takes up to 5.30% of the overall body weight. In the following motion simulation, these errors bring about difference in the calculated joint moment. Means of the difference of calculated joint moments are from 3.65% to 12.68%. This suggests that a careful specification of segment masses will increase the accuracy of the dynamic simulation.

5 Conclusions

This study aims at estimating the errors and their influences on dynamic analysis caused by the scaling method used in OpenSim. A 3D scan is used to construct subject's 3D geometric model, according to which segment masses are determined. The determined segment masses data is taken as the yardstick to assess OpenSim proportionately scaled model: errors are calculated, and influence of the errors on dynamics analysis is examined.

As a result, the segment mass error reaches up to 5.31% of the overall body weight (torso). Influence on the dynamic calculation has been found, with a average difference from 3.65% to 12.68% in the joint moments.

Conclusions could be drawn that (i) the use of segment volume and density data may be more accurate than mass distribution reference data in the estimation of body segment masses and (ii) a careful specification of segment masses will increase the accuracy of the dynamic simulation significantly. This current work is a study to determine inertial parameters of the human body segment in biomechanical simulation. It explores new, more precise and simpler ways to implement biomechanical analysis. This work is a step towards characterizing muscular capacities for the analysis of work tasks and predicting muscle fatigue.

Acknowledgement. This work was supported by INTERWEAVE Project (Erasmus Mundus Partnership Asia-Europe) under Grants number IW14AC0456 and IW14AC0148, and by the National Natural Science Foundation of China under Grant numbers 71471095 and by Chinese State Scholarship Fund. The authors also thank D. Zhang Yang for his support.

References

1. Eurogip: Déclaration des maladies professionnelles: problématique et bonnes pratiques dans cinq pays européens, p. 44 (2015). http://www.eurogip.fr/fr/produits-information/publications-d-eurogip/3906-declaration-des-mp-problematique-et-bonnes-pratiques-dans-cinq-pays-europeens
2. Chaffin, D., Andersson, G., Martin, B.: Occupational Biomechanics. Wiley, Hoboken (1999)

3. Delp, S.L., Anderson, F.C., Arnold, A.S., Loan, P., Habib, A., John, C.T., Guendelman, E., Thelen, D.G.: Opensim: open-source software to create and analyze dynamic simulations of movement. IEEE Trans. Biomed. Eng. **54**(11), 1940–1950 (2007)

4. Thelen, D.G., Anderson, F.C.: Using computed muscle control to generate forward dynamic simulations of human walking from experimental data. J. Biomech. **39**(6), 1107–1115 (2006)

5. Kim, H.K., Zhang, Y.: Estimation of lumbar spinal loading and trunk muscle forces during asymmetric lifting tasks: application of whole-body musculoskeletal modelling in opensim. Ergonomics **60**(4), 563–576 (2017)

6. Clauser, C.E., McConville, J.T., Young, J.W.: Weight, volume, and center of mass of segments of the human body. Technical report, Antioch coll yellow springs oh (1969)

7. De Leva, P.: Adjustments to zatsiorsky-seluyanov's segment inertia parameters. J. Biomech. **29**(9), 1223–1230 (1996)

8. Okada, H.: Body segment inertia properties of Japanese elderly. Biomechinsm **13**, 125–138 (1996)

9. Durkin, J.L., Dowling, J.J., et al.: Analysis of body segment parameter differences between four human populations and the estimation errors of four popular mathematical models. Trans.-Am. Soc. Mech. Eng. J. Biomech. Eng. **125**(4), 515–522 (2003)

10. Drillis, R., Contini, R., Bluestein, M.: Body segment parameters. School of Engineering and Science Research Division, New York University, NY (1966)

11. Delp, S.L., Loan, J.P., Hoy, M.G., Zajac, F.E., Topp, E.L., Rosen, J.M.: An interactive graphics-based model of the lower extremity to study orthopaedic surgical procedures. IEEE Trans. Biomed. Eng. **37**(8), 757–767 (1990)

12. John, C.T., Seth, A., Schwartz, M.H., Delp, S.L.: Contributions of muscles to mediolateral ground reaction force over a range of walking speeds. J. Biomech. **45**(14), 2438–2443 (2012)

13. Wei, C., Jensen, R.K.: The application of segment axial density profiles to a human body inertia model. J. Biomech. **28**(1), 103–108 (1995)

14. Lee, M.K., Le, N.S., Fang, A.C., Koh, M.T.: Measurement of body segment parameters using dual energy x-ray absorptiometry and three-dimensional geometry: An application in gait analysis. J. Biomech. **42**(3), 217–222 (2009)

15. Davidson, P.L., Wilson, S.J., Wilson, B.D., Chalmers, D.J.: Estimating subject-specific body segment parameters using a 3-dimensional modeller program. J. Biomech. **41**(16), 3506–3510 (2008)

16. Pearsall, D.J., Reid, G.: The study of human body segment parameters in biomechanics. Sports Med. **18**(2), 126–140 (1994)

17. Durkin, J.L., Dowling, J.J., Andrews, D.M.: The measurement of body segment inertial parameters using dual energy x-ray absorptiometry. J. Biomech. **35**(12), 1575–1580 (2002)

18. Lukaski, H.C.: Methods for the assessment of human body composition: traditional and new. Am. J. Clin. Nutr. **46**(4), 537–556 (1987)

Similarities and Differences in Posture During Simulated Order Picking in Real Life and Virtual Reality

Daniel Friemert[1,2]([⊠]), Florian Saala[2], Ulrich Hartmann[2], and Rolf Ellegast[1,2]

[1] Institute for Occupational Safety and Health of the German Social Accident Insurance, St. Augustin, Germany
friemert@hs-koblenz.de
[2] Department of Mathematics and Technology, University of Applied Sciences Koblenz, Remagen, Germany

Abstract. The study we present in this article investigates to which extent a virtual reality (VR) environment can replace a real physical mock-up for ergonomic analysis. For this purpose, we built both a physical mockup of a real order picking workplace (RE) and a corresponding VR environment using head mounted displays and haptic controller devices. We used state-of-the-art motion capturing tools in order to track the postures of our subjects during their picking activities in both conditions (VR and RE). The comparison of the measurements and the statistical analyses reveal the similarities and differences of movements and postures. For instance, a very high resemblance in posture was found in the thoracic spine lateral inclination, the head lateral inclination and the back flexion. Furthermore, we found that lateral movements and ranges of motion are very similar under all tested circumstances. However, looking at the sagittal head and neck flexion measurements, statistical analysis categorized a large majority of the data as dissimilar. Significantly higher sagittal head inclination angles are measured in VR. These differences might be caused by systemic traits connected to the VR environment, for example missing haptics or constrained field of view. Despite the fact that our VR environment could not perfectly mimic the real workplace, our study encourages the view that VR-HMDs have the potential to supplement physical mockups for ergonomic workload analysis or even become a *real* alternative once these traits are taken into account.

Keywords: Ergonomics · Computer-aided ergonomics
Virtual interactive design · Dynamic ergonomics analysis · Virtual reality
Posture analysis · Order picking

1 Introduction

Building real life mockups of workplaces has long been practice for the assessment of ergonomic risks [1]. Nowadays the planning, the construction and the testing of new workplaces are carried out with computer aided design risk assessment tools [2, 3].

© Springer International Publishing AG, part of Springer Nature 2018
V. G. Duffy (Ed.): DHM 2018, LNCS 10917, pp. 41–53, 2018.
https://doi.org/10.1007/978-3-319-91397-1_4

This implies using digital human models in order to get information about posture, movement speeds and efficiency of the workers. This approach is often preferred over the tedious setup of physical mockups because digital models are easy to modify, safe and cost-effective. However, one disadvantage of such models is their accuracy sensitively depending on the proper modelling of the human movement. This shortcoming might be healed by enabling more realistic human movements and postures in the digital world. This progress is achieved by introducing state-of-the-art Virtual Reality Head Mounted Displays (VR-HMDs) that come together with simple-to-use hand controllers. Such a VR environment can be programmed to enable the user to manipulate objects in virtual reality, thus allowing simple tasks to be performed. Although different approaches for the integration of VR into the risk assessment workflow have been proposed [4], this technology is not considered industrial standard at the time being.

Posture analysis is one of the well-established methods for the risk assessment of work-related musculoskeletal disorders and for the long-term assessment of occupational health and safety [5]. It is common sense that any physical workplace mockup must be as similar as necessary to the real workplace in order to arrive at similar movements and postures of the workers. Likewise, any VR mockup has to pass the same test. Therefore, the following research questions arise:

1. How accurate can a real-life workplace be simulated in VR?
2. Do postures differ in VR and RE?
3. Are there specific postures that have to be addressed in different ways?
4. Is low-cost VR finally suitable for the ergonomic analysis of posture?

2   Related Work

In addition to leisure and game industry where the use of VR is ubiquitous, many different use application cases for VR environments have emerged in the low cost segment. For example, VR-HMDs are utilized for therapy of burn victims that have to navigate themselves through different pleasing (icy) scenarios during treatment [6]. The immersive nature of VR is also used to treat mental disorders [7] or anxiety problems like aerophobia or claustrophobia [8, 9]. In surgery, VR is applied for training purposes. It has been shown that surgeons using VR work faster and more precisely than their colleagues trained by conventional methods [10–12].

Using VR for ergonomic analysis has also been tested. In 2004, Whitman et al. [13] published a study about a comparison between a mockup and a real life palletizing task. The experiment was carried out on both a real and a virtual mockup. It was investigated whether the results of both environments can be compared with each other. A lumbar motion monitor (LMM) was used for measurements of the spine and a HMD was used for depicting the virtual environment. A motion capture system was also used to represent the movements of the test persons in the virtual environment. The evaluation of the datasets showed that the velocities and accelerations of the movements in the virtual and real environment differ from each other. In the experiments with the HMD, the subjects moved more slowly than within the physical environment. However, there was no difference to be seen in the motion sequences. In 2013, Pontonnier et al. [14] investigated if assembly tasks can be analyzed using VR. Sixteen male volunteers with little experience in VR participated in the study. The workplace consisted of a crate with various openings, a storage box and twelve objects to be sorted. Depending on their shape, these objects should be sorted through the appropriate openings in the crate. If the object did not fit to any opening, it was placed in the storage box. This activity was carried out in a real and a virtual environment, whereby in the virtual environment the task was fulfilled with and without haptic feedback. The VR system used here was a high-resolution stereoscopic immersion room including a front-screen and a floor-screen. Besides analyzing various parameters, the Rapid Upper Limb Assessment (RULA) score was examined which indicated some resemblance.

To the best of our knowledge, plain posture data and its statistical distribution have not been thoroughly analyzed yet, although we think it is key for the assessment of more complex ergonomic evaluation methods.

3   Methods and Materials

For our study, we set up two different order picking environments. The first one is a real laboratory mockup (see Fig. 3) and the second one is realized as a VR model without any physical boundaries (see Fig. 1). The setup of both environments is derived from a real-life workplace located at our partner company 'wolfcraft', a hardware und tools manufacturer with self-established logistics. In this article, we focus on the similarities and differences of the workers' postures when measured in real physical space and then again in the virtual world. Furthermore, it is our goal to quantify the objective workload during the defined picking tasks.

3.1   Subjects

Eleven subjects (8 male, 3 female) participated in this study. The subjects were university students with a mean age of (23.7 ± 2.2) years, a mean height of (179.4 ± 7.6) cm and a mean weight of (81.9 ± 11.0) kg. No subject has worked in jobs similar to order picking in the past. All subjects have heard of VR-HMDs with respect to the gaming industry, while four subjects had prior knowledge about a different usage (science, education, ergonomics, work-related) as well. In addition, all subjects had used VR headsets at least once for gaming prior to this study, however all but two considered themselves novices in VR (1–2 on seven-point scale). Seven subjects considered themselves not prone (1–2) and four subjects mildly prone (3–5) to motion sickness during car or airplane rides on a seven-point scale.

3.2   Head-Mounted Displays for Virtual Reality

Prior to our study we evaluated different VR-HMDs. The HTC Vive was found most suitable for our purposes. Especially the precision of the tracking system and the provision of haptic feedback through vibration of the hand controllers were essential for our decision. Before each measurement, the VR environment was confined to a 4.5 m × 3 m rectangular area inside a room (5 m × 4 m) with blackened walls and floor for better tracking performance.

Fig. 1. Subject using the HTC Vive and hand controllers inside the tracking area

3.3   The Real-Life Workplace

Our laboratory workplace is based on a real-life order picking station at our partner company wolfcraft. Their workers, exclusively women, use this machine for fast, low-error and efficient order picking. The complete order picking system consists of three parts:

1. The storage facility

The warehouse is a fully automated high-bay storage facility with an area of several hundred square-meters. The system software knows how to process all orders from customers and puts the desired products (contained in yellow boxes) in an optimized order onto conveyer belts using warehouse robotics. The products finally arrive at the exchange port of the order picking machine. The storage facility has not been rebuilt in our lab because it is of no relevance for our investigation.

2. The interior

The interior of the machine is the entry point for new boxes and the exit point for boxes not used anymore and for completed customer orders. The latter is automatically transported to the appropriate loading dock. The machine interior can handle up to 48 customer boxes and up to 12 product boxes at any given time. The interior has been rebuilt in VR, but not in the physical mockup.

3. The frontend

The frontend (see Fig. 2) consists of five boxes that are present at the same time. The middle lane always contains the product box coming from the storage (Box M), while all other boxes (named Box LL, Box L, Box R, Box RR) are customer boxes. The monitor installed above Box M gives instructions to the workers. It tells them how many of the current products were ordered by which customer and how many products are left in the product box. Then the worker picks the correct number of products and places them into the appropriate customer box. After this work step has been finished

Fig. 2. (left) Schematic portrait of the interior of the picking maching (right) worker during order picking at wolfcraft company (Color figure online)

by pressing the green button next to the customer box the software checks, if any other customer has ordered the current product and displays the next command or respectively changes the products and the cycle repeats. Since all postures during work are dictated by the frontend, this part of the machine was rebuilt most realistically both in the laboratory and in VR.

3.4 Our Physical Mock-Up of the Picking Workplace

Our physical mockup (see Fig. 3) is built to scale, but is simplified with respect to the product provision and the objects that have to be picked. Our key requirement is to design the workplace interface for the subjects in such a way that it is as close as possible to the working environment of the real-life machine frontend. In order to automate and standardize the picking tasks we have chosen wooden balls of different weights (60 g, 150 g, 250 g, and 700 g) and diameters (40 mm, 60 mm, 80 mm, and 100 mm) as picking objects instead of real products. The parameter span of our fake products (i.e. the wooden balls) represents about 70% of all products picked by the workers. A single picking task is defined as follows: Our machine supplies a defined number of products in box M. According to the information on the monitor (see Figs. 2 and 3) that is mounted on the rack of the mock-up the products have to be correctly sorted into four boxes (LL, L, R, RR).

Fig. 3. Subject doing order picking on our physical mock-up while wearing the CUELA system

After having finished the picking task for one outgoing box the subject has to push a button thus indicating that this box is ready to be sent away. In our mock-up this step is realized by pneumatic pistons clearing all boxes mechanically. The complete setup is controlled and monitored by a customized software. All product sizes and boxes were equally distributed over the complete assignment (Fig. 4).

3.5   Our Digital Mockup of the Picking Workplace

The digital mockup is based on CAD files that are also built to scale. The task procedure is identical to that in the physical mockup with the one exception that the VR environment boxes are moved away when a task is completed. The products are handled using the VR controllers: when a VR controller touches a product in the virtual environment, the controller vibrates slightly indicating the product can be picked up. Pressing and holding the controller trigger allows the subject to move the object similar

Fig. 4. Overview of our digital mock-up

to using their own hands. The controllers are also used to complete a task using the buttons next to the appropriate box in the virtual environment.

3.6   Sensors and Recordings

Body postures are recorded by means of the CUELA system[1] [1, 5]. This ambulatory measuring system is based on a combination of IMUs (inertial measurement units) and potentiometers and includes a miniature data storage unit with a flash memory card, which can be attached to the subject's clothing. From the measured signals, the following body/joint angles and positions and their corresponding degrees of freedom are calculated resulting in direct parameters such as

– Head: sagittal and lateral inclination
– Thoracic spine: sagittal and lateral inclination at Th3

and derived parameters such as

• Neck flexion/extension: difference between head and thoracic spine inclination
• Back flexion/extension: difference between lumbar and thoracic spine inclination.

The data logger of the CUELA measuring system permits recording at a sampling rate of 50 Hz. The WIDAAN[2] software enables this data to be displayed together with the digitized video recording of the workplace situation and a 3D animated figure.

---

[1] German acronym for "Computer supported recording and long-term analysis of musculoskeletal workloads".

[2] German acronym for "Angle data analysis".

Subtasks can be defined and then be marked as intervals inside the software and can eventually be statistically analyzed separately or in bulk.

3.7 Procedure

Prior to the study the participants were asked to wear everyday clothing including pants and a t-shirt for the experiment. Before the experiment the participants were informed about the procedure. After giving informed consent, the participants filled out questionnaires about their experience with VR as well as some personal data e.g. age and education level. Weight and height were measured using an anthropometer and a personal scale. The CUELA-System was then fit to the subject ensuring that all sensors were aligned to the desired landmarks. Then the participants worked in randomized order on the physical or the virtual mockup. After this the participants received a brief theoretical introduction to the picking task and respectively to working in VR of about five to ten minutes. Prior to starting on one of the workplaces a participant performed a ten-minute practice phase during which they were allowed to ask questions concerning the task and getting used to the working procedure. After completing the introductory practice, the participants were asked to stand still in a relaxed I-pose with their hands next to their body. During this posture the measurement of the CUELA-System was started defining the zero position. All joint angles presented in this study are therefore measured relative to this position. The subjects had to work on their ordering tasks for 15 min. After this the participants were asked to reenter their neutral I-pose. While holding this posture the measurement was ended, in order to take into account possible offsets in sensor data due to potential sensor placement shifts during work. Then the participant switched to the workplace they have not worked on yet, e.g. from the VR to the physical mockup or vice versa. They were granted an additional ten-minute practice phase before starting the second measurement.

3.8 Data Analysis and Statistics

For body joint angle categorization, the ISO 11226 standard was used (Fig. 5, [15]). Usually, the data is displayed as a boxplot showing the distribution of the subjects' body angles and giving insight into the question of whether or not postures at specific workplaces tend to be more favorable or unfavorable [16]. For this purpose, the movement profile of the full working task was analyzed but as the posture strongly differs depending on which box the task takes place at, the data was additionally split into small subtasks allocated to the different boxes (LL, L, M, R, RR).

For analyzing similarities and differences, we identified the following derived parameters for each box and body angle:

- 5%-quantile (interpreted as minimum angle)
- 25%-quantile
- 50%-quantile (median)
- 75%-quantile
- 95%-quantile (interpreted as maximum angle)
- Interquartile range (interpreted as the average range of movement)

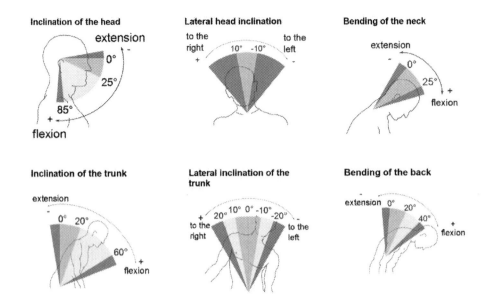

Fig. 5. Joint angle and posture definitions as described in the ISO 11226. Top to bottom, left to right: head sagittal inclination, head lateral inclination, neck flexion, thoracic spine sagittal inclination, thoracic spine lateral inclination, back flexion.

Table 1. Summary of test results for different upper and lower equivalency boundaries for all body parts (S = similar/rejected, D = dissimilar/not rejected)

	EU = EL									
	12.5°		10°		7.5°		5°		2.5°	
	S	D	S	D	S	D	S	D	S	D
Head sagittal inclination	8	28	6	30	4	32	0	36	0	36
Head lateral inclination	36	0	36	0	32	4	18	18	0	36
Neck flexion/extension	6	30	5	31	3	33	1	35	0	36
Thoracic spine sag. inclination	31	5	28	8	21	15	2	34	0	36
Thoracic spine lat. inclination	36	0	36	0	36	0	4	32	0	36
Back flexion/extension	36	0	36	0	31	5	23	13	1	35
Total	153	63	147	69	127	89	48	168	1	215

These parameters were tested using two on-sided tests for equivalence ($\alpha = 0.05$) [17, 18]. This test does not follow the standard t-test approach where the null hypothesis is stating similarity. Instead here, similarity to a certain degree is the *alternative* hypothesis, and the null hypothesis must be rejected. Because regularly this test has a high power, *not* rejecting the null hypothesis can carefully be interpreted as dissimilarity. For this reason, a value for an upper (EU) and a lower (EL) equivalence limit for similarity has to be introduced. Since there was no prior knowledge of what level of similarity could be expected, the tests were conducted using a sequence of values with EU = EL = {12.5°; 10°; 7.5°; 5°; 2.5°}. The changing of the test results due to these increasingly tighter boundaries will be discussed in Sect. 5. We chose this method instead of looking at the less accessible p-value. All data was tested for normal distribution using a Shapiro-Wilks-Test ($\alpha = 0.05$) and was additionally graphically analyzed using QQ-plots, which passed for all datasets. To address multiple testing all p-values were post-processed using a standard Benjamini-Hochberg-procedure [19]. All six quantile-parameters are tested for all 6 tasks (1 main task and the 5 subtasks) result in 36 tests per joint angle. Adding up over all joint angles yields 216 statistical tests which were conducted using the R software package.

4 Results

Table 1 shows the summary of all test results for different ELs and EUs. With increasingly tighter boundaries, more tests tend to fail. To get a better understanding of why the tests fail, we took a closer look at the test results for EU = EL = 7.5°. We picked this value because at this point, many tests begin to fail and we think that the 5° boundary starts to collide with the accuracy of body/joint angle recordings in our laboratory setup. In addition, boxplots for all subject and for all body parts were visually analyzed. Figures 6 and 7 show an example of the full task dataset for the all measured joint angles (Table 2).

5 Discussion

A very high resemblance in posture for VR and RE is found in the thoracic spine lateral inclination, the head lateral inclination and the back flexion. Here, nearly all tests indicate similarity between VR and RE postures.

The thoracic spine sagittal inclination data show high resemblance in the overall task and for the postures induced by working on box M. Subtasks in boxes RR, R, L and LL only show similarity for the lower flexion angles (5%- and 25%-quantile) and the IQR. By observing the subjects' movements during the experiment and analyzing the video footage, we made the following observation: the subjects hesitate to step close to the box they have to put products into when working in the VR environment. This results in a movement pattern similar in duration but different in joint angles. Connecting the CUELA motion analysis system with an avatar that makes the subjects see their body inside the VR environment might provide better results. Offering more training to the subjects could also lower the psychological barrier of walking through the VR environment.

Looking at the sagittal head data and the neck flexion for different EL- and EU-values, a large majority of the data is considered dissimilar even at higher values. The few parameters considered similar are the IQR, reflecting the average range movement relative to the median. Visually comparison of the subjects' boxplots suggests similarity in shape with an offset that shifts towards higher head sagittal inclination angles (see Fig. 6). As neck flexion angles are calculated from the differences of sagittal head

Table 2. p-values corrected with a Benjamini-Hochberg-procedure of all equivalency tests for EU = EL = 7.5°. Significant/similar values were marked in light gray. QXX is the XX% quantile, LL etc. are the box identifiers

Head sagittal inclination						
Tested parameter	LL	L	M	R	RR	overall
Q05	.99	.99	.99	.99	.99	.99
Q25	.99	.99	.99	.99	.99	.99
Q50	.99	.99	.99	.99	.99	.99
Q75	.99	.99	.99	.99	.99	.99
Q95	.96	.99	.99	.99	.79	.99
IQR	.02	<.01	.21	.01	.01	.23
Head lateral inclination						
Q05	.16	.11	<.001	<.001	<.001	<.001
Q25	.04	.04	<.001	<.001	<.001	<.001
Q50	<.01	.02	<.001	.01	<.01	<.001
Q75	<.001	.01	<.001	.04	.01	<.001
Q95	<.001	<.01	<.001	.12	.17	<.001
IQR	<.001	<.001	<.001	<.001	<.001	<.001
Neck flexion/extension						
Q05	.99	.99	.99	.99	.99	.99
Q25	.99	.99	.99	.99	.99	.99
Q50	.99	.99	.99	.99	.99	.99
Q75	.99	.99	.99	.99	.99	.99
Q95	.99	.99	.99	.99	.99	.99
IQR	.06	.01	.99	.99	.04	<.001
Thoracic spine sagittal inclination						
Q05	.03	.02	<.01	.02	<.01	<.01
Q25	.05	.05	.01	.09	.03	.03
Q50	.19	.26	.02	.37	.07	.03
Q75	.56	.66	.02	.80	.34	.02
Q95	.78	.75	.04	.94	.56	.07
IQR	.03	<.01	<.001	<.01	.06	<.01
Thoracic spine lateral inclination						
Q05	<.001	<.001	<.001	<.01	<.001	<.001
Q25	<.001	<.001	<.001	<.001	<.001	<.001
Q50	<.001	<.001	<.001	<.001	<.001	<.001
Q75	<.001	<.001	<.01	<.001	<.01	<.001
Q95	<.001	<.001	<.001	<.001	<.01	<.001
IQR	<.001	<.001	<.001	<.001	<.001	<.001
Back flexion/extension						
Q05	<.001	<.001	<.01	<.001	<.01	<.01
Q25	<.001	<.001	.03	<.001	<.01	.12
Q50	<.001	<.001	.04	<.001	<.01	.12
Q75	<.001	<.001	.02	<.01	<.01	.23
Q95	<.001	<.01	.19	<.01	<.01	.12
IQR	<.001	<.001	<.001	<.001	<.001	<.001

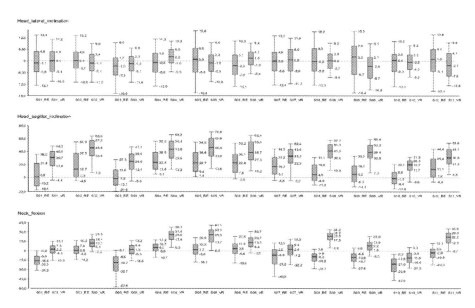

Fig. 6. Depiction of all participants' joint angle data for the complete task setup, shown in pairs for physical and digital mockup. Top to bottom: Head sagittal inclination, Head lateral inclination, Neck flexion

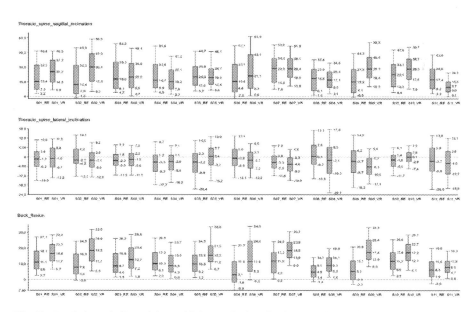

Fig. 7. Depiction of all participants' joint angle data for the complete task setup, shown in pairs for physical and digital mockup. Top to bottom: Thoracic spine sagittal inclination, Thoracic spine lateral inclination, Back flexion

and thoracic spine inclination angles, these differences can also be observed in the frequency distributions of neck flexion angles. Our observations of the subjects working in VR revealed that they are more frequently looking at their hands when performing the picks. Better haptics controllers or the provision of visual feedback for the subjects could resolve this problem and should definitely be considered if neck and head postures are important for the specific workload analysis. Increasing the field of view of the HMDs would also improve the subjects oversight in the VR environment, thus giving them more control.

6 Conclusion

In this study, we have shown to which extent spine and head postures are similar or dissimilar when performing workload analyses both in VR and on physical mockups. Our results imply that analyzing postures connected to head and neck movements show similar patterns. However, the results should be handled with care due to systemic errors caused by the limited overview and the missing haptics in the VR environment. We found that most notably lateral movements and ranges of movements are very similar under all tested circumstances. Future studies have to investigate the question if a precision of $\pm 5°$ to $\pm 7.5°$ per joint angle is of sufficient accuracy for ergonomic analyses in VR. We believe most of the critical issues we have just discussed will be resolved in the near future by the rapid development of novel VR equipment introducing for instance additional features like Realtime-VR-ready motion capturing devices. Taking into account the high flexibility and the cost-efficiency our study supports the point of view that VR-HMDs have the potential to become a *real* alternative to physical mockups for ergonomic workload analysis.

References

1. Glitsch, U., Ottersbach, H.J., Ellegast, R., Schaub, K., Franz, G., Jaeger, M.: Physical workload of flight attendants when pushing and pulling trolleys aboard aircraft. Int. J. Ind. Ergon. **37**(11/12), 845–854 (2007)
2. Mukhopadhyay, S., Das, S.K., Chakraborty, T.: Computer aided design in digital human modeling for human computer interaction in ergonomic assessment: a review. Int. J. Adv. Comput. Res. **2**(4), 130–138 (2012)
3. Tian, R., Duffy, V.G.: Computerized task risk assessment using digital human modeling based job risk classification model. Comput. Ind. Eng. **61**(4), 1044–1052 (2011)
4. Sacks, R., Perlman, A., Barak, R.: Construction safety training using immersive virtual reality. Constr. Manag. Econ. **31**(9), 1005–1017 (2013)
5. Ellegast, R., Hermanns, I., Schiefer, C.: Workload assessment in field using the ambulatory CUELA system. In: Duffy, V.G. (ed.) ICDHM 2009. LNCS, vol. 5620, pp. 221–226. Springer, Heidelberg (2009). https://doi.org/10.1007/978-3-642-02809-0_24
6. Hoffman, H.: Virtual-reality therapy. Sci. Am. **291**, 58–65 (2004)
7. North, M., North, S., Coble, J.: Virtual reality therapy: an effective treatment for psychological disorders. In: Virtual Reality in Neuro-Psycho-Physiology, pp. 59–70. IOS Press (1997)

8. Powers, M., Emmelkamp, P.: Virtual reality exposure therapy for anxiety disorders: a meta-analysis. J. Anxiety Disord. **22**, 561–569 (2007)
9. Parsons, T., Rizzo, A.: Affective outcomes of virtual reality exposure therapy for anxiety and specific phobias: a meta-analysis. J. Behav. Ther. Exp. Psychiatry **39**(3), 250–261 (2006)
10. McCloy, R., Stone, R.: Science, medicine, and the future: virtual reality in surgery. Br. Med. J. **323**, 912–915 (2001)
11. Haluck, R., Krummel, T.: Computers and virtual reality for surgical education in the 21st century. Arch. Surg. **135**, 786–792 (2000)
12. Seymour, N., Gallagher, A., Roman, S., O'Brien, M., Bansal, V., Andersen, D., Satava, R.: Virtual reality training improves operating room performance. Ann. Surg. **236**, 458–463 (2002)
13. Whitman, L.E., Jorgensen, M., Hathiyari, K., Malzahn, D.: Virtual reality: its usefulness for ergonomic analysis. In: Proceedings of the Winter Simulation Conference, Washington, D. C., pp. 1740–1745 (2004)
14. Pontonnier, C., Samani, A., Badawi, M., Madeleine, P., Dumont, G.: Assessing the ability of a VR-based assembly task simulation to evaluate physical risk factors. IEEE Trans. Vis. Comput. Graph. **20**, 664–674 (2013)
15. Delleman, N.J., Dul, J.: Internaational standards on working postures and movements ISO 11226 and EN 1005-4. Ergonomics **50**, 1809–1819 (2007)
16. Friemert, D., Ellegast, R., Hartmann, U.: Data glasses for picking workplaces. In: Nah, F.F.-H., Tan, C.-H. (eds.) HCIBGO 2016. LNCS, vol. 9752, pp. 281–289. Springer, Cham (2016). https://doi.org/10.1007/978-3-319-39399-5_27
17. Mara, C.A., Cribbie, R.: Paired-samples tests of equivalence. Commun. Stat.- Simul. Comput. **41**(10), 1928–1943 (2012)
18. Schuirmann, D.L.: On hypothesis testing to determine if the mean of a normal distribution is contained in a known interval. Biometrics **37**, 617 (1981)
19. Benjamini, Y., Hochberg, Y.: Controlling the false discovery rate: a practical and powerful approach to multiple testing. J. Roy. Stat. Soc. Ser. B **57**, 289–300 (1995)

A Growth Study of Chinese Ears
Using 3D Scanning

Fang Fu, Yan Luximon[✉], and Parth Shah

School of Design, The Hong Kong Polytechnic University,
Kowloon, Hong Kong SAR
yan.luximon@polyu.edu.hk

Abstract. Ears are important organs considering facial aesthetics and auditory function. Anthropometric data of ears can help in understanding the morphology, which can further be applied in medical and ergonomic research. The purpose of this study is to evaluate the variation of four selected ear dimensions along with other parameters such as gender, age and ear symmetry with the use of 3D scanned data. Sixty Chinese children (30 males and 30 females) aged 5 to 13 years were invited for the study. They were divided into three groups based on the age. Four dimensions (ear length, ear width, width from tragus to antihelix, and flipping angle from the base of the head to the helix) were measured for both ears from the point clouds data acquired from the 3D scans. Statistical analyses were performed to measure the growth and characteristics of ears' morphology. These results provide a better understanding of variation in ear morphology based on different demographic parameters. In addition, this research would assist in providing some basic 3D anthropometric data of ears for Chinese children, which can be helpful in deciding sizing, and grading parameters of ear related products for children.

Keywords: Growth study · Ear morphology · 3D scanning · Anthropometry
Ergonomics

1 Introduction

Ears play a very crucial role in facial aesthetics as well as auditory capability of an individual. With the physical growth and development of an individual, the morphology and the shape of ears changes along with the body shape. The understanding of dynamic changes in the ear morphology and shape along with age can be of great use for anthropometric research, medical research and product design applications. Hence, it is very important to understand the growth pattern of ear.

Various researchers have tried to conduct ear growth studies on different populations, such as Turkish [1], American [2], Italian [3], and Japanese [4]. As for Chinese population, growth studies have concentrated on height, weight and sexual maturity of the whole body mainly [5–7], whereas there is hardly any growth study focusing on ear morphology. Previous study has shown that the ear growth pattern may vary based on ethnic group and sociocultural environment [1]. Therefore, there is a need for such

© Springer International Publishing AG, part of Springer Nature 2018
V. G. Duffy (Ed.): DHM 2018, LNCS 10917, pp. 54–63, 2018.
https://doi.org/10.1007/978-3-319-91397-1_5

anthropometric study to be conducted on Chinese population to understand the change in ear's morphology.

To measure ear dimensions, researchers have widely used traditional measurement techniques, like using calipers [8] and scales [9]. Researchers have also used 2D data acquired from images to obtain the ear dimensions [10]. However, the selected dimensions in these studies were very restricted due to the complex structure of human ear [9] and the variety among different individuals [11]. Development of 3D scanning technology has provided a new opportunity for ear related anthropometric research. 3D scanning is now being used to acquire the 3D point cloud for part of human body [12, 13], and there are several applications of specific 3D scanning devices available [14]. This technology can provide highly accurate information which can help in analysis of shape variance as compared to traditional measuring techniques [15]. Some researchers have tried to use 3D scanning for ear related research [16–18], but still there is a huge need for research in this area, as with the advancements in technology it has been made easier to acquire accurate data even with the complexity in ear's contour.

The main aim of this study was to explore the variation in different morphological features of ear and deduce their relationship with parameters like gender, age and symmetry with the use of 3D scanning, which could in turn help in understanding the growth of external ears in Chinese children.

2 Methods

2.1 Participants

Sixty Chinese children (30 males and 30 females) within the age range of 5 to 13 years were invited to participate in this study. The participants were further divided into 3 groups equally: 5 to 7 years of age (Group 1), 8 to 10 years of age (Group 2), and 11 to 13 years of age (Group 3). Each group had equal amount (10) of male and female participants. The demographic description of the participants is shown in Table 1.

Table 1. The demographic information of the population in this study.

		Group 1 (N = 20)	Group 2 (N = 20)	Group 3 (N = 20)
Height (cm)	Male	116.75 ± 6.57	138.83 ± 4.06	158.11 ± 9.30
	Female	110.51 ± 6.58	138.35 ± 10.83	152.07 ± 7.79
Weight (kg)	Male	18.72 ± 1.79	33.75 ± 9.45	46.45 ± 10.15
	Female	20.56 ± 4.29	36.59 ± 9.62	46.00 ± 10.71

2.2 Procedure

An informed consent form was signed by the participant before conducting the 3D scanning procedure. Since 3D scanners cannot scan hair accurately, participants were made to wear a specifically designed latex cap [12]. Also to avoid head movements during the scanning process, a head rest was used, where the participants were made to rest their chin. 3D scanning was performed by using a handheld Artec Eva 3D scanner with an accuracy of 0.1 mm. A point cloud data of the head including the ear region was captured for each participant as shown in Fig. 1.

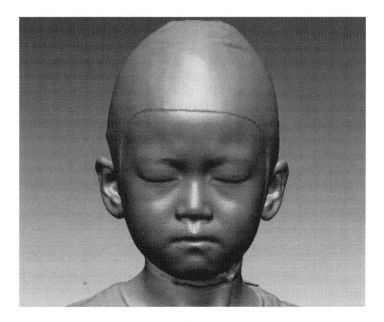

Fig. 1. A point cloud of the children head including the ear region.

Seven landmarks were selected on the surfaces of the 3D scanning model using Rapidform 2006 software. Four anthropometric dimensions were calculated based on the positions of the selected reference points. The landmarks and measurements are indicated in Fig. 2. The landmarks include (1) Superaurale, (2) Subaurale, (3) Postaurale, (4) Preaurale, (5) Lobule anterior, (6) Tragus, and (7) Strongest antihelical curvature. The dimensions involve (EL) ear length from superaurale to subaurale; (W_1) ear width from postaurale to the ear base line; (W_2) the width from tragus to the strongest antihelical curvature; and (FA) flipping angle from the base of the head to helix.

2.3   Data Analysis

Statistical analysis was performed to systematically analyze the acquired data using SPSS 20.0 software. A within group descriptive statistical analysis was performed to evaluate the mean values and standard deviations of all the measured anthropometric dimensions. Correlation analysis was conducted to understand the relationships between measured anthropometric dimensions and other demographic parameters, such as age, gender, symmetry, body height and weight. Paired t-test was used to understand the influence of right left symmetry on the dimensions. Two-sample t-test was used to determine the existence of gender based effects on the measured values. One-way ANOVA was performed between groups to examine the differences of the measurements of the three age groups for both the ears separately.

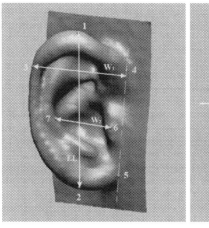 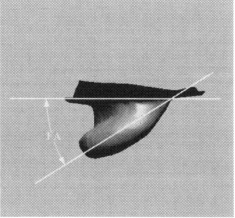

(a) Front view of the right ear;   (b) Top view of the right ear.

Fig. 2. Landmarks and measurements on the right ear.

3   Results

Tables 2, 3 and 4 provide general statistical description about all the measured dimensions under variables of gender, age and ear symmetry, respectively.

Table 2. General description of the dimensions for different gender groups (mm).

			Mean	Standard deviation	95% Confidence interval	
					Lower	Upper
EL	Right ear	Male	57.02	3.88	55.55	58.50
		Female	53.13	3.28	51.88	54.38
	Left ear	Male	56.90	3.23	55.67	58.13
		Female	53.86	3.29	52.61	55.12
W_1	Right ear	Male	33.90	2.31	33.02	34.78
		Female	31.84	2.22	31.00	32.68
	Left ear	Male	33.68	2.79	32.62	34.75
		Female	31.68	2.68	30.66	32.69
W_2	Right ear	Male	19.68	1.60	19.07	20.29
		Female	18.41	1.84	17.71	19.11
	Left ear	Male	19.46	2.02	18.69	20.23
		Female	18.85	1.84	18.15	19.55
FA	Right ear	Male	31.19	6.25	28.85	33.52
		Female	28.96	5.85	26.78	31.15
	Left ear	Male	32.09	7.80	29.17	35.00
		Female	30.99	6.76	28.46	33.51

Table 3. General description of the dimensions for different age groups (mm).

			Mean	Standard deviation	95% Confidence interval	
					Lower	Upper
EL	Right ear	Group 1	52.53	2.89	51.18	53.89
		Group 2	55.80	3.77	53.98	57.61
		Group 3	57.03	4.20	55.00	59.05
	Left ear	Group 1	53.32	3.02	51.91	54.73
		Group 2	55.79	3.04	54.33	57.25
		Group 3	57.14	3.68	55.37	58.91
W_1	Right ear	Group 1	31.92	2.24	30.87	32.96
		Group 2	33.15	2.58	31.90	34.39
		Group 3	33.60	2.40	32.44	34.75
	Left ear	Group 1	31.68	2.73	30.40	32.95
		Group 2	32.95	3.01	31.50	34.41
		Group 3	33.46	2.78	32.12	34.80
W_2	Right ear	Group 1	18.77	1.27	18.18	19.37
		Group 2	19.70	2.14	18.67	20.73
		Group 3	18.69	1.90	17.77	19.60
	Left ear	Group 1	19.21	1.79	18.37	20.05
		Group 2	19.59	2.04	18.61	20.57
		Group 3	18.66	1.99	17.71	19.62
FA	Right ear	Group 1	29.76	5.53	27.17	32.35
		Group 2	29.64	6.44	26.63	32.65
		Group 3	30.83	6.54	27.77	33.90
	Left ear	Group 1	30.96	7.50	27.45	34.47
		Group 2	31.42	5.93	28.64	34.19
		Group 3	32.23	8.44	28.28	36.19

Table 4. General description of the dimensions for right left symmetry (mm).

		Mean	Standard deviation	95% Confidence interval	
				Lower	Upper
EL	Right ear	57.02	3.88	55.55	58.50
	Left ear	53.13	3.28	51.88	54.38
W_1	Right ear	33.90	2.31	33.02	34.78
	Left ear	31.84	2.22	31.00	32.68
W_2	Right ear	19.68	1.60	19.07	20.29
	Left ear	18.41	1.84	17.71	19.11
FA	Right ear	30.08	6.11	28.50	31.65
	Left ear	31.54	7.26	29.66	33.41

Table 5. Correlation coefficients of morphological symmetry between the two ears.

	EL (right ear)	W_1 (right ear)	W_2 (right ear)	FA (right ear)
EL (left ear)	0.907**			
W_1 (left ear)		0.739**		
W_2 (left ear)			0.729**	
FA (left ear)				0.754**

**. $p < 0.01$; *. $p < 0.05$.

The correlation results in Table 5 suggested that there were strong relationships between right and left ear for all the measured dimensions. The correlation coefficients between the measured variables on each ear are separately presented in Tables 6 and 7. The correlation analysis showed that there were statistically significant relationships among dimension EL, W_1, W_2, body height and body weight, while dimension FA had little significant relationship with other variables. Considering the correlation coefficient values, there were significantly strong relationships between EL and W_1, between W_1 and W_2, between EL and body height, between EL and body weight, and between EL and age for both right and left ears, while the relationships between W_1 and body height, between W_1 and body weight, between W_1 and age were relatively weak with significance for both ears. It was also found that there were some relationships between EL and W_2 on right ear, W_1 and FA on right ear, as well as between EL and FA on left ear, but there was no significant relationship for the same dimensions on the opposite ear.

Table 6. Correlation coefficients between the dimensions on right ear.

	EL (right ear)	W_1 (right ear)	W_2 (right ear)	FA (right ear)
W_1 (right ear)	0.504**			
W_2 (right ear)	0.343**	0.580*		
FA (right ear)	0.190	−0.289*	−0.174	
Body height	0.512**	0.367**	0.093	0.129
Body weight	0.475**	0.308*	0.132	0.087
Age	0.445**	0.273*	0.014	0.098

**. $p < 0.01$; *. $p < 0.05$.

Table 7. Correlation coefficients between the dimensions for left ear.

	EL (left ear)	W_1 (left ear)	W_2 (left ear)	FA (left ear)
W_1 (left ear)	0.522**			
W_2 (left ear)	0.191	0.452**		
FA (left ear)	0.266*	−0.223	−0.212	
Body height	0.535**	0.338**	−0.050	0.078
Body weight	0.479**	0.290*	−0.114	0.015
Age	0.440**	0.326*	−0.142	0.066

**. $p < 0.01$; *p. < 0.05.

The results of paired t-test for the anthropometric dimensions under the variable of right left symmetry for are shown in Table 8. From the results, there was no significant difference between right and left ear on EL, W_1 and W_2. Only FA on right ear was significantly smaller than left ear.

Table 8. Comparison of the dimensions between left and right sides of ear.

	Mean difference[a]	Standard error	t	df	p
EL	−0.33	0.22	−1.52	59	0.14
W_1	0.12	0.25	0.50	59	0.62
W_2	−0.09	0.18	−0.51	59	0.61
FA	−1.46	0.62	−2.53	59	0.02*

*. $p < 0.05$
Mean difference[a] = mean on right ear − mean on left ear

Table 9 demonstrates the results of two-sample T-test for which gender was independent variable and anthropometric dimensions were dependent variables. It was indicated that gender had significant effects on the mean values of EL and W_1 for both ears. Dimension EL and W_1 were greater for males than females for both the ears. Dimension W_2 on right ear was significantly larger for males as compared to females, whereas there was no significant difference between both the genders for dimension W_2 of left ear. For dimension FA, there was unclear difference between males and females for both ears.

Table 9. Comparison of the dimensions between male and female.

		Mean difference[b]	Standard error	t	df	p
EL	Right ear	3.81	0.91	4.17	58	0.00*
	Left ear	2.17	0.59	3.47	58	0.00*
W_1	Right ear	1.21	0.44	3.65	58	0.00*
	Left ear	2.85	1.46	2.94	58	0.01*
W_2	Right ear	2.90	0.84	2.75	58	0.01*
	Left ear	2.05	0.70	1.01	58	0.32
FA	Right ear	2.23	1.56	1.42	58	0.16
	Left ear	1.10	1.88	0.58	58	0.56

*. $p < 0.05$
Mean difference[b] = mean of male − mean of female

The results of one-way ANOVA revealed the differences of the mean values of all the dimension among the three age groups as shown in Table 10. It showed the existence of statistical significant difference amongst the three age groups of dimension EL for both sides of ears, while different age groups had no statistically significant influence on dimension W_1, W_2 and FA. Specifically, Table 11 compares the differences of dimension

Table 10. Comparison of the dimensions among age groups.

		F	df^c	p
EL	Right ear	8.232	(2, 57)	0.001*
	Left ear	7.206	(2, 57)	0.002*
W$_1$	Right ear	2.203	(2, 57)	0.120
	Left ear	2.045	(2, 57)	0.139⁻
W$_2$	Right ear	1.955	(2, 57)	0.151
	Left ear	1.427	(2, 57)	0.248
FA	Right ear	0.227	(2, 57)	0.798
	Left ear	0.153	(2, 57)	0.858

*. $p < 0.05$
df^c = (df(Between Groups), df(Within Groups))

Table 11. Comparison of dimension EL among age groups.

		Mean difference	Standard error	p
EL (right ear)	Group 1–Group 2	−3.22	1.13	0.017*
	Group 1–Group 3	−4.46	1.13	0.001*
	Group 2–Group 3	−1.24	1.13	0.521
EL (left ear)	Group 1–Group 2	−2.54	1.01	0.040*
	Group 1–Group 3	−3.77	1.01	0.001*
	Group 2–Group 3	−1.23	1.01	0.448

*. $p < 0.05$.

EL between every age group. For both ears, dimension EL for Group 1 was significantly less than Group 2 and Group 3, while there was no significant difference between Group 2 and Group 3.

4 Conclusion and Discussion

Growth study about human ear provides a better understanding of the ear morphological changes which can be helpful for product design and medical applications. Previous ear growth studies have been performed on different populations [2, 3], but there are very few studies conducted on Chinese population. Hence, it is important to conduct similar research so as to help in better generalization and standardization of Chinese ear dimensions.

Previous studies [8, 19] indicated that male had significantly greater ear length and ear width than female in Turkish, Malaysian and Indian. Also in the current study, it was observed that ear length (EL) and ear width (W$_1$) for male were significantly greater than female for Chinese. Even though the relationships between right and left ear for ear length and width were similarly strong, the characteristics about the ear symmetry for different populations were not exactly the same [9, 20]. For Chinese population, a strong association between left and right side was found with coefficient of 0.91 in ear length (EL), 0.74 in ear width (W_1), 0.73 in ear width from the tragus to antihelix (W_2), and 0.76 in flipping angle from the base of the head to helix (FA), but no significant differences between the ear symmetry were discovered for all the dimensions in this study.

Liu [9] revealed that there was a weak association between ear length and body height among adults. Moreover, in this study, ear length (EL) appeared to be strongly related to body height, body weight and age, while ear width (W_1) had relatively weak relationships with these parameters. According to previous research [1, 2], there were continuous increments in ear length and width until the age of 18 years, and the growth rates became mild after certain ages with short period of no significant growth. In this study, the results were consistent with the past research. For both ears, there was a significant growth on ear length (EL) from group 1 to group 2 as well as from group 1 to group 3, but the increasing from group 2 to group 3 is not significant. Hence, the results showed that the ear length grew fast at earlier age and would turn slower after that. As to ear width (W_1) and the flipping angle (FA), the mean values were found to be increasing moderately without any significant differences from group 1, group 2 to group 3. Thus, the ear width and flipping angle were mildly growing. However, the width from the tragus to antihelix (W_2) was relatively stable without any trend of increase or decrease.

This study provides basic information about ear growth patterns for Chinese population. Based on these results, further studies can be conducted using large sample size which can help in better generalization of ear dimensions, which can help in understanding ear growth. This data can be very helpful for product design and medical application.

Acknowledgments. The research is funded by Hong Kong RGC/GRF project B-Q57F and Departmental General Research Fund of the Hong Kong Polytechnic University.

References

1. Kalcioglu, M.T., Miman, M.C., Toplu, Y., Yakinci, C., Ozturan, O.: Anthropometric growth study of normal human auricle. Int. J. Pediatr. Otorhinolaryngol. **67**(11), 1169–1177 (2003)
2. Farkas, L.G., Posnick, J.C., Hreczko, T.M.: Anthropometric growth study of the ear. Cleft Palate-Craniofac. J. **29**(4), 324–329 (1992)
3. Sforza, C., Grandi, G., Binelli, M., Tommasi, D.G., Rosati, R., Ferrario, V.F.: Age-and sex-related changes in the normal human ear. Forensic Sci. Int. **187**(1), 110.e1–110.e7 (2009)
4. Igarashi, M., Kajii, T.: Normal values for physical parameters of the head, face and hand in Japanese children. J. Hum. Genet. **33**(1), 9–31 (1988)
5. Leung, S.S.F., Lau, J.T.F., Xu, Y.Y., Tse, L.Y., Huen, K.F., Wong, G.W.K., Law, W.Y., Yeung, V.T.F., Yeung, W.K.Y., Leung, N.K.: Secular changes in standing height, sitting height and sexual maturation of Chinese—the Hong Kong growth study, 1993. Ann. Hum. Biol. **23**(4), 297–306 (1996)
6. Leung, S.S., Cole, T.J., Tse, L.Y., Lau, J.T.F.: Body mass index reference curves for Chinese children. Ann. Hum. Biol. **25**(2), 169–174 (1998)

7. Li, H., Ji, C.Y., Zong, X.N., Zhang, Y.Q.: Height and weight standardized growth charts for Chinese children and adolescents aged 0 to 18 years. Chin. J. Pediatr. **47**(7), 487–492 (2009)
8. Kumar, B.S., Selvi, G.P.: Morphometry of ear pinna in sex determination. Int. J. Anat. Res. **4**(2), 2480–2484 (2016)
9. Liu, B.S.: Incorporating anthropometry into design of ear-related products. App. Ergon. **39**(1), 115–121 (2008)
10. Liu, B.S., Tseng, H.Y., Chia, T.C.: Reliability of external ear measurements obtained by direct, photocopier scanning and photo anthropometry. Ind. Eng. Manag. Syst. **9**(1), 20–27 (2010)
11. Alvord, L.S., Farmer, B.L.: Anatomy and orientation of the human external ear. J.-Am. Acad. Audiol. **8**, 383–390 (1997)
12. Luximon, Y., Ball, R., Justice, L.: The 3D Chinese head and face modeling. Comput.-Aided Des. **44**(1), 40–47 (2012)
13. Zheng, R., Yu, W., Fan, J.: Development of a new Chinese bra sizing system based on breast anthropometric measurements. Int. J. Ind. Ergon. **37**(8), 697–705 (2007)
14. Shah, Parth B., Luximon, Yan: Review on 3D scanners for head and face modeling. In: Duffy, Vincent G. (ed.) DHM 2017. LNCS, vol. 10286, pp. 47–56. Springer, Cham (2017). https://doi.org/10.1007/978-3-319-58463-8_5
15. Kaushal, N., Kaushal, P.: Human earprints: a review. J. Biom. Biostat. **2**(129) (2011). https://doi.org/10.4172/2155-6180.1000129
16. Azouz, Z.B., Rioux, M., Shu, C., Lepage, R.: Characterizing human shape variation using 3D anthropometric data. Vis. Comput. **22**(5), 302–314 (2006)
17. Luximon, Y., Martin, N.J., Ball, R., Zhang, M.: Merging the point clouds of the head and ear by using the iterative closest point method. Int. J. Dig. Hum. **1**(3), 305–317 (2016)
18. Lee, W., Jung, H., Bok, I., Kim, C., Kwon, O., Choi, T., You, H.: Measurement and application of 3D ear images for earphone design. In: Proceedings of the Human Factors and Ergonomics Society Annual Meeting, vol. 60, pp. 1053–1057. SAGE Publications, Los Angeles (2016)
19. Barut, C., Aktunc, E.: Anthropometric measurements of the external ear in a group of Turkish primary school students. Aesthet. Plast. Surg. **30**(2), 255–259 (2006)
20. Ferrario, V.F., Sforza, C., Ciusa, V., Serrao, G., Tartaglia, G.M.: Morphometry of the normal human ear: a cross-sectional study from adolescence to mid-adulthood. J. Craniofac. Genet. Dev. Biol. **19**(4), 226–233 (1999)

Research on Ergonomics Design of the Height and Operation Force for Furniture Lockset

Huimin Hu[1], Yahui Bai[2], Yinxia Li[2(✉)], Haimei Wu[1],
Ling Luo[1], Rui Wang[1], and Pu Hong[2]

[1] Ergonomics Laboratory China, National Institute of Standardization, Beijing, China
{huhm,wuhm,luoling,wangrui}@cnis.gov.cn
[2] School of Mechanical Engineering, Zhengzhou University, Zhengzhou, Henan, China
1298687634@qq.com, liyxmail@126.com, 15090566727@163.com

Abstract. This study investigated the comfortable lockset height and the suitable force to open it. The experiment was designed and carried out with 14 participants. The data were measured by varied experimental tools. The factors that influence the comfort of lockset height such as the angle and body dimensions were analyzed. The results showed that the preferred/comfortable lockset height was below shoulder in 60 cm. The differences between male and female on comfortable force and maximum force were found. The capacity difference between male and male were significant, but the perception in comfort was almost unanimous. According to Chinese anthropometry data and ergonomics knowledge, the comfortable lockset height and the comfortable opening force were recommended.

Keywords: Lockset · Height · Force · Torques · Anthropometry · Ergonomics

1 Introduction

As one of the appliances to maintain the normal life and work, furniture appeared and developed by human, which can not only comfort daily life but also improve the work efficiency. In order to make the furniture more suitable for modern life, ergonomics need to be considered during the furniture design.

Ergonomics has been widely used in the field of furniture design. Lee and Merzenich [1] find that the anthropometric differences between the Turkish students and other nations by measuring 13 body dimensions of 1049 students with the standing posture and sitting posture. The data can be used to determine the limit values of designing classroom and laboratory design. Deros, Mohamad et al. [2] found that by using the anthropometric data of 1007 Malaysian respondents' physical body parts, the furniture would fit, appropriate, comfortable to at least 90% of the Malaysian population with respect to ergonomics, which helps to reduce the risks of injuries and pains among Malaysian home furniture users. Taifa and Desai [3] came up with exhaustive dimensions for designing adjustable classrooms furniture by collecting and analysing the health status of all students who have been using poorly designed furniture. The recommend furniture dimensions will help to create comfortability, safety, well-being, suitability, reduce Musculoskeletal disorders, and improve performance of students in terms

© Springer International Publishing AG, part of Springer Nature 2018
V. G. Duffy (Ed.): DHM 2018, LNCS 10917, pp. 64–74, 2018.
https://doi.org/10.1007/978-3-319-91397-1_6

of attentiveness. Hrovatin and Prekrat et al. [4]. used 3D modelling technology to simulate the optical depth and the height of storage capacities, and then provided advices for designing kitchen furniture that would meet the needs of the elderly based on the measurement analysis.

Most of the research used the anthropometry as the principle to guild the furniture design, furthermore, the anthropometry data are distinct differences between different areas. In China, the anthropometry and ergonomics were also widely used in the design of variety products, including furniture, vehicles and communal facilities, which has been improving the living quality. The domestic relevant researches were also significant for this study. Ai-ping, Xin, Guang et al. [5]. recommended the ergonomics value of the height shelf height of home bookshelf by using the VICON and JACK combined with the subjective evaluation, where the anthropometry are necessary for the conclusions.

The major aim of this study was to find the preferred lockset height and the force of opening the lockset, which can satisfy the ergonomic requirements when using the lockset. By using the BTE (Baltimore Therapeutic Equipment), the typical customer's preferred lockset height and force were collected and analyzed and then, the results provided a reference for the design of furniture lockset height and comfortable opening force.

2 Methods

2.1 Experimental Design

The experiment was designed to collect the data of opening the lockset. The comfort of lockset height, the elbow angle and shoulder angle, the comfortable and maximum opening force were measured and recorded simultaneously with changing the lockset's height. The lockset height was the only one factor that varied in the experiment, and the height varied from 60 cm to 170 cm, which included the comfortable control area on standing posture. The step size in this experiment was 10 cm, so there were 12 different experimental heights in all. Accordingly, the changes including angle, comfort score and force were collected in this research. By analyzing the relationships between the collected data, the correlation model may be established.

2.2 Subjects

The subjects were selected by taking into account of age, sex and body size. In this study, the subjects were 14 adults, right-handed, with ages ranging between 20 and 40 (M = 27, SD = 5) and heights varying from 152 cm to 180 cm (M = 167, SD = 8). All had no physical disability and they were evenly composed of men and women.

2.3   Apparatus

The BTE Primus RS was used to change the lockset height and collect the force when opening the lockset. which can give the power of objectivity and then capture the real-time data. All the main components of BTE Primus RS system were shown in Fig. 1 and the 202 tool was used as the key in this study. This system provided the device that can change the height of lockset, and the information about force can also be seen on the display. With the help of other tools like angular instrument and Martin measuring ruler, the data can be collected completely.

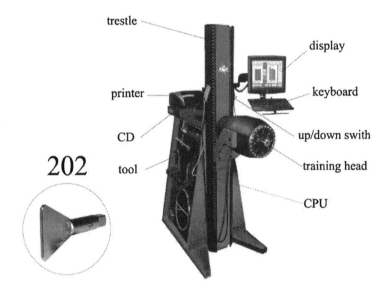

Fig. 1.   Components of BTE primus RS

2.4   Task and Procedure

The experimenter need to collect the basic anthropometry data of subjects, including height, weight and shoulder height. Each subject was required to take part in the following steps with the help of experimenters:

(1) Understand the basic purpose and process of the experiment;
(2) Stand his/her best comfortable distance from 100 cm away to the lockset when the tester adjusted the height of lockset by using the elevator mechanism of BTE;
(3) Open the lockset with a natural and comfortable posture with the elbow naturally drooping and unable to deviate inward or outward from the body excessively. Figure 2 shows the experiment scene. Meanwhile, the angles of shoulder and elbow were also recorded;
(4) Evaluate the comfort of locket height according to the comfort of shoulder and elbow by using the 7 levels subjective score, see Table 1;

(5) Open the lockset by using a comfortable force that the subject expected 3 times and the equipment can record the data. Likewise, use the maximum force to open the lockset after rest;

(6) Take a rest and then prepare for the next experimental height.

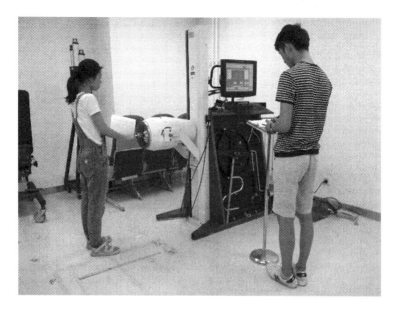

Fig. 2. Experimental scene

Table 1. 7 levels subjective score

1	2	3	4	5	6	7
Very uncomfortable	Uncomfortable	Less comfortable	General	More comfortable	Comfortable	Very comfortable

3 Data Analysis and Results

3.1 The Lockset Height

In this experiment, each subject gave a score about the comfort of different locket height and a total of 168 scores were collected from all the 14 subjects. At the same time, the angle of elbow and shoulder were also recorded to research the main factors that influence the comfort. Figure 3 shows the shoulder angle, where 1 to 14 represent the number of the subjects. It can be seen in the diagram, with the lockset height increasing from 60 cm to 180 cm, the angle of shoulder decreases firstly to the minimum at around 90 to 100 cm and then rises steadily. For certain height, for example, at the height of 120 cm. the shoulder angles of all subjects are totally different, which varies from 10° to 60°.

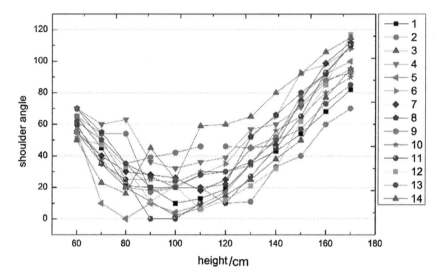

Fig. 3. Shoulder angle distribution on each height

Likewise, the elbow angle distribution is shown in Fig. 4, where the 1 to 14 represent the number of all subjects. In general, the elbow angle decreases to the minimum at 120 cm to 140 cm and then growing at a slow rate in the diagram. The changing trend is obviously the same for each subject, but the value of each subject was totally different at the same height.

The aim of this experiment in this part was to find the factors that may influence the comfort of lockset height. The arm is the main actor and the shoulder is the starting point during the movement of opening the lockset. The angle of elbow and shoulder will change when the lockset was at different heights However, the increment of angle was difficult to measurement and the variation trend was kind of different when the height of lockset changing. What's more, the comfortable angle was totally different for each subject. Figure 5 shows the range of elbow and shoulder angle when the sore was over 4, which shows that the statues of the arm with these angles was comfortable. It is a wide range and the distribution is even, which means the angle cannot be used to design the comfort height of lockset. There is a variation tendency that the range gets narrowed with the score increasing. It was difficult to find a regular pattern by using the elbow and shoulder angle. But the changing trend can be used for further research.

However, the correlation between lockset height and the subject height was more significant. The height of 14 subjects varied from 152 cm to 180 cm, so the relative position between the heights of lockset and each subject's shoulder was different.

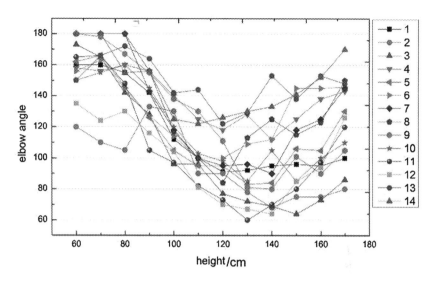

Fig. 4. Elbow angle distribution at each height

According to the movement of opening the lockset, the shoulder is the basic starting point. When the height of lockset changed in the experiment, the subject's shoulder was the original point. All the 14 subjects with different height can be put in one line by using the height of lockset from the subject's shoulders. In this study, the shoulder of each subject was seen as the original point, and the shoulder height minus the lockset height was the real variable, shown in Fig. 6.

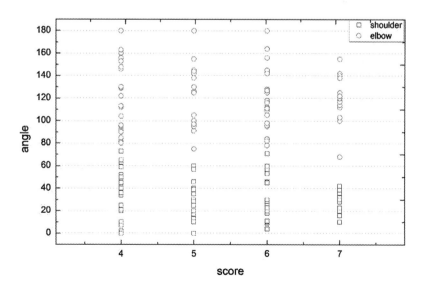

Fig. 5. The elbow and shoulder angle

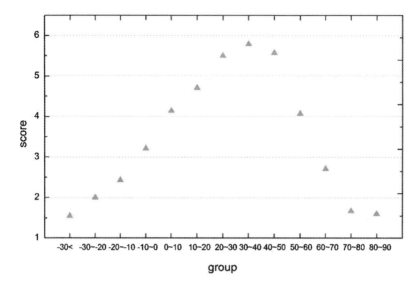

Fig. 6. The score distribution

The range of lockset height from the subject's shoulder was between -45 cm to 88 cm, which can be divide into 13 groups: −30<, −30~−20, −20~−10, …, 70~80, 80~90. Each group had an average score of the comfort of locket height, and the distribution of the score was shown in Fig. 6. The scores of 13 groups are distributed in a nearly normal fashion, which is consistent with the actual situation that people may be uncomfortable when the lockset is over high or low. As is shown in the graph, the scores of groups 0~10, group 10~20, …, group 50~60 are over 4, which means the heights are acceptable; the scores of groups 20~30, group 30~40 and group 40~50 are over 5, which means the heights are more comfortable; the scores of other groups are less than 4, which means the heights are uncomfortable. Results showed that the acceptable comfortable height of lockset was below shoulder in 60 cm.

3.2 The Opening Force

Both the comfort force and maximum force were collected 3 times during the experiment. Figure 7 shows the maximum force on each height, where the 1 to 7 represent the number of male subjects and the others were females. According to the average maximum force in different height of 14 subjects, there was no obvious change trend between the maximum force and the heights. The fact is when the height increases the maximum force of the subjects mainly varied from 50 N to 250 N. For a group, the maximum force of subjects 1 to 7 are bigger than that of subjects 8 to 14, which means that males are more powerful than females. For individual, the maximum force on each height is almost the same and the variation is small. According to the mentioned analysis, the average maximum force of each height can represent his/her maximum force.

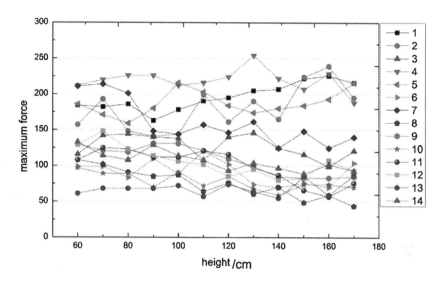

Fig. 7. Maximum force

The average maximum force of each subject is shown in Table 2. For male and female, the maximum force differences are significant and the maximum force of male is over female. The average maximum force of 7 males is 166 N and the 7 females is 92 N. The female maximum force is roughly half of male (55%). The data in the table shows the natural difference between male and female. The gender differences need to be considered during product design.

Table 2. Maximum force of different gender

| No. | Male | | | | | | | Female | | | | | | |
	1	2	3	4	5	6	7	8	9	10	11	12	13	14
Max force	196.3	179.7	127.9	219.8	187.1	91.4	159.9	74.6	108.0	78.1	100.0	105.4	68.1	107.1

The comfortable force on each height is shown in Fig. 8, where the variation on each height is lightly rambling in some line. It can be seen form the diagram, the comfortable force is mainly between 20 N~80 N, while some of the value was not stable. The changing trend shows that the comfortable force is irrelevant with the lockset height. For individuals, the comfortable force variation range is small, so the average comfortable force of 12 heights can represent all the subjects' comfortable force to open the lockset.

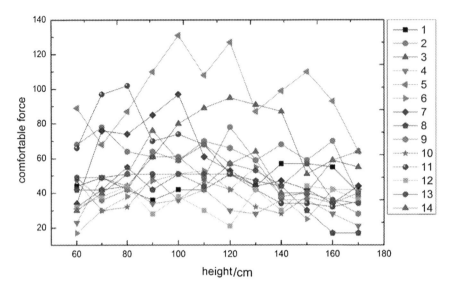

Fig. 8. Comfortable force

The average comfortable force in different height of 14 subjects is showing in Table 3, where the comfortable force is between 33.9 N to 97.7 N. The individual differences of comfort force was significant (M = 52, SD = 16.6), so the abnormal value need to be deleted when the value was lower 35.3 N or over 68.6 N [6]. The No. 4 33.9 N and No. 5 97.7 N were deleted. The average comfort force of male was 54.6 N, which was slightly over female with 46.2 N. The average of all subjects except two abnormal value was 49.7 N.

Table 3. Comfortable force of different gender

No.	Male									Female				
	1	2	3	4	5	6	7	8	9	10	11	12	13	14
Comfortable force	46.8	62.8	65.6	33.9	97.7	40.0	57.7	40.7	48.9	37.7	58.7	35.5	48.0	54.0

4   Discussion

4.1   The Acceptable Comfortable Lockset's Height

The comfortable height of lockset was below the shoulder in 60 cm, which can be used in the height design of lockset. The standard GB 1000-88 records 47 anthropometry data of different areas, including shoulder height [7]. The data of P5, P50, and P95 shoulder height of 18–60 years old is shown in Table 4. The comfortable lockset height can be calculated according to the anthropometry data and the experiment results.

Table 4. The shoulder height

	P5	P50	P95
Male	1281	1367	1455
Female	1195	1271	1350

When to satisfy at least 95% people, the shoulder height of P5 female is 1195 mm, adding 20 mm heel of shoes, so the upper limit of lockset height was 1215 mm. The shoulder height of P95 male is 1455 mm, adding 20 mm heel of shoes and deducting 600 mm, the lower limit of lockset was 875 mm. Finally, the rang of lockset height that satisfy 95% people should be 875 mm to 1215 mm from the floor.

Accordingly, we can get the small range, middle range and a large range that satisfy at least 5%, 50%, 95% respectively and the data is shown in Table 5. The recommended height value provides a reference for the ergonomic design of lockset height to satisfy the comfortable requirements.

Table 5. The comfortable range of lockset

Range	Lower limit	Upper limit
Small	877 mm	1202 mm
Middle	780 mm	1285 mm
Large	690 mm	1373 mm

4.2 The Comfortable Opening Force

For the maximum force of opening the lockset, the male was almost twice than female. For the comfortable force, the male was slightly over female. The capacity variance was caused by the gender difference, but it seems that the perception in comfortable was almost unanimous generally. The operation force is an important factor during the product design. If using the proper value in design, it can satisfy the need of most of the people.

In this study, the comfortable force result is around 50 N for all people. The diameter of the furniture key is around 20 mm, so the torque of opening the lockset was about 0.50 N.m, while the reference [8] said the torque should not over 0.65 N.m.

5   Conclusions

This study researched the two main factors that influence the user experience when opening the lockset. All the main factors were researched, and the results can be used in the furniture design to satisfy the ergonomics requirements. The comfort of product affected by many factors, and it is difficult to research all of them at the same time. It is proposed that the most important one should be set as the main object. The lockset height and the opening force were the main factors that influence the comfort of lockset, but they are also other factors, which depends on the real situations. There are some aspects which should be pay special attention during the experiment are as followed:

- The standard posture is necessary for different people during experiment;
- Enough rest is needed when it involves the maximum force;
- The multiple data acquisition is recommended during ergonomic experiment.

Furthermore, the experiment design can provide a reference for other study. The movement of opening key is familiar with the opening furniture by a pair of handles. The height design of handles can refer to the recommended lockset height though the objects are different. However, the results of this paper have certain limitations due to the difference of individuals and further verification experiment may be requisite.

Acknowledgement. This research is supported by 2017 National Quality Infrastructure (2017NQI) project *study on the key technology and standard for human-centred design and product user experience* (2017YFF0206603) and China National Institute of Standardization through the "special funds for the basic R&D undertakings by welfare research institutions" (522017Y-5278, 522016Y-4679, and 522015Y-3992).

References

1. Lee, C.C., Merzenich, M.M.: An analysis of biomechanical and anthropometric parameters on classroom furniture design. Afr. J. Biotechnol. **7**(8), 1081–1086 (2008)
2. Deros, B.M., Mohamad, D., Ismail, A.R., et al.: Application of malaysian anthropometric data in home furniture design (2009)
3. Taifa, I.W., Desai, D.A.: Anthropometric measurements for ergonomic design of students' furniture in india. Eng. Sci. Technol. Int. J. **20**(1), 232–239 (2016)
4. Hrovatin, J., Prekrat, S., Oblak, L., Ravnik, D.: Ergonomic suitability of kitchen furniture regarding height accessibility. Coll. Antropol. **39**(1), 185 (2014)
5. Ai-ping, Y., Xin, Z., Guang, C., et al.: Ergonomics Simulation of Furniture Structure Based on VICON and JACK. J. Ind. Eng. Manage. **18**(2), 136–140 (2013)
6. Chun-zhi, W., Qin, S.: A study of data statistical processing method of delphi method and its application. J. Inner Mongolia Univ. Financ. Econ. **09**(4), 92–96 (2011)
7. GB 1000-88. Human dimensions of Chinese adults
8. QB/T 1621-2015. Furniture lock

Study of Improving a Welfare Workplace by Surveying Good Standing Companies of Employment of People with Disabilities

Kanako Konno[1($\boxtimes$)] and Noriaki Kuwahara[2]

[1] Broadleaf Co., Ltd., Tokyo, Japan
kanako.konno@broadleaf.co.jp
[2] Kyoto Institute of Technology, Kyoto, Japan

Abstract. Employment of people with disabilities in companies and welfare facilities have been steadily increasing. However, welfare workshops usually have low productivity because of variation in abilities of welfare facility users. The authors consider ways to effectively standardize work with an analysis of a workshop for creating an environment where people with disabilities are able to work comfortably and maintain the production of quality products.

Keywords: Welfare workplace · Employment of people with disabilities

1 Introduction

Today, the number of employees with disabilities in domestic companies has reached record highs for the past 13 consecutive years. Moreover, private enterprises employ about 470,000 people with disabilities [1].

Since employment support personnel and living support personnel collaborate to provide work assistance for people with disabilities, the number of registrants at the Employment and Living Support Center, and the number of introductions for job placement at public employment security offices have also been increasing [1]. The Ministry of Health, Labor and Welfare, Japan divides the employment of people with disabilities into three categories (Regular Employment/Support for Continuous Employment Type A Service/Support for Continuous Employment Type B Service), shown in Table 1, announced the total number of disabled workers to be about 840,000 in 2008 fiscal year (FY2008) [2].

In this way, it is assumed that the employment of people with disabilities in companies is continuing to increase due to the legal employment rate of people with disabilities being raised, as well as the reasons mentioned above [3]. Furthermore, the number of users of employment-related services for people with disabilities is increasing; therefore, it appears likely that this trend will continue [1]. As I mentioned, we consider that both enterprises and welfare workplaces need to make improvements in their work environment for employees with disabilities. For this reason, we examined two different workplaces that employ workers with disabilities and compared the work environments.

© Springer International Publishing AG, part of Springer Nature 2018
V. G. Duffy (Ed.): DHM 2018, LNCS 10917, pp. 75–84, 2018.
https://doi.org/10.1007/978-3-319-91397-1_7

Table 1. Employment type of people with disabilities

Supporting type	Regular employment	Support for Continuous Employment Type A Service	Support for Continuous Employment Type B Service
Position of people with disabilities	Worker	Workers and service users	Service users
Number of workers and users	About 631,000 (Breakdown) Physical: 434,000 Intellectual: 150,000 Mental: 48,000	About 33,000 (Breakdown) Physical: 7,000 Intellectual: 133,000 Mental: 12,5000	About 175,000 (Breakdown) Physical: 226,000 Intellectual: 990,000 Mental: 535,000
Average monthly wage	Physical: About 223,000 JPY Intellectual: About 108,000 JPY	About 69,000 JPY	About 14,000 JPY
Valid term	For 2 years (*It is possible to renew for up to one year, only when there is need after individual examination.)	N/A	N/A

2   Method

2.1   Subjects

In this research, we examined the Regular Employment type company Sony Taiyo Co., Ltd. (hereinafter, referred to as S company) in Oita Prefecture. We compared it to the Y welfare workplace of Continuous Employment Type B Service in Kyoto Prefecture.

The reason why we decided on S company and Y workplace is that they have both similarities and differences. The common point is that they are both businesses that produce the final product, and have many people with disabilities employed.

The S company is held to the same manufacturing criteria as the other Sony manufacturing companies but employs people with disabilities at a much higher rate. They manufacture some of Sony's longest-standing high-quality products, such as professional microphones, high-end headphones etc.

On the other hand, Y workplace is a place where workers with disabilities produce rice crackers in a traditional, hand-baked process. We decided on Y workplace for our research because Y welfare workplace is in Kyoto which has the highest average wage increase rate in all Japanese prefectures for FY2004 and FY2005 [4].

A point of difference is the business type. S company is a Regular Employment type, and Y welfare workplace is a Continuous Employment Type B Service.

The average monthly wage should be taken into account to highlight this difference.

It is clear that S corporation, which is a private enterprises, pays workers a higher monthly wage on average as compared to Y workplace. This difference can be found in a report published by the Department of Health and Welfare for Persons with Disabilities [2].

2.2 Survey Overview

This study was made to clarify the differences in workplace environment between S company and Y welfare workplace.

We conducted a field survey in which we visited them and interviewed the people concerned. We used a semi-structured interview technique for both S company and Y welfare workplace in this survey. The details of the survey overview are below.

Interview Technique
We used a semi-structured interview technique.

Investigation Object

S Company
We interviewed a total of three people: one from the technical department, which advances improvement on manufacturing at the worksite; one from the manufacturing department; and one from the diversity and inclusion (D&I) supervision department, which advances diversity and inclusion at the company.
Y Welfare Workplace
We interviewed a total of three people: two management supporters who supervise the entire workplace, including spending for the disabled, and one on-site supporter who supervises the production of hand-baked rice crackers and teaches the method for manufacturing.

Visiting Day and Time

S Company
October 17, 2017 10:00–12:00
Y Welfare Workplace
October 31, 2017 10:00–12:00

Collecting Way of Study Contents
S Company and Y Welfare workplace personnel were interviewed using questions prepared beforehand based on information found in Sect. 3 Table 2. The interviewers in both workplaces told us about the way people with disabilities think and of their daily activities.

Table 2. Different levels of support for employing people with disabilities in S company and Y welfare workplace

Items	Subjects	
Support for people with disabilities working (workplace)	**S Company**	**Y Welfare Workshop**
1. Support for acquiring work skills	☑	☑
2. Support for compliance with workplace rules	☑	☑
3. Support for communication methods in the workplace	☑	☑
4. Support for workplace relationships	☑	☑
Support for employing companies (initial employment)		
5. Promoting internal understanding	☑	☑
6. Job selection and job development	☑	☐
7. Establishing an education and training system	☑	☐
8. Improving facilities and faculties	☑	☐
Support for employing companies (throughout employment)		
9. Understanding characteristics of people with disabilities	☑	☑
10. Learning of guidance and employment management know-how	☑	☑
11. Improvement of work process	☑	☐

We visited two workplaces for the study, spending a total of two hours at each place. Here is a breakdown of the time spent at each location: interview for the first hour, study the workshops with the interviewee for the next 45 min, then a question-and-answer session at the end for 15 min.

2.3 Survey Items

S company and Y welfare workplace were examined and compared in the following three categories based on the support system offered by the Ministry of Health, Labor and Welfare, Japan: Support for people working with disabilities (workplace); Support for employing companies (initial employment); Support for employing companies (throughout employment).

For each of these three categories, the employment and living support centers for people with disabilities offer support in collaboration with the employing enterprises.

3 Result

We compared the two surveyed enterprises described in Sect. 2.2. The results are shown in Table 2.

S Company had fulfilled all 11 items shown on the table, which means that the support system for regular employment has succeeded.

As for Y welfare workplace, 6. Job selection and job development, 7. Establishing an education and training system, 8. Improving facilities and faculties, and 11.

Improving the work process were not confirmed. Therefore, it has been concluded that Y workplace is not as comprehensive in their employment support as compared to S company. We consider each of the differences between enterprises in the four items listed above by using a specific example from the field study and interview results.

First, we will look at 6. Job selection and Job development. S Company respects the intention of the worker the most by actively supporting them in getting the kind of work they want to do. Moreover, they also implement changes to the workplace by varying the work and transferring workers to different sites to make use of the individual abilities of the workers.

Although Y welfare workplace respects the worker's preference in selecting a job, on-site support staff determine if the assignment is compatible with the worker's disabilities. Therefore, the workers often cannot do the work that they want.

Second, is 7. Establishing an education and training system. S company ranks workers according to skills and helps improve their skills through rank-based education and in-house skills tests.

On the other hand, in Y welfare workshop there are many jobs that the on-site supporters judge too difficult for workers due to their disabilities. For that reason, the supporters seldom offer the chance for the workers to be challenged by a new situation at work, which is usually a positive experience for employees. Thus a system for providing educational opportunities to workers with disabilities has not been designed in Y welfare workplace.

Third, is 8. S Improving facilities and faculties, S company provides devices to assist specific disabilities so all workers are able to work regardless of their disability. For example, when the job requires workers to inspect a product by handling it using their fingers, then they will provide a tool that has been redesigned so that those with impaired dexterity can perform the task, shown in Fig. 1 [5].

Fig. 1. Motion analysis software OTRS® used by S company

There is also a device for graphing sound, which displays the results in real-time on a monitor so that the process can be judged by sight in the case that a worker with a hearing impairment must do the sound inspection, etc., shown in Fig. 2 [5].

Fig. 2. Motion analysis software OTRS® used by S company

In addition, they make the environment so that workers in wheelchairs are able to work easily because the height of the work table can be tailored to meet each individual's needs.

Y welfare workplace improvement is not progressing because it is difficult for workers to change their work environment and tools are not made available for specific disabilities.

Last is 11. Improving the work process. S Company has systematically formulated standardized tasks performed by persons with disabilities as a work management method, a commonly used method from industrial engineering, shown in Fig. 3 [6].

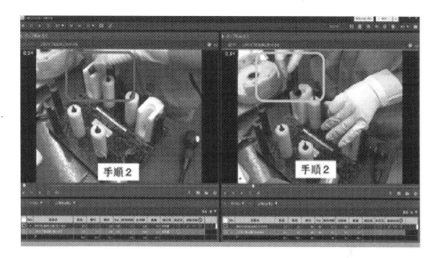

Fig. 3. Motion analysis software OTRS® used by S company

The improvement advances by seeing the difference in the standard work and then formulating it for each task. Regardless of the presence or absence of a disability, the time to do the standardized tasks is divided into two categories, value adding and non-value adding. The standardization takes into account the difference in degree and kind of disabilities of workers. Animations of the task are projected in the workplace so that all workers are able to see the formulation of the standard time, ideally, this keeps all the workers producing at the same rate.

Y welfare workplace as shown in Fig. 4 thinks that it is difficult to formulate standardized tasks because the type of the disability varies greatly. Although, there the support staff feel that both the facilities and the work content needs improvement. In addition, how to improve specifically what to do, and how to communicate the improvement measures to each of the workers, poses problem. The formulation of standardized tasks and the improvement of the work process do not address this problem.

Fig. 4. Workshop view in the Y welfare workplace facility

4   Discussion and Future Tasks

4.1   Discussion

In Table 2, Y welfare workplace was recorded as having 4 unconfirmed items. We thought that this was due to differences in their mindset toward the disabled people at each work site. S company aims to create a workplace environment where all employees in a company can work equally regardless of their disability and without special prejudice towards people with disabilities. On the other hand, Y welfare workplace is trying to create a workplace environment that allows each worker to work within the scope of differences in the degree and the type of individual disability. At Y welfare workplace, support staff consider the individual worker's degree of disability and decide what they can and cannot do. We believe there is a possibility that support staff are narrowing the potential of workers. The biggest challenge in the Y welfare workplace is increasing daily production volume. There is only one worker who can bake rice crackers among all eight workers, this has become a bottleneck in the process and productivity has fallen. Currently, there is no established system for workers to share their knowledge and train one another, so bottlenecks like this occur. In this case, the task involves hygienic standards that must be strictly adhered to so the worker must be reliable in this way. As was the case at S company, the Y workplace treats workers with disabilities equally to workers without disabilities, as independent individuals, and do their best to provide them with broader opportunities. This environment encourages the disabled worker and helps them expand their capabilities. With this approach, production bottlenecks like the rice cracker baking task, as shown in Fig. 5, can hopefully be eliminated in the future.

Fig. 5. The process view of crackers being baked

In addition, S company thinks that it is necessary to formulate standardized tasks to accommodate their workers with disabilities, this addresses item 11. Improvement of work process from Table 2. It is difficult to formulate standardized tasks for Y welfare workplace because of the degree and type of the disability vary widely for each individual. To address improving the work process, the standardized task formulation, using S company's idea of a video-guided process could be applied to Y welfare workplace. This concrete improvement plan could address a problem at the Y welfare workplace, making it possible to improve productivity.

4.2 Future Tasks

S company and Y welfare workplace were taken up as a study subjects because they are workplaces for Regular Employment and Support for Continuous Employment Type B Service users, respectively, and there are many cases where there is a severe difference of the worker's disabilities. It was understood through the interview that both companies are ready to employ individuals with a variety of disabilities while giving the theme that the individual ability can be utilized to their maximum potential, even if the worker of the Support for Continuous Employment Type B employment service increases in the future, although there are few workers with developmental disabilities in S company. Regarding work continuity support such as that provided by Y welfare workplace in the Support for Continuous Employment Type B facility, we would like to examine whether employing many people with widely varied disabilities can be applied to general enterprises in the future.

5   Conclusion

In conclusion, the present study has compared two workplaces: S company as a workplace of Regular Employment type of company for both people without and with disabilities and Y welfare workplace as a workplace of Support for Continuous Employment Type B Service for people with disabilities, and discussed the points in common and those that differed regarding their support for employment of people with disabilities.

S Company has a history of employing people with disabilities for 39 years and has been producing high quality products. In our opinion, by comparing S company and Y welfare workplace, it is clear that in order to improve the working environment for people with disabilities it is necessary that enterprises should not treat people with disabilities specially, and further, it is necessary to create a workplace environment where disabled people can demonstrate their intention as an individual. Further studies are needed in order to investigate that the same effect can be obtained at the Y welfare workplace when the productivity-increasing methods of S company are implemented.

Acknowledgement. This research was supported by MEXT COC+.

References

1. Teraoka, Z.: Future trends of employment services for people with disabilities, pp. 13, 15–16, 20. Ministry of Health, Labour and Welfare, Social Welfare and War Victims' Relief Bureau, Department of Health and Welfare for Persons with Disabilities, Welfare Division for Persons with Disabilities, Japan, 3 February 2017

2. Employment services for people with disabilities, p. 13. Ministry of Health, Labour and Welfare, Japan, 14 July 2010
3. The legal employment rate of people with disabilities is raising from April 1st, 2018. Ministry of Health, Labour and Welfare/Prefectural Labour Bureau/Public employment security office, Japan. (LL290630 Employment disabilities01) (2017)
4. Hattori, T.: Future trends of employment services in Comprehensive Services and Supports for Persons with Disabilities Act, pp. 13, 15–16, 20. Ministry of Health, Labour and Welfare, Social Welfare and War Victims' Relief Bureau, Department of Health and Welfare for Persons with Disabilities, Welfare Division for Persons with Disabilities, Japan, 26 May 2017
5. Sony/Taiyo Corporation. http://www.sony-taiyo.co.jp/index.html. Accessed 1 Feb 2018
6. Broadleaf Co., Ltd. OTRS. https://www.otrs.jp/overview/. Accessed 1 Feb 2018

Improving Occupational Safety and Health (OSH) in Human-System Interaction (HSI) Through Applications in Virtual Environments

Peter Nickel[✉] and Andy Lungfiel

Accident Prevention – Product Safety, Institute for Occupational Safety and Health of the German Social Accident Insurance (IFA), Sankt Augustin, Germany
peter.nickel@dguv.de

Abstract. Interactions between humans and system components of future work systems may be driven by digitalization, connectivity and agility. Though the design of future systems is not yet known or is not yet available or accessible, it would be desirable to ensure occupational safety and health (OSH) in early stages of development and design. It would also be helpful to learn about potential hazards and risks and prevent them before using work systems across their future life cycle. Since knowledge, experience and imagination might not be sufficient to predict human-system interactions (HSI) it should be possible to apply modeling and simulation such as virtual reality (VR) to overcome some of the challenges in analysis, design and evaluation of future work systems. Similar seems to be true for work systems too dangerous, too complex, or too resource demanding to investigate in reality. The concept on safety and usability through applications in virtual environments (SUTAVE) facilitates effective prevention through design in OSH to be addressed by means of innovative technology. Studies have been conducted to improve OSH in HSI supported by VR simulation; i.e. (a) risk assessments in planning stage, (b) task, interaction and information design in human robot interaction, (c) usability evaluation of safety measures in contexts of use, (d) near misses and course of events in accident investigations, (e) safety concept development. The results are encouraging to face future challenges in HSI as long as its design is taken into account early on and according to human factors and ergonomics principles.

Keywords: Occupational safety and health · Human system interaction
Virtual reality · Human information processing

1 Human-System Interaction

There is a growing concern due to digitalization in work systems design that occupational safety and health (OSH) requirements become less obvious and therefore less essential, although potential consequences may rather be sneaking in and become severe at the same time. Digitalization in smart manufacturing has a strong impact on human-system interaction (HSI) and seems to foster shifts in hazards (e.g. mechanical superimposed by mental) and in human task requirements (e.g. action implementation

© Springer International Publishing AG, part of Springer Nature 2018
V. G. Duffy (Ed.): DHM 2018, LNCS 10917, pp. 85–96, 2018.
https://doi.org/10.1007/978-3-319-91397-1_8

superimposed by perception and reasoning). Perspectives for prevention should adapt accordingly, in that design of human task and interaction interfaces referring to human factors and ergonomics principles become key performance indicators in mediating OSH. Modeling and simulation have a long tradition in research into future work systems as well as development of prospective design strategies and solutions. In the digital age it might be helpful to take simulations such as VR into account to facilitate prevention through design in future contexts of use while gaining experiences in introducing new technologies for the benefit of OSH in industry and services.

1.1 Occupational Safety and Health

According to the World Health Organization (WHO) occupational safety and health (OSH) refers to all aspects of health and safety in the workplace and should have a strong focus on primary prevention of hazards. Concepts on OSH may vary since OSH legislation differs across countries. The basis of the German social security system was formed in the 19th century and developed since to a comprehensive system with five pillars of insurances for health, pension, accident, long-term care and unemployment. OSH comprises all measures for safety and health of employees at work and other forms of activity. This includes the prevention of occupational accidents, occupational diseases and work-related health risks and the human centered design of working conditions. The national OSH system follows the conventions of the ILO and all legislation is harmonized with EU Directives [1].

Unlike legal requirements for OSH, the hierarchy of controls remains fairly similar across countries and provides some guidance for selecting effective measures for risk reduction and prevention in systems design. In Germany, a hierarchy of controls traditionally follows levels like (a) eliminating hazard (e.g. substitution), (b) technical measures (e.g. safeguard), (c) organizational measures (e.g. job rotation), (d) personal measures (e.g. personal protective equipment, PPE), and (e) instructional measures (e.g. warning sign). Albeit shorter, this hierarchy is similar to the ten level 'general principles of prevention' as listed in the EU OSH Framework Directive [2]. The hierarchy in OHSAS 18001 [3] also has five levels and contains similar content, however, with PPE listed lowest. Different perspectives on the hierarchy may also widen opportunities for interventions [4].

European and Australian OSH legislation with directives and guidelines are regarded especially useful in facilitating primary prevention. Manufacturers are required to design safe machinery that meet a set of minimal health and safety requirements and employers are held responsible for providing safe work equipment to employees [5]. As a consequence, technology and knowledge for designing safe equipment is accessible across countries; however, business decision makers and purchasers may not always value or request for it or manufacturers may not create demand for it by promoting it on the market [6]. Despite differences in OSH legislation across countries, OSH principles are equally important everywhere. The concept of primary prevention is a guiding principle for priority consideration of high level measures to combat hazards and risks at the work across the life cycle from early on with the consequence of lowering rates of occupational accidents and diseases.

1.2   Virtual Reality Simulation

Though work systems should not impair safety and health of humans interacting in these systems, they may not yet, readily, or easily available for investigating appropriate procedures for risk assessments or for developing and testing appropriate safety measures. Modeling and simulation of work systems seem to be solutions to provide support in terms of methods, tools and techniques. This opens up new and effective perspectives to face human factors and ergonomics challenges in work systems analysis, design and evaluation, in that it allows for systems to be investigated in temporal and spatial dynamics and across the life cycle from construction and development, over application in the context of use, up to modification and recycling [7, 8].

There is a long tradition also in OSH to use simulation techniques. Applications may refer to (a) procedures agreed on and established for testing product safety (e.g. laboratory heat stress testing for hydraulic pipes), (b) role plays in OSH trainings intending to simulate safety behaviour at the workplace, (c) retro-perspective accident analysis (e.g. cause effect and if what/when reasoning and analyses), and (d) investigations of unavailable, undesirable, inconvenient or future work scenarios (e.g. safety concept development to prevent from hazardous work equipment) [8, 9].

Over the past decades, VR has matured into a simulation tool for humans to interact with dynamic, three-dimensional virtual environments and into a methodology for different areas of applications. In industry and services VR allows applied research in human-machine system analysis, design, and evaluation for training, for demonstration, and for visualisation purposes [10]. VR has the potential to better bridge gaps between experimental research and traditional investigations at the shop-floor level while using specific advantages of simulation research [11] and being careful with human, material and financial resources. Improvements in technology and success stories from industrial applications attracted VR also to OSH. Applications often refer to rehabilitation and to qualification and training, with the latter placing an emphasis e.g. on safe behaviour at work or risk assessments [12, 13].

In OSH organisations VR is increasingly being used in studies on analysis, design and evaluation of task and interaction interfaces of work equipment such as machinery or tools with regard to improvements in human factors, ergonomics and safety [14–16]. Among these organisations, the Institute for Occupational Safety and Health of the German Social Accident Insurance (IFA) established the concept 'Safety and Usability Through Applications in Virtual Environments' (SUTAVE) to facilitate effective prevention through design of HSI in OSH to be addressed by means of innovative technology. Information about current activities in the SUTAVE laboratory in general and technical information is given elsewhere (www.dguv.de/ifa/sutave).

1.3   Occupational Safety and Health in Human-System Interaction

HSI focuses on the understanding of how humans interact within work systems [17] while emphasizing human factors and ergonomics design requirements with regard to human information processing [18]. The four stages of HSI are closely related to OSH investigations and procedures, starting with identification of situational characteristics (i.e. information acquisition, sensation, determination of limits of process under investigation), analysis (i.e. information analysis, perception, hazard identification), followed by assessments (i.e. decision making, action selection, risk evaluation) and may result in redesign (i.e. action implementation, intervention, risk reduction).

Linking the design of HSI more closely to procedures for risk assessments should improve both human factors and ergonomics design quality of HSI as well as OSH in HSI. Work system components and their interactions would be designed as to safeguard operational safety, effectiveness and efficiency of HSI as well as to optimize human operator workload, which in turn will contribute to operational safety and health in work systems. As a consequence, design flaws, hazards and risks could be reduced and prevent from health impairments, near accidents or accidents. Application of human factors and ergonomics design requirements for HSI thus does not merely reflect the necessary compliance with legal regulations but also the pursuit of basic system goals. Projects conducted at the IFA will be used to inform about activities to improve safety and health through design of HSI in virtual environments.

2   Occupational Safety and Health Applications in Virtual Environments

2.1   More OSH in HSI When Planning Work Environments

Standardization of future river looks has been given high priority by the German Federal Ministry of Transport and Digital Infrastructure (BMVI) since it allows OSH improvements for future operations while accelerating modernization of waterway transport infrastructure and reducing costs across the life cycle. OSH is seen most effective early in design because redesign due to safety issues would be resource-demanding, if not impossible, when river lock construction has already been completed. Therefore, the German Social Accident Insurance Institution of the Federal Government and for the railway services (UVB) launched a project to strengthen the impact of OSH on the standardization of river lock components in its future contexts of use. IFA and UVB in cooperation with partners from BMVI, German Federal Waterways and Shipping Administration (GDWS) and German Social Accident Insurance Institution for Transport and Traffic (BG Verkehr) are developing a dynamic VR planning model of the river lock standard in its future contexts of use [19].

The new standard comprises a kit of standardized objects covering river lock requirements for professional inland navigation in Germany (e.g. chamber construction, lock gates). As a consequence, the VR planning model on standardized river locks also provides variations with regard to rise of water level (e.g. gates and chambers for 4 m to 25 m), to length of river barges (e.g. for up to 135 m or even 185 m river barges), and to type of water way (e.g. canal locks may have economizing basins), to name but a few. VR-Model development in 1:1 scale (see Fig. 1) refers to drawings of ongoing implementation planning of the first river lock according to the new standard.

Fig. 1. VR simulation of maintenance work at standardized river lock for risk assessments.

With the aim to improve OSH, the VR model supports demonstration of about 75 different scenarios in a wide context of use across operational stages and the life cycle. Outcomes of risk assessments will result in documentations on

(a) design improvements of standardized objects to better match OSH requirements
(b) improved templates for conducting risk assessments [according to 20]
(c) new templates for conducting risk assessments [according to 2, 21, 22]
(d) design improvements for river locks currently under planning
(e) basic information for operation instructions for technical components
(f) basic information for working instructions for maintenance tasks at river locks
(g) references for risk assessments after successful construction.

Results have the potential to improve OSH in the process of standardization and in future work at river locks while at the same time immersing into future work scenarios in the context of use over next decades.

2.2 More OSH in HSI in Hazardous Work Environments

Investigations into work systems [17] should be conducted in protected simulation environments if these are too expensive to use in reality due to required downtimes or too dangerous or undesirable to face in reality. This also applies to empirical usability evaluations of prospective safety measures, as real contexts of use include hazardous and incident prone scenarios with near misses and accidents.

Mobile elevating work platforms (MEWP) enjoy increasing use and popularity and they provide flexible, easy and quick access to work places above ground level without setting up scaffolding. Unfortunately, the number of injuries and fatalities is still relatively high with most accidents referring to operators being crushed between MEWP rail guards and objects in the environment or being thrown from MEWP platforms [23].

Over the past years, efforts in MEWP safety [24] resulted in improvements, however, usable and effective safety measures are always required.

Among others, stop functions built into MEWP joysticks as new safety measure [25] have been assumed to be effective for accident prevention. Therefore the German DGUV Expert Committee 'Trade and Logistics', Subcommittee 'Goods Handling, Storage, and Logistics' in cooperation with the German Social Accident Insurance Institution for the trade and logistics industry (BGHW) as well as the German Social Accident Insurance Institution for the woodworking and metalworking industries (BGHM) have launched a research project at IFA to conduct a usability evaluation in VR before detailed recommendations for use of this additional protective measure would be given to manufacturers, rental companies or users.

In an industrial hall 22 naïve and experienced users performed on-site inspection tasks for about 2 h each [26]. Scenarios have deliberately been designed in a virtual environment to provoke accidents and near misses by constricting access to work places, reducing visibility in inspection areas, and adding obstacles in the environment. A MEWP in an industrial hall was set up in VR, except for MEWP controls and platform. MEWP drivers were required to perform driving and inspection tasks. Virtual near misses and accidents have occurred as rare events and as accidentally as in reality, i.e. collisions of the MEWP or its driver with objects in the hall.

As a result, near misses and collisions of the MEWP or the driver with objects in the environment occurred, similar to those reported in reality [23]. Surprisingly, the protective measure under usability evaluation has not been used in hazardous situations or during collisions. However, it has unintendedly been used in non-hazardous situations. Investigations into the use of controls in hazardous situations revealed that MEWP movements were always stopped by operators releasing their hands from the joysticks. In addition, system dynamics of joysticks with built-in safety function transformed linear joystick movements into exponential changes in MEWP movements, with the consequence that MEWP would always accelerate before coming to a stop, when using the safety measure. In conclusion, the given design of the measure has not been recommended for marketing, because the safety measure was not seen suitable to serve a measure for risk reduction and to prevent from severe accidents. Redesign suggestions have been documented accordingly.

Based on results of the VR usability evaluation, however, it has been possible to support accident investigations [27]. Post-hoc VR simulation of the VR usability study provided insights in the course of events by identification and reconstruction of near misses and accidents and by investigation of work system configurations, movements of the drivers and controls as well as MEWP movements in the work environment. Observations from variable locations and viewing angles disclosed potential impairments of human information processing through MEWP systems design during HSI. Recommendations for the development of measures of hazard and risk reduction could be given. In addition, the study illustrated how to detect potential accidents in future work scenarios and inform about development of measures for risk reduction early in design [28].

The IFA has also been requested by the German Social Accident Insurance Institution for Transport and Traffic (BG Verkehr) to develop a VR environment for accident investigations during unloading of vehicles with lifting platforms on loading ramps [29] (see Fig. 2). During unloading, the height of the vehicle body is adjusted continually, either automatically or manually, since the body of the vehicle would otherwise rise as the weight of the load decreases. Reports on slip, trip and fall accidents suggested that the lifting platform could shift horizontally causing the platform being in front of the loading ramp. A dynamic VR model was designed to foster reasoning, analysis and reconstruction of potential courses of events and may serve a basis for instructional support.

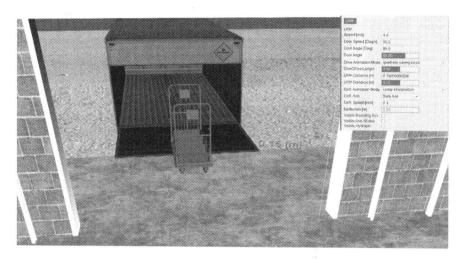

Fig. 2.   Unloading of vehicles with lifting platforms on loading ramp in virtual environment.

2.3   More OSH in HSI in Work Environments Not Yet Available

In future industry and services, work equipment is required that is more flexible to use while at the same time being specific and very effective for different purposes. In recent years human-robot interaction has evolved to provide solutions, however, implications for health, safety, and well-being are not always clear. Since workplaces with humans interacting or even collaborating with robots in time or space on common tasks are still rare [30], VR simulation studies have been conducted to investigate human factors and ergonomics issues with regard to OSH in future work environments [31]. Human factors requirements on human-robot collaboration (HRC) in industrial settings have been conducted in VR referring to spatial distances between humans and robots, robot speed in proximity of human collaborators, and predictability of robot movement [32–34].

A human operator workplace was set up in reality in front of the VR presentation wall and integrated in a VR manufacturing environment [32, 33]. Task performance in human-robot collaboration overlapped in time and space with both individual human operator and robot task performance, respectively. Results yielded effects of distance (300 mm versus 1400 mm) between an industrial robot and a human operator in combination with effects of robot movement speed (250 mm/s versus 1500 mm/s). At relatively shorter distances participants reported higher levels of anxiety, while relatively lower robot speed was associated with slower and less accurate task performance of participants [32].

Another HRC study in VR [33, 34] used a similar setting, however, investigated the impact of robot speed in combination with predictability of robot movements on human performance in spatiotemporally overlapping workspaces. A lower level of predictability was associated with a decrease in task performance, while faster movements resulted in higher-rated values for task load and anxiety, suggesting demands on the operator exceeding the optimum.

Function allocation in human-robot interaction with regard to human-automation taxonomy was also addressed in VR [35]. Different levels of automation in combination with different modes for signaling demands for interaction between a single human operator and two simulated industrial robots were investigated regarding their impact on human operator task performance and work load (see Fig. 3). Industrial robots either asked the human operator to interact whenever required or adapted the request for interaction to idle times between individual operator tasks. Requirement for interaction were either audio-visually indicated or not. Interactions indicated and adapted to operator task sequences resulted in relatively less operator distraction from task performance and less impairment in operator workload. In human-robot interaction OSH may improve when interaction is audio-visually indicated and work equipment is adapted to the human operator.

Fig. 3. Mixed reality manufacturing environment for human-robot interaction in STUAVE-Lab.

2.4   More OSH in HSI Through Safety Concept Development

With regard to safety concept development for HSI in manufacturing, VR studies have been conducted to investigate the design of tree-dimensional safety zones at work.

Electro-sensitive protective equipment (ESPE) such as safety light curtains, photoelectric switches, laser scanners and camera-based protective devices is used to protect workers from hazardous areas such as rotating parts of machinery [36]. Geometry of the detection zones and markings for identification by the human operator are among potential key differences in ergonomics design of ESPE with 3D and 2D safety zones. Therefore, a project has been launched by the German DGUV Expert Committee 'Woodworking and Metalworking' (FB HM), Subcommittee 'Machinery, Plants, Automation and Design of Manufacturing Systems' in cooperation with the German Social Accident Institution for the woodworking and metalworking industries (BGHM).

3D ESPE safety zones were explored in virtual manufacturing task scenarios on their effects on human performance, workload, and safety (see Fig. 4). Safety zones were varied in geometry (e.g. cuboid, spherical) and in modes for identification (e.g. warning zone, floor marking tape). Twenty participants performed manufacturing tasks on a machine with a rotary table. The machine was in operation while safeguarded by 3D ESPE when participants prepared materials for subsequent task sequences. Among others, results suggested that 3D safety zones in geometry should be adapted to contours of hazard zones (e.g. less edges and corners), as this yielded relatively fewer unintended breaches of detection areas for machinery safety. 3D ESPE floor marking tape is sometimes used to support operators in detecting invisible safety zones. Though useful in some situations to improve orientation for operators, it could not be identified as significantly increasing performance and improving workload in human system interaction [37]. In addition, VR revealed to be a helpful planning system for safety concept development and evaluation for a broad range of HSI settings at industrial workplaces.

Fig. 4. HSI in SUTAVE-Lab on machinery with rotary table; floor marking tape to support safety zone detection.

3   Improve OSH in HSI Through VR Applications

As demonstrated by examples presented, OSH becomes proactive and may draw benefits from VR in that a simulation environment facilitates analysis, design, and evaluation of HSI in work systems in industry and services for improving effective measures for prevention. Specific benefits refer to system interventions early in the design process (e.g. prevention through design) as demonstrated by the studies on risk assessments with regard to different perspectives in OSH legislation and different operational stages for work tasks at standardized river locks throughout the work system life cycle (see Sect. 2.1) [38]. VR has shown to support OSH in HSI design in situations too dangerous or undesirable to face in reality. Investigations in hazardous environments have extended the effective range of prevention in that realistic and more valid contexts of use could be applied in evaluation studies and in that the course of events in near misses and accidents could be investigated with regard to human information processing requirements (see Sect. 2.2) [28, 29]. Prevention in OSH intends to avoid detrimental consequences for operators before accidents are going to happen. VR modeling and simulation made this happen even though workplaces do not yet exist or have never been existed before and therefore predictions for potential hazards and risks are not necessarily met by knowledge, experience and imagination. In VR, systematic variations of standardized working conditions are available for investigations, even if testing is difficult, because their quality is subject to change (i.e. under heavy wear or degradation) (see Sect. 2.3). OSH in HSI will also improve when setting up new workplaces since reproduction of the same settings is as easy as it is to modify settings or scenario. Replication of contexts of use supports developing, testing and choosing among effective safety concepts for new interactions, machines and installations (see Sect. 2.4).

The presented studies go beyond VR simulations in that VR was used as a tool and method to improve OSH in HSI at work. OSH may take advantage of VR as future implementation of prevention measures can be accelerated early on. Given examples also provide support for the assumption that VR should be suitable to face future challenges for OSH in HSI in future systems evolving into smart factories, i.e. connectivity, optimization, transparency, proactivity and agility becoming main drivers that will be considered in OSH.

Acknowledgements. It is a pleasant duty to acknowledge all colleagues and participants for conducting the studies and for immersing in the virtual work environments. The author is very grateful to the efforts of Mr. Andy Lungfiel for technical development of the VR scenarios.

References

1. Froeneberg, B., Timm, S.: Country Profile of Occupational Health System in Germany. WHO European Centre for Environment and Health, Bonn (2012)
2. EU OSH Framework Directive 89/391/EEC of 12 June 1989 on the introduction of measures to encourage improvements in the safety and health of workers at work (with amendments 2008). Off. J. Eur. Union L **183**, 1–8 (1989)
3. BS OHSAS 18001: Managing Safety the Systems Way. BSI, London (2007)
4. Lehto, M.R., Cook, B.T.: Occupational health and safety management. In: Salvendy, G. (ed.) Handbook of Human Factors and Ergonomics, pp. 701–733. Wiley, Hoboken (2012)
5. Lin, M.-L.: Practice issues in prevention through design. J. Saf. Res. **39**, 157–159 (2008)
6. Schulte, P.A., Rinehart, R., Okun, A., Geraci, C.L., Heidel, D.S.: National prevention through design (PtD) initiative. J. Saf. Res. **39**, 115–121 (2008)
7. Meister, D.: Simulation and modelling. In: Wilson, J.R., Corlett, E.N. (eds.) Evaluation of Human Work, pp. 202–228. Taylor & Francis, London (1999)
8. Wickens, C.D., Hollands, J.G., Banbury, S., Parasuraman, R.: Engineering Psychology and Human Performance. Pearson, Upper Saddle River (2013)
9. Nickel, P., Nachreiner, F.: Evaluation arbeitspsychologischer Interventionsmaßnahmen. In: Kleinbeck, U., Schmidt, K. (eds.) Arbeitspsychologie (Enzyklopädie der Psychologie, D, III, 1), pp. 1003–1038. Hogrefe, Göttingen (2010)
10. Hale, K.S., Stanney, K.M. (eds.): Handbook of Virtual Environments: Design, Implementation, and Applications. CRC Press, Boca Raton (2015)
11. Chapanis, A., van Cott, H.P.: Human engineering tests and evaluations. In: van Cott, H.P., Kinkade, R.G. (eds.) Human Engineering Guide to Equipment Design, pp. 701–728. AIR, Washington (1972)
12. Miller, C., Nickel, P., Di Nocera, F., Mulder, B., Neerincx, M., Parasuraman, R., Whiteley, I.: Human-machine interface. In: Hockey, G.R.J. (ed.) THESEUS Cluster 2: Psychology and Human-Machine Systems – Report, pp. 22–38. Indigo, Strasbourg (2012)
13. Dźwiarek, M., Grabowski, A., Jankowski, J., Strawinski, T.: Analysis of usability of the VR technology for risk assessment in machinery design. In: EMET Proceedings, Venice, pp. 146–153 (2013)
14. Ciccotelli, J., Marsot, J.: Réalite virtuelle et prévention. Apports et tendances. Hygiène et sécurité du travail **199**, 99–111 (2005)
15. Määttä, T.J.: Virtual environments in machinery safety analysis and participatory ergonomics. Hum. Factors Ergon. Manuf. **17**, 435–443 (2007)
16. Marc, J., Belkacem, N., Marsot, J.: Virtual reality: a design tool for enhanced consideration of usability 'validation elements'. Saf. Sci. **45**, 589–601 (2007)
17. ISO 6385: Ergonomic Principles in the Design of Work Systems. ISO, Brussels (2016)
18. Nickel, P., Nachreiner, F.: Evaluation of presentation of information for process control operations. Cogn. Technol. Work **10**, 23–30 (2008)
19. Nickel, P., Janning, M., Wachholz, T., Pröger, E., Lungfiel, A.: Shaping future work systems by OSH risk assessments early on. In: Proceedings of the 20th Triennial Congress of the International Ergonomics Association (IEA), Florence, Italy, 26–30 August 2018
20. EU Machinery Directive 2006/42/EC of the European Parliament and the Council of 17 May 2006 on machinery, and amending Directive 95/16/EC (recast). Off. J. Eur. Union L **157**, 24–86 (2006)
21. EU Construction Directive 92/57/EEC on the implementation of minimum safety and health requirements at temporary or mobile construction sites. Off. J. Eur. Union L **245**, 6–22 (1992)

22. European Commission. Non-binding guide to good practice for understanding and implementing Directive 92/57/EEC 'Construction Sites'. Common, Frankfurt (2010)
23. De Cillis, E., Maida, L., Patrucco, M., Cirio, C.: Mobile elevating work platforms: a discussion on the main causes of accidents and some suggestions for prevention. In: Podofillini, L., Sudret, B., Stojadinovic, B., Zio, E., Kröger, W. (eds.) Safety and Reliability of Complex Engineered Systems (ESREL), pp. 3229–3236. Taylor & Francis, London (2015)
24. ISO 16368: Mobile Elevating Work Platforms – Design, Calculations, Safety Requirements and Test Methods. ISO, Geneva (2010)
25. Nischalke-Fehn, G., Bömer, T.: Use of a modified joystick for the avoidance of crushing accidents on elevating work platforms. Focus on IFA's work, no. 0332, pp. 1–2 (2011)
26. Nickel, P., Lungfiel, A., Bömer, T., Koppenborg, M., Trabold, R.-J.: Wirksamkeit einer ergänzenden Schutzmaßnahme in virtueller Realität zur Unfallprävention bei Hubarbeitsbühnen. In: GfA (ed.) Gestaltung der Arbeitswelt der Zukunft, pp. 85–87. GfA-Press, Dortmund (2014)
27. Dempsey, P.G.: Accident and incident investigation. In: Salvendy, G. (ed.) Handbook of Human Factors and Ergonomics, pp. 1085–1091. Wiley, Hoboken (2012)
28. Nickel, P., Lungfiel, A., Trabold, R.-J.: Reconstruction of near misses and accidents for analyses from virtual reality usability study. In: Barbic, J., D'Cruz, M., Latoschik, M.E., Slater, M., Bourdot, P. (eds.) EuroVR 2017. LNCS, vol. 10700, pp. 182–191. Springer, Cham (2017). https://doi.org/10.1007/978-3-319-72323-5_12
29. Naber, B., Lungfiel, A., Winter, G., Diedrich, W., Nickel, P.: Machbarkeitsstudie zur Modellierung von Gefahrenpotenzialen beim Entladen von Lkws über Hubladebühnen. In: GfA (ed.) Arbeit(s).wissen.schaf(f)t – Grundlage für Management & Kompetenzentwicklung. GfA-Press, Dortmund (2018)
30. ISO/TS 15066: Robots and Robotic Devices — Collaborative Robots. ISO, Geneva (2016)
31. Burdea, G.C., Coiffet, P.: Virtual Reality Technology. Wiley, New York (2003)
32. Naber, B., Lungfiel, A., Nickel, P., Huelke, M.: Human Factors zu Robotergeschwindigkeit und -distanz in der virtuellen Mensch-Roboter-Kollaboration. In: GfA (ed.) Chancen durch Arbeits-, Produkt- und Systemgestaltung – Zukunftsfähigkeit für Produktions- und Dienstleistungsunternehmen, pp. 421–424. GfA-Press, Dortmund (2013)
33. Naber, B., Koppenborg, M., Nickel, P., Lungfiel, A., Huelke, M.: Effects of movement speed, movement predictability and distance in human-robot-collaboration. In: XX World Congress on Safety and Health at Work 2014 'Sharing a Vision for Sustainable Prevention', Forum for Prevention, F02.26. ILO, ISSA, DGUV, Frankfurt (2014)
34. Koppenborg, M., Nickel, P., Naber, B., Lungfiel, A., Huelke, M.: Effects of movement speed and predictability in human-robot-collaboration. Hum. Factors Ergon. Manuf. Serv. Ind. **27**(4), 197–209 (2017)
35. Kaufeld, M.: Auswirkungen von Aufgabenpassung und Informationssignalisierung in der Mensch-Roboter-Interaktion auf die psychische Beanspruchung. Eine empirische Studie in virtueller Realität (Master thesis, Psychology). Universität, Bonn (2016)
36. ISO 12100: Safety of Machinery – General Principles for Design – Risk Assessment and Risk Reduction. ISO, Geneva 2010
37. Hauke, M., Naber, B.: Anordnung und Gestaltung dreidimensionaler Schutzräume an Maschinen. Focus on IFA's work, no. 0360, pp. 1–2 (2014)
38. Nickel, P.: Extending the effective range of prevention through design by OSH applications in virtual reality. In: Nah, F.-H., Tan, C.-H. (eds.) HCIBGO 2016. LNCS, vol. 9752, pp. 325–336. Springer, Cham (2016). https://doi.org/10.1007/978-3-319-39399-5_31

The Research on Layout and Simulation of Human-Machine Interface in Vehicle

Qing Xue, Jiawei Sun[✉], Jia Hao, and Minxia Liu

School of Mechanical Engineering, Beijing Institute of Technology,
Beijing 100081, People's Republic of China
{xueqing,haojia632,liuminxia}@bit.edu.cn, 895984926@qq.com

Abstract. In this paper, we analyzed the connotation of hip point, related ergonomics theories and industrial standard. Based on these analysis and hip point, this research outlined of man-machine relationships of operating device layout design in vehicle cab for improving safety, efficiency and comfort of the driver's operation. Moreover, we designed a simulation environment to analyze vehicle interface. With the development of the automobile industry and the maturity of the related technologies, the popularity of the automobile is more and more extensive. It is necessary to start designing from the perspective of "people oriented".

Keywords: Ergonomics · Hip point · Layout design · JACK simulation

1 Introduction

Ergonomics is a science that studies the interaction of human beings with other components of the system. Through its theories, principles and methods, we can optimize system efficiency, meet human's physiological and psychological characteristics. At the same time, it is necessary to study the relationship between human and the environment, so ergonomics is the basis of humanized design (Table 1).

Among these principles, we regard human safety and health as our primary goals. In general, there is exchange and interaction of information, material and energy between people and machines [1]. In the man-machine system, the man-machine interface plays a role of connecting the machine and the human which is the hub of information exchange. The relationship between the two can be seen from Fig. 1.

The layout of the cab is a key step in the process of car design, which directly affects the safety and comfort of the car. However, there are still methodological and technical difficulties in cab layout. With the improvement of automobile electrical degree, the car cab integrated LCD instrument, head-up display, central control screen and seat entertainment system, it enhances the driving experience. Therefore, the layout design play a very important role in the car design. At present, enterprises attach great importance to the application of ergonomics in the process of automobile development. Under the environment of intelligent manufacturing and people oriented, ergonomics promote the intelligent development of automobile interaction.

© Springer International Publishing AG, part of Springer Nature 2018
V. G. Duffy (Ed.): DHM 2018, LNCS 10917, pp. 97–108, 2018.
https://doi.org/10.1007/978-3-319-91397-1_9

Table 1. The design principles of ergonomics

Happiness	System effectiveness
Safety	Effectiveness
Healthy	Efficiency
Comfort	Reliability
User experience	

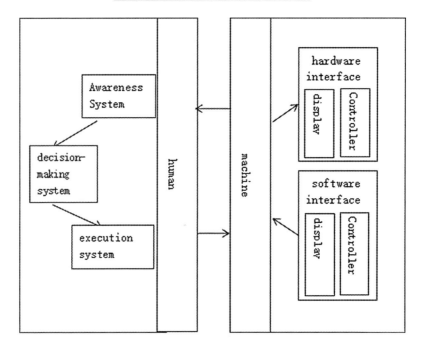

Fig. 1. The relationship between man-machine interface and human

The layout of the car cab should follow the following principles:

Based on above principles, considering the factors such as ride comfort, operation safety and SAE standard, it can be used to complete cab layout design combined with the digital simulation software (Table 2).

Table 2. The principle of cab layout

Ride comfort
Maneuverability
Vision
Convenience and safety
Relevant laws

JACK is an efficient software tool for crew simulation and automotive engineering design. 3D parametric human provided by the software [2] can be used in vehicle layout design and simulate the behavior of the driver. In order to avoid repeated changes in the design of the later stage, we can use it to do many ergonomics analysis in the early stage.

Based on the application of ergonomics in the layout of the car cab, this paper discussed the layout method for the car cab combining with the theory of ergonomics and tools of layout analysis, and provided a practical engineering case by JACK software [3].

2   Method

The Software simulation is based on the hip point and three ergonomics analysis tools [4], in which include visibility, accessibility and comfort analysis. The order of use of these tools is as shown (Fig. 2).

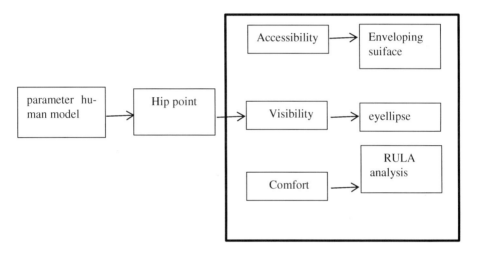

Fig. 2. Structure of ergonomics

2.1   Ergonomics Tools

Parameter Human Model
Parameter human model is an effective tool to describe human morphological and mechanical characteristics [5]. In the human-machine system, it is an necessary carrier for research, analysis and evaluation.

In this paper, we built 3D parameter human model through JACK software to check the ride comfort, the rationality of the layout of the pedal, the steering wheel, the seat and so on. Moreover, we made the motion simulation by driving the joints of the model (Fig. 3).

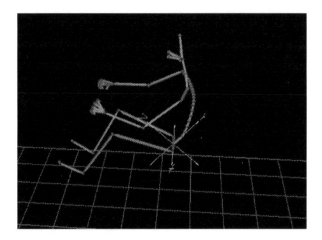

Fig. 3. The skeleton of 3D parameter human model

Hip Point

The hip-point is the theoretical, relative location of an occupant's hip: specifically the pivot point between the torso and upper leg portions of the body-as used in the cab layout design and vehicle regulation [6]. Hip point is the reference for evaluation of the car cab layout. The expression of hip points depends on the application, which mainly includes the actual-hip-points and the design-hip-points [7].

The H-point can be measured relative to other features, e.g. hip point to vehicle floor (H30) or hip point to pavement (H5). In other words, a vehicle said to have an hip point that is "high" relative to the vehicle floor, or road surface (Fig. 4). This method is called SAE Fit Line [8].

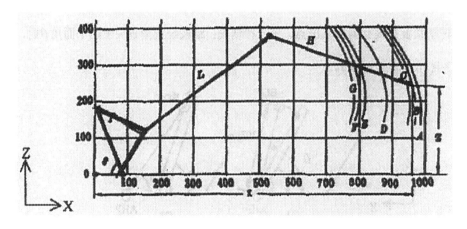

Fig. 4. Hip point position curve

There are 7 curves drawn by different percentile drivers in their respective driving position from a group of 2.5 percentile body to 97.5 percentile body.

$$X_{97.5} = 936.6 + 0.613879Z - 0.00186247Z^2$$
$$X_{95.} = 913.7 + 0.672316Z - 0.00195530Z^2$$
$$X_{90} = 885.0 + 0.735374Z - 0.00201650Z^2$$
$$X_{50} = 793.7 + 0.903387Z - 0.00225518Z^2$$
$$X_{10} = 715.9 + 0.968793Z - 0.00228674Z^2$$
$$X_5 = 692.6 + 0.981427Z - 0.00226230Z^2$$
$$X_{2.5} = 687.1 + 0.895336Z - 0.00210494Z^2$$

Eyellipse

Due to the input of visual information is more than 80% when driving, it should be ensured that the visual field is good. Eye ellipse is an elliptical distribution of the probability statistics of the coordinates of the position of the eye which takes elliptical distribution [9]. It is the main tool for visibility analysis that describe the position of the eye relative to the vehicle's interior reference point in field of cab layout (Fig. 5).

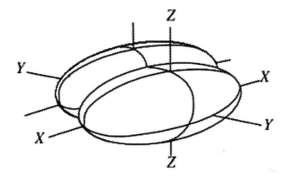

Fig. 5. Example of eyellipse

SAE standard gives two kinds of eyellipse size correspond to ninety-fifth and ninety-ninth percentile human body. One is when the horizontal adjustment stroke (L23) is in the range of 100–133 mm, one is when L23 is larger than 133 mm (Table 3).

Table 3. SAE eye ellipse size

Unit (mm)		95 percentile human body		99 percentile human body	
		100 < L23 < 133	L23 > 133	100 < L23 < 133	L23 > 133
Long axis		173	198	241	267
Short axis	Over head	105	105	149	149
	Side view	86	86	122	122

Enveloping Surface

The design of the car's indoor driving space is to be completed after ensuring ride comfort, visibility and accessibility, reasonable interior design makes driving experience safer and more comfortable. The main contents of the design of automotive interior space include hand space, head space before and after, knee space, abdomen space and leg space [10]. The main tools for the cab layout based on the human body parametric model include: human feature points, head envelope surface, around the lap envelope and abdomen envelope surface. Human body feature points are the locus of human joints and organs related to body layout, such as the head, eyes, abdomen, knee, hip feature points. The location of these feature points on the body in the car interior coordinate system can be determined by the driver's actual position after seating according to his wishes which are measured by photographic method. The connection of all the points in space has formed the human body characteristics distribution graph of different percentile men and women which is shown in Fig. 6.

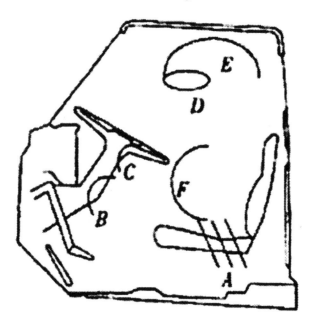

Fig. 6. Example of eyellipse

Notes A is the position line of hip point.
B, C   is the knee envelope of left and right
D   is the eye ellipse of driver
E   is the head envelope
F   is the abdomen envelope

Cab space design also includes all spatial layout design of components that may create constraints on the body's activities, such as space between arm and door guard, crew foot activity space design etc.

3   Discussion

3.1   Stage 1: Modeling and Positioning

First, we completed the modeling of the human body and the cab, which was the premise of visibility, accessibility and comfort analysis. During the process of modeling by JACK, we chose the database of Chinese to create the Chinese human body model and constructed the human body through 26 variables. As shown in the table, these variables could define a human body model (Table 4).

Table 4.   26 types of human body parameters in JACK

Stature	Hand length
Abdominal depth	Head breadth
Ankle height	Head height
Acromion height	Head length
Arm length	Hip breadth
Biacromial breadth	Interpupil distance
Bideltoid breadth	Shoulder elbow length
Buttock knee length	Sitting acromial height
Elbow rest height	Sitting eye height
Elbow-fingertip	Seated height
Foot breadth	Sitting knee height
Foot length	Length thigh clearance
Hand breadth	Thumbtip reach

After defining the size of the human model, we worked on creating and locating the driving attitude through driving the movement of each joint. In order to call directly, we saved the driving attitude to the database. At last, we imported the car CAD and bound it to the human model. As shown in the Fig. 7, we finished the modeling of the car cab and the driver.

3.2   Stage 2: Accessibility Check

When it came to accessibility check, we used the packaging guidelines (Automobile Design Guide) function provided by JACK software to verify the following aspects: push button max reach zone; three finger max reach zone; grasp max reach zone; wiper; shift area and thumb reach. The standard of inspection was the 5% female and 95% male human body model could meet the accessibility conditions.

Firstly, we ensured that the key components are within three reachable domains, which were the grasp maximum area, push button max reach zone; three finger max reach zone; grasp max reach zone; The radio and air conditioning knobs on the car must be controlled in this area. For example: Click Next > [Grasp Max Reach Zone] (the largest grab area), and the generated area was displayed on the screen in the form of curved boundary. As shown in Fig. 8, we could see the boundary surfaces.

Upon examination, we found that all buttons at the center console were in the push button max reach zone, hand brake, steering wheel, door handle and lever were in the grasp max reach zone.

Recently, with the increase of automobile functions, many functions such as driving mode switch buttons, shift paddles are integrated around the steering wheel to reduce the fatigue caused by frequent operation. Since JACK software doesn't give the accessibility criteria around the steering wheel, we reached a satisfactory solution.

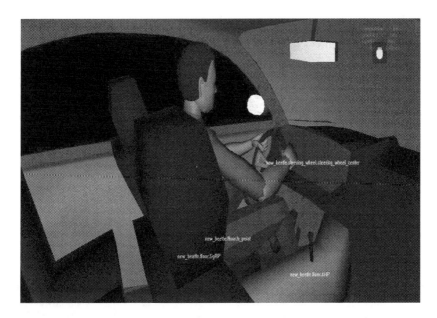

Fig. 7. 3D driving model

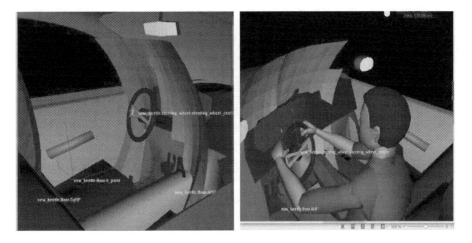

Fig. 8. Push button max reach zone and grasp maximum area

We simulated the position of our hands on the steering wheel by clicking the human control and manipulate function. and then, we generated reach zones including thumb domain and finger domain to check accessibility (Fig. 9).

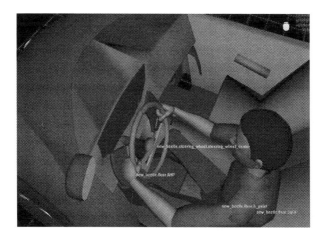

Fig. 9. Reach zones around steering wheel

3.3 Stage 3: Visibility Check

Visibility check is divided into two aspects

(1) Front view check

The front view includes the signal view, the view of the body barrier area, the bottom 30° view, and the wiper view.

(2) Rear view check

The rear view includes the inner mirror view and the side mirror view [11].

JACK's visibility field analysis tool was developed based on SAE eyellipse standard. Therefore, it can be directly applied to simulation without establishing visual simulation model.

In this paper, we used three functions including obscuration zones, reflection zones and packaging guidelines to calculate the scope of the vision field and finally the visibility check completed. As shown in the picture, there were results of visibility check about different checking item (Fig. 10).

3.4 Stage 4: Comfort Check

According to the driving conditions of the vehicle, driving comfort should include the following contents:

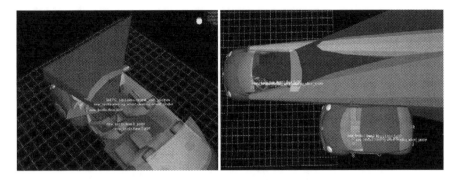

Fig. 10. Front view check and rear view check

(1) Static comfort: it refers to the influence of the seat on comfort related to the fit between the seat back and the human body when not considering the internal environment and the road condition of the vehicle.
(2) Dynamic comfort: it refers to the feeling of the driver when operating parts and interface interaction on comfort [12].

This was the process of comfort assessment:

Firstly, based on the data optimization algorithm, the most comfortable driving posture was quickly calculated by posture prediction module.

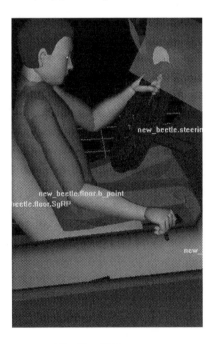

Fig. 11. Shift gesture

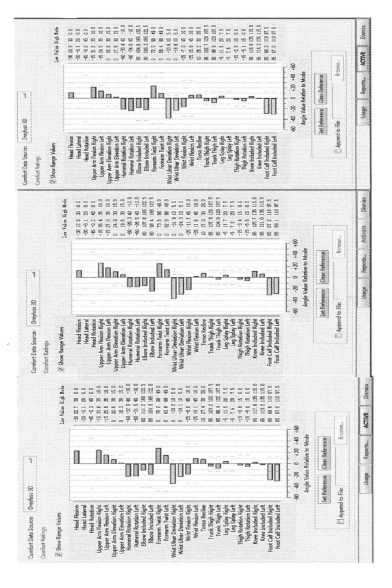

Fig. 12. Comfort evaluation results

Second stage, we established the driving operation gestures, including shifting, adjusting knobs, buttons, twisting and so on. For example, this picture showed shift gesture (Fig. 11).

Third stage, we achieved a comprehensive evaluation of comfort with comfort assessment module.

Finally, we got the comfort evaluation results (Fig. 12).

4   Conclusion

The main purpose of this paper is to study the layout of the cab based on ergonomics theory and JACK software. This paper is also the foundation for the future research of layout design in different kinds of vehicles.

In summary, the layout based on JACK could be a practical way to research the application of ergonomics theory in actual engineering. The main contents of this paper are as follows.

(1) According to ergonomics theory, we introduced three tools for accessibility check, visibility check and comfort check.
(2) Based on JACK software, we achieved cab layout analysis.

References

1. Milosevle, S.: Drivers' fatigue studies. Ergonomics **140**, 381–389 (1997)
2. Carsten, O.M.J., Lai, F.C.H., Barnard, Y., et al.: Control task substitution in semiautomated driving: does it matter what aspects are automated? In: Information Theory and Applications Workshop, pp. 1–9. IEEE Xplore (2011)
3. Townsend, F.E.: Bill validating apparatus: US, US 3481464 A (1969)
4. Maeda, K., Hünting, W., Grandjean, E.: Localized fatigue in accounting-machine operators. J. Occup. Med. Off. Publ. Ind. Med. Assoc. **22**(12), 810–816 (1980)
5. Park, S.J., Kim, C.B., Kim, C.J., et al.: Comfortable driving postures for Koreans. Int. J. Ind. Ergon. **26**(4), 489–497 (2000)
6. SAE J826-2002 H-Point Machine and Design Tool Procedures and Specifications
7. Miller, G., Parker, C.: Human engineering design for marine systems. Stand. News **4**(35) (2007)
8. SAE J941-2002 Motor Vehicle Drivers' Eye Locations
9. SAEJ1516 Accommodation Tool Referee Point, p. 3 (1998)
10. Mabbott, N.: Heavy Vehicle Seat Vibration and Driver Fatigue, Department of Transport and Regional Services Australian Transport Safety Bureau, July 2001
11. Chaffin, D.B.: Improving digital human modeling for proactive ergonomics in design. Ergonomics **48**(5), 478–491 (2005)
12. Beurier, G., Chevalot, N.: Simulation of digital human hand postures of car controls using a data based approach. Digital Human

Mapping System Between Passenger Experience and the Factors of Aircraft Cabin Design

Xinyi Tao, Siyu Ren, and Ting Han[✉]

School of Design, Shanghai Jiao Tong University, Shanghai, China
307175338@qq.com, {Vikey,hanting}@sjtu.edu.cn

Abstract. Nowadays, passenger comfort experience plays an increasingly important role in the design of aircraft. In order to further improve passengers' experience, systematical evaluation of the cabin of aircrafts is critical. And it's also the focus of airlines and aircraft manufacturers to promote their competitiveness to attract more customers.

In this paper, our target is quantitatively mapping influencing factors to the passenger comfort experience. Based on the factor model for passenger experience in the aircraft cabin design, which was presented in the previous research, we study the weight of influencing factors through expert interview. Then, we map each influencing factor to the passenger comfort experience using four kinds of methods: literature researching, questionnaire, experiment in the aircraft prototype and experiment with real size projection.

By weighting the relation function between the factor and the passenger experience, we obtain the whole quantitative mapping system. Also, we extended the system to an evaluation platform, which can quantitatively evaluate the comfort experience of aircraft cabin design.

Keywords: Mapping system · Passenger experience · Influencing factors
Evaluation platform

1   Introduction

Systematic and quantitative evaluation of passenger experience is of great significance to the aircraft cabin design. As the basic requirements of travel can be generally satisfied, passengers' experience during the trip, which largely depends on the aircraft cabin design, has a major impact on their choices of airlines. Studies on passenger comfort showed that vehicle (aircraft) with improved sense of comfort gain more popularity, which is compared with the unimproved ones [1–3]. In an effort to attract more passengers and promote their competitiveness, airlines and aircraft manufacturers focus on improving passengers' experience in the aircraft cabin. It is necessary to evaluate the passenger experience of aircraft cabin design systematically and quantitatively.

Prior literature mostly focuses on specific parts of aircraft cabin, such as the seat pitch [4], the color of light [5] and the cabin noise [6], and studies their relationships with passenger experience. Kremser who studied the influence of seat pitch on passengers' well-being developed a functional relationship among overall well-being,

© Springer International Publishing AG, part of Springer Nature 2018
V. G. Duffy (Ed.): DHM 2018, LNCS 10917, pp. 109–125, 2018.
https://doi.org/10.1007/978-3-319-91397-1_10

the subjects' anthropometry and seat pitch [4]. It was identified that there is a maximum overall well-being at a seat pitch of 34 inches to 40 inches. And a further enlargement of seat pitch, led to a reduction of well-being [4]. Winzen conducted a study aimed at analyzing the effects of four different lighting colors on the thermal experience in an aircraft-like environment [5]. In order to reveal optimisation potentials for an improved passenger noise acceptance, the effects of cabin noise on subjective comfort assessments were systematically investigated by Pennig [6]. The study of Ciloglu performed was performed to investigate and assess the whole body vibration (WBV) and the dynamic seat comfort of aircraft seats [7]. These researches focused on the specific part of aircraft cabin and figured out the exact relationship between these independent parts and passenger experience. However, the passenger experience of the entire aircraft remains unclear so far.

Although some researches demonstrated some factors which is influential to passengers' comfort and stand on holistic perspective, they usually don't map those factors to passenger comfort quantitatively, leave the exact relationship between factors and passenger experience unknown. Vink conducted a research to gather opinions from passengers, showing clear relationships between comfort and legroom, hygiene, crew attention and seat/personal space [1]. Patel worked out a model, which demonstrated what factors are affective and constitutive for aircraft passengers' comfort experience [8]. Ahmadpour's research characterized passenger experience in the form of eight themes and outlined their particular eliciting features [2]. His another study explored the factors underlying the passengers' experience of comfort and discomfort [9]. With these studies, airlines and aircraft manufacturers can figure out which factors are important, but not how they affect passenger experience.

Most of these researches evaluate passenger experience based on passengers' personal account for their flight comfort and analyze of the content of the data [2]. Generally, they investigate users and passengers via questionnaires and interviews. For example, the research of Brown collected the views and concerns from stakeholders in the aircraft industry, which illustrated the harmful aspects on passengers' health, comfort and safety of the aircraft cabin environment [10]. And in Vink's research, more than 10,000 online trip reports and 153 passenger interviews were used to gather opinions to evaluate passenger experience and explore the possibilities to improve the aircraft interior comfort experience [1]. Some researches assess user experience via objective measurement of physical parameters. The study of Ciaccia proposed a method to dynamically evaluate discomfort of a passenger seat by measuring the interface pressure between the occupant and the seat during the performance of the most common activities in a typical flight [11]. Li's research investigated and improved the method for simultaneous particle and gaseous contaminant fields measurement, which has a strong effect on the cabin environment and the comfort of passengers [12].

While there are several researches focused on passenger comfort in aircraft cabin, there is no method available that can not only evaluate passenger experience of aircraft cabin design holistically and quantitatively, but also conveniently. In order to improve passenger comfort, it is necessary to evaluate it systematically. Besides, experience is essentially subjective, which requires us investigate experts and passengers through questionnaires and interviews to evaluate it in this paper.

The previous research of our research group has presented the factor model for passenger experience in the aircraft cabin design. This model classifies the cabin hierarchically, including system, subsystem, high-level factors and underlying factors, and identifies the key underlying factors, which have major impact on passenger experience. In this paper, our goal is to conduct a mapping system between passenger experience and the factors of aircraft cabin design based on this model. We study the weight of influencing factors through expert interview. Then, each key underlying factor is further studied and mapped to the passenger comfort experience through user research and experiment. So that we got the quantitative mapping system with detailed parameters and relation functions.

What's more, we extended the mapping system to an evaluation platform, which can conveniently evaluate aircraft cabin design. Given the value of underlying factors, the platform can output scores of every part and the overall evaluation of the aircraft cabin design. This platform not only allows different design became comparable, but also enables us to see how the factors influence the design intuitively. It enables airlines and aircraft manufacturers to evaluate the passenger experience systematically, quantitatively and conveniently and to further improve the design of the aircraft cabin.

2   Factor Model for Passenger Experience in the Aircraft Cabin Design

The previous research of our research group has presented the factor model for passenger experience in the aircraft cabin design [13]. This model classifies the cabin hierarchically, including system, subsystem, high-level factors and underlying factors. Also, this model identifies the key underlying factors, which have main impact on passengers' experience. The framework and details of the factor model for passenger experience in the aircraft cabin design is shown in Figs. 1 and 2 [13].

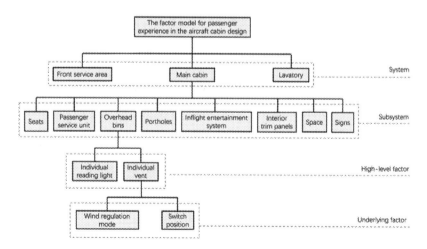

Fig. 1. Framework of the factor model for passenger experience in the aircraft cabin design.

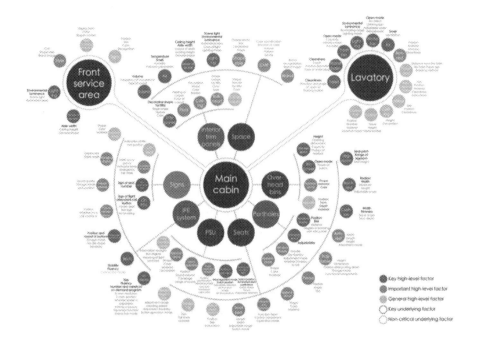

Fig. 2. The factor model for passenger experience in the aircraft cabin design with information of factor influence level.

Based on the factor model for passenger experience in the aircraft cabin design, we further study these key underlying factors in this paper. By studying the weights of these factors and their relationships with passenger experience, we map influencing factors in aircraft cabin design to the passenger comfort experience. Considering the large amount of all influencing factors and the passenger experience is mainly influenced by these key factors, we only focus on key underlying factors in this paper.

It should be noticed that crews on board are not under consideration in our model, since we only focus on the comfort experience of passengers. Here, we don't take cabin service into consideration.

3   Weights of the Factor Model

3.1   Method

The weights of influencing factors in the key influencing factor model are studied through expert interview. Participants of this research are experts on aircraft design from Commercial Aircraft Corporation of China Ltd, members of our research group, and expert users who travel by plane frequently. They would be compensated for their participation. We recruited passengers online, requiring them having more than 25 h of flight experience last year. These passengers with much flight experience are familiar with aircraft cabin and clear about how influencing factors affect their comfort experience.

The weight research contained 2 parts. In the first part, weights of systems, sub-systems and high-level factors are scored by participants, including 4 experts, 4 research group members and 4 passengers (7 males, aged 22–60, mean = 43). The second part is to score the key underlying factors. Participants are 7 research group members and 6 passengers (7 males, aged 22–46, mean = 32).

To begin the interview, the researcher explained the meaning of the factor model and these factors to make sure participants well understand the purpose of this research. Then participants are asked to score the weight of every part through a questionnaire. The researcher will be accompanied if the participant had any confuse about the meaning of factors. The researcher would be careful not to give any guidance that may have impact on the results. Finally, we collect and process the data. By averaging the data that all participants scored, we obtained the weight of these factors and systems.

3.2   Results

The weights of the factor model including four layers are shown in Table 1. For the three systems, the weights of the front service area, the main cabin and the toilet are 0.175, 0.656 and 0.169 respectively. It's obvious that the main cabin plays the most important role in the experience of passengers. And since seats and space give high weight in the evaluation system, they are critical for the main cabin.

Table 1. Weights of the factor model.

System		Sub-system		High-level factor		Underlying factor	
Front service area	0.175			Sense of space	0.60	Aisle width	1
				Lighting	0.40	Environmental luminance	1
Main cabin	0.656	Space	0.19	Sense of space	0.30	Ceiling height	0.42
						Aisle width	0.58
				Lighting	0.26	Scene light	0.58
						Environmental luminance	0.42
				Sound	0.22	Volume	1
				Air	0.22	Temperature	0.51
						Smell	0.49
		Passenger service units (PSU)	0.11	Individual reading light	0.46	Switch position	0.28
						Illuminated area	0.35
						Luminance	0.37
				Individual vent	0.54	Wind regulation mode	0.51

(*continued*)

Table 1. (*continued*)

System		Sub-system		High-level factor		Underlying factor	
						Switch position	0.49
		Overhead bins	0.10	Storage space	0.55	Height	1
				Overhead bin cover	0.45	Open mode	1
		Seats	0.22	Backrest	0.37	Radian (fit to body curve)	0.52
						Width	0.48
				Seat cushion	0.23	Width	0.50
						Firmness	0.50
				Legroom	0.40	Seat pitch	0.50
						Range of legroom	0.50
		Portholes	0.08	Transparency	0.48	Adjustability	1
				Window frame	0.52	Position	0.48
						Size	0.52
		Inflight entertainment system	0.16	HD display	0.36	Number and variety of on-demand program	0.36
						Fluency	0.35
						Size	0.29
				Wifi	0.33	Stability	0.50
						Fluency	0.50
				Passenger control unit	0.31	Position and layout of buttons	1
		Interior trim panels	0.07	Side panel	1	Decorative shape	0.55
						Tactility	0.45
		Signs	0.07	Sign on PSU	0.47	Sign of flight attendant call bottom	1
				Sign on overhead bin	0.53	Sign of seat number	1
Lavatory	0.169			Toilet	0.28	Toilet	1
				Hand basin	0.17	Hand basin	1
				Trash bin	0.14	Trash bin	1
				Water tap	0.10	Water tap	1
				Lighting	0.13	Lighting	1
				Air	0.18	Air	1

4   Mapping Relationship Research

To further study the mapping relationship between influencing factors and passenger experience, we investigated the experience of 31 key underlying factors in the aircraft cabin, trying to figure out how the passenger experience varies with the value of each factor.

Based on the factor characteristics and experimental conditions, we divided all the key underlying factors into four groups with different methods for further studying: literature researching, questionnaire, experiment in the aircraft prototype and experiment with full size projection. There is no recruited participant in literature researching. Using a 6-point scale, participants were asked to grade the experience of each key underlying factor (0 = extremely uncomfortable, to 5 = extremely comfortable).

4.1   Participants

We posted recruitment information on the internet. Participants are required to complete an online questionnaire about their background information including age, gender, height, number of previous flights, etc. We chose qualified participants base on the information they provided. And they would be rewarded for their participation. Considering that height and weight may affect the experience, we covered participants' heights in a wide range and kept well-proportioned. Also, participants should have flight experience last year and who with more flight experience would be preferred.

4.2   Literature Researching

3 factors in this part (Appendix 1) are based on literature researching. We adopted the results from literatures which have already worked out the mapping relationship we need. There are no recruited participants in literature researching.

For example, Lingying Ai conducted a research which figured out the relationship between the seat pitch and passenger experience (Fig. 3) [14]. We processed the data based on her research results.

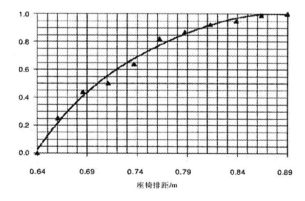

Fig. 3. Mapping relationship between the seat pitch and passenger experience.

4.3   Questionnaire

There are 11 factors that we studied through questionnaire (Appendix 1). These factors are explained clearly to make participants understand the exact meaning through the instructions and pictures in the questionnaire.

The questionnaire is elaborately designed, comprising three parts. The first part is a brief introduction of this questionnaire, including the purpose of this research and the instruction of how to complete the questionnaire. The second part is the main part, asking participants to evaluate the experience. Every factor was declared with its name, explanation and the system/sub-system it belongs to. Then, all options of this factor are listed and attached with statements and pictures about every option. And participants are asked to score the experience of every option of this factor (using a 6-point scale, 0 = extremely uncomfortable, to 5 = extremely comfortable). The third part concerned background information including age, gender, height, number of previous flights during last three years (1–10 times, 11–20 times, 21–30 times and more than 30 times), etc. The questionnaire was pilot-tested with three volunteers before distributing. It took roughly fifteen minutes to complete.

90 participants were recruited in a week. And we collected 86 valid responses (42 males, 44 females) in total. The age of the participants ranged from 18 to 55, averaged about 32 years old. The height of all the participants ranged from 155 cm to 180 cm. 56 participants had 1–10 flights during last three years, 18 had 11–20 times, 9 had 21–30 times and 3 had more than 30 times.

4.4   Experiment in the Aircraft Prototype

There are 11 factors that we studied through experiment in the aircraft prototype (Appendix 1). These factors are not easy for participants to imagine only with words or pictures, thus the simulated onsite experiment is necessary for participants to score the experience.

The experiment took place on the prototype of C919 at Commercial Aircraft Corporation of China Ltd. We set up the experiment environment to simulate the context of use of these factors. To begin the experiment, the researcher briefly introduced the purpose of this experiment and the tasks that participants need to complete, then collected the background information from participants. There were 11 tasks prepared, which are associated with 11 factors respectively. For example, we installed four displays of different sizes (7.9 in, 9.7 in, 10.5 in and 12.9 in) on the seat back and numbered them. Participants were asked to sit toward the display one by one to score the experience of each size (using a 6-point scale, 0 = extremely uncomfortable, to 5 = extremely comfortable). Participants were also encouraged to describe their feelings and how these influenced their sense of comfort.

There were 14 people that took part in this experiment (8 males, 6 females). The age of the participants ranged from 18 to 35, averaged about 27 years old. The height of the participants ranged from 155 cm to 188 cm. 3 participants had 4–7 flights last year, 7 had 8–11 times and 4 had more than 12 times (as the number of participants who can take part in the experiment was limited, we selected participants with more flight experience).

4.5 Experiment with Real Size Projection

7 factors in this part (Appendix 1), could not be simulated appropriately on the prototype, are studied by creating visually immersive scene. We held the experiment with a projection to simulate the environment on the plain.

The experiment took place in a laboratory at Shanghai Jiao Tong University with a projection wall larger than 24 m^2 (4 m high and 6 m long). The projector we used in this experiment is able to project the scene of simulated cabin to the screen with its real size. Pictures used to simulate the environment on the plain were exported from the 3D model which were supported by Commercial Aircraft Corporation of China Ltd and they were projected equally proportional to the real cabin. To begin the experiment, the researcher briefly introduced the purpose of this experiment and tasks that participants need to complete and then collected the background information of participants. There were seven groups of pictures which are correlated to seven factors. Participants were asked to stand in front of the projection wall. Before showing one group of pictures, participants were told which factor these pictures relating to. Participants will have a quick glance of every group of pictures, then will be asked to go through those pictures carefully and score the experience (using a 6-point scale, 0 = extremely uncomfortable, to 5 = extremely comfortable). There was 20 s' break between showing two groups of pictures.

There were 30 people that took part in this experiment (15 males, 15 females). The age of the participants ranged from 18 to 40 with the mean value equal to 24 years old. The height of the participants ranged from 155 cm to 180 cm. 20 participants had 1–3 flights last year, 9 had 4–7 times and 1 had more than 8 times.

5 Mapping Results

According to the features of the factors, all of the factors were categorized into three types: nominal, ordinal and interval. To discover the mapping relationships to the user experience, we processed and analyzed the data we collected based on their types.

5.1 Nominal

There are 13 factors (Appendix 1), each has several options. For example, the switch position of individual reading light (PSU – Individual reading light - Switch position) has three different options: integrated with the lamp, separate from the lamp and on the passenger control unit. This factor was tested in the experiment in the aircraft prototype. Participants were asked to use switches of those three kinds and then score the experience of each. By averaging the data of the options that all participants scored for respectively, and converting it to centesimal system, we obtained the experience value of each option (Table 2).

Table 2. Experience value of the switch position of individual reading light. (N = 14)

System/subsystem	Passenger service unit – Individual reading light – Switch position		
Option	01: integrated with the lamp	02: separate from the lamp	03: on the passenger control unit
Mean score (SD) from participants	2.73 (1.17)	3.13 (0.97)	4.27 (0.84)
Experience value	54.6	62.6	85.4

5.2   Ordinal

5 factors (Appendix 1) here are benchmarked by several degrees. For example, the fluency of the HD display (Inflight entertainment system - HD display - Fluency) is benchmarked by four degrees: very sluggish, sluggish, smooth and very smooth. This factor was tested in the questionnaire. Participants were asked to score the experience of each degree. By averaging the data that all participants scored for the degrees respectively and converting it to centesimal system, we obtained the experience value of each factor (Table 3).

Table 3. Experience value of the fluency of HD display in the inflight entertainment system. (N = 86)

System/subsystem	Inflight entertainment system - HD display - Fluency			
Degree	01: very sluggish	02: sluggish	03: sooth	04: very smooth
Mean score (SD) from participants	0.86 (1.37)	1.38 (1.28)	2.69 (0.99)	4.30 (0.92)
Experience value	17.2	27.6	53.8	86.0

5.3   Interval

There are 13 factors (Appendix 1). Values of these factors are on continuous within a certain range. For example, the height of aircraft ceiling (Space - Sense of space - Ceiling height) usually range from 1800 mm to 2250 mm [15]. This factor was tested in the experiment with real size projection. We simulated the cabin environment with six different heights of aircraft ceiling and asked participants to score each of them. By averaging the data that all participants scored for respectively, and converting it to centesimal system, we obtained the experience value of each height. The function was then fitted by six data point so that we can obtained the relationship between the height of aircraft ceiling and passenger experience (Table 4).

Table 4. Experience value of the ceiling height. (N = 30)

System/subsystem	Space - Sense of space - Ceiling height					
Height	01: 1800 mm	02: 1900 mm	03: 2000 mm	04: 2100 mm	05: 2200 mm	06: 2250 mm
Mean score (SD) from participants	2.27 (1.46)	3.23 (1.10)	3.10 (0.99)	3.20 (1.06)	2.67 (1.30)	2.43 (1.50)
Experience value	45.4	64.6	62.0	64.0	53.4	48.6
Relation function	$F(x) = -916.042 + 0.726x - 5.876E - 8)x^3$					

6 Results

6.1 Framework of the Mapping System

By combining the key factor model with the weight and the relation function we derived above, we obtained the mapping system between passenger experience and the factors of aircraft cabin design (Fig. 4). When there is a design proposal of aircraft cabin, the experience value of every underlying factor can be derived from the relationship function. Starting from the experience value, we cascaded the levels of our model by weighting. It's convenient for airlines and aircraft manufactures to evaluate the aircraft cabin design based on these scores.

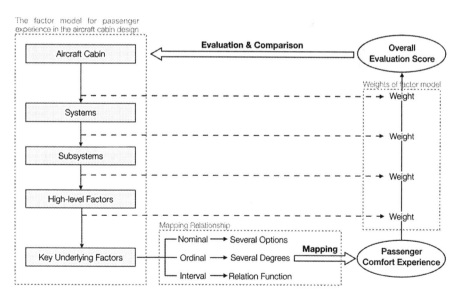

Fig. 4. Framework of the mapping system between passenger experience and the factors of aircraft cabin design.

6.2   Evaluation Platform

Based on the mapping system between passenger experience and the factors of aircraft cabin design, we developed an evaluation platform. This platform meet the needs of aircraft designers, airlines and aircraft manufactures, helping them to figure out the relationship between aircraft cabin design and passenger experience. To make it user friendly, factors of three types were input by check lists, text fields and sliders.

The platform is composed by five parts: model visualization (Fig. 5), scheme import (Fig. 6), scheme management, scheme detail and scheme comparison (Fig. 7). In the part of model visualization, the structures and details of the mapping system are showed visually. In the part of scheme import, users can input detailed parameters of factors to build a design scheme and scores of the scheme will be listed. In the part of scheme management, users are allowed to rename, copy, sort and label the schemes. Users can also check the details and scores of these schemes and export them to diagrams in the part of scheme detail. In the part of scheme comparison, users can generate the comparison chart by their own choice of schemes and factors, which can be exported easily and used for report and demonstration.

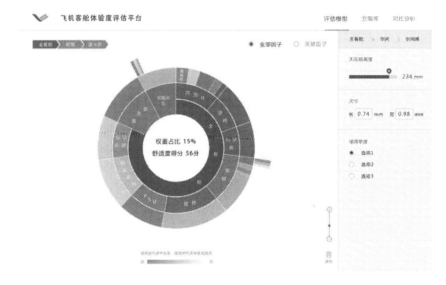

Fig. 5. Model visualization part of the evaluation platform, which visually shows the structures and details of the mapping system.

With this platform, users can easily evaluate and compare different design schemes of the aircraft cabin design. They can also figure out the advantages and disadvantages of these schemes and be clearer about what should they improve.

Fig. 6. Scheme import part of the evaluation platform, which enables users to input detailed parameters of factors to build a design scheme.

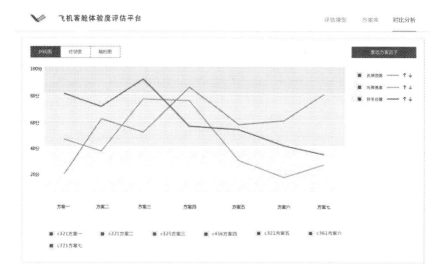

Fig. 7. Scheme comparison part of the evaluation platform, which can generate the comparison chart by users' choice of schemes and factors

7   Conclusion and Discussion

This paper describes in detail a mapping system between passenger experience and the factors of aircraft cabin design, and developed an evaluation platform. This mapping system can be used as a method that easily and systematically evaluates and compares design schemes of aircraft cabin. It's of great significance for airlines and aircraft manufactures to further improve aircraft cabin design and promote their competitiveness.

There are some limitations of this study, (1) the totality of the factors, (2) the relationship between some underlying factors and (3) the limitation of participants. Firstly, considering the large amount of all influencing factors and the passenger experience is mainly influenced by these key factors, we focused on key underlying factors in this paper. However, it should be admitted that the other factors also have impact on the passenger experience, though not considered highly relevant. Also, there were four key underlying factors (Temperature, Smell, Illuminated area and Luminance of the Individual reading light) that were not studied in this paper because of the limitation of experimental condition. And the experience of lavatory was not studied in this paper, which is considered as an relatively independent system. Secondly, we regarded these underlying factors as independent in this paper and evaluate their experience separately. However, in the real environment of aircraft cabin, the change of one factor may affect the experience of another factor, such as the seat pitch and the legroom. Finally, the number of participants is limited.

If any further searching is conducted, it should consider studying the factors more comprehensively, including the four key underlying factors (Temperature, Smell, Illuminated area and Luminance of the Individual reading light) and the factors with low impact. Also, enlarging the scale of the participants may make the relationship function more accurate and the background data of the platform can be updated. Furthermore, which factors have influences on others, how they affect each other, how they affect the overall evaluation of aircraft cabin design and how to combine them with the mapping system are interesting topics that deserve to be further studied.

Acknowledgements. This paper is sponsored by Shanghai Jiao Tong University Interdisciplinary among Humanity, Social Science and Natural Science Fund (13JCY02).

Appendix 1. Research Methods and Types of Mapping Results of the Key Underlying Factors

System	Sub-system	High-level factor	Underlying factor	Research method	Type of mapping result
Front service area		Sense of space	Aisle width	Experiment with real size projection	Interval
		Lighting	Environmental luminance	Experiment with real size projection	Interval

(continued)

(*continued*)

System	Sub-system	High-level factor	Underlying factor	Research method	Type of mapping result
Main cabin	Space	Sense of space	Ceiling height	Experiment with real size projection	Interval
			Aisle width	Experiment with real size projection	Interval
		Lighting	Scene light	Experiment with real size projection	Nominal
			Environmental luminance	Experiment with real size projection	Interval
		Sound	Volume	Literature researching	Interval
		Air	Temperature		
			Smell		
	Passenger service units (PSU)	Individual reading light	Switch position	Experiment in the aircraft prototype	Nominal
			Illuminated area		
			Luminance		
		Individual vent	Wind regulation mode	Questionnaire	Nominal
			Switch position	Experiment in the aircraft prototype	Nominal
	Overhead bins	Storage space	Height	Experiment with real size projection	Interval
		Overhead bin cover	Open mode	Questionnaire	Nominal
	Seats	Backrest	Radian (fit to body curve)	Experiment in the aircraft prototype	Ordinal
			Width	Literature researching	Interval
		Seat cushion	Width	Experiment in the aircraft prototype	Interval
			Firmness	Experiment in the aircraft prototype	Ordinal
		Legroom	Seat pitch	Literature researching	Interval
			Range of legroom	Experiment in the aircraft prototype	Nominal
	Portholes	Transparency	Adjustability	Questionnaire	Nominal
		Window frame	Position	Experiment in the aircraft prototype	Nominal
			Size	Experiment in the aircraft prototype	Interval

(*continued*)

(continued)

System	Sub-system	High-level factor	Underlying factor	Research method	Type of mapping result
	Inflight entertainment system	HD display	Number and variety of on-demand program	Questionnaire	Interval
			Fluency	Questionnaire	Ordinal
			Size	Experiment in the aircraft prototype	Interval
		Wifi	Stability	Questionnaire	Ordinal
			Fluency	Questionnaire	Ordinal
		Passenger control unit	Position and layout of buttons	Questionnaire	Nominal
	Interior trim panels	Side panel	Decorative shape	Questionnaire	Nominal
			Tactility	Experiment in the aircraft prototype	Nominal
	Signs	Sign on PSU	Sign of flight attendant call bottom	Questionnaire	Nominal
		Sign on overhead bin	Sign of seat number	Questionnaire & Experiment in the aircraft prototype	Nominal

References

1. Ciloglu, H., Alziadeh, M., Mohany, A., Kishawy, H.: Assessment of the whole body vibration exposure and the dynamic seat comfort in passenger aircraft. Int. J. Ind. Ergon. **45**(7), 116–123 (2015)
2. Ahmadpour, N., Lindgaard, G., Robert, J.M., Pownall, B.: The thematic structure of passenger comfort experience and its relationship to the context features in the aircraft cabin. Ergonomics **57**(6), 801–815 (2014)
3. Richards, L.G.: On the psychology of passenger comfort. In: Oborne, D.J., LevisHuman, J. A. (eds.) Factors in Transport Research, vol. 2, pp. 15–23. Academic Press, London (1980)
4. Kremser, F., Guenzkofer, F., Sedlmeier, C., Sabbah, O., Bengler, K.: Aircraft seating comfort: the influence of seat pitch on passengers' well-being. Work **41**(Suppl. 1), 4936–4942 (2012)
5. Winzen, J., Albers, F., Marggraf-Micheel, C.: The influence of coloured light in the aircraft cabin on passenger thermal comfort. Light. Res. Technol. **59**(46), 465–475 (2014)
6. Pennig, S., Quehl, J., Rolny, V.: Effects of aircraft cabin noise on passenger comfort. Ergonomics **55**(10), 1252 (2012)
7. Vink, P., Bazley, C., Kamp, I., Blok, M.: Possibilities to improve the aircraft interior comfort experience. App. Ergon. **43**(2), 354–359 (2012)
8. Patel, H., D'Cruz, M.: Passenger-centric factors influencing the experience of aircraft comfort. Transp. Rev. **38**(2), 252–269 (2017)

9. Ahmadpour, N., Robert, J.M., Lindgaard, G.: Aircraft passenger comfort experience: underlying factors and differentiation from discomfort. Appl. Ergon. **52**, 301 (2016)
10. Brown, T.P., Shuker, L.K., Rushton, L., Warren, F., Stevens, J.: The possible effects on health, comfort and safety of aircraft cabin environments. J. R. Soc. Promot. Health **121**(3), 177–184 (2001)
11. Ciaccia, F.R., Sznelwar, L.I.: An approach to aircraft seat comfort using interface pressure mapping. Work **41**(Suppl. 1), 240–245 (2012)
12. Li, F., Liu, J., Pei, J., Lin, C.H., Chen, Q.: Experimental study of gaseous and particulate contaminants distribution in an aircraft cabin. Atmos. Environ. **85**(2), 223–233 (2014)
13. Han, T., Ren, S., Tao, X.: Factor model for passenger experience in the aircraft cabin design, Commercial Aircraft Corporation of China Ltd. (2017)
14. Ai, L.: Evaluation of space comfort for civil aircraft cabin. China Sci. Technol. Inf. (13), 97–98 (2016)
15. A summary report of the design detail of the equipment and decoration of aircraft, Commercial Aircraft Corporation of China Ltd. (2017)

A Study on the Differences of Male Youth Physical Characteristics Between South China and Northwest China

Jiahui Xu[✉] and Xiaoping Hu

South China University of Technology, Panyu District, China
569306755@qq.com

Abstract. Many countries have established their own type database corresponding to the their country human body, and will regularly measure the specific size of the human body size. In particular, the differences in eating habits, environment, climate and other reasons will lead to a certain difference between people in various regions in China, with a vast territory and a huge population. Therefore, it is particularly urgent to do a physical characteristic survey on young people (this only for male youth as a research object).

The research objects are young men in southern China and the northwest. Firstly, questionnaires were used as a analyze survey in modern clothing market. The questionnaires collected the problems existing in the clothing market of the two regions both in the South China and the northwest, and analyzed the problems existing in the clothing market. It is a necessary step to interview the young men about the feeling when purchasing clothing in the South China and Northwest China. Later on the clothing design, designers can give a more special set and design in the non-fit parts. Secondly, selecting randomly 120 representative young men from South China or the northwest as objects to carry out body size measurement.

First, it provides a scientific and accurate theoretical basis for the prototype structure of clothes in different regions of China by the research and analysis of young men's the specific body differences in South China and Northwest China. Second, through a series of data analysis, the general trend and the regional difference of the characteristics of the young men in South China and Northwest China were obtained, which provided data for the establishment of regional database.

Keywords: Male youth · Region · Body measurement · Body difference
Clothing

1 Problems with Chinese Clothing Prototype

1.1 The Existing Data Is Old

In the late 1880s, China has carried on the massive body measurements and made basic data of human body size, respectively 1997 edition and 2008 edition, however, the two versions were based on a slight adjustment in the 1991 version, use the 2008 version has been in place for ten years now. With the improvement of living conditions, the

© Springer International Publishing AG, part of Springer Nature 2018
V. G. Duffy (Ed.): DHM 2018, LNCS 10917, pp. 126–134, 2018.
https://doi.org/10.1007/978-3-319-91397-1_11

changes in living environment and different dietary habits, the size of Chinese people has undergone great changes and varied greatly. Today's standard clothing size data appears to be aging, unable to meet the more requirements of today's consumers, at the same time the production of apparel companies also lack the corresponding value of reference and guidance.

1.2   Size Specification Is Not Detailed Enough

In many developed countries there are detailed standard clothing sizes classification. In Japan, for example, the size of a man's clothing is based on a classification of body size to indicate different clothing sizes. The size classification is determined by the difference between armpit circumference and waist circumference, including J, JY, Y, YA, BB, BE A, AB, B, E, A total of 10 kinds of body shape, in simple terms, they represent the person's obesity degree. In addition, in Japan, the standard of clothing size is also divided into different age stages. For example, men's clothing sizes are divided into two categories: boys and adults, and the classification is very detailed. However, in China, there are only four types of sizes for men's clothes, and the standard of clothes size is regardless of age. They are Y, A, B and C respectively. Among them, type A is the average body type of most people, type Y is small waist size, type B is slightly fat body type, and type C is obese body [1].

2   Body Measurement

2.1   Measurement Objects and Time

The measured samples from South China and northwest China were randomly selected 120 students from South China Technology University, all of which were represented in Guangdong Province and two places in northwestern Gansu province. Measurement time will be completed from December 2017 to January 2018.

2.2   Measurement Methods and Tools

First, the one-dimensional method of contact is used – the Martin measurement method, that is, manual measurement method. Second, the Heath-Carter method was used to measure. When measuring, the subjects need to keep upright, their eyes are straight ahead, their arms are naturally pendulous, palms facing the body side, and the left and right heel is aligned. When measuring one side, the uniform is subject to the right. At the same time, as the measurement time is winter, the subjects are asked to focus on the warm indoor laboratory, wearing close-fitting clothing for measurement.

Measuring tools include: altimeter, rod-shaped instrument, weight gauge, steel tape measure, soft tape measure, measuring instrument and so on.

2.3   Measurement Items

According to the human body measurements handbook, for the height, weight, cervical height, sitting cervical height, neck circumference, across shoulder, chest circumference, arm length, waist circumference, leg length, hip circumference 11 parts of the measurement. [2] In addition to the weight, according to the current Chinese clothing production and design needs and status quo, the remaining 10 items of the clothing model GB/T 1335.1 2008 platemaking and push board necessary parts, therefore, choose the above parts as measuring projects.

2.4   Analysis Method

The data analysis of this study was based on data integration analysis by Statistical Product and Service Solutions for Windows developed by the American SPSS Company in the early 1980s.

3   Data Extraction and Processing

According to the prescribed measuring position, each of the measurement objects measured the same specimen three times. If three times measuring range is in the range of deflection, then the data is available, take the average value as valid data, otherwise retest. Each measurement objects were measured by three surveyors, take the effective measure three data average as the experimental data (Table 1).

Table 1. Maximum allowable error and standard deviation for adult human body parts size.

Parts	Maximum allowable error/Δ (cm)	Standard deviation/s (cm)	S/Δ
Height	1.0	6.2	6.20
Chest circumference	1.5	5.5	3.67
Waist circumference	1.0	6.7	6.70
Hip circumference	1.5	5.2	3.47

4   Measurement Results and Data Analysis

It can be concluded from Fig. 1 that all the values listed in the picture, All body data of young men in Gansu province are larger than that of young men in Guangdong Province. In these projects, there were statistically significant differences in the height, chest circumference, waist circumference, abdominal circumference and hip circumference of male youth between Guangdong province and Gansu province. The results showed that the two regions of Northwest and South China were positively correlated with height, weight, high cervical point, cervical height, neck circumference, total shoulder width, chest circumference, arm length, waist circumference, leg length and hip circumference. In other words, the Northwest young men not only height, circumference and width size is also greater than the young men in South China. Young men in Northwest China than in South China young men are not only taller, the body outline is also more robust (Table 2).

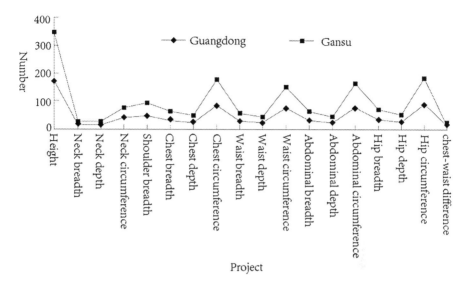

Fig. 1. .

Table 2. Chest circumference of male youth in Guansu province.

Height/cm	Chest circumference/cm	72	76	80	84	88	92	96
155	Number/60people				1			
160			1	2	2	1	1	
165		1	2	4	5	4	2	
170			1	4	6	5	3	1
175				2	3	3	2	1
180					1	1	1	

The following is an example of the chest circumference and waist circumference of the male youths in Gansu province in Northwest China and Guangdong province in South China (Tables 3 and 4).

Table 3. Chest circumference of male youth in Guangdong province.

Height/cm	Chest circumference/cm	72	76	80	84	88	92
150	Number/60people			1			
155				2	1		
160			1	4	4	2	
165			2	6	8	4	1
170			1	3	6	5	2
175				1	2	2	
180					1	1	

Table 4. Waist circumference of male youth in Gansu province

Waist circumference/cm	Height/cm					
	155	160	165	170	175	180
	Number/60people					
56						
58				1		
60			1	1		
62			1	1		
64		1	2	1		
66		2	3	2	1	
68	1	1	2	3	1	
70		1	2	3	2	1
72	1	1	2	3	2	
74		1	1	2	2	1
76			1	2	1	
78			1	1	1	
80				1	1	
82					1	

Figures 2 and 3 show the proportion of different body types in Gansu Province and Guangdong Province respectively. Type A is the average size of most people, the type Y is small waist size, type B is slightly fatter size, and type C is obese size. In this survey, the proportion of type A in Gansu province was the largest, ratio of 37.24%. Type C was the smallest, at 9.5%; In Guangdong province, the proportions of type A and type Y were almost the same, ratio of 37.27% and 37.04% respectively, while type C was the smallest, at 11.56%. This suggests that young men in Gansu province are more physically fit and less obese than men in the past. In south China, young men in Guangdong province are more well-proportioned and small waist size, and have less obese size (Table 5).

The body proportions(Gansu)

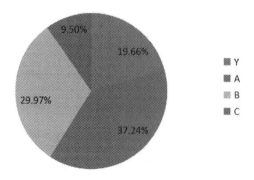

Fig. 2. .

The body proportions（Guangdong）

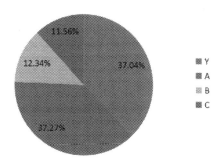

Fig. 3. .

Table 5. Waist circumference of male youth in Guangdong province.

Waist circumference/cm	Height/cm						
	150	155	160	165	170	175	180
	Number/60people						
58				1			
60			1	1			
62			1	2	1		
64	1	1	2	3	2	1	
66			2	4	3	1	
68		1	2	4	3	1	
70			1	2	2	1	
72		1	1	2	3	1	1
74				1	2	1	
76				1	1		
78					1		

A person's physique is often described in terms of body size, according to the physical classification developed by American psychologist W.h.sheldon, the body is roughly divided into three categories: endomorph (fat type), esomorphic (stout type), and ectomorphic (slender type), which can be divided into 13 body types. These 13 kinds are: ectomorphic endomorph, balanced endomorph, esomorphic endomorph, endomorph-mesomorph, endomorphic mesomorph, balanced mesomorph, ectomorphic mesomorph, mesomorph-ectomotph, mesomorphic ectomorph, balanced ectomorph, ectomorphic ectomorph, ectomorph-endomorph and central (Table 6).

The results show that: the average body size of young men in Gansu Province is 2.9-3.6-3.1 to 3.2-4.5-2.1, the overall majority of which belong to the endomorphic mesomorph, in 13 body types, with higher frequency of three body types are endomorphic mesomorph, endomorph-mesomorph and ectomorphic mesomorph, 18 persons(29.9%), 8 persons (14%) and 6 persons(10.3%) respectively. while the average

Table 6. The body proportions in Gansu and Guangdong province

The body proportions	Gansu	Guangdong
	Number/60people	Number/60people
Ectomorphic endomorph	0	0
Balanced endomorph	1	0
Mesomorphic endomorph	5	0
Endomorph-mesomorph	8	4
Endomorphic mesomorph	18	9
Balanced mesomorph	6	4
Ectomorphic mesomorph	6	13
Mesomorph-ectomorph	5	0
Mesomorphic ectomorph	6	7
Balanced ectomorph	2	12
Ectomorphic ectomorph	0	2
Ectomorph-endomorph	0	0
Central	3	9

figure of male youth in Guangdong province is 3.4-4.6-3.4, belonging to the endo-morphic mesomorph. In 13 kinds of body type, The highest frequency of the type is the ectomorphic mesomorph,13 people (21.7%), The highest frequency of the type is the balanced ectomorph,12 people (20%). The young men in Gansu province are tall and strong, while the young men in Guangdong province are mainly of ectomorphic and central type [3] (Table 7).

Figure 4 is the reference value of the male body average of height 170 cm [4].

Table 7. The reference value of the Chinese standard GBT1335.1-2008.

Parts of the	Height	Cervical height	Neck to waist	Arm length	Waist height	Chest circumference	Neck circumference	Across shoulder
The numerical	155	133	60.5	51	94	76	33.4	40.4
	160	137	62.5	52.5	97	80	34.4	41.6
	165	141	64.5	54	100	84	35.4	42.8
	170	145	66.5	55.5	103	88	36.4	44
	175	149	68.5	57	106	92	37.4	45.2
	180	153	70.5	58.5	109	96	38.4	46.4
	185	157	72.5	60	112	100	39.4	47.6
	190	161	74.5	61.5	115	104	40.4	48.5

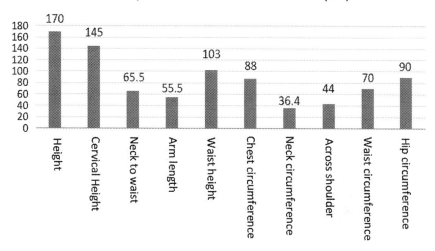

Fig. 4. .

5   Conclusion

The measured data are compared with the average of the data given by the Chinese men clothes standard GBT1335.1-2008], showing that at present China, chinese male body shape has become taller and stronger than the national average shape years ago, in the case of Gansu Province and Guangdong province.

This article through to male youth size in south China and northwest China comparative study, found that the two areas of young men overall size: young men in Guangdong province in southern China is relatively short and thin, and male youth groups in Gansu province in northwest China is relatively tall and burly, bones and muscles are more developed. Based on the differences between these two large areas of young men body sizes, therefore, the enterprises in the production of men's wear, should be divided according to different regions, different models in detail and make clothing structure targeted design more according with human body and wearing comfortable; At the same time, in the knowledge of these differences, to achieve reasonable production, can also bring cost savings to the enterprise.

As a result of funds, time and other objective conditions, this article only to the students of South China University of Technology from Gansu province and Guangdong province as a representative of the investigation, for further analysis and comparison, hope that the data can provide a reference for the relevant research field, and the results of the study also shows that t Chinese human body after more than 10 years of time, a certain change has taken place, and the conclusions of the data will make China's garment production more consistent with the human body, to adapt to the vast number of consumer groups.

References

1. Machiko, M., Rong, Z., Hao, Z.: Costume Modeling. China Textile Press, Beijing (2006)
2. Shao, X.: Human Measurement Manual, pp. 264–300. Shanghai Dictionary Press, Shanghai (1985)
3. Wan, X., Li, Q., Xu, F.: The application of Heath-Carter body type method. Med. Inf., **29**(36) (2016)
4. The State administration of quality Supervision, inspection and quarantine of the PRC. The People's Republic of China's national standard clothing size men: clothing size men. China Standard Press (2009)
5. Cui, J., Zhu, Q.: Study on the differences between male youth and other regions in western Guangdong. National College Track and Field Research Paper Reports (2010)
6. Pan, J.: Costume Ergonomics and Costume Design. China Light Industry Press, Beijing (2000)
7. Wu, R.K., Wu, X.Z., Zhang, Z.B.: Methods of Anthropometry, pp. 102–120. Science Publishing Company (1984). (in China)
8. Carter, J.E.L., Heath, B.H.: Somatotyping: Development and Applications, pp. 373–387. Cambridge University Press, Cambridge (1990)

3D Human Head Shape Variation by Using Principal Component Analysis

Yanling Zheng[1], Haixiao Liu[1], Jianwei Niu[1(✉)], Linghua Ran[2], and Taijie Liu[2]

[1] School of Mechanical Engineering, University of Science and Technology Beijing,
Beijing, China
`niujw@ustb.edu.cn`
[2] China National Institute of Standardization, Beijing, China

Abstract. In traditional anthropometry, people adopt the concept of percentile of some critical dimensions, e.g., height. However, percentile has been criticized and its applicability in product design is controversial. Another popular concept in fitting design is sizing, which means to classify human samples into pre-defined categories. Conventionally, sizing scheme usually adopt no more than four dimensions to set up dozens of complex grading charts. However, human head is in 3D form, and limited dimensions can't represent its whole morphologic variation. By the aid of 3D scan technology, there have appeared numerous large-scale 3D human body surveys, as an example, the latest and largest 3D human body survey of Chinese minors conducted by China National Institute of Standardization in the last decade. We used Principal Component Analysis (PCA) as our approach and analyzed 100 3D human head models (all males) and compared their shape variation. The sample data used for our study were taken from 3D human body survey of Chinese minors conducted by China National Institute of Standardization. Our results showed that four principal components described more than 90% of the total variation in the sample. Models of the 3D human head lying on the hyper-ellipsoid constituted by principal component axis have also been re-constructed, using the sample mean and principal components, and they are used to illustrate the variation in human head shape of the sample population, to generate new human head shapes and to reconstruct different human head shapes rapidly. Furthermore, the shape variation carried by each principal component combined distinct factors, e.g., height variation, width variation or depth variation. It is hard to differentiate the specific meaning of each principal component, which made PCA difficult to be used for product designers, tailors and other engineers. Therefore we extended PCA method with a novel regression model to explore the semantic attributes of each principal component. Our method can achieve 3D shape variation quantification efficiently, intuitively and accurately. Experimental results show that PCA on 3D point cloud to realize 3D human head shape variation is an effective method. This method can also find applications in parametric human body modeling, which will greatly reduce the cost of animation and the time of human modeling.

Keywords: Three dimensional (3D) · Human shape variation
Principal Component Analysis (PCA)

© Springer International Publishing AG, part of Springer Nature 2018
V. G. Duffy (Ed.): DHM 2018, LNCS 10917, pp. 135–144, 2018.
https://doi.org/10.1007/978-3-319-91397-1_12

1 Introduction

To quantify the variation of the human head shape is not easy. Traditionally, people adopt the concept of percentile of some critical dimensions, e.g., height. Percentile has been used in product ergonomic design. For instance, in automotive interior design, the 5th percentile of female and the 95th percentile of male are the two extreme interior dimension references. However, percentile has also been criticized and its applicability in product design is controversial. The opponents insist that not all the dimensions of human body will increase or decrease in the same extent simultaneously. In other word, there is no average man on the earth. Percentile only puts great emphasis on some key dimensions, and overlooks other dimensions, even though these dimensions are quite important for fitting design.

Another popular concept in fitting design is sizing, which means to classify human samples into pre-defined categories. Conventionally, sizing scheme usually adopt no more than four dimensions to set up dozens of complex grading charts. Human shape is in 3D form, and limited dimensions can't represent its whole variation. For instance, it's common to find out some persons who share the identical height, chest circumference and waist circumference, but actually their human shapes are not quite the same.

Due to the progress of 3D scan technology, it is easy to get a lot of 3D scanned data. There have appeared numerous large-scale 3D human body surveys in the world, as an example, the latest and largest 3D human body survey of Chinese minors conducted by China National Institute of Standardization in the last decade. In this survey, about 20,000 subjects (9,666 males and 9,699 females) participated. The population database has ages ranging from four to seventeen years old. Our previous work presented the preliminary statistical results of the database mentioned above [1]. Another large scale survey is the Civilian American and European Surface Anthropometry Resource (CAESAR) [2].

It's promising and challenging as well to quantify the human head shape variation directly on 3D human scanned point cloud, among which Principal Components Analysis (PCA) was believed as an attractive and focal method [3, 4]. We used PCA to analyze 100 3D human head models (all males) and compared their main shape variation. The sample data used for our study were taken from the senior high school students group of the 3D human body survey of Chinese minors conducted by China National Institute of Standardization. PCA offers a means of capturing the significant variations in a data sample. Our results showed that four principal components described above 90% of the total variation in the sample. Models of the 3D human head lying on the hyper-ellipsoid constituted by principal component axis have also been re-constructed, using the sample mean and principal components, and they are used to illustrate the variation in human head shape of the sample population, to generate new human head shapes and to reconstruct different human head shapes rapidly.

However, the main shape variation produced by PCA combined distinct factors such as length and width [5]. It is hard to differentiate the specific meaning of each principal component, which made this approach difficult to be used for product designers, tailors and engineers. Therefore we extended PCA method with a novel regression model to explore the space of semantic attributes. For each principal component, a linear mapping between semantic attribute parameters, such as height, and the corresponding shape variations is learned. Our method can achieve 3D shape variation quantification efficiently, intuitively and accurately.

2   Method

2.1   Sample Data

The sample data used for our research is from the latest and largest 3D human body survey of Chinese minors along with their age, weight, height and a key set of body measurements. This survey was conducted by Chinese National Institute of Standardization in the last decade. In this survey, about 20,000 subjects (9,666 males and 9,699 females) participated and 19 anthropometric dimensions were measured. 3D body scanning measuring technique was primarily used, while weight, stature and some other measurements were measured manually. Human Solutions Vitus 3D full body measuring equipment, Human Solutions 3D head measuring equipment, and weighing scales were used. The population database has ages ranging from four to seventeen years old. The children were classified into five age groups: preschool (4–6 ages), junior primary school (7–10 ages), senior primary school (11–12 ages), junior high school (13–15 ages), and senior high school (16–17 ages). The criterion of age stratification is based on ISO15535: 2003 General requirements for establishing anthropometric databases. The population database includes 2,117 pre-school students, 4,263 junior primary school students, 3,930 senior primary school students, 5,527 junior high school students, and 3,527 senior high school students. The subjects were recruited from six geographical areas in China: the northeast-north China, the central and western China, the lower reach of Yangtze River, the middle reach of Yangtze River, the south-east and the south-west China. The sample size in each area was determined based on the distribution of children's population reported by China National Bureau of Statistics. During the measuring process, twenty-one landmarks were stuck on the skin of the subjects to help distinguish these points more easily and conduct template fitting, because some anatomy landmarks can't be recognized by computer software and are not easy to be recognized manually on computer (Table 1).

Table 1. Distribution of sample size among age groups

Age	Male	Female	Total
4–6	1043	1074	2117
7–10	2113	2150	4263
11–12	1988	1942	3930
13–15	2795	2732	5527
16–17	1727	1800	3527
Total	9666	9699	1700

2.2   Pre-processing

Because of the light absorption and occlusions, there are holes and noise in the models from the database mentioned above. Besides, in order to apply the PCA to the 3D human head models, all the models must be in correspondence to each other. To be in correspondence means all models under consideration have to contain equal number of points and each point in one model must have a matching point in every other model. Inspired by the work of Anguelov et al. (2005), we used non-rigid template fitting to repair these models and bring all the models into correspondence [6]. This approach is to fit a generic mesh model called the template to every other scan data. The template has to be complete and has well-shaped and well-distributed triangles [7]. The fitting is done by minimizing a weighted combination of data error, smoothness error and landmark error. The data term is to ensure that each vertex of the transformed template is as close as possible to its correspondence vertex of the model. The smoothness term is to make sure that the transformed template is smooth and the landmark term is to avoid getting stuck in a local minimum. The landmarks used for template fitting are the ones placed manually during the measuring process. The ears have complicated geometry and have no effect on this study; therefore, we eliminated ears during pre-processing.

The template fitting requires a human head template as input. To get the template, we calculated the mean values of traditional dimensions, e.g., head length, head width, of the 100 models, and then calculated the Euclidean distance between the mean dimensions and the dimensions of the 100 models. We chose the model whose dimension distance is the closest to the mean dimensions as the template. To get a good trade-off between fitting quality and computational efficiency, we resampled the template to have 5901 points (Fig. 1).

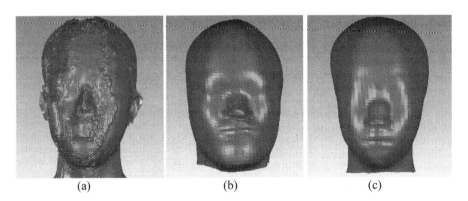

(a)   (b)   (c)

Fig. 1. Pre-processing of a head model.

2.3   PCA and Reconstruction

PCA is a statistical procedure that uses an orthogonal transformation to convert a set of observations of possibly correlated variables into a set of linearly uncorrelated variables. The objective of PCA is to find the most significant components and reduce dimensions, since the vectors with low variance can be discarded, and thus not full data needs to be retained to closely approximate the original sample [8]. The template fitting brought all the models in correspondence so that we are able to apply PCA to the point cloud of each model.

In this study, 100 subjects (all males) were chosen as our input. We stacked the points of the models into a $100 \times (5901 \times 3)$ matrix, Ψ. The deviation vector, Φ, is calculated by

$$\Phi_{i,j} = \Psi_{i,j} - \frac{1}{100} \sum_{i=1}^{100} \Psi_{i,j} \tag{1}$$

PCA of Φ yields a set of eigenvectors u and score p. Associated with each principal vector is a variance. The vectors are sorted according to the decreasing order of their variances. The deviation vector, Φ, is approximated as

$$\Phi = pu^+ \tag{2}$$

where u+ means the pseudoinverse of u. An unlimited number of new models who have a realistic appearance but do not look like any models from the example set can be reconstructed using Eq. 2. Experimental results showed that the first 4 principal components represent above 90% of the total variance.

2.4 Semantic Explanation

PCA helps us to characterize the space of human head variation. However, it does not provide an intuitive way to tell the specific meaning of each principal component, such as head length, head width and gender. In this case, this approach is difficult to be used for engineers. Inspired by Blanz and Vetter [9], we extended the existing PCA method with a novel regression model to explore the space of semantic attributes. For each principal component, a linear mapping between semantic attribute parameters, such as head length, and the corresponding shape variations is learned. Here we show how to learn a linear mapping between the attribute parameters and the principal components scores. Suppose we have l attribute parameters, the mapping can be represented as a $(k-1) \times (l+1)$ matrix, $\mathbf{M}$:

$$\mathbf{M} = [f_1 \cdots f_l 1]^{\mathrm{T}} = \mathbf{p} \tag{3}$$

where f_i are the attribute values of a model, and $\mathbf{p}$ are the corresponding PCA scores.

We can assemble the measurements from our database into an $(l+1) \times k$ attribute matrix $\mathbf{F}$ and get $\mathbf{p}$ by applying PCA. Thus we solve for $\mathbf{M}$ as

$$\mathbf{M} = \mathbf{PF}^+ \tag{4}$$

where $\mathbf{F}^+$ is the pseudoinverse of $\mathbf{F}$. After Eq. 4, we can change the value of attribute values, such as a desired weight, which means a new attribute matrix $\mathbf{F}'$. Then we calculate new corresponding PCA scores $\mathbf{P}'$ as

$$\mathbf{P'} = \mathbf{MF'} \tag{5}$$

We can reconstruct models using Eq. 2 with desired attribute parameters. We can either make them become taller or shorter, and/or fatter or thinner.

3   Results

The results showed that the first 4 principal components explain more than 90% of the shape variation-enough for most practical application. Statistical shape analysis provides intuitive visualization of the shape variation. We applied PCA directly to point cloud, and shape variation lying on each principal component can be visualized by varying the coefficient of the component. We implemented visualization using Matlab 2015 (Mathworks Inc., Natick, MA, U.S.). Figure 2 is a snapshot of the user interface for shape variation visualization. The slider controls the score of a principal component. Four components were provided. These scores determine the head shape. The users were allowed to control each slider to any specific percentile and then the digital head model will be changed accordingly. Thus head shape variation visualization was implemented. Figure 3 shows the shape variations on the first four principal components.

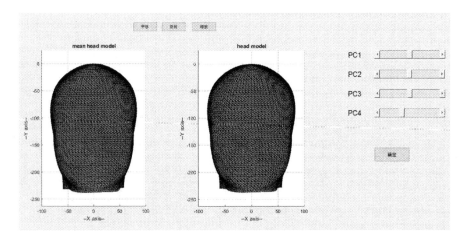

Fig. 2. User interface of the shape variation visualization

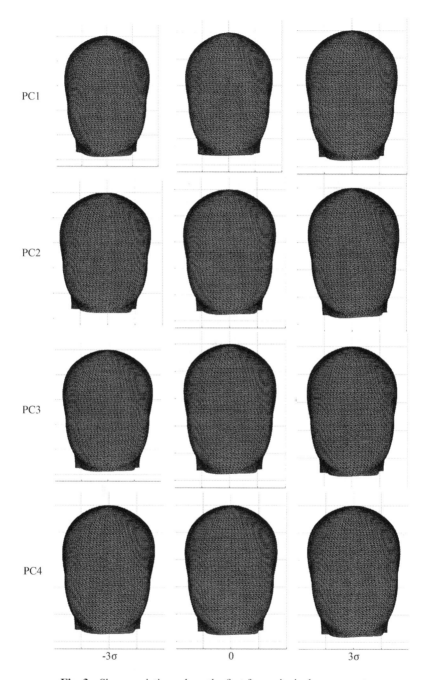

Fig. 3. Shape variations along the first four principal components

The principal components of variation produced by PCA combined distinct factors such as height, weight, girth, fitness, posture and other specific differences in human head shape. It is hard to differentiate the specific meaning of each principal component, which made this approach difficult to be used for engineers. We therefore extended PCA method with a novel regression model to explore the space of semantic attributes. We chose head height, head length, head width and the first four principal components to realize regression. The results of regression are as shown in Fig. 4.

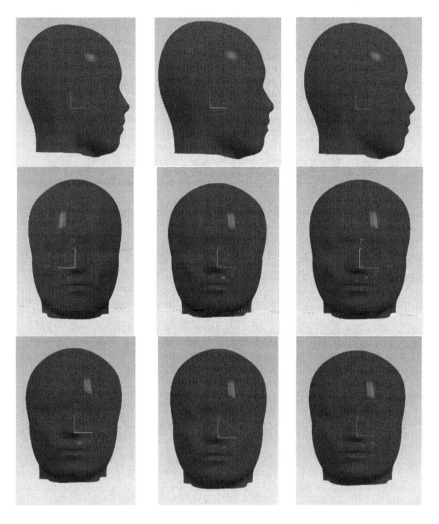

Fig. 4. The results of semantic explanation for head shape variation

4   Discussion

To establish a correspondence among all the models is a very important premise of analysis of 3D scan data. Ben Azouz et al. proposed a volumetric approach [10]. In this approach, every model is embedded in a regular grid and then they oriented and normalized the models carefully. By establishing a correspondence in the grid, a correspondence among the models is established. This method is easy to implement and does not need landmarks. However, the main drawback is that the correspondence is not accurate. Besides, holes have to be filled before correspondence, which consumes resources greatly and proved to be a difficult task because some parts have large holes. We adopted non-rigid template fitting to deal with the problem. The correspondence produced by this approach is accurate and most holes do not have to be filled manually before correspondence establishment.

PCA is believed as an attractive and focal method to quantify the human head shape variation directly on 3D human scanned data. PCA offers a means of capturing the significant variations in a data sample. Point cloud analysis of 3D head scanned data can reveal detailed shape variation among populations and be used for the design of related products. We analyzed 100 3D human head models (all males) and compared their principal modes of variation. Our results showed that four principal components described above 90% of the total variation in the sample. Through PCA analysis on the parameterized models, our results showed significant statistical variations between head shapes of Chinese senior high school students. Human head models lying on the hyper-ellipsoid constituted by principal component axis have also been re-constructed, using the mean sample and principal components, and they are used to illustrate the variation in human head shape. In the future, PCA may be used for three-dimensional sizing as well.

However, the principal components of variation combined distinct factors such as length, width, circumference, posture and other specific differences in human shape. Therefore, we extended PCA method with a novel regression model to explore the space of semantic attributes. We chose three traditional dimensions and the first four principal components to carry out regression. This method is a linear approximation; consequently it may not be completely accurate. Therefore, how to set up the relationship between the principal components and the traditional anthropometric dimensions needs further study.

Our method can achieve 3D shape variation quantification efficiently, intuitively and accurately. Experimental results show that PCA on 3D point cloud to realize 3D human head shape variation is an effective method. This method can also find applications in parametric human body modeling, which will greatly reduce the cost of animation and the time of human modeling.

Acknowledgments. This research is supported by Special funds for the basic R&D undertakings by welfare research institutions (522016Y-4680), National Key R&D Program of China (2017) YFF0206602, General Administration of Quality Supervision, Inspection and Quarantine of the People's Republic of China (201510042). The authors also appreciate the support from the State Scholarship Fund from China Scholarship Council (201208110144), the National Natural Science Foundation of China (51005016), and Fundamental Research Funds for the Central Universities, China (FRF-TP-14-026A2).

References

1. Zhang, X., Wang, Y., Ran, L., Feng, A., He, K., Liu, T., Niu, J.: Human dimensions of Chinese minors. In: Duffy, Vincent G. (ed.) ICDHM 2011. LNCS, vol. 6777, pp. 37–45. Springer, Heidelberg (2011). https://doi.org/10.1007/978-3-642-21799-9_5
2. Robinette, K., Blackwell, S., Daanen, H., Fleming, S., Boehmer, M., Brill, T., Hoeferlin, D., Burnsides, D.: Final Report. Civilian American and European Surface Anthropometry Resource (CAESAR), vol. I. Air Force Research Laboratory, Human Effectiveness Directorate, Bioscience and Protection Division. AFRL-HE-WP-TR-2002–0169 (2002)
3. Ben Azouz, Z., Shu, C., Lepage, R., Rioux, M.: Extracting main modes of human body shape variation from 3-D anthropometric data. In: International Conference on 3-D Digital Imaging and Modeling IEEE, pp. 335–342 (2005)
4. Zhuang, Z., Shu, C., Xi, P., Bergman, M., Joseph, M.: Head-and-face shape variations of u.s. civilian workers. Appl. Ergon. **44**(5), 775–784 (2013)
5. Ruto A., Lee M., Buxton B.: Comparing principal and independent modes of variation in 3D human torso shape using PCA and ICA. In: ICArn 2006, ICA Research Network International Workshop (2006)
6. Pishchulin, L., Wuhrer, S., Helten, T., Theobalt, C., Schiele, B.: Building statistical shape spaces for 3D human modeling. Pattern Recogn. **67**, 276–286 (2017)
7. Zhuang, Z., Shu, C., Xi, P., Bergman, M., Joseph, M.: Head-and-face shape variations of u.s. civilian workers. Appl. Ergon. **44**(5), 775–784 (2013)
8. Allen, B., Curless, B.: The space of human body shapes: reconstruction and parameterization from range scans. ACM Trans. Graph. **22**(3), 587–594 (2003)
9. Blanz, V., Vetter, T.: A morphable model for the synthesis of 3D faces. In: Rockwood, A. (ed.) Proceedings of ACM SIGGRAPH 99, Computer Graphics Proceedings, Annual Conference Series, pp. 187–194. ACM Press/Addison-Wesley Publishing Co., New York (1999)
10. Ben Azouz, Z., Rioux, M., Shu, C., Lepage, R.: Characterizing human shape variation using 3D anthropometric data. Vis. Comput. **22**, 302–314 (2006)

Motion Modelling and Rehabilitation

4 DOF Exoskeleton Robotic Arm System for Rehabilitation and Training

Siam Charoenseang[1(✉)] and Sarut Panjan[2]

[1] Institute of Field Robotics (FIBO), King Mongkut's University of Technology Thonburi, Bangmod, Thungkru, Bangkok 10140, Thailand
siam@fibo.kmutt.ac.th
[2] Department of Teacher Training in Electrical Engineering, Industrial Robotics Research and Development Center, King Mongkut's University of Technology North Bangkok, Wongsawang, Bangsue, Bangkok 10800, Thailand

Abstract. This paper presents a rehabilitation and training system with 4 DOF exoskeleton robotic arm. This proposed system can record a posture of physiotherapist and playback that posture to the patients. For the posture playback, the exoskeleton arm's motion was controlled with the recorded gesture and adjusted the level of an assistive motion. The GRNN method was used for predicting the static gravity compensation of each joint with accuracy of 94.66%, 97.63%, 87.02%, and 97.32%, respectively. Hence, the exact system modelling was not required in this system. The force controller with admittance control method was applied to control this exoskeleton robotic arm. The results of the usability test showed that the proposed system had an ability to enhance the muscle's strength and indicated that the purposed exoskeleton arm could be applied to the rehabilitation or training task.

Keywords: Exoskeleton · Rehabilitation · Force control · EMG based control
Admittance control

1 Introduction

According to the data from the Stroke Center at the University Hospital, stroke is the second worldwide leading of death which is about 4.4 million of the total 50.5 million deaths each year [1]. In the United States, more than 4 million people survived from a stroke were disabled. Ten percent of stroke patients can be recovered almost completely but 75 percent of stroke patients would lose or have impaired motor function and 15% die after the stroke. Rehabilitation cost per person is approximately $140,048 [2]. Because of very expensive rehabilitation cost, most of the patients were lack of opportunities for rehabilitation.

Generally, rehabilitation and training involving arm movement are types of repetitive tasks during period of time. This kind of task also requires the physiotherapist or trainer to spend the training times with the patient or trainee. The utilization of robot arm would be fit to do such a repetitive task and reduce the workloads of physiotherapist or trainer. Recently, many robots have been used in rehabilitation and training tasks. In general,

© Springer International Publishing AG, part of Springer Nature 2018
V. G. Duffy (Ed.): DHM 2018, LNCS 10917, pp. 147–157, 2018.
https://doi.org/10.1007/978-3-319-91397-1_13

robotic rehabilitation could be categorized into two styles which were wearable and non-wearable. For arm rehabilitation, joints and links of the wearable rehabilitation robot were usually designed correspondingly to the patient arm such as the cable-actuated dexterous exoskeleton for neurorehabilitation (CADEN)-7 [3]. The design of "CADEN" applied the cable-pulley to transmit torque/force from motor to each joint. This design can reduce weight of exoskeleton. ARMinIII [4] was designed to have three degrees of freedom for shoulder and one degree of freedom for elbow. Robotic Upper Extremity Repetitive Trainer (RUPERT) [5] had five actuated degrees of freedom for each joint which was driven by compliant pneumatic muscle actuators (PMA). The Mechatronics and Haptic Interfaces (MAHI) [6, 7] was designed to have 5 degrees of freedom for the elbow and forearm. The wrist of this exoskeleton was a 3-RPS (revolute-prismatic-spherical) joint. The non-wearable rehabilitation robots were usually adapted from the industrial robots but only one point of physical contact between patient wrist and the robot's end-effector such as MIT-MANUS [8] and MIME [9]. Both devices were designed for rehabilitation of shoulder and elbow joints. Benefits of wearable robotic rehabilitation were controlling and generating force feedback to each user arm's joint. Those rehabilitation robots were usually designed for right or left arm only. On the other hand, the advantage of non-wearable robot was flexibility for rehabilitation but it could not control or generate force feedback to all joints at the same time. All previous robotic devices for rehabilitation have mentioned limitations.

Hence, this project proposes the development of a robotic arm for rehabilitation and training. The proposed robot arm could hold and guide the user's through the predefined trajectory. Further, the user could wear this exoskeleton arm and move it to interact with the virtual object via the graphics user interface on a computer monitor or head-mounted display. This proposed robot arm supported the patient's arm during rehabilitation which is an repetitive task and takes a period of time.

2   System Design and Implementations

2.1   System Overview

Figure 1 shows configuration of the proposed system which consists of three main components. First, the four degrees of freedom exoskeleton arm [10] was used for supporting the arm motion during rehabilitation and training. This proposed exoskeleton could be used for left and right arm. The actuation and transmission system of the exoskeleton arm consisted of AC servo motors, planetary gearboxes, and steel cables. The steel cables were used to transmit the movement of the gearbox's output shafts to the exoskeleton joints. Force and torque sensors were mounted on each joint of the exoskeleton arm. Second component of this exoskeleton was the main controller which was used to receive the command from the main computer and control motion of the exoskeleton arm. Last component was used to control the exoskeleton with LABVIEW and MATLAB applications.

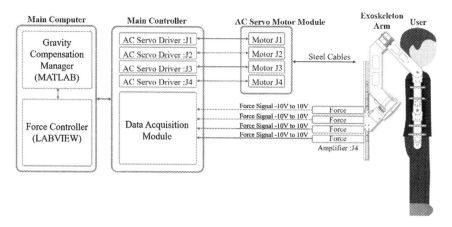

Fig. 1. System overview

2.2 Mechanic Section

The proposed robot arm was designed to have four degrees of freedoms. The first three joints represented the shoulder joints and the forth joint represented the elbow joint. The first link and second link were aligned with the upper limb. The design allowed the first and second joints to hold the position of shoulder while giving the shoulder some limited rotations in order to prevent any slips occurred at the shoulder. Furthermore, this robot arm was designed to be used with the left arm and right arm by rotating the second joint about 180° as shown in Figs. 2 and 3. In the design, the cable was used to transfer the power from the servo motor to each joint of the robot arm. Therefore, this robot arm had lightweight because the servo motors were not mounted on the robot arm.

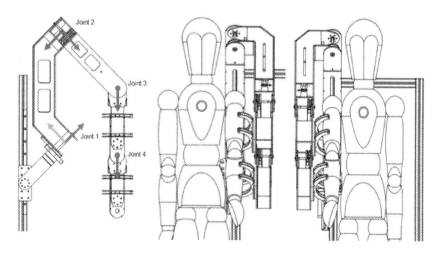

Fig. 2. Robot arm configurations

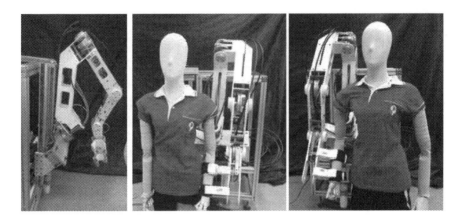

Fig. 3. Actual configuration of robot used with the left and right arm

2.3 Electronic Section

The upper limb exoskeleton arm received the desired position/velocity from the main computer. It also returned the current position/velocity and force data to the main computer. In Fig. 4, the upper limb exoskeleton received the desired position and velocity from the main computer via a motion control card. After that, the current position/velocity from the exoskeleton was sent to the main computer. Force sensor was installed on the exoskeleton joint for sensing the external force exerted on exoskeleton's joint in the clockwise and counterclockwise directions. The force sensor signal was amplified with a strain gauge amplifier module before being sent to the main computer. Limit switches were installed at each joint of exoskeleton arm for limiting the range of motion.

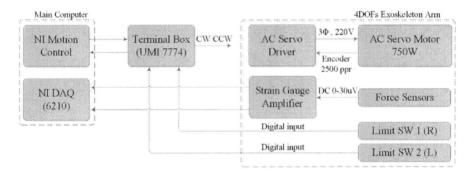

Fig. 4. Exoskeleton controller

2.4 Programming Section

Gravity compensation manager was used to calculate the static gravity force compensation. This compensation value was sent to the force controller for compensating the physical force input. In general, the physical parameters of the system were used to calculate the gravity force compensation. However, the exact physical parameters of this system were difficult to be modelled because the friction force in Bowden cable, which was applied to transmit the power of this exoskeleton, exhibited nonlinearity. As mentioned above, the proposed gravity compensation focused on the compensation without physical parameters of the exoskeleton arm. To solve this problem, the generalized regression neural network was applied to predict the gravity compensation value of given joint position because the training time of the GRNN was short and it could take care of a large input-output mapping.

2.5 Admittance Control

The admittance control was applied to calculate the joint motion. To describe the admittance control for this system, the Eq. 1 was used to calculate the desired robot velocity, where k_a is an admittance gain, F is a force exerted on each joint, and F_c is a gravity compensated value [11].

$$\dot{x}_d = k_a\left(F - F_c\right) \tag{1}$$

The force output could be calculated using Eq. 2, where k_p, k_d are the proportional and derivative gains. x_d and $\dot{x}_d$ are the desired robot position and velocity. x and $\dot{x}$ are current joint position and velocity of exoskeleton joint [11].

$$\tau_j = k_p\left(x_d - x\right) + k_d\left(\dot{x}_d - \dot{x}\right) \tag{2}$$

2.6 Posture Record and Playback

The exoskeleton arm was able to record posture from physiotherapist and playback that posture to the patient. The exoskeleton software consisted of joint controller, force controller, gravity compensation, user's database, and graphical user interface which were shown in Figs. 5 and 6. The joint controller was used to control exoskeleton joints motion with external force extern at each joint and record the joint's angle. The gravity compensation was used to calculate the gravity loads at each joint and send data to the force controller. Force controller with admittance control was used to control exoskeleton joints' motion when external exerted force at each joint of the exoskeleton arm. The user's database was used to store posture of each user. The graphics user interface was used to display the joint's targeted movement and the actual joint's movement.

There were two categories of an experiments. The first category was set to determine the system performance of the exoskeleton arm and the another one was to investigate the system usability. Six healthy people were asked to test the usability of this system.

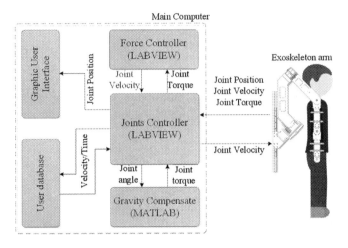

Fig. 5. Exoskeleton software overview

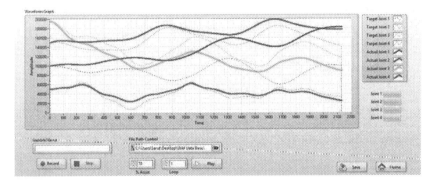

Fig. 6. Exoskeleton arm's graphical user interface

2.7 Repeatability

Repeatability is a measure of the ability of the exoskeleton arm to consistently and repeatedly reach a specified point. A dial gauge was used to measure the repeatability of the robot as shown in Fig. 7. The robot was moved to the dial gauge and moved out to the other position and returned to the dial gauge. The result of repeatability test was less than 0.11 mm as shown in Fig. 8.

Fig. 7. Repeatability test of exoskeleton arm

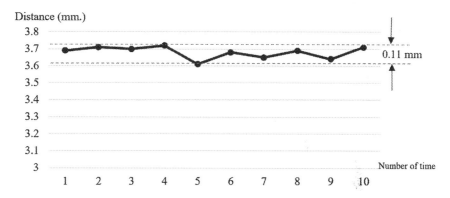

Fig. 8. Exoskeleton arm's repeatability

2.8 Gravity Compensation

The GRNN method was implemented and required the training data of joint angle-force mappings. To record the training data, each joint of the exoskeleton was set to rotate from lower limit to upper limit. Then, the force data was recorded as the output and the exoskeleton's joint angle as the input. The GRNN method was utilized to predict the gravity force output. The relationship between the gravity force and the exoskeleton's joint angle could be plotted as in Figs. 9, 10, 11 and 12.

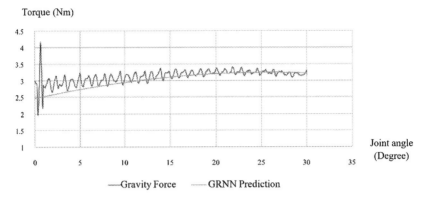

Fig. 9. Force data reading from joint 1 and GRNN's prediction

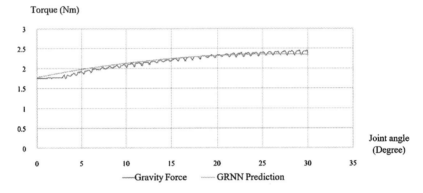

Fig. 10. Force data reading from joint 2 and GRNN's prediction

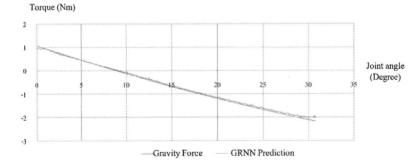

Fig. 11. Force data reading from joint 3 and GRNN's prediction

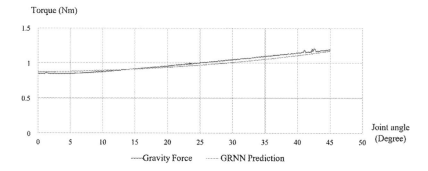

Fig. 12. Force data reading from joint 4 and GRNN's prediction

In Figs. 9, 10, 11 and 12, the horizontal axis represents the joint angle and the vertical axis represents force data. The force value of exoskeleton arm was plotted as a solid line and gravity force estimation value of the GRNN method was plotted as a dash line. The GRNN method could predict the gravity force at each joint with accuracy of 94.66%, 97.63%, 87.02%, and 97.32%, respectively, as shown in Figs. 9, 10, 11 and 12. Although the GRNN method could predict only static force, it was sufficient for this system.

2.9   Admittance Control Evaluation

The admittance control was the method to control the exoskeleton's movement accordingly to the external force. Therefore, the experiment presented the comparison between the torque which occurred at the exoskeleton joint and the joint motion response when the external force was applied to the robot. The result in Fig. 13 indicates that the admittance control method had an ability to response to the external force within 132 ms. So, this exoskeleton could response to the external force about real time.

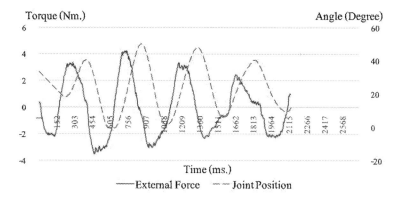

Fig. 13. Joint transient response by admittance controller

2.10   Usability Test

The system consisted of two operations which are record and playback modes. Record mode was used to record the user's posture. Playback mode was used to playback the posture which was recorded from the user's movement as shown in Fig. 14. The six participants were asked to wear the exoskeleton arm. Then, this system was tested with both modes by the users. After the experiment, the usability were collected by questionnaire which was in the form of the Google form. The results of the usability test indicated that the users were satisfied with this exoskeleton's motion. This exoskeleton arm had an ability to enhance their muscle strengths. They suggested that the purposed exoskeleton arm could be applied to the rehabilitation or training task. In their opinions, the design of this exoskeleton should be more friendly.

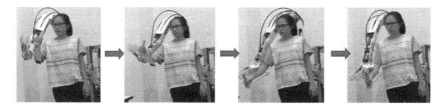

Fig. 14.   Robot arm moved accordingly to the user arm's movements

3   Conclusions and Discussions

The 4-DOF robotic exoskeleton arm was designed and built at the Institute of Field Robotics, King Mongkut's University of Technology Thonburi, Thailand. The exoskeleton arm could be configured by rotating joint 2 to 180° for the use of right and left arm. There were two control modes which are posture record and playback modes. For the posture record mode, the motion of the exoskeleton arm was controlled with forces exerting from the user and recorded the joint angles at the same time. For the posture playback, the exoskeleton arm motion was controlled with the recorded posture. The exoskeleton arm had ability to adjust the level of motion assistant. Graphical user interface was used to display the joint's target and actual joint's position. The neural network was used for predicting the static gravity compensation which mapped between the input joint angle and the output force at the elbow joint. The admittance controller was used to control motion of the exoskeleton joint. The GRNN could predict the static gravity force at each joint with accuracy of 94.66%, 97.63%, 87.02%, and 97.32%, respectively. The response time of the force controller could response about real-time. From the usability test, this proposed system had an ability to enhanced muscle strength. The users suggested that the purposed system could be applied to the rehabilitation or training task and the design of this exoskeleton should be more friendly. From the experimental results, this proposed system could be applied to the rehabilitation or training robot. In the future work, the virtual reality system would be implemented to provide the immersive and interactive graphical user interface for the upper limb rehabilitation using this robotic exoskeleton.

References

1. World Health Organization: World Health Organization disability assessment schedule: WHODAS II. Phase 2 field trials. Health services research (2000)
2. Gordon, N.F., et al.: Physical activity and exercise recommendations for stroke survivors: an American Heart Association scientific statement from the Council on Clinical Cardiology, Subcommittee on Exercise, Cardiac Rehabilitation, and Prevention; the Council on Cardiovascular Nursing; the Council on Nutrition, Physical Activity, and Metabolism; and the Stroke Council. Stroke **35**(5), 1230–1240 (2004)
3. Perry, J.C., Rosen, J., Burns, S.: Upper-limb powered exoskeleton design. IEEE/ASME Trans. Mechatron. **12**(4), 408–417 (2007)
4. Guidali, M., et al.: Assessment and training of synergies with an arm rehabilitation robot. In: IEEE International Conference on Rehabilitation Robotics, ICORR 2009. IEEE (2009)
5. Balasubramanian, S., et al.: RUPERT: an exoskeleton robot for assisting rehabilitation of arm functions. In: Virtual Rehabilitation. IEEE (2008)
6. Gupta, A., O'Malley, M.K.: Design of a haptic arm exoskeleton for training and rehabilitation. IEEE/ASME Trans. Mechatron. **11**(3), 280–289 (2006)
7. Pehlivan, A.U., Celik, O., O'Malley, M.K.: Mechanical design of a distal arm exoskeleton for stroke and spinal cord injury rehabilitation. In: 2011 IEEE International Conference on Rehabilitation Robotics (ICORR). IEEE (2011)
8. Dellon, B., Matsuoka, Y.: Prosthetics, exoskeletons, and rehabilitation [grand challenges of robotics]. IEEE Robot. Autom. Mag. **14**(1), 30–34 (2007)
9. Mao, Y., Agrawal, S.K.: A cable driven upper arm exoskeleton for upper extremity rehabilitation. In: 2011 IEEE International Conference on Robotics and Automation (ICRA). IEEE (2011)
10. Panjan, S., Charoenseang, S.: Design and development of a robotic arm for rehabilitation and training. In: Park, J.J.(Jong Hyuk), Pan, Y., Yi, G., Loia, V. (eds.) CSA/CUTE/UCAWSN-2016. LNEE, vol. 421, pp. 3–8. Springer, Singapore (2017). https://doi.org/10.1007/978-981-10-3023-9_1
11. Yu, W., Rosen, J., Li, X.: PID admittance control for an upper limb exoskeleton. In: American Control Conference (ACC). IEEE (2011)

A Novel Approach for Assessing Power Wheelchair Users' Mobility by Using Curve Fitting

Jicheng Fu[1(✉)], Fang Li[2], Marcus Ong[1], Tyler Cook[1], Gang Qian[1], and Yan Daniel Zhao[3]

[1] University of Central Oklahoma, Edmond, OK 73034, USA
{jfu,mong,tcook14,gqian}@uco.edu
[2] The University of Texas at Dallas, Richardson, TX 75080, USA
fxl171330@utdallas.edu
[3] University of Oklahoma Health Sciences Center, Oklahoma City, OK 73104, USA
daniel-zhao@ouhsc.edu

Abstract. It is important to assess power wheelchair users' mobility characteristics, which can provide insights about an individual's quality of life and health status. For practicality considerations, we propose to use smartphones (particularly, the built-in accelerometer) to collect wheelchair maneuvering data for assessing power wheelchair users' mobility characteristics. However, accelerometer data demonstrates a wide variety of patterns due to significant noise, which makes it difficult to process using traditional methods. To address these challenges, we developed a novel regression-based curve fitting approach that can transform the un-patterned raw sensor data into a sinusoid-like data curve to facilitate the analysis of wheelchair users' mobility. To evaluate the proposed approach, we have conducted a series of experiments in an indoor setting, which contains various types of terrains. Experimental results showed that our approach is promising in achieving accurate analysis of wheelchair users' mobility.

Keywords: Accelerometer · Bout · Jerk · Kernel regression · Mobility
Power wheelchair

1 Introduction

It has been proven that an active lifestyle can lower the risk of several chronic diseases, such as cardiovascular disease, cancer, diabetes, hypertension, etc. [1]. Unfortunately, more than 85% of Americans did not achieve a healthy level of physical activity [2]. As a result, physical inactivity has become a significant risk factor for premature morbidity and mortality [3]. The consequence of physical inactivity can be even more serious for power wheelchair users due to their limited mobility [1–4]. Although a power wheelchair can provide independent mobility to its users, research has shown that wheelchair users are more likely to live an inactive lifestyle than people without disabilities [5]. Since basic mobility activities are fundamental for more complex behaviors and social integration, it is important to assess power wheelchair users' mobility characteristics, which can provide insights about an individual's quality of life and health status [6, 7].

© Springer International Publishing AG, part of Springer Nature 2018
V. G. Duffy (Ed.): DHM 2018, LNCS 10917, pp. 158–168, 2018.
https://doi.org/10.1007/978-3-319-91397-1_14

To assess wheelchair users' mobility, the current practice typically attaches inertial sensors (e.g., accelerometers or gyroscopes) to the wheels of a wheelchair to collect wheelchair maneuvering data [8–10]. The advantage of such sensor placement is that it eases data analysis. For example, a tri-axis accelerometer measures acceleration in three axes. If the accelerometer is attached to a wheel, the acceleration from the axis aligned with the direction of wheel rotations resembles a sinusoid curve over time, which can be utilized to calculate the number of wheel revolutions. However, mounting inertial sensors to the wheel is impractical in daily life because wheelchair users can hardly set up the sensor by themselves, not to mention regularly maintaining the sensor (e.g., charging the sensor or downloading sensor data).

To provide a practical and effective approach for measuring wheelchair users' mobility, we propose to use a smartphone (particularly, its accelerometer) to effectuate wheelchair data collection. The challenge is that the collected accelerometer data does not have the sinusoid-like pattern because the smartphone will not be attached to the wheel of a wheelchair. Furthermore, the accelerometer is subject to both sensor and environmental noise, which may vary greatly from one place to another. As a result, sensor data demonstrates a wide variety of patterns, which are difficult for traditional methods to process.

To overcome the aforementioned challenges, we employed advanced mathematics and physics techniques to process and analyze data. Specifically, we process raw accelerometer data by calculating its derivatives, which are called jerks. Since jerk measures the change of accelerations, noise can be greatly reduced because noise tends to produce similar accelerations within a very short time period. Then, we propose to use a regression-based method to transform the un-patterned jerk data into a sinusoid-like curve. Although many regression methods (e.g., splines fitting, least square curve fitting, etc.) can be used, we selected the kernel regression method [11] because it only requires one parameter, i.e., bandwidth, which can be effectively tuned by using statistics methods.

Based on the kernel regression, we have developed a two-phase curve fitting algorithm to analyze jerk data. The goal of the first phase is to find the number of bouts (i.e., periods of continuous wheelchair movement), while the goal of the second phase is to determine the bout durations. The reason that we focus on bout and bout duration is that these are fundamental metrics for evaluating a wheelchair user's mobility. Among the mobility metrics for wheelchair users, the mobility bout is useful in measuring activity and social participation because a bout denotes a transition between locations. Hence, the number of bouts can reveal activities performed at different locations [6]. Research has shown that the number of bouts as well as the accumulated wheelchair maneuvering time have small variations for a wheelchair user and thus provide a reliable measure for mobility [6, 8]. The proposed two-phase curve fitting algorithm will provide a new way to accurately analyze the number of bouts and the accumulated maneuvering time.

To evaluate the proposed approach, we have conducted a series of experiments in an indoor setting, which contains various terrains, such as slope, curving floor, and flat floor. Experimental results showed that our approach correctly recognized all the bouts and achieved accurate measurements on accumulated maneuvering time, which are fundamental for evaluating a wheelchair user's mobility.

The rest of the paper is organized as follows. In Sect. 2, we present the proposed curve fitting approach. In Sect. 3, we show and discuss the experimental results. In Sect. 4, we conclude the paper and identify future research directions.

2 Method

In Sect. 2.1, we discuss how to collect and model wheelchair maneuvering data. In Sect. 2.2, we present how to reduce noise by transforming raw accelerometer data into jerk to facilitate data analysis. The obtained jerk data will be further processed by normalization and outlier removal. Based on the processed data, we develop a novel curve-fitting based algorithm to evaluate a wheelchair user's mobility, including the number of bouts, bout durations, and accumulated maneuvering time, in Sect. 2.3. Then, in Sect. 2.4, we present the experimental design for evaluating the proposed approach.

2.1 Data Collection

During data collection, we equipped a wheelchair with a smartphone holder since it is inconvenient for a user to drive the power wheelchair while operating the smartphone. We developed an Android app to control the accelerometer in a smartphone to collect wheelchair maneuvering data. The sampling rate of the accelerometer was set to the predefined SENSOR_DELAY_UI (14–16 Hz), which would not consume significant battery energy while still maintaining sufficient data precision [9]. During a time period $[t_1, t_2]$, the collected data is modeled as a sequence of accelerations:

$$D_R = \{r_1, r_2, \ldots, r_n\} \tag{1}$$

where $r_i = \langle \alpha_i^x, \alpha_i^y, \alpha_i^z, t_i \rangle$ ($1 \leq i \leq n$ and $t_1 \leq t_i \leq t_2$) and $\alpha_i^x, \alpha_i^y, \alpha_i^z$ are accelerations measured along three axes at time t_i.

2.2 Data Processing

In [12], we proposed to use jerk to mitigate the impact of noise. In physics, jerk is defined as the derivative of acceleration, i.e., $j(t) = d\alpha(t)/dt$, where $\alpha(t)$ is an acceleration function. For example, Fig. 1 shows a segment of raw acceleration data along one axis of the smartphone (i.e., the blue curve on the top) as well as the corresponding jerk curve (i.e., the red curve at the bottom). The initial portions of the curves represent a stationary period when the wheelchair stays put, while the subsequent portions denote a moving period. The raw sensor data curve was elevated above the X axis by the inherent sensor noise as well as the environmental noise, which is largely caused by gravity. Particularly, since the smartphone is arbitrarily placed into the smartphone holder, the gravity decomposes along three axes of the smartphone. As a result, even though the wheelchair is stationary, the sensor still detects significant accelerations. In comparison, the corresponding jerk curve is more accurate in illustrating the actual movements of the wheelchair.

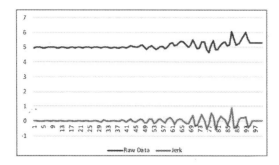

Fig. 1. Using jerk to reduce noise (Color figure online)

In general, the sequence of raw accelerometer data defined in (1) is transformed into the following jerk data set:

$$D_F = \left\{ f_1, f_2, \ldots, f_{n-1} \middle| f_i = \sqrt{f_{ix}^2 + f_{iy}^2 + f_{ix}^2} \text{ and } 1 \le i \le n \right\} \tag{2}$$

where $f_{ix} = d\alpha_i^x / dt \approx \alpha_{i+1}^x - \alpha_i^x$ (α_i^x is defined in (1)) because two consecutive accelerations are collected in a very short period of time. Correspondingly, we have $f_{iy} \approx \alpha_{i+1}^y - \alpha_i^y$ and $f_{iz} \approx \alpha_{i+1}^z - \alpha_i^z$.

In addition, we apply the quartiles and the interquartile range (IQR) method [10] to remove outliers, whose values could be much larger than the true wheelchair maneuvering signals. Figure 2 shows an example in which the raw jerk data is normalized first, followed by outlier removal. After outliers are removed, the jerk data curve demonstrates clearer patterns that reveal wheelchair maneuvering status.

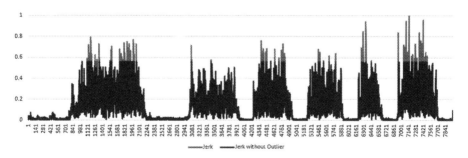

Fig. 2. Data processing with outliers removed

2.3 Data Analysis

Although the processed jerk data demonstrates clearer patterns, the large oscillations, as shown in Fig. 2, still make it difficult for data analysis. To obtain a smoother data curve, we propose to use a regression method to transform the un-patterned jerk data into a sinusoid-like curve. Although many regression methods can be used (e.g., splines fitting, least square curve fitting, etc.), we selected the kernel regression algorithm [11] because it only requires one parameter, i.e., bandwidth, to control the smoothness of the fitted curve. More importantly, bandwidth can be effectively tuned by using statistics methods.

Bandwidth Tuning. When using kernel-based methods, the resulting fit can be significantly influenced by the choice of bandwidth. Using a smaller bandwidth can lead to results with increased variability since fewer observations are used for estimation. Selecting a larger bandwidth can decrease variance by using more information, but this often comes with a cost of increasing bias. Several approaches have been proposed in the literature to handle this issue for both kernel density estimation and kernel regression. Basic rule-of-thumb estimators, including the popular estimator from Silverman [13], are perhaps the most straightforward approaches. These estimators are relatively easy to compute and are optimal provided that strong distributional assumptions are met. Unfortunately, it is often unrealistic to assume that the underlining data distribution is known. A class of estimators referred to as "plug-in" estimators provide an alternative technique without needing the same strong distributional assumptions. These plug-in estimators select the bandwidth by plugging in estimates of unknown quantities that appear in expressions for the optimal bandwidth [14]. While the plug-in methods are more flexible than rule-of-thumb estimators, they still have potential drawbacks since a pilot bandwidth is required [15]. Cross-validation is another popular approach for bandwidth selection that is also used in many other statistical contexts to find optimal values for unknown parameters. Estimates are chosen by finding values that minimize the cross-validation error, which results in a very flexible, data-driven approach. In our approach, we perform bandwidth selection using cross-validation by searching a grid of potential values for the one that minimizes the error. This is an attractive method because it allows for reliable bandwidth selection for a wide range of datasets by automatically choosing a value from the data. Loader [16] provides a detailed discussion on the benefits of methods such as cross-validation over plug-in estimates for bandwidth selection.

Specifically, to accomplish bandwidth tuning, we create a grid of possible bandwidth values evenly spaced between 0 and 1 in an increment of 0.1. For each value in the grid, a kernel smoother is fit to the data and the generalized cross-validation (GCV) score is calculated. This GCV statistic is an estimate of the test error. Therefore, the value of the bandwidth that minimizes the GCV is then selected for the final model fitting. In general, this approach works well in practice, but there occasionally are situations where the chosen bandwidth might not produce a curve that is smooth enough. This can happen, for instance, when the cross-validation error curve does not have a prominent minimum value resulting in several bandwidth values that have almost identical cross-validation errors. This phenomenon is seen throughout many cross-validation applications and a "one-standard-error rule" has been proposed to overcome this [17]. This involves selecting a value of the parameter that is within one standard error of the value that achieves the minimum error. In this spirit, we can modify our bandwidth selection algorithm by choosing the next largest value in the grid when it is desirable to increase the smoothness of the fitted curve.

The Two-Phase Curve Fitting Algorithm. After the kernel regression algorithm is applied to the processed jerk data, we obtain a smooth sinusoid-like curve as shown in Fig. 3 (i.e., the red curve). Every concave-down segment represents a continuous moving period (i.e., a bout), while each concave-up segment denotes a stationary period. Hence, the data analysis problem has been reduced to a problem of finding peaks and valleys in the curve. The number of peaks represents the number of bouts (segments of continuous movement). The boundary for each bout can be identified by finding the critical points (i.e., the start and end points) of a bout.

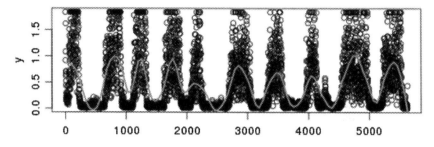

Fig. 3. Curve fitting (Color figure online)

Specifically, we have developed a two-phase curve fitting algorithm. In the first phase, we begin by fitting a kernel smoother to the jerk data. Model fitting is performed using the *locfit* package available in the R programming language [18]. The bandwidth is selected using cross-validation as described in the previous section by means of the *gcv* function. The *locfit* package has the ability to implement several different possible kernels, and we have elected to use the popular Epanechnikov kernel because it has compact support and has been shown to be preferred in many situations [16]. As a result, the kernel regression algorithm fits the data into a smooth curve as shown in Fig. 3. A smooth curve makes it easy to determine the peak location for each bout. This is important because the goal of the first phase is to find the number of bouts. We used the built-in function *findPeaks* provided by the *quantmod* package, which is also available in *R* [19], to determine the peak location for each bout. This package also provides the *findValleys* function that is used to find valleys.

The second phase of the proposed algorithm is to determine bout durations. This is equivalent to finding the critical points (i.e., the start and end points) of a bout. For example, Fig. 4-A shows a fitted curve that contains the peak points (marked in red), which are identified in the first phase, and critical points (marked in blue). To obtain the critical points, the second phase algorithm utilizes the following heuristic: A critical point can be heuristically determined by finding the point with the steepest slope from the fitted curve. The reason is that a critical point separates a static period from a moving one or vice versa, thus representing the most significant change in wheelchair maneuvers.

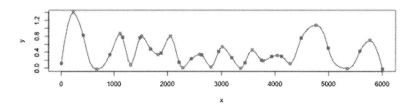

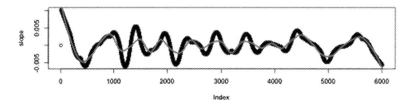

Fig. 4. Curve-fitting in the second phase (Color figure online)

To obtain the slopes, we derive another curve by calculating the derivatives (i.e., slopes) for the curve obtained in the first phase. Figure 4-B shows the resultant curve (i.e., the black curve), which represents slopes for the fitted curve in Fig. 4-A. Since the resultant curve is still ragged, we apply the kernel regression again to the ragged curve to make it smoother (i.e., the red curve in Fig. 4-B). Then, to determine the critical points is to find the peaks and valleys. Specifically, a peak represents the start point of a bout and the following valley represents the end point of the same bout. The reason is that the slopes are positive (i.e., going up) in the beginning of a bout while the slopes are negative (i.e., going down) by the end of a bout, as shown in Fig. 4-A.

2.4 Experimental Design

We evaluated the proposed approach in a multi-story building. This building was selected because it has various types of terrains, e.g., flat floor, curving floor, and slopes. Hence, we could evaluate whether the proposed approach could achieve accurate data analysis when the wheelchair was operating in different environmental settings. As discussed in Sect. 2.1, we equipped the power wheelchair (Invacare FDX) with a smartphone holder (Arkon Tab-802). An LG G2 (D800) smartphone was used to collect wheelchair maneuvering data.

Figure 5 shows the experimental setting in a bird's eye view. The building consists of two halves (i.e., left and right), which are connected by bridges on the second and third floors. The experiments were conducted on the second floor for 6 trials. Each trial was composed of 10 bouts. There was a 5-s pause (i.e., the wheelchair stayed put) in between two consecutive bouts. Specifically, all trials started from point *a* in the right half of the building, the research participant would:

1. Drive to the bridge
2. Turn left onto the bridge and continue to drive until it is halfway on the bridge

3. Drive to the left half of the building
4. Turn left (for even numbered trials) or right (for odd numbered trials), and then continue to drive until it is halfway to point *b* or *c*
5. Drive to point *b* or *c* depending on the even or odd numbered trial, and make a U turn
6. Drive back and stop when it is halfway toward the bridge
7. Continue to drive to the bridge
8. Turn left/right onto the bridge and continue to drive until it is halfway on the bridge
9. Drive to the right half of the building, and
10. Turn right and drive to point *a*.

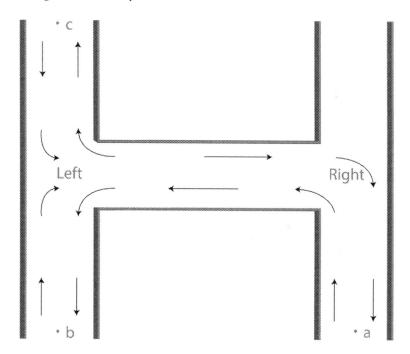

Fig. 5. Experimental setting.

In addition, we used a timer to record the duration of each bout as a baseline for the evaluation of the proposed algorithm.

3   Results

We found that the proposed curve fitting algorithm could correctly recognize all the bouts by finding the number of peaks (i.e., the outcome of the first phase of the proposed algorithm). Table 1 shows the experimental results on bout durations. The rows labeled with "Timer" were the baseline values recorded by the timer, while the rows labeled with "Calculated" were the results calculated by the proposed algorithm (i.e., the outcome of the second phase of the proposed algorithm). It can be seen that the average error on all the bouts is 19%, and the error for accumulated maneuvering time (i.e., the sum of all the bout durations) is 4%. To verify whether the calculated bout durations were correlated with the baseline values, we performed a chi-square test. The result showed the set of calculated bout durations fitted the set of baseline values ($p = 0.58$).

Table 1. Experimental results (unit: second)

Trial		Bout1	Bout2	Bout3	Bout4	Bout5	Bout6	Bout7	Bout8	Bout9	Bout10
1	Timer	12.53	17.92	13.92	19.90	13.60	25.20	18.73	13.73	31.28	23.87
	Calculated	17.50	15.55	18.32	22.20	13.17	22.84	18.03	23.18	24.28	24.79
2	Timer	12.07	16.07	12.78	16.38	13.68	21.99	18.95	13.09	29.86	23.80
	Calculated	12.48	13.58	12.93	19.98	14.80	19.34	14.49	12.68	23.12	24.64
3	Timer	12.12	14.80	12.83	16.64	10.13	14.58	11.62	10.56	27.88	24.29
	Calculated	15.66	17.74	10.95	12.38	10.18	16.97	11.48	12.11	24.32	23.18
4	Timer	12.27	14.78	13.02	15.60	15.14	21.12	17.80	15.00	29.62	24.05
	Calculated	15.21	11.75	11.14	21.81	21.12	19.25	16.65	13.54	25.35	23.49
5	Timer	12.38	14.96	12.93	15.52	10.18	15.82	10.74	10.49	28.02	24.36
	Calculated	19.16	18.81	13.70	17.76	16.64	18.98	17.97	11.72	21.29	25.63
6	Timer	12.42	14.49	12.60	15.83	10.66	14.87	12.04	10.28	27.73	24.13
	Calculated	15.63	12.94	13.70	21.57	12.80	16.46	20.20	11.20	20.64	27.05
Average error	19%					Error for accumulated maneuvering time			4%		

3.1   Discussion

The ability to determine the bout duration is important for analyzing power wheelchair users' mobility. For example, the mobility metric "maximum period of continuous movement" can be obtained by identifying the bout with the longest duration. The metric "accumulated maneuvering time" can be calculated by summing up all the bout durations. Based on the "accumulated maneuvering time" and the number of bouts, we can easily calculate the average maneuvering time.

The proposed two-phase algorithm achieved accurate analysis on the metrics of the number of bouts and accumulated maneuvering time, which can provide reliable assessment of a wheelchair user's mobility [6, 8]. However, Table 1 shows that the bout durations calculated by the proposed approach have large variations. Since the calculated and baseline bout durations were correlated ($p = 0.58$), the positive and negative deviations of the calculated durations cancelled out, resulting in accurate estimation of the accumulated maneuvering time. The variations in bout durations suggest that an adaptive method will be desirable, which can determine the bandwidth according to the characteristics of the slope curve in the second phase of the proposed algorithm.

4   Conclusion and Future Direction

In this paper, we proposed a novel regression-based approach, which exploits the curve-fitting technique to transform an un-patterned jerk data sequence into a sinusoid-like curve. Although existing approaches can also generate similar data curves, they have to be implemented at the cost of placing dedicated sensors to the wheels of a wheelchair, which is not convenient in practice. In comparison, our approach allows wheelchair users to easily use a smartphone to measure their mobility activities. Further, we have developed a two-phase algorithm to recognize bouts and estimate bout durations from the transformed jerk data. Experimental results showed that the first phase of the proposed algorithm could accurately recognize all the bouts. Meanwhile, the second phase of the proposed algorithm achieved satisfactory accuracy on the accumulated movement time.

In the next step, we will investigate an adaptive method to facilitate the determination of the critical points, which are the boundary points for bouts. Particularly, we will use machine-learning techniques to capture the characteristics associated with critical points. Thus, the curve-fitting based approach will achieve more stable and accurate analysis on wheelchair users' mobility.

References

1. Carlson, D., Myklebust, J.: Wheelchair use and social integration. Top. Spinal Cord Inj. Rehabil. **7**, 28–46 (2002)
2. Reznik, R.: Wheelchair facts, numbers and figures [Infographic] (2015). http://kdsmartchair.com/blogs/news/18706123-wheelchair-facts-numbers-and-figures-infographic
3. Postma, K., van den Berg-Emons, H.J., Bussmann, J.B., Sluis, T.A., Bergen, M.P., Stam, H.J.: Validity of the detection of wheelchair propulsion as measured with an activity monitor in patients with spinal cord injury. Spinal Cord **43**, 550–557 (2005)
4. Krause, J.S., Vines, C.L., Farley, T.L., Sniezek, J., Coker, J.: An exploratory study of pressure ulcers after spinal cord injury: relationship to protective behaviors and risk factors. Arch. Phys. Med. Rehabil. **82**, 107–113 (2001)
5. Tolerico, M.L., Ding, D., Cooper, R.A., Spaeth, D.M., Fitzgerald, S.G., Cooper, R., et al.: Assessing mobility characteristics and activity levels of manual wheelchair users. J. Rehabil. Res. Dev. **44**, 561–571 (2007)
6. Sonenblum, S.E., Sprigle, S., Harris, F.H., Maurer, C.L.: Characterization of power wheelchair use in the home and community. Arch. Phys. Med. Rehabil. **89**, 486–491 (2008)
7. Harris, F., Sprigle, S., Sonenblum, S.E., Maurer, C.L.: The participation and activity measurement system: an example application among people who use wheeled mobility devices. Disabil. Rehabil. Assist. Technol. **5**, 48–57 (2010)
8. Sonenblum, S.E., Sprigle, S., Caspall, J., Lopez, R.: Validation of an accelerometer-based method to measure the use of manual wheelchairs. Med. Eng. Phys. **34**, 781–786 (2012)
9. Coulter, E.H., Dall, P.M., Rochester, L., Hasler, J.P., Granat, M.H.: Development and validation of a physical activity monitor for use on a wheelchair. Spinal Cord **49**, 445–450 (2011)
10. Hiremath, S.V., Ding, D., Cooper, R.A.: Development and evaluation of a gyroscope-based wheel rotation monitor for manual wheelchair users. J. Spinal Cord Med. **36**, 347–356 (2013)
11. Takeda, H., Farsiu, S., Milanfar, P.: Kernel regression for image processing and reconstruction. IEEE Trans. Image Process. **16**, 349–366 (2007)
12. Li, F., Ong, M., Qian, G., Zhao, Y.D., Fu, J.: A feasible and terrain-insensitive approach for analyzing power wheelchair users' mobility. In: ICTAI, pp. 596–590 (2017)
13. Silverman, B.W.: Density Estimation for Statistics and Data Analysis, vol. 26. CRC Press, Boca Raton (1986)

14. Ruppert, D., Sheather, S.J., Wand, M.P.: An effective bandwidth selector for local least squares regression. J. Am. Stat. Assoc. **90**, 1257–1270 (1995)
15. Loader, C.R.: Bandwidth selection: classical or plug-in? Ann. Stat. **27**, 415–438 (1999)
16. Loader, C.: Local Regression and Likelihood. Springer Science & Business Media, New York (2006). https://doi.org/10.1007/b98858
17. Hastie, T., Tibshirani, R., Friedman, J.: The Elements of Statistical Learning: Data Mining, Inference, and Prediction. SSS. Springer, New York (2009). https://doi.org/10.1007/978-0-387-84858-7
18. Loader, C.R.: locfit: local regression, likelihood and density estimation, R package version 1.5-9.1. http://CRAN.R-project.org/package=locfit
19. Ryan, J.A.: quantmod: quantitative financial modelling framework, R package version 0.3-5 (2008). http://www.quantmod.com, http://r-forge.r-project.org/projects/quantmod

An Interactive Training System Design for Ankle Rehabilitation

Lu Liu, Zhanxun Dong$^{(\boxtimes)}$, and Ning Tang

School of Design, Shanghai Jiao Tong University, 800 Dongchuan Road,
Minhang District, Shanghai, China
{ibetray, dongzx}@sjtu.edu.cn, designingning@gmail.com

Abstract. Ankle sprain is a common trauma, most patients can recover by non-surgical treatments. However, prolonged immobilization of ankle sprains is a common treatment error. After ankle sprain, patients should keep rehabilitation exercises to recover to the same level as before. There are 3 stages of ankle rehabilitation training process. This paper focuses on the second stage - proprioceptive training of intermediate functional rehabilitation. The normal training exercise of the second stage is balance training, bilateral and unilateral stance on different surfaces, which has been verified effective by large experimental data. Although balance training is simple and convenient, people can hardly complete the required amount of training because of the monotonous process. Therefore, although the medical research in ankle rehabilitation is well developed, the ankle rehabilitation training is not effective nor efficient enough. This paper shows a way to improve the effects and experiences of ankle rehabilitation process through interactive design and gamification. The interactive training system consists of 2 parts, the multi-touch pressure sensor and the user interface. The sensor can acquire the data of users' feet pressure distribution, which can be used to judge if the user is doing the proper training action. The user interface can give users instant feedback by game elements. Users can control the movement of the game subject by feet force changes (The pressure data are processed to apply to the game control module) to win the awards and avoid the obstacles. Each time the users succeed a game, they complete a training task at the same time. A user test was implemented for the interactive training system. According to the effectiveness, efficiency and satisfaction result by questionnaires, the users showed high satisfaction of the training process and outcome.

Keywords: Gamification · Ankle rehabilitation · Balance training
Motivation

1 Introduction

Ankle sprain is a common trauma, 80%–90% patients can recover by non-surgical treatments. Prolonged immobilization of ankle sprains is a common treatment error [1]. Medical experts encourage patients to do proper rehabilitation training exercises after ankle sprains, which can reduce the risk of pain, swelling and effusion, prolonged recovery time, reinjury, and even chronic ankle instability (CAI). Therefore, patients should take active part in rehabilitation exercises after ankle sprains.

© Springer International Publishing AG, part of Springer Nature 2018
V. G. Duffy (Ed.): DHM 2018, LNCS 10917, pp. 169–182, 2018.
https://doi.org/10.1007/978-3-319-91397-1_15

Although medical theories and practices in ankle rehabilitation are well developed, many patients ignore the necessary exercises. Athletes who value their athletic ability usually have professional help from their physical therapists. Patients after CAI surgical treatments are monitored by clinicians to complete the rehabilitation training plan. But for other patients who take ankle sprains not a serious problem, they usually have a busy life and find the rehabilitation training monotonous and boring. Additionally, patients at home do not have a clinician's or a therapist's supervision and help, which may lead to wrong and inefficient exercises. As a result, although the medical research in ankle rehabilitation is well developed, the ankle rehabilitation training in practice is neither effective nor efficient enough.

In order to increase patients' motivation for ankle rehabilitation training after ankle sprains, this paper tries to provide an interactive training system by gamification design method. There are 3 stages of ankle rehabilitation training process, which are early functional rehabilitation, intermediate functional rehabilitation and advanced functional rehabilitation. Because the complete rehabilitation training program involves many different kinds of exercises, it is a heavy workload to build an overall training system that covers all the 3 stages. Thus, this paper focuses on balance training, which is extensively used in the second and third stage of ankle rehabilitation training. Balance training consists of bilateral and unilateral stance on different surfaces with or without resistance and perturbations. Balance training is simple and convenient for household training but balance training without variability and perturbation may not be adequate for forces that challenge neuromuscular system at the highest levels [2]. As patients are recovering gradually, balance training settings (different surfaces, postures and with perturbations, etc.) need to upgrade accordingly. However, most people will not prepare these devices and do not have professional help at home, so balance training at home lacks variability.

As discussed above, this paper intends to solve two problems of balance training of ankle rehabilitation: people can hardly keep daily training because of the monotonous process; for better rehabilitation effects, balance training requires variation which is convenient for household use. To solve the problems, the interactive training system introduces gamification design. With the help of sensors, it is easy to acquire related data of people's exercises. The training system can be used in personal computers which are convenient for household use. This paper shows a way to improve the effects and experiences of ankle rehabilitation process by turning the traditional training plan to an exergame for patients to do rehabilitation at home.

2   Design and Development of the System

2.1   Balance Training Model

Although it is important to individualize each rehabilitation program, medical experts have developed mature rehabilitation training templates that patients in different periods of recovery can adapt with. Therefore, the interactive training system for ankle rehabilitation is based on the research of the mature training templates.

As explained in the introduction, the interactive system is designed for users to keep balance training every day at home. Based on previous study, it appears that balance training after acute ankle sprain substantially decreased the risk of recurrent ankle sprains [3]. Balance training is bilateral and unilateral stance on different surfaces and devices and it requires repetitive exercises every day. According to Mattacola and Dwyer [4], in the intermediate functional rehabilitation training stage, patients can stand on the rotating wobble board and try to keep balance for a while. As the patient is recovering gradually, this exercise can be progressed by changing the size and surface of the board, visual input and weight-bearing. In the advanced functional rehabilitation stage, balance training can be progressed with rubber-tubing resistance or after light perturbations from the clinician. These perturbations caused by active movements or external push can provide more challenging exercises for ankle rehabilitation. The conditions and devices of balance training can vary vastly so that patients can be challenged constantly during the rehabilitation process. One major drawback of this training method is that people cannot have all the requested devices, nor the clinicians' help when training at home. For example, one advanced method of balance training is that the patient, standing on one leg on a trampoline, keeps throwing and catching a gym ball with the clinician. However, this kind of exercise is normally performed in a clinic with enough space and professional devices. As a result, although clinicians suggest taking exercises of balance training after ankle sprains, people cannot adhere to the rehabilitation training plan very well at home. A common mistake when performing proprioception and balance exercises is the lack of variability in speed and intensity [4]. In addition, people easily get tired of the monotonous training mode, unilateral stance on floor or on a wobble board.

As discussed above, the basic form of balance training is bilateral and unilateral stance on certain surface. Bilateral stance of balance training needs to be done on the wobble board and had better be performed under a clinician's supervision. Thus, this paper selects unilateral stance as the training contents (see Fig. 1). In Fig. 1, the person stands akimbo while in practice, the arms can be out to side or across chest according to individual conditions. After studying existing cases, it can be found that many commercial rehabilitation platforms are based on Kinect, a motion sensing input device. A classic example is one exergame for arm rehabilitation on the rehabilitation platform, MIRA. In this game, the user can control a bee by doing elbow extension and flexion to fly up and down to gather pollen to deposit in beehives, all while avoiding the other bugs. The game goal is not hard to achieve because the real goal of the rehabilitation game is to help the users to finish enough training exercises. But with the help of the game, the amount of arm rehabilitation exercises can be counted and shown on the user interface so that when users achieve the game goal, the training plan is executed at the same time. With the instant visual and aural feedback, users' attention can be attracted during the process. Many rehabilitation training software platforms use Kinect as input device because those exercises are repetitive movements and easily to be monitored by a motion capture camera, such as stand-up and sit-down. There are different kinds of sensors to acquire data of exercises and for ankle rehabilitation training system design, an input device is also necessary.

Fig. 1. Posture of unilateral stance of balance training

From the description of balance training above, it can be concluded as one's body standing straight for a short time, which is easy to be captured by Kinect. However, if the system is designed to only record users' training time daily and return some virtual rewards when the training task is done, the experience of gameplay is still not enough, and the design of progress path is monotonous (increasing the balance time and changing the posture of arms). In addition, without the help of multiple devices and clinicians, this balance training plan lacks the variability in speed and intensity. Because it is a training system used for household, internal perturbation is chosen to make the exercises more interesting and challenging. Internal perturbation can be linked with the design of video games. Users can break the balance state by shifting the center of gravity to control the game element on digital screen to achieve the game goal. When you stand on one leg, your standing foot forms your base of support. The center of gravity is above the center of your base to balance, hence acquiring the pressure center of your foot can describe the balance training exercises. And many external ankle support devices also provide feedback of pressure sensors during exercises. Therefore, pressure sensors are adopted as the input device in the system design.

In summary, to solve the problems of balance training of the traditional ankle rehabilitation, the system is designed for users to do unilateral stance training, to break and return to the balance state according to the prompts and feedback of the game interface. This newly designed system takes into account the basic method of balance training and necessary variability during the training process. Because it adopts the way of internal perturbation (the balance state is interrupted by the user's own movements), many different professional training devices are not needed. And with the game design, the balance training can be progressed by increasing the difficulty of the game. In the section that follows, the rules and progress path of the rehabilitation game will be elaborated.

2.2 Rules of the Game

The game rule design of balance training focuses on 2 purposes: (a) to encourage users to keep balance, and (b) to provide some perturbation to break the balance occasionally. Playing the game means to control a game element by keeping and breaking balance to interact with the other game interface according to game rules.

Gameplay. As the user receive feedback on how they perform from the game interface, the information provided on the interface will affect the user's next move and interest directly. Therefore, the game rules and the interface are designed to be intuitive and readily comprehensible, which conform to the context of ankle rehabilitation. Thus, when the user is in the state of balance, the player character in the game stays in the same position. Positive feedback and rapid rewards added at the right timing are indicators of success, which is an important feature for motivation [5]. Thereby when the user succeeds in keeping balance on one leg, there are awards in a line to be obtained (see Fig. 2), which can add game scores. The awards are moving down in a straight line and according to the theory of relative motion, it can be seen as the player character is moving up as well. When the player character runs into an award item, the scores of this round add 10. To add variability to the balance training, interferent items will come from the above randomly to hit the player character (see Fig. 2). If the player character was hit, the scores of this round will subtract 100 for each hit. Therefore, the user needs to shift the center of gravity to respond to the disturbing and the movements will invoke perturbation while maintaining balance. The player character can move in one dimensional. But when the users shift the center of gravity to left or right, their body cannot move straightly. In unbalanced state, people wobbles and as well as the center of gravity. Therefore, although the player character can only move to left or right, the users' ankle joint can be challenged in different angles and postures. Therefore, to minimize users' cognitive demand, one-dimensional control of the player character is applied.

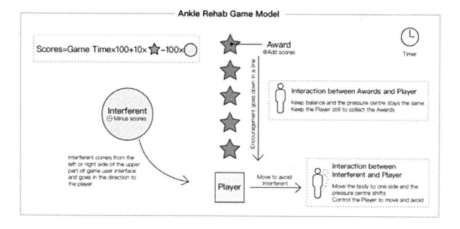

Fig. 2. Diagram of the game design of ankle rehabilitation

Game Goal. Balance training plan is usually designed as a round for a short time like 20 s. It is repeated 5–10 times as a set of exercises. And patients need to do 2–3 sets of the balance training exercises every day [4, 6]. The duration and frequency of balance training plan can be designed as game settings. The ankle rehabilitation game is designed in timing mode. When the time of one game is up, one time of balance training is completed. 5 times as a set so when 5 games are finished, a small prize will be provided to encourage users. Likewise, after achieving 3 small prizes, a big prize will be provided, which means today's training task is accomplished.

Progress Path. Thus far, the interactive system of ankle rehabilitation is generally shaped. In addition, it is important to design the progress path of the ankle rehabilitation game because during the recovering process, the difficulty of the game needs to be leveled up to meet the demand of training intensity. And according to the flow theory, the progress path can make users remain engaged during the rehabilitation process [7].

In consideration of different individual conditions, clinicians can choose and adjust the training plan for each patient because with the help of the e-platform, clinicians can view the patients' training logs, which are more accurate than patients' personal statement. When training at home, the training game will level up in accordance with the users' performance (e.g. game scores). The rehabilitation training system is progressed in 3 aspects (see Fig. 3): (a) the frequency of interferent items' occurrence increases, (b) the velocity of interferent items increases, and (c) time for one game prolongs. In this way, the users' ability of balance and response to perturbation improves.

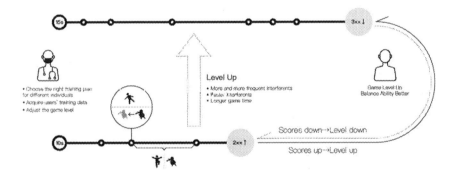

Fig. 3. Diagram of the progress path of the interactive system

The higher score of a game means better balance ability and better control of ankles. Therefore, when scores increase, the difficulty of the game should be increased. The score is calculated as followed.

$$Score = Game\,Time \times 100 + Award \times 10 - Interferent \times 100 \qquad (1)$$

Therefore, when the game levels up, the basic scores increase since the game time increases. And as time prolonged, more award items are available, so the scores will go up. But because of the more frequent and faster interferent items, it is more challenging for users to avoid them. Hence, the scores may decrease when the game becomes more difficult. The system can adjust the difficulty level of balance training gradually based on users' game performance. As seen in Fig. 3, it can be inferred that the progress path of the training game is an iterative process. By this means, people can do progressive balance training at home under guidance. Moreover, increase in difficulty of the game is an indicator of outcomes of rehabilitation exercises.

2.3   Hardware and System

As previously stated, the input data to describe the exercises is pressure center of the supporting foot. In order to simplify the development, Sensel Morph is used in this case (see Fig. 4). Sensel Morph is a multi-touch, pressure sensitive, and reconfigurable control surface for artists, musicians, coders, and other creative people. Because the foot pressure center cannot be calculated by single sensor, a multi-touch, pressure sensitive device is necessary. And Sensel Morph can meet the demands of the system development. Sensel Morph with different Overlays can adapt to many different tasks – playing music, editing video, drawing, playing games and so on. It also provides open source Sensel API for programmers to create new programs that interact with a Sensel. With the functions in Sensel library, the data acquisition and processing can be quickly set up. Sensel Morph can support systems of macOS, Windows, Linux, Android and iOS and languages of C, Python and C#. And because the game development is based on the pygame library of Python, the input coding also uses Python as the developing language. Sensel Morph can be connected with USB or wirelessly via Bluetooth 4.0LE.

Fig. 4. Sensel Morph – pressure sensitive pad used to acquire data

As explained earlier, the users control the game character by shifting the body, thereby the parameters used are Coordinates and Contact to calculate the y offset value. And initialization to identify the coordinates of the center of gravity in balance is designed. Before starting the training game, the users are asked to stay balance for 5–10 seconds for the system to record the initial coordinates of the pressure center (Fig. 5). People cannot keep absolutely still thus coordinates in a small wave range can be supposed in balance.

Fig. 5. Visualization of foot pressure

The algorithm of input data needs to be adjusted through user experiments so that the users can link the changes of gravity center with the displacement of the player character unconsciously. The unit length of displacement is designed in 3 levels and 10 users for each group. After experiments, they are asked to choose the experience (too fast, moderate, too slow). The experiment is repeated but narrowed down the range of the 3 unit lengths to optimize user experience.

The hardware of the system consists of 2 parts: a pressure sensor board and a computer (see Fig. 6). Personal computers and laptops are accessible to normal family.

Fig. 6. Hardware of the ankle rehabilitation system

2.4 User Interface

In this section, the user interfaces of a complete training process will be demonstrated. With the high-fidelity interfaces display, the gamification design of balance training can be better understood. To make the game goals and rules easily comprehended, the settings of story is applied. And ice skating can be linked with balance training. Additionally, story and character settings can make the training game more amusing and appealing.

Introduction and Task Table. When entering the system, a simple instruction of the training method is the first page. And you can tick the option of "not show again" then this page will not appear next time. After you click on the button "Got it", it jumps to the page of the task table. The task table illustrates the goal of today's training and current rate of progress. For example, in Fig. 7, the balance training plan is designed as 3 sets of 5 repetitions. The visualization of the training frequency can encourage users to carry out the plan.

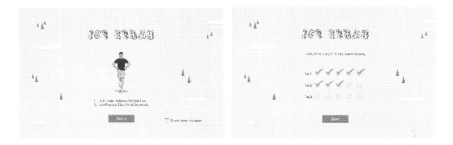

Fig. 7. User interface of introduction and training task table

Initialization and Countdown. After clicking on the button "Start", it jumps to the page of initialization. On this page, there are simple instructions of postures and a dynamic loading icon. The loading icon is filling with color to indicate the progress of the initialization. After the data of balance state is recorded, it will automatically jump to the countdown page. The countdown page is designed for users to get ready for the game start as it is a timer game and starts immediately (Fig. 8).

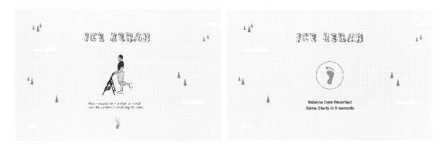

Fig. 8. User interface of Initialization and countdown

Game Interface. As mentioned previously, the game interface is designed on the basis of the diagram of the game design (see Fig. 2). The player character is set as a penguin slider (see Fig. 9), who can slide to left and right. The award items are set as fish, which can be easy to understand as rewards for the penguin. The big snowball represents the interferent items, which will slide from the above to hit the penguin. And as the snowball hits the penguin, animations of crushing into pieces are added to clarify the negative feedback. Furthermore, audible effects of obtaining the fish and being hit by the snowball are along with the visual effects to improve game experience. The shore side and fish are moving down so that it seems that the penguin is going forward. Story setting has a positive effect on comprehension of game rules and goals. Moreover, the game score is displayed with real-time changes as instant feedback.

Fig. 9. Game interface

Game Results. The game ends when time is up, then the page of results appears automatically. 3 number are listed (see Fig. 10): game scores, times that got hit, times of obtained fish. And the remained exercises of one set are reminded as well. And when one set of training exercises is finished, a grander congrats page will appear. Likewise, a new congrats page for one day's task is provided. The users can check their own rehabilitation outcomes by the game results. In contrast to traditional ankle rehabilitation training, the users can see the progress after exercises of each time.

Fig. 10. Interface of game results

3   Evaluation of the System

An initial evaluation of the system has been carried out with two patients after ankle sprains (Fig. 11). The participants' profiles are in Table 1. The two participants are asked to take the ankle training with the interactive system for one week (3 sets of 5 repetitions for one day). The training contents are explained ahead, but everyday task is not compulsory for them.

Table 1. Participant profiles

Participant	1	2
Age	22	24
Gender	Male	Female
Time of sprains	1 week	3 weeks
Foot	Right	Right

The two participants both show great interest in the training plan because they express that they have the problems of keeping rehabilitation exercises. The two participants completed all the training tasks willingly and showed evident progress during the experiment process. After insisting balance training for one week, they have been asked to evaluate the motivation and engagement for the interactive system by the Intrinsic Motivation Inventory (IMI, see Table 2). Four sub-scales are adopted in the questionnaire: Interest/Enjoyment, Perceived competence, Effort/Importance and Tension/Pressure. The statements are listed out of order for reliability.

Table 2. Intrinsic motivation inventory of interactive ankle rehabilitation system

	1 2 3 4 5 6 7
not at all true	somewhat true true very true

1. I enjoyed doing the rehabilitation training very much

2. I think I am pretty good at this activity

3. I put a lot of effort into this

4. It was important to me to do well at this task

5. I felt very tense while doing this activity

6. I tried very hard on this activity

7. This activity was fun to do

8. I would describe this activity as very interesting

9. I am satisfied with my performance at this task

10. I felt pressured while doing these

11. I was anxious while working on this task

12. I did not try very hard to do well at this activity

13. While I was doing this activity, I was thinking about how much I enjoyed it

14. After working at this activity for a while, I felt pretty competent

15. I was very relaxed in doing these

16. I was pretty skilled at this activity

17. This activity did not hold my attention at all

18. This was an activity that I could not do very well

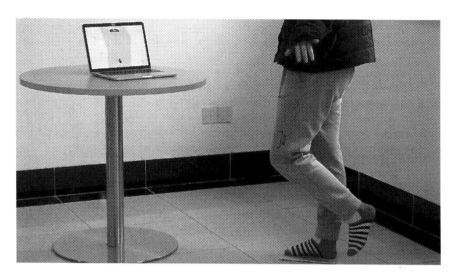

Fig. 11. Participants training in the experiment

The IMI scores shows a positive result of the interactive system (see Table 3). The two participants both thought that this training method was enjoyable, and they could feel the balance ability improved during the training process. Owing to the feedback, it could help them keep doing daily training exercises. They need some time to get acquainted with the game, but they could master the game after one game. Nevertheless, they proposed a complete training system covering all the stages and different exercises. And they also expressed worries on long-term effects since training of first week is still fresh and novel for users.

Table 3. Results on IMI of interactive ankle rehabilitation system

Sub-scale	1	2	Average
Interest/Enjoyment	6.43	7.00	6.72
Perceived competence	5.33	6.20	5.77
Effort/Importance	6.33	6.00	6.17
Tension/Pressure	3.20	2.60	2.80

4   Conclusion and Discussion

The interactive training system of ankle rehabilitation applies gamification design method to improve motivation and engagement, focusing on balance training. Meaningful feedback is provided to make the training process more interesting and interactive. In addition, the digital platform can help to record and reflect the training process as reference for both patients and clinicians. And the progress path is designed to provide the needed challenges for different periods of recovery. The result of the initial evaluation is positive generally.

How to ensure the contents and intensity of rehabilitation exercises are appropriate and effective is a significant issue in the research. Furthermore, with the accumulated training data, clinicians can optimize the training system and provide more diversified game experiences.

Acknowledgement. This paper was supported by Zhejiang Provincial Key Laboratory of Integration of Healthy Smart Kitchen System (Grant No: 2017F02) and the Fundamental Research Funds for the Central Universities of Shanghai Jiao Tong University (Grant No: 17JCYB07).

References

1. Kerkhoffs, G.M., Rowe, B.H., Assendelft, W.J., Kelly, K.D., Struijs, P.A., van Dijk, C.N.: Immobilisation for acute ankle sprain. Arch. Orthop. Trauma Surg. **121**(8), 462–471 (2001)
2. Ashton-Miller, J.A., Wojtys, E.M., Huston, L.J., Fry-Welch, D.: Can proprioception really be improved by exercises? Knee Surg. Sports Traumatol. Arthrosc. **9**(3), 128–136 (2001)
3. McKeon, P.O., Hertel, J.: Systematic review of postural control and lateral ankle instability, part II: is balance training clinically effective? J. Athl. Train. **43**(3), 305–315 (2008)
4. Mattacola, C.G., Dwyer, M.K.: Rehabilitation of the ankle after acute sprain or chronic instability. J. Athl. Train. **37**(4), 413 (2002)
5. Pereira, P., Duarte, E., Rebelo, F., Noriega, P.: A review of gamification for health-related contexts. In: Marcus, A. (ed.) DUXU 2014. LNCS, vol. 8518, pp. 742–753. Springer, Cham (2014). https://doi.org/10.1007/978-3-319-07626-3_70
6. Söderman, K., Werner, S., Pietilä, T., Engström, B., Alfredson, H.: Balance board training: prevention of traumatic injuries of the lower extremities in female soccer players? Knee Surg. Sports Traumatol. Arthrosc. **8**(6), 356–363 (2000)
7. Schell, J.: The Art of Game Design: A book of Lenses. CRC Press, Boca Raton (2014)

The Effect of Ankle Exercise on Cerebral Blood Oxygenation During and After Postural Change

Sachiko Nagaya[1(✉)] and Hisae Hayashi[2]

[1] Nagoya University Graduate School of Medicine, Nagoya, Aichi, Japan
nagaya@met.nagoya-u.ac.jp
[2] Seijoh University, Tokai City, Japan

Abstract. Orthostatic hypotension can cause dizziness, syncope, and falling when some individuals change their posture, due to the cardiovascular system improperly maintaining their blood pressure. The skeletal muscle pump plays an important role in adjusting hemodynamics. Ankle exercise has been proven as an effective intervention to increase venous velocity. If ankle exercise performed in a supine position is proven to have the effect of maintaining cerebral hemodynamics after postural change, it could prevent the symptoms of postural hypotension. The purpose of the present study was to determine the effect of active ankle exercise (60 s and 30 s) on postural change. Participants alternately performed plantar flexion and dorsiflexion movements of the ankle joint in the supine position. After the ankle exercise, we changed the participants' posture from supine to sitting and oxyhemoglobin levels were evaluated. Each ankle exercise was compared with the control condition. In the 60 s ankle exercise, the oxyhemoglobin level gradually increased in accordance with exercise. There was a significant interaction effect (exercise × time) for the oxyhemoglobin level in the 60 s ankle exercise. However, there were no significant differences before and after postural change in the 30 s ankle exercise. These results suggested that the duration of ankle exercise is important to attenuate the decreased cerebral oxygenation induced by postural change.

Keywords: Postural hypotension · Ankle exercise
Near-infrared spectroscopy

1 Introduction

Some people have symptoms resulting from hypotension when they change their posture, called orthostatic hypotension (OH). One of the main causes of OH is a shift in blood induced by postural change, commonly seen in transition from supine to standing. When people change their posture from supine to standing position, approximately 500–700 mL of blood shifts toward the lower extremities [1]. This blood shift leads to reduction in venous return. As a result, the cardiac output decreases, and subsequently, the mean arterial blood pressure (MAP) decreases. If there is a dynamic decrease in MAP, an adequate cerebral blood pressure cannot be maintained, causing syncope [2]. From

© Springer International Publishing AG, part of Springer Nature 2018
V. G. Duffy (Ed.): DHM 2018, LNCS 10917, pp. 183–192, 2018.
https://doi.org/10.1007/978-3-319-91397-1_16

this physiological mechanism, if an approach to promote venous return is identified, it can be a useful treatment for preventing OH.

Several physical counter maneuvers have been suggested to diminish OH symptoms. Leg crossing and squatting are representative examples of these interventions. They can contribute to the mechanical compression of veins in the lower extremities by stimulating muscles. This stimulus by muscles can reduce venous capacity and increase the total peripheral resistance. Consequently, increased venous return increases the mean blood pressure to a high enough level to maintain cerebral blood flow [3, 4]. However, these counter maneuvers are sometimes difficult for patients to perform immediately when they expect symptoms to occur. Therefore, we believe that there is room for discussion about a simpler approach to preventing OH.

Active ankle exercises have been proven to be an effective method to increase venous velocity by squeezing accumulated blood from the lower part of the body [5–7]. On the basis of these findings, we revealed that ankle exercise also increases cerebral oxygenation in the supine position [8]. We hypothesized that ankle exercise could be a simple and efficient intervention for preventing the symptoms related to postural changes. As counter maneuvers, we attempted to seek an easier exercise by changing the duration of exercise (60 s and 30 s).

The purpose of the present study was to determine the effect of active ankle exercise on postural change. The fundamental cause of OH is impaired cerebral hemodynamics [9]. Herein, we summarize our experiments with a focus on cerebral oxygenation and discuss the potential of ankle exercise as an intervention for preventing postural hypotension.

2   Experiment 1

2.1   Methods

Participants

This study consisted of 11 participants (5 men, 6 women) aged 46.2 ± 12.9 (range 31–74) years. Their mean height, weight, and body mass index were 160.6 ± 10.2 cm, 57.6 ± 8.8 kg, and 22.1 ± 2.5 kg/m^2, respectively. Participants with arrhythmias and/or impaired motor function were excluded. One of the participants was hypertensive and using antihypertensive medications. Before the study, the participants were instructed to abstain from alcohol for 12 h, not to eat a meal within 90 min of the experiment, and to get enough sleep.

Experimental Procedures

The experiments were conducted from September 2014 to October 2014. The room temperature was maintained at 25 °C with 50% relative humidity. Before the measurements, the experimental protocols were explained in detail to the participants. In addition, the participants practiced the ankle exercises with the researcher.

Figure 1 shows the protocol of the experiment. At the beginning of each measurement, the participant lay in supine on the bed for 120 s. For active ankle exercise, the participants alternately performed plantar flexion and dorsiflexion movements of the ankle joint for 60 s. The pace of ankle movements was 60 times/min. The manner of exercise was determined by referring to previous studies [7, 10]. After the exercise was finished, the participants changed their posture from supine to sitting. They maintained a sitting position for 60 s, and then the exercise protocol ended. The postural change was conducted passively. First, using the electric motor of a hospital bed, the participant's position was changed from supine to the high Fowler's position. Second, the researcher turned the participant's body 90° to a sitting position (sitting on the edge of a bed without leaning against the mattress). This sequence of postural changes took about 30 s. Subjects also completed a postural change without exercise as control data. For this test, subjects rested quietly for 180 s in supine prior to the postural change. The data of the first 60 s in supine position were used to obtain the baseline data of each participant. The order of the conditions varied in a balanced manner for each participant.

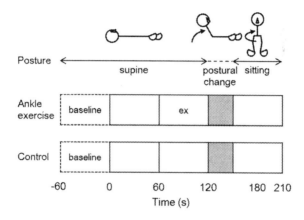

Fig. 1. Schematic representation of the experimental procedures (experiment 1).

ex = ankle exercise.

Measuring Physiological Responses

To estimate cerebral hemodynamic changes induced by postural change, continuous changes in the oxyhemoglobin (OxyHb) level were measured. The OxyHb level was measured by near-infrared spectroscopy (NIRS) (NIRO-200; Hamamatsu Photonics, Hamamatsu City, Japan) at a sampling rate of 2 Hz. Two optodes of the NIRO-200 were attached on the right and left sides of the forehead. The baseline value of OxyHb was determined for the first 60 s while the subject was in the supine position. The pulse rate (PR), systolic, and diastolic blood pressures were monitored by the HEM-7130 (Omron Colin, Tokyo, Japan). The PR and blood pressure were measured twice for each condition (at the time after the baseline data were obtained and again immediately after completion of the postural change). The MAP was calculated by adding one-third of the pulse pressure to diastolic blood pressure. Each condition was repeated twice to obtain stable data. However, due to the necessity to avoid a carry-over effect, neither of the conditions was repeated twice in a row.

Statistical Analysis

PR and MAP data between the supine and sitting positions were analyzed using the paired t-test. The signals before and after exercise were individually averaged for 60 s in two-way repeated measures (exercise × time) analysis of variance (ANOVA). The statistical significance was set at p < 0.05.

Ethical Considerations

The participants were told the purpose and methods of this study and were informed that they could refuse to participate or withdraw from it at any time. Informed consent was obtained in writing from all participants. The study protocol was approved by the Ethics Committee of Nagoya University Graduate School of Medicine in Japan.

2.2 Results

Table 1 describes the PR and MAP responses to postural change following 60 s of ankle exercise. Results are expressed as a mean ± standard error. The MAP showed a significant increase under both conditions (ankle exercise, p < 0.001; control, p = 0.003), from supine to sitting position. The PR also increased under both conditions. However, it was not significantly different between the conditions (ankle exercise, p = 0.07; control, p = 0.11).

Table 1. Pulse rate and mean arterial blood pressure response to postural change following 60 s of ankle exercise (n = 11).

	PR (bpm)		MAP (mmHg)	
	Supine	Sitting	Supine	Sitting
Ankle exercise	61.23 ± 2.41	65.18 ± 3.53	87.35 ± 2.98	93.76 ± 2.94**
Control	59.27 ± 1.81	61.68 ± 2.69	86.62 ± 2.85	91.85 ± 2.82**

Significant changes between supine and sitting positions are indicated by * (p < 0.05) and ** (p < 0.01).
PR = pulse rate; MAP = mean arterial pressure; bpm = beats/min.

Figure 2 shows the cerebral oxygenation responses to postural change following 60 s of ankle exercise performed in a supine position. The OxyHb level continually increased during active exercise. In contrast, the control condition showed little change from baseline. In both exercise and control conditions, the OxyHb level began to decrease after postural change.

Figure 3 shows changes in the OxyHb level caused by both conditions (60 s of ankle exercise and the control condition) before and after postural change. The data before postural change were obtained from 0 s to 60 s, and the data after postural change were obtained from 120 s to 180 s. Therefore, in the ankle exercise group, the data before postural change indicated that it was measured in supine position before performing ankle exercise. ANOVA revealed a significant interaction effect for OxyHb responses (p = 0.004).

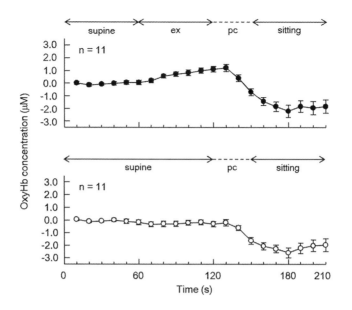

Fig. 2. Oxyhemoglobin responses to 60 s of ankle exercise and postural change (n = 11).

Top graph illustrates the response to 60 s of ankle exercise. The bottom graph illustrates the control condition. Each point represents data averaged over a 10 s period. Error bars are standard error of the mean.

OxyHb = oxyhemoglobin; ex = ankle exercise; pc = postural change.

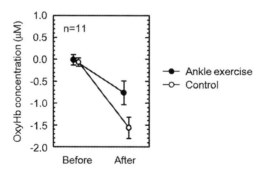

Fig. 3. Oxyhemoglobin responses to postural change following 60 s of ankle exercise (n = 11).

Figure 3 illustrates the OxyHb level averaged before and after position changes. The "Before" time point portrays the data averaged from a 60 s period in supine position without ankle exercise. The "After" data represent the OxyHb level obtained with 60 s of ankle exercise during and after postural change. Error bars are the standard error of the mean.

OxyHb = Oxyhemoglobin.

3   Experiment 2

3.1   Methods

Participants
The study consisted of 8 participants (4 men, 4 women) aged 71.3 ± 3.1 (range 65–75) years. Their mean height, weight, and body mass index were 160.1 ± 10.5 cm, 53.3 ± 9.4 kg, and 20.7 ± 2.2 kg/m^2, respectively.

Experimental Procedures
Figure 4 shows the protocol of the experiment. The experiments were conducted in November 2016. The participant lay supine in a reclining chair for 120 s and performed ankle exercise for 30 s. The data from the start to 60 s were used as the baseline data. After 90 s from starting the experiment, postural change was performed by raising the back of the chair using its reclining function. Postural change took about 10 s. The control condition was also assessed in each participant. In the control condition, participants rested quietly for 150 s in the supine position before postural change.

Measuring Physiological Responses
The OxyHb level was measured by NIRS (NIRO-200; Hamamatsu Photonics) in the same manner as in experiment 1.

Statistical Analysis
The OxyHb level during 30 s of ankle exercise was analyzed with a paired t-test. The signals before and after exercise were individually averaged for 60 s in two-way repeated measures (exercise × time) ANOVA. The statistical significance was set at $p < 0.05$.

Ethical Considerations
Informed consent was obtained from each participant in the same way as experiment 1. The study protocol was approved by the Ethics Committee of Nagoya University Graduate School of Medicine in Japan.

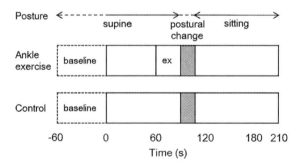

Fig. 4.   Schematic representation of the experimental procedures (experiment 2).

ex = ankle exercise.

3.2 Results

Figure 5 shows the cerebral oxygenation responses to postural change following a 30 s ankle exercise. In the control condition, the OxyHb level showed little change from the experiment start during supine position. In comparison, the OxyHb level seemed to increase slightly during 30 s of ankle exercise. However, there was no significant difference between the two conditions in the mean value from 60 s to 90 s (30 s of ankle exercise = 0.12 ± 0.17; control = −0.14 ± 0.16; p = 0.12). In both conditions, the OxyHb level began to decrease immediately after postural change.

Figure 6 shows changes in the OxyHb level caused by both conditions (30 s of ankle exercise and the control condition) before and after postural change. The data of before postural change was obtained from 0 s to 60 s and the data of after postural change was obtained 90 s to 180 s (during and after postural change period). The two-way repeated measures ANOVA revealed no significant differences exercise factor (p = 0.47) and time factor (p = 0.07).

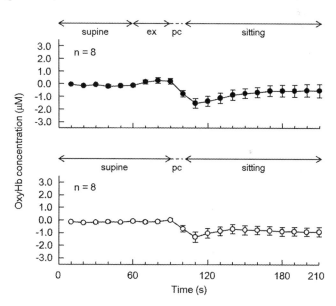

Fig. 5. Oxyhemoglobin responses to 30 s of ankle exercise and postural change (n = 8).

OxyHb = oxyhemoglobin; ex = ankle exercise; pc = postural change.

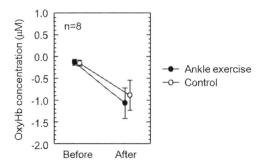

Fig. 6. Oxyhemoglobin responses to postural change following 30 s of ankle exercise (n = 8).

OxyHb = oxyhemoglobin.

4   Discussion

4.1   Responses of the PR and MAP to Postural Change After 60-s Ankle Exercise

In experiment 1, the PR increased slightly after postural change, but there were no significant differences between the data before and after postural change. However, the MAP showed a significant increase after postural change following both 60 s of ankle exercise and the control condition. This result indicates that participants tolerated the stress of postural change well. When the baroreceptor senses a decrease in the MAP by postural change, the sympathetic nerve is first activated to increase heart rate. Then, peripheral resistance increases to restore the MAP [11]. Our results may emphasize the point that the MAP increased after elevation of the heart rate.

We assumed that the experimental procedure also attributed to these results. In consideration of safety, we limited postural change from supine to sitting position. Therefore, in this study, we considered that the stress of postural change was lower than that needed to induce a drastic decrease in the MAP. Moreover, there were no participants with a diagnosis of OH. The participants' autonomic nerves were able to regulate their cardiovascular systems well in response to postural change. Previous studies have reported that a continuous measurement showed temporarily decreases in blood pressure caused by postural change, and the pressure recovered within 30 s. Sometimes the blood pressure recovers to a baseline level and reactively goes on to overshoot the baseline level [12–14]. Considering these reports, there is a possibility that the data after postural change show points of recovery from the stress of postural change.

4.2   The Difference in Cerebral Oxygenation Responses to Postural Change Based on the Duration Ankle Exercise Time

We revealed that compared with the control condition, active 60 s of ankle exercise can attenuate the decreased OxyHb level induced by postural change. However, in experiment 2, 30 s of ankle exercise did not affect the OxyHb level. On the basis of this results, we determined that the combination of exercise intensity and duration is important to obtain an appropriate counter effect of ankle exercise.

The beneficial effects of several physical counter maneuvers have been reported. However, to obtain the appropriate effect, some techniques are required. Galizia et al. proved that supine leg resistance exercise had a counteracting effect on OH. They tried to prevent OH by performing leg muscle exercises in supine before standing. They performed 10 full extensions of the ankle, knee, and hip joints of both limbs within 25 s against 6 kg of load using a resistance band [15]. The intensity of this exercise is much stronger than that of our active ankle exercise. Therefore, we concluded that our intervention in experiment 2 was not a high enough intensity to increase the OxyHb level effectively. Plantar and dorsiflexion ankle movements involve movements of the anterior tibialis, gastrocnemius, and soleus muscles. These muscles play important roles as pumps for returning pooling blood from the legs to the heart [1]. Figure 2 shows that exercise gradually increases the OxyHb level in accordance with the frequency of ankle movement. Low intensity exercise, such as ankle movement, may need more than 60 s or external resistance to elevate the OxyHb and counteract the postural change stimulus.

5   Conclusions

Active ankle exercise increases cerebral oxygenation and has a counteracting effect on postural change from supine to sitting. However, to achieve a sufficient exercise effect, the exercise intensity and duration need to be considered. We conclude that a 30 s about of active ankle exercise does not effectively increase cerebral oxygenation. To avoid and attenuate OH, ankle exercise in supine must be performed for more than 60 s.

Acknowledgements. We thank all participants in our study. Our study was supported by a Grant-in-Aid for Scientific Research (C) (no. 24593195) and Grant-in-Aid for Challenging Exploratory Research (no. 15K15790) from the Japan Society for the Promotion of Science. A part of data in experiment 1 in this article based on the first author's doctoral dissertation submitted to the Ishikawa Prefectural Nursing University.

References

1. Smith, J.J., Kampine, J.P.: Circulatory Physiology: The Essentials, 3rd edn. Williams and Wilkins, Baltimore (1990)
2. Costanzo, L.: Physiology, 5th edn. Saunders Elsevier, Philadelphia (2014)
3. van Lieshout, J.J., ten Harkel, A.D., Wieling, W.: Physical manoeuvres for combating orthostatic dizziness in autonomic failure. Lancet **339**(8798), 897–898 (1992)
4. Wieling, W., van Dijk, N., Thijs, R.D., de Lange, F.J., Krediet, C.T., Halliwill, J.R.: Physical countermeasures to increase orthostatic tolerance. J. Intern. Med. **277**(1), 69–82 (2015)
5. Kwon, O.Y., Jung, D.Y., Kim, Y., Cho, S.H., Yi, C.H.: Effects of ankle exercise combined with deep breathing on blood flow velocity in the femoral vein. Aust. J. Physiother. **49**(4), 253–258 (2003)
6. Sochart, D.H., Hardinge, K.: The relationship of foot and ankle movements to venous return in the lower limb. J. Bone Joint Surg. Br. **81**(4), 700–704 (1999)

7. Stein, P.D., Yaekoub, A.Y., Ahsan, S.T., Matta, F., Lala, M.M., Mirza, B., et al.: Ankle exercise and venous blood velocity. Thromb. Haemost. **101**(6), 1100–1103 (2009)

8. Nagaya, S., Hayashi, H., Fujimoto, E., Maruoka, N., Kobayashi, H.: Passive ankle movement increases cerebral blood oxygenation in the elderly: an experimental study. BMC Nurs. **14**, 14 (2015)

9. Harms, M.P., Colier, W.N., Wieling, W., Lenders, J.W., Secher, N.H., van Lieshout, J.J.: Orthostatic tolerance, cerebral oxygenation, and blood velocity in humans with sympathetic failure. Stroke **31**(7), 1608–1614 (2000)

10. McNally, M.A., Cooke, E.A., Mollan, R.A.: The effect of active movement of the foot on venous blood flow after total hip replacement. J. Bone Joint Surg. Am. **79**(8), 1198–1201 (1997)

11. Levick, J.R.: An Introduction to Cardiovascular Physiology, 5th edn. CRC Press, London (2010)

12. Bundgaard-Nielsen, M., Jørgensen, C.C., Jørgensen, T.B., Ruhnau, B., Secher, N.H., Kehlet, H.: Orthostatic intolerance and the cardiovascular response to early postoperative mobilization. Br. J. Anaesth. **102**(6), 756–762 (2009)

13. Imholz, B.P., Settels, J.J., van der Meiracker, A.H., Wesseling, K.H., Wieling, W.: Non-invasive continuous finger blood pressure measurement during orthostatic stress compared to intra-arterial pressure. Cardiovasc. Res. **24**(3), 214–221 (1990)

14. Thomas, K.N., Cotter, J.D., Galvin, S.D., Williams, M.J., Willie, C.K., Ainslie, P.N.: Initial orthostatic hypotension is unrelated to orthostatic tolerance in healthy young subjects. J. Appl. Physiol. **107**(2), 506–517 (2009)

15. Galizia, G., Abete, P., Testa, G., Vecchio, A., Corrá, T., Nardone, A.: Counteracting effect of supine leg resistance exercise on systolic orthostatic hypotension in older adults. J. Am. Geriatr. Soc. **61**(7), 1152–1157 (2013)

Motion Analysis of Simulated Patients During Bed-to-Wheelchair Transfer by Nursing Students and Skill Acquisition Based on the Analysis

Hiromi Nakagawa[1(✉)], Masahiro Tukamoto[1],
Kazuaki Yamashiro[2], and Akihiko Goto[3]

[1] Faculty of Nursing, Seisen University, 720 Hida, Hikone, Shiga 521-1123, Japan
nakaga-h@seisen.ac.jp
[2] Department of Advanced Fibro-Science, Kyoto Institute of Technology, Matsugasaki, Sakyo-ku, Kyoto 606-8585, Japan
[3] Faculty of Design Technology, Osaka Sangyo University, 3-1-1 Nakagaito, Daito, Osaka 574-8530, Japan

Abstract. The aging population in Japan is currently at 26.7% and is projected to reach 30.3% by 2025. This points to an increase in nursing care that involves transferring in and out of a wheelchair. Previous research has shown that the way a caregiver embraces the patient when transitioning her from bed to wheelchair contributes to lower back pain and has necessitated educational intervention to prevent occupational back pain. On the other hand, the patient is required to transfer into a wheelchair without falling and to maintain a seated position with the appropriate amount of body pressure. Both caregiver and receiver are asked to act in ways that are safe for both sides when transferring. In our own motion analysis of wheelchair transition, the non-experts bent forward more at the cervical and lumbar spine than the experts, creating greater body pressure distribution due to a smaller area of physical contact with the simulated patient. These results suggest that actions used for bed-to-wheelchair transferring influenced the seated position of the simulated patient. However, there are very few motion analysis studies that examine the patients' movements during a wheelchair transfer. Therefore, this study is based on a motion analysis of the simulated patients while they are being transferred from bed to wheelchair. The study involves 4 nursing students who completed their practical training, and 2 expert nurses. The goal of this study is to turn into explicit knowledge and quantify the tacit techniques of position changing performed in nursing care. Results of this study show that the simulated patients transferred by the non-experts were led through the seating phase faster than those transferred by the experts, and the increase in speed was related to the nurses' proximity to their simulated patients. Furthermore, we learned that motion analysis could be applied to skill acquisition.

Keywords: Motion analysis · Wheelchair transferring · Back pain · Acceleration
Interface pressure

© Springer International Publishing AG, part of Springer Nature 2018
V. G. Duffy (Ed.): DHM 2018, LNCS 10917, pp. 193–204, 2018.
https://doi.org/10.1007/978-3-319-91397-1_17

1   Introduction

According to the World Health Organization (WHO), the aging rate is defined as the percentage of elderly people aged 65 and over in relation to the total population. Furthermore, a society where the aging rate exceeds 7% is defined as an "aging society", that with over 14% as an "aged society", and that with over 21% is defined as a "super aging society" [1]. Japan became an aging society in 1970, and it became a super aging society in 2007. It has the highest aging rate in the world. The total population of Japan in 2014 was 127.08 million, and the number of elderly population was 33 million, the highest ever recorded, and its aging rate became 26.0%. It is estimated that by 2060, one out of 2.5 people will be 65 or over 65, further acceleration in the aging rate is expected [2].

Following the start of the super aging society in Japan, the number of the people aged 65 and over certified to require care reached 5.457 million by 2012, and this number has been increasing year by year. It resulted that the national medical expenses scored 40 trillion yen in 2014, and the cost required for the people aged 75 and over increased to about 11.5 trillion yen [3]. Moreover, by 2025, the national medical expenses for the elderly is expected to reach about 60% of the total medical expenses in Japan. The average health expectancy in Japan is 74.9, which is the highest in the world. In order to control the medical expenses for elderly people, it is necessary to maintain the health expectancy [4]. Sustainable Development Goals of WHO states as, "Ensure healthy lives and promote wellbeing for all at all ages", and it is required to maintain the healthy lives of elderly people at medical facilities, care facilities and private homes. The preventing the occurrence of sarcopenia or frailty is one of important factors to prevention of being bedridden. It is predicted that there will be further increase of transfer care by medical professionals, care workers and family members.

It is reported that transfer assistance causes lower back pain of nurses. Compare to the 43% occurrence rate in the UK [5] and 40–50% occurrence rate in the US [6], Japan has a high occurrence rate of 60% [7]. Especially the motion of holding and transferring patients to wheelchairs is proven to cause the lower back pain of nurses. It is reported that the factors of the high occurrence rate of lower back pain in Japan includes the lack of progress in prevalence of welfare equipment, assisting tools and educational training [8]. On the other hand, it is necessary to transfer patients safely to wheelchairs without them falling, and then to maintain their seated position with ensuring proper distribution of body pressure. Thus, a wheelchair transfer motion is required to be safe and easy for both a nurse and patient. However, as lower back pain prevention measures are not included in the transfer assistance trainings at nursing collages, and studies that compare the transferring motions of experts and non-experts are extremely rate, further examination is required regarding the training of non-experts.

In the past motion analysis of wheelchair transfer we conducted, it was clarified that nursing students (non-experts) bent forward more at the cervical and lumbar spine than the nurses (experts), which made the siting position the simulated patient (SP) shallower on the wheelchair, and resulted in greater body pressure of physical contact between the non-expert and the simulated patient (SP) [9]. This result suggested that the difference in wheelchair transfer motions among caregivers influences the contact area pressure and body pressure of SP when seating. The rule of the body mechanics encourages to "conduct in an appropriate movement speed" [10]. However, there are few studies that researched how the difference in wheelchair transfer motions between the expert and the non-expert affects the acceleration of SP. Thus, this study aims to clarify the influence of differences in wheelchair transfer motions between the expert and the non-expert on the acceleration of SP, for explicating the tacit knowledge hidden behind the nursing skill for body position change.

2   Methods

2.1   Participants

The participants were 4 students with four years of study in a university nursing science department with nursing clinical training and basic nursing course, and 2 certified nurses who have at least 20 years of experience.

The nursing students were called the non-experts, and the certified nurse were called the experts. The simulated patient (SP) was 1 healthy adult (Table 1).

Table 1. Attributions of participants.

		Expert (N = 2) Mean (SD)	Non-expert (N = 4) Mean (SD)	Simulated patient (N = 1) Mean (SD)
Age		49.5 (3.5)	21.8 (3.0)	24.0
Gender	M	0	2	1
	F	2	2	0
High (m)		1.6 (0)	1.7 (0.2)	1.7
Body mass index		24.1 (4.6)	21.0 (2.7)	20.8

2.2   Procedure

The movements to be studied were the transfer from bed to wheelchair. We used a height-adjustable bed that allowed the SP to sit in the center of the side frame of the bed with the soles of his feet touching the floor. The scenario was that the patient is unable to stand on his own and requires full nursing care. The participants were briefed on the conditions of the SP and were asked to transfer him from the bed to the wheelchair. As for the positions of the bed and the wheelchair, the latter was placed facing 30° toward the bed, with a slight adjustment to make the transition of the SP a little easier. As for the wheelchair transfer motions, we measured movements of each participant twice per single motion. We had a chair ready for the participants to rest if they got tired.

The bed-to-wheelchair motion was categorized into three phases. The first is "standing phases". The second is "assisting with direction change". And the third is "assisting to sit in the wheelchair," which covers the movement from the lowest point of the participant's hips while helping with sitting to the end of the seated position of the participant. These motions were analyzed, and each participant's phase was contrasted against the other (Table 2).

Table 2. Motion categories of transfer assistance motion from bed to wheelchair.

	Motion Categories	Scene	
1	Standing Phase	1) The point at which assistance starts. 2) The lowest point of the participant's hips while assisting standing. 3) The point at which standing ends.	
2	Turning Phase	1) The point at which direction changes.	
3	Seating Phase	1) Point at which the participant's hips are at the lowest point while assisting sitting down. 2) The point at which sitting ends.	

2.3   Recording Procedures

The reflector markers were attached to the body surface and movement during transfer assistance was recorded by six cameras to record 3-dimensional footage. Reflector markers were attached to the subject as shown in Fig. 1: The model had attachments on the head (top, front, right, left), neck (cervical nerve 7), shoulders, top, middle (lumbar nerve 5), trochanter major (TRO), elbows, wrists, thighs, knees, shins, ankles and toes (Fig. 1).

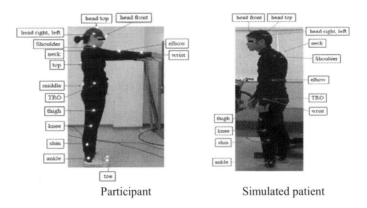

Participant   Simulated patient

Fig. 1.   The attached locations of the reflector markers.

The reflector markers were attached on his head front, neck (cervical nerve 7), shoulders, trochanter major (TRO), elbows, wrists, thighs, knees, shins, ankles and toes (Fig. 1).

For this research, we didn't attach reflective markers to the abdominal area since the patient would block the view. Instead, reflective markers were attached to the back of the participants to achieve a 3-dimensional analysis. The participants' movements that were assisting the patient from a seated position to the wheelchair. We used a MAC 3D System (motion analysis), sampling rate 100 Hz, creating stick figures to perform a three-dimensional motion analysis. The software was EvaRT Ver. 5.0.4 (motion analysis). We used it to calculate the participant's angle, acceleration per motion, as well as the time it took for each movement.

The section for acceleration measurement was chosen to be the head front section, as any stick picture data would not be missed from both the caregivers and the SP, and the transition data of acceleration during wheelchair transfer motions was collected. The interface pressure measurement sheet was set on the wheelchair to measure the interface pressure. ABW GmbH, ERGOCHECK was used for the interface pressure measurement.

2.4 Data analysis methods

As there was no normality in the statistical certification of each entry, Mann-Whitney's U test was used and the significant standard was set as 5% or less. SPSS for windows 21.0 J was used as the statistical analysis software. Each measurement value was expressed in mean ± standard deviation (mean ± SD).

3 Results

Following is the report regarding the results of the comparison between the experts and the non-experts of their cervical spines, lumbers, knees and elbow joints angles, transfer time, distance, acceleration and body pressure distribution during the wheelchair transfer.

3.1 Comparison Between the Experts and the Non-experts of Their Cervical Spines, Lumbers, Knees and Elbow Joints Angles During the Wheelchair Transfer

Table 3 shows the average angles of cervical spines, lumbers, knees and elbow joints angles during the wheelchair transfer (Fig. 2). The cervical spine angle of the experts was 170.2 (SD 9.6) degree (°) on the average and those of the non-experts was 159.1 (SD 8.5)° on the average. The non-experts flexed more toward the front than the experts at statistically significant level ($p < 0.001$). The lumber angle of the experts was the average 120.4 (SD 10.3)°, and those of the non-experts was the average 113.8 (SD 22.7)°. The non-experts flexed more than the experts at statistically significant level ($p < 0.001$). The knee angle of the experts was the average 141.6 (SD 19.8)°, and those of the non-experts was the average 154.5 (SD 17.1)°. The experts flexed more than the non-experts with statistically significant level ($p < 0.001$). The elbow joints angle of the experts was the average 125.6 (SD 40.8)°, and those of the non-experts was the average 95.5 (SD 42.4)°. The non-experts flexed more than the experts at statistically significant level ($p < 0.001$).

Table 3. Comparison between the experts and the non-experts of their cervical spines, lumbers, knees and elbow joints angles during the wheelchair transfer.

Angle (degree)	Expert (N = 2) Mean (SD)	Non-expert (N = 4) Mean (SD)	p
Cervical spine	170.2 (9.6)	159.1 (8.5)	<0.001
Lumber	120.4 (10.3)	113.8 (22.7)	<0.001
Knee	141.6 (19.8)	154.5 (17.1)	<0.001
Elbow	125.6 (40.8)	95.5 (42.4)	<0.001

Experts   Non-experts

Fig. 2. Comparison of joints angles between the experts and the non-experts at the end of turning.

3.2   Comparison of SP Wheelchair Transfer Time by the Experts and the Non-experts

The average time those the experts required for wheelchair transfers was 14.6 (SD 6.5) s (Table 4). Looking at the time required for each segment, the experts took 8.0 (SD 3.7) s during the standing phase, 4.3 (SD 2.1) s during the rotating phase, and 2.3 (SD 0.7) s during the seating phase. The average times those the non-experts required for wheelchair transfers was 10.2 (SD 2.3) s. Looking at the time required for each segment, the non-experts took 5.0 (SD 1.1) s during the standing phase, 3.1 (SD 2.2) s during the rotating phase, 2.1 (SD 1.0) s during the seating phase. Both the experts and the non-experts required most time during the standing phase, followed by the rotating and the

Table 4. Comparison of SP transfer time from the rotating phase to the seating phase between the experts and the non-experts.

Motion categories time (sec)	Expert (N = 2) Mean (SD)	Non-expert (N = 4) Mean (SD)
Standing phase	8.0 (3.7)	5.0 (1.1)
Turning phase	4.3 (2.1)	3.1 (2.2)
Seating phase	2.3 (0.7)	2.1 (1.0)

seating phases. There was no statistically significant difference between the wheelchair transfer times of the experts and the non-experts (p = 1.00).

3.3 Comparison of the Distance to SP During the Wheelchair Transfer by the Experts and the Non-experts

The distance from the head front of the experts and the head front of SP was 305.2 (SD 62.2) mm, and those of the non-experts was 322.9 (37.9) mm. The distance of the experts was closer to SP than the non-experts with statistical significance (Table 5).

Table 5. Comparison of the average distance to SP during the wheelchair transfer by the experts and the non-experts.

Participants	Expert (N = 2) Mean (SD)	Non-expert (N = 4) Mean (SD)	p
Distance of head front (mm)	305.2 (62.2)	322.9 (37.9)	<0.001

3.4 Comparison of the Average Accelerations Between the Experts and the Non-experts

The acceleration average of the experts and non-experts was calculated for each motion category, and X axis was set as time and Y axis was set as acceleration for the acceleration graph. The accelerations of the experts, the non-experts and SP repeated plus and minus values alternately, conducting reciprocating motions (Figs. 3 and 4).

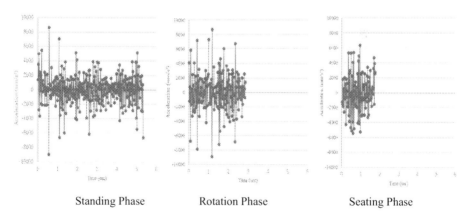

Standing Phase   Rotation Phase   Seating Phase

Fig. 3. The acceleration of the expert A.

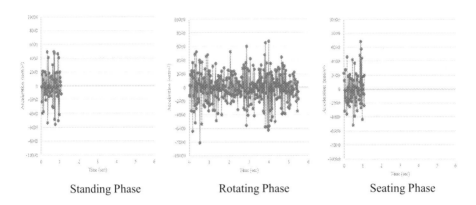

| Standing Phase | Rotating Phase | Seating Phase |

Fig. 4. The acceleration of the non-expert B.

The average acceleration of the experts during the standing phase was 16.2 (SD 2166.6) mm/s², and those of the non-experts was 41.1 (SD 3042.9) mm/s² (p = 0.82) (Table 6). The average acceleration of the experts during the rotating phase was –31.7 (SD 2129.9) mm/s², and those of the non-experts was –9.2 (SD 2477.7) mm/s² (p = 0.91). The average acceleration of the experts during the seating phase was 22.1 (SD 2447.9) mm/s², and those of the non-experts was 53.5 (SD 2517.4) mm/s² (p = 0.96).

Table 6. The average acceleration of participants.

Acceleration (mm/s²)	Expert N = 2	Non-expert N = 4	p
Standing phase	16.2 (SD 2166.6)	41.1 (SD 3042.9)	0.82
Turning phase	–31.7 (SD 2129.9)	–9.2 (SD 2477.7)	0.91
Seating phase	22.1 (SD 2447.9)	53.5 (SD 2517.4)	0.96

3.5   Comparison of the Average Accelerations of SP During Wheelchair Transfer Between the Experts and the Non-experts

The acceleration mean of SP during the standing phase by the experts was 15.1 (SD 2094.7) mm/s², and the acceleration mean of SP by the non-experts was 40.8 (SD 3034.4) mm/s² (Table 7). The acceleration mean of SP during the rotating phase by the experts was –12.5 (SD 3339.8) mm/s². The decrease in the speed was observed as the experts' cases (Fig. 5). The acceleration mean of SP by non-experts was 2.6 (SD 2293.1) mm/s², and its speed increased (p = 0.53). The acceleration mean of SP during the seating phase by the experts was –98.6 (SD 3137.7) mm/s², and its speed decreased. On the other hand, the average acceleration of SP by non-experts was 53.5 (SD 2517.4) mm/s², and its speed increased (p = 0.54).

Table 7. The average acceleration of the SP.

Acceleration (mm/s^2)	Expert N = 2	Non- expert N = 4	p
Standing phase	15.1 (SD 2094.7)	40.8 (SD 3034.4)	0.84
Turning phase	−12.5 (SD 3339.8)	2.6 (SD 2293.1)	0.53
Seating phase	−98.6 (SD 3137.7)	53.5 (SD 2517.4)	0.54

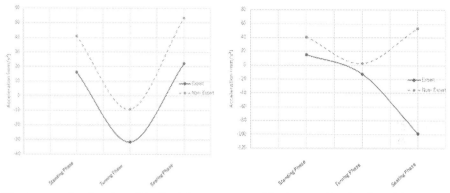

The Average Acceleration of the Participants.   The Average Acceleration of the SP.

Fig. 5. Comparison of average acceleration of SP during the wheelchair transfer by the experts and the non-experts.

3.6 Comparison of Body Pressure Distribution on the Contact Surface Immediately After Seating on the Wheelchair

The average body pressure of the SP immediately after the experts assisted his seating on the wheelchair was 92.8 (SD 8.4) mmHg, and immediately after seated the non-experts assisted his seating was 108.3 (SD 13.3). The number of the non-experts was higher.

4 Discussion

Following is the discussion on the comparison of the difference between the transfer motion by the experts and the non-experts during the wheelchair transfer through joint angles, transfer time and the distance to the SP, and its influence on the acceleration of the SP.

4.1 Comparison of the Angles of Cervical Spine, Lumber, Knees and Elbow Joints During the Wheelchair Transfer by the Experts and the Non-experts

The experts tended to stretch their necks, lower backs and elbow joints at statistically significantly more than the non-experts, held the body almost straight, and transferred the SP to the wheelchair while bending their knees. Their spines curved inwardly at the cervical spine and lumber. The lordosis of the cervical spine part worked as a spring to support their head, and the lordosis of the lumber part supported the weight of entire upper body, and worked as a fulcrum that gave mobility. Moreover, due to the physiological bowing, the lumber part evenly distributed the load of the upper body on the interspinal disk surface. [11] From this fact, it is inferred that the experts conducted a transfer movement without apply load on their lumber. On the other hand, the transfer motion done by the non-experts while they assisting the SP to a wheelchair in forward tilted posture showed smaller flexed angles of knees than those of the experts, and which may have increased the burden on their lower backs.

From the fact that the experts bent elbow joints less than the non-experts, it is inferred that the experts had smaller force moments of the elbow parts, leading to less burden on the arms. On the other hand, the average elbow angle of the non-experts was 95.5° and the upper arms were stretched. Thus, it is inferred that the non-experts were conducting transfer motions that burdened the arms.

4.2 Comparison of the Distance of Head Front During the Wheelchair Transfer by the Expert and the Non-expert

The experts had closer distance of head front to SP at statistically significant level than those of the non-experts. The experts came closer to the SP in order to bend the elbow joints shallower and to control the force moments during the rotating phase.

The non-experts stretched upper arms and bent the elbow joints while holding the SP. It is inferred that the bending of the elbow joints may have lessened the burden on the biceps, the forward bending of the upper body caused burden on the back muscle, which may lead to putting load on the lower backs.

4.3 Comparison of the Average Acceleration of SP During the Wheelchair Transfer by the Expert and the Non-expert

No statistically significant difference was observed when the average acceleration of the SP by the experts and the non-experts was compared. When being assisted by the experts, the SP seemed to accelerate more gently and stood up, in comparison to the cases of the non-experts. During the rotating phase, the experts changed the direction while controlling the motion speed. And during the seating phase, the experts helped the SP seated with gentle acceleration. It is inferred that the experts was controlling speed based on the rules of body mechanics. The experts swayed wider during the reciprocating motion of the rotating phase compared to those of the non-experts, because they moved their heads for checking the seating position on the wheelchair while changing the direction.

On the other hand, the acceleration of the non-experts during the standing phase was 3.9 times larger and faster than those of the experts. It is inferred that, because the non-experts was shortening the distance by pulling the SP closer with forward bending posture during the rotating phase, the negative acceleration was smaller than those of the experts. The acceleration during the seating phase of the non-experts was four times larger than those of the experts. It seemed that they couldn't adjust speed, which resulted in slightly faster in the seating time. It is inferred that the downward acceleration occurred at the beginning of the seating motion was large, and the stretching muscles moment of the hip joint and the knee joints of the SP did not fully function. Thus the downward acceleration was not suppressed, and the hip of the SP touched the seat surface with faster speed. This series of motions resulted in the higher body pressure.

Furthermore, the experts required longer average time for the wheelchair transfer than the non-experts. This is inferred that the experts evaluated the physical function and motion of the SP and adjusted the speed accordingly. It was suggested that this speed adjustment was one of nursing skill to reduce the body pressure immediately after seating and to offer more comfortable seating according to the SP's pace. The range of this study was the fact that we had small number of participants and therefore the results could not be generalized. We feel the strong necessity to continue further motion analyses.

5 Conclusion

Compared to the non-experts, the experts significantly stretched the cervical spines and the lumbers, held their bodies almost straight, and conducted the transfer motion that caused less load on the cervical spine, the lumber, the knee joints and the elbow joints. The non-experts conducted the transfer motion with forward bending posture, which brought burden on the lumber. There was no statistically significant difference in the influence on the acceleration of the SP between the wheelchair transfer motions of the experts and the non-experts. The experts accelerated gently, held the standing position, turned while adjusting acceleration and assisted the SP seated smoothly. As the experts gained the skill to control speed, knowledge and logical thinking through experience, quantification of the acceleration will be useful for the training of the non-experts.

References

1. World Health Statistics 2016: Monitoring health for the SDGs. http://www.who.int/gho/publications/world_health_statistics/2016/en/. Accessed 6 Jan 2018
2. Cabinet Office, Government of Japan. http://www8.cao.go.jp/kourei/whitepaper/w-2015/html/gaiyou/s1_1.html
3. Ministry of Health, Labour and Welfare: http://www.mhlw.go.jp/file/06-Seisakujouhou-12400000-Hokenkyoku/kiso26_teisei_1.pdf. Accessed 6 Jan 2018
4. Transforming our world the 2030 Agenda for Sustainable Development United Nations General Assembly (2015). https://sustainabledevelopment.un.org/content/documents/21252030%20Agenda%20for%20Sustainable%20Development%20web.pdf. Accessed 6 Jan 2018
5. Smedley, J., Egger, P., Cooper, C., Coggon, D.: Manual handling activities and risk of low back pain in nurses. Occup. Environ. Med. **52**, 160–163 (1995). https://doi.org/10.1136/oem.52.3.160
6. Edlich, R.F., Winters, K.L., Hudson, M.A., Britt, L.D., Long, W.B.: Prevention of disabling back injuries in nurses by the use of mechanical patient lift systems. J. Long Term Eff. Med. Implants **14**(6), 521–533 (2004)

7. Fujimura, T., Takeda, M., Asada, F., Kawase, M., Takano, K.: The investigation of low back pain among hospital nurse. JJOMT **60**, 91–96 (2012)
8. Japanese Nursing Association: Guidelines on Night Shift and Shift Work for Nurse. https://www.nurse.or.jp/nursing/shuroanzen/safety/yotu/index.html. Accessed 6 Jan 2018
9. Nakagawa, H., Mori, K., Takahashi, K., Yamashiro, K., Ogura, Y., Goto, A.: The motion analysis of transferring from bed to wheelchair conducted in the nursing field with focusing on the body pressure distribution. In: Duffy, V.G. (ed.) DHM 2017. LNCS, vol. 10286, pp. 141–159. Springer, Cham (2017). https://doi.org/10.1007/978-3-319-58463-8_13
10. Ogawa, K., Suzuki, R., Okubo, Y., Kunisawa, N., Konagaya, M.: Biomechanism Library Evidence-based Nursing Assisting. Society of Biomechanisms, Japan (2008)
11. Kelsey, J.L., Githens, P.B., White, A.A., Holford, T.R., Walter, S.D., O'Connor, T.: An epidemiologic study of lifting and twisting on the job and risk for acute pro-lapsed lumbar intervertebral disc. J. Orthop. Res. **2**(1), 61–66 (1984). https://doi.org/10.1002/jor.1100020110

Study of Factors that Lead to Falls During Body Position Change from a Dorsal Position to a Seated Position by Nursing Students

Hiromi Nakagawa[1](✉), Masahiro Tukamoto[1], Kazuaki Yamashiro[2], and Akihiko Goto[3]

[1] Faculty of Nursing, Seisen University, 720 Hida, Hikone, Shiga 521-1123, Japan
nakaga-h@seisen.ac.jp
[2] Department of Advanced Fibro-Science, Kyoto Institute of Technology, Matsugasaki, Sakyo-ku, Kyoto 606-8585, Japan
[3] Faculty of Design Technology, Osaka Sangyo University, 3-1-1 Nakagaito, Daito, Osaka 574-8530, Japan

Abstract. In Japan, medical accidents were defined as "accidents stemming from medical care provided by healthcare provider" in the 2014 revision to the Medical Service Law. 38.4% of medical accidents involve incidents that happen during recuperative care, such as falling or falling from the bed. These accidents occurred most frequently among various types of medical accidents. According to a report by the Japan Council for Quality Health Care (JCQHC), 1,590 falling incidents were recorded among 643 medical facilities in one year. Out of those, 7 incidents led to death. And 84 incidents out of the 1,590 falling incidents were caused by falling accident from the bed, and 6 incidents led to death. According to the analysis of JCQHC, most of these falling accidents were caused by actions initiated by the patient, and to this day, there is no clarity on the subject of falling accidents caused by healthcare providers. Furthermore, in terms of falls associated with position changing of the patient in bed, previous research based on action analysis was nowhere to be found, either in or outside of the country. In this research, we conducted a 3-dimensional action analysis using a MAC 3D SYSTEM on 13 non-expert nursing students and 2 expert nurses with 27 years of experience, as they performed a position change on patients from a dorsal to a seated position. Sudden falls from the bed were reported for simulated patients (SP) of 3, or 23.1%, of the nursing students. Our study attempts to address the factors that contribute to falling in the simulated patients when being transitioned from a dorsal to a seated position, and giving shape to the tacit skills employed in nursing care. The significance of this research is that it contributes to better medical safety, and to developing measures that help prevent falling incidents during position changing by caregivers. Results from this study revealed that non-expert nursing students moved faster and positioned themselves at a greater distance compared with the experts from their simulated patients when positioning them from a dorsal to a sitting position, and that these were contributing factors to the falling incidents of patients.

Keywords: Motion analysis · Jerk · Position-change · Falls · Nursing students

© Springer International Publishing AG, part of Springer Nature 2018
V. G. Duffy (Ed.): DHM 2018, LNCS 10917, pp. 205–216, 2018.
https://doi.org/10.1007/978-3-319-91397-1_18

1 Introduction

1.1 The Phenomenon and Problem of Falling in Medical Facilities

"The adoption of a definition for a fall is an important requirement when studying falls as many studies fail to specify an operational definition, leaving room for interpretation to study participants. This results in many different interpretations of falls. For example, older people tend to describe a fall as a loss of balance, whereas health care professionals generally define a fall as leading to injuries and ill health [1]."

A fall may be defined as an unintentional accident caused by an external force. Approximately 28–35% of people aged of 65 and over fall each year. And falls account for 40% of all injury deaths [2]. According to a report by the Japan Council for Quality Health Care (JCQHC) [3], there were 1,590 falling incidents at 643 facilities during a single year. Of those, seven incidents led to death. Of the 84 incidents that were caused by falling accident from the bed, 6 incidents led to death. Because of these incidents, additional medical expenses soared by 7 million yen a year [4]. The average health system cost per one fall injury episode for people 65 year and older in Finland and Australia was US$ 3611 (originally AUS$ 6500 in 2001–2002) and US$ 1049 (originally in €944 in 1999) respectively [2].

In a falling accident, patients may sustain injuries during a fall that extends their hospital stay or even become bed ridden. Falling accidents also reportedly add an average of 21 days to a patient's hospital stay due to fractures [4]. These accidents cause a myriad of other problems in addition to bodily harm—they instill fear in the patients, reduce their level of activity, and generally lower their quality of life. They have a strong correlation to head injuries and one of the biggest problems at hospitals requiring medical intervention. Head injuries are defined as injuries caused by their impact and acceleration [5]. But, until now, there has been no research on calculating jerk when it came to falls that occurred while the care receiver was being transferred.

Jerk refers to the rate of change of acceleration and a derivative with respect to time. It is used primarily to control vibrations or to assess impact. In other words, calculating jerk means to assess the vibrations caused in patients during their transfer. It is believed that it can be used as an educational tool for teaching nurses on techniques for safer and more comfortable position changing.

1.2 Falling Risk Factors and Preventative Measures

According to guidelines to prevent falling by the American Geriatrics Society, the British Geriatrics Society and the American Academy of Orthopedic Surgeons, anybody with one of the following symptoms—weak gluteal muscles, loss of balance and taking more than four types of medication—have a 12% chance, and anybody with all three have a 100% chance of falling within one year [6]. As seen here, the factors that contribute to falling are evident, and the guidelines stress the need for strength training, creating an environment that anticipates motion lines to prevent falling in facilities for the elderly. Furthermore, untrained staff can potentially cause patients to fall [7], and the guidelines advocate for the use of lifts and algorithms for safe patient handling [8].

In Japanese medical facilities, however, lifts and other such assisting tools are rarely used. In nursing education, transfer techniques focus mainly on body mechanics. There is a growing call for the use of assisting tools and acquiring position changing techniques that are safe for both patients and care givers.

1.3   The Work of Nurses Related Musculoskeletal Disorder and Posture Change

The term "musculoskeletal disorder" (MSD) is beginning to appear with greater frequency worldwide to describe various disorders that affect the muscles, bones and joints of the body. According to the World Health Organization, MSDs are caused by a variety of factors, the working environment and the nature of the work are significantly related. With regards to its causes, they are defined as one of the unspecified occupational diseases [9]. MSDs specifically refer to problems in the motor system; that is, the muscles, tendons, bones, cartilage, blood circulatory system, ligaments and the nervous system. Work-related musculoskeletal disorders (WRULD) are triggered by work or the nature of the work and includes all exacerbated conditions of MSDs. They include back pain, sciatica, rotator cuff injuries, epicondylitis and carpal tunnel syndrome. The occurrence of WRULD is particularly high worldwide within the nursing occupation, with transfers identified as the root cause of the problem [10–12]. Given the above, transfer work in the nursing occupation will focus on preventing WRULD and falling.

This time, we performed a 3-dimensional motion analysis study to compare the movements of 13 4-year nursing students (non-experts) and 2 nurses with 27 years of experience (experts) as they transferred a patient from a supine position to a sitting position on the bed. The analysis showed that three non-experts (23.1%) accidentally caused the falling of their patients. Therefore, this study determined the jerk between the patient and care giver during the transfer from a supine to sitting-up position in bed to examine the factors that caused the falling. The objective of this study is to take the jerk and examine the measures that prevent falling during position changes and contribute to improvements in medical safety.

2   Methods

2.1   Participants

The participants were 1 student with four years of study in a university nursing science department with nursing clinical training and basic nursing course, and 1 person who has at least 20 years of experience as a nurse and is a certified nurse.

The nursing student who couldn't prevent a falling of the simulated patient (SP) during the care assistance was called the non-expert, and the certified nurse with no fall was called the Expert. The simulated patient (SP) was 1 healthy adult (Table 1).

Table 1. Attributions of participants.

Participants		Expert (N = 1)	Non-expert (N = 1)	Simulated patient (N = 1)
Age		47.0	22.0	24.0
Gender	M	0	0	1
	F	1	1	0
High (cm)		155.0	160.0	170.0
Body mass index		20.8	20.3	20.8

2.2 Procedure

The reflector markers were attached to the body surface and movement during transfer assistance were recorded by six cameras to record 3-dimensional footage.

The scenario was that the patient is unable to stand on his own and requires full nursing care.

It was explained to the participants that the SP would start from a supine position on the bed and be transferred to an end sitting position on the bed on the right side. The hospital bed was adjusted so that the SP's feet could touch the ground when in an end sitting position on the bed.

To transfer from a supine position to an end sitting position, three movements were classified: from the supine position to a sitting position (finished sitting period); turning on the bed (revolving period); and after turning, taking an end sitting position (end sitting position on the bed period).

2.3 Recording Procedures

We used a MAC 3D System (motion analysis), sampling rate 100 Hz, and creating stick figures to perform a three-dimensional motion analysis. The software was EvaRT Ver. 5.0.4 (motion analysis). We used it to calculate the participant's angle, acceleration per motion, as well as the time it took for each movement.

When measuring the acceleration rates, the data wasn't lost because both the aide and the SP were measured from the head top with stick figures. Also data was recorded for acceleration changes when moving into a bed. Calculations were made from acceleration (a) through jerk (j) as follows.

The joint angle part of the cervical spine, lumbar, elbow and knee joint were measured. The distance between the participants and SP was measured from the head top. The angle, distance and acceleration data were collected at 60 frames a second. Measurements were calculated for the three categories from the supine position to a sitting position (finished sitting period); turning on the bed (revolving period), and after turning, taking an end sitting position on the bed period. The mean (standard deviation: SD) was shown, as the maximums (Max) and minimums (Min).

$$J = \frac{da}{dt}$$

The interface pressure measurement sheet was set on the bed to measure the interface pressure. ABW GmbH, ERGOCHECK was used for the interface pressure measurement. ERGOCHECK applies 712 sensors to the sheets. Each sensor detects pressure between human body and mattress per 5–10 cm square. It can serve as a measuring instrument to detect interface pressure.

This research received approval by Osaka Industrial University's Research Ethics Committee.

3   Results

3.1   Process of Posture Change Movements in Expert and Non-expert

The expert took 13.5 s to go from the finished sitting period, the revolving period and the end sitting position on the bed period. The expert took the weight with both legs, lifting the SP by the upper body, getting compact as they turn (Fig. 1). Also, transferring from the finished sitting period to the end sitting position on the bed period, the SP's cervical spine is supported. The expert explains the movements to the SP, vocalizing and timing his movements with the SP to execute the posture change.

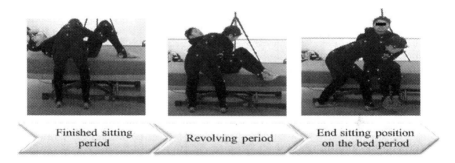

Finished sitting period   Revolving period   End sitting position on the bed period

Fig. 1. The expert's process for changing posture.

A fall happened during the assistance by the non-expert, and she took 10.3 s for the finished sitting period. The non-expert did not lift the SP by the upper body and bore the weight on the left leg side of her body, turning the lower half of the SP's body (Fig. 2). Also, the non-expert supported the SP by the thoracic vertebrae when transferring from the finished sitting position to the end of bed sitting position. The non-expert did not talk to the SP as she was changing the SP's posture.

The non-expert's waist is outside of the support area during the revolving period, end sitting position on the bed period and the falling period.

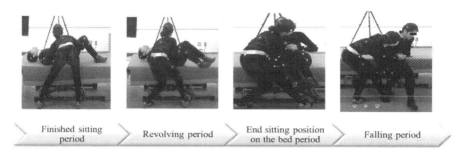

Finished sitting period | Revolving period | End sitting position on the bed period | Falling period

Fig. 2. The non-expert's process for changing posture

3.2   Process Joint Angles for Expert and Non-expert When Moving to Change Postures

The joint angle averages were calculated using 60 frames per second. The Expert's cervical spine was 168.4 (SD 5.8) degree (°); the Lumbar was 110.4 (SD 24.9)°, and the knee joint was 142.6 (SD 14.0)° (Table 2). The Non-expert's cervical spine was 159.3 (SD 8.5)°; the Lumbar was 121.5 (SD 28.9)°, and the knee joint was 160.0 (SD 11.4)°. The non-expert extended her knee joint during the rotating period.

Table 2. Average joint angles during posture changes.

Angle (degree)	Expert	Non-expert
	Mean (SD)	Mean (SD)
Cervical spine	168.4 (5.8)	159.3 (8.5)
Lumber	110.4 (24.9)	121.5 (28.9)
Knee	142.6 (14.0)	160.0 (11.4)

3.3   Comparison of the Distance Between the Feet of the Expert and Non-expert

The distance between the right ankle and left ankle of the expert was an average of 397.5 (SD 137.2) mm. For the non-expert, it was 630.0 (SD 94.8) mm (Fig. 3). The distance between the feet of the non-expert during the finished sitting period is wider than the expert's, but right before the fall that distance narrowed. On the other hand, the expert kept his feet at a consistent distance from each other from the finished sitting period to the revolving period.

3.4   Distance Between Participants' Head Tops and SP's Head Top

The average distance between the head tops of the expert and the SP was 752.1 (SD 398.7) mm (Fig. 4). The average distance between the head tops of the non-expert and SP was 758.8 (SD 390.4) mm.

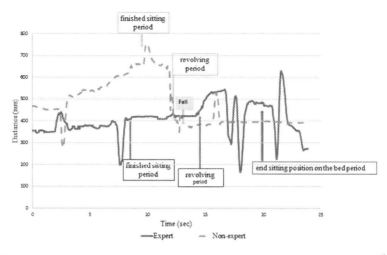

Fig. 3. Comparison of the distance between the feet of the expert and non-expert.

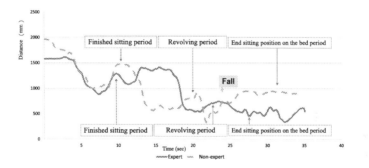

Fig. 4. Distance between participants' head tops and SP's head top.

3.5 Distribution of Body Pressure When SP Is in End Sitting Position on the Bed

Just after the revolving period, the maximum pressure on the buttocks was 36.8 mmHg for the expert and 35.3 mmHg for the non-expert. Right after the end sitting position on the bed, the pressure on the SP's buttocks was 61.6 mmHg for the expert and 91.3 mmHg for the non-expert. The non-expert exerted more pressure (Fig. 5). The interface of the non-expert with the buttocks was smaller than that of the expert, making the SP's buttocks slide off the bed.

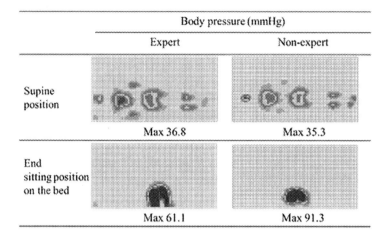

Fig. 5. Body pressure applied during end sitting position on the bed.

3.6 The Jerk of the Expert and the SP

The minimum (min.) jerk of the expert during the finished sitting period was –9086.1 mm/s^3 (Fig. 6). This was the jerk with the biggest burden recorded in the three movements. The maximum (max.) jerk in the revolving period was 9613.0 mm/s^3. The regular jerk was the biggest and the minimum was –7128.1 mm/s^3. The maximum jerk (max.) for the end sitting position on the bed period jerk was 5769.0 mm/s^3, and the minimum was –5911.8 mm/s^3.

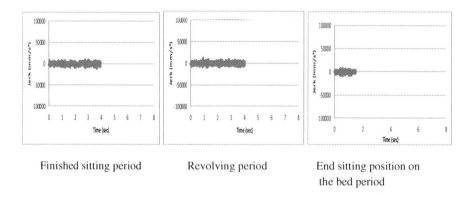

Fig. 6. Separate categories for the expert's jerk.

The maximum jerk when the expert helps the SP to the rising period was 7670.7 mm/s^3. The non-expert's jerk was 1.2 times more than that of the expert, and the expert's amplitude was smaller. The minimum jerk was –24424.3 mm/s^3. Of the three movements, the burden of the jerk was the biggest. The minimum for the end sitting position on the bed period jerk was –7586 mm/s^3, and the burden of the jerk was bigger than the Expert's. Looking at the mean of the expert's jerks, she slowed down during the revolving period and when the SP was in the end sitting position on the bed period (Fig. 7).

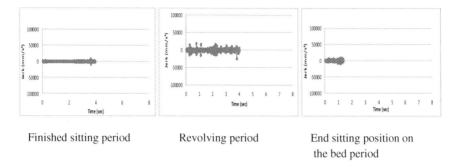

Finished sitting period   Revolving period   End sitting position on
                                                            the bed period

Fig. 7.   Separate categories for the SP's jerk.

3.7   The Jerk of the Non-expert and SP

The maximum jerk of the non-expert during the finished sitting period was 9425.4 mm/s^3. The maximum during the revolving period was 4391.8 mm/s^3, while the minimum was -5582.8 mm/s^3. The jerk for the end sitting position on the bed period was the biggest at 12271.9 mm/s^3, while the minimum was -12250.5 mm/s^3. The amplitude was the biggest (Fig. 8).

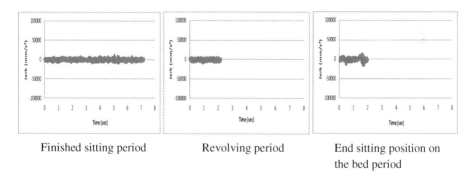

Finished sitting period   Revolving period   End sitting position on
                                                            the bed period

Fig. 8.   The separate categories for the non-expert's jerk.

The maximum jerk for the non-expert when with the SP in the finished sitting period rose suddenly to 67278.9 mm/s^3, it was 7 times more than the non-expert's typical jerk and with high amplitude. The maximum jerk in the revolving period was 67459.8 mm/s^3, and the minimum was -71613.9 mm/s^3 that was a large negative jerk. Of the three movements, the jerk of the revolving period was the biggest. In the end sitting position on the bed period when the SP fell, the maximum jerk was 9840.9 mm/s^3 (Fig. 9). Also, the Maximum jerk in the end sitting position on the bed was 12271.9 mm/s^3, while the Minimum was -12250.5 mm/s^3.

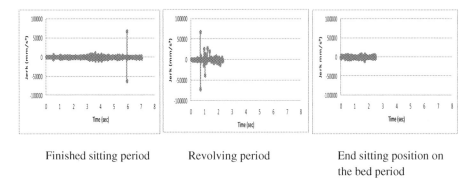

Finished sitting period	Revolving period	End sitting position on the bed period

Fig. 9. The separate categories for the SP's jerk.

3.8 Comparing Jerks of Expert and Non-expert

Regarding the number of jerks that went beyond –5000.0 mm/s^3 and 5000.0 mm/s^3, the highest expert's jerk was recorded in the revolving period, and followed with the second most in the finished sitting phase.

The non-expert's jerks did not surpass 5000.0 mm/s^3 in the revolving period, but the SP surpassed that level eleven times. Also, in the end sitting position on the bed period, the levels of 5000.0 mm/s^3 and –5000.0 mm/s^3 were surpassed more than five times, which is more than the expert.

4 Discussion

4.1 Comparison of the Joint Angles, Foot Distance and Head Top Distance of Expert and Non-expert

The non-expert flexed the cervical spine and lumbar region more than the expert and extended the knees. This is a stance that puts pressure on the intervertebral disc and knee joints. Also, during the finished sitting period, the distance between her feet was wide, and the lower support stabilization was not applied. Further, in the revolving period, the right knee joint was extended, and because the waist was outside of the support area, the centroid line was blurred, and it's thought that weight movement was insufficient.

The distance between the head tops of the expert and the SP was closer than with the non-expert on average. Because they were very close during the end sitting position on the bed period, it is thought that the expert can control the revolving at moments when strength is called for. Also, when the non-expert assumes a posture of assistance, she was perpendicular to the SP and did not make the SP's body compact, creating greater distance between the head tops. On the other hand, the expert struck a posture facing the SP, keeps the head top distance close, moved the SP's head first and then lower limbs to the proper direction, and the expert also moved in the direction of the rising patient. It is thought that these movements affect the weight movement and requires a minimum of strength.

This shows that the non-expert needs to learn the techniques of body mechanics to close the distance to the SP, provide a low base of support for stability and take the burden off the cervical spine and lumbar region by flexing the knee joints.

4.2   Comparison of SP Jerks with Expert and Non-expert

Flash et al. [13] reported that when people are in the process of moving their arms from the beginning until the goal is achieved, as the jerk is smaller, the movement becomes smoother.

The jerk can indicate a movement's awkwardness or smoothness. It is thought that the expert's jerk with the SP during the finished sitting position controlled the vibration and resulted in a smooth getting up motion. Also, it's thought that because the jerk in the revolving period for the expert and the SP was the largest, vibrations were formed. The reason the jerk was big in the revolving period was when the expert began the lifting with the SP facing up, he supported the SP's cervical spine, raised the head and flexed the upper body while rotating, and the vibrations in the head top were big. On the other hand, the non-expert supported the SP's thoracic vertebrae and rotated while extending the upper body, reducing the vibration from the head top.

The Non-expert produced a jerk with the SP during the finished sitting period of 67268.9 mm/s^3 (max.) $-$61630.4 mm/s^3 (min.) with rapid vibrations. This is because she extended the SP's upper body, it is though that rising up was conducted suddenly. The non-expert did not have a jerk bigger than 5000.0 mm/s^3 during the revolving period, but it had three jerks of at least $-$5000.0 mm/s^3. The SP had rapid jerks of 67459.8 mm/s^3 (max.) $-$71613.9 mm/s^3 (min.) and experienced jerks of more than 5000.0 mm/s^3 nine times, plus jerks of $-$5000.0 mm/s^3 eleven times. It's thought that the SP experienced continuing vibrations. Also, during the revolving period the SP's acceleration and deceleration went rapidly and repeatedly. Because the non-expert did not raise the SP's head when extending the upper body, the buttocks turned and it slipped to the end of the bed. Further, the SP's pelvis and trunk were pulled forward, and as the upper body started to fall during that moment, it is thought that this is what caused the fall. As the SP started to slip from the bed, the jerk grew larger.

From this, we presume that the non-expert is not ready to control the speeds, increasing the vibrations felt by the SP. It is thought that limits to the jerk during the finished sitting period and the revolving period are necessary. Also, by talking with the SP, the timing of movements can be coordinated, and the vibrations between the SP and the aide can be reduced, creating a comfortable posture change.

5   Conclusion

This research has clarified the jerk between the SP and aide when transferring from a supine position to an end sitting position on the bed. The jerk of the expert is smaller than that of the non-exert, and the amplitude of the motion is less when observed based on elapsed time. The results show that non-experts are not equipped with the body mechanics or speed control, and the resulting jerk becomes bigger. It is also clear that the vibrations can be the cause of a fall.

References

1. Zecevic, A.A., Salmoni, A.W., Speechley, M., Vandervoort, A.A.: Defining a fall and reasons for falling: comparisons among the views of seniors, health care providers, and the research literature. Gerontologist **46**, 367–376 (2006)
2. World Health Organization (WHO): WHO Global Report on Falls Prevention in Older Age. http://www.who.int/ageing/publications/Falls_prevention7March.pdf. Accessed 7 Jan 2018
3. Japan Council for Quality Health Care Homepage. http://www.med-safe.jp/contents/report/index.html. Accessed 7 Jan 2018
4. Egami, K., Hirose, M., Takemura, T., Okamoto, K., Tsuda, Y., Ohama, K., Honda, J., Shima, H., Imanaka, Y., Yoshihara, H.: Extra medical costs due to falls by using incident reporting and administrative profiling data at a teaching hospital in japan: a retrospective case study. J. Jpn. Soc. Healthc. Adm. **48**(3) (2011). https://doi.org/10.11303/jsha.48.157-169
5. Nakano, M., Matsuura, H., Tamagawa, M., Yukimasa, T., Yamanaka, M., Kubota, M.: Theoretical analysis of acceleration in brain at fall. In: LIFE 2012, pp. 1–4 (2012)
6. American Geriatrics Society, British Geriatrics Society, and American Academy of Orthopaedic Surgeons: Guideline for the prevention of falls in older persons. American Geriatrics Society, British Geriatrics Society, and American Academy of Orthopaedic surgeons panel on falls prevention. J. Am. Geriatr. Soc. **49**(5), 664–672 (2001)
7. Ganz, D.A., Huang, C., Saliba, D.: Preventing falls in hospitals: a toolkit for improving quality of care. (Prepared by RAND Corporation, Boston University School of Public Health, and ECRI Institute under Contract No. HHSA290201000017I TO #1). Agency for Healthcare Research and Quality, Rockville, January 2013. AHRQ Publication No. 13-0015-EF (2013)
8. Waters, T.R., Nelson, A., Hughes, N., Menzel, N.: Safe Patient Handling Training for Schools of Nursing Curricular Materials. Curriculum developed in partnership with the National Institute for Occupational Safety and Health (NIOSH), the Veterans Health Administration (VHA), and the American Nurses Association (ANA) N (2009)
9. World Health Organization, Protecting Workers' Health Series No. 5, Preventing Musculoskeletal Disorders in the Workplace (2003). http://www.who.int/occupational_health/publications/muscdisorders/en/. Accessed 7 Jan 2018
10. Smedley, J., Egger, P., Cooper, C., Coggon, D.: Manual handling activities and risk of low back pain in nurses. Occup. Environ. Med. **52**, 160–163 (1995). https://doi.org/10.1136/oem.52.3.160
11. Edlich, R.F., Winters, K.L., Hudson, M.A., Britt, L.D., Long, W.B.: Prevention of disabling back injuries in nurses by the use of mechanical patient lift systems. J. Long Term Eff. Med. Implants **14**(6), 521–533 (2004)
12. Fujimura, T., Takeda, M., Asada, F., Kawase, M., Takano, K.: The investigation of low back pain among hospital nurse. JJOMT **60**, 91–96 (2012)
13. Flash, T., Hogan, N.: The coordination of arm movements: an experimentally confirmed mathematical model. J. Neurosci. **5**, 1688–1703 (1985)

A Quaternion-Based Method to IMU-to-Body Alignment for Gait Analysis

Fabián Narváez[1]([✉]), Fernando Árbito[2], and Ricardo Proaño[3]

[1] GIByB Research Group, Department of Mechatronic Engineering,
Universidad Politéctica Salesiana, Quito, Ecuador
`fnarvaeze@ups.edu.ec`
[2] Faculty of Science and Technology, Universidad del Azuay, Cuenca, Ecuador
[3] Faculty of Health Sciences, Universidad Técnica de Ambato, Ambato, Ecuador

Abstract. Human gait analysis based on inertial measurement units (IMUs) is still considered a challenging task. This is because the accurate capture of human body movements depends on an initial sensor-to-body calibration and alignment process. In this paper, a novel sensor-to-body alignment method based on sequences of quaternions is presented, which allows to accurately estimate the joint angles from the hip, knee and ankle of the lower limbs. The proposed method involves two main stages, a sensors calibration and an alignment process for the body segments, respectively. For doing that, two different sequences of rotation based on Euler angle-axis factors are developed. The first rotational sequence is used to calibrate sensor's frame under a new general body frame by estimating the initial orientation based on its quaternion information. Then, a correction process is applied by factorizing the captured quaternions. Once the general body frame is defined, a second rotational sequence is implemented, which aligns each sensor frame to body frames, allowing to define the anatomic frames for obtaining clinical measurements of the joint angles. The proposed method was two-fold validated using both strategies, a goniometer-based measure system and a camera-based motion system, respectively. The obtained results demonstrate that the estimated joint angles are equal to the expected values and consistent with values obtained by the strategies widely used in real clinical scenarios, the goniometers and optical motion system. Therefore, the proposed method could be used in clinical applications and motion analysis of impaired persons.

Keywords: Inertial sensors · Quaternion-based calibration
Human motion analysis · Joint angular kinematics

1 Introduction

Human motion analysis is widely used to provide a quantitative description of movement patterns, which have been applied for biomechanical researches and

© Springer International Publishing AG, part of Springer Nature 2018
V. G. Duffy (Ed.): DHM 2018, LNCS 10917, pp. 217–231, 2018.
https://doi.org/10.1007/978-3-319-91397-1_19

clinical practices [1–3] as well as in many fields such as: development of humanoid robots [1], clinical gait analysis [4], sports motion analysis [5,6], human computer interaction (HCI) and augmented reality applications [7,8]. In clinical scenarios, it is considered an important clinical tool for quantifying normal and pathological patterns of locomotion, showing to be useful for prescription of treatments as well as in the evaluation of such treatments [2,9]. Several efforts have been made to develop strategies for a suitable measurement and data acquisition related to the kinematics of human gait [10], among these strategies, there are some systems based on goniometers, systems based on electromyography and systems based on computer vision techniques [11], which aims at capturing information related to position and orientation of the joints of body segments involved during any gait phases. Currently, computer vision-based gait analysis have reported to be the most advanced and accurate technique to provide clinical measures of the gait by using reflective markers placed in several parts of the lower limb of the person [10,11]. However, this strategy is quite expensive because it requires high frame rate cameras, advanced image or video processing techniques, an accurate position of markers in anatomical landmarks and high-structured laboratories. Currently, gait analysis based on inertial sensors technology has arisen as an alternative to traditional computer vision-based gait analysis systems due to its low-cost and usability in internal/external environments afford a wide range of remote applications [11,12]. This technology combines multi-axial accelerometers, gyroscopes and eventually magnetometers sensors to provide linear acceleration, angular velocity and magnetic field strength measurements, which are fused by a specific sensor fusion algorithm and are included in a single inertial measurement unit [5], usually referred to as IMU. In addition, IMUs are designed to be attached to different body segments. However, their use is limited due to the lack of standards for placing sensors on body segments and defining joint coordinate systems, a fundamental problem that directly affects the kinematic analysis [13]. In other words, IMUs local frames are not typically aligned with anatomically defined frames for each body segments, for which an initial sensor-to-body calibration procedure is required [5,6,14]. In consequence, human gait analysis based on inertial measurement units (IMUs) is still considered a challenging task and the accuracy of those systems is still debated [13,15].

2   Related Works

Several strategies have been proposed to solve this fundamental problem [16,17] by attempting to align the IMUs local frames respect to the body segment frames [18]. Some calibration techniques are based on special sequence of predefined user movements to define the axis of joint motion [5,15], or by including supplementary devices such as video cameras [19], anatomical landmark or exoskeleton harnesses [20]. Nevertheless, the use of those additional tools requires experienced personnel. Basically, each IMU provides an estimate of the body segment orientation relative to a global frame of reference (the Earth's coordinate systems) but they do not measure position directly, for which a second general frame related to anatomical coordinate system (Body Frame) must be established, the same that is suggested by the international society of biomechanics (ISB) and defined as a mutual coordinate system, named, the joint coordinate system (JCS) [14]. However, the initial location between the sensors and body segments is eventually unknown, a problem that has been faced as a transformation of coordinate issue, for which have been evolved some strategies based on rotational matrix [6], Euler angles [21], a quaternion strategy [16–18] and optimization techniques. Those strategies expect to accomplish the axis of joint motion and, consequently, measure 3D joint angles [18].

This paper presents a novel sensor-to-body alignment method based on quaternions strategy for estimating the joint angles of the hip, knee and ankle of the lower limbs during the gait. For doing that, two different sequences of rotation based on Euler angle-axis factors are developed. The first rotational sequence calibrates sensor's frame under a new general body frame by estimating their quaternions of the initial orientation. Then, a correction process is applied by factorizing the captured quaternions. Once the general body frame is defined, a second rotational sequence is implemented, which aligns each sensor frame to body frames, allowing to define the anatomical frames. Unlike other approaches, we do not attempt to exactly establish certain orientations and specific placement in which the sensors must be mounted with respect to the body segments but instead, alignment process of sensor-to-body frames is carried out using relevant information from the anatomical axis of major importance involved in the motion of each joint.

The rest of this article is organized as follows: after this introduction and related works, next section presents the methods, then results are shown and last section discusses conclusions.

3   Methods

The method pipeline is illustrated in Fig. 1. The method starts by assuming that different coordinate systems are associated to each IMU sensor (Sensor Frame), then its aims is to define a mutual coordinate system with the same orientation for each body segments, beginning at the Pelvis. In this method, seven IMU sensors are used, setting a rigid body model, for which each IMU is attached to the lateral position of each body segment, as well as the superior position of the mid-foot, with an additional IMU sensor positioned over the pelvis, at the level of the L5S1 joint. Finally, an common coordinate system for the body segments is obtained and established as the anatomical body frame (Body Frame), which is used to compute the joint angles, such as: flexion-extension, abduction-adduction and internal-external rotation. The proposed method includes two stages: a sensor's calibration and an alignment process, respectively, by introducing a quaternion strategy based on two Euler angles-axis sequence, as described below:

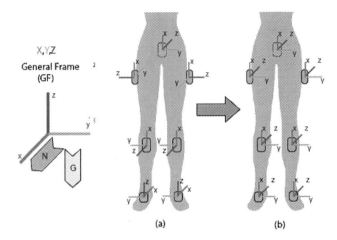

Fig. 1. The pipeline of our proposed method is illustrated. Panel (a) illustrates the sensor local frames (SF) according to an initial location of sensors. Panel (b) illustrates the results of alignment process between sensor to body frames (BF), respectively. The General Frame (GF) corresponds to Earth's coordinate system.

3.1   Calibration Algorithm and Definition of General Body Frame

First, a new coordinate system is defined by using an initial orientation in quaternion format (q) from the sensor placed at Pelvis. The problem is herein formulated as the decomposition into quaternion factors from a quaternion associated with some rotation in R^3, those factors provide meaningful and useful rotation about to their principal axes and are used for calibrating and aligning some coordinate systems. We consider that any two independent coordinate frames can be related by a sequence of rotations about coordinate axis, as well-known as Euler angle-axes sequence [22]. Thus, the corresponding quaternion (q) is considered as a rotation operator related by the sequence of rotations (abc), as follows:

$$q = a^i \otimes b^j \otimes c^k \tag{1}$$

where $i, j, k = 1, 2, 3$ describe the rotation about the principal axes. In this work, a first sequence of rotation was defined by $a^3b^2c^1$, whose sequence order is established according to the importance of movements at the pelvis [23]. Therefore, our rotation operator is defined as: $q = a^3 \otimes b^2 \otimes c^1$. To decompose into its quaternion factors, a factorizing process is formulated applying some criteria established by quaternion algebra [22]. For instance, the product of two rotation sequences may be depicted by a rotation operator. In this case, a new rotation operator is included and defined as: $p = a^3 \otimes b^2$, simplifying the rotation respect to a single axis (c^1) as:

$$q = a^3 \otimes b^2 \otimes c^1 = p \otimes c^1 \tag{2}$$

where c^1 is the rotation respect to $x\hat{i}$ -axis. Provided that only its angle need to be computed, the principal axes are defined according to their unit vector for each rotation as:

$$c^1 = c_0 + \hat{i}c_1 = \cos\frac{\phi}{2} + \hat{i}\sin\frac{\phi}{2} \tag{3}$$

$$b^2 = b_0 + \hat{j}b_2 = \cos\frac{\theta}{2} + \hat{j}\sin\frac{\theta}{2} \tag{4}$$

$$a^3 = a_0 + \hat{k}a_3 = \cos\frac{\psi}{2} + \hat{k}\sin\frac{\psi}{2} \tag{5}$$

where c_0, c_1, b_0, b_2, a_0 and a_3 are the components of each sequence of rotation, a, b, c, respectively. In the same way, q and p quaternions may be to depict as: $q = q_0 + \hat{i}q_1 + \hat{j}q_2 + \hat{k}q_3$ and $p = p_0 + \hat{i}p_1 + \hat{j}p_2 + \hat{k}p_3$, where (q_0, q_1, q_2, q_3) and (p_0, p_1, p_2, p_3) are the components of those quaternions, respectively. Therefore, each angle of rotation is obtained by:

$$\tan\phi = \frac{-2(q_0q_1 + q_2q_3)}{-q_0^2 + q_2^2 + q_1^2 - q_3^2} \tag{6}$$

where ϕ angle is used to obtain the factor c^1 from Eq. 3, thus p is also obtained replacing c^1 in Eq. 2. Finally, the obtained p factor is decomposed into its components: $p_0 = a_0b_0$, $p_1 = -a_3b_2$, $p_2 = a_0b_2$ and $p_3 = a_3b_0$ by multiplying the obtained quaternion factors, p and c^1. Those relationship among quaternion components are used to establish their angles respect to their principal axes, as follow:

$$\frac{p_2}{p_0} = \frac{b_2}{b_0} = \tan\frac{\theta}{2} \tag{7}$$

$$\frac{p_3}{p_0} = \frac{a_3}{a_0} = \tan\frac{\psi}{2} \tag{8}$$

In consequence, ϕ, θ and ψ angles are estimated from the initial orientation of sensor placed at pelvis. Finally, both values, rotation angles and each quaternion factors are used as correction factors for calibrating and adjusting the new Sensor Frame (SF) according to Earth's coordinate system.

- **Calibration algorithm:** A first stage of the proposed method consists in canceling any rotation angle respect to Earth's coordinate system, this is due to the initial position of the IMU at pelvis. For doing that, an initial posture for our rigid body model is suggested when this is evaluated in volunteers. This pose is commonly well-known as N-pose (straight back, feet aligned respect to upright shoulder) and is suggested to avoid any flexion-extension angle of the hip and lower limbs. Then, a new sensor coordinate system is established (named Sensor Frame) where the z-axis is agreed to direct towards the front of volunteer and the xy-plane is perpendicularly considered respect to horizontal plane. This is formulated as the following set-zero calibration problem:

$$^0q_0' = r_{\hat{j}90} \otimes {}^0q_0 \tag{9}$$

$$p_0 = c_{0q'}^* \otimes r_{\hat{i}180}^* \otimes {}^0q_0' \tag{10}$$

where $^0q_0$ is the quaternion's component due to initial orientation of sensor at the pelvis, $^0q_0'$ corresponds to orientation respect to vertical plane, $c_{0q'}$ is the c

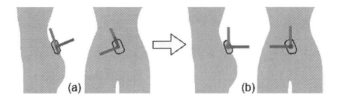

Fig. 2. The proposed calibration process is illustrated. Panel (a) illustrates an initial coordinate system of sensor located at the pelvis. Panel (b) illustrates the obtained result of calibration and alignment process.

component defined in the sequence of rotation $a^3b^2c^1$, this component describes the rotation respect to magnetic field vector, p_0 defines to correction factor respect to vertical-axis around this y-axis and r_{j90} corresponds to a rotation of 90^0. (*) is its complex conjugate. The result of this process is illustrated in Fig. 2.

3.2 IMUs Alignment Process and Definition of Body Frame

Once the new general frame (SF) was established at the pelvis, each inertial sensor requires to be aligned to its body segment (see Fig. 1). This problem is herein formulated as the following sensor-to-body alignment problem:

$$^0q'_n = p_0 \otimes {}^0q_0^* \otimes {}^0q_n^* \tag{11}$$

where $^0q'_n$ depicts the corrected quaternion of any $n-$IMU, at a time $t = 0$. This rotational correction is computed respect to general sensor frame (SF). Thus, $p_0 \otimes {}^0q_0^*$ defines the improved rotation of the pelvis' sensor frame (SF). Then, body frames are aligned to the principal axis of body segments by using the corrected quaternion $^0q'_n$, defining a common body frame, here named, the Anatomical Frame (BF). In this process, the quaternion factors obtained from our sequence of rotation are included, as follow:

$$p_n = {}^0q'_n{}^* \otimes r_{y180} \otimes b_{c^*_{0q'_n}} \otimes c^*_{0q'_n} \tag{12}$$

where p_n defines the corrected position for each IMU. This value depends on quaternion factor $c^*_{0q'_k}$, which is obtained by improved rotation about body $x-$axis, and $r_{y180} \otimes b_{c^*_{0q'_k}}$ defines an improved rotation about body $y-$axis.

Since the anatomical frame (BF) was aligned, those improved quaternion are used to estimate some rotations of the body segment respect to our proposed rigid body model, as follow:

$$R_n = p_0^* \otimes {}^0q_0^* \otimes q_n \otimes p_n \tag{13}$$

where R_n is the rotation of any $n-$IMU, at a time $t \neq 0$. Basically, we estimates the joint rotation combining two rotations of continuous body segments by:

$$\Theta_n = R_{n-1} \otimes R_n \tag{14}$$

where Θ_n is the joint rotation between two continuous body segments. Finally, the angles from hip, knee and ankle joints, such as: flexion/extension, internal/external rotation and abduction/adduction, are estimated. For doing that, a second sequence of rotations is implemented as $a^1 b^3 c^2$. The order of this sequence of rotation corresponds to the agreement suggested by the international biomechanics society [14], establishing a general reporting standard for joint kinematics. This sequence of rotation is also factorized for yielding some factors and component of quaternions related to the rotation about the anatomical axes. This process is similar to the formulation process used for the first sequence of rotation $a^3 b^2 c^1$.

4   Results

The performance of our proposed method was two-fold evaluated using a comparative analysis respect to two different approaches: an goniometer system and a camera-based motion system, respectively. For doing that, the method was implemented in an IMU-based motion capture system from the well-known XSens Technology[1], namely, the MVN AWINDA system, a commercial IMU-based motion capture for motion tracking applications in real time [5]. This system includes a set of seven IMU sensors. Each IMU measures the acceleration, angular rate and the magnetic field vector in its own three-dimensional local coordinate system. The axes of this local coordinate system represent an orthonormal base that is typically well aligned with the outer casing of the sensor and it incorporates algorithms for estimating sensor's orientation with respect to a global fixed coordinate system (GF). Its orientation is provided in quaternions format (q). Sensor data were collected at a sampling frequency of 60 Hz. The experimental evaluation process was implemented in MATLAB R17, running on a Linux PC with 2 Intel Quad Core i7 at 3.07 GHz and 24 GB of RAM.

4.1   Comparative Evaluation Respect to a Goniometer System

First, the aptness for estimating the joint angles was assessed, for which a kinematic chain assembled by two goniometers was implemented. Then, three consecutive inertial sensors were placed and unaligned respect to the principal axes of the implemented kinematic chain, as is illustrated in Fig. 3.

Then, a consecutive sequence of angles for each goniometer was performed. Angles from -30^0 to 120^0 with steps of $\pm 30^0$ were assigned for the first goniometer (G_1). In addition, for each assigned angle of the first goniometer, other sequence of angles from -30^0 to 120^0 with steps of $\pm 30^0$ were also assigned for the second goniometer (G_2). This evaluation compared the measured joint angles, when the IMUs were manually aligned, respect to our proposed alignment method, for which the IMUs were misaligned. In order to compare the joint angle obtained from both aligned and misaligned approaches, the well-known Root Mean Square Error (RSME) was calculated. This metric was used

---

[1] https://www.xsens.com.

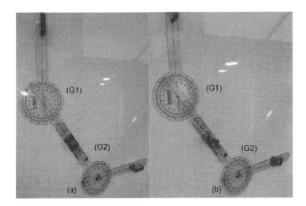

Fig. 3. Overview of the proposed kinematic chain by two goniometers, G_1 and G_2. Panel (a) illustrates the sensor local frames aligned respect to the goniometer's principal axes. Panel (b) illustrates the sensor local frames unaligned respect to the goniometer's principal axes.

to quantify the difference of the value of the angles between the goniometers model and the estimate using the both alined and misaligned sensor approaches, respectively. The error was obtained by:

$$e(n) = \Theta_{Goniometer}(n) - \Theta_{sensor}(n) \tag{15}$$

$$RMSE = \sqrt{\frac{1}{k}\sum_{n=1}^{k} e^2(n)} \tag{16}$$

where k represents the number of angles taken with both schemes and n represents a defined angle in a specific goniometer position. The results obtained for this evaluation are presented in Table 1.

Table 1. Performance evaluation: manual sensor alignment respect to the proposed alignment method.

	Manual alignment		Proposed alignment	
	G_1	G_2	G_1	G_2
RMSE	2.02	4.14	**1.12**	**2.28**

The first two columns correspond to results obtained when the IMUs were manually aligned according to the segments of goniometers, being the RMSE average of each assigned angle for both goniometers, G_1 and G_2, respectively. In this same way, the last two columns correspond to obtained results when IMUs were misaligned and our proposed method was implemented. Overall, results shown a reduced error rates of 1.12^0 and 2.28^0 respect to 2.02^0 and 4.14^0 for each joint, G_1 and G_2, respectively. These were yielded when our alignment approach was used, which reflects a high accuracy with the proposed alignment method.

4.2 Comparative Analysis Respect to Camera-Based Motion System

On the other hand, the proposed IMU-to-body alignment method was also evaluated in a real scenario with some volunteers, by using the joint angles data captured from the IMU-based motion capture system respect to data captured by a camera-based motion system. Basically, camera-based motion system provides information of the joint angles, which is computed and extracted from a sequence of video using the open-source software "KINOVEA", a semi-automated tracking tool to follow points or trajectories from optical tracking systems [2]. An example of this evaluation process is illustrated in Fig. 4.

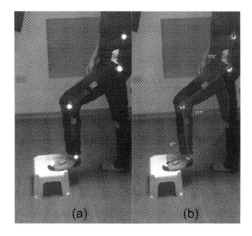

Fig. 4. Example of a predefined movement (trial) to compute the joint angle in sagittal plane using both motion capture systems is illustrated. Figure (a) illustrates IMUs sensor and optical markers position. Figure (b) illustrates the joint angles measured by KINOVEA software.

For this experiment, a sequence of movements was defined, as follows: the subject starts moving from a stationary position (seating-down), then the subject takes a step and the leg climbs a stool. In order to conduct this evaluation, the flexion-extension angle for the hip, knee and ankle joint were estimated using the sagittal plane, this is due to the configuration of the camera-based motion capture. For which, a set of optical markers were placed and setup on the volunteer

---

[2] https://www.kinovea.org.

to define some anatomical landmarks according to ISB recommendations [23], in the same way, the IMUs were placed and unaligned in each body segments of the volunteer. Therefore, both IMU and video information are captured together for comparative purpose. The IMU-based motion capture was configured to capture joint angle data to a rate of 60 Hz and the camera-based motion system captured sequences of videos to a rate of 30 Hz (30 fps). In order to compare the joint angle trajectories during the sequence of movements, a similarity metric was calculated, which allows to quantify the similarity between trajectories (curves). This metric is the well-known as the coefficient of multiple correlation (CMC), taking values between 0 and 1; with a value of 1 for indicating an exact similarity. CMC was computed as shown in [13]:

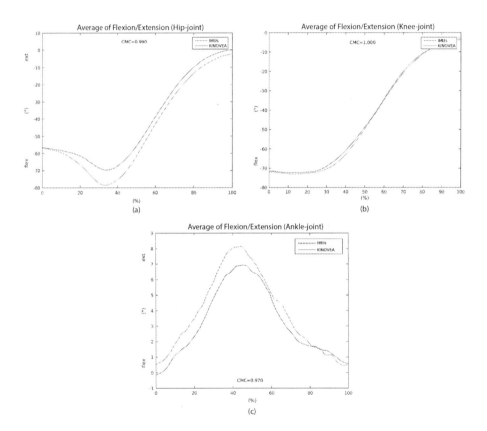

Fig. 5. Average curves of flexion-extension during the first sequence of movements. Figure (a) corresponds to the obtained curves for hip-joint. Figure (b) corresponds to the obtained curves for knee-joint. Figure (c) corresponds to the obtained curves for ankle-joint. (Color figure online)

$$CMC = \sqrt{1 - \frac{\sum_{g=1}^{G}[\sum_{p=1}^{P}\sum_{f=1}^{F}(\theta_{gp}(f) - \bar{\theta}_{gf})^2/GF_g(P-1)]}{\sum_{g=1}^{G}[\sum_{p=1}^{P}\sum_{f=1}^{F}(\theta_{gp}(f) - \bar{\theta}_g)^2/G(PF_g - 1)]}} \qquad (17)$$

where θ_{gpf}, is the joint angle at frame f that is measured by method p (IMU or camera system) at sequence cycle g; $\bar{\theta}_{gf}$ is the mean angle at frame f between angles measured by the two systems for the sequence cycle g:

$$\bar{\theta}_{gf} = \frac{1}{p}\sum_{p=1}^{2}\theta_{gpf} \qquad (18)$$

$\bar{\theta}_g$ is the grand mean for the sequence cycle g among these two methods:

$$\bar{\theta}_g = \frac{1}{2F}\sum_{p=1}^{2}\sum_{f=1}^{F}Y_{gpf} \qquad (19)$$

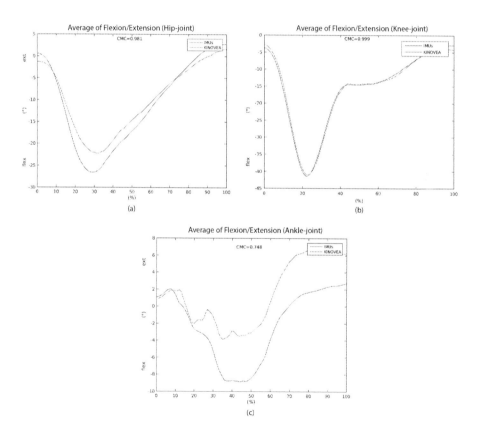

Fig. 6. Average curves of flexion-extension during the second sequence of movements. Figure (a) corresponds to the obtained curves for hip-joint. Figure (b) corresponds to the obtained curves for knee-joint. Figure (c) corresponds to the obtained curves for ankle-joint.

where $P = 2$ corresponds to the number of methods evaluated. $F = 103$ is the total number of video frames. G is the number of cycles corresponding to a procedure (trial), which is one cycle for all trials in this evaluation.

In this evaluation, a group of 10 normal healthy subjects (age range of 22–27 years, 5 males and 5 females) with no previous history of musculoskeletal problems were evaluated. To assess the repeatability of motion data, the subjects were evaluated three times with both the IMU system and optical system. This evaluation aimed to establish the behavior of the joint angles from a lower limb when three stages of movements were carried out.

The results of this preliminary evaluation, during the first movement (seating-down stage) report an average of $CMC = 0.99$, $CMC = 1.00$ and $CMC = 0.97$ for the hip, knee and ankle joints, respectively. Figure 5 shows the average curve of Flexion-Extension angle vs. (%) Percentage of movement, obtained during the first stage for the hip, knee and ankle joints. Overall, the curves show how

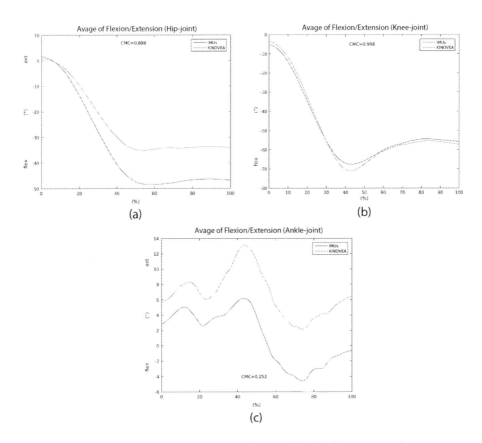

Fig. 7. Average curves of flexion-extension during the third sequence of movements. Figure (a) corresponds to the obtained curves for hip-joint. Figure (b) corresponds to the obtained curves for knee-joint. Figure (c) corresponds to the obtained curves for ankle-joint.

our aligned method applied to the IMU-based motion capture (blue line) system coincide when knee-angles and hip-angles are estimated by the optical tracking system (red line).

The obtained results, during the second phase of movement (takes a step), report an average of $CMC = 0.98$, $CMC = 0.99$ and $CMC = 0.74$, approximately. These for the hip, knee and ankle joints, respectively. These results are presented in Fig. 6, In the same way, Fig. 6 shows the average curve of Flexion-Extension angle vs. (%) Percentage of movement, obtained during the second stage for the hip, knee and ankle joints, which reveal that ankle angles measurements are sensitive when they are captured with the IMU-based motion capture, as is shown is Fig. 6(c).

Figure 7 show the obtained results, during the third phase of movements, reporting an average of $CMC = 0.88$, $CMC = 0.99$ and $CMC = 0.25$ for the hip, knee and ankle joints, respectively. In this case, Fig. 7(c) show that ankle-angles measurements are the most variable when fine movements of the ankle joint are required, this is to say, when ankle-angles involves small displacements. This is the case of our third phase of movements when the upper limb was raised. Possibility, the optical system used in this evaluation, requires to use more anatomical markers at the foot.

Conclusions

Unlike to conventional calibration procedures described in the literature [5], the herein proposed method provides an easy and fast sensor placement, for which no need any additional tools or special calibration movements performed by the user. The obtained results demonstrate that the estimated joint angles are equal to the expected values and consistent with the values obtained by strategies widely used in real clinical scenarios, both goniometers and optical motion system, respectively. Also, obtained results indicate that the method is suitable to measure angles of the hip, knee and ankle of the humans joints during physical activities. Therefore, the proposed method could be used in applications such as functional movements rehabilitation, that requires motion analysis of impaired persons.

Acknowledgment. This work was partially funded by the Ecuadorian Consortium for Advanced Internet Development (CEDIA) through the CEPRA projects. Specifically, under grants CEPRA-X-2016 project; "Tele-rehabilitation platform for elderly with dementia disorders, based on emerging technologies". [Grant number: X-2016-02].

References

1. Díaz, I., Gil, J.J., Sánchez, E.: Lower-limb robotic rehabilitation: literature review and challenges. J. Robot. **2011**(i), 1–11 (2011)
2. Charalambous, C.P.: Measurement of lower extremity kinematics during level walking. In: Banaszkiewicz, P.A., Kader, D.F. (eds.) Classic Papers in Orthopaedics, pp. 397–398. Springer, London (2014). https://doi.org/10.1007/978-1-4471-5451-8_100

3. Lebel, K., Boissy, P., Hamel, M., Duval, C.: Inertial measures of motion for clinical biomechanics: comparative assessment of accuracy under controlled conditions - effect of velocity. PLoS ONE **8**(11), e79945 (2013)

4. Makino, Y., Tsujiuchi, N., Ito, A., Koizumi, T., Nakamura, S., Matsuda, Y., Tsuchiya, Y., Hayashi, Y.: Quantitative evaluation of unrestrained human gait on change in walking velocity. In: Conference proceedings : ... Annual International Conference of the IEEE Engineering in Medicine and Biology Society. IEEE Engineering in Medicine and Biology Society. Annual Conference 2014, pp. 2521–2524 (2014)

5. Roetenberg, D.: Xsens MVN : Full 6DOF Human Motion Tracking Xsens MVN : Full 6DOF Human Motion Tracking Using Miniature Inertial Sensors. Technical report, XSENS TECHNOLOGIES, January 2009

6. Jakob, C., Kugler, P., Hebenstreit, F., Reinfelder, S., Jensen, U., Schuldhaus, D., Lochmann, M., Eskofier, B.: Estimation of the knee flexion-extension angle during dynamic sport motions using body-worn inertial sensors. In: Proceedings of the 8th International Conference on Body Area Networks (2013)

7. Antón, D., Goñi, A., Illarramendi, A.: Exercise recognition for kinect-based telerehabilitation. Methods Inf. Med. **54**(2), 145–155 (2015)

8. Ye, M., Yang, C., Stankovic, V., Stankovic, L., Kerr, A.: A depth camera motion analysis framework for tele-rehabilitation: motion capture and person-centric kinematics analysis. IEEE J. Sel. Top. Signal Process. **10**(5), 877–887 (2016)

9. Narváez, F., Marín-Castrillón, D.M., Cuenca, M.C., Latta, M.A.: Development and implementation of technologies for physical telerehabilitation in Latin America : a systematic review of literature, programs and projects Desarrollo e implementación de tecnologías. TecnoLógicas **20**(40), 155–176 (2017)

10. Ali, A., Sundaraj, K., Ahmad, B., Ahamed, N., Islam, A.: Gait disorder rehabilitation using vision and non-vision based sensors: a systematic review. Bosn. J. Basic Med. Sci. **12**(3), 193–202 (2012)

11. Muro-de-la Herran, A., García-Zapirain, B., Méndez-Zorrilla, A.: Gait analysis methods: an overview of wearable and non-wearable systems, highlighting clinical applications. Sensors (Switzerland) **14**(2), 3362–3394 (2014)

12. Narvaez, F., Fernando, A., Luna, C., Merchan, C., Cuenca, M.C., Diaz, G.: Kushkalla: a web-based platform to improve functional movement rehabilitation. In: Valencia-García, R., Lagos-Ortiz, K., Alcaraz-Mármol, G., Del Cioppo, J., Vera-Lucio, N., Bucaram-Leverone, M. (eds.) Technologies and Innovation. CCIS, vol. 749, pp. 194–208. Springer, Cham (2017). https://doi.org/10.1007/978-3-319-67283-0_15

13. Zhang, J.T., Novak, A.C., Brouwer, B., Li, Q.: Concurrent validation of Xsens MVN measurement of lower limb joint angular kinematics. Physiolog. Meas. **34**(8), N63–N69 (2013)

14. Wu, G., Cavanagh, P.R.: ISB recommendations in the reporting for standardization of kinematic data. J. Biomech. **28**(10), 1257–1261 (1995)

15. Laudanski, A., Brouwer, B., Li, Q.: Measurement of lower limb joint kinematics using inertial sensors during stair ascent and descent in healthy older adults and stroke survivors. J. Healthc. Eng. **4**(4), 555–576 (2013)

16. Sun, T., Liu, Q., Li, W., Lu, Z., Chen, H., Chen, P., Lu, Z.: Hip, knee and ankle motion angle detection based on inertial sensor. In: Proceedings of the IEEE International Conference on Information and Automation, pp. 1612–1617, August 2016

17. Wang, Y., Xu, J., Wu, X., Pottie, G., Kaiser, W.: A simple calibration for upper limb motion tracking and reconstruction or reconstruction upper limb motion tracking and reconstruction. In: Conference of Proceedings of the IEEE Engineering in Medicine and Biology Society, pp. 5868–5871 (2014)
18. Vargas-Valencia, L., Elias, A., Rocon, E., Bastos-Filho, T., Frizera, A.: An IMU-to-body alignment method applied to human gait analysis. Sensors **16**(12), 2090 (2016)
19. Qi, Y., Soh, C.B., Gunawan, E., Low, K.S., Thomas, R.: Lower extremity joint angle tracking with wireless ultrasonic sensors during a squat exercise. Sensors (Switzerland) **15**(5), 9610–9627 (2015)
20. Li, G., Liu, T., Yi, J., Wang, H., Li, J., Inoue, Y.: The lower limbs kinematics analysis by wearable sensor shoes. IEEE Sens. J. **16**(8), 2627–2638 (2016)
21. Seel, T., Raisch, J., Schauer, T.: IMU-based joint angle measurement for gait analysis. Sensors (Basel, Switzerland) **14**(4), 6891–6909 (2014)
22. Kuipers, J.B.: Quaternions and Rotation Sequences: A Primer With Applications to Orbits, Aerospace, and Virtual Reality. Princeton University Press, New Jersey (1999)
23. Wu, G., Siegler, S., Allard, P., Kirtley, C., Leardini, A., Rosenbaum, D., Whittle, M., D'Lima, D.D., Cristofolini, L., Witte, H., Schmid, O., Stokes, I.: ISB recommendation on definitions of joint coordinate system of various joints for the reporting of human joint motion–part I: ankle, hip, and spine. J. Biomech. **35**(4), 543–548 (2002)

Research on Motor Function of the Elderly in Guangzhou Based on Anthropometry

Fenghong Wang[(⊠)], Zhenwen Zeng, and Lin Lin

School of Design, South China University of Technology,
Panyu District, Guangzhou, China
fhwang@scut.edu.cn

Abstract. Taking the elderly in Guangzhou as an example, this paper collects the data of elderly upper limb range of motion by manual measurement. After analyzing the data of elderly upper limb range of motion, the anthropometry database of older people in Guangzhou was established, and the upper and lower limits of the range of motion of elderly products can be get from this database. Also, the anthropometry database can provide the valid date as a design basis for the outdoor fitness products which are tailored to the elderly in Guangzhou.

Keywords: Guangzhou · Elderly · Anthropometry measurement
Range of motion

1 Introduction

With the development and improvement of social living standards and the aggravation of the aging of society, the awareness of fitness of the elderly in urban areas are increasing constantly. According to a survey, more than 60% of the elderly in urban areas are exercising, and more and more elderly people have a strong sense of fitness and are actively involved in the exercise [1].

Many communities in the city are equipped with a variety of fitness equipment for elderly, however, these fitness equipment are designed according to the Chinese adult human body size (for example, national standard GB/T10000-88, its human body data was collected from male not over the age of 60 and female not over the age of 55) as the design standard, thus does not conform to the human activity scale and meet the fitness requirement of the elderly. With the improvement of the health consciousness of the elderly, more and more elderly people are actively participating in the fitness activities, which puts forward more stringent requirements on the design of fitness products.

Guangzhou fully entered the aging society in 2005, and more and more elderly joined in the fitness team. Although anthropometric measurement is difficult, time-sensitive, and there are obvious differences among different regions, however, with the increasing of the aging population and the products designed for elderly,

Fund project: Design of sports and fitness product for the elderly in the pearl river delta region based on anthropometry. Guangdong science project. Project number: 2015A020219002.

© Springer International Publishing AG, part of Springer Nature 2018
V. G. Duffy (Ed.): DHM 2018, LNCS 10917, pp. 232–241, 2018.
https://doi.org/10.1007/978-3-319-91397-1_20

conducting the elderly anthropometry in a region is at the opportune moment. Therefore, this paper randomly selected the elderly in the community and collected their human body data and analyzed the data in order to provide a data reference for the design of the elderly fitness product in Guangzhou.

2 Guangzhou Elderly Anthropometric Sample Selection

This paper selects the elderly between 60 to 70 years old in Guangzhou as the research object, because according to the survey, more than half of the elderly in Guangzhou are between 60–70 years old. Elderly at this age also has stronger activity ability and more likely to choose to exercise with the fitness equipment [2].

This paper adopts the simple random sampling method and set up the small data sample by means of sampling measurement. A reasonable sample size can ensure the validity of the data. According to the sample estimation method recommended by the international standard ISO15535 [3], the following formula is obtained:

$$n = \left(\frac{Z \times CV}{\alpha}\right)^2 \times 1.534^2 \tag{1}$$

In the formula: Z is a normal value. To ensure the accuracy of the measured data, select the 95th percentile value $Z = 1.96$; α is relative error percentage; CV is the coefficient of variation ($CV = SD/M \times 100$, SD is the standard deviation, M is the mean value). Because of the lack of relevant data reference to determine the CV value, considering the manpower and time factor, we preliminarily determine the sample as 50 elderly men and women. The CV value can be calculated according to the actual measured sample size. Using formula (1) to calculate the relative error percentage α, if the value of α is acceptable, then the effective sample size is reasonable, otherwise the sample size is small. The measured data should be used carefully.

3 Measure Content and Method

3.1 Measure Content

This paper mainly aimed at Guangzhou elderly upper limbs motion range measurement. According to the literature, the current outdoor fitness equipment, such as running trainers, elliptical machine, riding machine are focusing on the exercise of lower limbs. They require a large range of movement and a good sense of balance and mobility. Therefore, only the elderly with better physical quality will use the equipment. The exercise equipment that focuses on the upper part of the limbs such as arm extension apparatus, the suspension loop, the tractor back massager, big wheel, tai chi wheel and push plate, however, are more popular among the elderly as they do not consume much physical strength and do not need a large range of movement but can also achieve exercise effect [4]. In consequence, this paper selects the elderly upper limbs motion range as the research object.

Dynamic joint range of motion refers to the angle parameters of the limbs and the rotation angle of the center of gravity location (near the center of the body joints) of human body parts in active position. This paper studies and measures the human upper limbs joint range of motion, including the head, neck, shoulder, elbow and the waist. The measure contents are listed in Table 1.

Table 1. Measure contents of range of motion.

Body parts	Joint	Activity
Head to the trunk	Head joint	Bowed head, raise head Tilt to left, tilt to right Turn left, turn right
Trunk	Chest joints, waist joints	Bend forward, bend backward Bend to left, bend to right Turn left, turn right
Upper arm to trunk	Shoulder joint	Sway outward, sway inward Sway upward, sway downward Sway forward, sway backward
Lower arm to upper arm.	Elbow joint	Sway outward, sway inward Sway upward, sway downward sway forward, sway backward
Hand to lower arm	Wrist joint	Sway outward, sway inward Bend, stretch
Hand to the trunk	Shoulder joint, lower arm	Turn left, turn right

3.2   Methods of Motion Range Measurement

Anthropometric can be conducted by manual measurement, two-dimensional non-contact body measurement and 3d human body measurement technology [5]. During the measurement, the body posture change will make human body parts contour change, which will cause larger deviation if use two-dimensional or three-dimensional measurement method. Meanwhile, some places cannot be scanned by the machine, which will cause inconvenience for the data collection. After analyzing the existing conditions and comparing the above methods, this paper chooses the manual measurement method, and the contact measurement is carried out by using the joint range of motion meter. In the measurement, the fixed arm of the meter is fixed at the fixed point of the volunteer horizontally or vertically; Then let the volunteer sway their arm to their best efforts, record the value on the angle dial, that is, to get the range of motion [6].

Before conducting the contact measurements, we told the details of the measurement to the elderly, and began to measure after reaching consensus with the elderly. Due to the obvious differences between the mobility and the maximum motion range of the elderly, we took the maximum range of motion that they willing to exert as the final measurement results.

4   Collection and Analysis of Measurement Data

4.1   Statistics of the Range of Motion of Elderly Upper Limb

This paper processes the measured data according to the gender and analyzes the data by using the statistical software SPSS23.0. The average motion range values (M), the minimum (min), the maximum (Max), the standard deviation (SD) and coefficient of variation (CV) of the elderly can be obtained [7]. While the motion range of different individuals is distributed in a certain range, we can only use a certain value but not the average value in the design. So this subject adopts the percentile (divided the total number of people by the number of people that equal to or less than the range of motion) to describe the data. The results are listed in Tables 2, 3, 4 and 5.

Table 2.   Table of Guangzhou male elderly range of motion measurement (°).

Measure content	N	Min	Max	M	SD	CV (%)
Bow head+	48	25	59	40	9	22.5
Raise head–	48	16	52	32	10	31.3
Tilt head leftward+	48	25	52	38	6	15.8
Tilt head rightward–	48	25	52	38	6	15.8
Turn head leftward+	48	32	62	44	9	20.5
Turn head rightward–	48	32	62	44	9	20.5
Bend trunk forward+	48	68	105	93	10	10.8
Bend trunk backward–	48	20	54	38	12	31.6
Bend trunk leftward+	48	27	50	38	7	18.4
Bend trunk rightward–	48	27	50	38	7	18.4
Turn trunk leftward+	48	28	55	41	8	19.5
Turn trunk rightward–	48	28	55	41	8	19.5
Bend hip joint forward+	48	80	130	106	12	11.3
Bend hip joint backward–	48	10	30	18	6	33.3
Bend hip joint outward+	48	20	44	31	7	22.6
Bend hip joint inward–	48	9	21	14	3	21.4
Turn hip joint outward+	48	95	119	104	6	5.8
Turn hip joint inward–	48	57	75	64	5	7.8
Sway shoulder joint outward+	48	170	180	178	3	1.7
Sway shoulder joint inward–	48	20	43	27	6	22.2
Sway shoulder joint upward+	48	175	180	179	2	1.1
Sway shoulder joint downward–	48	15	51	39	9	23.1
Sway shoulder joint forward+	48	125	162	137	8	5.8
Sway shoulder joint backward–	48	25	60	38	9	23.7
Bend elbow joint+	48	102	153	134	146	109.0
Stretch elbow joint	48	0	0	0	0	–
Sway wrist outward+	48	20	61	35	10	28.6
Sway wrist inward–	48	15	32	24	5	20.8
Bend wrist+	48	50	82	71	6	8.5
Stretch wrist–	48	30	68	58	7	12.1

Table 3. Percentile of Guangzhou male elderly range of motion measurement (°).

Measure content	1	5	10	50	90	95	99
Bow head+	25	26	29	40	53	57	59
Raise head–	16	18	19	29	50	52	52
Tilt head leftward+	25	26	30	38	45	47	52
Tilt head rightward–	25	26	30	38	45	47	52
Turn head leftward+	32	33	35	41	57	60	62
Turn head rightward–	32	33	35	41	57	60	62
Bend trunk forward+	68	69	74	95	102	104	105
Bend trunk backward–	20	21	23	39	52	53	54
Bend trunk leftward+	27	28	29	38	48	49	50
Bend trunk rightward–	27	28	29	38	48	49	50
Turn trunk leftward+	28	29	31	43	51	53	55
Turn trunk rightward–	28	29	31	43	51	53	55
Bend hip joint forward+	80	84	86	104	120	128	130
Bend hip joint backward–	10	11	13	18	28	29	30
Bend hip joint outward+	20	21	23	30	40	43	44
Bend hip joint inward–	9	10	11	13	19	20	21
Turn hip joint outward+	95	96	97	104	113	118	119
Turn hip joint inward–	57	58	59	62	72	74	75
Sway shoulder joint outward+	170	170	175	180	180	180	180
Sway shoulder joint inward–	20	21	23	28	35	42	43
Sway shoulder joint upward+	175	175	176	180	180	180	180
Sway shoulder joint downward–	15	22	23	42	48	50	51
Sway shoulder joint forward+	125	126	128	136	150	152	162
Sway shoulder joint backward–	25	26	27	36	54	58	60
Bend elbow joint+	102	103	108	138	151	152	153
Stretch elbow joint	0	0	0	0	0	0	0
Sway wrist outward+	20	25	26	32	50	60	61
Sway wrist inward–	15	16	17	25	29	30	32
Bend wrist+	50	59	60	71	78	80	82
Stretch wrist–	30	49	51	58	65	67	68

4.2   Sample Size Verification

The elbow bend coefficient of variation of male elderly is 109, the sample size is 50, the 95th percentile corresponding Z value is 1.96. The a % is 47.5% calculated by the formula, but this data should be use cautiously. In addition, the other a % of the male elderly men motion range is less than 15%, among the acceptable range. The maximum variation coefficient of female elderly is 29.4, the sample size is 50, the 95th percentile corresponding Z value is 1.96. Calculated by the formula, the a % is 12.5%, less than 15%. The rest of the data are also in the acceptable range.

Table 4. of Guangzhou female elderly range of motion measurement (°).

Measure content	N	Min	Max	M	SD	CV (%)
Bow head+	52	20	60	42	9	21.4
Raise head–	52	15	50	31	8	25.8
Tilt head leftward+	52	20	52	37	8	21.6
Tilt head rightward–	52	20	52	37	8	21.6
Turn head leftward+	52	25	70	44	10	22.7
Turn head rightward–	52	25	70	44	10	22.7
Bend trunk forward+	52	60	120	90	11	12.2
Bend trunk backward–	52	20	55	40	11	27.5
Bend trunk leftward+	52	20	70	40	9	22.5
Bend trunk rightward–	52	20	70	40	9	22.5
Turn trunk leftward+	52	28	65	41	8	19.5
Turn trunk rightward–	52	28	65	41	8	19.5
Bend hip joint forward+	52	83	126	107	10	9.3
Bend hip joint backward–	52	9	30	17	5	29.4
Bend hip joint outward+	52	18	50	34	8	23.5
Bend hip joint inward–	52	9	25	15	3	20.0
Turn hip joint outward+	52	94	125	106	6	5.7
Turn hip joint inward–	52	56	80	65	5	7.7
Sway shoulder joint outward+	52	160	180	179	4	2.2
Sway shoulder joint inward–	52	19	50	30	6	20.0
Sway shoulder joint upward+	52	175	180	179	1	0.6
Sway shoulder joint downward–	52	20	70	43	11	25.6
Sway shoulder joint forward+	52	125	170	142	10	7.0
Sway shoulder joint backward–	52	28	65	42	10	23.8
Bend elbow joint+	52	100	160	137	13	9.5
Stretch elbow joint	52	0	0	0	0	–
Sway wrist outward+	52	23	60	37	9	24.3
Sway wrist inward–	52	16	45	27	7	25.9
Bend wrist+	52	60	80	71	5	7.0
Stretch wrist–	52	50	70	58	5	8.6

4.3   Compare Male and Female Data by ANOVA

The differences between the genders cause differences between the data. And the difference degree determines whether the design size differences between men and women should be considered. In order to determine the degree of data difference between men and women, we have collected the single factor analysis of variance (ANOVA) of the joint range of motion to test the difference degree of the elderly human body data caused by the gender. Its principle is: the difference between the mean of different group are caused by the experimental condition and random error. Through the analysis of different sources of variation of total variation of contribution, we can know the influence of controllable factors on the results [8]. Group the men and

Table 5. Percentile of Guangzhou female elderly range of motion measurement (°).

Measure content	1	5	10	50	90	95	99
Bow head+	20	24	30	42	54	56	60
Raise head–	15	16	19	30	41	46	50
Tilt head leftward+	20	24	26	38	46	51	52
Tilt head rightward–	20	24	26	38	46	51	52
Turn head leftward+	25	31	32	43	56	65	70
Turn head rightward–	25	31	32	43	56	65	70
Bend trunk forward+	60	63	70	92	102	104	120
Bend trunk backward–	20	21	22	43	53	54	55
Bend trunk leftward+	20	24	27	39	50	60	70
Bend trunk rightward–	20	24	27	39	50	60	70
Turn trunk leftward+	28	29	30	42	48	64	65
Turn trunk rightward–	28	29	30	42	48	64	65
Bend hip joint forward+	83	84	92	106	121	124	126
Bend hip joint backward–	9	10	11	17	23	25	30
Bend hip joint outward+	18	19	22	34	48	49	50
Bend hip joint inward–	9	10	12	15	19	20	25
Turn hip joint outward+	94	95	99	105	113	115	125
Turn hip joint inward–	56	57	59	63	72	75	80
Sway shoulder joint outward+	160	170	178	180	180	180	180
Sway shoulder joint inward–	19	20	22	30	36	41	50
Sway shoulder joint upward+	175	176	178	180	180	180	180
Sway shoulder joint downward–	20	23	31	42	57	64	70
Sway shoulder joint forward+	125	127	133	139	153	164	170
Sway shoulder joint backward–	28	29	34	39	60	63	65
Bend elbow joint+	100	102	125	137	151	152	160
Stretch elbow joint	0	0	0	0	0	0	0
Sway wrist outward+	23	25	28	35	50	59	60
Sway wrist inward–	16	18	19	26	35	43	45
Bend wrist+	60	63	64	72	78	79	80
Stretch wrist–	50	51	53	59	65	69	70

women data, establish the test hypothesis H0: The mean of all the samples is the same. The inspection level is 0.05. If the significance value > 0.05 means accepting H0 assumption, shows that there are little data differences between men and women; Otherwise the difference is significant. Results are shown in Fig. 1.

The figure of significant coefficient analysis shows that there are significant differences in the motion range of swaying shoulder joint upward and backward. Beyond that, there are little difference between the male and female data in the upper limb motion range comparison, which shows the consistence in the elderly people upper limbs motion range. Therefore, designers can use the same size to design upper limb movement fitness products to Guangzhou elderly man and woman.

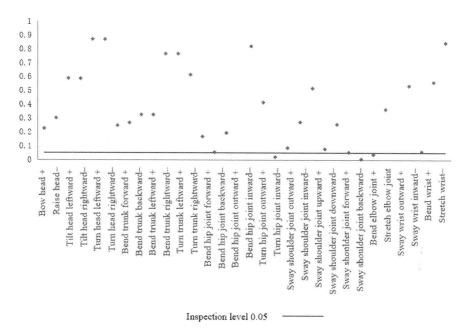

Inspection level 0.05   ———————

Fig. 1. Figure of significant coefficient distribution of Guangzhou elderly men and women upper limbs motion range.

While the motion range of different individuals is distributed in a certain range, we can only use a certain value but not the average value in the design. According to national standard GB/T12985-1991 general principles of the application of human body size percentile in product design, it needs two human body size percentile as the upper limit value and the lower limit value for the design of fitness products. To ensure consumers' health and safety, and reduce the production cost and simplify the manufacture principle, we should choose male size P95 as the upper limit size, and choose women size P5 as the lower limit [9].

We manage to get the size design basis after constructing the Guangzhou elderly upper limbs motion range database: the 5th percentile of female and 95th percentile of male, the results are shown in Tables 4, 5 and 6, it can be used as a data reference for related fitness products design.

4.4   Analysis of the Elderly Upper Limb Motor Function

Through the observation and statistics of the measurement, we found that the motion range of multiple joint of the elderly decreased. This is due to the decline in the elasticity of soft tissue around the joints as the age increases, and the extensibility and elasticity of the muscles around the joints decrease, leading to the inability of the joints to fully extend or contract. When doing posture such as raising head, swaying shoulder joint backward, bend trunk leftward, rightward and backward, many elderlies feel

Table 6. The 95 percentile value of Guangzhou male and female elderly motion range measurement.

Measure content	Female P5	Male P95
Bow head+	24	57
Raise head–	16	52
Tilt head leftward+	24	47
Tilt head rightward–	24	47
Turn head leftward+	31	60
Turn head rightward–	31	60
Bend trunk forward+	63	104
Bend trunk backward–	21	53
Bend trunk leftward+	24	49
Bend trunk rightward–	24	49
Turn trunk leftward+	29	53
Turn trunk rightward–	29	53
Bend hip joint forward+	84	128
Bend hip joint backward–	10	29
Bend hip joint outward+	19	43
Bend hip joint inward–	10	20
Turn hip joint outward+	95	118
Turn hip joint inward–	57	74
Sway shoulder joint outward+	170	180
Sway shoulder joint inward–	20	42
Sway shoulder joint upward+	176	180
Sway shoulder joint downward–	23	50
Sway shoulder joint forward+	127	152
Sway shoulder joint backward–	29	58
Bend elbow joint+	102	152
Stretch elbow joint	0	0
Sway wrist outward+	25	60
Sway wrist inward–	18	30
Bend wrist+	63	80
Stretch wrist–	51	67

difficult or fail to stretch properly, because these are not our common daily actions and we neglect to practice targeted exercise for a long time [10].

5   Conclusion

Through the actual measurement and the analysis of the Guangzhou elderly upper limbs range of motion data, this paper comes up with the data scope of the fitness products designed for the elderly in Guangzhou according to the national design standard, provides an effective data basis for the Guangzhou elderly fitness products design. At present the elderly fitness products cannot set a reasonable range of motion for the elderly. To achieve the reasonable fitness effect and make fitness products more suitable for the elderly, more accurate human body data are needed in order to provide the reference for the design.

References

1. Yu, W.: Reflections on population aging and provision for the aged in Guangzhou. TAN QIU **02**, 13–18 (2010)
2. Wang, T.: Analysis of the characteristics and causes of population aging in Guangdong Province. J. Nanchang Jr. Coll. (2), 14–15, 22 (2011)
3. ISO15535: International Organization for Standardization. General requirements for establishing anthropometric database, Switzerland (2003)
4. Zheng, W.: Improved Design for Public Outdoor Fitness Equipment and Thoughts on the Application of Universal Design Principles. Tongji University (2008)
5. Hai-tao: Anthropometric Measurement of The Elderly. Tsinghua University, Beijing (2005)
6. Hu, C.: Design and realization of precision measurement system for joint activity. Nanjing University, Nanjing (2015)
7. Wu, Z., Ma, X., Li, Y.: Introduction of statistical analysis software SPSS. J. Hebei North Univ. **22**(6), 67–69, 73 (2006)
8. Hou, H.: Ergonomics-based Design and Analysis for an upper/lower Limb Rehabilitation Training Apparatus. Yanshan University (2013)
9. Lv, J., Chen, J., Xu, J.: Ergonomics, pp. 21–25. Tsinghua University Press, Beijing (2009)
10. Wang, M., Ji, W., Yuan, S., Huang, K.: The effect of Chinese traditional fitness programs on improvement of body function in middle aged and older persons—a balance function-based pointcut. Contemp. Sports Technol. **17**, 11–13 (2015)

Perception of Floor Slipperiness
Before and After a Walk

Caijun Zhao[1] and Kai-Way Li[2(✉)]

[1] School of Safety and Environmental Engineering, Hunan Institute of Technology,
Hengyang, People's Republic of China
646004531@qq.com
[2] Department of Industrial Management, Chung Hua University, Hsin-Chu, Taiwan
kaiwayli@qq.com

Abstract. Nowadays, Slips and falls have become the leading causes of deaths and injuries at both workplaces and public sectors. Perception of floor slipperiness has been considered as one of the important item affecting the gait pattern of a walker and thus affects the risk of slip and fall. For investigating the factors affecting the perception of floor slipperiness and the relationship between the perception rating of floor slipperiness before and after a walk, a gait experiment was conducted. Two walkways, each of 5.4 m long, were installed. The floors on these walkways were polished granite and ceramic tile. There were two floor surface conditions: dry and water-detergent solution contaminated conditions. Two types of shoes were tested: rubber-soled and EVA-soled. In addition, the illumination conditions included light and dark. In the experiment, the subject stood in front of the walkway and reported his perception rating of floor slipperiness though a five-point scales from 1 extremely slippery to 5 not slippery at all. He, then walked through the walkway and gave his perception rating of floor slipperiness again. In addition, he also gave a perceive sense of slipperiness. The results indicated that the perception rating of floor slipperiness both before and after walk and the perceive sense of slip were all affected significantly by floor ($p < 0.0001$) and floor surface conditions ($p < 0.0001$). Details of the results were discussed. The information in this study is helpful in understanding human behaviors when walking on slippery and non-slippery floors.

Keywords: Floor slipperiness · Perception rating of floor slipperiness · PSOS

1 Introduction

Slips and falls often occur. They are leading causes of deaths and injuries at workplaces [1]. Slip and fall accidents have accounted for 14.6% of the total cost of the occupational incidents in the USA, the cost was more than USD 7.7 billion in 2007 [2]. In 2009, the cost of slip and fall accidents was USD 6.2 billion, which was lower than that in 2007. But slips and falls have been ranked second among the top 10 causes and direct cost of the most disabling workplace injuries in the USA [3]. In Taiwan, falls are common occupational hazard for service workers, which were next only to traffic accidents [4].

© Springer International Publishing AG, part of Springer Nature 2018
V. G. Duffy (Ed.): DHM 2018, LNCS 10917, pp. 242–252, 2018.
https://doi.org/10.1007/978-3-319-91397-1_21

More than two thousands same level falls has been reported in 2013, which has accounted for 17.89% of all job-related injuries [5].

Reducing the occurrence of slipping has become one of the major issues in the scientific community. When the friction coefficient between the shoe and the ground is lower than the friction required to balancing the body, a fall could occur. Friction on the floor has been widely used as an index of the risk of slips and falls. Li et al. [6] compared the performances of the Brungraber Mark II (BM II) and Mark III (BM III) slipmeters in assessing the friction of the floor. Although there were certain differences in the values measured by two instruments on the coefficient of friction (COF) and normal force, the BM III was found to be equivalent to the BM II on the measurement of friction. Chang et al. [7] investigated the friction mechanisms between shoe and four different floor interfaces which included dry, liquid, icy and solid contaminated surfaces. They pointed out that static friction measurement can be only used for dry surface and clean surface, and dynamic and transition friction methods are required to properly estimate the potential risks of the contaminated surface. Liu et al. [8] studied the effects of shoe sole, floor, floor contamination and inclined angle of the floor surface on the COF. They reported that all the four factors have significantly effect on friction coefficient.

Floor slipperiness is one of the most important parameters in evaluating the risk of slips and falls. Before stepping on the floor, people judge the floor slipperiness through the observation of the floor. Then they adjust the forces applied on the floor so as not to exceed those limits. Tisserand [9] suggested that there is a mental model of friction limits when a person is walking. Some scholars studied the floor slipperiness by measuring subjective response of human subjects. Swensen et al. [10] investigated the subjective ratings and rankings of the slipperiness about the steel beams. They reported that the subjective ratings had a high correlation ($r \geq 0.75$) with the measured COF.

Chang et al. [11] used friction measurements as the objective measurement and the employees' ratings of floor slipperiness as the subjective measurement to investigate the floor slipperiness in 7 kitchen areas of 10 western-style fast-food restaurants in Taiwan. They found that the Pearson's correlation coefficients between the averaged COF and subjective ratings was 0.49 and Spearman's was 0.45 ($p < 0.001$). Bang et al. [12] used two subjective rating methods to evaluate floor slipperiness on seven floor surfaces contaminated with detergent solution. They found a higher correlation ($r = 0.99$) between the two tests results except for the ground steel. These studies showed that the perception of slipperiness not only could be used to assess the floor slipperiness but also be the subsidiary measurement of the friction on the floor.

Cohen et al. [13] requested their subjects to slid their barefoot on the test titles and compared the slipperiness of these tiles with a standard tile whose value COF value was 0.5. They found disagreements between the COF values and the subjects' ratings of the tiles. In a subsequent research, Cohen et al. [14] conducted an experiment to test the subjects' perceptions in conditions closer to real life. This experiment contained 10 outdoor walking surfaces and each had two conditions (dry and wet), and the subjects were asked to look at each floor and ranked its perception of slipperiness (observed), then walked on each surface under each condition and ranked the slipperiness of the floor again (experienced). They found that no matter on dry surface or wet surface, the difference between the "observed" and "experienced" ratings was not statistically significant. They reported that subject evaluated the slipperiness of one surface condition when they observing it, then tended to evaluate it after a walk. This implied that prior observation may affect the following perception of the floor slipperiness after a walk.

Both floor slipperiness and floor roughness affect the happen of slips and falls. Li et al. [15] compared the perception of floor roughness and the perception of floor slipperiness, which was evaluated based on tactual sensations from different body segments for males and females. They found that both the perception of floor roughness and floor slipperiness were predicted better by using the floor roughness parameter R_a than that using the COF of the floor. Yu et al. [16] compared the perception of floor slipperiness with and without shoes for males and females. They found that the subjects made more adjustments on the rating of the perception of floor slipperiness when they were wearing shoes than when they had bare foot. The adjustment of the perception of floor slipperiness was affected by gender, floor, surface conditions, and footwear conditions.

Floor slipperiness, floor roughness, and shod conditions are all believed to have effects on the happen of slipping and falling during a gait. Perception of floor slipperiness and floor roughness are important measures in understanding the risk of slipping and falling [15]. This study aimed to compare the perception of floor slipperiness before and after a walk on the floor.

2   Methods

A gait experiment was carried out in the ergonomics laboratory at Hunan Institute of Technology. The mean (SD) temperature and humidity were 21.12 °C (±3.29) and 78.2% (±7.05), respectively.

2.1   Human Subjects

Six adult males participated in the experiment. Their age, height, body weight, and length of lower extremity were 20.17 yrs (±0.37), 169.00 cm (±5.03), 63.83 kg (±6.73), and 89.92 cm (±3.34), respectively. All the subjects was asked to read the instructions carefully and sign the experimental protocol before the experiment (Table 1).

Table 1. Fundamental data for human subjects

Item	Mean	Std	Min	Max
Age (yrs)	20.17	0.37	20.0	21.0
Height (cm)	169.00	5.03	160.0	177.0
Body weight (kg)	63.83	6.73	55.0	75.0
Length of lower extremity (cm)	89.92	3.34	83.5	93.0

2.2   Experimental Conditions

The experimental conditions included floor, floor surface, shoes, and level of illumination. There were two walkways, each of 5.4 m long, were installed. The floors on these walkways were polished ceramic tile and granite (see Fig. 1). Ceramic tile ($R_a = 14.95$) had higher surface roughness than granite ($R_a = 0.05$). A suspension rail was installed over-hear to support a safety harness along the walkway to provide safety precaution for the gait.

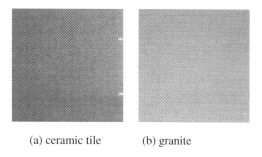

(a) ceramic tile   (b) granite

Fig. 1. Tested floors

The floor surface condition included dry and water-detergent solution contaminated surface. For dry condition, the test floors' surfaces were clean and dry. For water-detergent solution, the target area (the final 1.2 m floor, see Fig. 2) of the test trail was covered by a detergent solution which was mixed with water and detergent according to the proportion of 1:30, and other floors of the test trail were clean and dry as the dry condition.

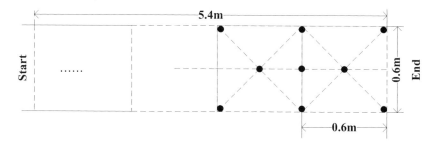

Fig. 2. Illumination measurements spots on the walkway

The illumination conditions included light and dark. The illumination was measured at 9 locations (see Fig. 2) on the test floor using a TES1336A light meter. For light condition, the illumination was 366.07 ($\pm$70.47) lx. For dark condition, the illumination was 0.05 ($\pm$0.02) lx.

The shoes condition included rubber-soled shoes and Ethylene-vinyl acetate (EVA)-soled shoes (see Fig. 3). The left shoe sole was EVA and the right shoe sole was rubber.

Fig. 3. Shoes

2.3 Experiment Procedure

When the subjects first entered the laboratory, his fundamental data were collected by the research personnel. In the light condition, the subject was requested to stand at the starting point of the walkway and wore the safety harness (see Fig. 4). For dark condition, the subject was waiting in a preparation room next door to the laboratory, and wore an eye mask before entering the lab. Then the research personnel led the subjects to the starting point of the walkway and removed their eye mask. When the subjects adapted to the dark condition which approximately takes five minutes, the research personnel continued the same procedure as in the light condition. The subject looked at the target area of floor and gave a subjective rating of floor slipperiness before the gait trial start. This rating was termed RFS_{before} (perception rating of floor slipperiness before a walk). Then he was asked to put on the suitable laboratory shoes and walked at a speed following the sound of a metronome toward the end of the walkway and stopped. The metronome pace of the metronome was 100 per minute and it was closest to the normal gait frequency which was determined after repeated tests. The subject gave a subjective rating of floor slipperiness after the gait trial. This rating was termed RFS_{after} (perception rating of floor slipperiness before a walk). In addition, a perceived sense of slip (PSOS) rating was also collected.

Fig. 4. Trial experiment

2.4   Dependent Variables

In the experiment, the following dependent variables were collected: RFS_{before}, RFS_{after}, and PSOS. A five-point scale was adopted for both the RFS_{before} and RFS_{after}: from 1 extremely slippery to 5 not slippery at all. The PSOS [17] was composed of the following four questions:

(1) How much did you feel yourself slip?
(2) Did you have any difficulty in maintaining balance?
(3) Did you feel at any time that you would slip?
(4) What would you say was the overall difficulty of this task?

Each of the questions required a five-point responses from 0 (not at all) to 2 (a lot) with an increment of 0.5. The final score of PSOS was addition of the scores from these four questions.

2.5   Experiment Design and Data Analysis

A factorial randomly block design experiment was performed. The illumination condition was the block. The total trial was 96 (6 subjects × 2 shoes × 2 floors × 2 surfaces × 2 illumination conditions). Analysis of variance (ANOVA) was performed. Duncan's multiple range tests were performed for factors with more than two levels if the main factor reached the significance level of 0.05. The statistical analyses were performed using the SAS®14.0 software.

3   Results

3.1   Descriptive Statistics

Figure 5 shows the RFS_{before} under floor, surface conditions, and illumination conditions. Figure 6 shows the RFS_{after} under floor and surface conditions. Figure 7 shows the PSOS under shoes, floor and surface conditions.

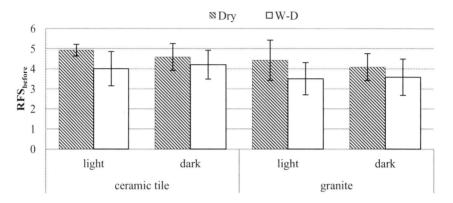

Fig. 5. RFS$_{before}$ under floor, surface, and illumination conditions, Note: RFS$_{before}$ = perception of floor slipperiness before a walk; W-D = water-detergent solution

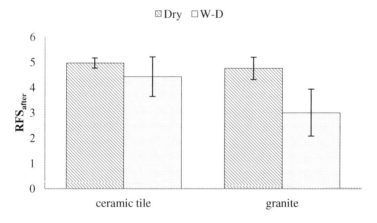

Fig. 6. RFS$_{after}$ under floor and surface conditions, Note: RFS$_{after}$ = perception of floor slipperiness after a walk; W-D = water-detergent solution

3.2 Analyses of Variance

The ANOVA results of the RFS$_{before}$ indicate that the effects of floor ($p = 0.0016$) and surface conditions ($p < 0.0001$) were significant. The results of Duncan's multiple range test showed that RFS$_{before}$ (4.23) of EVA-soled footwear was not significantly different from that (4.08) of Rubber-soled footwear. RFS$_{before}$ (4.21) of light condition was not significantly different with that (4.10) of dark condition. The effects of shoes and illumination conditions were not significant. The Duncan's multiple range test results for the floor, surface conditions are shown in Tables 2 and 3.

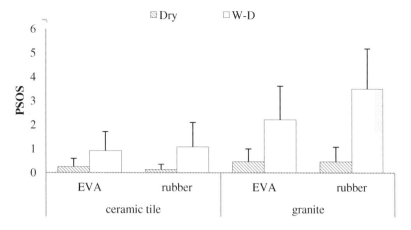

Fig. 7. PSOS under shoes, floor and surface conditions, Note: W-D = water-detergent solution

Table 2. Results of Duncan's multiple range test for RFS$_{before}$ of floor conditions

Floor	Mean RFS$_{before}$	Duncan's grouping*
Ceramic tile	4.42	A
Granite	3.90	B

*different letters indicating they are statistically significant at $\alpha = 0.05$.

Table 3. Results of Duncan's multiple range test for RFS$_{before}$ of surface conditions

Surface conditions	Mean RFS$_{before}$	Duncan's grouping*
Dry	4.50	A
Water-Detergent	3.81	B

*different letters indicating they are statistically significant at $\alpha = 0.05$.

The ANOVA results of the RFS$_{after}$ indicated that the following effects were significant: floor ($p < 0.0001$), surface conditions ($p < 0.001$), shoes $\times$ surface conditions ($p < 0.05$), floor $\times$ surface conditions ($p < 0.0001$). The effects of shoes were not significant. Neither were the effects of illumination significant. The Duncan's multiple range test results for the floor and surface are shown in Tables 4 and 5.

Table 4. Results of Duncan's multiple range test for RFS$_{after}$ of floor conditions

Floor	Mean RFS$_{after}$	Duncan's grouping*
Ceramic tile	4.67	A
Granite	3.88	B

*different letters indicating they are statistically significant at $\alpha = 0.05$.

Table 5. Results of Duncan's multiple range test for RFS$_{after}$ of surface conditions

Surface conditions	Mean RFS$_{after}$	Duncan's grouping*
Dry	4.85	A
Water-Detergent	3.71	B

*different letters indicating they are statistically significant at $\alpha = 0.05$.

The ANOVA results of the PSOS indicate that the following effects were significant: floor ($p < 0.0001$), surface conditions ($p < 0.0001$), floor × surface conditions ($p < 0.001$). The effects of illumination conditions and shoe were not significant. The Duncan's multiple range test results for the floor, and surface conditions are shown in Tables 6 and 7.

Table 6. Results of Duncan's multiple range test for PSOS of floor conditions

Floor	Mean PSOS	Duncan's grouping*
Granite	1.66	A
Ceramic tile	0.60	B

*different letters indicating they are statistically significant at $\alpha = 0.05$.

Table 7. Results of Duncan's multiple range test for PSOS of surface conditions

Surface conditions	Mean PSOS	Duncan's grouping*
Water-Detergent	1.93	A
Dry	0.33	B

*different letters indicating they are statistically significant at $\alpha = 0.05$.

3.3   Analyses of Correlation

The results of correlation analyses between the variables were calculated and are shown in Table 8.

Table 8. Correlation analysis between the variables

	RFS$_{before}$	RFS$_{after}$	PSOS
RFS$_{before}$		0.594	−0.651
RFS$_{after}$			−0.924

4   Discussion

Before the experiment, illumination was considered an important factor affecting the perceived floor slipperiness. One of the illumination conditions represents the ordinary daylight condition and the illuminations of the target area of the test floors were more than 300 lx. The dark condition was at night and with all the curtains in the laboratory pulled up to prevent the outside light in, the illuminations of the target area of the test floors were less than 0.10 lx. The RFS_{before} was the rating of floor slipperiness based on visual judgment. Therefore, the floor and floor conditions we had observed would have an impact on the RFS_{before}. The experimental results confirm this version. Table 2 shows the RFS_{before} of ceramic tile (4.42) was significantly different from that of the granite (3.90). Table 3 shows RFS_{before} of dry condition (4.50) was significantly different from that of the water-detergent (3.81). For illumination conditions, it was anticipated that the subjects would reluctant to give a NOT SLIPPERY rating when they could not see clearly the walkway. Li et al. [18] confirmed this hypothesis. However, the ANOVA results in the current research indicated that the effects of illumination was not significant ($p > 0.05$) on the RFS_{before}.

For the RFS_{after}, the subjects gave their ratings of floor slipperiness based on their perception during the gait. Therefore, the subjects used the traction of their foot on the floor to make judgment instead of the vision. Our ANOVA results showed that the effect of illumination on RFS_{after} was not significant ($p = 0.6390$), and the RFS_{after} was significantly affected by the interaction between the shoes and surface conditions ($p < 0.05$), floor and surface conditions ($p < 0.0001$). However, prior observation could influence later experience in the perception of floor slipperiness [14]. Table 8 shows there was a significant positive correlation between the RFS_{after} and RFS_{before} ($r = 0.594$, $p < 0.0001$).

Chiou et al. [17] proposed the PSOS to indicate the risk of slip and fall when walking. The final score of PSOS was the addition of the scores from the four questions. As each of the response of the question was in the range of 0 to 2, the final score of PSOS was between 0 and 8. Chiou et al. [17] indicated that a fall will occur if the PSOS exceeds 4.5. In our experiment, the PSOS ranged from 0 to 5.5. However, 95% of the PSOS values were lower than 4.5 and most of them were 1.0 or lower. This infers that the overall risk of slip and fall in our experiment was low. For the floors, the PSOS of granite (1.66) was significantly ($p < 0.05$) higher than those of ceramic tile (0.60). This infers that the granite floor provided higher risk of slip and fall than the ceramic tile floors. For the surface conditions, the PSOS of the water-detergent condition (1.93) was significantly ($p < 0.05$) higher than that of the dry (0.33) surface conditions. The subjects certainly perceived higher risk of slip and fall when they were walking on detergent contaminated surfaces than the dry surfaces. For shoes conditions, the PSOS difference between the rubber (1.29) and EVA (0.96) was not significant ($p > 0.05$). This implies that rubber and EVA have a small difference on the risk of slip and fall. However, Fig. 5 shows that the mean PSOS of rubber soled were higher than that of EVA soled no matter which conditions. The inconsistency between Fig. 5 and the ANOVA results may be due to the small sample size of the study.

5 Conclusion

A gait experiment was carried out to test the subjective ratings of human subjects concerning their perception on floor slipperiness. It was found that the RFS_{before}, RFS_{after} and PSOS were all affected significantly by floor and floor surface conditions. In addition, the RFS_{after} and PSOS were significantly affected by the interaction between floor and floor surface condition. For RFS_{after}, there was also interaction between shoe sole material and floor surface conditions. There are significant correlations between $RFS_{before,}$ RFS_{after} and PSOS.

References

1. Chang, W.R., Leclercq, S., Lockhart, T.E., et al.: State of science: occupational slips, trips and falls on the same level. Ergonomics **59**(7), 861 (2016)
2. Chang, W.R., Courtney, T.K., Huang, Y.H., et al.: Safety in fast-food restaurants: factors that influence employee perceptions of floor slipperiness. Prof. Saf., 56 (2011)
3. Liberty Mutual Group.com (Internet). Hopkinton, MA, USA. https://www.libertymutual group.com/about-lm/research-institute/commu. Accessed 15 Aug 2016
4. Huang, Y., Feng, C.-A., Hsu, Y.-Y., et al.: Risk factors of occupational slip-and-fall injuries. J. Occup. Saf. Health **21**(1), 38–52 (2013)
5. Occupational Safety and Health Administration (Internet). Taipei, Taiwan. Chinese. http://www.osha.gov.tw/1106/1164/1165/1168. Accessed 10 Aug 2016
6. Li, K.W., Chang, W.R., Chang, C.C.: Evaluation of two models of a slipmeter. Saf. Sci. **47**(10), 1434–1439 (2009)
7. Chang, W.R., Grönqvist, R., Leclercq, S., et al.: The role of friction in the measurement of slipperiness, part 1: friction mechanisms and definition of test conditions. Ergonomics **44**(13), 1217–1232 (2001)
8. Liu, L.W., Li, K.W., Yunghui, L., et al.: Friction measurements on "anti-slip" floors under shoe sole, contamination, and inclination conditions. Saf. Sci. **48**(10), 1321–1326 (2010)
9. Tisserand, M.: Progress in the prevention of falls caused by slipping. Ergonomics **28**(7), 1027–1042 (1985)
10. Swensen, E.E., Purswell, J.L., Schlegel, R.E., et al.: Coefficient of friction and subjective assessment of slippery work surfaces. Hum. Factors **34**(1), 67 (1992)
11. Chang, W.R., Li, K.W., Huang, Y.H., et al.: Assessing floor slipperiness in fast-food restaurants in Taiwan using objective and subjective measures. Appl. Ergon. **35**(4), 401–408 (2004)
12. Bang, C.H., Kim, J.S.: Comparison between subjective and objective measurement of slipperiness. Key Eng. Mater. **627**, 433–436 (2015)
13. Cohen, H.H., Cohen, D.M.: Psychophysical assessment of the perceived slipperiness of floor tile surfaces in a laboratory setting. J. Saf. Res. **25**(1), 19–26 (1994)
14. Cohen, H.H., Cohen, D.M.: Perceptions of walking surface slipperiness under realistic conditions, utilizing a slipperiness rating scale. J. Saf. Res. **25**(1), 27–31 (1994)
15. Li, K.W., Yu, R., Zhang, W.: Roughness and slipperiness of floor surface: tactile sensation and perception. Saf. Sci. **49**(3), 508–512 (2011)
16. Yu, R., Li, K.W.: Perceived floor slipperiness and floor roughness in a gait experiment. Work **50**(4), 649–657 (2015)
17. Chiou, S., Bhattacharya, A., Succop, P.A.: Evaluation of workers' perceived sense of slip and effect of prior knowledge of slipperiness during task performance on slippery surfaces. AIHAJ A J. Sci. Occup. Environ. Health Saf. **61**(4), 492 (2000)
18. Li, K.W., Zhao, C., Peng, L., et al.: Subjective assessments of floor slipperiness before and after walk under two lighting conditions. Int. J. Occup. Saf. Ergon. Jose, 1 (2017)

User Diversity and Well-being

Privacy Pirates - The Key Role of User Diversity in V2X-Technology

Teresa Brell[✉], Ralf Philipsen, and Martina Ziefle

Human Computer Interaction Center, RWTH Aachen University, Aachen, Germany
{brell,philipsen,ziefle}@comm.rwth-aachen.de

Abstract. Success of novel products and services depends on a profound understanding and integration of the consumers wants and needs. Privacy is one major contributor that influences the acceptance, use, and efficiency of novel technologies. To understand, if the usage-context of technologies shapes the privacy perception, we conducted an empirical user study with n = 157 participants and two different considered domains: First, internet usage as a generalized topic. Second, autonomous driving as a more specialized field of interest. One key finding of the presented study is that privacy perception depends on the specific usage-context of a technology. Furthermore, several user diversity factors, such as technical self-efficacy and gender were identified as significant and profound levers on privacy perception.

Keywords: Autonomous driving · Privacy · User-Diversity

1 Acceptance of Novel Technological Development and Privacy Concerns in a Connected World

The steadily increasing technological developments in the mobility sector are key factors in todays society. Promising research approaches such as Volvos Vision 2020 [20] aim for zero traffic accidents due to autonomous driving functions or smartening the infrastructure to secure traffic situations like the CSIC [6]. By implementing smart communication systems into vehicles (V2X; Vehicle-to-everything), problems like the increasing number of traffic fatalities or heavy pollution are addressed. Currently, technical issues are mainly focused in research, e.g. development of specialized network technology [18, 21], whereas an awareness that novel technology is not always capable being seamlessly integrated into customers' and public perception should be raised.

Out of a pragmatic perspective, it could be assumed that novel technologies naturally evoke concerns and criticism in the launching phase. Due to adjusting the technology, these concerns decrease over time. Also, persuasive marketing is in fact a powerful tool, that might solve or camouflage most of public concerns, even after the technological devices or products are already positioned in the market. Both assumptions seem to be not far-reaching enough, out of a social science perspective. Especially large-scale technologies are critically viewed or at least ambivalently perceived by the public [13]. In contrast to technical artefacts (e.g. mobile devices), people have difficulties to

© Springer International Publishing AG, part of Springer Nature 2018
V. G. Duffy (Ed.): DHM 2018, LNCS 10917, pp. 255–267, 2018.
https://doi.org/10.1007/978-3-319-91397-1_22

comprehend or control large scale technologies, which leads to feelings of insecurity, aloofness and ultimately in rejection of the technology [16]. It has been shown that the users' perceived risk of a novel technology and the rejection probability are negatively correlated with the familiarity, the knowledge and the information depth [3]. It was also found that personal factors as age or gender do considerably impact risk perceptions towards large scale technologies [24]. Thus, public perception and users' acceptance should be implemented as early as possible within the technology development in order to adapt technology decisions in line with the fears and wishes of the customers.

The research field of automated vehicles requires more personal data of both active (e.g. driver) and passive traffic participants (e.g. pedestrian passenger), bringing privacy as crucial factor to the topic [7, 12]. Concluding, a profound understanding of the users' acceptance or reluctance towards the technology is essential for future research. The constant increase of privacy concerns can be seen in various research fields for developing technologies as the internet itself [2, 11], social media [5, 17] or medical technology [22, 25]. However, there is a lack of research on privacy issues on autonomous driving out of a social science perspective. Seen from a legal point of view, sharing personal information like position, medical status or type of vehicle to others makes all entities with access automatically co-owners of that information [1]. This underlines that benefits of data sharing and the guarantee of protecting (and not imposing) personal data is an important and fragile part that needs to be transparently communicated to potential users – especially in automated technology. Otherwise, future scenarios like fully automated driving are hardly to be realized without public protest. Previous and current experience as well as domain knowledge can be important drivers for trust; as was displayed in internet research [4] or information technology [19].

2 Questions Addressed and Experimental Design

From the presented development level, it becomes clear that the user has only been involved in a few studies, especially regarding the codetermination, which data transmission is approvable and what happens with the data. To investigate relevant user factors for a wide-spread dissemination of autonomous vehicle technology, the attitude towards privacy as influential factor will be focused, to determine whether there is a difference between privacy perception with data embedded in the internet context versus privacy perception with data embedded in autonomous driving context. Also, a closer look on the user diverse requirements on privacy context-bound to autonomous driving will be given following these main research questions:

1. **Which user-specific factors have an influence on privacy perception?**
2. **Does (technical) context play a crucial role in the perception of privacy?**

Based on a profound literature review and prior qualitative studies (expert interviews), the experimental design for answering the questions mentioned above will be laid out. As can be seen in Fig. 1, the methodological concept shows that user factors (age, gender, technical self-efficacy and prior experience) are examined further. First, they are analyzed towards a general privacy disposition. Further, a contextual embedded question-block about internet and autonomous driving privacy perception gives insights of the contextual dependence. The increase or decrease of the participants' intention to use autonomous driving technology is also identified.

3 Methodological Approach and Survey

Building on the results of former acceptance-centered V2X-technology research [14], we identified relevant user factors in order to test their influence on the perception of privacy. Further, we divided the empirical approach of the privacy perception assessment in two context based question blocks to test a possible influence on the intention to use autonomous driving features. A brief overview of the study design will be reported:

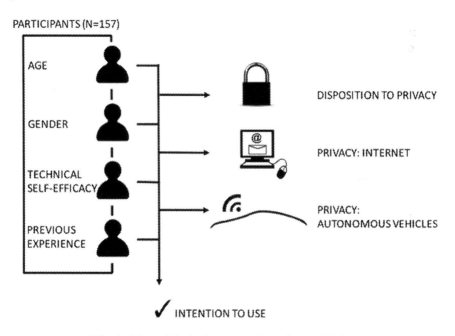

Fig. 1. Methodological concept of experimental design.

3.1 Survey

Demographical Questions. Demographical details (age, gender, etc.) and previous mobility experience as driver (professions such as public transport, cab or ambulance driver etc.) were questioned first.

Mobility Profile. Further, the participants were questioned about their drivers' license and their willingness to use autonomous driving. As a next part, the frequency of different means of transport and the experience with driver assistance systems was questioned (e.g. park assistant, lane assistant etc.).

Privacy and Technical Profile. The next part measured the technical self-efficacy (KUT) [8], the individual confidence in one's capability to use technical devices. Also, the general disposition towards privacy was questioned (see Table 1). The participants also rated privacy perception statements in the context of internet usage (compare [10, 9]).

Table 1. Item example of participants' general disposition of privacy.

How do you evaluate the following statements? (1 = do not agree, 6 = totally agree)
– I am comfortable telling other people, including strangers, personal information about myself
– I am comfortable sharing information about myself with other people unless they give me a reason not to
– I have nothing to hide, so I am comfortable with people knowing personal information about me
– Compared to others, I am more sensitive about the way other people or organizations handle my personal information
– Compared to others, I see more importance in keeping personal information private
– Compared to others, I am less concerned about potential threats to my personal privacy

Privacy in Autonomous Driving. The last part included the rating of privacy perception statements in the context of autonomous driving (see Table 2; compare [23, 15]). Further the participants were invited to think of certain traffic situations in which autonomous driving could be used. At last, the participants had the possibility to give feedback about the topic in general.

Table 2. Item example of participants' privacy perception of autonomous driving.

How do you evaluate the following statements? (1 = do not agree, 6 = totally agree)
– As a result of my usage of autonomous vehicles, others know more about me than I am comfortable with
– As a result of my usage of autonomous vehicles, information about me, that I consider private will be more easily available to others than I would like to
– As a result of my usage of autonomous vehicles, information about me is out there that, if used, will invade my privacy
– As a result of my usage of autonomous vehicles, my privacy will be invaded by others, who collect all data about me
– I feel I will have enough privacy when using autonomous vehicles
– I am comfortable with the amount of privacy I will have when using autonomous vehicles in the future
– I think my privacy is preserved when I use autonomous vehicles
– The above use of personal information for autonomous driving is an invasion of privacy

3.2 Sample/Participants

In total 157 participants took part with an age range of 16 to 67 years (**Mean** = 31.7; **S**tandard **D**eviation = 12.3). The gender distribution is slightly asymmetrical with 106 men (67.5%) and 51 women (32.5%). Most participants hold a driving license (97.5%). The sample contains 48.1% with a university degree or higher (n = 76), 33.1% with a technical college degree (n = 52) and 12.1% did vocational training (n = 19). All participants reported a rather high technical self-confidence with 4.43/6 (SD = 0.79). Cronbachs alpha for the 12 self-efficacy items were .85 respectively.

   Here, men are significantly more technical affine (M = 4.59; SD = 0.75) than women (M = 4.11; SD = 0.80) (t(155) = 3.61, p < .001). For further research, users had to classify if they used technical support systems (lane assistant, distance control, automatic parking, cruise control and brake assistant) in vehicles before. Here, the overall sample has rather little experience M = 2.10 (scale form 0 = no experience to 5 = experience with all systems). Participants, who use(d) none or one of the questioned driver assistance systems before, were classified as *laypeople* (n = 69, 43,9%), whereas participants, who have experience with two or more driver assistance systems were classified as *experienced* (n = 88, 56,1%). The distance control was used/is used by 40,8% (n = 64) participants, the lane assistant by 33,8% (n = 53) and the automatic parking by 26,8% (n = 42).

4   Results and Data Analysis

First, the findings for both privacy contexts on the complete sample will be reported. Afterwards, the effects of age, gender, previous experience with assistance systems and technical self-efficacy will be introduced extensively. The resulting data were analyzed by descriptive analysis and, with respect to the effects of user diversity, by uni- and multivariate analyses of variance ((M)ANOVA) as well as non-parametric counterparts. The level of significance was set to $\alpha = 0.05$. We report the perception of privacy related to the internet and autonomous driving.

4.1 Overall Findings

We report that the overall sample would in fact drive autonomous vehicles (75,2%; n = 118), while a smaller part would not drive such a vehicle (24,8%; n = 39). A closer look into the reasons against autonomous driving shows that out of the 39 non-drivers, 53,8% (n = 21) like driving themselves too much. Also the distrust in the technology was a highly anticipated reason (25,6%, n = 10). The sample's general disposition on privacy was rather indifferent (M = 3.60; center of scale at 3.50, SD = 0.07), while the privacy perceptions in the two technology contexts were just slightly higher (see Fig. 2.), with higher values indicating greater concerns about the preservation of privacy aspects.

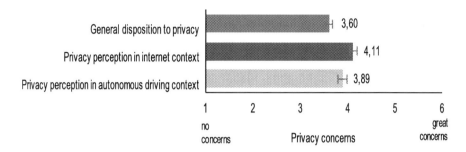

General disposition to privacy   3,60
Privacy perception in internet context   4,11
Privacy perception in autonomous driving context   3,89

1   2   3   4   5   6

no concerns   Privacy concerns   great concerns

Fig. 2. Means and standard deviations of privacy concerns regarding general disposition and technology usage contexts (min = 1, max = 6).

Looking at the relations between the personal disposition and the perception of privacy in both the internet and the autonomous driving context, it becomes clear that all factors were significantly positively intercorrelated (see Table 3).

Table 3. Pearson correlation coefficients and p-values of the general disposition on privacy and privacy perception in technology contexts.

		General disposition on privacy	Privacy perception in internet context	Privacy perception in autonomous driving context
General disposition on privacy	r	1	.239	.204
	p		.003*	.011*
Privacy perception in internet context	r		1	.603
	p			<.001*
Privacy perception in autonomous driving context	r			1
	p			

There was only a small correlation between the personal, general attitude towards privacy and the privacy perception in the different technology contexts. In contrast, the privacy perception of internet usage was highly correlated with the one of autonomous driving. Figure 3 gives a more detailed insight into the differences between the contexts regarding the agreement to privacy perception statements. Following, we report a general evaluation about which attitude towards privacy the user has in both, the context of internet usage and the theoretical context of driving autonomously (see Fig. 3).

There are several caveats in both context-based privacy perception results. The feeling of having "enough privacy when using internet/autonomous driving" results in a small agreement (M = 2.52, SD = 1.13/M = 2.73, SD = 1.28) whereas the fear, that the usage of either the internet or autonomous vehicles is an invasion in one's privacy results in a stronger agreement (M = 4.18, SD = 1.32/M = 4.03, SD = 1.53). Overall, the internet privacy concerns (Fig. 3 light blue bars) have a higher approval rate compared to the autonomous driving privacy concerns (Fig. 3 dark blue bars), except for the possible "invasion by others", who collect all the data about the user (internet: M = 3.78, SD = 1.40/autonomous driving: M = 3.85, SD = 1.54). Also, some approval

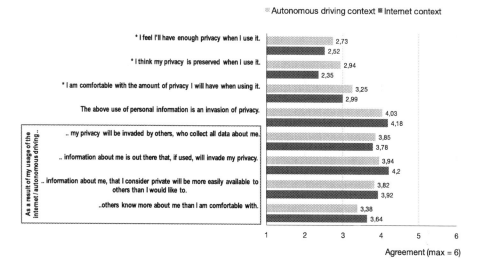

Fig. 3. Average agreement to privacy perception statements in both internet and autonomous driving context (min = 1, max = 6). (Color figure online)

rate differences between the contexts were statistically significant, namely the disparities regarding the belief that privacy will be preserved (F(1,156) = 28.844, p < .001), the satisfaction with the amount of privacy during use (F(1,156) = 5.088, p = .025), and the feeling to have enough privacy (F(1,156) = 4.007, p = .047), indicating an influence of context in the privacy perception of technology.

4.2 Effects of Age

In the following section, age is the first examined user factor considered in detail. First, no connection between age and the intention to drive autonomous vehicle was found. Although, age is a critical factor for experience with driver assistance systems (r = .318, p < .001, n = 157). Age had no influence on the disposition of privacy in general. There were also no significant differences/results in the agreement to the privacy perception statements in both contexts compared to the overall sample.

4.3 Effects of Gender

Gender appeared to be more formative influential. Although, an influence on the intention to drive autonomously could not be identified and the disposition of privacy in general was not significantly different between both sexes. Gender showed several significant effects on the privacy perception in the internet context (see Fig. 4).

As a result of my usage of the internet ...

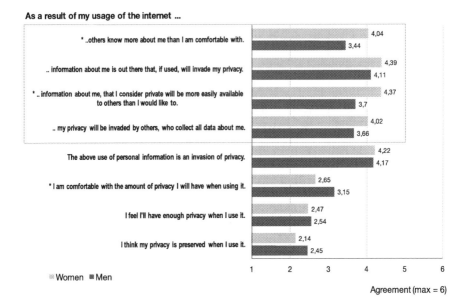

Fig. 4. Arithmetic means of statement agreements for internet-based perceived privacy differentiated by gender (N = 155), significant differences marked with * (min = 1, max = 6).

Women agree (M = 4.04, SD = 1.43) significantly more on the statement, that due to their usage of the internet, others know more about them, than they are comfortable with (t(155) = −2,374, p = .019) compared to men (M = 3.44, SD = 1.49). They also agree (M = 4.37, SD = 1.50) significantly more on the possibility that the information, which is considered as private, is more easily available to others due to their usage of the internet (t(155) = −2,663, p = .009) than men (M = 3.70, SD = 1.50). At last, a significantly lower agreement towards the comfort of the amount of privacy when using the internet (t(155) = 2,243, p = .026) could be identified for women (M = 2.65, SD = 1.32) compared to men (M = 3.15, SD = 1.32). Further, no significant differences could be identified concerning the perceived privacy statements in the autonomous driving context.

4.4 Effects of Technical Self-Efficacy

A close evaluation of the results shows a positive correlation between the technical self-efficacy and the intention to use autonomous driving (r = −.366, N = 157, p < .001). The higher the technical self-efficacy scores, the more likely is the intention to use autonomous vehicles. In contrast, it had no influence on the disposition of privacy in general. As to the significant differences of the privacy perception in internet contexts, see Table 4 (only significant results are shown):

Table 4. Overview of significant results in internet-based privacy perception and KUT.

As a result of my usage of the internet...	N	M (SD)	Result	Sig.
.. others know more about me than I am comfortable with	[157]		t(155) = 2,180, p = .031	*
Low KUT	83	3.88 (1.52)		
High KUT	74	3.36 (1.43)		
.. information about me, that I consider private will be more easily available to others than I would like to	[157]		t(155) = 2,677, p = .008	*
Low KUT	83	4.22 (1.53)		
High KUT	74	3.58 (1.43)		
I am comfortable with the amount of privacy I will have when using it	[157]		t(155) = −3,067, p = .003	*
Low KUT	83	2.69 (1.36)		
High KUT	74	3.32 (1.23)		
I think my privacy is preserved when I use it	[157]		t(155) = −2,710, p = .007	*
Low KUT	83	2.11 (1.12)		
High KUT	74	2.62 (1.26)		

The technical self-efficacy has also a significant influence on the privacy perception in autonomous driving contexts, see Table 5:

Table 5. Overview of significant results in automated driving-based privacy perception and KUT.

As a result of my usage of autonomous driving...	N	M (SD)	Result	Sig.
.. information about me, that I consider private will be more easily available to others than I would like to	[157]		t(155) = 2,646, p = .009	*
Low KUT	83	4.12 (1.53)		
High KUT	74	3.47 (1.53)		
I feel I'll have enough privacy when I use it	[157]		t(155) = −3,179, p = .002	*
Low KUT	83	2.43 (1.22)		
High KUT	74	3.07 (1.28)		
I am comfortable with the amount of privacy I will have when using it	[157]		t(155) = −2,199, p = .029	*
Low KUT	83	3.01 (1.49)		
High KUT	74	3.51 (1.35)		
I think my privacy is preserved when I use it	[157]		t(155) = −2,668, p = .008	*
Low KUT	83	2.66 (1.41)		
High KUT	74	3.26 (1.38)		

4.5   Effects of Previous Experience

With regard to previous experience, the intention to use autonomous vehicles did not show any significant differences compared to the overall sample. Further, no influence of previous experience on the disposition of privacy in general could be identified. There was also no significant difference/result in the agreement to the privacy perception statements in the internet context. Moreover, there were a few significant effects in the autonomous driving context, namely, the experienced group agreed stronger $(t(155) = -1,897, p = .060)$ on the statement "As a result of my usage of autonomous driving, information about me, that I consider private, will be more easily available to others than I would like to." $(M = 4.02, SD = 1.47)$ than the laypeople $(M = 3.55, SD = 1.64)$. Also the experienced group agreed stronger $(t(155) = -2,597, p = .010)$ on the statement "…information about me is out there, if used, will invade my privacy." $(M = 4.24, SD = 1.59)$ than the laypeople $(M = 3.57, SD = 1.64)$.

5   Discussion

Aiming a first impression of how context influences the perception of privacy in different technology contexts, we worked with a well-educated, highly technical affine, but diverse sample in terms of previous experience with driver assistance systems. A solid age range, but slightly asymmetrical gender distribution made a close look on the user specific factors possible. Further, the participants were analysed due to their general disposition to privacy. All questioned characteristics could be relevant corner stones for privacy perception in technological contexts. Also, the intention to use automated driving (in future) was questioned to identify two of the main groups (according to Rogers 2003): possible deniers or early adopters – which was not the case due to the overall high approval of using automated driving functions. Context-dependency was a former key factor of the willingness to share (private) data with V2X-technology [14], also the FIA (Federation Internationale de l'Automobile) reported similar outcomes in their report 2016 [26]. Therefore, one of the research questions addressed context as possible influential factor of privacy perception. Addressing the first research question, which user specific factors have influence on privacy perception, it can be stated that several results can be highlighted. Whereas age had almost no effect at all on the privacy perception or the intention to use autonomous vehicles, the consequence arises that privacy is a crucial factor of all age (timeless). This fact could be explained by a closer look on the age-range of the sample. Here, all participants could have been involved with either internet based applications or web-enabled devices. A general sensitivity for privacy (concerns) can be identified throughout the age of a user.

The intention to drive autonomous vehicles – which is overall present – is in general not influenced by any of the user factors, except the technical self-efficacy. A higher technical confidence relates to the agreement to use automated vehicles. Generally speaking, ones' capability to use technology is identified as the main key factor for privacy perception. Therefore, technology – especially data sensitive technology like connected or autonomous vehicles – should have the opportunity to train ones' capability, by different automation modi for example. The analysis revealed, that the less affine to technology a user is, significantly more concerns arise – in both the internet and the autonomous driving context. This could lead to the conclusion, that a profound understanding of how the technology works, overall experience and self-confidence with technology results in less concerns about the own privacy. Here, a transparent communication and information model could help educating people about their privacy options.

Speaking of previous experience, contrastingly, participants who used driver assistance systems in the past, have significantly stronger privacy concerns, but only in the autonomous driving context. Experience as such is according to that an intensifying factor in both directions.

, Another influencing factor seems to be gender. Women have significantly stronger concerns about their privacy in the internet context – also in the automated driving context, but not significantly – especially when it comes to what others may be able know about them.

Here, a more frequent use of different services could lead to a higher experience level or a higher frustration about the terms and conditions provided. Therefore, a questioning about general (previous) experience with internet-based services should be focused in future studies, to help identify, if this discrepancy is connected to usage and experience with the technology or gender.

Addressing the second research question, context can be characterized as driving factor for privacy perception. Here, several significant differences in privacy perception of the two domains were displayed. An overall scepsis towards both context-based privacy scenarios could be revealed, opening questions about privacy terms and conditions in general. Interestingly, the concerns of the autonomous context were not as strong as the concerns of the internet context, leading to the consideration that the more generalized topic (internet) is known for years and the use of autonomous vehicles is mostly a theoretical scenario. The disposition of privacy intercorrelated strongly with both context-based perceptions, indicating that concerned people do not put their attitudes aside, but the manifestation varies context-wise. The identified privacy concerns are also an indicator for a possible overall distrust in technology and the data handling of todays services and applications.

6   Conclusion and Outlook

The findings revealed interesting insights into effects of user diversity and even more the effects of context dependent technology perception. Although, the results show only a small part of the diversity of user types and only two different technology contexts, the identification of technical self-efficacy as one of the key factors, which influence the privacy perception of technology was possible. A replication of the study with a larger and more diverse sample should be a next step. Another limitation was the online-based study method, due to a difficult accessibility of e.g. hands on experience with the technology. Context is a crucial factor for a users' perception of privacy. Further research with technology-involving topics like medical care, communication tools confirm the users' need of a transparent communication model about privacy handling.

Acknowledgment. Many thanks go to Sarah Völkel, Florian Groh and Philipp Brauner for research assistance. This project was supported by the Center of European Research on Mobility (CERM) – funded by both strategy funds at RWTH Aachen University, Germany and the Excellence Initiative of German State and Federal Government. Further, thanks go to the project I2EASE, funded by the German Federal ministry of Research and Education [under the reference number 16EMO0142K].

References

1. Acquisti, A., Brandimarte, L., Loewenstein, G.: Privacy and human behavior in the age of information. Science **347**(6221), 509–514 (2015)
2. Akhter, S.H.: Privacy concern and online transactions: the impact of internet self-efficacy and internet involvement. J. Consum. Mark. **31**, 118–125 (2014)
3. Arning, K., Kowalewski, S., Ziefle, M.: Health concerns vs. mobile data needs: conjoint measurement of preferences for mobile communication network scenarios. Int. J. Hum. Ecol. Risk Assess. **20**(5), 1359–1384 (2014)
4. Blank, G., Dutton, W.H.: Age and trust in the Internet: the centrality of experience and attitudes toward technology in Britain. Soc. Sci. Comput. Rev. **30**(2), 135–151 (2012)
5. Boyd, D., Hargiattai, E.: Facebook privacy settings: who cares? First Monday **15**(8), 1–14 (2010)
6. Cambridge Centre for Smart Infrastructure and Construction. University of Cambridge (2017). http://www-smartinfrastructure.eng.cam.ac.uk. Accessed 16 Jan 2017
7. Goel, S., Yuan, Y.: Emerging research in connected vehicles (guest editorial). Intell. Transp. Syst. Mag. IEEE **7**(2), 6–9 (2015)
8. Karrer, K., Glaser, C., Clemens, C., Bruder, C.: Technikaffinität erfassen – der Fragebogen TA-EG. Online: Deutsches Zentrum für Luft- und Raumfahrt e.V (2015). https://www.re searchgate.net/profile/Carmen_Bruder/publication/266876811_Technikaffinitat_erfassen_-_ der_Fragebogen_TAEG/links/563c526708ae45b5d286f7d0.pdf?inViewer=0&pdfJsDown load=0&origin=publication_detail. Accessed 10 Jan 2017
9. Li, Y.: The impact of disposition to privacy, website reputation and website familiarity on information privacy concerns. Decis. Support Syst. **57**, 343–354 (2014). https://doi.org/ 10.1016/j.dss.2013.09.018. Accessed Dec 2016
10. Morton, A.: Measuring inherent privacy concern and desire for privacy-A pilot survey study of an instrument to measure dispositional privacy concern. In: 2013 International Conference on Social Computing (SocialCom), pp. 468–477. IEEE (2013)
11. Nissenbaum, H.: A contextual approach to privacy online. Daedalus **140**(4), 32–48 (2011)
12. Othmane, L.B., Weffers, H., Mohamad, M.M., Wolf, M.: A survey of security and privacy in connected vehicles. In: Benhaddou, D., Al-Fuqaha, A. (eds.) Wireless Sensor and Mobile Ad-Hoc Networks, pp. 217–247. Springer, New York (2015). https://doi.org/ 10.1007/978-1-4939-2468-4_10
13. Renn, O.: Three decades of risk research: accomplishments and new challenges. J. Risk Res. **1**, 49–71 (1998)
14. Schmidt, T., Philipsen, R., Ziefle, M.: User diverse privacy requirements for V2X-technology - quantitative research on context-based privacy aspects. In: Proceedings of the International Conference on Vehicle Technology and Intelligent Transport Systems (VEHITS 2016), pp. 60–67 (2016)
15. Schwaig, K.S., Segars, A.H., Grover, V., Fiedler, K.D.: A model of consumer's perception of the invasion of information privacy. Inf. Manag. **50**(1), 1–12 (2013). Accessed 15 Jan 2017

16. Siegrist, M., Keller, C., Cousin, M.-E.: Implicit attitudes toward nuclear power and mobile phone base stations: support for the affect heuristic. Risk Anal. **26**, 1021–1029 (2006)

17. Thelwall, M., Wilkinson, D., Uppal, S.: Data mining emotion in social network communication: gender differences in MySpace. J. Am. Soc. Inf. Sci. Technol. **61**(1), 190–199 (2010)

18. Trivisonno, R., Guerzoni, R., Vaishnavi, I., Soldani, D.: SDN-based 5G mobile networks: architecture, functions, procedures and backward compatibility. Emerg. Telecommun. Technol. **26**(1), 82–92 (2015)

19. Vance, A., Elie-Dit-Cosaque, C., Straub, D.W.: Examining trust in information technology artifacts: the effects of system quality and culture. J. Manag. Inf. Syst. **24**(4), 73–100 (2008)

20. Volvo Group.: Vision 2020 (2016). http://www.volvocars.com/intl/about/our-stories/made-by-sweden/vision-2020#. Accessed 15 Jan 2017

21. Klappstein, J., Vaudrey, T., Rabe, C., Wedel, A., Klette, R.: Moving object segmentation using optical flow and depth information. In: Wada, T., Huang, F., Lin, S. (eds.) PSIVT 2009. LNCS, vol. 5414, pp. 611–623. Springer, Heidelberg (2009). https://doi.org/10.1007/978-3-540-92957-4_53

22. Wilkowska, W., Ziefle, M.: Privacy and data security in E-health: requirements from the user's perspective. Health Inform. J. **18**, 191–201 (2012)

23. Xu, H., Teo, H.H., Tan, B.C.Y., Agarwal, R.: Effects of Individual Self-Protection, Industry Self-Regulation, and Government Regulations on Privacy Concerns: A Study of a Location-Based Services, Institute for Operations Research and the Management Sciences. https://faculty.ist.psu.edu/xu/papers/isrxu2012.pdf. Accessed 15 Jan 2017

24. Zaunbrecher, B., Ziefle, M.: Social acceptance and its role for planning technology infrastructure. A position paper, taking wind power plants as an example. In: 4th International Conference on Smart Cities and Green ICT Systems (SMARTGREENS 2015), pp. 60–65 (2015)

25. Ziefle, M., Himmel, S., Wilkowska, W.: When your living space knows what you do: acceptance of medical home monitoring by different technologies. In: Holzinger, A., Simonic, K.-M. (eds.) USAB 2011. LNCS, vol. 7058, pp. 607–624. Springer, Heidelberg (2011). https://doi.org/10.1007/978-3-642-25364-5_43

26. Federation Internationale de l'Automobile.: What Europeans Think About Connected Cars. http://www.mycarmydata.eu/wp-content/themes/shalashaska/assets/docs/FIA_survey_2016.pdf. Accessed 10 Jan 2017

From *Hörspiel* to Audio Fiction: Sound Design Perspectives for Blind and Visually Impaired People

Andrea Catropa[✉], Sergio Nesteriuk, and Gilbertto Prado

Graduate Program in Design, Anhembi Morumbi University, São Paulo, Brazil
andreacatropa@gmail.com, nesteriuk@hotmail.com,
gttoprado@gmail.com

Abstract. Since the emergence of radio, the *hörspiel* (audio drama) has demonstrated the possibility of incorporating the narratological inheritance to the technical specificities of sound language. The growing demand for accessible content expanded the audio narrative production through new technologies. Audiobooks and screen reader applications also have improved this process. However, they focus primarily on the semantic and verbal aspects of the text. This article endorses that sound design is a way to broaden the narrative potentialities for Blind and Visually Impaired People (BIVP) and at the same time to attract people with all levels of vision to the universe of innovative audio fiction.

Keywords: Accessibility · Inclusion · Sound design · Audio fiction
Well being

1 Introduction

If we consider the number of people affected by damages to the sight, we are dealing with a significant portion of the population. The International Classification of Diseases divides vision into 4 basic types: (1) normal vision; (2) moderate vision impairment; (3) severe vision impairment and (4) blindness. According to the World Health Organization, in 2017 an estimated 253 million people live with vision impairment; among them, 36 million are blind and 207 million are moderate to severe vision impaired [1].

In a society where the visual input is rapidly increasing, with all kinds of images emerging from digital media, the life quality of people with visual loss has new challenges as well as new possibilities. If technology brought new ways of carrying on our daily lives, we could not fail to include this significant amount of the population in the scenario of these changes.

In addition, when we think about creating a more inclusive and accessible society for people with visual impairment and blindness (BVIP), we must defend their right to art and entertainment. Regarding this matter, we consider that narrative constitutes one of the most fruitful artistic fields to exploit for people with vision loss, as for its importance in culture, as for the potential that sound design brings to the development of audio plays.

Oral narratives are of ancient origin but recording and broadcasting technologies only have gained momentum from the first decades of the 20th century. Artists such as

© Springer International Publishing AG, part of Springer Nature 2018
V. G. Duffy (Ed.): DHM 2018, LNCS 10917, pp. 268–279, 2018.
https://doi.org/10.1007/978-3-319-91397-1_23

Kurt Schwitters and Hugo Ball, for example, created poetic compositions using the sound in an innovative and irreverent way. If the European vanguards had opened the way for sound experiences with words, the *hörspiel* (or audio drama) consolidated, from the earliest days of the radio, a path to explore sound narratives.

Almost one hundred years after the birth of *hörspiel*, we have achieved technological resources that the first audio dramas' authors never dreamed of. Nowadays, with the diffusion of digital media and the internet, sound narratives can be produced, stored and listened to in different ways, allowing people to access it more efficiently.

The pioneering experience and consistent production of numerous audio dramas in the past have facilitated the creation of concepts and an entire field of study about the particularities of sound in a narrative structure. One of the modalities of sound narrative that is becoming more and more popular is the audiobook. This kind of adaptation of texts written for the audio environment has several uses because it allows a book to be enjoyed in conditions that are impossible to read (such as when someone is driving or washing dishes). More importantly, it also promotes accessibility for those who are visually-impaired as for other disabilities.

Nowadays France leads the way on the production of book adaptations, allowing BVIP to access several kinds of publications, such as fiction, non-fiction, and cookbooks. Since 2006, French law makes it possible to transcribe them into braille or sound just after they have been launched.

"In the past few years, new technology has brought about major changes in the daily life of blind and severely visually impaired people - 1.2 million in France, 285 million worldwide. Services for downloading audiobooks have appeared in many countries. There are also special players for listening to books. PCs and smartphones now offer similar functions. Braille terminals are available too, with scope for reading and input" [2].

Among the BVIP, sound narratives have the advantage of not needing any special learning, such as Braille books, to be enjoyed. As a tactile reading system, based upon cells composed of dots, Braille has two forms: non-contracted (alphabetic) or contracted (literary). The first one, easier to learn, is used to make brief notes or read urban signs. But the second one, used for reading books and magazines, according to The American Foundation for the Blind, takes an adult one year of weekly lessons to be learned. In this sense, the diffusion of narratives by audio becomes more universally accessible than the texts in Braille.

However, if a pleasant and clear voice-over, along with the use of sound effects can make enjoyable the experience of listening to an audiobook, we argue that sound narratives have specific resources to be used. These enrich the experience of the listener and, for the BVIP can mean the contact with works as complex and instigating as the best achievements of other areas, such as opera, cinema, dance and the visual arts.

If an adaptation of self-help book or detective novel can fit well into a mimetic structure, based on oral interpretation, it may not apply to formally challenging literary works such as *Orlando: A Biography*, by Woolf [3]; *Finnegan's Wake*, by Joyce [4] or *A Clockwork Orange*, by Burgess [5]. How can we allow BVIP to have an experience when listening to such adaptations that is compatible with the impact that these literary works may cause on the reader?

In this case, a more appropriate relationship between form and content would benefit from an inventive exploration of the voice and effects used. To do so is necessary to emphasize the sound specificities that allow exploring its creative potential widely. Thus, in this article we will return to the story of the emergence of audio dramas, from the conception of what was *hörspiel*, to describe the main elements of sound design that can be used in the composition of quality audio fiction.

2   Audio Drama: From Radio and Beyond

The creation and the future consolidation of the radio during the 1920's and the 1930's made this medium develop in its various technical and aesthetic aspects. Radio stations created and experimented, in addition to the musical and journalistic programming - evidenced in most of today's broadcasts - grids with a diverse range of programs.

One of the genres that had significant development in this period was the radio play. According to Scheffner, the first audio dramas (*hörspiel*) came together with the first official broadcast of the medium in Germany on October 29, 1923 [6]. At that time, theater pieces were adapted, called "radio plays." Regarding the genesis of this genre, we must consider a peculiar aspect:

"The new acoustic art - the radio drama - did not arise as painting or architecture, from an organically born necessity - emerged, like cinema, from a technical invention. Few traditional artistic forms had such a synthetic birth. No other, with such a comprehensive transmission system" [7].

The radio play can be defined as a genuinely radiophonic genre (since it emerges and develops at the core of the radio) with the capacity to assume the most diverse narrative forms, from the police novel to the documentary and the children's story. It is evident that, at first, this genre justified itself by remediating media [8] such as theater and literature, especially novels with serialized narrative structure. In the same way as, later, it ended up influencing television genres, such as sitcoms and soap operas.

Over time autonomy was achieved, allowing *hörspiel* to develop its own language, dialoguing with the intrinsic characteristics of the radio medium, but also surpassing it and migrating to other media, where it will be called audio drama, audio play or audio fiction (a term that we prefer for its versatility). This autonomy does not, however, invalidate the existence of hybridizations with forms of literature, music, and dramatic art; but always without being confused with these, since audio fiction has developed as a genre of its own and not as a kind of recorded text or sound theater, for example.

In this sense, one of the leading characteristics of the genre lies in its broad synesthetic and creative potential. By not working with visual images, the narrative sound can stimulate sensations and the imagination of each listener - without giving up their collective task, capable of simultaneously reaching a group of people (audience). Thus, it has the function not only of entertaining or representing a given immediate reality but of overcoming it, reaching the universe of meaning, the imaginary and the adventure of language, which makes it a particularly interesting medium for BVIP.

Audio fiction must be understood, not only as a finished product but complex process, a phenomenon. We will cover here some of the leading aspects present in this process in their dimensions of production [9] and reception.

3 Principles and Elements of the Sound Language

The creation and analysis of an audio fiction presuppose an understanding of what Schafer called the soundscape: the diegetic or extradiegetic (re)creation of a sound environment ("real" or "virtual") in its physical and synesthetic aspects [10]. Just as we can create, describe, and illustrate an environment through words and visual images, we are also able to use the sound to do so. The soundscape of an environment should not only be descriptive but also to capture its sensorial atmosphere.

The design of sound ambiance is vital to establish the setting of a narrative to BVIP. We can compare the soundscape of an audio fiction to the scenario of a movie for a sighted person. It is something that can act as a support to the plot, or it can be so crucial that it is developed as a character of the storyline. An example of this last case, in cinema, is *The Shining* (1977), a film adaptation of Stephen Kings' book directed by Kubrick [11]. In this classic horror picture, the hotel where Jack Torrance's family gets stuck in after a winter storm (called Overlook Hotel) is as important as the story's leading roles.

Each soundscape is composed of two elements, layers, and sound textures. By sound layers we can understand the different layers of sounds that appear in an environment, that is, the number of distinct sounds that can be heard and identified at the same time. Usually, the sounds come in different intensities of volume, and they can be understood as background or as foreground.

The sound designer's sensibility is fundamental to decide how to choose between the varieties of resources. Not always the excess of distinct sonorities works in the soundscape; on the contrary, it can often result in noise pollution. Likewise, the intensity of the different volumes (measured in decibels) is fundamental to reinforce an idea of likelihood, when this is the case.

We can also identify a proper tone, a specific low or high tessitura, at each layer of sound that is called the sound texture. In other words, it is the characteristic or set of gathered features that make a given sound to be understood as such and not like any other.

Creating elaborate soundscapes requires extensive knowledge of sound design, besides the simple use of foley and sound effects. By sound design, we must understand the whole process of research, selection, application, and adequacy of a sound element. Some people nowadays use the term sound designer, rather than audio technician, to designate the professional responsible for this task, because, in a way, the sound designer makes with sound, what the designer traditionally does with the visual. In addition to sensitivity and technical mastery, the professional responsible for sound design should understand the characteristics and relationships between the five different elements of sound design: voice, music, foley, sound effects and "silence."

By voice we understand all types of intelligible or unintelligible sound (above or below the semantic level) emitted by the human speech apparatus - and therefore, not only "speech." Each voice is unique and depends mainly on three factors: physical, psychological and sociocultural. The first factor is defined in part by genetic inheritance, in part by different training techniques; the second, by the very way of being or acting of a person and its personality; and the third one is defined by the relationship of the self with specific groups in their life in Society.

Voice is undoubtedly one of the leading elements of audio fiction since it allows a rescue and an update of orality, mediated by sound technologies [12]. The voice on the radio is a mediated orality because in the first instance the microphone picks up the voice in a way different from what the human ear will do, what explains the strangeness of hearing one's own voice when recorded. Secondly, once recorded and stored, the voice can become raw material for further manipulation in its most diverse spectra. It can be thought and used in three different ways: speech, vocal possibilities and other sounds of the voice.

According to Klippert [13], up until the early 1960s, *hörspiel* was considered a work of art because it lacked many post-production resources. The use of music in the sound narratives was expanded until it came to be used in three main ways: as "ambient," incidental music or as a leitmotiv. In the first case, the music serves to create or to reinforce a certain developed atmosphere:

"Composers dedicated to *hörspiel*, such as Hugo Pfister and Winfried Zillig, understood music in its dramaturgical function as a means of complementing, intensifying or structuring processes of spoken dramatic action. Hugo Pfister wrote that Hörspiel's music has the power to give atmosphere to a scene, staying in the background, perhaps almost inaudible. (…) There was a consensus that the music of radio drama should never be an end in itself" [13].

Incidental music is the music that is "playing" in the scene, and that can be confused with the other sonorities of a given scene (diegetic). It differs from the previous category in its essence because in this case, it represents the sonority of a sound body present in the scene and not of a soundtrack "evoked" by the director (extradiegetic), although it can be used with a similar function.

Music as leitmotiv has the function of associating a musical sonority to a specific dramatic situation, returning, usually, countless times during history, whenever this situation (re)appears. Thus, the same narrative can present more than one leitmotiv, which, in turn, can be performed with different executions. However, it is not a standard procedure in radio plays, unlike television, the presence of numerous leitmotivs in the same story, because the listener does not count with the support of visual images to facilitate these associations about a dramatic situation.

The foley is equivalent to what many call sound effects - we shall see later the distinction between the terms - that is, the sounds emitted by the sound sources present in a given dramatic scene.

"The first and main difference between the various sounds our ears hear is the difference between noise and musical sounds… We realize that, generally, a noise is accompanied by rapid alternation between different kinds of sound. Think, for example, in the rattling of a carriage, in the granite of the pavement, in the water spreading and swarming in a waterfall or the waves of the sea, in the rustling of leaves in a forest. In all these cases we have fast and irregular, but distinctly perceptible, alternations between various kinds of sounds, which manifest intermittently" [10].

Two different categories can be thought about the use of foley: natural or artificial. The natural foley corresponds to the use of a sound whose actual sound reference exist "outside the studios" (diegetic sound). It may have, in this case, a figurative function, that is, the sound is used as an immediate correspondent to that sound source; in a scene that happens in a farm, it is heard the neighing of a horse, for example. Already as a function of metaphor, we use a sound recognized as a natural foley, outside its original context.

Artificial foley correspond to the creation of a sound whose immediate referent did not exist "outside the studios" (non-diegetic or extradiegetic sound). It is used as a sound representation of an unknown object or else merely as a more abstract and formal function, without being associated with a specific sound source, and yet not confused with music.

Sound effects are any intentional type of filter, distortion or manipulation that significantly changes the final shape of the sound in its physical constitution (wavelength). Currently, sound effects are numerous and can be produced and combined with each other *ad infinitum* in soundboard, mixer or specific software. The echo, for instance, is one of the most well-known sound effects: it's a reflection that makes the sound arrive at the listener with a delay when we consider the moment of its emission.

The absence of audible sounds, that is, silence can also be considered as a form of expression, as we find it in minimalist works, notably in John Cage's work. The American musician and composer, influenced by the teachings of Zen Buddhism, had two significant experiences to think about the role and importance of silence in a sound piece.

Absolute silence can only exist in situations in which sound cannot propagate - as in a vacuum, for example. Humans can listen to frequencies between 20 and 20,000 Hz, which means that no natural environment provides absolute silence for the human being. Even the quietest environment or situation that we may know or have experienced has a minimal sound unit, identified by audio professionals as "breath," and varies at each specific location. In searching for the characteristics and possibilities of silence, John Cage remained for some time in an anechoic chamber, which prevents the reflection of sound waves and is isolated from any noise. About this experience, he tells:

"I thought there was something wrong with the room, some leak. I looked for the sound engineer and told him that the anechoic chamber had some problems: 'I can hear sounds inside. How is it possible?'. Then he asked me to describe them; I described them as a bass and treble sounds. 'Well,' he said, 'the treble sound is your nervous system, and the bass sound is the noise in your bloodstream.' So, it became clear to me that silence does not exist, that it is a mental matter. The sounds you hear are probably silent if you do not want them. But they're always ringing. There is always something to listen" [14].

In the second experiment, Cage composed, in 1952, a work entitled 4′33″, whose score has only time comments, without musical notes, which shifted the focus of interest out of work itself. In this manner, the composition incorporated the external characteristics of its surrounding reality, the sound to which attention is paid during its performance. The music is always the same, what changes is precisely the sound environment around you. This work will produce, each time it is executed, a different result depending on the time and space. About 4'33", the composer stated:

"(…) Has changed my mind, of course, in the sense of appreciating all those sounds that I do not compose. I discovered that this piece is the one that is happening all the time. I wanted people to find out that ambient sounds are often more interesting than the sounds we hear in a concert hall" [14].

Therefore, silence in audio fiction should always be considered in its figurative sense, because in the studio and the reception environment of the listener, there will always be sound, desirable or not (unwanted noise). The "silence" can, therefore, appear in different forms with different functions. In principle, every form of speech (and sound, in a general way) is understandable only by the presence of "silence." If speech were to form an eternal continuum, we would probably not be able to distinguish the changes and nuances present in its dynamics. Pauses during speech may still represent characteristics of the character with nervousness, anxiety, doubt, sadness, hesitation, etc. Also, "silence" can also be used as an element of absence, allowing the creation of an idea of the passage of time, of reflection by the listener or of expectation of a fact that will occur, creating a climate of suspense that precedes the action.

The use of these five elements of the sound design of an audio fiction usually takes place via the use of electronic or digital equipment, such as the soundboard, mixers, and, more recently, the computers. The art of audio fiction is born into this equipment through the intermediation of a technical-creative process between its first conception and its final transmission.

Besides this technical knowledge, that is essential to building a repertoire of possibilities to the sound designer; he must also consider the available data about BVIP sensory perception. To create exciting art pieces for people with disabilities, authors and producers must take this public into account from the beginning of the conception of audio fiction. "People who are blind use parts of their brain that normally handle for vision to process language, as well as sounds – highlighting the brain's extraordinary ability to requisition unused real estate for new functions." [15]

The concept of neuroplasticity in the blind demonstrates that sensory deprivation can cause the brain to modify itself to perfect its behavioral adaptation. In an experiment to investigate an alternative approach to visual rehabilitation, Ella Striem-Amitt used a sensory substitution device (SSD) to translate visual information using sounds. "A neuroimaging investigation of the processing of SSD information showed that despite their lack of visual experience during development, the visual cortex of the congenitally blind was activated during the processing of soundscapes (images represented by sounds)" [16].

Therefore, art can dialogue with science to create potentially playful audio fictions, but also stimulate the senses of BVIP audience. If the brain structure that is usually responsible for vision is used to process the sounds for blind people, we might think of audio fiction as a potential substitute to audiovisual entertainment for those who have vision loss. Working the soundscape with layers, textures, voice, and music - all of it punctuated by silence - can build audio fictions that reach BVIP in extraordinary ways, amplifying their sensibility and helping to expand their imagination.

Thus, after dwelling on the specificities of the audio fiction genre, we need to think about its current situation and consider its future transformations that may contribute to increasing its interest not only for BVIP but also for a wider audience.

4   State of the Art and Perspectives

The fields of entertainment and information in the contemporary world seem to point out to two main approaches. The first of them lies on the fictionalization of the real and the creation of fantastic universes, tasks that are facilitated by the technological resources of the present. The second is based on the search for truth, anchored in the reality of the facts. Whether through an audio fiction or news broadcast on the radio, both of them have a mediation of the language that is crossed by the medium where this information will be transmitted.

This same technical-technological feature in the making of audio fiction also permeates the process of transmitting the audio itself. Thus, audio fiction could assume the character of *ars multiplicata*, which allowed the appropriation and subversion of the radio as a means of mass communication. It was possible, then, to take advantage of the learning process achieved by radio production to make works of sophisticated quality and great cultural and social potential.

It was precisely those possibilities that attracted authors such as Eugene Ionescu, Bertold Brecht, Walter Benjamin and Orson Welles, among countless others, to write and direct their radio plays. This significant moment in radio became known as its "Golden Age," with a program schedule full of good quality pieces coupled with an extreme diversity of genres. Moreover, in most countries, the radio played the role of the central means of mass communication. All this made the radio count, in addition to a broad reach, with a large staff of professionals and with substantial financial incomes to support this structure.

The arrival and the popularization of television caused that, in most parts of the world, the radio lost its hegemonic post for the audiovisual rival and, more recently, for the internet. When the broadcasters lost part of their audience and resources, they had to gradually adjust themselves to a new reality, represented mainly by a decrease in their costs and structures - which, in principle, should not necessarily justify a creative and experimental limitation of the medium.

As the private and public capital diminished in the radio, most of the artists and professionals migrated to the television, lending their knowledge and experiences to the construction of the language of the new environment. In addition to some technical innovations in its history - such as the cassette tape, the effect table, the transistor and the headset - the radio starts to be rethought and begins to restructure itself. However, in this process of rebirth, the radio has renounced the kind of programming that made its glory in the past, the narrative genre and its various formats, such as radio soap opera, documentary, sketches, series and the *hörspiel*.

However, this reorganization of the vehicle represents, in addition to the abandonment of many of its formats, the abandonment of many of its potentialities, since radio broadcasters have given up studios, artists, writers, producers, to operate within much more restricted perspectives than those of the period of its apogee.

Some may argue that this is due to a change in the public's taste or the fact that television has occupied that space. But to maintain a "24-hour on-air" schedule and at the same time to operate with a shortage of funds has limited the radio to a production structure that does not allow it to perform this type of production. At least, not in the same way and with the same frequency as it has been done previously. Even in the news media, so crucial in today's radio, there are almost no documentaries and reports of more massive scale and formal elaboration. The communication is usually limited in these cases to coverage of events and live commentary.

The reduction of productions such as radio soap operas, radio documentaries, and sound adaptations does not necessarily mean disinterest of the public about these productions, but the inability, for various reasons, of the radio to realize them. As rare as they are praiseworthy are the spaces within the stations destined for the production and transmission of the narrative genre, and even of other modalities considered more experimental. Thus, conventional radio is, unfortunately, less and less the space for innovation or even the production of more elaborate and sophisticated works.

In this sense, in recent years, besides community and state radios, new alternatives have appeared for an expanded performance of the radio medium. Educational and university projects, in addition to a plethora of actions for the third sector, are demonstrating that there are perspectives on the creative use of sound language. The advent of digital and new technologies, such as Web radios and podcasts, offers new possibilities for the production and dissemination of the genre in sound media. Here we cite the example of BBC audio dramas, where we find potent adaptations of books such as Gibson's *Neuromancer* [17] and Bradbury's *Fahrenheit 451* [18].

These potentialities make viable the idea of a "possible radio," as imagined by Brecht [19], who defended the end of the bourgeois radio and its transformation into a weapon of a democratic society. The author believed in the effective bidirectionality in broadcasting and that, therefore, the medium could no longer be an instrument controlled by a privileged minority: producers and owners of radio stations. We can speculate that this non-hierarchical conception, from a many-to-many production, in which all could be simultaneously emitters and receivers, has some structural similarity to what is nowadays called potential of the internet.

Thus, bidirectionality becomes possible not only within the equation "listener-listener," but also in the sense that the distance between "producer-consumer" becomes smaller and smaller. As in the musical field, sound productions of a more independent character can already be performed with a more straightforward and more accessible structure than before. It is already within reach to listen to sound narratives, sound poems and other more experimental works produced within studios and structures much smaller than those of radio stations.

Once the desired bidirectionality is achieved, it is still the moment, according to Brecht [19], to think of creating quality pieces that are effective with the intrinsic characteristics of that media. That is, works designed, produced and transmitted exclusively for sound language, and that know how to explore the expression forms of each audio medium.

Moreover, if we consider the research in which Agnieszka Walczak and Louise Fryer tested the impact of audio description (AD) on dimensions of presence, we can state that the creative and detailed narratives provide more immersive experience to BVIP than the objective descriptions. Thus, the sound design used with excellence to produce good audio fictions from an artistic point of view can also contribute to enhance the understanding of space and location for people with vision loss [20].

5 Conclusion

The traditional radio play is also known as *hörspiel* constitutes a link between narrative, one of the most traditional elements of our culture, and radio, one of the most interesting and democratic technological achievements of humankind. The narrative forms initially transmitted by the radio waves today can be expanded by the most diverse media and diffuse sound codes through the internet.

One must also consider that the act of narrating facts and events, of storytelling, accompanies man long before the emergence of the radio. The desire to record these narratives reveals itself in diverse forms, from the first cave paintings to the video games that use technological supports of the last generation.

"Moreover, under these almost infinite forms, the narrative is present at all times, all places, in all societies and begins with the history of humanity. There is nowhere, no people without narrative. All human groups have their narratives, and often these narratives are shared by men of different and even opposing cultures. Narrative ridicules good and bad literature. International, transhistorical, transcultural, the narrative is there, with life" [21].

In this way, the sound narrative, while dialoguing with an entire narratological heritage, incorporates characteristics of sound language and its means of production, transmission, and reception. It is necessary not only to rescue the genre but also to update it for the new generations in the face of the profound social and technological changes experienced in the last decades.

Such changes have raised some possibilities already pointed out by Schöning regarding the development of *hörspiel* as an "(…) autonomous artistic product and disconnectable from the medium in which it was born" [7]. Today, audio drama can overcome the limits inherent in radio, thus exceeding the boundaries of its home environment. With this, the genre came to be called audio fiction, sound narrative or even audio play, which are broader and generic designations, capable of accounting for the new scope reached.

Regardless of its transmission or distribution support, the narrative sound is a possible way to shelter and disseminate, either for specific niches or millions of people, the most diverse folkloric, mythical, romantic or popular narrative modalities. This genre helps to rescue, stimulate, research, exchange and recreate stories that have always fascinated man.

The audio fiction can still reach a portion of the population that can't access content in other media, such as the blind and the visually impaired people. Because BVIP doesn't find in audiovisual vehicles, like television or internet sites, for instance, independence from the visual aspect, they are discriminated by the mainstream culture. Watching a movie or navigating through Facebook can be defying and frustrating at the same time because those who lack vision misses most of the content.

Beyond BVIP, audio fiction also reaches a public who already establish relations with other media and supports, but who do not know the constitutive forms of sound language. It should be noted that, in this case, audio fiction does not represent a "threat" to other forms; it is "old news" capable of (re) teaching people to listen. It is not, therefore, a matter of seeking to rescue the past, but to reinvent the future.

If the sound designers are familiar with the concept of universal design [22, 23], they must pursue its principles and apply them to achieve an amplified notion of accessibility. Particularly about perceptible information (principle four), which reinforces the importance of redundancy and provides compatibility with devices used by people with sensory limitations [22]. As previously stated, audio narratives have both cognitive enhancement and entertainment potentialities for BVIP. Considering the development of audio-fiction not only the elements of sound but also of accessibility, is fundamental. Therefore, universal design can inspire the delivery of content in various audio formats, which can be accessed online or downloaded to the listener's smartphone, for example. Also, information and additional material on each production can be disseminated in different ways, considering the four officially classified types of vision [1]. Why not create, for example, a site about an audio fiction, which brings the details of this work in audio, but also in images and letters that can be enlarged?

Decentralized distribution and collaborative possibilities not restricted to the geographical proximity afforded by digital media can amplify the diversity of audio fiction. We hope, therefore, that alongside the adaptations, specific narratives for the sound medium will also be produced, whose contents may be relevant to the BVIP with themes and scripts motivated by their reflections and experiences. Ideally, these pieces could hire BVIP as consultants, actors, and directors of content to increase the employ ability of people with visual disabilities. The more creative these audio fictions are, the higher the audience they will attract, and may even include transmedia elements to enable interaction with relatives and friends of BVIP, making the society more aware of the specific challenges they face in the world.

References

1. World Health Organization (2017). http://www.who.int/mediacentre/factsheets/fs282/en/
2. Cabut, S.: France leads the way on audiobooks for blind and visually impaired people - new technology and download services allow for fast and easy access. In: The Guardian, London (2013). https://www.theguardian.com/society/2013/dec/31/digital-audiobooks-visually-impaired-download-france
3. Woolf, V.: Orlando: A Biography. Harvest House, Eugene (2016)
4. Joyce, J.: Finnegans Wake. Important Books Press, London (2013)
5. Burgess, A.: A Clockwork Orange-Burgess Tribute Edition. Independently Published (2018)
6. Scheffner, H.: For a radio play theory. In: Sperber, B.G. (org.) Introduction to the Radio Play, pp. 111–164. EPU – Editora Pedagógica e Universitária (Martins Fontes), São Paulo (1980). (in Portuguese)

7. Schöning, K.: Listen to radio play: in defense of an abandoned child. In: Sperber, B.G. (org.) Introduction to the Radio Play, pp. 167–188. EPU – Editora Pedagógica e Universitária (Martins Fontes), São Paulo (1980). (in Portuguese)
8. Bolter, J.D., Grusin, R.A.: Remediation: Understanding New Media. MIT Press, Cambridge (2000)
9. McLeish, R., Link, J.: Radio Production. Focal Press, New York (2016)
10. Schafer, R.M.: Soundscape: Our Sonic Environment and the Tuning of the World. Destiny, Rochester (1993)
11. Kubrick, S.: The Shining. Distributed by Warner Bros, 144 minutes (1980)
12. Silva, J.L.O.A.: Radio: Mediated Orality. The Spot and Elements of the Radio Language. Annablume, São Paulo (1999). (in Portuguese)
13. Klippert, W.: Elements of the radio play. In: Sperber, B.G. (org.) Introduction to the Radio Play, pp. 11–110. EPU – Editora Pedagógica e Universitária (Martins Fontes), São Paulo (1980). (in Portuguese)
14. Cage, J.: Interview. In: Garcia, R.L. (org.) Voices & Visions: An Overview of American Art and Culture. Iluminuras, São Paulo (1996). (in Portuguese)
15. Hamzelou, J.: Blind People Repurpose the Brain's Visual Areas for Language. New Scientist, London (2017). https://www.newscientist.com/article/2147696-blind-people-repurpose-the-brains-visual-areas-for-language/
16. Striem-Amit, E.: Neuroplasticity in the blind and sensory for vision substitution. Ph.D. thesis. Hebrew University of Jerusalem, Department of Neurobiology (2014). https://scholar.harvard.edu/striemamit/publications/neuroplasticity-blind-and-sensory-substitution-vision
17. Gibson, W.: Neuromancer. Penguin Random House, New York (2016)
18. Bradbury, R.: Fahrenheit 451 – 60th Anniversary Edition. Simon & Schuster, New York (2012)
19. Brecht, B.: Radio as a means of communication. Screen **20**(3–4), 24–28 (1979). https://doi.org/10.1093/screen/20.3-4.24. Society for Education in Film and Television, London (Translated by Hood S)
20. Walczak, A., Fryer, L.: Creative description: the impact of audio description style on presence in visually impaired audiences. Br. J. Vis. Impairment **35**(1), 6–17 (2017). https://doi.org/10.1177/0264619616661603
21. Barthes, R.: Introduction to the Structural Analysis of the Narrative. Hill and Wang, New York (1974). (Translated by Miller R)
22. Connell, B.R., Jones, M., Mace, R., Mueller, J., Mullick, A., Ostroff, E., Sanford, J., Steinfeld, E., Story, M., Vanderheiden, G.: The Principles of Universal Design. The National Institute on Disability and Rehabilitation Research, U.S. Department of Education/NC State University, The Center for Universal Design (1997). https://projects.ncsu.edu/design/cud/about_ud/udprinciplestext.htm
23. Lidwell, W., Holden, K., Butler, J.: Universal Principles of Design, Revised and Updated: 125 Ways to Enhance Usability, Influence Perception, Increase Appeal, Make Better Design Decisions, and Teach through Design. Rockport Publishers, Beverly (2010)

SEE BEYOND: Enhancement – Strategies in Teaching Learning as a Stimulus to Creativity in Fashion Design

Geraldo Coelho Lima Júnior[✉] and Rachel Zuanon

Sense Design Lab, Graduate Program in Design, Anhembi Morumbi University,
São Paulo, Brazil
glimadesign58@gmail.com, rzuanon@anhembi.br,
rachel.z@zuannon.com.br

Abstract. The creative capacity of the brain is a valuable aid to learning. Studies of the Neurosciences when applied to the area of teaching/learning, provide an understanding of the cognitive processes of the brain; the mapping and formation of images; human behaviour; and the support tools for teachers and students. This kind of assistance, to a great extent underpins the assimilation of information that is conveyed in the classroom and the consolidation of knowledge in the memory, so that it can be elicited by the students on future occasions. Against this background and based on the Neuroeducation' studies, the SEE BEYOND method has been incorporated as a means of including sensorimotor stimuli in the progressive stages of the project and as a result, enlarging the methodological framework that is traditionally employed for higher education training courses in fashion design. This paper addresses the main results and benefits obtained from the application of this method to the "Enhancement" module. This module covers studies of shapes and volumes as well as colours and surface textile design. Its parameters were determined by the course taught to a group of students with visual impairment in the city of Sao Paulo (Brazil), in the period August–December 2015.

Keywords: Fashion design · Neuroeducation · Creativity
SEE BEYOND method · Visual impairment

1 Introduction

Learning takes place as a result of the formation and consolidation of links between the nerve cells. It is the outcome of chemical and structural alterations in an individual's nervous system which require energy and time to be fully manifested. It is a personal and private phenomenon which conforms to individual historical circumstances [1].

According to Damásio [2], mental maps are not static as in classical cartography. They are unstable and shifting all the time to reflect the changes that are occurring in the neurons which supply them with information. These maps, in turn, also reflect the changes that occur within our bodies and in the world around us, as well as the fact that we ourselves are also constantly in a state of movement.

© Springer International Publishing AG, part of Springer Nature 2018
V. G. Duffy (Ed.): DHM 2018, LNCS 10917, pp. 280–294, 2018.
https://doi.org/10.1007/978-3-319-91397-1_24

This means that it can be said that learning takes place by means of the same changes that occur in the neurons, as well as in an awareness of our surroundings and everything that forms a part of it.

The study of neuroscience is becoming an essential research endeavour for the understanding of the mechanisms of learning insofar as it throws light on the following: the cognitive processes of the brain; mapping and image formation; human behaviour; and support tools for teachers and students.

The field of neuroeducation combines research in the areas of neuroscience, neurology, psychology, pedagogical studies and teaching methodologies concerned with planning lessons and offering a wide range of opportunities for the application of lesson content from the subjects of the students. These studies have emerged as a continuous activity and subject of interest for an increasingly large number of teachers devoted to assessing the effectiveness of a new teaching model.

It is against this background that the "SEE BEYOND" method is employed. This method seeks (a) to broaden the scope of stimuli experienced by the students, whether with or without visual impairment; (b) enhance the teaching/learning process; and (c) raise an awareness of the design features needed for compiling collections in fashion design. Didactic materials are employed that are of a wide-ranging nature and generally not adopted in higher education institutions in Brazil. In other words, there is a recognition of the value, conception and application of instruments and activities that are geared towards the sensorimotor and cognitive stimulation of the students (whether blind or with normal sight), for teaching the methodology required for the fashion design project. For this reason this study is structured in three modules: (A) Foundation; (B) Enhancement; (C) Materialization. In the domain of (A) (Foundation), the aim is to concentrate on outlining the basis of the knowledge of design and fashion in a way that it can represent a theoretical framework for undertaking projects. With regard to (B) (Enhancement), this is devoted to teaching all the stages related to carrying out projects in fashion design. In the case of (C) (Materialization), all the knowledge acquired in the two previous stages is summarized and applied to a fashion collection project [3].

This paper focuses on the main results obtained and the benefits of the Enhancement module for (a) the training of the students with visual impairment and the students with normal sight; (b) the inclusion of the results in Higher Education Fashion Design courses in Brazil; and (c) the recognition of the value of self-esteem and attainment of well-being.

2   Neuroeducation: Strategies for Active Learning

During the teaching/learning process, passive students who do not take part in the set activities in the classroom, will definitely achieve unsatisfactory results. "Learning is partly based on the capacity of the brain to create" [4]. In view of this, it is essential for students to be stimulated to creativity and proactivity or rather to become players in a process that encourages them to stimulate their own learning with a view to nurturing the mental states related to pleasure and achievement. These are directly linked to the limbic cortex and play an essential role in the area of teaching.

In these conditions, the teacher is not just someone who simply transmits the lesson content of the classes; what is required is cooperation between the teacher and students in devising teaching methods and techniques to ensure the learning objectives of the course are carried out effectively.

In light of this, the recognition of the value of individual features can also foster learning. The particular nature of each individual and his/her most pressing needs are of paramount importance. In other words, if certain conditions or skills cannot be properly explored in the face of pressing needs that arise, the teacher must be aware of how to adapt the teaching method in an appropriate way so that the knowledge is provided to all the students in the same class in an equitable manner.

Tokuhama-Espinosa [4], draws attention to 14 key drivers of Neuroeducation as providing an essential framework in the teaching-learning process, and should be combined with closely related studies on neuroscience, psychology and education. These are as follows:

(a) students learn better when they are highly motivated than when they have little or no motivation; (b) stress impacts learning; (c) anxiety blocks learning opportunities; (d) depressive states can impede learning; (e) other people's tones of voice are quickly judged in the brain as either threatening or non-threatening; (f) people's faces are judged nearly instantaneously in the brain (i.e. as good or bad intentions); (g) feedback is important for learning; (h) emotions play a key role in learning; (i) using movements can enhance learning; (j) humor and laughter can enhance our learning experience; (k) nutrition impacts learning; (l) sleep is vital for memory consolidation; (m) learning styles (cognitive preferences) are due to the unique structure of individual brains; (n) differentiation (allowing students to learn at different levels and paces) in classroom practice can be justified by the fact that students have different intelligences and cognitive preferences".

It can be seen that to some extent the principles are narrowly confined to teaching models because they show that the active involvement of the teachers in effect interferes with the learning of the students, as expressed in principle 'a'. Some of the other principles - 'e', 'f', 'g', 'i', 'j' - are closely linked to how the degree of attention and observation of the teacher in the classroom is able to alter the way a class is handled and hence, affect the behavior of the students.

Every student has his/her own perceptions and by addressing the question of learning styles, principle 'm', underlines a number of different points bound up with cognitive absorption and memorizing capacity or conversely, the difficulty of retaining what has been learnt. With regard to this last point, weariness, sleepiness and anxiety can also lead to poor student achievement, as highlighted in 'l'. Finally, principle 'n' is worth pointing out as a means of understanding how abilities and skills can be added to the factors of intelligence and creativity to assist in carrying out activities.

Damásio [5] underlines the importance of body-brain-object interactions, "mapped in neural patterns and constructed in accordance with the capacities of the organism", on the basis of four domains which can bring about reactions and attitudes in the body and brain that can be either positive or negative to the students [2]. These are as follows: (i) sensitive motor patterns when looking at the object (such as movements of the eyes and neck or the movement of the whole body, when applicable); (ii) the sensitive motor pattern linked to touching and handling the object (if applicable); (iii) the sensitive motor pattern resulting from the evocation of previously acquired memories related to the object; (iv) the sensitive motor patterns caused by the triggering of emotions and feelings associated with the object.

In summary, sensations, motor reactions and emotional stimuli interfere with behavior and, as a result, in the learning process, as is indicated by principle 'h', since "emotions are essential for pattern recognition" [4]. In other words, learning can be supported as a body and brain-based skill for detecting patterns, "if it involves self-correction and learning by experience through data analysis and self-reflection" [4].

In this physiological recruitment order, in which the body/brain have a mutual effect and control on each other, creativity plays a crucial role in the consolidation of learning and hence, in the enhancement of the subjectivity and identity of the individual.

3   Strategies of the Mind for Creative Learning

Creativity has always captured the attention and interest of authors in various fields of knowledge. Abraham [6] points out that there have been a significant number of research studies in this area, although they have not managed to narrow down the concept to a definition that can cover such diverse areas as "musical creativity, visual creativity, synesthesia and creativity, divergent and convergent thinking, insight, scientific creativity, problem solving"; among others. With regard to research studies concerning the Neurosciences, the concept of creativity has followed several directions, some of which are divergent [6–10].

Dietrich [8] believes that "creativity is a fundamental activity of human information processing", and in her view, two features define the term as a productive act which includes shaping something new that can be appropriated by the individual. This position is shared by Fink et al. [9] whereas in the case of Pinheiro [10], creativity is regarded "as an attribute and process that is determined and evolves at both an individual and social level". On the basis of the definitions of these authors, creativity can be understood as the capacity of the individual and this is also expressed in the results of the activities he/she carries out.

Despite the need for further advances in this investigation, Dietrich [8] sets out from a neurophysiological perspective and highlights the prefrontal cortex as the important region to observe with regard to creative thinking, since it "harbors a person's cultural system, values and beliefs" [11].

In the opinion of Dietrich [8], "novelty production can occur in emotional structures or in cognitive structures and crossing the type of information with the two modes of processing (deliberate or spontaneous) yields the four basic types" which are an intrinsic part of her concept of creativity. On the basis of these crossings, the following descriptions can be noted: (a) Deliberate mode – cognitive structures; (b) Deliberate mode – emotional structures; (c) Spontaneous mode – cognitive structures; and (d) Spontaneous mode – emotional structures [8]. It should be stressed that as well as the prefrontal cortex, the working memory and the interconnection with the Parietal-Temporal-Occipital lobes, act together to shape what is described as creativity.

Damásio [11] broadens this brain-creativity relationship to another sphere between the mind and body and states that the mind carries out several tasks that are useful to the body. These include (i) the controlled execution of automatic responses with regard to a determined goal, (ii) previews and the planning of new replies, (iii) the creation of more varied circumstances and the presence of objects that can be beneficial to the survival of the body [5].

This kind of body-mind-brain interconnection ensures that the contacts of this body are embedded in the surroundings and stimulate the creative process, as well as the survival of the body itself, on the basis of a dialogue between an individual's memories and all the objects, space and time that nurture this knowledge and these emotions or feelings [5, 8].

Munari [12] links this perspective to design processes and believes that when carrying out a project, creativity should take account of all the necessary operations that must be followed for the data analysis, before deciding on a solution. Moreover, with regard to this field of knowledge, creativity can be harnessed to aesthetics, which "stems from the Greek word aisthesis which means some kind of sense perception" [13].

The path followed here lays emphasis on the complexity of the concept of creativity and provides clear evidence of an equivalence between the body-mind-brain relationship and the design process, since "some of the ideas of the body (…) are to a great extent determined by the prior design of the brain and by the general needs of the organism" [5]. In other words, when creativity is viewed as something that is planned in the context of design, it takes place as a result of a continuous interaction between the mind of the designer, cerebral mechanisms and all the stimuli – whether external or internal - that react on or affect its organism.

From this perspective, it can be understood that combining the principles of neuro-education with the stages of a fashion design project, can enhance the skills and the creative abilities of a new generation of university undergraduates, especially with regard to the inclusion of people with visual impairments in the higher education training courses. It is against this background and aligned to this objective, that the SEE BEYOND method is put forward, as outlined in the following section.

4   Body-Brain-Object: Strategies for Creation and Creativity in Fashion Design Based on the "SEE BEYOND Method: Enhancement"

Designing a collection project follows clearly distinguished stages. Fashion Design students are expected to have certain knowledge before they embark on creating and producing garments. In the opinion of Rech [14], the clothing supply chain consists of six stages, which can be categorized as: "(a) the production of raw material; (b) spinning; (c) weaving; (d) processing/finishing; (e) manufacturing; (f) the market-place".

The fashion designer can begin the process of carrying out the project in different ways. Generally, it takes place by determining a particular subject based on research studies centering on the collection. The fashion designer follows a sequence in defining the planned formal features which are wide-ranging and varied, as well as being interwoven. Jones [15] describes the key features of creation in fashion as being silhouettes, lines and texture, and the forms as those features that can be used – repetition, rhythm, shades, radiation, contrast, harmony, balance and proportion.

The embodiment of these features takes place in parallel with the choice of fabrics - color displays, modelling techniques, sewing, and processing/finishing for each planned garment. This choice is made together with the definition of the target public or the person who will wear the product, while taking account of their attitudes, values and life-style. This means that "the ideas should be creative based on the conceptual principles and in line with a profound analysis that involves a diagnosis of the problem and corresponds to (…) a genuine demand" [16].

Before the project reaches its end, the designer must follow each stage. The sequence of these stages might vary on account of the different features of each collection. On the basis of a definition of the formal design features, the following are generally taken into account: (a) model design; (b) modelling; (c) piloting; (d) garment testing standards; (e) model approval; (f) showcase replication; (g) sales; (h) production (in accordance with the specifications regarding size, color, fabric and processing); (i) distribution for the retail sector. There may also be intermediary stages if improvements are made to the garments.

The purpose of the SEE BEYOND method that is being examined here, is to broaden the structure of the planned methodology that is conventionally employed for higher education training courses in fashion design so that sensorimotor stimuli can be embedded in the planning of each stage.

In the case of the students, a clear understanding of the stages of a project sometimes requires a teaching model that can assist in their data abstraction [3]. Moreover, this is a stimulus to creativity or rather can make it more comprehensible with regard to the particular features of the project and hence provide a wider range of potential solutions to the problem that has been detected. Encouraging students to learn to think like designers is probably the key motivational factor. Thinking like a designer means noticing, analyzing and understanding the reality of situations so that products and processes can be created that address real needs [17].

With regard to the application of the SEE BEYOND method in particular, a continuous stimulus leading to abstraction and creativity represents a strategy that is essential for the consolidation and evocation of memories throughout the whole design process.

The focal point of this paper is on the results obtained from the Enhancement module, when this was applied to students with visual impairment who took part in fashion design training course in the city of Sao Paulo, Brazil, in the period August–December 2015.

4.1   Results and Discussion

The main results that make up the Enhancement Module are organized in two sets, and comprise studies related to: [1] forms and volumes; [2] colors and textile surface design, as follows.

4.1.1   Shapes and Volumes
(a) The Achievement of the Two-Dimensional Plane

According to Damásio [2], the human brain maps any object outside it, any activity that takes place outside it and all the interrelations that objects and activities form in time and space, and relatively to each other, as well as with regard to the organism.

Traditionally, the teaching of fashion design has adopted distinct ways of representing garments, in particular free-hand design drawing based on visual studies of shape. This method has proved to be effective when applied to a class that is wholly made up of students with normal sight. However, this is not the case when the class includes students with some kind of visual impairment, such as low vision or blindness (Fig. 1).

Fig. 1. The recognition of shape and counter shape, as identified in E.V.A plates. Source: the author's collection.

Since it is faced with the challenge of including this group in the learning, the SEE BEYOND method is concerned with other modes of perception such as touch, which can allow the recognition of lines, points, angles, contours and texture. As well as ensuring that the two-dimensional plane can be achieved by the students with visual impairment, this strategy also enhances the creativity of the students with normal sight by heightening their sensory awareness through tactile perception. With regard to both types of students, this merging of the senses of touch and sight (the latter in the case of students with normal sight), is essential for carrying out future projects which will combine design, shape, fabrics and texture to create garments for a collection.

Thus the first stage of the procedure involved working with E.V.A. sheets already outlined with geometrical removable shapes. By doing this, it was possible to study the shape and counter shape, as well as the handling of the objects (both separately and in sets), in a way that can reveal the inner lines or those of the contours, as well as the angles and texture.

After these had been recognized, these shapes were enlarged on paper by using string and pins so that they could be filled in with colors (Fig. 2).

Fig. 2.   The study of shape from a design made of yarn and pins. Source: author's collection.

(b) Shapes that Drape Bodies

Souza [18] believes that reproducing the physical dimensions of the human body - on either a natural (1:1) or reduced scale – has been extremely useful for the sizing of the products since it (i) allows a greater control and knowledge of the body; (ii) helps make one familiar with its proportions and morphology; and (iii) provides a clearer idea of scale.

The modelling of garments is generally carried out through different techniques, the most common being flat patterns and molding. Regarding the latter, the item of clothing is created directly from a bust or someone's body, which means it is worked on a human scale. In the case of someone with visual impairment and who relies on touch the sense to assist in identifying objects, the proportions of a bust very often make it very difficult to fully recognize the object itself and hence create a mold from the bust (Fig. 3).

At the same time, the students with normal sight also faced a difficulty in the process which was largely linked to the problem of recognizing the body as a means of supporting the creation of a garment. With the aim of overcoming these kinds of limitations, which are evident in both situations, the SEE BEYOND method, first and foremost, envisages modelling an item of clothing when it is carried out on an articulated dummy which represents the proportions of the human body on a smaller scale. This miniature figure allows both students with impaired vision and normal sight, to recognize the proportions with regard to the shape-object-body and on this basis, try out different ways of draping the body of the articulated dummy, before carrying out the task of converting it to a

Fig. 3. Two-dimensional and three-dimensional features - the study of parts of the mould of a garment on a body. Source: author's collection.

human scale. The successful two-dimensional plane which is obtained in the previous stage, is an essential factor in enabling the students to understand how this kind of surface plane is able to wrap round and drape a body, while bearing in mind its use in the future production of molds for garments.

(c) Silhouettes Under Construction

Sacks [19] argues that some objects may be recognized immediately after birth or soon afterwards, such as, for example, faces. Apart from these however, the world of objects has to be learnt from experience and activities: looking, touching, handling, and correlating the impressions given by objects through their appearance.

During the teaching/learning process in fashion design, forming the silhouette of a body basically takes place by means of observation and by making drawings of the human figure. In this situation, the silhouette is represented from the standpoint of the two-dimensional nature of the design. In the case of the students with normal sight, this represents a constraint to the perception of the three-dimensional nature of the body that must be dressed (Fig. 4).

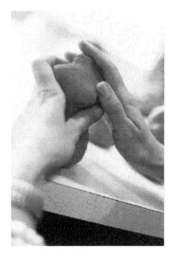

Fig. 4. Modelling technique for constructing a body on a small scale. Source: author's collection.

However, with regard to the students with impaired vision, this limitation is imposed by the impossibility of visual perception or of making a representation by means of a drawing.

In the light of these kinds of constraints, the SEE BEYOND method provides a modelling technique for constructing a body on a small scale (i.e. mini sculptures), through the use of plastic material with the aim of making a tactile and visual perception of the body feasible at 360°.

This allows the creative process to abandon the two-dimensional figure and move towards the three-dimensional plane, which is an essential domain for students when creating items of clothing for a collection. It is important to understand the relationship both inside and outside and that introducing three-dimensional concepts provides an opportunity that cannot be ensured by the drawing.

The two exercises (b, c) are planned to be complementary within studies of shape and volume. In this sphere, the perception of the silhouette of the female body was given priority because the group of students involved only comprised women.

After completing each of the exercises (a, b, c), the students shared the results they had obtained with each other. Everyone was able to touch and note the following: (a) in the first exercise – that the designed shapes were still only outlined by string and pins, together with a texture obtained from crayons; (b) in the second exercise – the different ways of dressing a body; (c) in the third exercise – the volumes of the mini sculptures (Fig. 5).

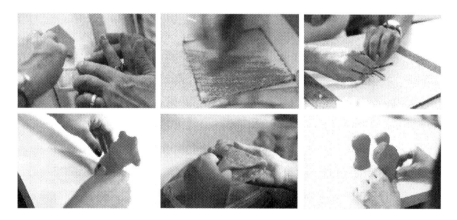

Fig. 5. Studies of shapes represented in upper images and studies of volumes represented in lower images. Source: author's collection.

4.1.2   Colors and Surface Textile Design
(d) Sensory Color Perception

The study of colors is an essential feature of design projects. In the case of fashion, colors are indicators of the nature of a collection and establish a key relationship with a particular epoch since, together with shapes, fabrics and texture, they are able to define the distinguishing characteristics of a historical period (Fig. 6).

Fig. 6. Mosaic of images with objects selected to represent the magenta color. Source: author's collection (Color figure online)

According to Guimarães [20], "the objects of our sensory world, particularly those that are chromatic, preserve their appearance in a latent state and are conveyed to the eyes by rays and beams of light". But, of course, the perception of light is impossible for someone with total visual impairment. What at first is characterized as a constraint on the apprehension of visual features, or rather, the image of a garment, can be overcome through a broadening of the concept of the image itself. Damásio [11] stresses the fact that images are not only of a visual kind but can also be auditory, visceral or tactile.

On the basis of this understanding, the SEE BEYOND method provides both students with normal sight and with visual impairment, the opportunity to form sensory panels geared towards the study of colors. The sensory panels consist of objects of different kinds and trigger tactile, olfactory, auditory and taste stimuli with the aim of heightening their perceptions and broadening the domain of the chromatic scales for the students (Fig. 7).

An interpretation of the theoretical framework with regard to the physical factors involved in the visual perception of color, is suggested as an initial stimulus [20]. Following this, the choice of the objects is made by the students themselves who are guided by the link between the theoretical framework and its individual reference-points for an understanding of each color in the principal scale – cyan, yellow, magenta – and of the secondary scale – green, violet and red.

By carrying out this exercise, the students managed to learn the meaning of the concepts of hue, saturation and intensity with a view to defining the palette of colors in a collection which would determine the course of the surface textile design and their choice of trimmings and finishings.

(e) The Textile Surface Undergoing Change
The impossibility of students with visual impairment seeing the fabrics or the difficulty experienced by those with normal sight in feeling and differentiating them, should not

Fig. 7. Sensory panel for yellow color. Source: authors' collection (Color figure online)

be regarded as an obstacle to identifying the range of textile products and the opportunities for changing them. In the opinion of Saltzman [21], texture is linked to the sense of touch as much as vision and thus can be created either by visual effects or by being definitely tactile.

Fig. 8. Studies of printing by hand, with a stencil (upper images) and free hand print (lower images). Source: authors' collection.

Thus when touch is regarded as the key factor in this process, the SEE BEYOND method recommends the study of stamping as an initial strategy for tactile perception and hence visual perception, since it allows the surface fabric to be identified and transformed by both students with normal sight and those with visual impairment.

In the light of this, two exercises involving hand-painted designs were carried out to enable students to recognize the differences between the prints - rapport and localized distribution patterns. The first consisted of a stencil which involves using a kind of mask made from a plaster cast which is covered with ink by means of paint rollers or airbrushing – often found in graphite in the street (Fig. 8).

The other technique, which is freer, entails painting with a brush and seeking to make use of the expressive gestures of the students to explore geometric shapes. Learning both techniques can significantly heighten the awareness of the students with regard to the opportunities for creation provided by a direct intervention with the fabrics, which to some extent, involves making alterations to both the visual and tactile appearance of the garment.

5   Conclusion

By making use of the resources available for undertaking all the exercises put forward to stimulate the sensorimotor system of both students with normal sight and those with visual impairment, the Enhancement Module of the SEE BEYOND method is able to achieve its first objective. This is to include higher education students with visual impairment in fashion design, as well as, to set out strategies for stimulating creativity by immersing students (with normal sight or otherwise) in the teaching/learning processes required for this field of knowledge.

These strategies are intertwined with patterns of repetition, that is of doing a particular exercise or activity again and again so that the students assimilate the information in their brain, consolidate it in their memory and are able to draw on it when required.

Creativity plays a significant role in this module. According to Damásio [5], "once you form an idea of a certain object, you can form an idea of the idea, and an idea of the idea, and so forth", which suggests that creativity can result from a process that once set in motion, can be continuously expanded.

The notion of the 'idea of ideas' lies at the heart of the creative process. Forming ideas of ideas paves the way to the awareness of countless opportunities for interaction between the designer, design features and the potential capacities of the surroundings.

Dietrich [8] states that perception assessment can be employed to make sophisticated representations that serve as the basis for cognitive processing.

Thus, by drawing on the theories of the Neurosciences, it can be said that the creative processes are not confined to the act of designing or creating an object or garment. Creativity is shaped through a continuous interaction between the individual, his/her body (understood in terms of the body-mind-brain triad) and the surrounding environment. During this interactive process, the stimuli triggered by the body and surroundings act by nurturing and advancing the creative processes, either in the sphere of fashion design or other areas of knowledge.

These kinds of interactions – body-brain-surroundings – pervade all the pedagogical activities set out in the Enhancement module.

By experiencing these interactions in the different processes involved in modelling the body, while studying shape and volume, the students with visual impairment or normal sight can gradually assimilate the increasing complexity of the two-dimensional and three-dimensional shapes that represent the body. This corroborates the fact that this experience has been consolidated in their memory. The knowledge acquired in this way strengthens the neural architecture which is an essential requirement for planning the structures, forms and volumes that will comprise the collection projects in the future.

Together with the studies of colors and surface textile design, the body-brain-surroundings interactions engender sensorimotor dialogues between the students (whether with normal sight or not) and the sensory panels, as well as the textile substrates. By supporting the personal body of work of these students, the memory of these dialogues can be enlarged and bear fruit in the planning of ideas which when instigated, can be turned into a project collection.

Both the studies follow a pattern of gradually building up the self-esteem of the students – those with normal sight as well as those with visual impairments. Little by little, the feelings of fear, shyness, vulnerability and insecurity are turned into self-confidence, loss of inhibitions, satisfaction and well-being. In other words, the commonly observed patterns of stress, anxiety and depression which are all responsible for negative and pent up feelings and are obstacles to learning, are gradually replaced by a positive kind of behaviour that is relaxed, light-hearted and carefree and this leads to significant benefits for the health of the students.

As a result, the particular and personal constraints that each of them face are at the same time overcome in the successive repetition of exercises and when this is applied to the activities of their everyday lives. This means that they follow a pattern that begins within the context of a classroom but then spreads out so that each individual is strengthened when confronted with the everyday challenges of human survival.

In further investigations in the future, the research will examine the stages that comprise the Materialization module of the SEE BEYOND method, and the way it can provide guidance to the students on creation and what is strictly speaking, the correct way of carrying out a fashion collection.

References

1. Cosenza, R.M., Guerra, L.B.: Neurociência e educação: como o cérebro aprende. Artmed, Porto Alegre (2011)
2. Damásio, A.R.: E o cérebro criou o homem. Companhia das Letras, Sao Paulo (2011)
3. Lima Júnior, G.C., Zuanon, R.: The foundation of the SEE BEYOND method: fashion design and neuroeducation applied to the teaching of the project methodology to students with congenital and acquired blindness. In: Streitz, N., Markopoulos, P. (eds.) DAPI 2017. LNCS, vol. 10291, pp. 528–546. Springer, Cham (2017). https://doi.org/10.1007/978-3-319-58697-7_40

4. Tokuhama-Espinosa, T.N.: The scientifically substantiated art of teaching: a study in the development of standards in the new academic field of neuroeducation (mind, brain and education science). Capella University (2008). http://pqdtopen.proquest.com/doc/25088 1375.html?FMT=ABS
5. Damásio, A.R.: Em busca de Espinosa: prazer e dor na ciência dos sentidos. Companhia das Letras, Sao Paulo (2004)
6. Abraham, A.: The promises and perils of the neuroscience of creativity (2013). http://journal.frontiersin.org/article/10.3389/fnhum.2013.00246/full, https://doi.org/10.3389/fnhum.2013.00246
7. Aldous, C.R.: Creativity, problem solving and innovative science: insights from history, cognitive psychology and neurosciences (2007). http://files.eric.ed.gov/fulltext/EJ834201.pdf
8. Dietrich, A.: The cognitive neurosciences of creativity (2004). https://www.ncbi.nlm.nih.gov/pubmed/15875970
9. Fink, A., Benedfek, M., Grabner, R.H., Neubauer, A.C.: Creativity meets neuroscience: experimental tasks for the neuroscientific study of creative thinking (2007). https://goo.gl/6xyxr0, https://doi.org/10.1016/j.ymeth.2006.12.001
10. Pinheiro, I.R.: Modelo geral da criatividade. In: Psicologia: Teoria e Pesquisa (2009). https://goo.gl/RUfq1g
11. Damásio, A.R.: Descarte's Erros: Emotion, Reason and the Human Brain. Putman, New York (1994)
12. Munari, B.: Das coisas nascem coisas. Martins Fontes, São Paulo (1998)
13. Löbach, B.: Design industrial: bases para a configuração de produtos industriais. Editora Edgard Blücher, São Paulo (2001)
14. Rech, S.: Estrutura da Cadeia Produtiva da Moda (2008). https://goo.gl/x4Krkk
15. Jones, S.J.: Fashion design: manual do estilista. Cosac & Naify, São Paulo (2005)
16. Fiorini, V.: Design de Moda: abordagens conceituais e metodológicas. In: Pires, D.B. (org.) Design de Moda: olhares diversos. Estação das Letras e Cores Editora, Barueri SP (2008)
17. Fornasier, C.B.R., Martins, R.F.F., Demarchi, A.P.P.: O ensino da disciplina de desenvolvimento de projetos como sistema de gestão de conhecimento. In: Pires, D.B. (org.) Design de Moda: olhares diversos. Estação das Letras e Cores Editora, Barueri SP (2008)
18. Souza, W.G.: Modelagem no design do vestuário (2007). http://fido.palermo.edu/servicios_dyc/encuentro2007/02_auspicios_publicaciones/actas_diseno/articulos_pdf/A6045.pdf
19. Sacks, O.: O olhar da mente. Companhia das Letras, Sao Paulo (2010)
20. Guimarães, L.: A cor como informação: a construção biofísica, linguística e cultural da simbologia das cores. Annablume, Sao Paulo (2000)
21. Saltzman, A.: El cuerpo diseñado: sobre la forma em el proyecto de la vestimenta. Paidós, Buenos Aires (2004)

Inclusive Design and Textile Technology in the Everyday Lives of Wheelchair Dependent

Veridianna Cristina Teodoro Ferreira[1] and Agda Carvalho[1,2(✉)]

[1] Graduate Program in Design, Anhembi Morumbi University, Sao Paulo, Brazil
[2] Graduate Program in Arts, UNESP, Sao Paulo, Brazil
veridiannaf@gmail.com, agdarcarvalho@gmail.com

Abstract. This paper discusses the benefits of textile technology to inclusive design, focusing on aspects that prioritize comfort and health for wheelchair dependent individuals. To this end, the focus of this paper is the ergonomics of products designed for the disabled, as well as their conception. It investigates the development of a form of technological processing based on applying microcapsules to textile materials, in addition to exploring its many functionalities and the possibilities for widening its scope of application, particularly relating to the contact of the fabric with the skin. The process reported here deals with people with mobility difficulties, specifically wheelchair dependents, having as its goal the prevention of pressure ulcers. To exemplify these possibilities, the research work carried out by designer Elisa Marangon Beretta is presented, wherein microcapsules of eicosane are applied onto polyurethane foam, used in wheelchair seats, with the purpose of contributing to the comfort and well-being of wheelchair dependents. New possibilities of textile processing are further explored, relating to the use of microencapsulation for offering greater comfort, preventing pressure ulcers and providing better adaptation approaches to increase the ability of physically disabled people to participate in everyday life, and hence improve their general health.

Keywords: Inclusive design · Textile technology · Microencapsulation
Wheelchair dependent

1 Introduction

Since the 19th century, with the advent of studies of pathologies in medicine and the social sciences, disabilities became an object of study. Pathology is understood as the field that studies anatomical or physiological deviations that constitute or characterize a given disease. Initially deficiencies were classified according to their pathological features, divided into the following categories: mental, physical and sensory-perceptual, which in turn enabled diagnosis and determined a course of treatment in the medical field. This way, the disable person was seen as an individual that had some form of incapacity or suffered a disadvantage relating to their body [1].

The word "disabled", when applied to people who suffer physical, sensorial or mental limitations, is the opposite in meaning to "able", and this very conception explains the

© Springer International Publishing AG, part of Springer Nature 2018
V. G. Duffy (Ed.): DHM 2018, LNCS 10917, pp. 295–307, 2018.
https://doi.org/10.1007/978-3-319-91397-1_25

difficulty of adapting built space, from housing to work environments, to the needs of the users with particular limitations and difficulties. Thus, many disabled people become incapable of performing everyday tasks, from the maintenance of their personal hygiene to their ability to work and engage in leisure activities, a situation that can result in the social exclusion of these people. It is important to remember that the fundamental principles of exclusion of disabled people from social life were shaped by the influence of the Greek culture, and as a result were ultimately adopted by the peoples of Western society exposed to it. For these people, physical beauty is frequently associated with character, whereas the disabled are frequently seen as subjects to be pitied, who suffer the consequences of a God-sent punishment, or as a form of entertainment for society's 'normal' and accepted citizens [2].

Generally speaking, people with motor deficiencies resent a variety of neurosensory conditions that affect them in terms of mobility, speech or general motor coordination, as result of nerve, neuromuscular and osteoarticular lesions, or even congenital or acquired malformation. Depending on the case, people with difficulty of locomotion can move themselves with the aid of prosthesis, wheelchair or other auxiliary appliances.

The need for an interface for the locomotion of disabled users and which can also aid them in carrying out everyday activities denotes that the products developed to this end must be based on ergonomic concepts. "Between the people with physical disabilities and non-disabled people, there are evident differences in the living states. [...] people with limb disabilities have special needs for the aesthetic and functional structures of clothing, distinct from non-disabled people, and consequently their garments have specific design requirements [3]".

It is important to emphasize that principles of ergonomics prescribe that the product must be adapted to the user's body and not otherwise, seeing that if the product is inadequate the body must modify its posture in an effort to adapt to it, which in turn can lead to varying degrees of discomfort, aches and pains and major health problems. Consequently, it is advisable that the development of such products be based on three elements, responsible for satisfying certain needs of users, such as technical, ergonomic and aesthetic qualities [4].

The precision in human body measurements increases the chances of developing an ergonomic product with increased usability that provides a greater measure of comfort for the user. Measurements must meet anthropometric criteria, wherein a number of techniques are employed in obtaining accurate static and dynamic measurements of the human body. That is to say, they must include both simplified measurements taken of the human body standing up and measurements of detailed parts of the body when sitting, bending down, kneeling, crouching etc., and/or making different types of movements [4].

The body must be the starting point for any and all products developed, from clothing to tools to physical environments. Design projects must also take into account that bodies change over the course of a lifetime and are different according to each age group, and also differ according to race and climate. Finally, different types of disabilities also define specific body characteristics, as considered in this paper.

On this account, the development of products aimed at disabled people should seek to provide physical comfort and well-being and to promote better health, but is also important in improving everyday situations, facilitating personal autonomy in daily life.

In this context, this research examines textile technology and the processing of textiles with the use of microcapsules, focusing on skin protection for disabled individuals who are wheelchair users, thus avoiding the formation of skin injury that can become severely aggravated if untreated. In other words, the relevance of this investigation lies in the application of textile technology in the remit of inclusive design. In this particular case, it centers on contexts that deal with the physical adaptation of individuals with motor disabilities for appropriate everyday wheelchair use. Even though the benefits for wheelchair users are many, due to their wide variety of needs, this research looks specifically at the prevention of pressure ulcers, thus contributing to improving the quality of daily activities for wheelchair users.

This paper takes as a case study a research work on a microencapsulation technique developed in Rio Grande do Sul, Brazil, in 2015, aimed at decreasing the intensity and frequency of the pressure and shearing force between the disabled individual's body and the wheelchair. The research project, carried out by designer Elisa Marangon Beretta, was chosen for its use of technological processing of textiles based on microcapsules, with the aim of decreasing the formation of sores and abrasions on the skin of wheelchair users when in a static position for a considerable length of time.

The case study foregrounds one of the greatest scourges of wheelchair users is remaining in a single position for a long period of time. This situation is aggravated when the wheelchair dependent actively participates in the labor market, as they are often unable to take pauses to the adjust their posture or shift positions in the wheelchair, therefore preventing any single area of skin from being under constant pressure, further exacerbated due to heat from the wheelchair-seating. This condition can result in skin breakdown and even in sores called pressure ulcers. According to a definition provided by Rocha [5], these ulcers consist in "localized areas of ischemia and cellular necrosis that tend to occur due to prolonged compression of soft tissue between a bony prominence and a firm surface".

In this way, the contribution of this paper lies in its analysis of the application of phase change materials encapsulated in textile materials for body temperature control and prevention of pressure ulcers, caused by constant pressure of an area of the skin against the wheelchair due to everyday use of the chair, further worsened by an unfavorable ergonomic condition and lack of thermal comfort.

2 Technology Applied to the Textile Product

Researches aimed at the discovery, development and processing of new technological fabrics are conducted in laboratories that manipulate chemical substances, with applications of physics and investigating technological possibilities of materials and processes. This framework enables the creation of textiles for different uses, namely adaptive, curative, ecological, sportive and also designed for physically disabled people with the objective of improving their well-being and health [6].

Intelligent fabrics were introduced in the early 1990s, strongly influenced by military investigation and wearable technology in general. In this context, it is worth highlighting an interactive garment called the "wearable motherboard", a pioneering project with adaptive and responsive structures such as integrated sensors and communication ability. The piece aimed to rescue soldiers, monitoring their health status in real time [7].

Technology has offered contributions for the better adaptation of clothing to the body. A new type of smart clothing developed by researchers from the University of Bath's Centre for Biomimetics, England, coordinated by Professor Julian Vincent in 2004, employs microtechnology to present thermal comfort for the user. Using principles of biomimetics[1], the piece of clothing comprises a cooling function, thus controlling the ideal temperature of the user's body when the ambient temperature rises, and providing heat retention when the external temperature falls [8].

Ergonomic clothing design projects seek to fulfill an array of different purposes, such as fabrics that protect the body from weather interference or performance fabrics in sportswear that maximize athletic performance, and high-end moisture management fabrics that allow sweat to pass through from the inside out and evaporate, keeping the skin and clothing dry, but preventing rain droplets from penetrating from the outside. Fabric science is frequently incorporated into athlete uniforms, so as to maximize prevent sweat and the actual costume from adversely affecting their performance [9].

Smart textiles are based on researches into different disciplines such as: textile design, technology, chemistry, physics, material science, engineering, biochemistry, computer science and technology.

These textiles are possible due to the following three developments: the first relates to the introduction of new types of mechanically and electrically high-performing textile fibers and structures, specifically conductive materials. Secondly, the miniaturization of electronics that enables the integration of electronics into textile structures and into various products. The third one refers to the capability of making technology be used and worn while and also being interconnected with other devices, such as computers and mobile phones. "In addition, there are experimental textiles that do not arise from the influence of existing textiles, but from references obtained in different areas, such as the architecture, arts, contemporary culture, such as the nature itself. In an emerging era of biotechnology, nature is not only being copied by biological imitation (biomimetics), nor just being exploited in the development of bioactive materials, but mostly collaborating with the emergence of other 'natural' versions through textile engineering" [10].

The developments of products that apply intelligent textiles generally stem from a concern with providing users with elements of protection, wellness and optimization of comfort, as well as easy care, durability, and resistance to washing and wind. Developments are also taking place in researches and projects that seek to heighten and sharpen our senses, as is the case of the Co-Evolving Smart Textile project, by the Brazilian

---

[1] According to Bar-Cohen [17] and Allen [18], biomimetics consists in the development of novel technologies through the distillation of principles from the study of biological systems. Biomimetic technologies arise from a flow of ideas from the biological sciences into engineering, benefiting from the millions of years of design effort performed by natural selection in living systems.

researchers Rachel Zuanon and Geraldo Lima. In this research work, "(…) the textile acts as an interface, through which the individual interacts with the surrounding environment and stimulates its sensory device in different ways, in a dialogical relationship with numerous references capable of association and recognition by this body. In this mediation, co-evolving smart textile appears as a possibility to simultaneously promote and expand the scope of sensations to the human body and, thus, provide the differentiated management of body-environment communication [10].

The project conceived by designer Elisa Marangon Beretta employs textile technology to a technique of microencapsulation applied to the fabric used in wheelchair seating so as to create a low-friction interface, and avoid skin injury problems, a common problem for wheelchair users due to prolonged pressure and shear forces that contribute to the formation of pressure ulcers.

Recent data obtained from the National Health Survey, conducted by the Brazilian Institute of Geography and Statistics - IBGE (2015), among a Brazilian population of 200.6 million people, 6.2% of people over the age of 18 had at least one of the four impairments: intellectual, physical, hearing and visual. In Brazil, 0.8% or 1.6 million people live with intellectual disabilities, while 1.3%, or 2.6 million cope with physical disabilities. Hearing impairments, in turn, represents 1.1%, or 2.2 million people and the greatest number, representing 3.6% or 7.2 million people, relates to people with visual disabilities. This panorama demonstrates the relevance of this study just to begin identifying the benefits already provided by textile technology for the everyday life of these people, and in turn, to propose new applications for this technology to benefit wheelchair dependents. Among these types of disabilities, the physical disability is that which causes most harm to skin health, because of patient's static position in a wheelchair or bed, which, as previously mentioned, can result in superficial sores or more severe injuries [11].

The major cause for the formation of pressure ulcers is the inadequate supply of blood and nutrients in a particular part of the body, due to external pressure exerted by an object against bony or cartilaginous prominences. Humidity and friction further aggravate the condition, as the sores appear in parts of the body that support its weight. For this reason, wheelchair dependents are more susceptible to developing pressure ulcers in the ischial region, which supports the weight of the body when a person is in a sitting position [5–12].

The first stage of development of pressure ulcers consists in a mild skin alteration, normally indicated by the appearance of a red spot on fair skin and a bluish or purple one on darker-colored skin. As the change is not abrupt, it frequently passes unnoticed, but there are other properties that indicate that they are pressure sores: the temperature of the skin being either hotter or colder; the skin's consistency or texture, which can be either firmer and thicker or lighter and softer; and for those with more sensitive skin, there can be physical pain or itching [13].

The second stage involves a decrease of the skin thickness (epidermis and/or dermis). The ulcer presents itself as a blister or small wound on the skin, though still superficial. The third stage is characterized by a significant loss of skin thickness with damage or necrosis of the subcutaneous tissue, almost reaching the underlying fascia. In the fourth stage, the tissue is extensively destroyed, presenting necrosis and even muscular and bone lesions, with or without loss of the whole thickness of the skin. In case the ulcer is not identified from the outset, it can evolve rapidly to the next stages, wherein the later stages are more difficult to treat. The image below shows the depth of ulcers in each stage [13] (Fig. 1).

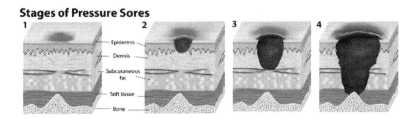

Fig. 1. Stages of pressure ulcer development (Source: https://mangarhealth.com/uk/news/new-mangar-health-websites-launched/)

The main of preventing the formation of pressure ulcers is to change positions every two hours, in the case of patients confined to a bed, in order to alleviate the skin pressure points in areas of greater risk. For people in wheelchairs who remain in a sitting position for a long time should shift their position with increased frequency, every ten to fifteen minutes. However, this is often unfeasible for wheelchair dependents who actively participate in the labor market, which underscores the importance of Beretta's research, in which textile technology is employed for the protection of the wheelchair user's skin.

3   Inclusive Design in the Daily Lives of Wheelchair Dependents

From the 1970s onwards, design began moving towards a more human-centered approach with Victor Papanek, industrial designer and design director of the California Institute of the Arts. Since that time, Papanek encouraged a more solidary attitude in the attempt of abandoning 'design for profit' in favor of human desires and needs. To this day, the designer continues appeal to designers to stop working within a culture of consumerism and in a superficial way, and to start developing research projects aimed at solving the problems of the society, and to cater to the need all kinds of people, regardless of their social and economic circumstances. In the 1980s and 1990s, an increase in the number of research work in the field of design centered on issues related to sustainability and consumer education can be observed. In that same period accessibility and social inclusion also become matters of interest for designers [14].

As of the 1970s, the first signs of inclusive design begin to appear, even though at present the number of research projects that associate design and technology to improve the life of disabled individuals is still limited. Many wheelchair dependents have joined the labor market, working the same number of hours as individuals without disabilities, which only enhances the importance of this study.

The principle reason that led a much greater number of disabled individuals to find employment is the existence of a Quotas Law, passed in 1991[2], which established that any company with more than hundred or more employees must fill between 2% to 5% of their positions with people with a disability. Currently, there already are 9.3 million disabled people working and who fit the criteria, in addition to 827 thousand vacant positions. However, the working hours of a wheelchair dependent is no different from that of a person without a disability, being an average of eight hours a day, Monday to Friday, and four hours on Saturdays, totaling forty-four hours of work per week.

Many wheelchair dependents are fully capable of working, and these activities play a crucial role in restoring and enhancing their self-esteem, promoting their independence and social inclusion. As they enter the labor market, these individuals begin to feel the need to visually identify themselves according to the normative guidelines of the company they work in, having to dress appropriately in formal attire, sportively or even wear uniforms. Besides, upon joining the workforce and having to remain seated in the same position for long hours, the chances of developing pressure ulcers increase. This scenario provides the main motivation for seeking solutions in the domain of textile technology capable of contributing to the well-being and health of disables persons in these conditions.

Therefore, the project developed by Elisa Marangon Beretta in 2015 significantly contributes to reducing the formation of pressure ulcers in disabled users due to long permanence in a sitting position without physical movement. The designer employs the technique of microencapsulation applied to the fabric and introduces a personalized wheelchair seating system finely adjusted to the individual user's anatomy. It is important to point out that this option improves the user's positioning, but could also negatively impact on thermal discomfort, as it increases the contact surface area. That being the case, the designer applies a textile substance using phase changing technology to the textile cover of the wheelchair seat, adjusted to the wheelchair user's skin temperature. This way, the appearance of pressure ulcers is avoided as temperature control is established in the areas of friction between the body and the wheelchair [15].

The PCMs are based on the absorption or liberation of heat when a change of physical state occurs - from solid to liquid, or liquid to gas, or vice-versa. Hence they can be defined in a simplified way as substances with the capacity of altering their physical state at a given temperature interval, absorbing or liberating heat energy from the surrounding environment. When the phase change is completed, the continued heating/cooling results in a gradual temperature increase/reduction, which in turn is defined by a thermo-regulating property known as sensible heat [16].

The casing material in the process of encapsulation can be polymeric, ceramic or gelatin. The encapsulation can also be classified as porous or non-porous, being that the porous gradually releases the material within the core while the non-porous acts as a protective layer to the phase change material. Furthermore, the microcapsules can be permanent or temporary. The temporary ones also gradually release the material in the core when the protective shell is broken. The permanent ones, on the other hand, are designed to protect the core as long as possible [15].

---

[2] Brazilian Law N° 8.213, enacted on July 24, 1991.

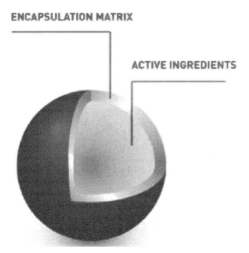

Fig. 2. Structure of a microcapsule (Source: http://capsularis.com/capsularis-expert-microen capsulation/?lang=en)

The image above represents the structure of a microcapsule (Fig. 2). The encapsulation matrix, referred to as the coating material, protects the material from external influences, while the active ingredients, also referred to as the core, holds the substance that characterizes the textile substrate's functionality.

The definition of the protective casing in the microencapsulation process occurs according to the specific characteristics of the material being encapsulated and its potential application, such as fibers and textile substrates, surface coatings, physiotherapy equipment, isolating panels, among others.

The image below shows each stage of the development of the personalized wheelchair seat. The study consists in obtaining the shape of the user's body through the use of molds made by health professionals using both plaster and vacuum mattresses and also through

Fig. 3. Production process of personalized seats Source: (BERETTA, 2015)

direct scanning of the patient. The plaster molds (Fig. 3A) are scanned by a using a 3D scanner (Fig. 3B). The data collected is transposed to a CAD/CAM program (Fig. 3C) and processed so as to customize the form for manufacturing using CNC-controlled precision machine tools (Fig. 3D). The seat is directly manufactured in foam (Fig. 3E), which guarantees the precision of its forms. In Fig. 3F it is possible to visualize the structure of the personalized seat, fitted into the wheelchair. [15, 16] Next, the textile substrate containing microcapsules with PCM embedded into their core is applied onto this structure. These microcapsules act as a shell, which avoids PCM leakage in its liquid phase.

Once this stage of the process is finalized, the designer performs validation tests, verifying the latent heat energy emanating from the seat surface by conducting a thermography analysis. This requires that the user remains seated on the seat for 20 min. As soon as they rise from the seat the temperature of the surface is measured by thermography to obtain a mapping of the heat energy on the surface. In Fig. 4 it is possible to observe that the manually shaped seat leads to a concentration of heat energy in its central area, and consequently to the production of temperature peaks in the area of the buttocks and back upper and inner thighs of the user's legs in contact with the surface of the seat. Figure 4 (below) the optimum distribution of heat throughout the seat, resulting from the application of textile substrate with phase change thermal storage.

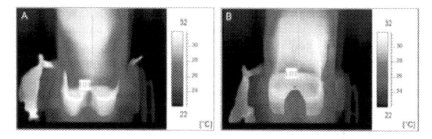

Fig. 4. Temperature measurement of the seat Source: (BERETTA, 2015)

Beretta's project demonstrates that the eicosane microcapsules can reduce the heating effect of the wheelchair seat on the wheelchair user's skin, namely by thermoregulation provided by foam and textile material. In other words, the microclimate between the seat surface area and the user's body reaches an equilibrium state and ceases the production of sweat resulting from excessive heat, also preventing localized damage to the skin.

Over the last years, phase change materials have been used to manufacture thermoregulating textiles and provide greater thermal comfort for wheelchair dependents. At present, PCM microcapsules are integrated into acrylic fibers and polyurethane foam, and used in various textile-related applications, such as ski garments, gloves, socks, nightwear, shoes, protection equipment, medical textile products, among others [15].

In other words, the development of new fabrics with the use of microencapsulation has been assisting many people with a range of different needs, particularly including: sun protective fabrics, insect-repellent textiles for users who are allergic to insect bites and/or use in high-risk insect-transmitted disease areas or periods. Microencapsulation is also used for applications such as controlled release of various types of fragrance, maintain the scent on items of clothing and/or user for longer periods of time. Such processing techniques can effect a potentialization of products and their functions, and also significantly extend the reach of inclusive design.

4   Results and Discussions

In Elisa Marangon Beretta's investigation and subsequent tests, this paper identifies the results of the application of textile technology, more specifically that of encapsulation articulated with certain materials and procedures such as the 3D modeling in conjunction with the manufacturing process on a CNC machine, used in the production of an inclusive design-oriented product. The fact is that these resources and processes demonstrate the intrinsic importance of both an interdisciplinary and a transdisciplinary approach to inclusive design. The major contributions to improving the everyday quality of life of disabled persons who depend on the use of a wheelchair provided by Beretta's research work can be summed up as follows:

4.1   Ergonomics, Comfort and Inclusion

Beretta's project emphasizes the way in which design can contribute to develop inclusive and ergonomic interfaces and, in the case of the disabled individual's body, highlights that it is necessary to research materials and processes that can provide and ensure the comfort of the user for an unlimited amount of time.

The previously listed project-based actions present the benefits of a personalized seat, once every disabled individual has a different body structure, with distinct variations relating to their impairment of movement. The fabrication of a mold of the user's body provides a better understanding of the specificities of each body, and supplies relevant and valuable information for the decisions related to the project. The mold is used as a basis for digital modeling, and the fabrication process is rendered directly using the foam material. This process is crucial to ensure precision and ergonomic correspondence between the seat and the wheelchair dependent's body. In other words, a product design that is oriented towards the physical needs of each individual user is a fundamental aspect in dealing with a project that centers on adapting and producing inclusive interfaces.

4.2   Textile Materials and Thermoregulation of the Human Body

Ergonomic comfort is not sufficient to ameliorate the effects of heating for the wheelchair user. However, by way of inclusive interfaces it is possible to identify the ideal distribution of the pressure of the user's body onto the seat during the use of the wheelchair.

The completion of the production process and the subsequent testing that ensued demonstrated a higher level of tactile comfort for the user, due to the seat's ability to mold itself to the contours of the user's body, minimizing the friction between the body and the seat, and hence preventing the appearance of pressure ulcers. In this regard, the domain of textile technology can be considered a fundamental field of research in the context of attaining thermal and ergonomic comfort for disabled users in their daily lives. Beretta's investigation emphasizes the use of Phase Change Materials (PCMs) with the aim of achieving thermoregulation. As shown by the designer, the PCM's capacity for absorbing and releasing heat point to a method of working that is consistent to the design of inclusive interfaces. This potential presents itself as directly proportional to the needs arising from each individual body/lesion, which in turn denotes a vast field of possibilities awaiting to be explored and put into use, ultimately offering considerable benefits for the health and well-being of disabled users.

4.3 Beyond the Prevention of Pressure Ulcers

A thorough understanding of the microencapsulation process opens up a vast field of application. In Beretta's case, the option for microencapsulation with an eicosane nucleus seeks to reduce the formation of pressure ulcers by ensuring a thermal balance between the wheelchair dependent's skin and the wheelchair seat. To this end, determining the fabric's qualities (less or more permeable, for example) has direct impact on the fabrication of the seat, whereby the permeability of the fabric to air is an essential factor in achieving thermal comfort, as is the textile's thickness, weight and density and the type of processing that should be applied. According to [15], attaining a balance between the breathability rate and the thermal transference in the production of a textile for this end is of crucial importance. In this way, in addition to proposing a project-oriented approach to the prevention of pressure ulcers, the microencapsulation studies developed by Beretta also point to fertile perspectives vis-à-vis an inclusive approach in product design.

5   Conclusions

This paper foregrounds textile technology an effective means to optimize the relation between the wheelchair dependent's body and the surrounding environment, based on designer Elisa Marangon Beretta's research work. The benefits derived from the project directly impacts the quality of everyday activities of the wheelchair user, as they promote the prevention of pressure ulcers by way of textile encapsulation, aimed at providing the user with thermal and ergonometric comfort.

This discussion foregrounds the significance and meaning of design with an inclusive approach, as although a number of research studies and actions aimed at improving the daily lives of wheelchair dependent individuals have already been performed, there still exists a substantial number of products, work conditions and physical environments that are partially or totally inadequate for the disabled individual and require further study, adaptions and solutions. That being said, the need for projects that include more through investigation pursued in conjunction with other fields of knowledge is paramount. Clearly a trans and interdisciplinary approach to research can offer a wider frame of reference for the exploration of materials and processes, which, added to analog and digital procedures, can provide a broader perspective for the consolidation of inclusive design.

With future development, the research aims to use make use of the results obtained by Baretta [15] and expand them in the development of an assistive interface directed at reducing the appearances of pressure ulcers in wheelchair dependents. In this way, the ultimate objective is to evaluate the potential for other substances (in addition to the use of eicosane) in microencapsulation applied to textile materials, thus enabling the production of even more consistent results for the aforementioned context.

References

1. Roncoleta, M.R.: Design de Calçados para pessoas com deficiência física: os prazeres do belo e do conforto. Ph.D. thesis, Universidade de São Paulo. Faculdade de Arquitetura e Urbanismo, Sao Paulo (2014)
2. Qualharini, E.L., Anjos, F.C.: Ergonomia no espaço edificado para pessoas portadoras de deficiência (1998). http://www.abepro.org.br/biblioteca/ENEGEP1998_ART086.pdf. Accessed 15 Oct 2015, 2018
3. Chang, W.M., Zhao, Y.X., Guo, R.P., Wang, Q., Gu, X.-D.: Design and study of clothing structure for people with limb disabilities. J. Fiber Bioeng. Informatics 2(2), 61–66 (2009). https://doi.org/10.3993/jfbi06200910
4. Iida, I.: Ergonomia: projeto e produção, 2nd edn. Blucher, Sao Paulo (2005)
5. Rocha, J.A., Miranda, M.J., Andrade, M.J.: Abordagem Terapêutica das Úlceras de Pressão: Intervenções Baseadas na Evidência. Acta Médica Port. 19, 29–38 (2006)
6. Chataignier, G.: Fio a fio: tecidos, moda e linguagem. Estação das Letras e Cores, Sao Paulo (2006)
7. Berglin, L.: Smart Textiles and Wearable Technology – a study of smart textiles in fashion and clothings. In: Diva Digitala Vetenskapliga Arkivet (2013). http://www.diva-portal.org/smash/record.jsf?pid=diva2:884011. Accessed 15 Jan 2018
8. Tecido inteligente mantém temperatura do usuário. http://www.inovacaotecnologica.com.br/noticias/noticia.php?artigo=010160041015#.WrVO8ih4VV4. Accessed 15 Jan 2018
9. Avelar, S.: Moda: globalização e novas tecnologias, 2nd edn. Estação das Letras e Cores, Sao Paulo (2011)
10. Zuanon, R., Júnior, G.C.L.: Design of co-evolving textiles applied to smart products. In: Streitz, N., Markopoulos, P. (eds.) DAPI 2015. LNCS, vol. 9189, pp. 461–470. Springer, Cham (2015). https://doi.org/10.1007/978-3-319-20804-6_42
11. Souto, L.: Cresce o número de pessoas com deficiência no mercado, mas preconceito persiste (2002). https://oglobo.globo.com/sociedade/cresce-numero-de-pessoas-com-deficiencia-no-mercado-mas-preconceito-persiste-20128635. Accessed 7 Jan 2018
12. Sprigle, S., Sonenblum, S.: Assessing evidence supporting redistribution of pressure for pressure ulcer prevention'. J. Rehabil. Res. Dev. 48(3), 203–214 (2011). https://doi.org/10.1682/JRRD.2010.05.0102
13. Dealey, C., Lindholm, C.: Pressure Ulcer Classification. In: Romanelli, M., Clark, M., Cherry, G.W., Colin, D., Defloor, T. (eds.) Science and Practice of Pressure Ulcer Management, pp. 37–41. Springer, London (2006)
14. Papanek, V.: Design for the Real World: Human Ecology and Social Change, 2nd edn. Thames & Hudson, London (1995)

15. Beretta, E.M.: Obtenção e Aplicação de Microcápsulas de Eicosano em Espumas de Poliuretano Visando Conforto Térmico em assentos para Cadeira de Rodas'. Ph.D. thesis, Universidade Federal do Rio Grande do Sul, Porto Alegre (2015)
16. Silva NTDF: Incorporação de materiais de mudança de fase em materiais de construção. Masters Dissertation, Universidade do Minho, Braga (2009)
17. Bar-Cohen, Y.: Biomimetics: Biologically Inspired Technologies. CRC Press, Boca Raton (2006)
18. Allen, R.: Bulletproof Feathers: How Science Uses Nature's Secrets to Design Cutting-Edge Technology. University of Chicago Press, Chicago (2010)

Game Design and Neuroscience Cooperation: Perspectives to *Cybersickness* Reduction in Head Mounted Displays Experiences

Felipe Moreno[✉] and Rachel Zuanon

Sense Design Lab, Graduate Program in Design, Anhembi Morumbi University, São Paulo, Brazil
felipe.smoreno@gmail.com, rachel@all-affective.com

Abstract. The technological evolution of HMDs is responsible for making devices available that are lighter, cheaper and more operational, as well as being aware of the risks of *cybersickness*. *Cybersickness* involves a range of symptoms similar to those of motion sickness, which affects a significant number of users and is currently regarded as one of the main obstacles to virtual reality helmets in the market. The focal point of this paper is on merging the fields of knowledge of Neuroscience and Games Design as a strategy for mitigating the symptoms of *cybersickness*. It sets out the results obtained from an experiment carried out with two groups of volunteers – heavy and low users of games for HMDs. These results underpin the sensory rearrangement theory and point out the kind of design choices that can trigger the symptoms of *cybersickness*. As a result, it is becoming possible to design games by predicting the design decisions required to overcome the problem of this malady.

Keywords: Game design · Neuroscience · *Cybersickness*
Head mounted displays · Virtual reality

1 Introduction

Virtual reality has formed a part of the everyday lives of human beings since the time of primitive designs and has always been employed as a kind of expression through paintings, cinema, theatre, opera, illusionism and other artistic activities [35]. Technology is being integrated with virtual reality in an attempt to surround the spectator with images through an expanded kind of cinema, CAVE and HMDs [9].

The increase of processing speed and reduction in the size of computer components, are making it increasingly feasible to develop technologies for the improvement of HMDs (Head mounted display). These consist of helmets or glasses that have two screens – one for each eye – that produce images from an application produced by the computer.

Virtual reality with HMD is one of the emerging interactive media that is attracting most attention from the large technology companies [29]. Following considerable financial expenditure and research in the area, Facebook, Google and HTC have invested in

© Springer International Publishing AG, part of Springer Nature 2018
V. G. Duffy (Ed.): DHM 2018, LNCS 10917, pp. 308–325, 2018.
https://doi.org/10.1007/978-3-319-91397-1_26

the creation of their own virtual reality devices with the aim of launching HMDs as products that can be accessible to the general public.

In technological terms, the consolidation of virtual reality in HMD (with cheaper, lighter and more operational devices) has not been enough to overcome what currently represents one of its most serious challenges - *cybersickness*, one of the main obstacles to the success of these helmets in the market.

Cybersickness induces an array of symptoms that affect the experience of virtual reality. These symptoms include nausea, sweating, motion sickness, headaches, increased saliva, blurred vision and ocular fatigue [29]. It does not represent a disease but is a natural response of the human body to unaccustomed stimuli, and it affects 50% of those involved in the experience of virtual reality.

There are several theories about the physiological causes of *cybersickness*, in particular the following: (a) sensory conflict [13, 15–17, 19]; (b) postural instability [4, 30] (c) poisoning [5, 24, 36]; and (d) sensory rearrangement [28].

In the domain of virtual reality games, *cybersickness* is also called virtual reality sickness (VRS) and occurs largely as the conflict between three sensory systems: visual, vestibular and proprioceptive [19]. VRS constrains the planning capacity of the designers of games, who are responsible for deciding about all the features, rules and dynamics of a game. The games currently being designed for this platform show significant reductions in the complexity of these mechanisms and dynamics.

In light of this problem, this paper seeks to combine the field of knowledge of Neuroscience with Games Design, in an attempt to find possible design strategies that are able to mitigate the symptoms caused by *cybersickness* in games made for virtual reality helmets. This involves setting out the results obtained from an experiment on the experience of games involving virtual reality helmets, which was carried out with two groups of volunteers made up of heavy and low users in the 18–35 age range. The purpose of this experiment was to identify and analyze the planned decisions made for this game and their ability either to increase or reduce the presence of symptoms of *cybersickness* among the users. As a result, the study sought to point out the main design features of the game that should be avoided when devising games of this nature, as well as assisting in the development of games that are increasingly more aware of the perceptive and cognitive system of the users.

2   Simulator Sickness and *Cybersickness*: The Main Differences

The condition called Simulator Sickness became well known at the end of the 1950s, when virtual reality was still restricted to training helicopter pilots. Its symptoms were recorded for the first time by Casali and Frank [4], and described as discomfort, drowsiness, pallor, sweating, nausea and occasional vomiting, which were the cause of distraction and impaired the effectiveness of the simulators [18]. In view of its complex and polysymptomatic features, (with significant variations from one person to another which made its diagnosis and treatment difficult), Kennedy and Fowlkes [17] decided to recognize it as a syndrome.

As the scope of its field broadened, with a more extensive use of laboratories and simulators, virtual reality reached the general public and the condition of Simulator Sickness began to be called *Cybersickness*, since it was no longer confined to the world of simulators. The distinction between both conditions also extended to the kind of technology used. Whereas cases of Simulator Sickness generally involve stationary virtual reality devices, those related to *Cybersickness* stem from the use of HMDs, in which movements of the user´s head have already been detected [27].

Cybersickness is a condition very similar to Motion Sickness[1], the symptoms of which include vomiting, sickness, nausea, headaches, increased salivation, fatigue, cold sweats, and pallor [8, 16, 19]. Although, motion sickness and *cybersickness* have similar symptoms, they are not necessarily the same thing [19]. Motion sickness is caused by movements of the body, while the eyes are focused on a static point; in contrast, *cybersickness* is caused by the inability to simulate the movements of the body while the eyes follow its movements. On account of this feature, some researchers describe *cybersickness* as visually induced motion sickness (VIMS).

Cybersickness can also be defined as an affliction that is usually caused by immersing someone in virtual environments, which makes a large number of the users of virtual reality devices suffer from the range of symptoms and types of discomfort described above [29]. Jones et al. [14] list the following factors that can lead to either an increase or mitigation of the causes of *cybersickness*:

1. **System:** level of distortion of the image; amplitude of the field of vision; flickering on the screen; mobility of the users provided by mobile platforms; screen frequency; resolution; input delays of the player with regard to head movements; and the upgrading frame speed per second;
2. **Personal features and experiences:** sex, age, illnesses, degree of postural stability and propensity to motion sickness;
3. **Time:** duration of the user´s experience in virtual reality;
4. **Number of experiences:** frequency of the user´s experience with virtual reality;
5. **Cinematic features:** degrees and levels of user interaction in the virtual reality experience.

Rolnick and Lubow [31] stated that when the user makes an unexpected movement, this represents one of the key factors that cause *cybersickness*. So et al. [32] suggested that acceleration is one of the main factors that cause *cybersickness* in a navigation of virtual reality environments with HMDs. Since the vestibular human system, which is responsible for the detection of these kinds of stimuli, does not respond to constant speed, the continuous movements represent fewer sensory conflicts. At the same time, linear or angular accelerations cause greater discomfort, owing to the sensory conflict caused by the fact that the body is stopped. For this reason, shorter accelerations are more comfortable to users than those that are more extensive.

---

[1] It is characterized by the intolerance to the movement resulting from a sensory conflict between the vestibular, visual and proprioceptive systems. This results in a physiological response related to the stimuli of unfamiliar movements [28].

In contrast, Palmisano [27] argues that the developers of software must take care when making representations of movements of the head for people wearing virtual reality helmets, because alterations in the desynchronization of the movements of the head or even delays in response, can lead to *cybersickness*.

Detecting the exact cause of *cybersickness* is a difficult task because as well as suffering from polysymptomatic distress, the users have different experiences and react in an individual way to the stimuli. The stimuli can be delayed over a period of minutes or hours and the question of human adjustment is another key factor that can make it hard to determine the exact cause of the problem [15]. Users with a tendency to feel sick in rides at amusement parks or cars, also tend to be more sensitive.

In the past, researchers believed that an improvement in the hardware of VR devices would mitigate the symptoms and allow a better human adjustment [33]. On the other hand, studies such as those of Mon-Williansm, Wann e Rushton [23] argued that an upgrading of the hardware of stereoscopic screens caused an increase of the symptoms.

There is a wide range of methods for measuring and assessing *cybersickness*, which include the following: galvanic skin response; electroencephalograms; and the Simulator Sickness Questionnaire (SSQ). The SSQ was devised by Kennedy [15], together with other researchers, and was based on the MSQ (Motion Sickness Questionnaire). It covers 3 different categories of symptoms: Nausea; Oculomotor Movements; and Disorientation (Chart 1). Each of these categories has different weights and constants. The weights of the SSQ-N, SSQ-O and SSQ-D categories are multiplied to the value assigned by the participant of the virtual reality experience himself, for each symptom mentioned in the questionnaire, in a scale of 0 to 3 (0.0 = no symptom; 1.0 = few symptoms; 2,0 = moderate symptoms; 3 = many symptoms). The weight of the SSQ-T category is multiplied by the sum of the total number of values obtained from the SSQ-N, SSQ-O and SSQ-D categories. Despite the limitations of a questionnaire, where the users might record symptoms that have not really occurred or even lie, the SSQ is the only method that does not require special equipment and its data are easy to interpret.

3   *Cybersickness*: The Main Theories

Research in the field of neuroscience has investigated *cybersickness* by means of the sensory rearrangement theory of [25, 28, 36], through an approximation of neuromechanisms responsible for vection, vertigo and motion sickness [1, 10, 19, 27] and through a hypothetical neural pathway of visual, vestibular and proprioceptive senses [11, 12].

Most of the studies related to *cybersickness* cite the sensory conflict theory as an explanation of the problem. However, after 1990, new theories were advanced by researchers in the field of psychology. These sought to explain motion sickness as being induced by visual stimuli, knowledge, the theory of postural instability and poisoning. The clash between these theories led to an investigation of the possible neural mechanisms and etiology of *cybersickness*. To understand the neural mechanisms, it is essential to follow strategies to find possible solutions to the malady.

3.1 The Sensory Conflict Theory

Since *cybersickness* has characteristics similar to motion sickness, theories about the causes of both problems have been correlated. This theory was formulated in an attempt to explain the cause of motion sickness and takes account of the sensory conflict between the information that is being processed by the eyes, semicircular canals, otoliths, proprioceptors and somatosensory data, compared with the existing patterns in a neural network of past experiences. The comparison between the two memories leads to inconsistency and causes the symptoms of motion sickness/*cybersickness*, at the same time that someone experiences an adjustment to these stimuli [13].

The vestibular system is responsible for transmitting information about movement and head orientation so that the brain can process it. This occurs in the inner ear, which contains the receptors responsible for the position of the head. The signals produced by this positioning are converted into neural signals that are transmitted to the nuclei by means of vestibular nerves. These nuclei are situated in the encephalic trunk and their predictions provide information about the movement of the head and its position relative to gravity, the stability of the eyes during the movements of the head, postural adjustment, autonomous functions and awareness [21].

Reason and Brand [28] concluded that there are several kinds of sensory conflict that can cause motion sickness. Although 'visual without the vestibular' sensory conflict is widely accepted as the cause of *cybersickness*, there are other sensory conflicts such as 'vestibular disorder without vision', which cause symptoms of motion sickness, that resemble the symptoms of *cybersickness* (Table 1).

Table 1. Types of conflict found in real situations [28]

Type of conflict	Example of situation
Visual and vestibular	Using a virtual reality helmet with a different calibration for head movements in the real world
Visual without vestibular	Movement in virtual reality while stopped in the real world
Vestibular disorder without vision	Reading a book while travelling in a moving vehicle
Otolith and canal	Quickly swinging the head in microgravity[a]
Canal without otolith	Caloric stimulation of the inner ear[a]
Otolith without canal	Low frequency oscillations in a vertical plane[a]

[a]Experiments that can be verified only in experiments conducted in laboratories

Although this is the most widely accepted theory, researchers such as Riccio [30] and Money [24] argue that sensory conflict does not exist and that the non-redundant multisensory patterns can be regarded as complementary and not conflicting. Moreover, Stroffregen and Riccio [30] and Frank and Casali [4] stated that the sensory conflict theory fails to predict increases in intensity or when the *cybersickness* will occur and cannot even determine how severe will be the difference between the senses.

3.2 Theory of Postural Instability

Riccio and Stoffregen [30] put forward the theory of postural instability, which regards a stable posture, or rather, balance, as a natural part of human behavior. Having stable posture can be defined as a situation when someone´s uncontrollable movements are restricted to those caused by factors in the surrounding environment. The body naturally seeks postural stability as shown in the example in Fig. 1, and a person attempts to correct the posture of his body by bending. In the situation represented, as the gravity remains low, the posture will be unstable owing to an incorrect visual stimulus. The more unstable the posture, the more prolonged will be the period of instability or adjustment and the more likely will be the occurrence of *cybersickness*.

Fig. 1. Image illustrating an incorrect visual stimulus [29].

For example, in a virtual reality application, not all the information related to gravity is the same as in the real world and hence while the body perceives gravity in one way, the vision is perceiving it in another. In an attempt to keep its balance, the body ends up by inducing the symptoms of *cybersickness*. It is worth noting that it is for this reason that authors such as Rebenitch [29] state that postural instability has not ceased to be a type of sensory conflict.

3.3 Theory of Poisoning

The theory of poisoning was suggested by Claremont [5] and later formalized by Treisman [36]. Measured from a perspective related to biological evolution, the theory of poisoning seeks a way of explaining the reason why a movement, or illusion of a movement, in the context of virtual reality, can cause nausea and vomiting.

This theory suggests that motion sickness and *cybersickness* are the result of an evolutionary process, according to which the intake of poison causes an alteration in the vestibular system that causes sickness and makes one disgorge what is in the stomach

[5]. Thus, virtual reality will act in a psychological way and make the body think it has ingested some kind of toxic substance and react in an instinctive way, resulting in symptoms of nausea and vomiting. Money [24] regards motion sickness as an evolutionary abnormality that can be found in several other species and is thus not a condition confined to human beings but also recognizable in other animals.

3.4   Theory of Sensory Rearrangement

The theory of sensory rearrangement is described by Reason and Brand [28] and puts forward the idea that the cause of motion sickness originates from sensory inputs that diverge from the "normal". Unlike the sensory conflict theory, the theory of sensory rearrangement is supported by the question of human adaptability.

Virtual reality makes use of sensory stimuli to create a world that does not exist. Whatever attempts are made to replicate the physical features of reality, the HMDs are still unable to reproduce the physical world as a whole, with fidelity and hence simple alterations, such as changes in the field of vision, type of navigation and even the lack of gravity, can trigger the symptoms of motion sickness.

Those who wear glasses that include prismatic lenses, have symptoms similar to *cybersickness* when they alter the angle of the lenses. This is due to the need for sensory adaptation.

When a movement is planned, and the copy of sensory stimulation caused by the brain is compared with the actual stimulation prompted by one of the senses, the brain initiates a sensory rearrangement and produces new information for future movements in accordance with what is occurring (Fig. 2).

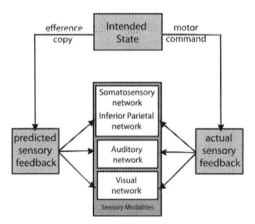

Fig. 2. Cerebral sensory model of the estimated states in which a general control reaches a state in which the efference copy is withdrawn. This copy is compared with the complete sensory response in multiple regions of the brain [6].

The cerebellum plays a key role in the creation of internal models that are designed to control the arms, legs and other parts of the body. It has neurons called Purkinje fibers, and these acts to stabilize the movements of the head. In recent research in the field of neuroscience, Oman and Cullen [25] suggest that there is a connection between the neurons of the vestibular nucleus in the encephalic trunk and the integrated sensory network of the brain. Researchers such as Dennison [6] state that this connection might be the key to finding the origins of the symptoms of *cybersickness*.

4   *Cybersickness* in Virtual Reality Games of HMDs

Cybersickness is a condition that affects the whole process of producing a virtual reality game. According to Carmack [2], *cybersickness* is one of the main problems facing the virtual games industry in its desire to adopt a greater degree of virtual reality. Other researchers like Mammen et al. [22] think that *cybersickness* should be viewed as a part of the enjoyment but in a way that does not spoil the experience of the game.

The high latency of the user´s head movements is mentioned as one of the main causes of *cybersickness*. This was found in old generations of HMD and made it difficult to produce games for the general public. However, even after a significant improvement in virtual reality technology, to the point of almost eradicating the problems of latency, there are still many reported cases of players suffering from *cybersickness* [29].

The recent virtual reality helmets have corrected several of the problems caused by the old versions; however, the problems cannot only be attributed to technology. A large proportion of the problems that cause *cybersickness* in virtual reality are linked to the application design [26].

Virtual reality helmets such as Oculus Rift and Playstation VR are intended to provide the user with an experience of virtual reality, while comfortably seated [20]. This position is suited to sessions of the game that last a long time, and reduce the dangers caused by falls.

However, before the designers can provide the player with a satisfactory experience while seated, they must introduce innovations for the time when the navigation of this experience is planned. Shooting games like DOOM[2] and QUAKE[3], which make use of cameras with an inner focus lens, require the users to make constant backwards and sideways movements, which are prone to lead to *cybersickness*. Another factor that impairs the experience of the games of this nature is the need to rotate the virtual body of the user, so he can interact with what takes place in the part behind his field of vision. This requires a physical rotation or the use of an input in a gamepad, which will make the digital camera of the game move.

In other words, most of the experiences of virtual reality games are spoilt by attempts to prevent sensory conflict, since they result in limited navigations or require a great deal of physical space for locomotion. This is also the case with games created for the Vive virtual reality helmet produced by HTC, which employs INAV (In-place Navigation Technique). The game captures the movements of the body by means of sensors and reproduces them from translations to rotations, as a means of embedding the user

---

[2] Games published by Bethesda Softworks and designed by Id Software. First launched on 13th May 2016.

[3] Game first launched on 5th December 1999 published and developed by Id Software.

in the virtual world. However, the rotation of the user´s body through a joystick, allows the camera of the game to move without the user having to move his head and this causes a great disparity between the visual and vestibular information and hence *cybersickness*.

Another outcome from the creation of virtual reality games lies in the limitations *cybersickness* causes to the level design, as in the example of the version of virtual reality SUPERHOT[4]. Whereas the version for personal computers and video games allows users to cross over the levels by navigating with a joystick, to carry out the translation and rotation movements, the virtual reality version of the game had all the levels redesigned, so that no navigation of any kind was necessary during each of the levels. The player can only move his body in a way that can allow him to hide from, or shoot at, the enemies spread out in his field of vision.

This makes it clear that despite all the advances in hardware and software technology, until now *cybersickness* has remained a significant problem in the development of virtual reality games. The fact that it involves both technical constraints and the creative process, makes it difficult to achieve progress in this area.

5   The Experiment

This research study carried out an experiment with the aim of finding possible design strategies that could mitigate the symptoms caused by *cybersickness* in virtual reality games made for helmets. This involved a sample of two groups of volunteers made up of *heavy-users* and *low-users*, in the age range of 18–35. The experiment detected, analyzed and interpreted the design decisions found in the game that was tested and determined whether they were able to increase or reduce the incidence of symptoms of *cybersickness* among the users.

5.1   Game for the Virtual Reality Helmet

The platform selected for the application of the prototype was the Samsung Galaxy S7 smartphone together with the HMD Samsung Gear VR. With a resolution screen of 2560×1440 and processing capacity sufficient to maintain an upgrading rate of 60 fps, the cellular device is coupled to the HMD by an entry micro-USB, capable of receiving information from the gyroscope and the accelerometer of the helmet.

The interface used for the interaction with the prototype was the wireless joystick which comes with the 2017 version of Gear VR. The control has six different buttons. Only the Button located in the region of the thumb was used for the experiment, which apart from being pressable, selects the touch position on the surface (Fig. 3).

---

[4] Independent distributed and developed by SUPERHOT Team. Its virtual reality version has been released in 6th December 2016, while its PC version has been released 25th February of 2016.

Fig. 3. Samsung Gear VR and its joystick.

The video processing capacity (GPU) of the cell device has limitations during the development process of the application. Adjustments are necessary, as well as a reduction in the consumption of the device resources to keep the rate at 60 fps. There is a need for this to avoid any lowering of the application performance and hence, resulting in symptoms of *cybersickness*.

The engine Unity 3D game was used for designing the game employed in the experiment, together with the official library, which is provided free of charge to developers on the official page of the Oculus Company. Small alterations were made to the codes of the basic library to adapt the movements of the character in a way that could avoid the physical movements of the player, particularly when handling curves (Fig. 4).

```
Vector2 primaryTouchpad = OVRInput.Get(OVRInput.Axis2D.PrimaryTouchpad);
Vector3 euler = transform.rotation.eulerAngles;

if (OVRInput.Get(OVRInput.Button.One))
{
    if (primaryTouchpad.y > 0.5f)
    {
        moveForward = true;
        dpad_move = true;
    }
    else if (primaryTouchpad.y < -0.5f)
    {
        moveBack = true;
        dpad_move = true;
    }

    if (primaryTouchpad.x > 0.5f)
    {
        euler.y += 1;
    }
    else if (primaryTouchpad.x < -0.5f)
    {
        euler.y -= 1;
    }
}
```

Fig. 4. Alteration of the *Updated* method of the OVRController.cs script, found in the basic library of Oculus VR.

5.2   The User's Experience

The application of the experiment took place in five stages: (a) the first involved a survey of information related to the physical condition and health of the user; (b) the second is devoted to the random assignment of participants in the sequence of the game being played, before the beginning of the experience; (c) the third consisted of putting on the virtual reality helmet for the calibration and adjustments; (d) the fourth covered the virtual reality experience. This was carried out in a session lasting a total of 30 min, −10 min being devoted to being immersed in 'Level 1' of the game; a 10 min interval; and 10 min for immersion in 'Level 2' of the game. We emphasize here the random order for the beginning of the experience at 'Level 1' or 'Level 2', as indicated in Item 'b' and described in Item 4.2.3; (e) the fifth corresponds to the application of the Simulator Sickness Questionnaire (SSQ).

Participants
The participants were all native Brazilians who are residents of the urban regions of the State of Sao Paulo, and came from several professional areas. The experiment comprised 24 male participants and this sample was divided into two groups: 12 *low users* and 12 heavy users of digital games. The criterion for categorizing and dividing the respective groups took account of the level of experience the users had of virtual reality games for helmets: none, little [*low-users*] or considerable [*heavy users*].

The Simulator Sickness Questionnaire
In making an assessment of the symptoms of *cybersickness*, the experiment relied on the Simulator Sickness Questionnaire, devised by Kennedy et al. [15]. This questionnaire has been adopted for most of the investigative studies of *cybersickness*. A review of the literature by Carvalho [3] revealed that between 40 and 50 studies have used it as an assessment method.

The 16 items listed on the left show the potential symptoms of the user during the experience of virtual reality. Added to these are three categories that show the possible causes of each of the symptoms mentioned. These are: Nausea; Oculomotor; and Disorientation. The scores are shown through each of the following abbreviations: SSQ-N, SSQ-O, SSQ-D, SSQ-T (Total) (Table 2).

Stages of the method

(a) In the first stage of the experiment, the users answered short questions related to their physical condition and health, in particular any possible history of cardiac problems or in the vestibular system such as labyrinthitis.
(b) In the second stage, a random allocation of the order of the game ('Sequence A' or 'Sequence B') was made to begin the experience in the virtual reality helmet. At this time, the amount of information given to the user was restricted with the aim of avoiding making any suggestions.

In 'Sequence A' of the game, the player began his navigation from Level 1, followed by Level 2; while in 'Sequence B', the player began his experience at Level 2, so as to follow Level 1 afterwards in a reverse order. The purpose of altering the design of these levels was to determine the possible effects on the checked results that originated from the sequence in which the features of the game were displayed to the user and hence find out the possible symptoms of *cybersickness* related to them (Table 3).

Table 2. SSQ: indication of the symptoms assigned to each category and the weights for each category

SSQ Symptom[a]	Weight – Nausea (SSQ-N)	Weight – Oculomotor (SSQ-O)	Weight – Disorientation (SSQ-D)
Fatigue		1	
Headache		1	
Eyestrain		1	
Difficulty in focusing		1	1
Increased salivation	1		
Sweating	1		
Nausea	1		1
Difficulty in concentrating	1	1	
Fullness of head			1
Blurred vision		1	1
Dizziness (Eyes open)			1
Dizziness (Eyes closed)			1
Vertigo			1
Stomach awareness	1		
Burping	1		
TOTAL	[1]	[2]	[3]
Weighting score for each category	9.54 × [1]	7.58 × [2]	13.92 × [3]
Total Score (SSQ-T)	([1] + [2] + [3]) × 3.74		

[a]For each symptom, the participant assigned a score in the intensity scale of 0 to 3 (0.0 = no symptom; 1.0 = a mild symptom 2,0 = moderate symptoms; 3 = high symptom).

(c) In the third stage, the participant put on the virtual reality helmet and was given instructions about how to move and control the avatar in the space of the game. At this time, the user was also told to avoid moving his body during the curves; the aim of this was to encourage him to use the control as an interface for interaction. In addition, the player was requested to memorize the effects of the experience on his body and note the differences between the two levels, in particular with regard to possible symptoms caused by *cybersickness*.

(d) The fourth stage covers the experience of the user in two levels of the game. The experience at each level lasts 10 min with an interval between them of the same length of time. The order for the beginning of 'Level 1' or 'Level 2' is random.

Throughout this stage, the participant is questioned about the occurrence of any symptom related to *cybersickness*, and about what aspect of the game he thinks is responsible for triggering it. It is worth mentioning that the user is granted the right to abort the experiment at any time, especially if the symptoms of *cybersickness* too much to bear.

(e) The fifth and final stage occurs soon after the end of the experience, which the player has of both levels of the game and involves the user being given the questionnaire (SSQ) to fill in. The experience at each level is recorded by the user in separate Tables. As well as the Table, the form includes a section for information regarding the identity of the volunteer, as well as space for possible comments about the experience he has undergone.

Table 3. Differences in the displayed order of the levels of the game established by the experiment

Experiment	First level	Second level
Sequence A	Level 1	Level 2
Sequence B	Level 2	Level 1 (Reversed)

5.3 Results and Discussions

The data collected from the Simulator Sickness Questionnaire was divided into the following categories: SSQ-N [Nausea]; SSQ-O [Oculomotor]; SSQ-D [Disorientation]; and SSQ-T [Total]. The scores of each participant were calculated in accordance with the guidelines indicated by the referred method. Graph in Fig. 5 shows the results obtained from all the participants of the experiment, who were classified as '*Heavy Users*' and '*Low Users*'.

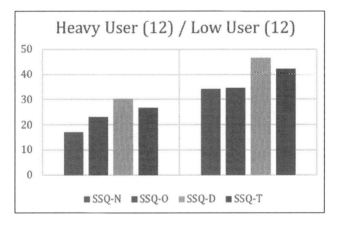

Fig. 5. Results of the SSQ: a comparison between 'heavy users' and 'low users'.

The comparison between the results obtained for the group of '*Heavy Users*' and '*Low Users*', give evidence of a striking difference between the scores for all the categories, that observed in the SSQ-D category being the most significant: with 17.05 for the low users and 34.22 for the heavy users. SSQ-T also showed a significant difference: with 26.80 for the low users and 42.38 for the heavy users.

Table 4. Comments made by the participants during the experiment.

Problem noted	Participants	Sequence
Joining walls (Corners)	1	A and B
Staircase	3	A and B
Strong light	4	A
Rotation with control	2	A and B
Downward movement	3	B
Swinging round rapidly	3	A and B
Difference between the internal and external lighting	1	A
Saturated colors	1	A
Curves	1	A
Movements without acceleration	1	A and B
Ramps	1	A and B
Flickering due to a lack of anti-aliasing[a]	1	B

[a]Filter present in 3D applications, which cause an illusion "flattening" at the borders of 3-dimensional models. This filter is only an illusion, a blur that gives the impression of a "mountain range" or "teeth" because of a lack of pixels in the objects, which are found on the diagonal. This technique requires a high processing of the video card (GPU) of the device, in which the application is embedded.

On the basis of these results, it is possible to identify, analyze and interpret the main design decisions that increase the symptoms of *cybersickness*, in each of the sequences A and B, and particularly, for each group (Table 4).

(A) **The main difference in the performance of heavy users and low users**

The differences observed in the results obtained for the groups of heavy users and low users suggest that the low users have more symptoms related to *cybersickness*, especially with regard to the SSQ-D [Disorientation] category.

These results strengthen the theory of sensory rearrangement, put forward by Reason and Brand [28]. This means the players who are heavy users of digital games end up by having efference copies for situations that are repeated in environments reproduced by virtual reality helmets – for example, through the rotation of the camera by using leveraged analogical skills in joysticks. This very common technique in video games is used in the experiment and has proved to be one of the main causes of the disorientation experienced by the participants. Other uncommon factors among the low users such as irregular movements when climbing stairs or involuntary movements of the head of the avatar, are also commonly found among heavy users, a fact which leads the more experienced users to adapt more quickly to the stereoscopic screen of the HMD.

(B) *Cybersickness* **originating from luminous stimuli**

The comments of the participants referred to which of the design decisions that are common in video and computer games, lead to an increase in the symptoms of *cybersickness*, when applied to virtual reality games.

The strong light in the corridor (Fig. 6), used as a kind of distraction to prevent the player from noticing a hidden key, features as one of the main complaints of the participants in the experiment as being associated with symptoms of *cybersickness*. A smaller number of users also noted the difference of the lighting in the inner environment and the outer environment, which was exposed to the skybox as a cause of these symptoms. In both situations – the sudden change in the intensity of the lighting caused a significant increase in *cybersickness*.

Fig. 6. Source of shining light in Level 1 of the game designed and applied in the experiment

(C) ***Cybersickness* caused by the movement of climbing stairs: conflicts between the experience and efferent copies**

Another result observed was the difference between people who had symptoms of *cybersickness* when they climbed or went down ramps or stairs. According to Dorado and Figueroa [7], ramps lead to better results with regard to mitigating *cybersickness* when compared with those obtained from people using stairs with natural movements (Fig. 7).

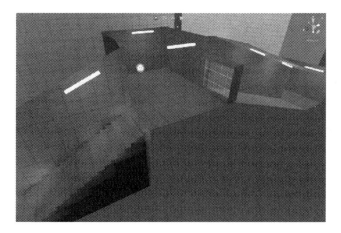

Fig. 7. Ramp and staircase at a moment in the game designed and applied to the experiment

This result provided evidence that the action of climbing stairs with natural movements causes instability in the movements of the camera. The link between instability and this situation is uncommon in the vestibular system of the human beings, which already has efferent copies of vertical movements related to 'climbing stairs', stored in its nervous system. In an experience with virtual reality helmets, the vestibular system is not stimulated during this kind of movement. This means it is not feasible to make an ideal comparison between the situation experienced by the player and the existing reafference, which leads the user to suffer from symptoms of *cybersickness*.

6   Conclusion

Cybersickness has arisen as a limiting factor for the creation of games that require greater complexity in the handling of the avatar (virtual character) of the player. In light of this, when compared with computer games and videogames, games for virtual reality helmets are being simplified.

This paper investigates the close alliance between the design of games and the fields of neuroscience by seeking to understand the crucial importance of overcoming *cybersickness*. When carried out from the perspective of the operational sensorimotor and cognitive systems of the user, (and from the neurophysiological mechanisms that cause *cybersickness*), a planning strategy can open up secure ways of exploring the design of games for HMDs, by providing evidence of design features that are able to maintain the navigational complexity for the users through different levels of the game, while at the same time, mitigating the symptoms of cybersickness.

This potential capacity is borne out by the results obtained from the application of the experiment set out here and can be carried out with both heavy users and low users of games for virtual reality helmets. The main results and benefits for the mitigation of the symptoms caused by *cybersickness* emerge from the following design decisions:

- Avoiding the use of ladders in designing the "levels";
- Avoiding sharp contrasts in the lighting when applied to different settings and effects;
- Taking account of the sensory adaptation of the user in designing different levels. In other words, situations capable of causing *cybersickness* should only be shown to the player after he/she has fully adapted to the virtual reality interface;
  Ensuring the design of games involving a complex navigation system are aimed at heavy users, since their previous experiences with regard to interaction in virtual reality systems, strongly corroborates the fact that they are able to make a faster and more effective sensory adaptation to the interface of this game.

It should be noted that currently *cybersickness* represents one of the most limiting factors for high investment in the development of complex games for HMDs. This fact puts in the shade the current games for HMDs, which are designed for traditional platforms.

In view of this, the future development of this research study seeks to carry out and apply new experiments aimed at broadening the range of design solutions described here. In this way an attempt will be made to overcome the symptoms caused by *cybersickness*, in both low and heavy users of games for virtual reality helmets.

Thus, it is believed that by following the recommendations for this purpose in a systematic way, a significant contribution can be made to the games industry for everyone concerned.

References

1. Brandt, T.: Vertigo: its multisensory syndromes, n. 2 (1999)
2. Carmack (2014). https://www.youtube.com/watch?v=nqzpAbK9qFk
3. Carvalho, M.R., Da Costa, R.T., Nardi, E.A.: Simulator Sickness Questionnaire: Tradução e adaptação transcultural. Jornal brasileiro de psiquiatria **60**(4), 247–252 (2011)
4. Casali, J.G., Frank, L.H.: Manifestation of visual/vestibular disruption in simulators: severity and empirical measurements of symptamotology. In: AGARD Conference, n. 433, pp. 11–18 (1988)
5. Claremont, C.A.: The psychology of sea-sickness. Psyche **11**, 86–90 (1931)
6. Dennison, M.: Motion sickness in virtual environments, p. 101. Tese (Doutorado) em Psicologia, California (2017)
7. Dorado, J.L., Figueroa, P.A.: Ramps are better than stairs to reduce *Cybersickness* in applications based on a HMD and a gamepad. In: IEEE Symposium on 3D user Interfaces, Minneapolis, pp. 29–30 (2014)
8. Ehrlich, S.D.: Motion Sickness. Pennstate Hershey (2014). http://pennstatehershey.adam.com/content.aspx?productId=107&pid=33&gid=000110
9. Grau, O.: A arte virtual: Da ilusão à imersão. UNESP e Senac, São Paulo (2007)
10. Hettinger, J., Berbaum, K.S., Kennedy, R.S., Dunlap, W.P., Nolan, M.D., et al.: Vection and simulator sickness. Mil. Psychol. 2, 171–181 (1990)
11. Ji, J.J., So, R.H.Y., Cheung, T.F., Howarth, P., Stanney, K.: A search for possible neural pathways leading to visually induced motion sickness. Vision **2**, 131–134 (2005)
12. Ji, J.J., So, R.H.Y.: Visually induced motion sickness: an insight from neurosciences. In: First International Symposium on Theoretical Issues in Ergonomics Science, San Diego, pp. 18–21 (2004)
13. Johnson, D.M.: Introduction to and review of simulator sickness research. Research report (U.S. Army Research Institute for the Behavioral and Social Sciences), Fort Rucker (2005)
14. Jones, M.B., Kennedy, R.S., Stanney, K.M.: Toward systematic control of *Cybersickness*. Presence: teleoperators and virtual environments, vol. 13, Massachusetts, pp. 589–600 (2004)
15. Kennedy, R.S., Lane, N.E., Berbaum, K.S., Lilienthal, M.G.: Simualtor sickness questionnaire: an enhanced method for quantifying simulator sickness. Int. J. Aviat. Psychol. **3**(3), 203–220 (1993)
16. Kennedy, R.S., Lanham, S., Drexler, J.M.: A comparison of incidences, symptom profiles, measurement techniques and suggestions for research. Presence **6**, 638–644 (1997)
17. Kennedy, S.R., Fowlkes, J., Berbaum, K.S., Lilienthal, M.G.: Use of motion sickness history questionnaire for prediction of simulator sickness. Aviat. Space Environ. Med. **63**, 588–593 (1992)
18. Kolasinski, M.E.: Simulator Sickness in Virtual Environments, p. 68 (1995)
19. LaViola, J.: A discussion of *cybersickness* in virtual environments. ACM SIGCHI Bulletin **32**, 47–56 (2000)
20. Luckey Patcher. https://www.youtube.com/watch?v=-YCBadIVro8&list=PLckFgM6dUP2 hc4iy

21. Lundy-Ekman, L.: Neurociência: Fundamentos para a Reabilitação, 2nd edn. Elsevier, Rio de Janeiro (2004)
22. Mammen, S.V., Knote, A., Adenhofer, S.: Cyber sick but still having fun. In: VRST 2016 Proceedings of the 22nd ACM Conference on Virtual Reality Software and Technology, New York, pp. 325–326 (2016)
23. Mon-Williams, M., Wann, J.P., Rushton, S.: Design factors in stereoscopic virtual-reality displays. Soc. Inf. Disp. **3**, 207–210 (1995)
24. Money, K.E.: Motion and Space Sickness. CRC Press, Boca Raton (1990)
25. Oman, M.C., Cullen, E.K.: Brainstem processing of vestibular sensory exafference: implications for motion sickness etiology. Exp. Brain Res. **232**(8), 2483–2492 (2014)
26. Porcino, M.T., Clua, E., Trevisan, D., Vasconcelos, C.N., Valente, L., et al.: Minimizing cyber sickness in head mounted display systems: design guidelines and applications. In: IEEE 5th International Conference on Serious Games and Applications for Health (SeGAH), Perth (2017). ISSN 978-1-5090-5482-4
27. Palmisano, S., Mursic, R., Kim, J.: Vection and *cybersickness* generated by headand- display motion in the Oculus Rift. Displays **46**, 1–8 (2017)
28. Reason, J.T., Brand, J.J.: Motion Sickness. Academic Press, London (1975)
29. Rebenitch, L., Owen, C.B.: Review on *cybersickness* in applications and visual displays. Virtual Real. **20**, 101–125 (2016)
30. Riccio, G., Stroffegen, T.: An Ecological Theory of Motion Sickness and Postural Instability. Ecol. Psychol. **3**, 195–240 (1991)
31. Rolnick, A., Lubow, R.E.: Why is the driver rarely motion sick? the role of controllability in motion sickness. Ergonomics **34**, 867–879 (1991)
32. So, R.H.Y., Lo, W.T., Ho, A.T.K.: Effects of navigation speed on motion sickness caused by an immersive virtual environment. Hum. Factors **43**(Edição 3), 452–461 (2001). The Journal of the Human Factors and Ergonomics Society, Hong Kong
33. Stanney, K., Salvendy, G.: Aftereffects and sense of presence in virtual environments: formulation of a research and development agenda. Int. J. Hum. Comput. Interact. **10**, 135–187 (1998)
34. Talban, R.J., Cardulo, F.M.: Neural mechanisms of motion sickness. J. Med. Invest. **41**, 44–59 (2001)
35. Tori, R., Kirner, C.: Fundamentos de realidade virtual. In: Fundamentos e tecnologia de realidade virtual e aumentada. Belém: VIII Symposium on virtual reality. Cap. 1, pp. 2–22 (2006)
36. Treisman, M.: Motion sickness: an evolutionary hypothesis. Science **197**, 493–495 (1977)

Generating Personalized Virtual Agent in Speech Dialogue System for People with Dementia

Shota Nakatani[1]($\boxtimes$), Sachio Saiki[1], Masahide Nakamura[1], and Kiyoshi Yasuda[2]

[1] Graduate School of System Informatics Kobe University,
1-1 Rokkodai, Nada, Kobe, Japan
shota-n@ws.cs.kobe-u.ac.jp, sachio@carp.kobe-u.ac.jp,
masa-n@cs.kobe-u.ac.jp
[2] Chiba Rosai Hospital, 2-16 Tatsumidai-higashi, Ichihara, Japan
fwkk5911@mb.infoweb.ne.jp

Abstract. Our research group has been studying a speech communication system with a virtual agent (VA), to support person-centered care (PCC) of people with dementia (PWD). The current system uses the 3D model based on an unreal character for the VA. Because the unfamiliar appearance is to be a mental obstacle to PWD, PWD hardly accept advice and which causes a limitation in the care effects. In this paper, we develop a novel system that dynamically creates a VA based on a given facial image of real person. The proposed system constructs a three-dimensional model based on facial landmarks within the image. It then stretches and transforms some portions of the 3D model to generate facial expressions. From just a given picture, the proposed system easily generates a communication agent familiar with individual PWD. Hence, it can implement (virtual, but effective) conversations with familiar partners. We implement the prototype based on the proposed system and conduct the experiment targeting to the elderly.

Keywords: Virtual agent · Home elderly care · Person-centered care

1 Introduction

Japan is facing a hyper-aging society. The number of people with dementia (PWD) will reach 7 million in 2025, where one-fifth of five elderly people in Japan will suffer from dementia [1]. Hence, a care and a support for PWD are socially needed.

The person-centered care (PCC) is an ideal care for PWD, which monitors and understand individual circumstances, and plans and executes optimized care. The PCC is different from the conventional care and needed to watch care subject sufficiently, which poses heavy physical and mental burden on family and caregivers. In practice, however, the PCC completely relies on human effort.

© Springer International Publishing AG, part of Springer Nature 2018
V. G. Duffy (Ed.): DHM 2018, LNCS 10917, pp. 326–337, 2018.
https://doi.org/10.1007/978-3-319-91397-1_27

To cope with the problem, our research group has been studying a PCC support system for PWD, exploiting the latest IoT and cloud technologies [12]. Gathering and analyzing sensor data from the home of PWD, the system understands activities and contexts of PWD at home [11]. The system then generates dialogues, and talks to PWD through the virtual agent technology [9]. The virtual agent (VA) is a human-looking animated chat-bot program operated on a lap-top PC. Using the speech recognition and synthesis technologies, a PWD can communicate with the VA as if (s)he talks to a human partner.

However, the current system uses an unreal and artificial avatar for the VA. In social psychology, the faces have a large effect on partner in communication between humans. It is considered the same thing in communication with the VA, since you communicate. Hence, because of unacceptance of the VA's appearance in current system, the care and advices from unfamiliar avatar does not motivate the PWD very well. It poses limitations on concentration and engagement of the PCC.

This paper develops a new technology that introduces more familiar agent as the VA, in order to achieve more concentrated and effective care within the PCC system. We use just a picture of face in method to generate the VA. As a result, the system can easily display the avatar of the person as the VA, who is familiar with PWD or influential in PWD.

We generate a three-dimensional model from a given picture of a face of a familiar person of a PWD, and integrate the 3D facial model as the VA of the PCC support system. More specifically, for a given picture of a face, the system extracts landmark points of the face using a face recognition algorithm. Based on the landmark points, the system then stretches and transforms some portions of the 3D model, to dynamically generate facial expressions. Also, for a given voice data, the system synchronizes the lip motions, as if the 3D model speaks to the PWD. By integrating the generated model to the PCC system, we expect to relieve PWD of resistance to care and communication in an existing PCC support system.

From just a given picture, the proposed method can dynamically generate a communication agent according to preference of individual PWD. Hence, it can implement (virtual, but effective) conversations with familiar partners of PWD, such as close relatives, child, close friends and so on. As a result, the proposed system contributes to the implementation of more effective PCC support system.

2   Preliminary

2.1   Person-Centered Care Support System with Virtual Agent

Our research group has been studying how the ICT can support a person with dementia (PWD) at home. The concept of person-centered care (PCC) defines an ideal care for PWD, which monitors and understand individual circumstances, and plans and executes optimized care. Our current aim is to provide person-centered communication for PWD using the virtual agent (VA) technology. The VA is a human-looking animated chat-bot program operated on a PC. Using the

Fig. 1. VirtualCareGiver

speech recognition and synthesis technologies, PWD can communicate with the VA as if (s)he talks to a human partner.

In our previous research, we have developed a system, called Virtual Care Giver (VCG), using the VA [12]. Figure 1 shows the image of VCG. VCG was designed to be able to cooperate with Web services, to integrate IoT, smart home and cloud. Because of this design, VCG can generate personalized cares and conversations from activities and contexts estimated based on sensor data gathered from the home of a PWD. VCG then can provide a care and conversation for the PWD via VA, which supports the PCC. Delegating the communication care with VCG, a human caregiver can concentrate on human-centric tasks that cannot be done with ICT.

Our preliminary experiment shows that VCG can achieve useful context-aware care for PWD, including, daily greeting, schedule reminder, and prompting medication.

However, there is also a limitation caused by the looking of VA. Currently, the VA of VCG is implemented by MMDAgent [7], which displays a 3D animation character like Fig. 1. So, the care and advices from unfamiliar avatar do not always motivate the PWD very well. This poses limitations on concentration and engagement of the PCC.

2.2 Face Recognition in Cognitive Computing

Cognitive computing is a computing paradigm where a system imitates the human brain and learns itself to derive answers. It often refers to the emerging technologies that can analyze non-numerical data, such as language, picture and voice, which were difficult to understand by the conventional computing.

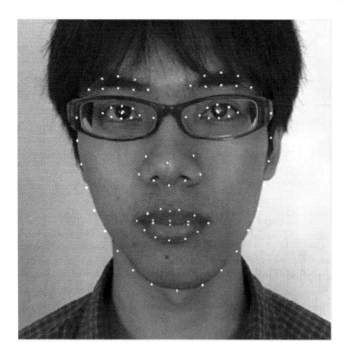

Fig. 2. Facial landmarks derived by Face++

Face recognition and analysis are the major technologies within the cognitive computing. Recently, several companies have published Web API for face recognition. For instance, Microsoft provides Face API and Emotion API [6] within the Azure Cloud Services.

Most face recognition technologies (e.g., [2,10,13]) use machine learning to detect characteristic points on a face such as eyes, nose, mouth and so on. Such points of the face are called facial landmarks. When a new picture is given to the machine, it tries to extract the facial landmarks within the picture. Figure 2 shows that facial landmarks which are extracted from my picture using the API of Face++ [4] are overlaid on the picture. Face++ API is developed based on [2]. It can derive 83 landmarks as coordinates on a picture. Moving position of these extracted landmarks to stretch and transform the picture, we can perform operations to move any specific parts of the face in the picture.

2.3 Related Work

Hinds reported the impression of the robots in case when people do group work with human-like robot or machine-like robot [3]. Hinds mentioned the more the robot of partner is human-like, people become to accept achievement and put confidence in the robot. The evaluation of Hinds's experiment was the impression on physical robots, which is different from the VA, the focus of this study. However, supposed it is the same in the point of the personification of robots, it is considered that how personified the appearance of robots is influencing the contents of communication with robots. The VA of Fig. 1 is an animation character modelled after human, but by the VA getting more human-like appearance, there is some possibility of improving the communication between the VA and human.

3 The Proposed System

We referred to the problem of current PCC support system in Sect. 2.1. Accordingly, in this paper, we propose the system that is aimed to solve the problem, which is not conducted efficient cares for PWD by the faces of VA because the users cannot choose the VA based on his/her preferences in the existing PCC support system.

3.1 Key Idea

As a key idea to achieve more interesting communication care for a PWD, we aim to easily generate a VA based on the preferences of the individual PWD. Using the face recognition and analysis technologies, we generate a 3D facial model from a picture of the person whom the user wants to display as the VA. We then integrate the generated model to the PCC system, and create a situation where the PWD talks with the person whom the PWD want to talk with. As a result, we can implement more quality PCC, compared to the conventional artificial VA.

The existing system which is replaced by proposed system is constituted with application software which the VA is implemented in and Web API to control the application of VA. In the following sub-sections, we describe the functional requirements of the proposed system, and design of the application of VA and the service API. We also illustrate how the proposed system is integrated with the PCC support system.

3.2 Functional Requirements

Based on the analysis of the previous system, we identified that the proposed system must implement following three key features.

Feature F1 (generate a VA):
    For a given picture of a face, the system can dynamically generate a VA with the face.
Feature F2 (instruct the VA to speak):
    For a given text, the system can instruct the generated VA to speak the text.
Feature F3 (instruct the VA to change expression):
    For a given command, the system can change the facial expression of the generated VA.

F1 implements a fundamental requirement of the system to create a VA of a familiar person of PWD. With this feature, every PWD can generate his/her own VA.

F2 implements an ability of speaking in the VA. With this feature, the VA is able to be a conversation partner.

F3 implements an ability of emotion in the VA. With this feature, the VA can behave like a human being, and produce friendly conversation with non-verbal communication.

3.3 Design of Service API and Application

Considering replacement of the previous VA system, we intend to integrate the VA with IoT and smart home. Hence, we deploy Web APIs to control the VA application in which implements the features mentioned in Sect. 3.2 as a Web service. By doing this, external applications within the PCC system can easily use the features **F1**, **F2**, **F3** via Web API. Here we define three Web APIs that define **F1**, **F2** and **F3**, respectively, and explain how to work in the VA application.

createVA(faceImageFile)
> Generates a VA from an image file which is specified by *faceImageFile*. For a given picture of a face, the system extracts landmark points of the face using a face recognition algorithm, and generates a 3D facial model. By default, we suppose that the VA does natural motions such as blink, swaying its face, and so on.

speak(type, text)
> Instructs the generated VA to speak (read) a text sentence specified by *text* with a type of voice specified by *type*. The type of synthesized voice is a parameter that is specified based on generated VA's gender and user's language. We suppose, within the API, that voice data (wav, mp3, etc.) should be synthesized from the text using a text-to-speech technology. As the VA plays back the voice data, we also suppose that the VA should synchronizes the lip motions, by stretching lips within the 3D facial model.

changeExpression (expression)
> Changes the facial expression of the generated VA by a label specified in *expression*. Based on the extracted facial landmark, the system stretches and transforms some portions of the 3D model, which change facial expressions. Typical expressions include normal, smile, angry, sad, surprised, and fear.

3.4 Integrating into PCC Support System

We suppose to deploy the above Web APIs on a Web server called *VAManager*. Figure 3 shows a sequence diagram showing how *VAManager* works within the PCC support system. Here we assume a scenario that a user creates a VA and greets to it.

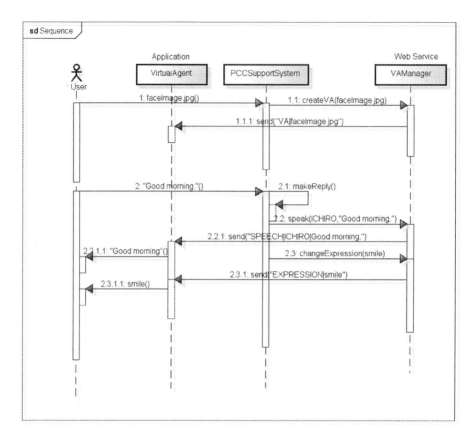

Fig. 3. The sequence of integrated system.

The user first registers an image file (*"faceImage.jpg"*) to the PCC support system. The PCC support system then executes *createVA(faceImage.jpg)* to generate the VA. The VA looking like the person in *faceImage.jpg* is displayed on user's PC.

Suppose that the user says to the VA "Good morning". The PCC system recognizes the user's voice by speech recognition, generates the reply *"Good morning"*, and executes *speak(ICHIRO, "Good morning.")* to instruct the VA to say, *"Good morning"* with the synthesized voice type, *"ICHIRO"*. At the same time, the system executes *changeExpression(smile)* to instruct the VA to smile. As a result, the VA on the PC screen replies to the user, "Good morning" with smile.

4   Implementation of Prototype

Based on the proposed system, we have implemented a prototype system. Technologies used in the implementation are as follows.

Fig. 4. Images of a virtual agent produced by the prototype system.

VAManager
- Development Language: Java
- Web Server: Apache Tomcat
- Web Service Frameworks: Apache Axis2

VirtualAgent(MPAgent)
- Development Language: C#
- MotionPortrait SDK [8]
- Bing Speech API [5]

VAManager is a Web API that is implemented by Java, and deployed on a Tomcat Web server. Based on requests from the PCC support system, it controls Virtual Agent application.

MPAgent is an application software that is implemented by C# using Motion-Portrait SDK. This SDK provides powerful libraries for generating and operating 3D facial model. With the SDK, we were able to implement features **F1** to **F3** very efficiently in C#. We also use Bing Speech API within Microsoft Azure Service to synthesize voice for VA. You can get a synthesized voice with this API by specifying text and voice type defined gender and language. With this API, the system can synthesize different voice based on VA's gender and user's language. The application receives commands *VAManager* and then executes **F1** to **F3**.

Figure 4 shows example facial images in the prototype system. The images show, from left to right, the original face picture, the VA with "happy" expression, the VA with "sad" expression, the VA that is speaking.

Figure 5 shows a scene of the demonstration video talking with the VA generated with the picture of *Albert Einstein*.

The generated movie file can be watched in https://youtu.be/sXaSQJpXojc.

5   Experiment

The purpose of this experiment is to evaluate whether the faces of VA have an influence on receptivity to the care by PCC support system.

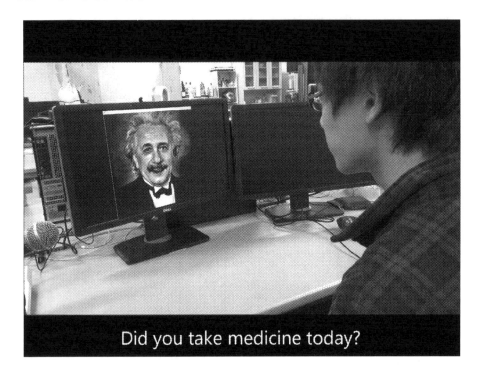

Fig. 5. A scene of the demonstration video.

5.1 Outline of Experiment

At nursing facility, we conducted evaluation experiments with the proposed system, which targets the five elderly from 74 to 99 years old, including person with dementia and person needed care/support.

In the experiment, first, we execute care program for subjects by VCG using character VA which is shown in Fig. 1, then we generate the VA by the proposed system from a picture of familiar person for each subject based on answer in advance questionnaire, "Who is your favorite singer?". After the subjects experience a short conversation with VA about three minutes, we interview subjects and get answer orally.

5.2 Result of Experiment

We got the answers to the interview from four out of five subjects. The other one was not interested in this system, so we could not get answers from her. Questions of the interview and answers for that are as follows. The same answers from different subjects are omitted.

1. What do you feel the impression of the VA generated from a picture (ex. locution, expression, accord with between voice and face)?

- Locution and expression are not on my mind, but accord with between the voice and face of VA is a little.
- I feel strange about it, but locution is not unnatural and accord with between the voice and face of VA is not on my mind.
- I feel surprised and interested. Locution and expression are normal.

2. The system can create a VA if there is even a picture, whom do you want to talk with?
    - There is no one whom I talk with especially.
    - No one occurs to my mind now.

3. Which is it to talk with existing VA in Fig. 1 or real VA generated from a picture?
    - I prefer to the generated with a picture. I can also speak with the previous VA, but I want to use the new VA in the sense that I can see my family or spouse.
    - I prefer to the generated VA with a picture.
    - In the past, there is not being with faces like the previous VA. So, because the previous VA is a strange being, I prefer to the generated VA with a picture which has a human-like and familiar face.

5.3   Discussion

The discussion about each particle of the interview are as follows.

Impression of the VA

Because a voice of VA is generated by Bing Speech API, it is different from a natural voice of person in picture. There is also some possibility that some people feel uncomfortable in intonation and timing of speaking because of the synthesized voice. Compared with the previous VA based on character, it is considered that how to feel a face and expression of the VA differs by individual. In this point, according to result of the experiment, there are both opinions to concern about accord with face and voice of the VA and not to concern. Therefore, we need to improve the system by using more comfortable voice.

Person who want to display as the VA

The subjects did not mention who they want to display as VA. However, from the opinion that the user can see his family or spouse, according to the person, it is considered that the better effects can be gotten by displaying the person who is closer to user as a VA.

Easiness to talk with the VA

In comparison previous VA and proposed VA, the experiment shows the VA which has a human-like appearance by generating with picture is more acceptable than the unfamiliar character VA. All of the subject who answered the interview preferred to the VA generated with picture. However, it is considered that there is a generational problem about this from the answer of subjects. From the answer that he had not ever seen the face of the previous VA, we might be able to get different opinions from a relatively young generation that have some opportunity to see 3D the character model as the computer spreads. That is to say, when the current young generation become to the elderly in the future, how acceptance for the appearance of the VA is different from that by the current elderly, as a result, it is considered that strangeness of the VA generated with picture might be emphasized.

According to the above, there is the case to feel uncomfortable about accord with face and voice of the VA. However, in the point of system, because the method to use a picture is highly effective, this method is expected to be useful in the scene of the care.

6   Conclusion

In this paper, we propose a system that aims more efficient person-centered dementia care with the virtual agent (VA) technology. Using the face recognition technology, the proposed system generates a 3D facial model from a given picture, integrates the model as a personalized VA of the PCC support system. Since every user can easily generate his/her own VA with a preferred face, the system can be expected to achieve more effective PCC. Then, we implemented the prototype system based on the proposed system, and experimented about effect on the face of the VA.

Acknowledgements. This research was partially supported by the Japan Ministry of Education, Science, Sports, and Culture [Grant-in-Aid for Scientific Research (B) (16H02908, 15H02701), Grant-in-Aid for Scientific Research (A) (17H00731), Challenging Exploratory Research (15K12020)], and Tateishi Science and Technology Foundation (C) (No. 2177004).

References

1. Cabinet Office, Government of Japan: Annual Report on the Aging Society, June 2017. http://www.cao.go.jp/
2. Fan, H., Cao, Z., Jiang, Y., Yin, Q., Doudou, C.: Learning Deep Face Representation. CoRR abs/1403.2802 (2014). http://arxiv.org/abs/1403.2802
3. Hinds, P.J., Roberts, T.L., Jones, H.: Whose job is it anyway? A study of human-robot interaction in a collaborative task. Hum. Comput. Interact. **19**(1), 151–181 (2004)
4. Megvii: Face++. https://www.faceplusplus.com
5. Microsoft: Bing Speech API. https://azure.microsoft.com/ja-jp/services/cognitive-services/speech/
6. Microsoft: Emotion API. https://azure.microsoft.com/en-us/services/cognitive-services/emotion/
7. MMDAgent Project Team: MMDAgent - Toolkit for Building Voice Interaction Systems. http://www.mmdagent.jp
8. MotionPortrait Inc.: MotionPortrait. https://www.motionportrait.com

9. Sakakibara, S., Saiki, S., Nakamura, M., Yasuda, K.: Generating personalized dialogue towards daily counseling system for home dementia care. In: Duffy, V.G. (ed.) DHM 2017. LNCS, vol. 10287, pp. 161–172. Springer, Cham (2017). https://doi.org/10.1007/978-3-319-58466-9_16

10. Taigman, Y., Yang, M., Ranzato, M., Wolf, L.: DeepFace: closing the gap to human-level performance in face verification. In: The IEEE Conference on Computer Vision and Pattern Recognition (CVPR), pp. 1701–1708, June 2014

11. Tamamizu, K., Sakakibara, S., Saiki, S., Nakamura, M., Yasuda, K.: Capturing activities of daily living for elderly at home based on environment change and speech dialog. In: Duffy, V.G. (ed.) DHM 2017. LNCS, vol. 10287, pp. 183–194. Springer, Cham (2017). https://doi.org/10.1007/978-3-319-58466-9_18

12. Tokunaga, S., Tamamizu, K., Saiki, S., Nakamura, M., Yasuda, K.: VirtualCare-Giver: personalized smart elderly care. Int. J. Softw. Innov. (IJSI) **5**(1), 30–43 (2016). https://doi.org/10.4018/IJSI.2017010103. http://www.igi-global.com/journals/abstract-announcement/158780

13. Zhang, Z., Luo, P., Loy, C.C., Tang, X.: Facial landmark detection by deep multi-task learning. In: Fleet, D., Pajdla, T., Schiele, B., Tuytelaars, T. (eds.) ECCV 2014. LNCS, vol. 8694, pp. 94–108. Springer, Cham (2014). https://doi.org/10.1007/978-3-319-10599-4_7

Audiogames: Accessibility and Inclusion in Digital Entertainment

Sergio Nesteriuk[✉]

Graduate Program in Design, Anhembi Morumbi University, São Paulo, Brazil
nesteriuk@hotmail.com

Abstract. Video games represent one of the most popular forms of digital entertainment, but people who are blind or visually impaired end up having restricted
access to these games. Discussions about digital accessibility and inclusion often
end up leaving this question aside, in favor of some discourse considered more
"utilitarian" or "productivist". However, video games have a relevant role in
contemporary culture and can bring cognitive, motivational, emotional, and social
benefits, as well as contribute to the well-being of their players. Audiogames are
a specific type of digital game that have sound and sometimes tactile stimuli as
their central element, rather than visual graphics. Thus, audiogames can create
atmosphere, mechanics, and unique gameplay, while making digital entertainment more accessible to people with all levels of vision. It is also necessary to
consider (and charge) the need for other types of digital games to comply with
accessibility guidelines and to guarantee the right to play for everyone. Digital
games that promote universal design and that are capable of captivating their
players can ensure that people with different levels of vision can interact, collaborate, and even compete on equal terms with the same game - a situation that can
not always be observed in other everyday situations.

Keywords: Videogames · Audiogames · Accessibility · Digital inclusion
Well being

1 Introduction

It is estimated that there are 250 million blind or visually impaired people (BVIP), about
3.3% of the world's population [1]. When talking about digital inclusion and accessibility for this group, one usually thinks of ways of accessing information, education, or
work [2]. Approaches that prioritize forms of leisure and entertainment are often cast
aside in this discussion for a more "utilitarian" or "productivist" discourse.

This text, therefore, starts from the premise that the issue of digital inclusion and accessibility and welfare for BVIP must - within the contemporary context - also consider the
digital forms of leisure and entertainment. Video games have become the primary entertainment industry, moving a market of $116 billion in 2017 [3] with an estimated audience
of 2.21 billion active players - about a third of the planet's population [4].

In addition to its economic relevance, authors such as Huizinga [5] and Callois [6]
emphasize the importance of playfulness for the constitution of the social subject. In the

© Springer International Publishing AG, part of Springer Nature 2018
V. G. Duffy (Ed.): DHM 2018, LNCS 10917, pp. 338–352, 2018.
https://doi.org/10.1007/978-3-319-91397-1_28

particular dimension, playing contributes to the processes of structure and well-being of the individual. Collectively, playfulness inserts people into cultural dynamics that ultimately shape their perceptual judgments and the very society in which we live.

We must also consider that video games are the gateway to digital culture. Children traditionally learn to play video games before using a computer just as they learn to draw before writing [7]. Likewise, the use of video games makes the digital literacy process more comfortable and faster [8]. This fact may be particularly relevant for BVIP since they often have to overcome additional barriers in these processes due to the technical and technological limitations of digital equipment and contents - which do not always meet the norms and demands of accessibility [2].

Video games also represent an essential form of socialization in the contemporary world. MMOs (Massive Multiplayer Online games), for example, require the creation of groups of players from established relationships within or outside the game universe. In the same way, other types of games stimulate the creation of communities, even if not necessarily to play. Such is true in the case of production of complementary content, sharing of tips, comments, and other experiences and collective constructions [9].

Furthermore, several studies indicate that video game can enhance well-being and have cognitive, motivational, emotional, and social benefits, even in the case of games not explicitly designed for such purposes [10].

Audiogames is the term that has been used to define video games that contemplate this demand for BVIP. In the sequence, we will present some definitions and questions related to the audiogames, followed by a survey on the state of the art of research in this field. In the end, we present the results and discussions obtained from the study carried out, with the primary objective of corroborating the inclusion and digital accessibility, the right to digital entertainment, and the welfare of this public.

2 Audiogames: Trajectory, Typology, and Characteristics

According to this research, an audiogame is a type of digital game that has sound as its central element, that is, as its chief mechanics, interfaces, output and feedback. Sometimes, these games may contain also tactile stimuli rather than visual graphics. Thus, audiogames can create atmospheres, mechanics, and unique games while making digital entertainment more accessible to people with all levels of vision.

At the beginning of the commercialization of digital games, BVIP that had access to a computer paradoxically found fewer accessibility problems and fewer difficulties to play some of the regular commercial games. Interactive fiction, RPG (Role Playing Games), and adventure games had more elaborate narrative plots such as "Colossal Cave Adventures" (1977) and "Zork" (1977). As the digital resources of sounds and images were insufficient at this time, the use of written language better accommodated such narrative demands. The same was true for the first MMOs known as MUD (Multi-User Dungeon, Multi-User Dimension or Multi-User Domain), for example, "MUD1" (1978). These games, based on written text, were part of a type of digital game known as "text-based games". Although not designed to meet the BVIP, such games could (and still can) be played by using assistive technologies such as screen reader and speech recognition software and devices [11].

Over time, as the hardware capacity grew, the use of the written text gave way to graphic images and audiovisual language. At the same time, mainstream games (aka "AAA" or "triple-a") have significantly increased the complexity of their gameplay, their interfaces, and their controls, making it even more challenging to access BVIP [11]. On the other hand, the technological advance also favored that new solutions arose for inclusive games.

"Touch Me" (1974) was one of the first games whose technology allowed the inclusion of BVIP [12]. The game consisted in reproducing, in the same order executed by the device, a random sequence that was generated from four sound tones. The objective of the game was to memorize and reproduce the largest possible sequence of sounds. Although each color (red, green, blue, and yellow) related itself to a specific sound tone, the visual element was not essential for its gameplay. In 1978, Atari released a portable version of the game, "Touch Me Handheld Version." BVIP can now use mobile devices to play collections of accessible games, such as Audio GameHub [13]. Despite the distance of forty years, the mechanisms responsible for running these games still have some ergonomic and design similarities (Fig. 1).

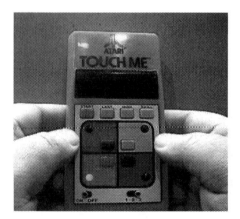 

Fig. 1. On the left, image of the portable device "Touch Me," released in 1978. The right, smartphone running "Audio Game Hub," [13] released in 2016. (Source: author)

Games like "Touch Me" or even text-based games, although not specifically designed to be accessible, allowed BVIP to play and also to compete and interact with any player, including sighted people. This fact is particularly relevant if we consider that BVIP regularly lives in their personal and professional relationship circles with sighted people, who are also, sometimes, video game players.

Archambault et al. [14] identify three distinct types of audiogames: those that predominantly use audio, although associated with a visual interface, those linked to experiments of musical artists, and those that use "only" sound elements to play.

The "Game Accessibility Project" understands that games accessible to BVIP can be classified as text-based games, mainstream video games, audiogames, video games accessible by their original design, and mods-accessible video games (MODs) [11].

Regarding text-based games, in addition to what has been commented previously, although there are several examples of this type of product, they have become less popular these days. It might occur because they do not offer the same diversities or other attractive resources if compared to the most wanted games by the players.

In mainstream games, it is worth pointing out that some BVIP develop considerable skills in games that had been designed, initially, for sighted people, becoming "hardcore gamers". One of the cases that gained media notoriety was that of blind player, Brice Mellen, who was considered a major competitor in the "Mortal Kombat" fighting game.

"Skullgirls" (2012) is an example of a fighting game that had not been originally developed to be accessible but is played by BVIP, mainly because of its feedback and its specific use of sound language. From the detected demand, the developer studio, Reverge Labs, provided customizations that favored the gameplay by BVIP. As a result, "Skullgirls" is often referred to in specialized forums as one of the most accessible mainstream games and one of the favorites among the blind and visually-impaired players [15].

Audiogames are understood by "The Game Accessibility Project" as games that use "only" sounds and are without any visual output. Although they can be played by sighted people, they are, very often, more attractive for BVIP. Therefore, they end up being developed by enthusiasts, by academic projects, or by the blind community itself. "Most audio games are elementary games (compared to conventional games) and lack many of the properties of conventional games, such as diversity, multiplayer functionality and good replayability" [11]. One exception is the popular "TopSpeed" car racing series, an audiogame that features three sequences developed by Playing in the Dark Studio.

Even when sound-based audiogames reach a broader audience, they continue to be received peculiarly by BVIP. As an example of this statement, we can cite the horror audio games, such as "Papa Sangre" (2010). In these types of games, the emphasis is much more on the absence of a sense, the vision, than on the empowerment of hearing [16].

Regarding the category of video games originally designed to be accessible, perhaps this is the one that best represents the proposal to develop an inclusive (and not exclusive) project. "The Blind Eye" (2010) was a pioneering effort that aimed to explore the potential of developing a 3D game for BVIP focused on the development of skills related to navigation and spatial cognition. Like "The Curb Game" (2005) and "Terraformers" (2003), the game is also considered "hybrid," which means that it has visual graphic representation. This pioneering work has led to the exploration of technologies unheard of at the time, such as an interactive binaural sound. The focus on auditory navigation was the exploration of binaural (3D sound) sound environments. In the game, the avatar controlled by the player must locate a series of musical instruments that are placed in different places of a city - each with a characteristic sound landscape. The instrument starts playing when the avatar approaches. When locating all the instruments, the player has to find a garage where a man is playing a kind of barrel organ. There is a time limit of 60 min to complete the game, and collisions with cars and walls are obstacles that draw energy from the avatar. Directional buttons give control to the player, while the step sounds function as a location reference; if they can be heard more clearly, the avatar is close to a wall; if they are not so clear, it is because the avatar is walking in an open area. Although in some moments the game uses voice over narration, it is a good example of a more expressive exploration of sound design in video games and the potential of audiogames.

Modifications in games, also known as "MODs," are changes made by players and enthusiasts who bring some modification to the original game - be it more superficial or structural [17]. Thus, some modifications are made with the aim of adding accessible features, enabling BVIP to play such modified games. An example is "Accessible Quake," also known as "AudioQuake" (2007), an accessible version of the popular First Person Shooter (FPS) "Quake".

The portal "Audiogames.net", one of the primary references on this subject on the Internet, classifies this sort of accessible games in a way that resembles the ordinary video games' genres. These categories are action games, adult games XXX, adventure games, audio adventures, arcade games, card games, first-person adventures, FPS, gamebooks, incremental games, interaction fiction, interactive fiction interpreter, Japanese games, MUD, MUD clients, MMORPG, puzzle games, racing games, role-playing games; educational games, side-scrollers, space invaders games, strategy games, trivia games, traditional games, sports, simulation games, word games, compilations, and miscellaneous [15].

This same portal has a very active forum [18] and a repository of audiogames [19] in which it is possible to have access to about 650 titles classified among the 30 categories listed in the previous paragraph. The site comments that it includes only a few interactive fictions because there is already a specific (and more complete) site about this genre called "The Interaction Fiction Archive" [20]. In the repository, it is also possible to check audiogames' descriptions, comments, and records, as well as an updated list of projects under development and credits of 75 developers.

As we look more closely at this list of developers, we can see that they are small teams - sometimes made up of a single person - consisting, predominantly, of enthusiasts, independent studios ("indies") or members of projects that are carried out by universities or sector organizations.

The "Audio Game Hub" is an example of a project that is the result of an international cooperation between the Gamification Lab of the Leuphana University of Lüneburg and the University of Technology's School of Computer and Mathematical Science at Auckland University of Technology. The team was composed of thirteen people, who held the roles of the project leader (Jarek Beksa), design, programming, sound effects, graphics and website; three testers and six voice actors are also credited. This number can be considered quite small, considering the size of video game development teams, the fact that they belong to two different institutions, and the number of games implemented. In total, there are, available for free download, twelve audiogames: casino games, bomb disarmer, Super Simon, archery, hunt, samurai tournament, samurai dojo, labyrinth, memory, blocks, animal escape, and runner [13]. The project, supported by "The Able Gamers Charity" [21], had more than 80.000 downloads with a good average rating (4.8/5.0) and has won important awards, such as "The Play by Play Festival" and the "Royal National Institute of Blind People".

3   Audiogames: State of the Art

This study, to overlook state-of-the-art audiogames, examined books and databases like Scopus, SpringerLink, Mendeley, Scielo, Project MUSE, Web of Science, Google Scholar, and the Academia.edu platform.

Although it is possible to locate the first experiences related to audio games in the 1970s, it was only at the turn of this century that this theme's first theoretical references appeared [22, 23]. Between 1999 and 2016, sixty-five articles were identified that directly addressed audiogame - average of less than four (3.6) texts per year. The Graph 1 below shows this output categorized per year and by type of approach. The first one is theoretical, with thirty-nine papers, which presents theories, concepts, and eventual analyses of audiogames and their benefits. The second one has twenty-six texts about development, which predominantly reveals project documentation and the audiogame implementation process, eventually reporting results from user (player) testing.

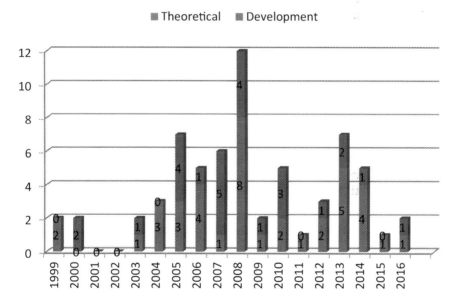

Graph 1. Division by type of approach and year of publication of articles on audiogames. Seven of the eighteen years surveyed were above average (3.6) of texts produced per year, while two years (2001 and 2002) had no publication. (Source: author)

Another issue raised concerns the country of origin of these publications. The sixty-five texts were published by authors linked to teaching and research institutions in thirteen different countries - an average of five texts per country. Only four countries produced above this average: the United States, Brazil, France, and Austria. We note that, compared with data for the thirteen most significant gaming-consuming countries in the world - which, together, represent 84% of the global market [3] - about half of them are in the two lists (China, United States, Germany, United Kingdom, France, Canada, and Brazil). Also, it is possible to repair a non-alignment between percentage and position of these countries in the respective rankings, as we can see in the comparison below (Graph 2 and Table 1).

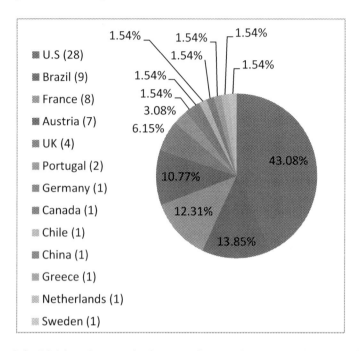

Graph 2. Division of text production on audiogames by country. (Source: author)

Table 1. Largest gaming consumer markets in the world [3]. When comparing the data of the graph with those of the table, it is possible to observe the mismatch between the percentage, the position, and even the absence of some countries between the two rankings.

Country	U$ M
China (28,05%)	32,536
US (21,92%)	25,426
Japan (12,11%)	14,048
Germany (3,82%)	4,430
UK (3,65%)	4,238
South Korea (3,62%)	4,203
France (2,57%)	2,977
Canada (1,70%)	1,968
Spain (1,65%)	1,918
Italy (1,62%)	1,881
Russia (1,32%)	1,531
Mexico (1,22%)	1,418
Brazil (1,14%)	1,324

The survey also identified the keywords associated with the authors themselves and their articles. The five most cited keywords were accessibility (33 times), video games (24 times), audiogames (20 times), visual impairment (16 times), and blindness (15 times). At the other end, among the less cited keywords, one observes the diversity and the high number of terms that were mentioned twice (14 different names) and only once (59 different words) among all the articles surveyed as shown in Graph 3.

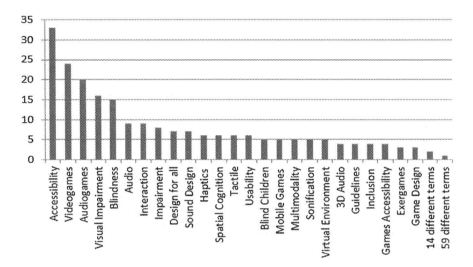

Graph 3. Descending order of the most present terms in the relations of the keywords indicated by the authors in their respective articles. (Source: author)

Other terms that appear most often are audio and interaction (nine times each); impairment (eight times); design for all and sound design (seven times each); haptic, spatial cognition, tactile, and usability (six times each); blind children, mobile games, multimodality, sonification, and virtual environment (five times each); 3D audio, guidelines, inclusion, and accessible games (four times each); exergames and game design (three times each). To better visualize this data, we present a cloud of words (Fig. 2) representing the recurrence of these terms.

Of the sixty-five texts surveyed, twenty-one (about one-third of the total) presented information on the development of one or more skills. In total, twenty-eight mentions correspond to a total of eight distinct abilities. Audiogame players showed improvements in spatial cognition skills (ten occurrences); navigation (nine events); memory (three appearances); physical conditioning (two occurrences); and tactile perception, sound perception, academic knowledge, and Braille knowledge (one incident each).

Fig. 2. Cloud of words representing the terms mentioned in the keywords by the authors themselves in the respective texts. (Source: author)

In this way, it is possible to infer that a little more than two-thirds of the skills are related to spatial cognition and navigation. However, it was not possible to determine if this predominance was due to the identification of a direct demand of the users or for other reasons inherent to the respective projects [22–42] (Graph 4).

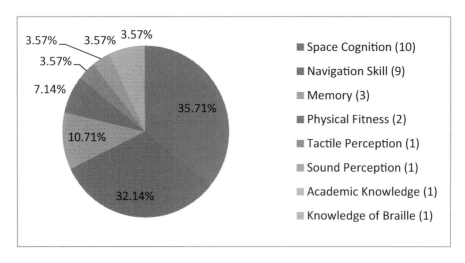

Graph 4. Percentage and number of mentions of skills developed. (Source: author)

4   Results and Discussions

The issue of digital inclusion and accessibility, well-being, and even the development of skills for BVIP should consider audiogames as a relevant form of digital leisure and entertainment. As seen, audiogames can serve as a gateway to digital culture, thus, favoring forms of inclusion, socialization, and digital literacy for this audience [7, 8]. From the design perspective, game designers and other audiogame developers should pay attention to the points and possibilities that we highlight below.

(a) The participation of BVIP as specialists, testers, and team members during all stages of project development must be considered. Thus, it is possible to understand better the profile of this audience, their demands, and preferences rather than to establish assumptions or preconceptions;

(b) It is essential to know the highest quantity and diversity of audiogames, including projects with better and worse acceptance by the public. In both cases, identifying possible reasons for such receptions may provide relevant inputs for the development of new games;

(c) It is necessary to take into account the limitations or technological restrictions of the domestic user (player). In the case of BVIP, there are often additional costs for the acquisition of assistive interfaces, such as adapted keyboards and mice, Braille display and printer, pressure trigger, and tabletop scanner, among others. Thus, it is not possible to assume that the final public will have state-of-the-art equipment such as high-performance sound cards or 7.1 surround headphones;

(d) In potentiating the field of sound design, which is often limited to the soundtrack and sound of images or environments, the sound project and its implementation pass to play a central role in the project. The game is thought from sound, not the contrary. It is, therefore, a form of empowerment of hearing [16] and not suppression of vision;

(e) This is a fertile field for experimentation. Projects that prioritize the sound dimension can also be thought of as works of art and technology or experimental games, as pointed out by Archambault et al. [14]. An example is the project "PHASE – Haptic Sound Application Platform for Musical Awakening (in French)" exposed in the museum Georges Pompidou [43]. In this way, it is possible to expand digital inclusion and accessibility to the field of the arts through playful and interactive projects;

(f) Experimentation also often plays the role of the precursor of innovations that will later be incorporated by the gaming industry. New technological developments, sound language, and sound design can be assimilated into the universe of digital games in general. Cases such as the "Blind Eye" project, which utilizes interactive binaural sound like a game mechanic, favor a more creative exploration of sound as a game design element, not as a mere aid in the sonorization of graphic images in digital games;

(g) Projects with state-of-the-art equipment and technologies not accessible to the home user (player) can be developed for controlled environments such as laboratories, institutions, or schools focused on BVIP. Such projects, although not available to a broader audience, can be used to develop ideas and prototypes that may eventually be incorporated into other situations;

(h) Inclusive games are better than "exclusive games," but more difficult to develop. We understand that one of the main design challenges is the creation of games that can not only be played by BVIP, but also expand their niche and attract sighted players. Universal games favor ways of integrating BVIP not only with other BVIP but also with sighted players - who are part of their everyday relationship circles. From the design point of view, the challenge of the game design is in the development of a game that is not only accessible to both audiences; an inclusive game should also, ideally, be equally attractive, fun, and challenging (motivational) for both audiences. It should favor the flow, the balance and the fairness of the game, allowing BVIP and sighted people to interact, collaborate and compete on equal terms within the game - a situation that can not always be observed in other everyday situations. Cases, such as "Skullgirls" seen earlier, validate this hypothesis and make the possibility of developing such games more economically viable (or attractive) for mainstream developers;

(i) The guidelines for accessibility in the development of digital games should be considered. The "Game Accessibility Guidelines" site presents the results of collaborative work in progress between studios, researchers, and players to establish referrals, with the goal of making games accessible to as many people as possible. These guidelines are divided into three categories: basic, intermediate, and advanced. The levels of this categorization are based on balancing three factors: reach (number of people who benefit), impact (the difference made to those people), and value (cost to implement). It is also recommended to follow a six-step process: familiarize, evaluate & plan, prioritize and schedule, inform, and review & learn [43].

Another site that provides accessibility guidelines is "Blind Computer Games" which provides over fifty items to be checked, classified into six main categories: absolutely critical features, general feature checklist, screen reader feature checklist, self-voicing feature checklist, suggested feature checklist, and subtle factors [44].

Cheiran presents in his master thesis a more comprehensive compilation of several other guidelines, in addition to promoting a comparative study among his recommendations. The research concludes that the vast majority of the instructions studied are applied in a limited way or even not observed in most commercial video games. This conclusion is also corroborated by many of the authors consulted in this research. Cheiran points out that in addition to social responsibility, considering accessibility guidelines is also a strategic way to achieve, from the same game, a new niche of consumers disregarded in the digital gaming market [45];

(j) In the same way that game design is composed of many design elements such as level design, character design, and sound design it is necessary to consider the establishment of an "audiogame design." This new specialty should deepen the discussions presented briefly in this article, to consolidate as a new discipline within the field of digital games;

(k) Develop teaching-learning methods that include BVIP in game design courses, as it already happens in other fields of design, such as fashion, for example [46]. This way, it can allow the access and the inclusion of this public and the formation of game designers who are blind and visually impaired. Such a professional would develop unique expertise that would transcend both the performance of a game designer and the participation of BVIP as an enthusiastic developer or tester.

5   Conclusion

The issue of digital accessibility and inclusion for blind or visually impaired people (BVIP) is usually thought from perspectives considered "utilitarian" or "productive". Such a discourse often leaves aside the question of digital entertainment - equally relevant in contemporary times. Also, digital games promote and favor the well-being of players, as well as can bring different benefits [10].

Access to these games can represent a significant challenge for BVIP, since, despite the existence of accessibility guidelines, there are still few cases of mainstream games that seek to follow them [43–45]. Despite proper qualification and the market's small interest in applying these guidelines, audiogames have been gradually gaining more space in recent years. This can be perceived through the mapping of the research done, the games developed and the community engagement in various projects and actions [11, 13, 15, 18–21, 45–47].

In this sense, audiogames are offered as an alternative for the inclusion of players in the universe of digital entertainment. However, this type of video game is, in most cases, being developed by enthusiasts or small groups with training and resources more restricted when compared to the mainstream games. Thus, although developed voluntarily and well received by BVIP, many audiogames end up being limited to this group of players.

Considering that BVIP regularly cohabit with sighted persons, inclusive digital games should not be "exclusive." This is true not only for poorly accessible mainstream games but also for audiogames that do not have the same attractiveness of other games for sighted players [11]. Thus, we believe that as important as promoting the accessibility of mainstream games is the development of audiogames capable of including both BVIP and sighted people who regularly play other games.

By meeting the accessibility guidelines, indies and mainstream games can reach an expanded audience and a new niche market formed by BVIP excluded from this type of production. In the same way, when thinking about audiogames capable of captivating sighted players, it is possible to reach a wider audience, which can make feasible the investment of more resources in the development of this type of digital game. In both cases, the search for a universal game design should seek to satisfy the points and possibilities highlighted in the previous section of this paper. These points and possibilities were derived from the literature review and suggest avenues for promising developments in this field.

Acknowledgment. The author would like to thank Anhembi Morumbi University and the CNPq (National for Scientific and Technological Development) for the PIBITI (Institutional Program for Initiatives in Technological Development and Innovation). This grant was awarded to Vitor Monteiro Chioccola, a game design undergraduate researcher, who assisted in the collection of data, sources, and other references for this paper.

References

1. Bourne, R.R.A., Flaxman, S.R., Braithwaite, T., Cicinelli, M.V., Das, A., Jonas, J.B., Vision Loss Expert Group, et al.: Magnitude, temporal trends, and projections of the global prevalence of blindness and distance and near vision impairment: a systematic review and meta-analysis. Lancet Glob. Health. **5**(9), e888–e897 (2017). https://doi.org/10.1016/s2214-109x(17)30293-0

2. Lazar, J., Goldstein, D.F., Taylor, A.: Ensuring Digital Accessibility through Process and Policy. Morgan Kaufmann, Waltham (2015)

3. Newzoo Global Games Market Report. https://newzoo.com/resources

4. Number of Active Video Gamers Worldwide from 2014 to 2021 (in millions). https://www.statista.com/statistics/748044/number-video-gamers-world

5. Huizinga, J.: Homo Ludens: A Study of the Play-Element in Culture. Martino Fine Books, Kettering (2014)

6. Caillois, R.: Man, Play and Games. University of Illinois Press, Champaign (2001)

7. Prensky, M.R.: From Digital Natives to Digital Wisdom: Hopeful Essays for 21st Century Learning. Corwin, Thousand Oaks (2012)

8. Lankshear, C., Knobel, M.: Digital Literacies: Concepts, Policies and Practices. New Literacies and Digital Epistemologies, vol. 30. Peter Lang Publishing, New York (2008)

9. Johnson, S.: Everything Bad is Good for You: How Today's Popular Culture is Actually Making Us Smarter. Riverhead Books, New York (2006)

10. Granic, I., Lobel, A., Engels, R.C.: The benefits of playing video games. Am. Psychol. **69**(1), 66–78 (2014). https://doi.org/10.1037/a0034857

11. The Game Accessibility Project. http://game-accessibility.com

12. Reinhard, B.: A sound solution: history of audio games for the visually impaired. In: Artistry in Games (2014). http://artistryingames.com/sound-solution-history-audio-games-visually-impaired

13. Audio Game Hub. http://www.audiogamehub.com

14. Archambault, D., Ossman, R., Gaudy, T., Miessenberger, K.: Computer games and visually impaired people. Eur. J. Inform. Prof. **8**(2), 43–53 (2007)

15. Audiogames. http://www.audiogames.net

16. Webber, J.E.: Video Games Which Open the Door for the Blind to Play. The Guardian, London (2014). https://www.theguardian.com/technology/2014/oct/13/video-games-that-let-blind-people-play

17. Champion, E.: Game Mods: Design, Theory and Criticism. Lulu.com, Raleigh (2013)

18. Forum Audiogames. http://forum.audiogames.net

19. Audiogames Archive. https://www.agarchive.net

20. The Interaction Fiction Archive. http://ifarchive.org

21. The Able Gamers Charity. http://www.ablegamers.org

22. Lumbreras, M., Sánchez, J.: Interactive 3D sound hyperstories for blind children. In: Proceedings of the SIGCHI Conference on Human Factors in Computing Systems (CHI 1999). ACM International Conference Proceeding Series, New York, pp. 318–325 (1999). https://doi.org/10.1145/302979.303101

23. Lumbreras, M., Sánchez, J.: Virtual environment interaction through 3D audio by blind children. CyberPsychol. Behav. **2**(2), 101–111 (1999)

24. Afonso, A., Katz, B.F.G., Blum, A., Jacquemin, C., Denis, M.: A study of spatial cognition in an immersive virtual audio environment: comparing blind and blindfolded individuals. In: Proceedings of the Tenth Meeting of the International Conference on Auditory Display. ICAD – International Community for Auditory Display, Limerick, pp. 228–235 (2005)

25. Paterson, N., Naliuka, K., Søren, K.J., Carrigy, T., Haahr, M., Conway, F.: Design, implementation and evaluation of audio for a location aware augmented reality game. In: Proceedings of the 3rd International Conference on Fun and Games. ACM International Conference Proceeding Series, New York, pp. 149–156 (2010). https://doi.org/10.1145/1823818.1823835

26. Morelli, T., Foley, J., Columna, L., Lieberman, L., Folmer, E.: VI-Tennis: a vibrotactile/audio exergame for players who are visually impaired. In: Proceedings of the Fifth International Conference on the Foundations of Digital Games. ACM International Conference Proceeding Series, New York, pp. 147–154 (2010). https://doi.org/10.1145/1822348.1822368

27. Rector, K., Bennett, C.L., Kientz, J.A.: Eyes-free yoga: an exergame using depth cameras for blind & low vision exercise. In: Proceedings of the 15th International ACM SIGACCESS Conference on Computers and Accessibility. ACM SIGACCESS Conference on Computers and Accessibility, New York, pp. 12–20 (2013). https://doi.org/10.1145/2513383.2513392

28. Bargerhuff, M.E., Cowan, H., Oliveira, F., Quek, F., Fang, B.: Haptic glove technology: Skill development through video game play. J. Vis. Impair. Blind. **104**(11), 688–699 (2010)

29. Milne, L.R., Bennett, C.L., Ladner, R.E., Azenkot, S.: BraillePlay: educational smartphone games for blind children. In: Proceedings of the 16th International ACM SIGACCESS Conference on Computers and Accessibility. ACM SIGACCESS Conference on Computers and Accessibility, New York, pp. 137–144 (2014). https://doi.org/10.1145/2661334.2661377

30. Rassmus-Gröhn, K.: Enabling audio-haptics. Licentiate Thesis, Certec 2. Division of Rehabilitation Engineering Research, Department of Design Sciences, Faculty of Engineering. Lund University, Lund (2006). http://portal.research.lu.se/ws/files/6053626/3045994.pdf

31. Sánchez, J., Guerrero, L., Sáenz, M., Flores, H.: A model to develop videogames for orientation and mobility. In: Miesenberger, K., Klaus, J., Zagler, W., Karshmer, A. (eds.) ICCHP 2010. LNCS, vol. 6180, pp. 296–303. Springer, Heidelberg (2010). https://doi.org/10.1007/978-3-642-14100-3_44

32. Merabet, L.B., Connors, E.C., Halko, M.A., Sánchez, J.: Teaching the blind to find their way by playing video games. PLOS ONE **7**(9), e44958 (2012). https://doi.org/10.1371/journal.pone.0044958

33. Connors, E.C., Yazzolino, L.A., Sánchez, J., Merabet, L.B.: Development of an audio-based virtual gaming environment to assist with navigation skills in the blind. J. Vis. Exp. (JoVE) **73**, e50272 (2013). https://doi.org/10.3791/50272

34. Sánchez, J., de Borba Campos, M., Espinoza, M., Merabet, L.B.: Audio haptic videogaming for developing wayfinding skills in learners who are blind. In: Proceedings of the 19th International Conference on Intelligent User Interfaces. ACM International Conference Proceeding Series, New York, pp. 199–208 (2014). https://doi.org/10.1145/2557500.2557519

35. Sánchez, J.: User-centered technologies for blind children. Interdiscip. J. Hum. ICT Environ. **4**(2), 96–122 (2008). https://doi.org/10.17011/ht/urn.200810245832

36. Raisamo, R., Patomäki, S., Hasu, M., Pasto, V.: Design and evaluation of a tactile memory game for visually impaired children. Interact. Comput. **19**(2), 196–205 (2006). https://doi.org/10.1016/j.intcom.2006.08.011

37. Targett, S., Fernstrom, M.: Audio games: fun for all? All for fun! In: Proceedings of the 9th International Conference on Auditory Display (ICAD), pp. 216–219. Georgia Institute of Technology, Boston (2003)

38. Nogueira, T.D.C.: Comparative study of the blind and sighted users experience in responsive and non-responsive web design. Master thesis in Computer Science. Federal University of Goiás (UFG), Goiânia (2015). http://repositorio.bc.ufg.br/tede/handle/tede/5215. (in Portuguese)

39. Ossmann, R., Miesenberger, K., Archambault, D.: A computer game designed for all. In: Miesenberger, K., Klaus, J., Zagler, W., Karshmer, A. (eds.) ICCHP 2008. LNCS, vol. 5105, pp. 585–592. Springer, Heidelberg (2008). https://doi.org/10.1007/978-3-540-70540-6_83

40. Gaudy, T., Natkin, S., Archambault, D.: Pyvox 2: an audio game accessible to visually impaired people playable without visual nor verbal instructions. In: Pan, Z., Cheok, A.D., Müller, W., Rhalibi, A.E. (eds.) Transactions on Edutainment II. LNCS, vol. 5660, pp. 176–186. Springer, Heidelberg (2009). https://doi.org/10.1007/978-3-642-03270-7_12

41. de Voogt, A., Linders, L., van den Broek, E.: Mancala games and their suitability for players with visual impairments. J. Vis. Impair. Blind. **104**(11), 725–731 (2010)

42. Pereira, M.L.D.: Inclusive design - a case study: play to see - toys for blind and low vision children. Master thesis in Design and Marketing – Textile Option. School of Engineering of the University of Minho (EEUM), Guimarães (2009). https://repositorium.sdum.uminho.pt/bitstream/1822/10741/1/tese.pdf. (in Portuguese)

43. PHASE: Haptic Sound Application Platform for Musical Awakening. Interactive music installation. Exposition Écoute, Musée d'art Contemporain. Museum Georges Pompidou, Paris (2004). (in French)

44. Game Accessibility Guidelines: A Straightforward Reference for Inclusive Game Design. http://gameaccessibilityguidelines.com

45. Guidelines for Building Blind-Accessible Computer Games. http://www.blindcomputergames.com/guidelines/guidelines.html

46. Cheiran, J.F.P.: Inclusive games: accessibility guidelines for digital games. Master thesis in Computer Science. Federal University of Rio Grande do Sul (UFRGS), Porto Alegre (2013). http://www.lume.ufrgs.br/handle/10183/77230. (in Portuguese)

47. Lima Júnior, G.C., Zuanon, R.: The foundation of the SEE BEYOND method: fashion design and neuroeducation applied to the teaching of the project methodology to students with congenital and acquired blindness. In: Streitz, N., Markopoulos, P. (eds.) DAPI 2017. LNCS, vol. 10291, pp. 528–546. Springer, Cham (2017). https://doi.org/10.1007/978-3-319-58697-7_40

Landscape Design and Neuroscience Cooperation: Contributions to the Non-pharmacological Treatment of Alzheimer's Disease

Rachel Zuanon$^{(\boxtimes)}$ and Barbara Alves Cardoso de Faria

Anhembi Morumbi University, Sao Paulo, Brazil
rachel@all-affective.com, barbara.acff@gmail.com

Abstract. Research studies on neuroplasticity suggest that architecture and design have the potential capacity to alter the brain structure and its functions. With regard to constructed healing spaces, the landscape design project acts as a key feature in clinics that treat patients with Alzheimer's disease. The relationship between the patients and nature is essential because living in a green area has a number of positive effects such as the following: adjustment of the patients to their circadian rhythm; an increase in the production of Vitamin D; basic notions of time; better quality air and a wide range of stimuli. Thus the landscape and architectural features of a green environment play a key role in the sensorimotor and cognitive stimulation of the patients. Against this background, this paper seeks to investigate how there can be the collaboration between the area of landscaping and neuroscience, especially with regard to a comprehensive list of recommendations involving therapeutic design gardens, with a view to offering non-pharmacological treatment to patients suffering from Alzheimer's disease. The 38 proposed recommendations that were set out, are based on a review of the literature and a research field carried out in the wards of a center for elderly people requiring care called 'Recanto Monsenhor Albino' [Monsignor Albino's Rest Home], located in the town of Catanduva (Sao Paulo – Brazil). The main benefits that can be highlighted include the set of guidelines for the project, together with an analysis of therapeutic gardens and the quality of life and well being of the people in this environment.

Keywords: Landscape design · Neuroscience · Alzheimer's disease
Non-pharmacological treatment · Therapeutic gardens · Guidelines on design

1 Introduction

The first links made between the fields of knowledge of Neuroscience and Architecture occurred at the end of the 1950s, in response to the need for an understanding of how human beings perceive, experience and interrelate with constructed space.

As an example of this, it is worth drawing attention to the work of the doctor Jonas Salk. At this time, which was for him a decisive moment for undertaking research, Salk discovered and developed one of the first vaccines against poliomyelitis. This achievement was made while he was staying at a 13th Century monastery in Assisi in Italy. Salk

© Springer International Publishing AG, part of Springer Nature 2018
V. G. Duffy (Ed.): DHM 2018, LNCS 10917, pp. 353–374, 2018.
https://doi.org/10.1007/978-3-319-91397-1_29

claimed that being able to interact with the setting of that locality proved to be a stimulus for new methods of thinking and research. Since he was persuaded of the capacity of architecture to alter a human being's way of acting and thinking, and the influence that the features of one's surroundings can exert on someone's physical and mental health [1], Salk invited the architect Louis Kahn to set up the Salk Institute in La Jolla – California. This was a place designed to act as an incentive to creativity and to stimulate advances in Science [2].

As a result, the link between these areas began to be strengthened as a means of finding a response to the kind of questions that emerge in investigations of this nature and bringing benefits to those who design or dwell in the created space.

Currently, there are several research studies which are within the scope of neuro-science, architecture and design and these have gathered momentum with the increasing importance of this field of knowledge. Research studies of this kind [1, 3–21] are devoted to studying the complexity of the human brain and how it is influenced by different spaces and interfaces.

Among the significant contributions made by neuroscience to architecture and to design, it can be stated that Neuroplasticity is related to the way that the environment models and modulates the human brain throughout our lives. Neuroplasticity is the capacity of the brain to be molded and adapted both in the structural and functional spheres either during its development or when subject to new experiences and sur-roundings. This feature of the nervous system ensures that the neural circuits are malleable and interfere directly in forming and establishing the memories and learning as well as adjusting to lesions and traumatic events [22, 23].

This capacity for transformation continues in the brain even after the specific stages of its formation and is closely bound up with (i) the surroundings in which it is embedded; (ii) the substances with which the brain is nourished; and (iii) the degree of neural stimulation by means of which this potential capacity for alteration and adjustment is either increased or neglected [10].

All internal and external stimuli shape the behavior of any living being, from the simplest to the most complex organisms, such as human beings. According to Pallasmaa [18], the brain controls human behavior, whereas the genes control the brain structure. The environment can modulate the function of the genes and ultimately the brain structure. In other words, changes in the environment alter the brain and hence change the behavior of the individual. It is within this analytical framework that architecture and design play a crucial role in shaping the experience of the individual within his/her world. In other words, the architecture and design mediate a bond between the body and the environment and within this mediation, the space that is formed acts as one of the main interfaces that assist in the process of neuroplasticity.

Thus if "the architecture is the constructed mental space" [18], the project exter-nalizes the human mind. At the same time, owing to the neuroplasticity, the human brain is sensitized and designed by these materializations of the mind. Everything that is constructed is supplied by the human mind while the brain is altered with regard to everything that is constructed. The spaces formed by the architects/designers explore the opportunities that go beyond these functionalities and everyday uses. They are the embodiment of the wishes and needs of those who inhabit them. These kinds of expectations are present in human minds and they are externalized by architects and designers through the different opportunities they offer for constructions, while at the same time, the inhabitants internalize all the opportunities that the spaces offer [19].

Farlling [20] states that, "when designing spaces, we alter our behavior and the capacity of our brains". Hence, understanding the brain functions and how an individual perceives, understands and acts in space, is becoming essential when designing environments that are suitable and congenial to their users. Exploring what neuroscience is able to offer can provide architects/designers with the capacity to design even more complex models with regard to environmental-perceptual-behavioral interaction.

This means that, apart from their scientific added value, investigations that focus on human behavior with regard to constructed space, can lead to significant benefits: (a) the project process of architects/designers; (b) project analysis; and (c) to the users of these environments, especially when they are suffering from neurological diseases that impair their cognitive functions, such as that caused by Alzheimer's disease.

Currently, the number of people diagnosed with Alzheimer's disease or other types of dementia, exceeds 47 million throughout the world, more of a million of whom are living in Brazil. Alzheimer's disease is a progressive brain disorder and although it unfortunately has no known cause or cure, it can be treated.

The main objectives of pharmacological and non-pharmacological treatments are to alleviate existing symptoms by stabilizing them or at least allowing a large proportion of patients to progressively slow down the disease so as to preserve their independence in daily activities for as long as possible.

In the context of non-pharmacological treatments, constant and diversified cognitive stimulation throughout the individual's life is a way to slow down the disease process, once it can bring benefits to the maintenance of skills that are still preserved. The purpose of this type of stimulation is to minimize patients' difficulties from compensatory strategies so that they can make consistent use of intellectual resources still available.

Against this background, this paper seeks to make a contribution by investigating the degree of cooperation between the areas of the landscape design and neuroscience, especially with regard to a comprehensive list of recommendations for designing therapeutical gardens, with a view to offering a non-pharmacological form of treatment for patients afflicted with Alzheimer's disease.

The results obtained cover a total of 38 drawn up recommendations and are based on a review of the literature and research field carried out in the precincts of the center of care for the elderly called 'Recanto Monsenhor Albino' [Monsignor Albino's Rest Home], located in the town of Catanduva (Sao Paulo – Brazil). In the sphere of the landscape design, the extent of the list of recommendations indicates which design features are essential for the sensorimotor and cognitive stimulation of these patients.

2 Man-Nature-Landscape Design: Widening Constructed Space

There is an intrinsic relationship between human beings and nature, which pervades the whole of existence [24]. It is an almost unconscious affinity, which has been called as Biophilia [25], and leads man to appropriate all the features that nature can offer and make them form a part of his own history. Grinde and Patil [26] argue that an individual's need to make use of the resources of nature in his day-to-day life is caused by the biophilic design of his mind.

At the same time, the responses to stimuli prompted by nature, are linked to the memories formed during one's own life. Colors, smells, flavors, textures and all the sensations caused by nature, are factors that enhance the affective memory, as well as the memories that are stimulated through experiences that arouse emotions and feelings. This means the individual is biologically prepared to feel secure and relaxed in natural environments and in spaces laid out with green areas. Differences in culture can explain the preference for natural spaces but the deepest and almost unconscious relationship the human being can have with nature, seems to be genetic [27].

Through its restorative, soothing and therapeutic qualities [27], nature is able to provide a state of well being for man in many ways such as through: the fragrance of a flower; the rustling of the breeze blowing through the trees; the awareness of different textures when touching the surface of plants; the influence of a microclimate which is responsible for mitigating humidity and improving the purity of the air [26]; a considerable reduction in levels of stress compared with those experienced in urban environments [28]; and cognitive improvements of a high order.

As well as the numerous pharmacological and non-pharmacological benefits that nature provides (the former confirmed by scientific studies), there is an interaction of human beings with the area of architecture related to nature – landscape design.

Landscape design is a vital part of architecture, which is directly related to the person who experiences it. It is the area of architecture that is closest to the primitive relationships of human beings or more precisely, what allows an encounter between the individual and his/her origins [29].

Landscape design covers areas that are free and not built for residential purposes, work or services and appropriates these spaces to shape a new landscape based on the interpretation of the social behavior of a community. In this context, the landscape design is a form of language, an element of communication that acts directly on the individual's awareness of space, involving their five senses [30]. For this reason, understanding the relations that the human being establishes with nature is essential to ensure that the constructed space meets the needs of the people who inhabit it [19].

The planning of a landscape project entails both arranging natural features such as plants, rocks, water, light etc., and incorporating architectural features such as roads, pergolas, outdoor furnishings, and kiosks which assist in creating space that is formed in a natural setting. In reality, the raw material of a landscape design project "does not consist of flowers, stones or trees but feelings" [30]. Moreover, it is by articulating the design features – lines, shapes, texture, colors, movements, sounds, smells and the main aesthetic attributes, that the emotional experiences are constructed and provided to human beings. In other words, when a landscape design project includes the relationship human beings forge with nature, as well as meeting the needs of the people who inhabit this respective space, the planned decisions covered there, will be responsible for inducing positive emotional and cognitive changes, as well as benefiting people's health and well being [31].

In this area, landscape design projects are included for therapeutical purposes and devoted to the treatment and recovery of patients, either temporarily or permanently suffering from illnesses or health syndromes.

3   Health and Well Being: Landscape Design Projects for Therapeutical Purposes

The monastic spaces found in Europe in the 15th Century which were generally surrounded by cloisters and arches, characterize the first dwellings in which gardens were deliberately included as a part of the healing process. Two examples of these are the hotels-Dieu ("hostels of God") and the Cistercian abbey of St. Bernard de Clairvaux (in France). Kaufman and Warner [32], argue that this indicates the intuitive perception of the sensory information that gives Nature its meaning as a significant factor of the healing process for the well being of those who inhabited these environments.

From 1450 onwards, the concern with contagious infectious diseases that could be transmitted through the air, restricted the monastic gardens to being used as infirmaries, as a strategy to control the spread of diseases. Moreover, it was only at the end of the 15th century and beginning of the 16th Century that the architects of the infirmaries tried out a new conception of therapeutic space, which included the use of sunlight, the circulation of air and green areas. This idea was directly influenced by the set of aesthetic features introduced by the Arabs, which included arcades, patios and windows that allowed the air to circulate and shed sunlight on the patients - all of which resulted in an improvement in their state of well being.

Apart from their spatial configuration, these changes even went so far as to train personnel to work in these hospitals. As a result, activities in the fresh air, physical exercises and socializing, began to form a part of the everyday routine of the patients.

However, the first attempt to make recommendations for designing hospital gardens only appeared in the 18th Century when Christian Cay Lorenz stated that: "[…] a hospital garden should have everything to enjoy nature and to promote a healthy life […] it should be close to the hospital or even better surround it […] a view from the window onto blooming and happy scenes will invigorate the patient […] a nearby garden also encourages patients to take a walk […] the plantations should wind along dry paths that offer benches, […] colored leaves and blossoming and fragrant shrubs and flowers […]" [32].

During the First World War (1914–18) significant benefits were obtained from open and green areas in the treatment of the wounded which is borne out by the significant recovery rates and an exponential reduction in the mortality rates in hospitals that used therapeutic gardens as a part of their treatment.

Since then, there has been an understanding of the value of the landscape design project in healing environments. This has been strengthened by advances made in a number of research studies [6–9, 24, 29, 31, 33–36] which been able to attest to the positive effects that the stimuli of outside spaces and therapeutical gardens exert on the brain and hence on the restoration of health to human beings.

3.1 The Landscape Design Project in the Non-pharmacological Treatment of Alzheimer's Disease

Each person understands designed space in different ways. Moreover, in this area, memory plays a key role in guiding people to these spaces and forwarding the meanings to them. On this basis, it can be understood what damage has been caused to the perceptions and spatial experience of people with brain injuries resulting from neurological syndromes and ailments, which affect the memory, like Alzheimer's disease.

Alzheimer's disease was first described in 1906 by the German psychiatrist and neurophysiologist, Alois Alzheimer. It concerns a progressive neurological illness and is still fatal. It is responsible for slowly and gradually impairing the functions of the brain and is characterized by its harm to two or more of the following cognitive functions: memory, language; attention; logical reasoning; judgment; planning; visual and spatial skills. Moreover, it is sufficiently serious to have an adverse effect on the everyday life of someone afflicted with it. Among the high levels of cognitive failure, behavioral problems and psychiatric symptoms that the patients of Alzheimer's disease are subject to, hallucinations, depression, physical aggression and alterations in sleep patterns are conditions that should be highlighted.

In other words, the damage to the brain caused by Alzheimer's disease is, at the moment, something that is irreversible and in a significant way, can alter the whole intellectual, affective, behavioral and ultimately physical functioning of the individual concerned. Gradually, the patient loses his/her capacity to think, learn, remember, communicate or carry out everyday activities in an effective and independent way, as well as to manage his/her life in an autonomous way, since this person requires constant care [37].

Age is the major risk factor for the development of Alzheimer's disease. After 65 years of age, the risk of developing the disease doubles every five years.

According to the Alzheimer's Association [38], nearly 47 million people are believed to be living with Alzheimer or dementia worldwide. This number is predicted to increase to almost 75 million by 2030 and almost 132 million by 2050. And according to the Center for Disease Control and Prevention [39], an estimated 5.1 million Americans, aged 65 or older, may currently have Alzheimer. This estimate may rise to 13.2 million by 2050. In Brazil, there are about 1.2 million cases, most of which are still undiagnosed [40].

Although there is still no cure for Alzheimer's disease, some studies [9] suggest that if the illness is treated in its early stages, soon after the first symptoms have been detected, measures can be taken to control its progression. There are two kinds of treatment for Alzheimer's disease – pharmacological and non-pharmacological.

Whereas pharmacological treatment is based on the use of medication to ease the advance of the disease, non-pharmacological treatment makes use of several kinds of therapies, which entail exposing the brain to several kinds of stimuli. The purpose of this is to arrest the advance of the disease and provide a sense of well being for patients with these conditions.

It is worth drawing attention to the concern with projected space – for inside and outside places - when offering non-pharmacological treatment. According to Zeisel [8], people suffering from Alzheimer's disease need to live in secure and carefully planned environments because among other problems linked to the disease, they have great difficulty in remembering the spaces they have visited as well as being able to locate these environments. Patients with Alzheimer's disease have difficulty in remembering the place where they were only a few minutes before.

On the other hand, those affected by the disease (and other patients too) tend to be healthier when support is given to making them feel secure and interact in a friendly way. This is because the environments planned for this purpose create the right conditions and sensorimotor stimuli for the enhancement of cognition and sensitizing the spatial perception of these patients and hence enable them to get their bearings in this space. These kinds of stimuli allow the brain to respond in a positive way to the created space and as a result, the patients are able to walk from one point to another with the aim of arriving at a particular place and knowing exactly where they are. As well as triggering a stimulus to spatial perception, environments of this kind also provide areas devoted to a wide range of activities with therapeutical goals such as physiotherapy, music therapy, gardening, and painting. They are also geared to enabling the patients to socialize between them and with their families.

This means that these kinds of environments can assist the patients in being conscious of who they are and what they are doing and this is a strong support to the independence and health of people in these conditions. Thus the landscape design project of clinics that offer homes to patients with Alzheimer's disease plays a crucial role in their care and non-pharmacological treatment by providing them with a healthy period of residence in this healing space. This includes the positive emotions and feelings aroused by the outside environment and gardens which are responsible for: (i) the significant reductions in stress, agitation and aggressive behavior; (ii) a greater production of Vitamin D; (iii) a significant improvement in sleep patterns, hormonal balance and the quality of life of these patients. Examples of this are: the healthy sensations caused by sunshine, fresh air, breeze and the temperature of the skin; a view of nature, colors and the textures of plants and flowers; the pleasures of gardening and the chance to go for walks, feed the birds, take exercise and socialize with friends [24, 31, 33, 34] among other kinds of stimuli that are able sensitize the physical and psychological domains of a person in a satisfactory way.

In this sphere, the spatial configuration of the healthcare centers for patients with Alzheimer's disease and other forms of dementia are altered and molded with a view to offering them environments that resemble a residential dwelling. Relatively small clinics which recreate the feeling of a home, are the opposite of what is found in large impersonal hospitals and are becoming increasingly common because patients suffering from dementia tend to behave better and have a more pleasurable life in this type of accommodation [41].

The feeling of home is increased by the presence of therapeutical gardens in the landscape design projects of these clinics. They allow patients suffering from Alzheimer's disease to take up gardening as a form of therapy. In general, plants significantly benefit the physical and psychological well being of the residents. In particular, plants or flowers familiar to the patients play a key role in evoking affective memories. In addition, the need to take care of plants which is involved in gardening, assists in the maintenance of motor skills and offering positive forms of sensory stimuli, as well as being a topic of conversation between the patients and personnel who take part in this activity. Through the active interaction between patients with limited motor skills, it is recommended that plants should form the project of a therapeutic garden that should also take account of tolerance to rough treatment or excessive irrigation of the plants [29].

There are a number of suggestions in the literature [6–9, 29, 31, 35], which make a wide range of recommendations for designing therapeutic gardens and take account of different levels of neurological and physical involvement for patients with Alzheimer's disease. With regard to the scope of this research study, these recommendations can be divided into eight categories: (a) access; (b) pathways; (c) uses; (d) particular activities; (e) comfort; (f) planting/sensory stimulation; (g) spaces/stimuli; (h) security and conservation – as set out in Table 1:

Table 1. Scope of recommendations for designing therapeutic gardens.

Access	Pathways	Uses	Particular activities
Number of doors/gates giving access to the garden	Complexity of the paths for the patients	Gardens separated owing to the different levels of Alzheimer's disease	Areas set aside for manual activities that involve horticulture and tilling the soil
Bathrooms near the garden	Signs of landscape features that can attract the attention of the patients during their walks	Factors that encourage the residents to help in looking after the garden	Areas suitable for physical activities like physiotherapy and organized walks
Freedom of access to the garden	Layout to indicate the pathways	Uses of the garden by the staff at the Center	
		Uses of the garden by the families	
		Uses of the garden at nighttime	

Comfort	Planting/sensory stimulation	Space/stimuli	Security and conservation
Location of the chairs and benches to allow patients to rest	Existence of plants with shapes/aromas that can provoke irritability	Architectural features that can evoke memories or types of behavior that can stimulate the brain	The existence of emergency exits
Presence of seats and shade for the hot period after midday	Plants and flowers with vivid colors	Landscape features of the garden that linger in the past of the patients and can evoke memories	Ensuring the patients are able to see the perimeter surrounding the garden
	Plants that undergo seasonal changes and seasonal plantation	Shape of plants, structures, shade, statues and suchlike that can provoke hallucinations or illusions	View of the garden from within the building
			Existence of poisonous plants
			Existence of plant species with sharp edges that can hurt the patients

Source: the authors.

Setting out from this range of recommendations, an investigation is carried out into the 'Recanto Monsenhor Albino' [Monsignor Albino Rest Home] clinic, which is specialized in the treatment of elderly people with dementia, such as that caused by Alzheimer's disease, and located in the town of Catanduva (Sao Paulo – Brazil), as described in the following section.

4 The 'Recanto Monsenhor Albino' Landscape Design Project

This research field study was carried out during December 2017, in the precincts of the 'Recanto Monsenhor Albino' rest home located 4 km from the Dr. Alberto Lahós de Carvalho highway in the town of Catanduva, in the Northeast region of the State of Sao Paulo (Brazil), and 384 km from the capital, Sao Paulo.

Currently, the clinic is run by the Sister Anália Nunes, and includes a staff of doctors, nurses, a nutritionist, an occupational therapist, a psychologist, a physiotherapist and a social assistant. The place seeks to welcome elderly people over the age of 60 of both sexes and offers them apartment suites or simple bedrooms. It has the capacity to accommodate 50 elderly people and is divided into female and male wards.

The method for gathering data entailed the practice of regular visits to the space in question and conducting interviews with the staff of health cares. Moreover, as in the case of the method employed for the analysis and interpretation of the results obtained, the study followed the full range of recommendations for designing therapeutic gardens based on the ideas of Zeisel [6–9] Marcus e Sachs [29]; Pappas [31]; and Hernandéz [35].

The 'Recanto Monsenhor Albino' possesses a farm that was donated by the Rotary Club of Catanduva. This covers an area of 240.220 m^2, where buildings have been erected for both men and women, which are sites for nursing and visiting rooms. There are also buildings with offices for administration, social services and psychology, together with a canteen, toilet facilities, a kitchen a room fitted for physiotherapy, and a chapel for prayers and religious services. In addition, there are spaces for doing physical exercises and socializing with the patients, as well as green areas for walks and gardens where vegetables are grown for their own consumption.

The clinic was opened in the middle of February 2001. The families of the elderly guests are allowed to take part by making daily visits between 10:00 and 17:00 h. The patients usually have meetings with their families in the outside area of the rest home in Praça da Amizade [Friendship Square].

The main access to the place was through a gate, which remained open the whole day and was the place where pedestrians and cars entered the premises. The cars were parked in front of Praça da Amizade [Friendship Square]. This is the square where the families stay during their visits and it includes a grotto dedicated to the Blessed Virgin Mary.

There is a pathway covered with awnings which has handrails throughout its length and leads the visitor or patient (both male and female) to their wards where are situated their sleeping quarters, the dining-room, the chapel and the physiotherapy rooms.

Both the women's ward and the men's ward are similar and have either individual suites or rooms for two people. These bedrooms have windows that open out to an expansive green area. The building for the female ward has a larger area because the number of women with Alzheimer's disease tends to be larger than that of men [43].

The chapel, physiotherapy rooms and dining-room were built separately and interlinked by walkways as a means of encouraging walking, since the topography of the site is designed to make it possible to walk without difficulty.

At the back of the dining room, there is a large kitchen garden enclosed by a hedge, where several kinds of vegetables, greens and other produce are grown with the assistance of the patients, for their own consumption.

The free and green area of the center is significantly larger than the covered area. In addition, the presence of animals such as cats, hens, turkey and various birds helps to give a greater spatial resemblance to a farm and this distinguishes the 'Recanto Monsenhor Albino' from other clinics that offer homes to patients with Alzheimer's disease.

The types of flora that can be seen mainly consist of green foliage. The uniform green area is suited to walking, making observations and the time spent there by the patients and their families. However, there is no garden for activities to be carried out together with the residents.

The activities that take place in the open air usually involve special events on commemoration days. The other everyday activities of the patients are carried out in closed environments such as the physiotherapy room. However, all indoor environments are connected directly to the green area. In the same way, access to these places necessarily requires the elderly people to walk through green areas.

5   Results and Discussion

This section sets out the results obtained from the analysis of the landscape design project that centered on the 'Recanto Monsenhor Albino' rest home, and includes a discussion based on the features that make up the list of recommendations for designing a therapeutic garden (Table 1) and the contribution made to this project made by practice in the field.

(a) Access to the Garden

Following the research studies carried out by Zeisel [6–9] and Marcus and Sachs [29], the recommendations for the project in the 'Access' category include: (1) the number of doors/gates that give access to the garden; (2) the bathrooms closest to the garden; (3) freedom of access to the garden. At the same time the work undertaken in the field study broadened the scope of this inquiry by incorporating two new features: (4) ease of access to the garden by the patients; (5) accessibility as outlined below (Table 2):

The exits from the wings providing the patients with access to the garden are indicated in a satisfactory way. However, this pathway might be confusing for the residents because of the various outbuildings and gates. In light of this, it is recommended that the paths should have pointers that can serve as guides for the patients, with colored floors and handrails for identification (for example, red for the dining-room, blue for the chapel, and yellow for the physiotherapy rooms). These pathways are quite extensive for the patients.

For this reason, it is recommended that sanitary facilities should be installed that are separate from the huts and set up along the paths. This would allow the residents to make use of the bathrooms without having to enter the huts. This measure is of crucial importance since patients with Alzheimer's disease suffer from incontinence soon after the beginning of the second phase of the disease [29, 37].

Table 2. Scope of recommendations for the 'Access' category.

Access	Results	Commentary
Number of doors/gates with access to the garden	**[Partly addressed]**	There is a door that gives access to the garden in each wing (make and female). However, owing to the fact that the outhouses or huts are detached from the wings, the patients can feel confused when following the path that provides access to the garden
Bathrooms close to the garden	**[Partly addressed]**	Each hut provides toilet facilities. However, owing to the distance between each of the huts, there is an insufficient number
Freedom of access to the garden	**[Fully addressed]**	The doors of the wings remain open for the whole of the day
Ease of access to the garden by the patients	**[Fully addressed]**	The green area of the clinic covers a significant part of the terrain and the way it is designed allows the patients to have ease of access to the garden
Accessibility	**[Fully addressed]**	Ramps and handrails can be found in all the pathways giving access

Source: the authors.

The way the clinic is designed meets all the requirements with regard to accessibility and allows the patients, visitors and staff of cares to enter the green area without any difficulty. Since contact with nature is immediate and extended to the whole terrain, anybody can easily enjoy the benefits of the garden of the clinic. The doors and gates providing access to the garden are kept open so as to encourage the patients to make use of the green area, as well as to be able to walk about freely.

(b) **The Garden Paths**

Following the suggestions made by Zeisel [6–9] and Marcus and Sachs [29], the design recommendations for the 'Paths' category cover: (6) the complexity of the paths for the patients; (7) Signs of landscape features that might attract the attention of the patients during their walks; (8) Layout that suggests what pathways can be taken. And as a result of the procedure followed in the field survey, a new factor has been added to this: (9) the gentle topography for both walking and resting patients, in accordance with the description given below (Table 3):

Table 3. Scope of recommendations for the 'Paths' category.

Pathways	Results	Comments
Complexity of the paths for the patients	[Partly addressed]	The pathways are set out with clearly defined areas, awnings and handrails
Signs of landscape features that might attract the attention of the patients during their walks	[Partly addressed]	There are features such as: a grotto for Nossa Senhora Aparecida [Our Lady of the Appeared Conception (one of the titles of the Virgin Mary)]; and species of tall plants that stand out
Layout that suggests what pathways can be taken	[Fully addressed]	The whole pathway is created by a different layout
Gentle topography for both walking and resting patients	[Fully addressed]	The terrain is sufficiently flat and relaxing for the patients

Source: the authors.

The design of the clinic includes an arrangement of pathways fitted with handrails, differentiated floors and awnings that connect one hut from another so that both the staff and residents can clearly make out which path to follow. However, owing to the monotony of the colors, textures and shapes, the patients can easily be confused. It is recommended that these paths are distinguished more clearly and have contrasting features so that they can guide people more effectively. In addition, distinguishing marks in the landscape are essential to enhance the stimuli provided by the pathways since these can be understood by the patients as reference-points of their location. This means increasing the number of distinguishing features spread around the garden such as fountains, statues, benches, and large-sized plants.

With regard to its topography, the terrain of the clinic was found to be flat enough and congenial and allowed the patients autonomy and ease of movement when walking. As it grew, it was suggested that occasional, gentle slopes could be included as a means of helping the residents do exercises.

With regard to the layout, the pathways are indicated by the concrete floor, iron handrails and awnings made of translucent polystyrene tiles. These paths link one hut to another and are in direct contact with the garden. For the benefit of the residents, a new feature should be added to this layout, which is the idea of having a pathway in the middle of the garden with the use of comfortable wooden duckboards.

(c) The Uses that can be Made of Gardens

With regard to the 'Uses' category, Zeisel [6–9]; Marcus and Sachs [29]; Pappas [31]; and Hernandéz [35] make the following recommendations: (10) separate gardens for different levels of Alzheimer's disease; (11) features that encourage the patients to help in taking care of the garden; (12) uses of the garden by members of the staff; (13) uses of the garden by families; (14) uses of the garden at nighttime. On the basis of the procedure followed in the field research, a new factor us put forward for this area: (15) design of the garden for therapeutical and socializing purposes and a number of activities involving all the patients such as the following (Table 4):

Table 4. Scope of recommendations for the 'Uses' category.

Uses	Results	Comments
Gardens separated to take account of different levels of Alzheimer's disease	[Not addressed]	All the patients are free to enjoy the same areas of the garden
Factors that encourage patients to help with looking after the garden	[Partly addressed]	Apart from the kitchen garden at the back of the clinic, the patients do not actively take part in looking after the garden
Uses of the garden for members of the staff at the center	[Fully addressed]	All the staff stated that they made use of the garden for purposes of relaxation, contemplation and socializing
Uses of the garden by the families	[Fully addressed]	It was noted that it was widely used by the families during their visits
Uses of the garden at nighttime	[Not addressed]	The garden is not used at nighttime
Shaping of the garden for therapeutic practice socializing and various activities with all the patients	[Partly addressed]	Although the area is suitable for distinct activities, these are carried out in closed environments

Source: the authors.

Since all the patients with Alzheimer's disease respond to stimuli in different ways during the different stages of the disease, it is recommended that there should be specific areas in the garden devoted to differentiated types of cognitive stimulation that are aligned to the stages that apply to the residents of the clinic.

With regard to the question of looking after the garden, this was shown to be essential since it acts as sensory therapy and assists in establishing a daily routine for the patients. In view of this, features should be included in the green area that allow residents to react in an active way to this space.

In the case of physical, therapeutic and socializing activities, although the green area of the clinic offers good prospects for these uses, it is restricted to the space allotted for meetings between the residents and visitors by the 'Praça da Amizade' [Friendship Square], which provides the features of rest and relaxation, such as benches and shade. Thus, in light of its potential uses and significant benefits, it is strongly recommended that activities focused on encouraging the patients to linger in the garden should be expanded.

This can be extended to the use of the green area at nighttime. At all events, it is essential to renew the current installations and a scheme for illuminating the gardens could be put into effect. At the time of the field research, the existing lighting system proved to be insufficient to allow patients to walk about at night.

(d) **Carrying out Specific Activities in the Garden**

With regard to the 'Specific Activities' category, Marcus and Sachs [29] and Pappas [31] make the following recommendations: (16) there should be areas devoted to manual activities that involve horticulture and tilling the soil; (17) areas suitable for physical activities such as physiotherapy and walks. On the basis of the process followed in the field research, two new items are included: (18) involvement of the patients in looking after particular garden species; (19) gathering species for uses that entail manual activities such as those described in the following chart (Table 5):

Table 5. Scope of recommendations for the 'Specific Activities' category.

Particular activities	Results	Comments
Areas designated for manual activities that involve vegetable gardens and tilling the soil	**[Fully addressed]**	There is a large kitchen garden for one's own planting and consumption, with a significant variety of vegetables and greens and the patients assist in its maintenance
Areas suitable for physical activities like physiotherapy and going for walks	**[Partly addressed]**	No physiotherapy activities are carried out in the green area, although the patients are encouraged to go for walks
Interactions of the patients through taking care of garden species	**[Partly addressed]**	The patients with only slight cognitive impairment help in looking after the garden, although this activity does not form a part of a program of sensory therapy
Gathering species for manual activities	**[Partly addressed]**	The manual activities regarding the care of vegetable species involve horticulture and picking flowers to decorate the indoor environments

Source: the authors.

The activities involving horticulture are essential to enable the residents to live in the midst of nature, work out or socialize. Horticultural activities can be shaped as a strategy for the evocation of affective memories by the patients.

In the case of activities carried out in the open air, these are mainly devoted to walking and enjoying the views. The scope of these should be broadened by integrating the physiotherapy activities in the green area. As well as having a closer contact with nature, interaction between the patients and health carers can be strengthened through physical activities carried out in the garden.

Moreover, as well as horticulture, there are patients who can help look after the vegetable species that are found in the garden. This dynamic does not form a part of the planning of activities that can be carried out by the patients but depend on the curiosity and wishes of the residents. This means the gardening activities are mainly concentrated on the kitchen garden, apart from picking flowers in the garden which is done by the patients with the assistance of the staff of health carers at particular times of the year, with the aim of making floral arrangements for decorating the rooms for indoor events. It is a very good idea to include a schedule of everyday activities for the residents with the aim of broadening the range of sensorimotor and cognitive stimuli for the patients. These might involve both looking after the garden and gathering species for use in manual activities.

(e) The Feeling of Comfort Provided by the Garden

According to Hernandéz [35], the recommendations for the 'Comfort' category include the following: (20) location of seats that can allow the patients to rest. "Layout" which involves deciding which spots are suitable for rest; (21) the existence of seats and shade for periods after midday. In this context there are some new benefits that arose from the field study: (22) recreation rooms for the patients with a view of the garden, as in the following chart (Table 6):

Table 6. Scope of recommendations for the 'Comfort' category.

Comfort	Results	Comments
Location of seats where patients can rest. Layout which involves deciding which spots are suitable for rest	**[Fully addressed]**	There are fixed benches in the green area
Existence of seats and shade for periods after midday	**[Fully addressed]**	There is a square with ample shade the whole day
Recreation rooms for patients with a view of the garden	**[Fully addressed]**	The recreation rooms of the two wards are arranged so that they are open to the green area

Source: the authors.

In the case of both the horticultural activities and the walks, it is essential for the patient to be able to decide to remain in the green area and feel comfortable, as allowed by the presence of suitable seats in spaces of this kind. As well as the patients, the families and staff of carers can also benefit from the opportunities of social interaction and rest provided by these seats.

However, just having seats is not enough to ensure that the patients can remain in the outside area in a state of comfort. Patients with Alzheimer's disease gradually lose any idea of temperature and for this reason, cannot remain directly exposed to the sun, especially in the period after midday. This means that during the season of the year when the sun is really hot, there must be areas with shade in the garden to ensure their well being.

With regard to the recreation rooms, owing to storms and sudden changes of weather, at times, it is impossible for patients or the staff of health carers to be in direct contact with the garden. At these times, the inside environment of the recreation room allows the patients to have an idea of the changes of weather throughout the day.

(f) Plantations and the Sensory Stimuli Fostered by the Garden

With regard to the 'Plantation/Sensory Stimulation' the recommendations of Marcus and Sachs [29] and Hernandéz [35] take account of the following: (23) the existence of plants with shapes/aromas that can provoke irritability; (24) plants that show signs of changes in their shape during the seasons – seasonal plantations;

(25) plants and flowers with vivid colors. At the same time, the findings of the research field include: (26) popular species that can be included in the planting carried out in the residential gardens; (27) species that can be found by the patients to stimulate touch, smell and vision, as shown in the chart below (Table 7):

Table 7. Scope of recommendations for the 'Plantation/Sensory Stimulation' category.

Plantation/sensory stimulation	Results	Comments
Existence of plants with shapes/aromas that can provoke irritability	**[Fully addressed]**	There are no plants that act as a trigger for irritability
Plants that show signs of changes in their shape during the seasons – seasonal plantations	**[Not addressed]**	Homogeneous plantations, which do not recognize the value of species that change with the seasons and the changes in the shape of the garden caused by them
Plants and flowers with vivid colors	**[Partly addressed]**	The configuration of the garden is predominantly green
Popular species that can be included in the planting carried out in the residential gardens	**[Fully addressed]**	There are species that are well-known by the patients such as bromelias, orchids, ferns and palm trees, as well as the vegetables and greens planted in the kitchen garden
Species that can be found by the patients to stimulate touch, smell and vision	**[Partly addressed]**	Patients can access all existing species. However, low diversity of species capable of stimulating patients' sight and smell is identified

Source: the authors.

The species used in the plantation of the therapeutic garden are often employed in gardens and for the decorations of residential dwellings. This arouses a feeling of familiarity in the residents and enables them to evoke affective memories from their interaction with the plants and at the same time, avoid provoking irritability.

As well as the affective memory, the question of the perseverance of the sensory stimuli is an essential factor in the stimulation of the neural activities of patients with Alzheimer's disease.

The landscape design project of the 'Recanto Monsenhor Albino' rest home benefits the tactile stimulus. This means the sense of vision and smell are less stimulated by the therapeutic garden.

Thus, what is recommended as a stimulus to vision is a heterogeneous plantation where there are striking alterations between the different seasons of the year. For example, azaleas, carnations and begonias are resistant to wintry conditions, while dahlias, geraniums and periwinkles are resistant to the high temperatures of summer. In addition, the planting of flowers and shrubs can attract the attention of the patients because of their colors and striking presence such as roses, dracaenas [female dragons] and crotons.

And to stimulate the sense of smell, plants and flowers should be planted that exhale strong aromatic scents, such as lavender, roses, jasmine at night and dama da noite [lady of the night].

(g) Stimuli Triggered by Features Found in the Garden

With regard to the 'Space/Stimuli' category, Zeisel [6–9] and Marcus and Sachs [29] make the following recommendations: (28) architectural features which can stimulate the brain and behavior; (29) features that form the landscape of the garden and reflect the cultural traditions of the patients; (30) the shape of the plants, structures, shade, statues and so forth which can induce hallucinations or illusions, as set out in the following chart (Table 8):

Table 8. Scope of recommendations for the 'Space/Stimuli' category.

Space/stimuli	Results	Comments
Architectural features that can stimulate the brain and behavior	[Not addressed]	There are few features that stimulate the brain and behavior of the patients. The landscape proves to be monotonous and pastoral
Features that comprise the landscape of the garden and reflect the cultural traditions of the patients	[Partly addressed]	The grotto with the religious image represents an important cultural feature for the patients
Shape of plants, structures, shade, statues and so forth which can induce hallucinations or illusions	[Fully addressed]	There are no features that can provoke irritability

Source: the authors.

The architecture together with the landscape design of the 'Recanto Monsenhor Albino' rest home, endow the landscape with local features that are pastoral and monotonous. These features confine the inducement of key stimuli to the sensorimotor and cognitive system of patients suffering from Alzheimer's disease. In view of this, it is recommended that new features should be included in the landscape that are able to induce positive stimuli to the brain and behavior of the residents, while taking account of the different stages of the disease.

The cultural link with space is another essential factor for the evocation of the affective memories of the patients [8]. The grotto with a religious image carries out in isolation the role of representing a cultural feature that is important for the residents and hence acts as a "trigger" for activating memories. In light of these benefits, more features should be included in the landscape of the garden that are closely linked to the cultural traditions of the patients.

Thus the architecture and landscape design project can provide positive stimuli to the individual. At the same time, there might be features or configurations that can act as "triggers" that can provoke irritability and stress or even hallucinations and illusions in patients with Alzheimer's disease such as shapes, noises, shadows, labyrinthian paths, and unclear access among other factors. When necessary, it is essential to detect these features so that they can be immediately removed.

(h) Safety Features and the Preservation of the Garden

With regard to the 'Safety and Conservation' category, the recommendations of Zeisel [6–9]; Marcus and Sachs [29]; and Pappas [31] are as follows: (31) the presence of emergency exits; (32) the perimeter fence of the garden should be visible to the patients; (33) the garden should be made visible from within the building; (34) checking the existence of poisonous plants; (35) checking the existence of species with sharp edges that can injure the patients. Thus the contributions made to the field include: (36) handrails to assist the patients when walking in the green areas; (37) a direct link of the inside environment with the garden; (38) maintenance of the garden, as follows (Table 9):

Table 9. The scope of the recommendations for the project in the 'Safety and Conservation' category.

Security and conservation	Results	Comments
Presence of emergency exits	**[Not addressed]**	There were no emergency exits
Ensuring the perimeter fence of the garden is visible to the patients	**[Partly addressed]**	The landscape is extensive and the residents may have difficulty in knowing the garden in its entirety
The visualization of the garden from inside the building	**[Fully addressed]**	The garden can be seen from all sides of the outbuildings
Existence of poisonous plants	**[Fully addressed]**	There are no poisonous plants
Existence of plants with sharp edges that can injure the patients	**[Partly addressed]**	There are plant species such as agave and Phoenix palm trees that can injure the face or hands of the patients
Handrails to assist the patients when walking in the green areas	**[Partly addressed]**	There are handrails on the walkways that pass through the green areas; however, they do not give assistance for walking by the grass verges
Direct link of the inside environment with the garden	**[Fully addressed]**	The entrances to the wings and huts are directly connected to the green areas
Maintenance of the garden	**[Fully addressed]**	There is a team of gardeners who carry out maintenance on a daily basis

Source: the authors.

The emergency exits are not properly signposted. As well as following correct safety standards, the emergency exits must be visible and accessible. However, they should not contrast with the atmosphere of the landscape to avoid causing "triggering effects" and agitating the patients.

It is essential to know the landscape in its totality to prevent the patients sounding out places that are unauthorized or inaccessible. Similarly, it is essential for the residents to be able to see the garden as a whole so that their walks are not the cause of stress, anxiety or uncertainty [44].

Since the space of the clinic is pervaded by a green area, it is recommended that mobile grab bars should be made available so that they can be used in the gardens during walks, physical activities and visits from the families.

In the clinic, the garden can be seen from all sides of the huts. The entrances of the wards and huts are directly connected to the green areas. All the men's and women's bedrooms are open to the green areas too. These bedrooms have a small balcony where the patients can sunbathe without having to leave their apartments.

The lack of judgment that characterizes patients with Alzheimer [8], can lead to hazardous situations such as tasting and chewing poisonous plants. The daily maintenance of the green areas of the 'Recanto Monsenhor Albino' rest home ensures that there are no poisonous plants throughout the whole area, as well as helping to preserve the therapeutic garden in a good condition. However, to ensure the protection of the health of the residents, health carers and visitors, species of plants with sharp edges, such as agaves and Phoenix palm trees should be replaced with other plants since they might injure the face or hands of the patients.

6 Conclusions

This paper has sought to demonstrate the importance of the landscape design project as a means of assisting the non-pharmacological treatment of Alzheimer's disease. It is based on knowledge of neuroscience and the assistance that this research can provide in a created space. Studies devoted to neuroplasticity provide evidence of how someone's brain is closely linked to his/her surroundings and how the external stimuli caused by this environment can alter the brain structure. Thus the designed space is able to stimulate the brain capacity to interfere in the behavior of human beings.

Against this background, the landscape design project can be regarded as a key aspect of constructed space. The presence of green areas has proved to be significant during the whole process of transforming the individual-architecture relationship. In the environment required for healing, it acquires an even more significant value insofar as it combines both the treatment and therapeutical domains of the patients. This can make us fully aware of the relationship established by the landscape design project with human beings and the assistance that the planned green areas can offer to the non-pharmacological treatment of dementia such as Alzheimer's disease.

The results obtained here pinpoint 38 recommendations for the design of therapeutic gardens which are outlined here and divided into 8 basic categories: (a) access; (b) pathways; (c) uses; (d) particular activities; (e) comfort; (f) planting/sensory stimulation; (g) spaces/stimuli; (h) safety and conservation. Out of all the recommendations, 26 emerged from the research carried out by Zeisel [6–9]; Marcus and Sachs [29]; Pappas [31]; Hernandéz [35], which were discussed in the review of the literature; and 12 originated from the investigation conducted in the field study at the 'Recanto Monsenhor Albino' rest home. 18 of the recommendations were fully addressed; 15

partly addressed and 5 not addressed at all. In other words, almost 53% of the requirements either needed to be reinforced or fully implemented.

On the basis of these results, it can be inferred that the official recommendations for the design of therapeutical gardens aimed at the non-pharmacological treatment of Alzheimer's disease have been of significant value. They can be represented to healthcare centers treating patients with this illness, particularly since they provide clear guidelines and increase the range of sensorimotor and cognitive stimuli to help improve the well being and quality of life of the residents.

In future developments, the research will broaden the scope of the investigation in the field and examine other clinics in the State of Sao Paulo (Brazil), that are dedicated to caring for patients with Alzheimer's disease. The aim of this is to extend the current set of recommendations based on the landscape design project to other centers of this nature and make further contributions to these patients.

References

1. Eberhard, J.: Neuroscience & Architecture of Health Care Facilities. In: 2nd Workshop Neuroscience & Architecture. Woods Hole, Massachusetts (2014)
2. Anthes, E.: Building around the mind. Sci. Am. Mind **20**, 52–59 (2009)
3. Ulrich, R.: Aesthetic and affective response to natural environment. Human Behavior and Environment, pp. 85–125. Plenum Press, New York (1983)
4. Ulrich, R., Simons, F., Losito, B., Fiorito, E., Miles, M., Zelson, M.: Stress recovery during exposure to nature and urban environments. J. Environ. Psychol. **11**, 201–230 (1991)
5. Ulrich, R.: How design impacts wellness. Healthc. Forum J. **30**, 20–25 (1992)
6. Zeisel, J., Hyde, J., Levkoff, S.: Best practices: an environment behavior (EB) model for Alzheimer special care units. Am. J. Alzheimer's Care Relat. Disord. Res. **9**, 4–21 (1994)
7. Zeisel, J., Raia, P.: Nonpharmacological treatment for Alzheimer's disease: a mind-brain approach. Am. J. Alzheimer's Dis. Other Dement. **15**, 331–340 (2000)
8. Zeisel, J.: Inquiry by Design: Environment/Behavior/Neuroscience in Architecture, Interiors, Landscape, and Planning. W.W. Norton, New York (2006)
9. Zeisel, J.: Improving person-centered care through effective design. Gener. J. Am. Soc. Aging **37**(3), 45–52 (2013)
10. Mallgrave, H.: The Architect's Brain. Wiley, United Kingdom (2010)
11. Zuanon, R.: Bio-Interfaces: designing wearable devices to organic interactions. In: Ursyn, A. (ed.) Biologically-Inspired Computing for the Arts: Scientific Data through Graphics, pp. 1–17. IGI Global, Hershey, Pennsylvania (2011)
12. Zuanon, R.: Designing wearable bio-interfaces: a transdisciplinary articulation between design and neuroscience. In: Stephanidis, C., Antona, M. (eds.) UAHCI 2013. LNCS, vol. 8009, pp. 689–699. Springer, Heidelberg (2013). https://doi.org/10.1007/978-3-642-39188-0_74
13. Zuanon, R.: Using BCI to play games with brain signals: an organic interaction process through NeuroBodyGame wearable computer. In: Huggins, J.E. (ed.) Fifth International Brain-Computer Interface Meeting 2013, 66th edn, p. 64. Graz University of Technology Publishing House, Austria (2013)
14. Zuanon, R.: Design-Neuroscience: Interactions between the Creative and Cognitive Processes of the Brain and Design. In: Kurosu, M. (ed.) HCI 2014. LNCS, vol. 8510, pp. 167–174. Springer, Cham (2014). https://doi.org/10.1007/978-3-319-07233-3_16

15. Lima Jr., G.C., Zuanon, R.: Fashion design and tactile perception: a teaching/learning methodology to enable visually handicapped people to identify textile structures. In: Streitz, N., Markopoulos, P. (eds.) DAPI 2016. LNCS, vol. 9749, pp. 233–244. Springer, Cham (2016). https://doi.org/10.1007/978-3-319-39862-4_22

16. Zuanon, R.: Game design and neuroscience cooperation in the challenge-based immersion in mobile devices as tablets and smartphones. In: Streitz, N., Markopoulos, P. (eds.) DAPI 2016. LNCS, vol. 9749, pp. 142–153. Springer, Cham (2016). https://doi.org/10.1007/978-3-319-39862-4_14

17. Lima Jr., G.C., Zuanon, R.: The foundation of the SEE BEYOND method: fashion design and neuroeducation applied to the teaching of the project methodology to students with congenital and acquired blindness. In: Streitz, N., Markopoulos, P. (eds.) DAPI 2017. LNCS, vol. 10291, pp. 528–546. Springer, Cham (2017). https://doi.org/10.1007/978-3-319-58697-7_40

18. Pallasmaa, J., Mallgrave, H., Arbib, M.: Architecture and Neroscience. Tapio Wirkkala - rut Bryk Foundation, Finland (2013)

19. Pallaasma, J.: Body, mind and imagination: the mental essence of architecture. In: Pallasmaa, J., Robinson, S., Farlling, M. (eds.) Mind in Architecture Neuroscience, Embodiment, and the Future of Design. MIT Press, Massachusetts (2015)

20. Farlling, M.: From intuition to immersion: architecture and neuroscience. In: Pallasmaa, J., Robinson, S., Farlling, M. (eds.) Mind in Architecture Neuroscience, Embodiment, and the Future of Design. MIT Press, Massachusetts (2015)

21. Robinson, S.: Nested bodies. In: Pallasmaa, J., Robinson, S., Farlling, M. (eds.) Mind in Architecture Neuroscience, Embodiment, and the Future of Design. MIT Press, Massachusetts (2015)

22. Lundy-Ekman, L.: Neurociência: fundamentos para reabilitação. Elsevier, Rio de Janeiro (2004)

23. Lent, R.: Neurociência da Mente e do Comportamento. Guanabara Koogan, Rio de Janeiro (2008)

24. Kaplan, R., Kaplan, S.: The Experience of Nature: A Psychological Perspective. Cambridge University Press, Cambridge (1989)

25. Wilson, O., Kellert, S.: Biophilia and the Conservation Ethic: The Biophilia Hypothesis. The Island Press, Washington DC (1993)

26. Grinde, B., Patil, G.: Biophilia: does visual contact with nature impact on health and well-being? Int. J. Environ. Res. Public Health 6, 2332–2343 (2009)

27. Ulrich, S., Kellert, S., Edward, W.: Biophobia and Natural Landscapes in The Biophilia Hypothesis. The Island Press, Washington DC (1993)

28. Ulrich, S.: Effects of Gardens on Health Outcomes: Theory and Research. Wiley, New York (1999)

29. Marcus, C., Sachs, A.: Therapeutic Landscapes: An Evidence-Based Approach to Designing Healing Gardens and Restorative Outdoor Spaces. Wiley, Hoboken (2013)

30. Filho, J.: Paisagismo: elementos de composição e estética. Aprendefácil, Viçosa (2002)

31. Pappas, A.: Exploring therapeutic restoration theories of nature and their application for design recommendations for an Alzheimer's garden at Wesley Woods Hospital. Master Thesis in Architecture, University Of Georgia, Athens (2006)

32. Gerlach-Springgs, N., Kaufman, R., Warner, S.: Restorative Gardens: The Healing Landscape. Yale University Press, New Haven (1998)

33. Olmsted, F.: Civilizing American cities: writings on city landscapes. Paperback, New York (1971)

34. Nightingale, F.: Notes on Nursing: What it is and What it is Not. Knopf, New York (1980)

35. Hernandez, R.: Effects of therapeutic gardens in special care units for people with Dementia. J. Hous. Elder. **21**(1–2), 117–152 (2007)
36. Garcia, J.M.: Clinica SeniorVit, Campinas. Presential interview held in August 2017 (2017)
37. Instituto Alzheimer Brasil. http://www.institutoalzheimerbrasil.org.br
38. Alzheimer's Association. https://www.alz.org/
39. Center for Disease Control and Prevention. http://www.cdc.gov/aging/healthybrain/index.htm
40. Associação Brasileira de Alzheimer. http://www.abraz.org.br
41. Kuller, R.: Familiar design helps dementia patients cope. Design Intervention: Toward a more humane Architecture, pp. 255–267. Van Nostrand Reinhold, New York (1991)
42. Instituto Alzheimer Brasil. http://www.institutoalzheimerbrasil.org.br
43. Nitrini, R., Herrera, J., Carmelli, P.: Estudos epidemiológico populacional de demência na cidade de Catanduva, estado de São Paulo. Rev. Psiq. Clin. **25**, 70–73 (2014)
44. Kaplan, R., Kaplan, S.: With People in Mind: Design and Management of Everyday Nature. Island Press, Washington DC (1998)

Drawing Memories: Intersections Between the Sites of Memory and the Memories of Places

Rachel Zuanon[1(✉)], Melissa Ramos da Silva Oliveira[1], Haroldo Gallo[2], and Cláudio Lima Ferreira[2]

[1] Anhembi Morumbi University, Sao Paulo, Brazil
`rachel@all-affective.com, melinerso@gmail.com`
[2] UNICAMP, Campinas, Brazil
`{haroldogallo,claudiol.f}@uol.com.br`

Abstract. This paper explores the relationships between people, place and memory and involves discussing the links between the "sites of memory" and the "convergence-divergence zone", which is bound up with the processes of perception and evocation/recognition of fleeting memories, as experienced by the residents of the central district of the town of Campinas - Sao Paulo - Brazil. A field research was carried out with a sample of 266 participants from the central area of this town, who agreed to take part in interviews and produce drawings on the basis of which it was possible to identify places of memory. These places were appropriated and preserved through shared feelings, which distinguished them from others, and the memory of these places was undertaken there. The results show the close ties between the individual, the urban/architectural space created and the recognition of the value of the constructed urban identity that is based on the memory that the participants had of their city, cultural heritage, symbolic reference points and representations. These representations underpin the discussions about the way cultural heritage and memory are endowed with legitimacy and preserved in the present.

Keywords: Neuroscience · Architecture · Drawings · Sites of memory
Memory of places

1 Introduction

Memory is an evocation of the past. St Augustine [1] showed that memory is not simply a way of recalling and recording things, but rather a manner of evoking past ties which can no longer be accessed. He also stressed that the past is our history, while at the same time it lingers on into the present and explains many of the current events that take place.

St Augustine [1] also states that human beings learn about time in three phases: past, present and future. The past is something far away and refers to events that simply once occurred but still influence what we are at present. The present corresponds to what is here and now – the period when our lives and experiences are happening at this moment. The future is the place where all events that are taking place will reach a conclusion and the time when the determined period of what is going to happen arrives. This being the case, the past constitutes an abstraction, which only materializes through the evocation of the living experiences of the present, and this generally occurs by envisaging and making predictions about what the future will be like.

In other words, the brain creates records of memory through sensory maps and reproduces an approximation of its original facts. This process is known as 'recall' or 'evocation'. Remembering a person or an event or telling a story requires evocation, that is, it involves recognizing the objects and situations around us. This procedure is of value since it allows us to think about the objects with which we interact and the events we witness, as well as the whole imaginative process through which we plan our future [2]. In the present, we are able to reconstruct memory. This process of reconstruction is fundamentally mediated by memory. Halbwachs [3] stated that memories always originate from a collective process and are embodied in a precise social setting.

According to Damásio [2], our memories are preconceived, in the strict sense of the term, by our history and prior beliefs. The notion of an infallible memory is a myth and can only be applied to trivial matters. The idea that the brain retains something that seems an isolated "memory of the object" reveals to be unsustainable. The brain retains a memory of what occurred during an interaction and what is crucial is that this inter-action includes our past and even very often the past of our biological species and culture. This means that remembering does not exactly entail reconstituting the experiences or events of the past but rather recognizing things that have value and being able to embody them in our present circumstances.

Value, in the sense derived from economics, is the quality through which something is roughly estimated and determines its importance for people. Thus, cultural heritage is something that has value insofar as its assets are of a cultural and non-monetary order: it is something formed and created that constitutes a legacy of past generations. This heritage belongs to both individuals and society and its legacy is an intrinsic part of the life of communities. A community can be defined as a particular group of human beings who share common features such as ethnicity, territory and beliefs – and it is the outcome of a common social pattern; they also share a common history and heritage. Hence, the fact that they perceive things through a form of interaction and appropriation and not through a passive receptivity may be the secret of the "Proust effect" in memory and the reason why we often remember situations and not simply isolated things [2].

Pollak [4] underlines the fact that memory is selective. Being a first-rate editor, the brain creatively manipulates "multimedia" records of images, sounds, tactile sensations, smells and other perceptions of this kind. Each mind abstracts and discards to what does not interest it and focuses and records what most attracts it, while always being guided by value judgements. The assigning of a significant value to the capacity of something (whether tangible or intangible) is a way of responding to a human need and means people are compelled to make choices that are mediated by feelings and meanings.

Damásio [2] argues that what we remember from our encounter with a particular object is not only its visual structure, which is mapped through optical images on the human retina. A key additional factor is that there is a real governance controlling the sensorimotor patterns which makes the formation of memories possible. This involves: "the sensory-motor patterns associated with the view of the object; the sensory-motor pattern associated with touch and handling the object (if this is the case); the sensory-motor patterns resulting from the evocation of previously acquired memories related to the object; the sensory motor patterns involved in triggering the emotions and feelings associated with the object".

In view of this, the selection based on a judgement value is always bound up with feelings of esteem – positive feelings that we nurture for something - which is a key factor in the formation of memory and identity. There is no relationship of belonging unless there has been affectivity and appropriation or in other words, "unless we nurture a positive feeling that we can be identified with or it is related to us" and without which the conservation will not be justified. These feelings are expressed in the values and meanings that the things have for us but which are not an intrinsic part of them. They are the results of the relationships maintained with them and vary in accordance with each individual, community, temporality and spatiality [5].

Menezes [6] believes that value is not inherent to goods and things. It can fluctuate and can be divided into the following categories: cognitive value (associated with the opportunities provided by knowledge), formal value (which allows the construction of a world of meaning), affective value (with regard to a heavy symbolic weight) and pragmatic value (i.e. a utilitarian value). Finally, it is the result of the relations people have with themselves and not only of their direct relations with objects. The assigning of value calls for a distinction and allows the retrieval of memory.

Halbwachs [3] stated that there is no collective memory that does not occur in a spatial context. He argued that space offers an image of permanence and stability through signs left by social groups. These signs can assist in arousing memories and evoking the past and thus represent valuable testimony since they involve the retrieval of information about people and significant social facts about the groups. In this way, the places of memory can be shaped – places that are appropriated and preserved by the existence of a shared meaning that distinguishes them from others.

At the same time, the 'physical' sites of memory are connected to the 'neurophysiological' places of memory, described by Damásio [2] as 'convergence-divergence zones'. These zones can be defined as a set of neurons where a large number of handle signals make contact in *feedforward-feedback loops*, which assist the neural architecture responsible for the evocation of memories and hence the recognition of all our surroundings.

In light of this, this paper collates information about the relationship betweeen the history and significant memories of the central area of the city of Campinas - Sao Paulo – Brazil. The purpose of this is to identify the "places of memory" recognised by the inhabitants and mediated by the "convergence-divergence zones", which constitute the spaces for images and dispositions that are bound up in the perception and evocation/recognition of these memories.

2   Sites of Memory

"Sites of memory" [les lieuz de mémoire] is a term coined by the French historian Pierre Nora [7] to designate places in every sense of the word, from the material and concrete object to the most abstract, symbolic and functional entities which show vestiges that are recalled and transformed by the history of a society.

The site of memory that covers a territory corresponds to the records and everything that goes beyond them, which is another way of saying that it encompasses the symbolic meaning inscribed in its own record. These territories are places where memory is established and look like a new unnatural way of confining memory since we do not experience more than what they mean and what history, as a source, appropriates from them. In this way they are 'material' (tangible) and 'non-material' (intangible) stopping points where memory is solidified by a community, country and places where groups or peoples can be identified or make their mark; this gives rise to a feeling of identity and belongingness.

Even a place, which has a purely material appearance like a filing cabinet, is only a site of memory if the imagination bestows on it a symbolic aura. Even a purely functional place like a classroom textbook, a will or a group of former combatants, only enters the category if it is an object of ritual. Even a minute's silence, which has the ultimate symbolic significance, is at the same time the material form of a temporal unit, which periodically serves as a vivid reminder of the need to remember. The three factors always coexist (...). It is (a) material for a demographic profile; (b) hypothetically "functional" since it ensures, at the same time, the crystallization of memory and its transmission while (c) it is symbolic by definition, since it is characterized by an event or vivid experience [7].

Running in parallel with this, neuroscience has made a considerable effort to understand the neural basis of the representation of objects and how knowledge of an object can be stored in the memory, categorized in terms of conceptual and linguistic factors and retrieved through an evocation or recognition [8]. From this perspective, Damásio [2] extended the 'site of memory' concept to the area of neurophysiology to define the theory of convergence-divergence zones. The purpose of this was to set out a neural architecture of cortical connections, endowed with converging and diverging node markers, closely related to perception and memory. This theory assumes there are two cerebral spaces: (a) images and (b) dispositions.

The space of the image designs clear maps of objects and events during the perception and redesigns them during the evocation. Both in the perception and the evocation, there is a display in which the properties of the object correspond with the map. This space consists of an aggregate of primary sensorimotor cortices, or in other words, regions of the cerebral cortex situated at the entrance point of the visual, auditory, and other types of sensory signals in the nearby areas. It also includes the nucleus of the solitary tract, the parabrachial nucleus and the superior colliculus, which are provided with the capacity to create images.

In contrast, instead of maps, the space of the dispositions includes mechanisms, which consist of implicit formulas about how to reconstitute the maps in the space of the image. This space consists of an aggregate of associative cortices. This means it is situated in the cerebral cortices, which are not occupied by the space of the image (the higher-order association cortices and the limbic cortices) and in the large number of subcortical nuclei. In this space, the mechanisms maintain the basis of knowledge and the means for reconstituting this knowledge in the evocation. It is the source of the images in the imagination and reasoning process and is also used to activate movement.

The two spaces show the different ages in the evolution of the brain – one in which the dispositions are strict enough to ensure a suitable behavior and the other in which the maps form images and make an improvement in the standard of the behavior. Today the two are inextricably intertwined. And at the intersection, the sites of memory of Nora [7], and the convergence-divergence zones of Damásio [2], coexist in their potential capacity and can be found in the spaces that design and shape the concept of the city.

The cities are formed of built and natural spaces which being constituted of meaning, turns them into an empowered region and allows them to integrate this symbolic community of meanings called the imaginary world. Above all, they are places endowed with a symbolic weight which distingushes them and gives them an identity. These entities can be represented by a monument, museum, well-known character, file or even a symbol, event or an institution. However, not all of them are characterized as sites of memory.

For this reason, these territories must possess a "desire for memory" and be able to show in their origins a memorialist purpose that ensures their identity. What constitutes them is an interplay between memory and history which is an interaction of the two factors that lead to their own mutual determination. Without this will, places of memory are only places of history. It should be remembered that memory and history are not synonymous, while, at the same time, they are narratives of the past that reshape episodes that have occurred and are not subject to repetition.

It is not correct to say that in order to remember, it is necessary to be transported in our thoughts outside space because, on the contrary, it is precisely the image of constructed or natural space that, owing to its stability, gives us the illusion of not being changed by another time and finding the past in the present – "but it is exactly in this way that we can define memory, and only space (whether created or natural) is stable enough to last without aging and without losing any of its parts" [7].

Every city is the owner of its history and memories and, equally, of the community of meaning which entitles it to its identity. Finally, memory is something evoked and vivid and its intellectual reconstruction is history.

3   The Center of Campinas

In the context of this discussion the central area of the municipality of Campinas, located in the State of Sao Paulo – Brazil, can be dubbed as a "site of memory"; this is appropriate since the city itself is renowned for the transformations it has undergone throughout its history. It represents a place where people can be identified, remembered and feel nostalgic about the experiences it has given them. Hence, what should be remembered represents both known memories and an infinite number of anonymous stories about the people who have passed through it. Even though these spaces have undergone radical changes and deterioration, they have left their traces and memories, and these can act as benchmarks for identifying the evolving pattern of the city.

Until the end of the 19th Century, Campinas was the largest producer of coffee in the State of Sao Paulo and one of the main bases for the expansion of its coffee industry. This was partly due to the social and economic history that characterized the city itself and partly on account of its ideal position as a key staging post for transport and communications. This central location has always been one of the permanent features required for the structuring of this town and shaping the formal and cultural features of its urban landscape.

In the opinion of Lapa [9], since the original foundation of the city, it has always been a center of commerce with stores for both wet and dry products, and sales outlets for foodstuffs, clothing and footwear. It was also a thoroughfare for carts drawn by animals alongside the Sao Carlos Theatre, which was demolished in 1922. In the center, the first tramways of Campinas could be found.

According to Badaró [10], the change of Campinas into the main center for coffee production, led to a wide range of alterations to the city that changed its appearance. From an urban standpoint, the changes brought about by coffee resulted in several improvements, which included the following: public gas lighting (1875) and animal-drawn trams installed by the Companhia Carris de Ferro [Steel Railway Company] (1879). Several buildings arose in the urban environment which served the public, such as hospitals, schools and markets - these created a more public life in the city that was embedded in middle-class and urban values. A new neo-classical style of architecture emerged which was adopted for several residential dwellings and public constructions and led to alterations in many colonial buildings. The location of the railway station served as a new central hub of the city - with the cathedral at one of its extreme points, and beyond that the Sao Carlos Theatre; and, at the other end, the station itself. Thus, the station attracted to itself the extension of the commercial area of Campinas, already established in the border areas to the central centers of the city. This explains the trend for a "North-South occupation", which followed the pre-urban axis of the way known as Guaiases at that time.

Fig. 1. Campinas in 1929. Source: Oliveira, 2012 [11]

Following the industrial expansion, which gave an impetus to Campinas at the beginning of the 20th Century, there began to be other urban requirements. The narrow streets and colonial appearance of the buildings were not in tune with the modern "progressive" spirit of the upper classes in Campinas. Thus, in 1934, an urban plan for redesigning the city, called the Urban Refurbishment Plan was implemented and the civil engineer Francisco Prestes Maia undertook this project (Fig. 1).

Badaró [12] believes that the historic center was treated in an appropriate way since it was redesigned, when there was a great concern about its aesthetic and civic features. On the question of traffic circulation, Prestes Maia suggested building two orthogonal avenues at a right angle, which crossed the regular network of the central area. In the North-South divide of the city, an alternative choice was the enlargement of the Francisco Glicério Street between Luzitana and José Paulino streets. In the East-West direction, it was decided to enlarge Campos Salles Street. As a result of the broadening of this street, it was turned into a new link between Fepasa Station Square and the main center, which is connected to an avenue that intersects the center at Francisco Glicério Street.

One of the design features that emerged in the first half of the 20th Century was verticalization. This is revealed by the technological and formal evolutionary patterns of society and the new styles of living and working, as well as the attempt to break up the landscape in the central area. This led to a social/spatial segregation that is witnessed by the physico-aesthetic appearance of the buildings. These had advanced and sophisticated levels of construction, as well as being both comfortable and functional, with extensive areas for leisure activities and large verandahs, and were sold at high prices.

The center of the city includes the remains of many buildings, which bear all the hallmarks of their construction, alterations, adaptations, appropriations and re-appropriations undergone over a long period of time. In view of this, how can one single out the significant memories that can be recognized as a cultural heritage? What are the historical places, sites of memory and memory of places in the central area of Campinas?

4   Results: The Sites of Memory and the Memory of the Places in the Center of Campinas

As a means of providing a clearer understanding of the sites of memory and memory of the places in the town of Campinas – Sao Paulo – Brazil, an attempt was made to interpret the representation of the people who make use of this municipality, by means of a field research that was carried out in 2011. The methodology of this research involved both a qualitative and quantitative analysis which addressed individual issues that affected the residents and their relationship with the memory of the city. A sample of 276 people was interviewed[1] and they answered a questionnaire in which they expressed the main things they could remember about key features of the city, with an emphasis on memory and cultural heritage.

---

[1] Residents, passers-by and users, in short, people who experience space in their activities, in the center of Campinas. Different profiles of social class, age, occupation, income, origin and races were considered, in order to observe the differences between the referentials of the center identified by the interviewees.

The undertaking comprised open-ended and semi-structured questions, which the interviewees answered by hand; they were free to write about anything they wished without any type of restriction. There was also space for the participants to express themselves freely by means of designs. They were requested to design a representation of their view of the center of Campinas without the imposition of any time constraints or control of their technique. This took account of the fact that memories that are made up of events, can be evoked from the representation of any one of the factors that form the event [2].

The memory of an object is stored in a dispositive way. As explained earlier, the dispositions are dormant, implicit, and non-active and explicit records like images. These dispositive memories do not just store aspects of the physical structure of an object but have the capacity to reconstruct its shape, color, sounds, characteristic movements, smells etc. In addition, the dispositive memories also store the features of the motor involvement of the organism in the process of learning about key factors such as: the emotional reactions to the object; and the physical and mental state that are shaped at the time when the respective object is apprehended. As a result, the evocation of an object and clear formation of its image in the mind, are accompanied by the reconstruction of at least some of the images that represent these features. This means that the evocation of an object sets in motion the convergence-divergence zones and their respective spaces of the dispositions and of the image. The reconstruction of this set of adjustments to the organism that is evoked creates a situation similar to what occurs when someone directly perceives an outside object [8].

Thus on the basis of the answers of the interviewees, subcategories were established which guided the analysis and were devoted to an understanding of the relationship between memory, the city and the cultural heritage such as: religious buildings; buildings/monuments; and streets/squares. This formed the basis of the Table 1 below in which the question asked to the interviewees is in the first column, the classification of categories is in the second and a general tabulation of the replies obtained, is shown in the third.

When obtaining the immediate results of the analysis of this investigation, it was observed that the group comprised by the youngest members (under 40 years of age), was the group with the fewest items with regard to the memory of place, regardless of social class or gender considerations. An additional factor in this result is the finding that people with incomes above 10 minimum salaries were more representative[2].

[2] At the time when this research was conducted, the minimum monthly salary in Brazil was R$622,00, which at that time was roughly equivalent to $270,00 [US dollars].

Table 1. Answers to the questions of the questionnaire that was applied in the research field study. Source: Oliveira, 2016 [14]

Questions	Subcategories	Specific Subcategories/Directions
When one speaks of the center, what is the first thing that comes to your mind?	Religious buildings (18)	Cathedral (14), churches (4)
	Buildings/monuments (8)	Old buildings (4), the demolished theatre (2), the central market (2)
	Others (10)	Tradition/history/cultural heritage (7), childhood (2), trams (1)
What do you most like in the center?	Religious buildings (11)	Cathedral (11)
	Buildings/monuments (12)	Historic building (6), Fepasa Railway Station (4), monuments (2)
	Others (8)	Architecture (7), the railway (1)
What things that have been lost did you like in the Center?	Religious buildings (1)	Igreja do Rosário [Rosário Church] (1)
	Buildings/monuments (10)	Fepasa Railway Station/passenger trains (3), the Carlos Gomes Theatre (3), the Public Library (1), historic buildings (1), the Hotel Terminus (1), monuments (1)
	Streets/squares (3)	Rua Treze de Maio [13th May Street] (2), streets with paving stones (1)
	Others (10)	Romanticism (3), traditions (2), history (1), trams (1), the Fountain of Rua Treze de Maio (1), Ezekiel living dead dolls (1), the Umbrellas of Rua Treze de Maio (1)
What would you like to see in the Center?	Buildings/monuments (12)	Buildings/preserved history (9), things as they were in the past (9)
Which spaces/places in the Center do you make most use of?	Religious buildings (11)	Churches (11)
	Buildings/monuments (4)	Centers of culture (4)
	Streets/squares (3)	Areas with shade from trees (3)
What kind of cultural heritage is there in the Center at present?	Religious buildings (122)	Cathedral (90), Churches (20), Rosário Church (2), Universal Church (1)
	Buildings/monuments (169)	Culture of the FEPASA station (30), Palace of Azulejos [glazed tiles] (22), Palace of Jequitibás (19), Jockey Club (12), Statue of Carlos Gomes (12), monuments (11), buildings (10), the Town Market (8), Carlos Gomes College(7), The Forum (5), Museums (5), PUC Central [Catholic University](5), CCLA [Latin American Cultural Center] (4), Carlos Mendes Theater (4), the Post Office (3), MACC Building [Medical/Scientific Computing Center] (3), Health Center (3), Mogiana (2), Headquarters of the Carlos Gomes Band (1), Carlos Salles Monument (91), Giovanetti (1), Niemeyer Building (1)
	Streets/squares (64)	Carlos Gomes Square (24), Community Center (17), Squares (10), Carmo Square/Bento Quirino Square (5), Rosário Place (3), Jequitibás Wood (2), Pará Place (2), Parks (1)
	Others (16)	Railway (10), Bars (2), Hotels (2), Pedestrian tunnel (1), Bandstand (1)

This Table will be examined in greater detail in this section with a view to revealing some of the key features of significance to the sites of memory and the memory of places in the central area of Campinas. These are related to thoughts, affectivity, imagination or losses in the center of Campinas (Question 1, 3, 4 and 5 of the questionnaire), the Cathedral was mentioned 25 times and the other churches 5 times. With regard to the buildings/monuments, the old and historic buildings, in general terms, were referred to 20 times. Items with a low frequency (a maximum of four mentions) were: the demolished theatre (Sao Carlos), the Railway Station (Fepasa), the Carlos Gomes Theatre, and monuments, among others. The features in the subcategory streets/squares were not often mentioned. Seven interviewees showed concern about the loss of their history and seven with the loss of their architecture.

On the particular question of the presence of signs of cultural heritage in the central space, the research determined that 22 respondents mentioned the churches. The Metropolitan Cathedral of Campinas was remembered by 90 of the interviewees, Carmo Church by nine, Rosário Church by two, Universal Church by one and churches generally by 20. These results raise the following question: were the churches remembered because of their historic and artistic value or the fact that religious feelings prevailed?

With regard to the drawings designed by the participants, the places of memory in the central region of Campinas were also not clearly distinguished. Only in some of them there was an allusion to the cultural assets that the city possesses. The following stood out in some of the designs: Design 1 (Fig. 2) designed by Aline (aged 23, 3–5 minimum salaries, secretary), six cultural assets of great importance were mentioned: the Community Center, Metropolitan Cathedral, Town Market, Municipal Civic Center, Bento Quirino College and Progresso College. Although it was represented in a symbolic way, the design of the Cathedral drew attention to the Church Tower, which is an important landmark in the local landscape.

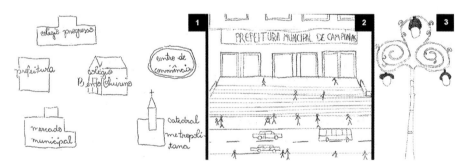

Fig. 2. Cultural assets of significant value for the city of Campinas: buildings, churches, the stairway in front of the Municipal Civic Center and the lamppost in front of the Jockey Club building. Source: Oliveira, 2016 [13]

Leonardo (aged 14 anos, 3–5 minimum salaries, student), in Design 2 (Fig. 2), displays the stairway that leads to the square in front of the Jequitibás Palace, the headquarters of the Municipal Civic Center which is constantly used as a platform for demonstrations and protests. An urban feature - the cast iron lamppost in front of the

Jockey Club building in Bento Quirino Square - was highlighted by Rosana (aged 41–50, 5–10 minimum salaries, teacher), in Design 3 (Fig. 2).

Thus, as in the answers to the questions in the questionnaire, the Cathedral was the most prominent feature in the drawings. Design 1 (Fig. 3) by Fernando (aged 29, 3–5 minimum salaries, advertising salesman) found a symbiosis between the vertical lines marked by the skyline of the tall buildings and church tower, and the horizontal line of a street that cuts through the drawing. The large number of people shown in the image leads us to believe that it refers to Treze de Maio Street and that the church represented is Campinas Cathedral. It is worth noting that the tall buildings designed at the same height as the church tower, are evidence that this symbolic landscape feature no longer stands out in the midst of the tall buildings surrounding it. Design 2 of Fig. 3, drawn by José (aged 46, 1–3 minimum salaries, caretaker) shows Francisco Glicério Avenue, also in perspective, with a suggestion of the Cathedral Square and Matriz Church with its towers, on the right-hand side.

Fig. 3. Glicério Avenue: skyline of tall buildings and the Cathedral tower. Source: Oliveira, 2016 [13]

In Fig. 4, the Cathedral Square, bordered by the high constructions surrounding it, is recorded in the foreground of Design 1, drawn by Sandra (aged 39, 5–10 minimum salaries, architect). The Cathedral Tower forms the initial point of an axis that terminates at Fepasa Station, parallel to the outline of Treze de Maio and Costa Aguiar Streets, as can be seen in the image 2 shown on the right.

Set against the verticilization of the center, the Cathedral towers and Railway Station show this axis in visual terms and shape the visual features of the central area. At present, the two towers are hidden by the patchwork of buildings that delineate the landscape at the center. However, the axis for the circulation of traffic remains at Treze de Maio and Costa Aguiar Streets.

In Fig. 5, Design 1 Letícia, (aged 24, 3–5 minimum salaries, designer) displays a decorative picture between posts, which supports the idea that the space in front of the Cathedral, can serve as a meeting place for events and festivals. Design 2 (Rafael, aged 17, 5–10 minimum salaries, office assistant) shows the neighborhood in the precincts of the Cathedral, bordered by Treze de Maio Street, Costa Aguiar Street and Francisco Glicério Avenue. A crowd of people and several shops represents Treze de Maio Street,

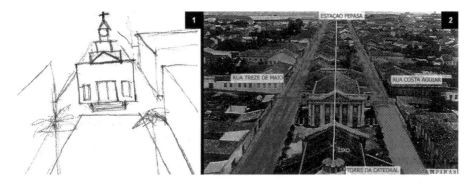

Fig. 4. The Cathedral Square and Cathedral-Fepasa Station. Source: Oliveira, 2016 [14]

while Glicério Avenue conveys the idea of congestion, judging from the large number of cars that have been drawn. The Cathedral is delineated with its front towers and the Cathedral Square (labelled "square" in the design) highlights an everyday public space with a large concentration of people.

Fig. 5. Cathedral Square with space for meeting and socializing. Source: Oliveira, 2016 [13]

These designs are notable for showing the steady flow of people and traffic that circulate around the central area. They testify to the fact that it is a center where contact can be made by people driving cars or travelling by public transport, as well as by the physical contact of people walking along the pavements, thus demonstrating that they identify themselves with the center and appropriate it in a distinct manner.

The streets, avenues, squares, gardens and pavements are spaces for collective activities, and a blending of people, customs, opinions and joint ownership. […] They are spaces for existing, seeing and feeling and are far removed from a purely functional system that can lead to social displacement [14].

The clock shown in Design 1 of Fig. 6 (male participant, aged 31–41) leads us to believe that the building in the picture refers to Fepasa Station, which is now called the Cultural Station, an important vestige of the heritage of the railways. Design 2 (Fig. 6) by Julio (aged 46, 5–10 minimum salaries, designer) highlights Carlos Gomes Square with its bandstand and a row of imperious palm trees at the central corner of Anchieta Avenue, adjacent to the square.

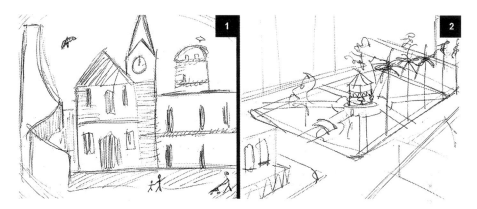

Fig. 6. Building of Fepasa Station and its tower with a clock and Carlos Gomes Square with its bandstand and imperious palm trees. Source: Oliveira, 2016 [13]

5   Discussions

Both the narratives and drawings of the interviewees raise a number of points for discussion, including the following:

(a) **Inconsistency between the memories of the people and the memories of the State**

The sites of memory highlighted by the people do not show a correspondence with the cultural assets and memory recognized by the State. As the choice of assets usually entails compiling an inventory of the cultural heritage[3] through the techniques of the government itself, and the final opinion[4] is strongly influenced by them, it can be argued that, generally speaking, this memory is more closely linked to the hegemonic powers and not to the memory found in the discourse of those who frequent or live in that place. In this way, the public authorities filter and select the cultural assets and lay down their own criteria for their preservation, without always taking account of the effective places of memory and the "vivid memories" of the people in their everyday lives. Thus, it is worth noting that the State should pay more attention to the memory expressed by the inhabitants of the place in seeking a greater resonance between the people and the assets

---

[3] The inventory of the cultural heritage is a declaration of value of a good, expressed by a law that prevents, through administrative restrictions, its destruction and ensures the protection of cultural heritage. It is the means by which the state recognizes cultural assets of significant relevance to the history and memory of a place.

[4] It is carried out by representative Councils of society and traditionally constituted of notables and specialists in the area.

that are legally preserved by the inventory, even while being aware that memory is formed over a period of time.

(b) The lack of education on matters concerning the heritage undermines the sense of "belonging"

What we generally describe as the memory of an object is memory consisting of sensory and motor activities related to the interaction between the organism and the object over a given period of time. Moreover, the set of sensorimotor activities varies in accordance with the circumstances and value of the object and even take place through the retention of these kinds of activities. Our memories of certain objects are governed by our previous knowledge of comparable objects or similar situation [2].

Many of the cultural places and assets, as well as the symbolic landmarks that can be found in the center of the city, were not mentioned by most of the interviewees, particularly the youngest of them, even though they are constituted as historically and socially created objects. This is a clear demonstration that there is little knowledge of the cultural heritage and memory that can be found in the center of Campinas.

It can be inferred from this that there is a lack of resonance between the sites of memory in the memories described by the interviewees, which results from a lack of education in heritage matters. This is evidence of the need to improve the extent of belonging and forge affective links with the people, so as to endow the cultural heritage, historical places and memory of places with a greater legitimacy. It should be stressed that the sense of "belonging" is a two-way street because it belongs to us and, at the same time, we merge with it; in a dialectical relationship, it transforms us since it is transformed by us.

In this way, we feel that a cultural treasure passed down to us by our ancestors belongs to us, insofar as we value it, identify ourselves with it and acquire added materiality or significance from it. From this notion of identity, things or signs, which we are able to adjust to and form a reference-point that is dear to us, we value the things that we want to conserve and do not want to lose. But none of this can occur unless we know something.

(c) The loss of memories of place and hence identity as a result of urban renewal

Another dimension of the discussion concerns assigning a negative value to place. In the opinion of Espinosa [15], a person is as affected, either pleasantly or adversely, by the image of something in the past or future, as by the image of something present. Thus most of the objects surrounding us and the respective flows of ideas, trigger emotions that are either powerful or weak, good or bad, conscious or unconscious, that occur in the domain of the body or its cerebral maps and hence affect out feelings.

The main regions of the brain responsible for triggering emotions, involve the amygdala, which is located in the temporal lobe; the ventromedial prefrontal cortex; and the frontal part of the cingulate cortex and in the supplementary motor area. In the domain of social emotions, the ventromedial prefrontal cortex responds to the detection of objects and situations, whether natural or acquire, which trigger feelings such as the discomfort caused by a particular place [2].

In the case of some buildings in the central area, their lack of use can cause their physical deterioration. Hence, people assign a negative value to the place because the traditional and social values are forgotten or given lower priority.

The image of the center as an important and secure place is also tarnished. It was confirmed that, in general terms, the central area acquired negative associations in the popular imagination of most of the inhabitants who were accustomed to beauty, opulence, security and cleanliness in the shopping centers in other central locations.

Urban renewal which in recent years has transformed the center into a place for consumer goods (particularly down-market), may have also aggravated the degree of negative emotions and hence led to a loss of identification among the people for whom these new spaces have been created.

(d) **The lack of synchronization between different dynamics of time as a significant factor in the loss of memories of place**

In consolidating memories of place, the question of time is being turned into a fundamental benchmark through its intervention in the substance, tangibility and materiality of the place. Time is not a static concept. There is no consensus about the ideas of time, which are wide-ranging and pluralistic and can be differentiated for each religious, cultural and social system. Nonetheless, it is the notion that is altered through the unfolding of life and in the face of historico-cultural mutations. The view and meaning of past phenomena are altered by time itself; different times give rise to different views of the past.

In the dimension of time, our age is affected by the rapid "speed" of flows of information in communications systems and technological change. This exceptional speed is today leading us to a sensation of temporal densification: as a result, time is compressed in a space, which is condensed and depersonalized like systems on the "Internet". Our historical background and constructed environment are formed of much slower dynamics and it is evident that there is no synchronization between the slow and static rhythms of the cultural heritage with the fast and dynamic rhythms of the vital process. The collision between two temporal strata – one tangible and one intangible – is determining a new kind of reality for human beings. Rapid changes of subject are making this reality more prevalent: the visual image is thus being superimposed on the concepts. As "visuality" is prevailing over ideas, human awareness is becoming fragmented, with a loss of integrity in our perception of the surrounding world [5].

Thus the acceleration of changes in time that lead to a disintegration of the memory of place (whether individual or collective), can still be another cause that distances the individual from his/her origins, past and memories. This is because the memory of entities and unique events which are, at the same time, unique and personal, require a highly complex context. In other words, the more the reconstituted sensorimotor context concerns the determined entity or event, the more complex it is and hence, the time for action will evolve. In a hierarchical progression, the following can be observed: (a) entities, unique and personal events require greater complexity; (b) entities, unique events and not personal then follow; (c) entitites and events that are not unique require less complexity [2].

6 Conclusion

The human brain is an inborn cartographer. It can map any object or activity that occurs outside it as well as all the relations that the objects and activities forge in time and space both with each other and with regard to their own organism. The brain also creates maps for the evocation of memories.

The memories of things and its properties, people and places, as well as events and relationships, skills and the management of life – in short, all the memories inherited from evolution and already made available at birth or acquired from learning – exist in the brain in an dispositive way. They are stored there so that they can be evoked and become explicit images or actions in these maps [2].

Thus the results obtained from this research provide evidence of the way that the interviewees revealed their personal accounts and designs. Moreover, they showed a clear connection between the 'places of memory', put forward by Halbwachs [3], and the 'convergence-divergence zones', coined by Damásio [2].

These connections also support discussions on the manner by which the heritage and memory have come to be recognized, preserved and valued at the present time. As Nora [7] makes clear, memory is life and something that is always borne by living groups and, to this extent, it is in a permanent state of evolution and open to the dialectic of remembering and forgetting. Moreover, it is unaware of its successive distortions, vulnerable to all its uses and manipulations, and susceptible to protracted latencies and sudden renewals.

In time, the evocation can lose intensity [2]. In other words, changes, transformations and deterioration gradually affect people's memory and cut them off from their origins, past and all they can remember. With regard to this problem, this research provides evidence of a lack of "resonance" [16] between the places of memory that tell the history of Campinas and the memories of places retained by the inhabitants of that city and suggests that the most likely motivational factors are as follows: (a) a lack of an education in heritage and cultural traditions; (b) the loss of an ability to identify with the created space and hence a failure to recognize the value of this place owing to a urban renewal; (c) the mismatch between the memories preserved by the State and the memories evoked by the local inhabitants; (d) the negative effects that the different dynamics regarding the concept of time, can have on consolidating the memories of place.

In a future development of this research, an attempt will be made to broaden the discussion by following the procedures clearly laid out in this paper, as well as in other places and cities. It is expected that this will entail: [i] seeking to make the conclusions outlined here more universal and representative - but always in the light of new inter- and transdisciplinary benchmarks, such as those referred to here; and [ii] providing new conceptual instruments and methodologies that can enable measures to be taken for cultural preservation and the training of memory and identity, an area that is currently undergoing a dramatic expansion.

References

1. Agostinho, S. (St Augustine): *Confissões* (Confessions). Trad. J. Oliveira e Ambrósio Pina. Coleção os Pensadores. Nova Cultural, Sao Paulo (1999)
2. Damásio, A.: E o cérebro criou o homem (And the brain created man). Companhia das Letras, Sao Paulo (2011)
3. Halbwachs, M.: A memória coletiva (Collective memory). Trad. Laurent Leon Schaffer. Vértice/Revista dos Tribunais, Sao Paulo (1990)
4. Pollak, M.: Memória e identidade social (Memory and social identity), vol. 5, no. 10. Estudos Históricos, Rio de Janeiro (1992)
5. Gallo, H.: Arqueologia, arquitetura e cidade: a preservação entre a identidade e a autenticidade (Archaeology, architecture and the city: preservation of the difference between identity and authenticity). In: *Patrimônio:* atualizando o debate, 9ª SR, 2ª Edição Ampliada. IPHAN, Sao Paulo (2015)
6. Menezes, U.T.B.: Os usos culturais da cultura. Contribuição para uma abordagem crítica das práticas e políticas culturais (The cultural uses of culture: contribution to a critical approach to cultural practices and policies). In: Yázigi, E. (ed.) Turismo: espaço, paisagem e cultura. Hucitec, Sao Paulo (1999)
7. Nora, P.: Entre memória e história: a problemática dos lugares (Between memory and history: the question of places). Revista Projeto História, no. 10. PUC-SP, Sao Paulo (1993)
8. Damásio, A.: O mistério da consciência (The mystery of consciousness). Companhia das Letras, Sao Paulo (2009)
9. Lapa, J.R.A.: A cidade: os cantos e os antros (The City: the nooks and crannies) Campinas 1850-1900. Edusp, Sao Paulo (1996)
10. Badaró, R.S. Campinas: o despontar da modernidade (the emerging dawn of modernity), Coleção Campiniana, no. 7. Centro de Memória/UNICAMP, Campinas (1996)
11. Oliveira, M.R.S.: Intervenções urbanas e representações do centro de Campinas/SP: convergências e divergências (Urban interventions and representations at the Center of Campinas: convergences and divergences) Tese (Doutorado em Geografia) – Instituto de Geociências da Universidade Estadual de Campinas, Campinas (2012)
12. Badaró, R.S.: O Plano de Melhoramentos Urbanos de Campinas: (The Plan for the Improvement of Campinas) 1934-1962. Dissertação (Mestrado em Arquitetura e Urbanismo) - Faculdade de Arquitetura e Urbanismo da Universidade de Sao Paulo, Sao Paulo (2002)
13. Oliveira, M.R.S.: Intervenções urbanas e representações do centro de Campinas/SP: as inter-relações entre as verticalidades e as horizontalidades nos processos de refuncionalização urbana (Urban interventions and representations at the Center of Campinas – the interrelations between vertical and horizontal features in the process of urban renewal) Novas Edições Acadêmicas, Saarbrücken (2016)
14. Ferrara, L.D.A.: Os significados urbanos (Urban meanings), Acadêmica, 31. EdUSP/FAPESP, Sao Paulo (2000)
15. Damásio, A.: Em busca de Espinosa: prazer e dor na ciência dos sentimentos (In search of Espinosa: pleasure and pain in the science of feelings). Companhia das Letras, Sao Paulo (2004)
16. Gonçalves, J.R.S.: Ressonância, materialidade e subjetividade: as culturas como patrimônio (Resonance, materiality and subjectivity: the cultures as a heritage), vol. 11, no. 23, pp. 15–36. Horizontes Antropológicos, Porto Alegre (2005)

Nursing and Medical Applications

Pedicle Screw Insertion Surgical Simulator

Zhechen Du[1], Reihard Zeller[2], David Wang[1(✉)], and Karl Zabjek[3]

[1] University of Waterloo, 200 University Avenue West,
Waterloo, ON N2L 3G1, Canada
dwang@uwaterloo.ca
[2] Toronto SickKids Hospital, 555 University Avenue, Toronto,
ON M5G 1X8, Canada
[3] University of Toronto, 27 King's College Circle, Toronto, ON M5S 1A1, Canada

Abstract. Scoliosis is a sideway spinal deformity. If the curvature is measured to be more than $50°$, surgery is required to straighten the spine. Pedicle screw insertion is a procedure that requires the placement of screws from the pedicle into the vertebral body. A rod is used to connect all the pedicle screws. The spine is straightened during the connection process. One of the most common techniques used for pedicle screw insertion is called the free hand technique, where the surgeon creates a screw channel by manually probing into the spine. The surgeon relies strongly on haptics feedback. However, small changes in force or direction can cause the probe to breach out of the spine. If the breach reaches the spine medial, the spinal cord could be damaged. Even experienced surgeons can not prevent breach.

In this paper, a pedicle screw insertion simulator is developed which combines visual and haptics sensation to recreate the channel creation process of the surgery. The device includes a linear actuator and a rotary motor. The simulator is tuned to four different surgical scenarios by 2 expert surgeons. Ten additional surgeons are asked to participate in the clinical study. Four research questions were examined: 1. Can experience help the surgeon improve correct breach recognition rate? 2. Can experience help the surgeon improve overall correct scenario recognition rate? 3. Is there any performance difference between surgeons with different experience levels? 4. Can the simulation trials become a learning tool for the simulation tasks? It was concluded that there is no statistically significant relationship between the wrong breach or total wrong recognition rate and surgical experience. Furthermore, there is statistical significance in the hard probing scenario between surgical experience and vertical force variance. Lastly, ANOVA analysis is used to examine breach force and velocity performance between three trials to evaluate learning with increase trials. The results are close to being statistical significant.

Keywords: Virtual reality · Scoliosis · Haptic · Surgical simulator
Surgery · Pedicle screw insertion

© Springer International Publishing AG, part of Springer Nature 2018
V. G. Duffy (Ed.): DHM 2018, LNCS 10917, pp. 395–409, 2018.
https://doi.org/10.1007/978-3-319-91397-1_31

1   Introduction

More than 54% of adults will experience back pain during some part of their life [1,2]. Scoliosis is a sideway spinal deformity. The deformity causes the spine to form into a "S" or "C" shape. Scoliosis is determined if the curvature is bigger than 10° [3]. Scoliosis itself generally does not cause any pain. However, the lateral curvature can cause balance issues which can lead to problems such as back pain. If the curvature between any two point of the spine is measured to be more than 50°, the patients can feel significant discomfort. In such cases, surgery is required to straighten the spine [4].

1.1   Pedicle Screw Insertion

Pedicle screw insertion is a common procedure for scoliosis surgery [6]. The technique requires the placement of pedicle screws from the pedicle into the vertebral body (see Fig. 1). After all screws are placed into the spine, a rod is used to connect the screws together (see Fig. 2). Like all spine related surgery, this technique has many risks such as spine fluid leakage, nerve damage, and spine fracture.

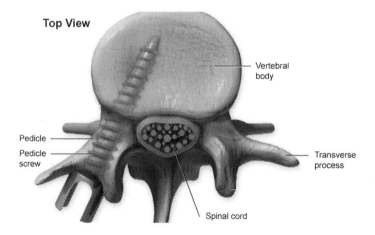

Fig. 1. Pedicle screw inside the pedicle [5]

One of the most common technique used for pedicle screw insertion is called the free hand technique [6,8]. During the free hand surgery, the surgeon has to probe manually into the spine without any visual feedback. It requires tactile haptics feedback, particularly because the bone structure is often deformed due to scoliosis [9]. In order to place the screw into the vertebra, a channel has to be created in the spine first. This procedure is called the channel creation procedure.

A curve or straight pedicle probe is used to channel though the cancellous bone. The surgeon requires haptics feedback to identify the position of the probe.

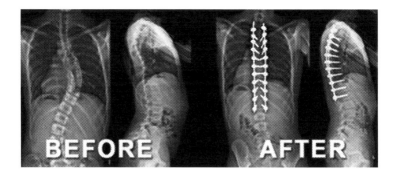

Fig. 2. Pedicle screw insertion before and after surgery [7]

Sudden changes in resistance could indicate breaking out of the pedicle bone and into the soft tissue. This event is called a breach [10]. If the breach is in the direction of the vertebral foramen, it is called medial breach. Due to the limited operating space, this is by far the most challenging part of the surgery. After removing the pedicle probe, the surgeon has to make sure only blood is flooding out of the spine. Any other fluid would indicate a breach.

There have been many studies on the accuracy of pedicle screw insertion. In one review conducted from 21 studies with 4570 pedicle screws in 1666 patients [6], the reported screw misplacement rate is around 11%. Revision surgery was performed on 12 patients for misplaced or loose screws. In another review, the reported accuracy rate from different studies for free hand pedicle screw insertion ranged from 69% to 94% [11].

Surgeon experience is an important factor that can affect the accuracy of free hand pedicle screw insertion. In a study conducted by Samdani et al. [12], 856 samples was collected and reviewed. The breach rate for surgeons with less than 2 years experience is 12.7%, 2–5 years experience is 12.9%, and 5 or more years of experience is 10.8%. There is no statistically significant difference between the three groups. However, for more serious medial breach, the breach rate for surgeons with less than 2 years experience is 7.4%, 2–5 years experience is 8.4%, and 5 or more years of experience is 3.5%. This is correlated by another study conducted by Lehman et al. [13], where it has shown that the surgeon's medial breach rate using the free hand technique decreases over an 8 year period. Due to the complexity of channel creation procedure, a simulator is developed as a training tool for the surgery. This is the main focus of this paper.

2   Previous Work

Luciano et al. [14] have developed a simulator that combines haptics with virtual reality. A CT scan is used to form the basic model for 3D spine. As for the haptics sensation, the group used an ImmersiveTouch haptic stylus to create force feedback. A lumber Sawbones spine model was used to evaluate the effectiveness of the simulator [15]. Although the haptics feedback force is minimal, the study did show the simulation can be helpful for training a non-expert in complex tasks [16].

In another study, Xing et al. [17] used the Phantom haptics device as the probe to simulate the pedicle insertion process. Spine modelling and collision detection are two important aspect of this paper. However, there was no clinical testing for this approach.

The main drawback of the existing haptics simulators is the lack of large force simulation. In order to simulate breach, a sudden change in force and velocity is required. All the existing simulators are unable to provide enough force in such an event.

3   Experimental Apparatus

The haptics surgical simulator developed by University of Waterloo in conjunction with SickKids Hospital is shown in Fig. 3. There is a rotary stage and a vertical stage. The rotary stage provides surgeon with a sense of pedicle density and the vertical stage can simulate the depth of the pedicle.

The rotary stage of the haptics simulator is a 1DOF haptics simulator for probe channelling during pedicle screw insertion surgery [19]. The simulation

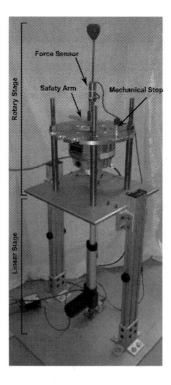

Fig. 3. Surgical simulator after phase two [18]

is performed by the surgeon from a probe at the top of the simulator. A force sensor is attached to the bottom of probe. It is used to measure the surgeon's applied force and torque on the probe. A servo DC motor is positioned at the bottom of the simulator. The motor is used to simulate the force and torque feedback of the probe's rotational movement inside the pedicle.

The linear stage is added underneath the rotary stage to provide the vertical movement [18]. The vertical probing process requires high speed motion with precision control. The actuator should be able to handle the large downward force created by the surgeon. The typical force created by a surgeon is around 150N [20]. Moreover, the surgeon is required to pick up subtle changes in force and dynamic. Quick response is important in such situations. A Bimba linear actuator with stepper motor and integrated driver was chosen, and the actuator is able to provide an initial thrust of 667N and top speed of 0.23 m/s. At 0.15 m/s, the actuator has an thrust of 180N [21].

The linear actuator is designed to run in real time closed loop control. The actuator is set to velocity mode, which the actuator is driven by a velocity command. The controller frequency is set to 1 kHz, which is also the human haptics resolution limit [22]. Since motor speed is directly related to the input current from the driver, the actuator controller can automatically increase operation current to account for the additional external force and friction applied on the actuator. Due to the fast response time of the driver, a sudden increase in external force should not affect actuator's performance.

4   Controller

The rotary stage involves a gain-scheduling PD controller strategy to create viscous friction and detent effects [19]. For the linear stage, the admittance controller uses external force to manipulate the movement of the surrounding environment or the virtual surface.

When the surgeon is probing inside the pedicle, one important detail is that the surgeon has to start rotating the pedicle before applying any vertical force. Therefore, a switch condition is added to the linear stage admittance controller. The admittance controller is only active after the rotary velocity is more than 10 degrees per second.

For the linear stage admittance controller, a virtual mass spring damper system is used to simulate pedicle insertion dynamics. The behaviour of the actuator is determined by a linear second order system.

$$M(\ddot{x} - \ddot{x}_0) + D(\dot{x} - \dot{x}_0) + K(x - x_0) = F_{ext} \tag{1}$$

where: M is the Virtual Inertia Coefficient, D is the Virtual Damping Coefficient, K is the Virtual Stiffness/Spring Coefficient, $x, \dot{x}, \ddot{x}$ are the Actuator Position, Velocity, and Acceleration, $x_0, \dot{x}_0, \ddot{x}_0$ are the Equilibrium Position, Velocity, and Acceleration, and F_{ext} is the External Force.

Because of the high stiffness and damping of the pedicle, the relatively small mass of the pedicle is assumed to be zero. The actuator position is also assumed to be same as the desired actuator position. This is due to the fast response of the linear actuator, where the difference between desired position and actuator position is very small. The external force is said to be equal to the control force F assuming the inertial force are small. Assuming a virtual mass spring damper system have zero velocity at the surface of the system, the equilibrium velocity can be assumed to be equal to zero. Thus, the desired velocity feed into the actuator can be obtained from the following controller:

$$\dot{x}_d = (F - K(x_d - x_0))/D \qquad (2)$$

Under normal pedicle screw insertion surgery, the probing process can be described as breaking though layers of a lattice. From the haptics perspective, the sensation can be described as a series of strong vibrations. This is due to the non-uniform density distribution of the pedicle bone. To simulate this effect, the vertical probing length is broken into many small layers, each layer represented by its controller in Eq. (2). An illustration of the probing process can be seen in Fig. 4(A). The spring and damping coefficient is unique to that layer. A switching controller is added to change the parameter for each layer (see Fig. 4(B)). Each layer is assigned with its own depth. The system will switch to a new layer once the probe reaches the end of the previous layer. A sudden change in resistance is felt by the operator.

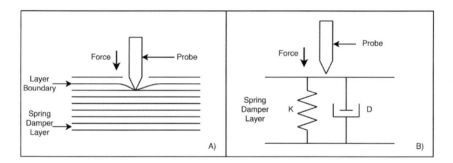

Fig. 4. Spring damper model of the pedicle bone. (A) Probe drilling into the pedicle layer. (B) Spring and damper inside each layer

Breach simulation is an extension to the normal pedicle probing procedure. In most cases, the breach haptics sensation is different compared to normal probing. The breach simulation procedure can be split into two parts. The first part is before the breach, where the probe is experiencing increased resistance. The second part is after the breach occurred, where the resistance is minimum. The controller uses two different sets of parameters to simulate the haptics sensation.

In most surgery conditions, there are obvious warnings before breach occurs. Surgeons have to recognize these warnings in order to avoid breach. The most important warning is the increasing probing resistance. This indicates the probe have reached the outer cortical of the pedicle (see Fig. 5). More often then not,

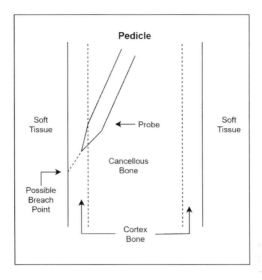

Fig. 5. Illustration of breach reaching cortex bone of the pedicle

the increase in resistance is due to narrow pedicle size. If the surgeon is determined to continue probing without stopping, then the surgeon has to increase the navigation force to overcome probing resistance or correcting the probe position. If the probe reaches past the pedicle wall, breach will begin. The breach resistance is decreased significantly. The breach point is identified as breach threshold in the simulation. This is the largest possible force exerted on the probe before breach. The breach velocity is determined by the breach force.

For the implementation, a reference location is used as a starting point for the increase in probing resistance. A parameter called resistance interval R_i is used to model the distance travelled by the probe between the reference location and the actual breach location. When the probe is travelling during this interval, the probing resistance is increased linearly. A scaling parameter, resistance factor R_f, is used as the slope of the change. The spring and damping coefficient from Eq. (2) will increase based on the resistance factor and probe location.

The most common breach scenario is breaching into surrounding soft tissues. This haptics sensation is much softer than probing inside the pedicle. In order to adapt to this change, the vertical direction admittance controller's parameters are readjusted for the simulation. If a breach has occurred, then the resistance of simulator will drop dramatically, which results in sudden drop in the vertical resistance. The low breach resistance is accomplished by setting the stiffness coefficient to zero, and the damping coefficient to a much smaller number. The desired velocity feed into the actuator from Eq. (2) is now simplified to the following equation:

$$\dot{x}_d = F/D_b \tag{3}$$

where D_b is the breach damping coefficient.

During breach, the soft tissue and body fluid can reduce rotational resistance, in most cases, the rotational resistance is close to zero. A rotational switch is implemented to shut down the rotational motor after breach has occurred. Since the rotational motor is a servo motor, shutting down is motor does not lock the rotation. Therefore, the rotational resistance is close to zero.

In total, four scenarios were created for the clinical study. These scenarios are hard bone probing, soft bone probing, lateral breach, and in-out-in probing. The illustration of these scenarios is shown in Fig. 6. The first two scenarios (hard probing and soft probing) are variation of normal probing inside the pedicle. The simulation is achieved by scaling the vertical tuning parameters according to the bone density. Each scenario has its own specific spring damper system. The lateral breach scenario is breach to soft tissue as explained in the previous paragraph. The in-out-in probing is an extension to lateral breach. In this case, after the probe breaches into the soft tissue, due to the curvature of the pedicle, the probe can be navigated back inside the pedicle. The implementation of this part is repeat of the lateral breach but includes a restoration to the previous bone probing scenario [20].

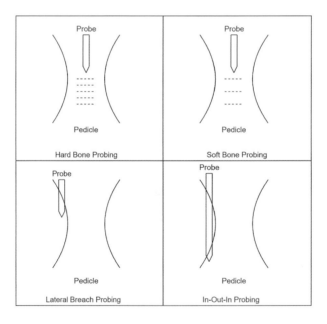

Fig. 6. Four simulation scenarios developed by the surgeons

In order to simulate real surgical procedure, 8 unique parameters have to be tuned in the linear stage. The parameter are shown in Table 1.

The simulator tuning session was conducted by Dr. Zeller and Dr. O'Shea from Toronto SickKids Hospital. Dr. Zeller is a world class spine surgeon with over 25 years of experience [23]. And Dr. O'Shea has more than 5 years of

Table 1. Linear stage tuning parameters

Normal probing parameters	Breach parameters
Spring Coefficient K	Resistance Interval R_i
Damper Coefficient D	Resistance Factor R_f
Equilibrium Point x_0	Breach Interval L_b
Equilibrium Interval Scale L	Breach Damping Coefficient D_b

experience [24]. Details of the tuning process can be found in [25]. This will be considered to be the benchmark or true parameter values. The other participants will be studied in comparison to these expert's tuned parameter values.

5   Experimental Procedure

In order to evaluate the effectiveness of the simulator, a clinical study is conducted with 10 other surgeons. All of them are orthopedic surgeons from Toronto SickKids Hospital. The surgeons are composed of 2 senior surgeons, 4 fellows, and 4 residents. Participants were asked to complete a set of 12 trials on the surgical simulator. The trials can be broken down into four different scenarios with each scenario performed three times. The order of the trials was randomized.

For each trial, the participant's objective is to create a screw channel using the probe in a single motion. Ideally, the participant should reach the designated probe stop point without any motion pause. This includes breach scenarios.

For the study, the participants are blind to the number of scenarios and the trial order. However, the participant is informed that the test scenarios are free hand pedicle screw insertion simulation that includes potential breach simulation. After each trial is completed, the participant is asked whether they experienced a breach during the trial. If the answer is yes, then a additional question is asked to confirm the location of the breach. The simulation is completed when the participant completes all 12 trials.

6   Discussion

6.1   Research Question No. 1

Can experience help the surgeon improve correct breach recognition rate?

H_0: The surgeon's experience background has no effect on breach recognition rate.

The summary of the study results on number of incorrect breach identifications is shown in Table 2. The wrong breach identification number is retrieved from the incorrect breach recognition from lateral breach and in-out-in breach. In total, the surgeons performed 6 breach trials. The average correct breach

Table 2. Incorrect identification results from lateral breach and in-out-in breach.

Surgeon experience (years)	# of wrong breach identifications/ total breach trials
6	2/6
3	1/6
1	0/6
1	1/6
0.5	0/6
0.33	0/6
0.1	0/6
0	3/6
0	1/6
0	1/6

identification rate for the 10 surgeons is 85%. In order to analysis the results, a linear regression t-test is conducted on number of wrong breach identification results with respect to the surgeon's experience (Table 3).

Table 3. Regression analysis results for surgeon's experience vs number of wrong breach identification.

Predictor	Coefficient (β_m)	SE coefficient ($SE(\beta_m)$)	$T(t_m)$	$P(p_m)$
Constant ($m=1$)	0.7105	0.3796	1.8717	0.0981
Years of experience ($m=2$)	0.1588	0.1744	0.9106	0.3890

By following the standard procedure of regression analysis, a p-value is obtained from the test. The results of the test is shown in Table 5. It was found that the p-value number of wrong breach identification test is 0.3890. In this test, the p-value is significantly larger than the typical significant level of 0.05. Therefore, the null hypothesis is not rejected. Based on the results, surgeon's experience has no effect on the number of wrong breach identifications.

6.2 Research Question No. 2

Can experience help the surgeon improve overall correct recognition rate?

H_0: The surgeon's experience background has no effect on overall wrong recognition rate.

The summary of the study results on number of incorrect identifications is shown in Table 2. The number of wrong identifications is retrieved from all four scenarios, this includes the wrong breach identifications. In total, the surgeons

Table 4. Total number of incorrect identification results

Surgeon experience (years)	Total # of wrong identifications/ total trials
6	3/12
3	3/12
1	2/12
1	1/12
0.5	3/12
0.33	0/12
0.1	0/12
0	5/12
0	2/12
0	4/12

performed 12 trials. The average correct identification rate for the 10 surgeons is 81.8%. Similar to research question 1, a linear regression t-test is conducted on number of wrong identification results with respect to the surgeon's experience. The results are shown in Table 5. It was found that the p-value for total number of wrong identification test is 0.6920, which is not statistically significant. Therefore, the null hypothesis is not rejected. It is interesting to note that the p-value is higher in wrong breach identification test than the wrong identification test (Table 4).

Table 5. Regression analysis results for surgeons experience vs total number of wrong identification.

Predictor	Coefficient (β_m)	SE coefficient ($SE(\beta_m)$)	T (t_m)	P(p_m)
Constant (m = 1)	2.1537	0.6494	3.3164	0.0106
Years of experience (m = 2)	0.1225	0.2983	0.4107	0.6920

6.3   Research Question No. 3

Is there any performance difference between surgeons with different experience levels?

H_0: Surgeon's experience has no effect on the measured data such as operation time, breach time, velocity variance, mean force and force variance.

In order to evaluate the difference in the surgeon's performance with different experience level, the collected data was examined and processed to retrieve numerical values such as operation time, velocity variance, mean force, and force variance. In order to account for the variation between trials, the mean of each surgeon's three trials results was taken. Because there is no sudden motion change in the soft probing and hard probing scenario, the complete duration of the trial was examined. For the breach scenario, due to the short length of normal probing travel in breach scenarios, only the breach section of the trial was examined.

Due to the small sample size, possible outliers may have strong affects on the regression test. A modified Z-score test is conducted before each regression analysis [26]. A outlier is identified if the absolute value of the modified z-score is bigger than 3.5. The M-estimation robust regression using bisquare estimator is used for the analysis.

The result p-value of the robust regression analysis is shown in Table 6. In most of robust regression analysis conducted, no trend or significance was discovered from the data. However, the force variance does provide some interesting results. First, The p-value of robust regression analysis for hard probing force variance is 1.34e−4. Because the p-value is less than 0.05, the null hypothesis is rejected. For the soft probing, surgeon 10 is removed from the data set due to high z-score value of 8.72. The p-value of the robust regression analysis is 0.1049. Although this is the above the 0.05 statistically significant level, more data samples could potentially reject the null hypothesis. All other p-values are much bigger than 0.05, which is not statistically significant.

The results of such a small force variance p-value is probably because experienced surgeons are more comfortable with the surgery. They are able to change their applied force according to the simulation haptics feedback. The inexperience surgeons are more focused on completing the task, which means they are more mechanical with less force variance. It is also interesting to note that from research question 2, experienced surgeons did not perform better compared to inexperienced surgeons in overall recognition rate. This indicate that improving force variance performance can not help surgeons in better recognition rate. The large variance may prevent surgeon from recognizing the drop in resistance during breach event. It could be interesting to find if lowering expert's force variance can lead to better recognition rate.

Table 6. Robust regression analysis p-value.

	Soft probing	Hard probing	Lateral breach
Operation time	0.5784	0.9792	0.3269
Velocity variance	0.629	0.8164	0.2707
Force variance	0.1049	1.34e−4	0.3424
Mean force	0.9233	0.3969	0.3838

6.4 Research Question No. 4

Can the simulation trials become a learning tool for the simulation tasks?

H_0: Simulation trial cannot be a learning tool for the simulation tasks.

The main goal of the simulator is to help new surgeons prepare for breach event. One effective way is to examine if there are any progress in participant's results over the course of the study. In the analysis for breach event, the data was split into three groups based on each participant's trial sequence. One way ANOVA was used to evaluate between the three trials. The main goal is to find out if surgeons is able learn or adapt during the study and if there is any difference in performance between first, second, and third trial. The resulting p-value is shown in Table 7. One of the most importance information for breach is the breach velocity. The p-value from ANOVA for breach velocity is 0.0627, which is close to statistically significant. The p-value for breach mean force is at 0.0693. Because both p-value is above statistically significant of 0.05, the null hypothesis is not rejected. Although the above two numbers are not statistically significant, it is interesting to further analyse these data with a larger sample size as they are very close to significant. This potentially can prove there is performance difference from the first trial to the third trial and the simulator is a great learning tool for the tasks.

Table 7. One way ANOVA p-value

	Breach velocity	Velocity variance	Force variance	Mean force
p-value	0.0627	0.2064	0.1008	0.0693

7   Conclusion and Future Research

Pedicle screw insertion surgical simulator is a new kind of training simulator. It is able to simulate the hardest and most dangerous part of the pedicle screw insertion surgery, which is the pedicle channel creation process. A simulator tuning session was conducted with help of 2 expert surgeons and four scenarios were created to simulate the complex events that can happen in a real surgery. There were 10 other surgeons who were asked to conduct in a clinical study.

By using linear regression analysis on incorrect recognition and incorrect breach recognition with respect to surgeon's experience, it was concluded that there is no statistically significant relationship between the wrong breach recognition rate and surgical experience. In addition, there is no statistically significant relationship between the total wrong recognition rate and surgical experience.

Further analysis was conducted using the collected measurements. In the hard probing scenarios, it was found that surgical experience has an effect on vertical force variance, where the more experienced surgeons tend to have a larger operating range. The soft probing's force variance is also very close to statistically significant. With help of more data, it may be possible to reject the null hypothesis.

The difference between the trials of the same scenario were also analysed. This was used to evaluate whether the simulator is an effective training tool and if the surgeons did adapt over the study time. One of the most important indicator for this analysis is the breach data. By using ANOVA, it was found that the p-value for breach velocity is 0.0627. The p-value for breach mean force is at 0.0693. Although both are not considered statistically significant, they are close and could be interesting to further analyse the data with a larger sample size.

In terms of future research, this project should continue collecting data from more surgeons. Currently, there are only 10 participants conducted the clinical study. Many analyses such as the breach velocity regression analysis are close to statistically significant. A larger sample size could potentially help reject the null hypothesis. Furthermore, the larger sample size could lead to new finding that were previously ignored due to Type I error. Lastly, it would be interesting to re-conduct the study with the participants after a certain period of time. Since many participating surgeons currently have minimum experience in the pedicle screw insertion surgery, it may be interesting to find if there is any progression or regression in their surgical skill after a period of study in pedicle screw insertion.

The current haptics sensation tuning and scenario design was only completed by two expert surgeons. From the clinical study, it was clear that many surgeons operate differently, and even expert surgeons can have significant different operating techniques. The simulator could be greatly improved if more expert surgeons were involved in the tuning process. This can lead to creation of a universal scenario.

References

1. Cassidy, J.D., Carroll, L.J., Côté, P.: The Saskatchewan health and back pain survey: the prevalence of low back pain and related disability in Saskatchewan adults. Spine **23**(17), 1860–1866 (1998)
2. Manchikanti, L., Singh, V., Datta, S., Cohen, S.P., Hirsch, J.A.: Comprehensive review of epidemiology, scope, and impact of spinal pain. Pain Physician **12**(4), E35–E70 (2008)
3. Scoliosis. www.hopkinsmedicine.org/healthlibrary/conditions/orthopaedic_disorde rs/scoliosis_85,P07815/
4. Sud, A., Tsirikos, A.I., et al.: Current concepts and controversies on adolescent idiopathic scoliosis: Part I. Indian J. Orthop. **47**(2), 117 (2013)
5. Pedicle screw fixation. https://www.linkedin.com/pulse/pedicle-screw-fixation-howard-cotler-md-facs-fabos/
6. Hicks, J.M., Singla, A., Shen, F.H., Arlet, V.: Complications of pedicle screw fixation in scoliosis surgery: a systematic review. Spine **35**(11), E465–E470 (2010)
7. Scoliosis. http://www.bcchildrens.ca/our-services/clinics/orthopaedics/spine-con ditions/scoliosis
8. Silbermann, J., Riese, F., Allam, Y., Reichert, T., Koeppert, H., Gutberlet, M.: Computer tomography assessment of pedicle screw placement in lumbar and sacral spine: comparison between free-hand and O-arm based navigation techniques. Eur. Spine J. **20**(6), 875–881 (2011)
9. Mattei, T., Meneses, M., Milano, J., Ramina, R.: "Free-hand" technique for thoracolumbar pedicle screw instrumentation: critical appraisal of current "state-of-art". Neurol. India **57**(6), 715–721 (2009). http://www.neurologyindia.com/article.asp?issn=0028-3886;year=2009;volume=57;issue=6;spage=715;epage=721; aulast=Mattei;t=6

10. Kim, Y.J., Lenke, L.G., et al.: Thoracic pedicle screw placement: free-hand technique. Neurol. India **53**(4), 512 (2005)
11. Gelalis, I.D., Paschos, N.K., Pakos, E.E., Politis, A.N., Arnaoutoglou, C.M., Karageorgos, A.C., Ploumis, A., Xenakis, T.A.: Accuracy of pedicle screw placement: a systematic review of prospective in vivo studies comparing free hand, fluoroscopy guidance and navigation techniques. Eur. Spine J. **21**(2), 247–255 (2012)
12. Samdani, A.F., Ranade, A., Sciubba, D.M., Cahill, P.J., Antonacci, M.D., Clements, D.H., Betz, R.R.: Accuracy of free-hand placement of thoracic pedicle screws in adolescent idiopathic scoliosis: how much of a difference does surgeon experience make? Eur. Spine J. **19**(1), 91–95 (2010)
13. Lehman Jr., R.A., Lenke, L.G., Keeler, K.A., Kim, Y.J., Cheh, G.: Computed tomography evaluation of pedicle screws placed in the pediatric deformed spine over an 8-year period. Spine **32**(24), 2679–2684 (2007)
14. Luciano, C.J., Banerjee, P.P., Sorenson, J.M., Foley, K.T., Ansari, S.A., Rizzi, S., Germanwala, A.V., Kranzler, L., Chittiboina, P., Roitberg, B.Z.: Percutaneous spinal fixation simulation with virtual reality and haptics. Neurosurgery **72**, A89–A96 (2013)
15. Sawbones. https://www.sawbones.com/
16. Gasco, J., Patel, A., Ortega-Barnett, J., Branch, D., Desai, S., Kuo, Y.F., Luciano, C., Rizzi, S., Kania, P., Matuyauskas, M., et al.: Virtual reality spine surgery simulation: an empirical study of its usefulness. Neurol. Res. **36**(11), 968–973 (2014)
17. Xing, Q., Chen, J.X., Li, J., Moshirfar, A., Theiss, M.M., Wei, Q.: A real time haptic simulator of spine surgeries. In: Proceedings of the 21st ACM Symposium on Virtual Reality Software and Technology, pp. 121–124. ACM (2015)
18. Moafimadani, S.: Haptic training simulator for pedicle screw insertion in scoliosis surgery. Master's Thesis, University of Waterloo
19. Leung, R.: Design of a haptic simulator for pedicle screw insertion in pediatric scoliosis surgery. Master's thesis, University of Toronto
20. Zeller, R.: Scoliosis surgery experiment and test data. http://www.sickkids.ca/AboutSickKids/Directory/People/Z/Reinhard-Zeller.html
21. Bimba actuator. http://www.bimba.com/Products-and-Cad/Electric-Actuators/Inch/Rod-Style/Standard-Duty/Original-Line-Electric-Actuator/
22. Klatzky, R.L., Lederman, S.J., Reed, C.: There's more to touch than meets the eye: the salience of object attributes for haptics with and without vision. J. Exp. Psychol. Gen. **116**(4), 356 (1987)
23. Reinhard. http://www.sickkids.ca/AboutSickKids/Directory/People/Z/Reinhard-Zeller.html
24. Dr. Ryan O'Shea. https://health.usnews.com/doctors/ryan-oshea-1123399
25. Du, Z.: Pedicle screw insertion surgical simulator. Master's thesis, University of Waterloo
26. Natrella, M.: NIST/SEMATECH e-Handbook of Statistical Methods (2010)

Characteristics of Eye Movement and Clinical Judgment in Nurses and Nursing Students During the Sterile Glove Application

Shizuko Hayashi[1](✉), Asumi Sugaike[2], Akino Ienaka[2], Rieko Terai[1], and Naoko Maruoka[1]

[1] Ishikawa Prefectural Nursing University, Kahoku, Ishikawa, Japan
hayashiz@ishikawa-nu.ac.jp
[2] Public Central Hospital of Matto Ishikawa, Hakusan, Ishikawa, Japan

Abstract. The purpose of this study is to elucidate differences between nursing students and nurses in obtaining visual information while performing sterile technique and thought processes when making judgments on sterility.

Study methods: The subjects were nine nursing students and eight nurses. Data collection was (1) View a video at sterile gloves, (2) Measure eye movement with eye camera, (3) Interview. The analysis calculated each time and number of times that they watched closely. The details of the interviews for each subject were recorded verbatim. The interview parts describing the observation details were extracted and analyzed qualitatively and inductively.

Result & Discussion: The analyzed target people are 7 Nursing students and 8 Nurse. Sight information was frequent in the domain indicating all seven action scenes [border part of cleanliness area and the pollution area]. For the talk of the sterilization gloves wearing action, [cleanliness area and boundary drawing] and [consciousness of the securing of cleanliness level] and three intentions of [confirmation of the wearing situation] were extracted.

Keywords: Eye movement · Clinical judgment · Nurse · Germfree operation

1 Introduction

Much of nursing care starts with observation, generally with the five senses. Visual data accounts for the largest proportion of the data obtained from the five senses, so it is possible to "overlook" any crucial point that nurses should pay careful attention to.

One illustration is aseptic technique, one of the nursing skills which prevents pathogenic microorganisms from entering patients' body. Since pathogenic microorganisms are invisible to the naked eye, nurses are required to perform aseptic technique while visually confirming that sterility is maintained. When any crucial point is "overlooked," it is impossible to confirm that a clean state is maintained, which is likely to increase the risks of infection. Therefore, it is important to use visual observation while employing this technique to confirm that sterility is being maintained properly.

Maintaining sterility requires nurses to be aware of the boundaries between clean and unclean areas. In spite of all the lectures and practice time for aseptic technique

© Springer International Publishing AG, part of Springer Nature 2018
V. G. Duffy (Ed.): DHM 2018, LNCS 10917, pp. 410–418, 2018.
https://doi.org/10.1007/978-3-319-91397-1_32

provided for nursing students, they often find it difficult to understand and make correct judgments on the boundaries between the two areas.

In the clinical settings, one of the occasions where aseptic technique is required the most is in the operating room where nursing skills are necessary. Since the operating room requires particularly accurate judgment on clean and unclean areas, many institutions have adopted the system in which several nurses cross-check the sterility without relying on one nurse making the judgment alone. Even though the cross-checking system involves multiple nurses in the operating room, the fact that checking process relies on visual confirmation can make objective evaluations of the sterility difficult. What makes objective evaluations is using eye movement trackers. Previous studies conducted in the operating room using eye movement trackers include studies on surgeons' intraoperative gaze (Khan et al. 2012; Atkins et al. 2012) and nurses' gaze during surgery (Ranieri et al. 2011). These studies were conducted in the actual operating rooms. Thus, they did not focus exclusively on aseptic technique.

One of the common aseptic techniques, sterile glove application includes not only the simple act of putting on gloves, but also applying them while nurses are constantly conscious about sterile and non-sterile zones so as to maintain sterility. However, sterile gloves must be tightly fitted to the hands, which is rather difficult. Furthermore, nursing students cannot make judgment on what is clean and what is not easily by visual observation alone. Therefore, they often have great difficulty learning to apply sterile gloves using the correct techniques.

On the other hand, experienced nurses are able to apply sterile gloves quickly while maintaining sterility, which leads us to believe that nurses' visual information and abilities to judge sterility while performing aseptic technique vary depending on the nurse's experience level. Thus, the present study aims to elucidate differences between nursing students and nurses in visual observations during sterile glove application and thought processes when making judgments on sterility.

2 Purpose

The purpose of this study is to elucidate differences between nursing students and nurses in obtaining visual information while performing sterile technique and thought processes when making judgments on sterility.

3 Study Methods

3.1 Protocol

The subjects were nine nursing students and eight nurses with more than five years of experience. Data collection was conducted in the following three steps:

Step 1: Subjects were asked to view a video on applying sterile gloves.
Step 2: Subjects were asked to wear an eye camera (Talk-Eye2, Takei Scientific Instruments, Co., Ltd., Niigata, Japan), viewing 17 still images depicting sterile glove application for three seconds each.

Step 3:   Subjects were shown the visual data obtained by the eye camera, and an interview was conducted.

In the interview the subjects were asked to describe what they were thinking while replaying the visual data on their tracked eye movements. The interviews were recorded with an IC recorder.

3.2   Methods of Analysis

For the eye movements, 12 of the 17 [A1] images, capturing the process from opening the wrap of the sterile gloves until putting on the gloves, were analyzed. An analysis area was determined for each image, and the total duration and number of gaze were counted. The analysis areas were established so as to include the [sterile zone] and [boundary between the sterile and non-sterile zones].

The 12 images were classified into seven sterile glove application steps: [inspecting the pack], [opening the outer wrap], [opening the sterile inner wrap], [unfolding the wrap], [pulling out a sterile glove and putting it on one hand], [putting on the other sterile glove], and [completing the sterile glove application].

The details of the interviews for each subject were recorded verbatim. The parts describing the observation details were extracted and analyzed qualitatively and inductively.

3.3   Ethical Considerations

The purpose and methods of the study, voluntary nature of participation, data management methods, and confidentiality were explained to the participants verbally and in writing, and their signatures were obtained on the consent forms.

This study was approved by the institutional review board of the Ishikawa Prefectural Nursing University (Nursing University approval No. 460) (Nursing University approval No. 871).

4   Results

Consent to participate was obtained from nine nursing students. Of these, two were excluded after the device stopped tracking their pupils halfway through the experiment. All eight nurses' data were included in the analysis.

We checked the gazed areas in the 12 images. There were no differences in the areas gazed by the nursing students and those gazed by the nurses.

In all seven steps, there was a high number of both nursing students and nurses who focused on the areas that included the [boundary between the sterile and non-sterile zones], and they observed them for long durations at high frequencies.

From the narratives describing the acts of sterile glove application, the following three intentions were identified: [delineating the sterile zone from the boundary], [awareness of securing the sterile zone], and [checking the application status].

For [delineating the sterile zone from the boundary], nursing students described that they were thinking "whether the boundaries between the sterile and non-sterile zones were being maintained" and "whether or not the boundary was contaminated." Nurses described that they were thinking they "might cross the boundary into the contaminated zone" or that they "paid attention to the boundary." However, there were some nurses who did not mention this at all.

In terms of [awareness of securing the sterile zone], nursing students explained that they were careful about "minimizing the contaminated zone" and "avoiding touching the clean part to prevent contamination while pulling on the fold." Nurses described that they "opened the wrap so that it did not become unclean" or "did not perform any tasks above the sterile gloves." There were also some nurses who did not mention this at all.

With regards to [checking the application status], nursing students described that they "checked to make sure that all fingers were inserted properly" and "made sure that the folded part was completely unfolded," while nurses said that they "inspected for pinholes" or "made sure that the gloves were fitted tightly between the fingers." Again, there were some nurses who did not mention this at all.

Regarding the seven steps in applying sterile gloves, nursing students tended to speak more about [delineating the sterile zone from the boundary] and [checking the application status].

For the preparatory steps such as [inspecting the pack], [opening the outer wrap], [opening the sterile inner wrap], and [unfolding the wrap], nursing students described that they "inspected whether the gloves had been sterilized," "checked the expiration date," "inspected for tears or contamination," and "tried to minimize the contaminated zone." Nurses said that they "checked the glove size" or "did not normally care about anything in particular."

During the steps of [pulling out a sterile glove and putting it on one hand] and [putting on the other sterile glove], nursing students visualized the steps of sterile glove application to avoid contaminating the sterile gloves. There were some nursing students who spoke less on these two images compared to the other images. Similarly to the nursing students, some nurses said that they visualized the steps. However, they also gave details on their own tricks used when they were applying sterile gloves. Furthermore, the narratives from both nursing students and nurses indicated that they were thinking about what to do next. Nursing students' narratives predicting what may happen next included abstract thoughts, such as "possibility to become contaminated," while nurses described in detail how certain movements could cause contamination. Nurses' narratives further indicated that they inspected from a wider perspective as seen in "observing the process as a whole" and "paying attention to their surroundings." Their narratives also included a judgment aspect, such as "assuming that it was clean." However, some nurses made almost no mention of [delineating the sterile zone from the boundary] or [awareness of securing the sterile zone].

Moreover, when viewing the videos and still images of sterile glove application that were presented to the nurses, some nurses commented, "This method is different from mine, and it might cause uncleanness," or "New nurses and nursing students are doing it slowly like this, but I don't do it this way," without reflecting upon their own glove application.

5   Discussion

5.1   Tendencies in Eye Movements During Aseptic Technique

No differences were observed between nursing students and nurses in terms of the number of subjects who looked at certain categories or the duration or number of their gaze. In particular, many subjects gazed at the [boundaries between the clean and unclean zones] for all 12 images, and they also gazed them for long durations at high frequencies. Textbooks on nursing skills state that "it is important to recognize the boundaries between clean and unclean zones" in performing aseptic technique. Furthermore, nurses are required to be conscious of these boundaries when performing the technique. Developing this awareness requires nurses to determine the clean and contaminated areas by actual visual observation. That is, the "boundaries between clean and unclean zones" are very important observation points in aseptic technique, and our results demonstrated that both nursing students and nurses were able to direct their gaze at these important observation points. The "boundaries between the clean and unclean zones" at which many nursing students and nurses looked are areas where visual verification is highly necessary during sterile glove application. Thus, this study clarified the zones where verification is highly necessary. Furthermore, an eye movement tracker can verify the presence or absence of gaze. This may increase the likelihood of making objective assessments and detecting "overlooking." Also, objective assessments gained by this study method may help develop new teaching methods.

5.2   Thought Processes During Aseptic Techniques

Three intentions of [delineating the sterile zone from the boundary], [awareness of securing the sterile zone], and [checking the application status] were identified for aseptic technique.

Many narratives obtained from the interviews with nursing students included frequent use of technical terms, such as "clean," "contamination," and "boundaries, used in textbooks." This demonstrated that they had a good understanding of specialized terms such as "clean" and "contamination" and that they were able to use the knowledge on aseptic technique that they learned from the textbooks.

Nursing students spoke about [delineating the sterile zone from the boundary] and [awareness of securing the sterile zone] in all steps of sterile glove application. This demonstrated that they were aware that [delineating the sterile zone from the boundary] and [awareness of securing the sterile zone] were very important details in performing aseptic technique.

Nurses also used technical terms, such as "clean," "contamination," and "boundaries" in their interviews. However, there were no verbal descriptions on [delineating the sterile from the boundary] or [awareness of securing the sterile zone], and some nurses only nodded while watching the movements of the gaze. This is presumed to be due to the fact that nurses had much experience in applying sterile gloves and were checking the boundaries without being aware of making these observations.

In the subjects' narratives on [checking the application status], nursing students talked about "checking to make sure that all fingers were inserted properly," while nurses talked about checking on specific and predictable details such as "inspecting for pinholes." For the nursing students, the purpose of their observations was likely to be able to put on the sterile gloves properly, while the nurses' thought processes included predicting risks, as it was demonstrated by some subjects who discussed possible "contamination through pinholes" during the glove application. Nursing students also demonstrated predictive thought processes during sterile glove application by stating, "The fingers might touch it." However, their narratives likely reflected their practice experience on sterile glove application. Nurses' predictive thought processes involved foreseeing risks for contamination and choosing behaviors to avoid it, which included tricks they used during sterile glove application. Nurses have likely made mistakes and caused contamination in their career, enabling them to not only predict risks, but also develop tricks to avoid them and even think about measures taken in case of contamination. On the other hand, nursing students have had little experience in sterile glove application; thus, their thought processes did not go beyond predicting the risks for contamination.

There were many instances in which nurses were unable to describe their thought processes. This may be due to the fact that much of the nurses' knowledge became "tacit knowledge," that is, intentional or conscious thought processes became inexpressible or inexplicable after years of clinical experience.

Nursing students may perceive aseptic technique difficult. However, as observed in nurses, nursing students will be able to visualize clean and contaminated zones and their boundaries through experience. Although it is a skill that should be practiced carefully, it is a fundamental skill that does not apply to other tasks. Therefore, nurses have mastered this as a fundamental skill and are able to perform it unconsciously.

Among the nurses in this study, some viewed the videos and still images capturing the steps of sterile glove application not through a first-person perspective but through the perspective of somebody evaluating the steps. This requires a pre-determined set of points to check, as well as a set of criteria on which the actions are evaluated. Mastering the fundamental skill of aseptic technique through experience enables nurses to predict risks, which new nurses and nursing students are prone to having, and have a viewpoint that allows them to evaluate actual performance.

Going forward, we hope to apply this experience-based knowledge and evaluative perspective to educating nursing students and new nurses.

Appendix

See Table 1.

Table 1. Nurse and nursing student gazing contents when wearing sterile gloves

Nurse n=8 , Student Nurse n=9

Situation*1 · Images		Area	N (%) Nurse	N (%) St Nurse	Gaze time M±SD (ms) Nurse	Gaze time M±SD (ms) St Nurse	Number of gaze M±SD (Times) Nurse	Number of gaze M±SD (Times) St Nurse
No.1		①	8 (100)	9 (100)	1349.9 ±321.4	1118.5 ±200	9.3 ±5.3	7.4 ±3.4
No.2		①	8 (100)	9 (100)	1020.8 ±463.3	1066.6 ±324.3	7.8 ±3.4	7.2 ±2.3
		②	4 (50.0)	6 (66.6)	450.0 ±259.8	261.1 ±107.9	2.5 ±1.7	2.3 ±0.9
		③	4 (50.0)	6 (66.6)	583.3 ±177.7	205.6 ±91.2	3.5 ±0.5	2.0 ±1.0
No.3		①	3 (37.5)	2 (22.2)	222.2 ±62.9	50.0 ±16.7	1.7 ±0.5	1 ±0
		②	1 (12.5)	0 (0.0)	166.7	0	1	—
		③	3 (37.5)	6 (66.6)	288.9 ±103.0	300.0 ±214.2	3.3 ±1.2	3.7 ±2.6
		①	8 (100)	8 (88.8)	970.8 ±359.2	716.6 ±511.5	6.9 ±1.9	5.4 ±3.2
		②	2 (25.0)	2 (22.2)	166.7 ±66.7	433.4 ±366.7	2.5 ±1.5	2.0 ±1.0
		③	6 (75.0)	7 (77.7)	472.2 ±245.2	780.9 ±639.9	5.2 ±3.3	5.3 ±2.5
No.4		①	8 (100)	8 (88.8)	1062.5 ±527.7	1091.6 ±571.2	8.9 ±2.9	8.0 ±3.4
		②	5 (62.5)	4 (44.4)	366.6 ±425.3	258.3 ±83.0	2.2 ±1.0	2.5 ±1.1
		③	7 (87.5)	8 (88.8)	728.5 ±474.5	658.3 ±433.9	6.9 ±3.4	5.0 ±2.8
		①	8 (100)	5 (55.5)	566.6 ±290.5	526.6 ±226.5	4.8 ±4.3	3.4 ±1.6
		②	0 (0.0)	2 (22.2)	—	166.7 ±33.4	—	2.5 ±0.5
		③	8 (100)	6 (66.6)	520.8 ±393.7	733.2 ±626.1	4.9 ±2.9	5.3 ±3.6

(continued)

Table 1. (*continued*)

Nurse n=8 , Student Nurse n=9

Situation[1] · Images		Area	N (%) Nurse	N (%) St Nurse	Gaze time $M \pm SD$ (ms) Nurse	Gaze time St Nurse	Number of gaze $M \pm SD$ (Times) Nurse	Number of gaze St Nurse
No.5		①	6 (75.0)	5 (55.5)	677.7 ±595.8	533.3 ±304.8	5.8 ±2.7	4.8 ±2.0
		②	5 (62.5)	4 (44.4)	173.3 ±106.2	208.4 ±95.4	1.4 ±0.5	1.8 ±0.4
		③	8 (100)	7 (77.7)	658.3 ±263.4	819.0 ±588.8	6.0 ±2.1	7.3 ±3.2
		①	7 (87.5)	6 (66.6)	550.4 ±258.7	472.2 ±386.1	4.6 ±2.6	2.8 ±1.3
		②	5 (62.5)	2 (22.2)	213.3 ±77.7	100.0 ±33.3	1.6 ±0.5	1 ±0.0
		③	6 (75.0)	9 (100)	788.8 ±536.6	592.5 ±486.3	6.2 ±2.9	5.3 ±2.7
		①	3 (37.5)	4 (44.4)	411.0 ±193.0	383.3 ±356.2	4.7 ±3.1	3.0 ±2.3
		②	4 (50.0)	6 (66.6)	325.0 ±266.0	177.8 ±125.7	3.0 ±1.9	2.0 ±1.4
		③	8 (100)	9 (100)	637.4 ±380.6	537.0 ±342.7	6.0 ±2.4	5.0 ±2.2
No.6		①	3 (37.5)	3 (33.3)	288.8 ±83.1	111.1 ±68.5	3.0 ±0.8	1 ±0.0
		②	2 (25.0)	1 (11.1)	283.3 ±183.3	300	1.8 ±0.5	2
		③	1 (12.5)	1 (11.1)	133.4	33.3	2	1
		④	6 (75.0)	6 (55.5)	827.7 ±243.7	485.7 ±259.3	7.8 ±3.3	3.6 ±1.6
		①	1 (12.5)	2 (22.2)	333.3	383.3 ±150.0	1	3.0 ±2
		②	1 (12.5)	0 (0.0)	100	—	1	—
		③	6 (75.0)	6 (66.6)	661.1 ±609.9	611.1 ±416.7	5.0 ±2.9	5.0 ±3.1
		④	3 (37.5)	4 (44.4)	200.0 ±0.05	166.7 ±74.5	3.0 ±0.8	2.0 ±1.0
		⑤	8 (100)	9 (100)	991.6 ±379.6	766.6 ±418.3	9.25 ±2.4	8.3 ±4.4
No.7		①	2 (25.0)	2 (22.2)	116.6 ±50.0	49.5 ±16.7	3.0 ±1.0	1.5 ±0.5
		②	0	0	—	—	—	—

*1   Situation
No.1 [Inspecting the pack]
No.2 [Opening the outer wrap]
No.3 [Opening the sterile inner wrap]
No.4 [Unfolding the wrap]
No.5 [Pulling out a sterile glove and putting it on one hand]
No.6 [Putting on the other sterile glove]
No.7 [Completing the sterile glove application].

References

Khan, R.S., Tien, G., Atkins, M.S., et al.: Analysis of eye gaze: do novice surgeons look at the same location as expert surgeons during a laparoscopic operation? Surg. Endosc. **26**(12), 3536–3540 (2012)

Atkins, M.S., Tien, G., Khan, R.S., et al.: What do surgeons see: capturing and synchronizing eye gaze for surgery applications. Surg. Innov. **13**, 241–248 (2012)

Ranieri, Y.I., Kho, T.P., Christopher, D.W.: Differences in attentional strategies by novice and experienced operating theatre scrub nurses. J. Exp. Psychol. **17**(3), 233–246 (2011)

Development of Safety Testing Technologies of Defecation Assist Devices

Bibliographic Survey and Development of a Rectum Model Sheet

Keiko Homma[✉], Kiyoshi Fujiwara, Isamu Kajitani, and Takuya Ogure

National Institute of Advanced Industrial Science and Technology (AIST),
Central 2, 1-1-1 Umezono, Tsukuba, Ibaraki 305-8568, Japan
keiko.homma@aist.go.jp

Abstract. In Japan, the increase in the number of elderly persons needing long-term care has become a serious problem. Caregiving for elderly persons requiring intensive care is a severe burden. In particular, excretion care is one of the most demanding tasks for caregivers.

Elderly persons tend to suffer from constipation; and constipation is a particularly critical problem for bedridden patients, since chronic constipation is a potential cause of intestinal diverticulitis. Thus, mechanical intervention methods may be required to remove fecal impaction.

The aim of this study was to develop safety test methods, and determine safety test device specifications, for defecation assist devices. To this end, a bibliographic survey was conducted.

In addition, we developed a rectal model sheet for use in the abovementioned safety testing. The sheet is a single-layered square of silicone rubber, whose Young's modulus and thickness were determined with reference to the properties of the human rectum. In future, we will assess the validity of the developed model through experimentation.

Keywords: Elderly care · Defecation assist device · Safety test · Hazardous event
Bibliographic survey

1 Introduction

In Japan, the increase in the number of elderly persons needing long-term care has become a serious problem.

According to the Annual Report on the Aging Society in Japan [1], at the end of FY2014, the number of people aged 65 and over who were certified as requiring long-term care was 5.918 million, 1.39 times more than at the end of FY2006; and the ratio of elderly people certified as care level 4 or 5, to the total number of those certified, was 21.9%. (Under the Japanese long-term care insurance system, nursing care level is classified between 1 and 5 based on assessment of care requirements, where level 5 is the highest.)

© Springer International Publishing AG, part of Springer Nature 2018
V. G. Duffy (Ed.): DHM 2018, LNCS 10917, pp. 419–428, 2018.
https://doi.org/10.1007/978-3-319-91397-1_33

More than half of those certified as requiring long-term care, who are living at home, are living with their families, who are also their main caregivers. According to a governmental survey [1], more than half of the main caregivers of those certified as care level 4 or 5 spend "almost the entire day" taking care of them, which means that the care of such people is a severe burden; and excretion care is one of the most demanding tasks for caregivers.

The Japan Science and Technology Agency (JST) is funding the Impulsing Paradigm Change through Disruptive Technologies (ImPACT) Program. One of the R&D projects in the ImPACT Program is the Innovative Cybernic System for a ZERO Intensive Nursing-care Society project [2]. This project aims to develop an innovative cybernic system that combines the human brain-nerve-muscular system with robots and other devices. Cybernics is an interdisciplinary research field established by Sankai [3]. The developed system will improve, extend, amplify, and assist the residual functions of human beings. As part of this project, technologies for safety testing of defecation assist devices, as well as such devices themselves, are being studied.

In this study, based on a bibliographic survey, we investigated safety criteria which may be used to develop safety testing technologies for defecation assist devices. In addition, we developed a rectal model sheet for use in safety testing.

2   Target Care Task

We focused on excretion care as our target care task, and investigated in detail the difficulties experienced in this form of care.

Gallagher and O'Mahony summarized relevant statistics, etiology, complications, evaluation criteria, and treatment of constipation in the elderly [4]. According to this study, 30–40% of elderly people living in their communities, and over 50% of the residents of nursing homes, experience chronic constipation. The study also indicated that fecal impaction following constipation causes complications such as diarrhea, intestinal obstruction, stercoral ulcers, etc.

Knight et al. noted that constipation is a critical problem for bedridden patients, and that chronic constipation is a potential cause of intestinal diverticulitis [5].

Efforts for the prevention or relief of constipation in everyday life include dietary modification and physical exercise. Laxatives are also used to relieve constipation [4].

In some cases, mechanical intervention methods are required to remove fecal impaction. Popular methods include enemas and manual disimpaction, but both are burdensome tasks for caregivers.

Several devices have been developed to assist defecation. Coloplast, Ltd. offers the Peristeen® anal irrigation system [6], which introduces water into the bowel through a rectal catheter, using a manual pump. The water stimulates the bowel and encourages defecation.

Centurion Medical Products Corporation offers the DisImpactor® [7], which penetrates fecal impactions and makes them easier to remove.

Several Japanese researchers have also studied defecation assist devices. Yagata et al. proposed an "evacuation care system" [8], which is inserted into the rectum, crushes a fecal impaction using ultrasound, and suctions out the impaction with water. Nakamura et al. proposed a "feces suctioning catheter", with two different types of design [9].

In spite of such efforts to develop useful devices, defecation assist devices are not popular in Japan, one possible reason for which is that no methods have yet been established for testing and evaluating the safety of such devices.

Therefore, we have been investigating safety tests and evaluation of defecation assist devices.

3   Identification of Safety Hazards

3.1   Incidents in Excretion Care

Safety incidents in excretion care, especially those involving the use of enemas, have been reported by several researchers.

Paran et al. reported cases of perforation of the rectum and/or sigmoid colon caused by irrigation enemas [10]. Thirteen patients with perforation of the rectum and/or sigmoid colon, caused by irrigation enemas, were admitted to the surgical department of their hospital over a three-year period, and three of these patients died of sepsis and multi-organ failure.

Niv et al. conducted a two-phase study [11], the first phase of which was a retrospective study, based on which they formulated guidelines that governed patient treatments in the study's second phase. In the first phase, they studied 269 patients referred to the Emergency Department of their hospital because of severe constipation, over a one-year period. They reviewed the medical records of the patients, and monitored return visits within one week, as well as 30-day mortality. Of the 269 patients, 207 (76.9%) were treated with a cleansing enema, and three (1.4%) suffered colorectal perforation. The authors suggested that the rigid tip of the enema device was a possible cause of the perforations.

Christensen et al. evaluated the long-term outcome of transanal irrigation for constipation and fecal incontinence [12]. Over a ten-year period, 348 patients suffering from defecation disturbances, and with differing background pathologies, were treated with transanal irrigation, and two suffered bowel perforations as a result of the treatment.

The prevalence of enema-related perforation varies among the studies; however, perforation is one of the serious concerns associated with enema device use, as well as with the use of other transanal defecation assist devices.

3.2   Safety Hazards for Prospective Defecation Assist Devices

As a specific target method, we focused on transanal bowel irrigation; and as prospective target devices, we focused on those that are inserted into the rectum and assist defecation in a fully-automated manner, to alleviate some of the caregiver's burden through the use of robotic technology. Moreover, the prospective devices must achieve a high level of safety, which requires appropriate testing methods. Therefore, we conducted a bibliographic survey to develop methods and device specifications required for effective safety testing.

First, through brainstorming, we explored potential safety hazards associated with use of the prospective automated transanal bowel irrigation devices. Five mechanical hazards were identified: (1) perforation of the rectum by jet flow, (2) laceration of the rectum by suction, (3) rupture of the rectum by hydraulic pressure, (4) perforation of the rectum by contact between the defecation assist device and the rectal wall, (5) laceration due to the repetitive insertion or removal of the device.

We then estimated the pressure range within which the human rectum may be harmed, for each of these five hazards, based on a bibliographic survey.

Below is a description of the various hazards.

(1) Perforation of the rectum by jet flow. Here, the jet flow from the defecation assist device perforates the rectal wall. Since no reports of such perforation or ablation of rectal tissue by jet flow were found in the survey, we referred in this case to the literature on the strength of the relevant body tissues.

(2) Laceration of the rectum by suction. Here, the device sucks and tears the rectal wall when it tries to remove feces from the rectum. The literature offers a possible case, in which the authors infer that colonic perforation was caused by the rapid transanal decompression and continuous suction of the device [13].

(3) Rupture of the rectum by hydraulic pressure. Here, water from the defecation assist device increases the pressure in the rectum to the bursting point. The literature offers a case in which the rectum was perforated due to enemas or spouting hot water in a spa facility [14, 15].

(4) Perforation of the rectum by contact between the device and the rectal wall. Here, the tip of the nozzle of the device strikes and perforates the rectal wall. Possible cases have been reported involving the use of endoscopes during inspection or surgery [16].

(5) Laceration of the rectum due to the repetitive insertion or removal of the device. Here, the nozzle of the device comes into contact with and lacerates the rectal wall, possibly by the sharp tip or edge of the nozzle.

4   Bibliographic Survey

A promising method for evaluating the safety of defecation assist devices is simulation of the respective hazardous events: pressure caused by contact between the nozzle or water and the rectal wall is measured, and the pressure on the rectal wall is determined to be above or below a safe level with reference to pressure data from the literature.

4.1   Perforation of the Rectum by Jet Flow

A high-pressure water stream is used for incision and ablation in surgery [17]. According to [17], the biomedical effects of this stream in water jet surgery include: (1) perforating, (2) crushing and fracturing, (3) ablating, (4) cleansing and spraying or infusing a drug in tissue.

Repici et al. studied the efficacy and safety of colorectal endoscopic submucosal dissection (ESD) using a device called a HybridKnife [18], which combines a water jet and an electrocautery needle. The maximum pressure of the water jet is 80 bars (8 MPa).

If the flow pressure from a defecation assist device is too high, using a water jet device such as this, perforation may result.

Work-related abdominal perforation by the high-pressure water jet gun has been repeatedly reported [19, 20]. In these cases, patients failed to handle a water jet gun properly in cutting or cleaning tasks, and struck their abdomen with the jet from outside. In each case, the pressure of the water jet was 40 MPa or more.

Repici et al. specified the maximum water jet pressure of the device, but the pressure actually used in ESD is not available, and our survey found no other report on perforation or laceration of the rectum by such water jets. Thus, the safety threshold was determined based on the literature on the mechanical properties of the related human body tissue.

Yamada and Evans reported the results of various material tests on various organs from fresh cadavers [21]. For the expansive properties test, specimens from 75 individuals were used. Before the experiments, the test materials were soaked in a saline solution overnight for stabilization. Then the specimens were cut into $15 \text{ mm} \times 15 \text{ mm}$ squares, attached to a Mullen tester with a test hole of 7 mm, and subjected to pressure. The mean value of the ultimate expansion strength of rectal specimens from those between the age of 70 and 89 was 6.1 kg/cm^2 (0.598 MPa). As the mean value of ultimate expansion strength declines with age (except for those under 10 years of age), the safety threshold for expansive strength should be determined based on the value of those between the age of 70 and 89.

4.2 Laceration of the Rectum by Suction

Here, the device sucks the rectal wall when it suctions feces.

Hyodo et al. reported a case possibly involving a similar mechanism [13]. In this case, a transverse colon cancer patient required intestinal tract decompression using a transanal decompression tube. The applied pressure of continuous suction was 10 cm H_2O (0.98 kPa). Four days after insertion of the tube, it was observed that it had penetrated into the mesentery in the area containing the tumor. A possible cause of the perforation was thought to be the continuous suction by the tip of the tube in contact with the intestinal tract.

Tracheal suction would appear to be another medical practice involving such a hazard. According to the "Tracheal aspiration guidelines 2013" published by Japan Society of Respiratory Care Medicine [22], the intensity of negative pressure for tracheal suctioning should be limited to 20 kPa.

The case described in Hyodo et al. suggests that far less suction pressure than is used in tracheal suction may cause tissue damage, though the damaged area in this case was not intact but affected by cancer.

4.3   Rupture of the Rectum by Hydraulic Pressure

Here the water spouting from the device accumulates in the rectum, which increases the intrarectal pressure, and finally causes a rupture of the rectum due to hydraulic pressure. This kind of accident, involving a similar mechanism, is often reported. Choi, for example, reported two cases of rectosigmoid colon perforation caused by the hydrostatic pressure of tap water during unauthorized anal irrigation or enemas [14], and Takei et al. reported a case of rectal perforation due to spouting hot water in a spa [15]. Many cases have also been reported involving watercraft accidents.

Burt investigated the pressure necessary for the intestinal tract to be ruptured [23]. He prepared specimens of the gastrointestinal tract, from the rectum to the esophagus, of 18 cadavers, attached these to an accumulator and a manometer, and subjected them to pressure sufficient to rupture them. Among the results, we focused on the rectal data for three adults: a 21-year-old female, a 45-year-old female, and a 78-year-old male, for whom the pressure at which perforation of the mucosa occurred was 4.94 psi (34.1 kPa), 2.09 psi (14.4 kPa), and 3.80 psi (26.2 kPa), respectively.

Either the mean or the minimum value of the above results could mark the safety threshold for the risk of rupture by pressure.

4.4   Perforation of the Rectum by Contact Between the Device and the Rectal Wall

Here, the tip of the nozzle of the device makes contact with and perforates the intestinal wall when inserting the nozzle into the rectum. Niwa noted that the intestinal canal can be perforated when using an endoscope for inspection or surgery [16]. According to his survey, 68 cases of perforation were reported among 54463 cases of colonoscopy inspection.

Uno evaluated the contact force generated by a large intestine endoscope, using a model [24]. He assumed three types of mechanism for perforation of the large intestine by the endoscope; and based on the results reported by Yamada [25], he determined that the threshold pressure likely to cause perforation was 3–4 kg/cm^2 (294–392 kPa). In Uno's study, various regions of the large intestine were considered in determining this threshold.

4.5   Laceration of the Rectum by the Repetitive Insertion or Removal of the Device

Here, the nozzle of the defecation assist device lacerates the intestinal wall as it is inserted or removed from the intestine. As the sharp tip or edge of the nozzle is possible source of this harm, safety evaluation will be done based on stress concentration as well as the pressure applied on the intestinal wall. Since the sharp edges or protruding parts should be avoided at the design stage, no report was found concerning the cases involving a similar mechanism.

5   Development of the Rectal Model Sheet

We aim to develop safety testing technologies for defecation assist devices, in which physical interaction between the device and the rectum is evaluated. Though ideal samples used in safety tests will be tissues from human or animals, they are not easily available because of deviation in properties, difficulty in handling and issues in bio-ethics. Therefore, the model which reflects the properties of tissues are required to conduct safety tests. In order to conduct safety evaluation tests for the hazards described in Sect. 4, we developed a rectal model sheet. The properties of the sheet, such as the Young's modulus and thickness, were determined based on the literature.

5.1   Young's Modulus of the Rectal Wall

Riken and the Industrial Research Institute of Shizuoka Prefecture offer "the body tissue physical properties value database" for computational biomechanics [26]. Based on this database, we determined the relevant value of Young's modulus to be 0.5 MPa, which corresponds to Young's modulus for the large intestine in the circular direction.

5.2   Thickness of the Rectal Wall

Tsuga et al. evaluated the colorectal wall in normal subjects and patients with ulcerative colitis, using an ultrasonic catheter probe [27].

In order to determine the proper thickness of the rectal model sheet, we focused on the data on the study's 36 normal subjects (25 men and 11 women), and determined that the mean value of total rectal wall thickness was 2.14 mm.

5.3   Specifications of the Rectal Model Sheet

Figure 1 shows the developed rectal model sheet. The sheet is made of silicone rubber, with a Young's modulus of 0.5 MPa and thickness of 2.15 mm as target specifications, based on 5.1 and 5.2.

The model is a single-layered, smooth, fringeless, square (200 mm × 200 mm) sheet. The sheet can be cut into pieces for use in strength testing. We will examine the validity of the developed model through experimentation.

Currently, we are planning tensile tests using the developed rectal model sheet to validate it. In the future, safety testing methods will be established corresponding to the hazards identified in Sect. 3, the safety tests using the rectum model sheet will be conducted, and the safety test results will be evaluated based on the criteria investigated in Sect. 4.

Fig. 1. Photo of the developed rectal model sheet

6   Conclusion

We conducted a bibliographic survey to investigate safety criteria for the development of safety test methods, and safety test device specifications, for defecation assist devices.

Prior to a bibliographic survey, the target devices were assumed as the defecation assist devices to be inserted into the rectum, and a primitive inspection of expected harms was conducted. Five mechanical hazards such as (1) perforation of the rectum by jet flow, (2) laceration of the rectum by suction, (3) rupture of the rectum by hydraulic pressure, (4) perforation of the rectum by contact between the defecation assist device and the rectal wall, (5) laceration of the rectum by the repetitive insertion or removal of the device were assumed.

Aiming to be used for safety evaluation test, we have developed a rectum model sheet. Properties of the rectum model sheet were determined with reference to the properties of human rectum.

For future work, we will establish safety testing method and conduct the safety tests using the rectum model sheet, and then evaluate the safety test results based on the criteria investigated in this study.

Acknowledgment. This work was funded by the ImPACT Program of the Council for Science, Technology and Innovation (Cabinet Office, Government of Japan).

References

1. Annual Report on the Aging Society 2017, Cabinet Office, Government of Japan. http://www8.cao.go.jp/kourei/whitepaper/w-2017/html/zenbun/index.html. Accessed 9 Feb 2018. (in Japanese)
2. "Innovative Cybernic System for a ZERO Intensive Nursing-care Society" project, ImPACT Program. http://www.jst.go.jp/impact/en/program/05.html. Accessed 5 Feb 2018
3. Sankai, Y., Suzuki, K., Hasegawa, Y. (eds.): Cybernics: Fusion of Human, Machine and Information Systems. Springer, Tokyo (2014). https://doi.org/10.1007/978-4-431-54159-2
4. Gallagher, P., O'Mahony, D.: Constipation in old age. Best Pract. Res. Cl. Ga. 23(6), 875–887 (2009). https://doi.org/10.1016/j.bpg.2009.09.001
5. Knight, J., Nigam, Y., Jones, A.: Effects of bedrest 2: gastrointestinal, endocrine, renal, reproductive and nervous systems. Nurs. Times 105(22), 24–27 (2009)
6. Peristeen® anal irrigation system. https://www.coloplast.co.uk/peristeen-anal-irrigation-system-en-gb.aspx. Accessed 5 Feb 2018
7. DisImpactor®. http://disimpactor.centurionmp.com. Accessed 5 Feb 2018
8. Yagata, K., Harada, A., Higuma, M., Ohnishi, T., Demoto, M., Tanda, Y.: Development of an evacuation care system (ultrasonic fecal disintegration and suction device). Jpn. J. Med. Instrum. 63(Suppl. 1), 59–60 (1993). (in Japanese)
9. Nakamura, E., Enomoto, H., Ohgoe, Y., Takahashi, C., Hirakuri, K., Takai, N., Nonomura, N., Yasukawa, Y., Niitsuma, J.: Study on functionalization of an intestinal infusion catheter. Jpn. J. Med. Instrum. 69(10), 534–535 (1999). (in Japanese)
10. Paran, H., Butnaru, G., Neufeld, D., Magen, A., Freund, U.: Enema-induced perforation of the rectum in chronically constipated patients. Dis. Colon Rectum 42(12), 1609–1612 (1999). https://doi.org/10.1007/BF02236216
11. Niv, G., Grinberg, T., Dickman, R., Wasserberg, N., Niv, Y.: Perforation and mortality after cleansing enema for acute constipation are not rare but are preventable. Int. J. Gen. Med. 6, 323–328 (2013). https://doi.org/10.2147/IJGM.S44417
12. Christensen, P., Krogh, K., Buntzen, S., Payandeh, F., Laurberg, S.: Long-term outcome and safety of transanal irrigation for constipation and fecal incontinence. Dis. Colon Rectum 52(2), 286–292 (2009). https://doi.org/10.1007/DCR.0b013e3181979341
13. Hyodo, M., Sekiguti, C., Tsukahara, M., Nagai, H.: A case of penetration caused by transanal decompression tube in an obstructive transverse colon cancer. Jpn. J. Gastroenterol. Surg. 33(11), 1839–1843 (2000). https://doi.org/10.5833/jjgs.33.1839. (in Japanese)
14. Choi, P.W.: Colorectal perforation by self-induced hydrostatic pressure: a report of two cases. J. Emerg. Med. 44(2), 344–348 (2013). https://doi.org/10.1016/j.jemermed.2012.02.076
15. Takei, H., Ishikita, T., Roppongi, T., Fujii, T., Morishita, Y.: Rectal perforation due to the spouting hot water: a case report. Prog. Acute Abdom. Med. 13(1), 131–134 (1993). https://doi.org/10.11231/jaem1984.13.131. (in Japanese)
16. Niwa, H.: Adverse events and control measures of gastroenterological endoscopy. Gastroenterol. Endosc. 27(Suppl.), 2510–2513 (1985). https://doi.org/10.11280/gee1973b.27.Supplement_2510. (in Japanese)
17. Nishisaka, T.: Current situation and future development of water jet surgery. BME 8(1), 1–6 (1994). https://doi.org/10.11239/jsmbe1987.8.1. (in Japanese)
18. Repici, A., Hassan, C., Pagano, N., Rando, G., Romeo, F., Spaggiari, P., Roncalli, M., Ferrara, E., Malesci, A.: High efficacy of endoscopic submucosal dissection for rectal laterally spreading tumors larger than 3 cm. Gastrointest. Endosc. 77(1), 96–101 (2013)
19. Neill, R.W.K., George, B.: Penetrating intra-abdominal injury caused by high-pressure water jet. Brit. Med. J. 2(5653), 357–358 (1969). https://doi.org/10.1136/bmj.2.5653.357

20. De Beaux, J.L.M.: High-pressure water jet injury. Brit. Med. J. **280**(6229), 1417–1418 (1980). https://doi.org/10.1136/bmj.280.6229.1417-a
21. Yamada, H., Evans, F.G.: Strength of Biological Materials. Robert E. Krieger Publishing Co., Inc., Huntington (1973)
22. Japan Society of Respiratory Care Medicine: Tracheal aspiration guidelines 2013 (for adult patients with an artificial airway). Jpn. J. Respir. Care **30**(1), 75–91 (2013). (in Japanese)
23. Burt, C.A.V.: Pneumatic rupture of the intestinal canal with experimental data showing the mechanism of perforation and the pressure required. Arch. Surg. **22**(6), 875–902 (1931). https://doi.org/10.1001/archsurg.1931.01160060003001
24. Uno, Y.: Newly devised sigmoidoscopy, type CF-SV-evaluation of safety. Jpn. J. Med. Instrum. **67**(7), 289–292 (1997). (in Japanese)
25. Yamada, H.: Strength of Human Bodies and Aging: Measurements Based on the Strength of Biological Materials. Japan Broadcast Publishing Association, Tokyo (1979). (in Japanese)
26. Human organs property database for computer simulation. http://cfd-duo.riken.go.jp/cbms-mp/index.htm. Accessed 5 Feb 2018
27. Tsuga, K., Haruma, K., Fujimura, J., Hata, J., Tani, H., Tanaka, S., Sumii, K., Kajiyama, G.: Evaluation of the colorectal wall in normal subjects and patients with ulcerative colitis using an ultrasonic catheter probe. Gastrointest. Endosc. **48**(5), 477–484 (1998). https://doi.org/10.1016/S0016-5107(98)70088-4

Increasing Safety for Assisted Motion During Caregiving

Comparative Analysis of a Critical Care Nurse and a Care Worker Transferring a Simulated Care-Receiver

Yasuko Kitajima[1(✉)], Ken Ikuhisa[2], Porakoch Sirisuwan[3], Akihiko Goto[4], and Hiroyuki Hamada[2]

[1] Faculty of Nursing, Tokyo Ariake University of Medical and Health Sciences, 2-9-1 Ariake, Koto-ku, Tokyo 135-0063, Japan
kitajima@tau.ac.jp
[2] Department of Advanced Fibro-Science, Kyoto Institute of Technology, Matsugasaki, Sakyo-ku, Kyoto 606-8585, Japan
ikuhisaken@yahoo.co.jp, hhamada@kit.ac.jp
[3] Rajamangala University of Technology Thanyaburi, 39 Moo1, Rangsit-Nakhon Nayok Road, Khlong Hok, Khlong Luang 12120, Pathum Thani, Thailand
porakoch.s@en.rmutt.ac.th
[4] Faculty of Design Technology, Osaka Sangyo University, 3-1-1 Nakagaito, Daito, Osaka 574-8530, Japan
gotoh@ise.osaka-sandai.ac.jp

Abstract. It is said that nurses and care workers take different approaches when assisting the transfer of patients or care-receivers. For example, even on the same purpose, in case of the transfer assistance of a patient or care receiver from a bed to a wheelchair, they take different approaches. In our previous study, the transfer assistance motions of a care worker and a critical care nurse were observed when they were assisting a simulated care-receiver (hereinafter referred to as SCR) or simulated patient (hereinafter referred to as SP) to be transferred from a bed to a wheelchair using a slide board. Their motions were measured by the motion capture to comparatively analyze the differences. As a result, the both care worker and critical care nurse assisted the transfer the SCR and the SP using the same care-assistance device, but they took different approaches in each phase. The reason for the differences is attributed to their daily working circumstance or style how to assist care-receivers or patients. Care workers usually conduct the transfer assistance at elderly nursing facilities or individual homes of care-receivers, whereas nurses usually assist patients at hospitals. We arrived at the conclusion that environmental factors such as the difference in room sizes, room layouts, or whether the place where they are working is for medical treatment or daily life, are likely the main cause for the care workers and the nurses in each situation to create their own unique transfer assistance method [1]. As aforementioned, although care workers and nurses take different approaches, their purpose is the same, just to assist care-receivers or patients to be transferred safely. This is the most important thing what they have to bear in their mind. The purpose of this study is to clarify what kind of safety measures care workers or nurses take in

© Springer International Publishing AG, part of Springer Nature 2018
V. G. Duffy (Ed.): DHM 2018, LNCS 10917, pp. 429–439, 2018.
https://doi.org/10.1007/978-3-319-91397-1_34

their transfer assistance. We assigned one care worker and one nurse who is specializing in the critical care as test subjects and asked them to assist a simulated care-receiver (SCR) or a simulated patient (SP) to be transferred from a bed to a portable toilet. Their motions were measured and analyzed by motion capture. Transferring a care-receiver or a patient to a portable toilet is a daily task carried out in various assisted-motion environments, such as elderly care facilities, individual homes and hospital wards. One difference is that care workers mainly assist elderly care-receivers, while nurses, especially critical care nurses assist patients who just recovered from critical care, but both care workers and nurses are engaged in this task on the daily basis, we therefore chose this movement for the test situation.

Even though they may take different approaches, their main purpose is the same: assist the transfer safely. If we can specify the particular actions that are used to guarantee the patient's safety, it will help us to connect how to safely assist in any working environment. Moreover, this study is not limited to care-receivers or patients' safety, it is extended to concerns about the patient's comfort. By measuring the jerk from the markers set on the SCR or SP's head, we examined how and when the subjects were burdened, and consider what sort of movements are difficult for the patient. In order to cope with the upcoming super aging society, we hope the study will contribute to develop flexible, tailored made transfer assistance techniques that can be adapted to any working environments.

Keywords: Jerk · Motion capture · Critical care nurse · Care worker

1   Introduction

In Japan, both roles that nursing and nursing care have been carried out by specialists referred to by the name of the certified care worker (kaigo fukushishi) and the nurse (kangoshi) respectively. According to Ministry of Health, Labour and Welfare, the certified care worker is a nationally licensed practitioner who uses the appellation "certified care worker" to engage in the business of providing care for a person with physical disabilities or mental disorder and intellectual disabilities that make it difficult to lead a normal life, and to provide instructions on caregiving to the person and the person's caregiver based on Certified Social Worker and Certified Care Worker Act (Act No. 30 of 1987) [2]. On the other hand, the nurse refers to a person under licensure from the Minister of Health, Labour and Welfare to pro-vide medical treatment or assist in medical care for injured and ill persons or puerperal women, as a profession, according to the Article 5 of Act on Public Health Nurses, Midwives, and Nurses (Act No. 203 on July 30, 1948) [3]. Thus the difference is clearly stated in the legal language.

In our previous study, we evaluated the difference between care workers and nurses on their specialties, work contents, or what they have to observe on the legal basis [4]. In this study, we focus on the care assistance movements of a care worker and a critical care nurse when they support a care-receiver or a patient.

In the previous study, the transfer assistance motions were comparatively analyzed between the care worker and the critical care nurse by a motion analysis system. We examined the transfer of the care-receiver or patient from a bed to a wheelchair using slide board. It was found that they took different approaches in each phase, and the reason for the difference was attributed to their regular working environment. On the one hand, care workers usually conduct the transfer assistance at elderly nursing facilities or care-receivers' homes, whereas nurses usually assist patients at hospitals. Due to the difference in room sizes and room layouts, among other environmental causes, we believe that they are naturally drawn to differing methods of assistance. When comparing the motions taken by the care worker and the critical care nurse, the most notable difference is that the care worker tended to take the postures to bear the physical burden on his lower back, while the nurse did not. Nurses are usually taught to assist patients based on the body mechanics theory as a foundational part of their education. The body mechanics principle is to apply the kinetics theory onto a human body and help to achieve the task safer and more efficiently. The technique based on the body mechanics shows effective human motions and movements related to postures and holding postures. It is considered to reduce physical burden of care workers and nurses and is incorporated widely in the field of nursing and elderly care facilities [5]. Therefore, when nurses are engaged in transfer assistance, their particular approach is based on body mechanics theory. For securing the safety and comfort of patients, when a patient's condition is beyond the range of a single nurse's capacity, they usually ask others for help or use care assistance devices.

On the other hand, care workers are mostly required to support the transfer of care-receivers in such a limited environments. In some cases, care workers work alone with their care-receivers striving to maintain safety and comfort, even if that sometimes means they must use postures that put undue stress on their own bodies. This study is intended to comparatively analyze the movements involved in supporting a care-receiver or patient as they move to a portable toilet, as performed by a care worker and a nurse specializing in critical care, using a motion capture system. Transferring a care-receiver or a patient to a portable toilet is one of the daily tasks performed in a variety of environments, including elderly care facilities, individual homes and hospital wards. Since this assistance is applied not only to elderly care-receivers, but also to patients recovering from the critical care, and both care workers and nurses provide it on a daily basis. We chose this task as a test situation believing that is most suitable for comparison analysis.

We attempted to clarify the essential movements for maintaining the safety and comfort of care-receivers and patients through comparative analysis of the motions performed by the care worker and the critical care nurse. We hope that the outcome of this study will contribute to developing flexible, tailored made transfer assistance techniques that can be adapted to any working environments. Furthermore, by measuring the jerk of the head top movements of the care-receiver or patient, we attempted to verify how and when undue physical stress was imposed on the care-receiver or patient during transfer. A sense that humans perceive changes in exercise, jerk is higher than the acceleration. In recent years it has been used for research on the measurement of movement of nursing care [6].

Care workers experiencing lower back pain has spurred the ongoing problem of care worker shortages. By taking full advantage of body mechanics theory, they can not only protect their own bodies, but also ensure the safety and comfort of care-receivers. Currently in nursing, "body mechanics theory" is the standard, however; we may have to reconsider if the safety and comfort of care-receivers and patients are completed secured under this practice. Very few studies in nursing research focus on patients' discomfortability, and quantify human discomfort using numerical values. In this study, we aimed to verify what kind of actions help to secure the safety and comfort of care-receivers and patients by making use of these methods.

2   Method

2.1   Participants

In this study, we designated one skilled care worker and one nurse, specializing in critical care, as test subjects. The care worker has 23-year working experience, stands at 160 cm in height, 69 kg in weight. The nurse has over 20-year working experience at a hospital (but no working experience at elderly care facilities), stands at 164 cm in height, 52 kg in weight, and 48 years of age. One simulated care-receivers (SCR) is assigned for the care worker, and one simulated patient (SP) is for the nurse, respectively. Both the care worker and the critical care nurse assisted the SCR or SP from a bed to a portable toilet. At the beginning of the study, both the SCR and SP were asked to take a sitting posture on the bed. During the test, the both groups were asked to repeat the same transfer assistance motions several times, and their motions was recorded and analyzed by the motion capture system.

2.2   Recording Procedure

The transfer assistance motions carried out by the care worker and the critical care nurse were recorded by digital video camera. Simultaneously, coordinates captured by each marker were measured by the optical motion capture system MAC3D SYSTEM (Motion Analysis Co., Ltd.). The sampling frequency was set at 120 Hz for the care worker, 60 Hz for the nurse. Since the sampling frequency were different, we took the footage from every other frame of the care worker, and matched each frame to the footage of the nurse for equal comparison. The infrared reflective markers were attached 26 locations on the both care worker and the nurse, and 16 locations for the SCR, and 20 locations for the SP. In the coordinate system, the movement in the vertical direction (left-right) was set as the X-axis, the front-back direction was set as the Y-axis, and the up-down direction was set as the Z-axis. Focusing on the jerk at the moment just before and after the SCR and SP were seated on the portable toilet, the sitting condition was visually judged based the footage of the digital video camera and three-dimensional data.

3   Results and Discussion

There was a difference in the time required for completing a series of transfer assistance action between the care worker and the critical care nurse. After making contact with the patient, the nurse took 8.484 s before transitioning to support the SP in standing up, whereas the care worker only took 3.191 s (Table 1). Because the nurse took more time to adjust the SP's position on the bed before moving, the SP was easily helped to stand up from the bed. First, the nurse assisted the weight shift of the SP on the bed in the right-left direction while supporting the buttock, in order to reduce the surface contact between the SP and the bed, making standing up easier through a shallower sitting position (Fig. 1). Similar actions taken by the care worker were not observed. Moving the SP left and right reduces the physical stress on the nurse when standing-up, but it might impose some physical stress on the SP from rocking on the bed. Moreover, reducing the contact surface of the SP on the bed makes it easier for the nurse to move him toward the edge, but conversely, less surface contact makes the SP unstable, and in combination with rocking the patient back and forth, these methods could actually increase the danger of an accident from falling over in bed or even falling off of the bed.

Table 1. The time required for transfer assistance.

		Care worker		Critical care nurse	
		Frame	Time (s)	Frame	Time (s)
1	Start touching	390	3.242	220	2.833
2	Prepare to stand up	773	6.433	680	11.317
3	Completion of stand up movement	1068	8.892	780	12.983
4	Move in front of portable toilet	1988	16.558	900	14.983
5	Completion of undress movement	2400	19.983	1250	20.817
6	Seated on the portable toilet	2800	23.325	1395	23.233
7	Final adjustment	3260	27.15	1460	24.317

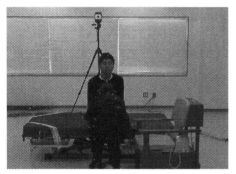 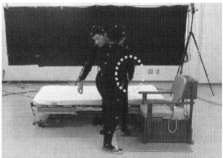

Fig. 1. Critical care nurse making a shallower sitting position.

Fig. 2. Care worker touching the SCR's body part to be moved.

After the nurse supported the SP to stand up completely, she took only 2.0 s for changing the direction of the SP's body and guiding him to be positioned in front of the portable toilet, while the care worker spent 7.666 s for this phase. The care worker spent time explaining the upcoming movements to the SCR. Not merely giving a verbal explanation, but touching the SCR's body part to be moved, this helped in shifting smoothly to the next movement (Fig. 2). This sort of explanation is thought to be valuable for not only securing the safety and comfort of care-receivers and patients, but also for preventing the occurrence of an accident caused by unexpected movements.

The common movements observed in both the care worker and the critical care nurse was securing a wide area for their base of support. Both the care worker and nurse kept their stance wider in the front-back direction, and stepped in between the SCR' or the SP's legs (Figs. 3 and 4). While keeping a wider base of support with this posture, they kept their knees engaged and their gravity center lower for securing the stability. This posture enables a smooth transfer for both who provide and received assistance [7]. Moreover, both the care worker and the nurse set their leg behind them without disturbing the course of motion. Both the care worker and the nurse faced toward the direction of motion to make sure the course was safe and clear of obstruction (Figs. 5 and 6), just as when parking a car. Both the care worker and the nurse kept a close distance to the SCR or the SP, enabling an efficient transfer. The above can perhaps be considered techniques for maintaining safety when assisting a transfer.

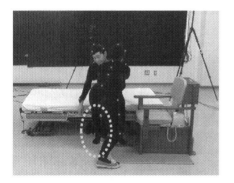

Fig. 3. Stance wider in the front-back direction, and stepped in between the SCR's legs.

Fig. 4. Stance wider in the front-back direction, and stepped in between the SP's legs.

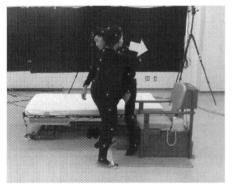

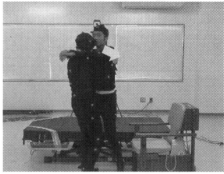

Fig. 5. Care worker faced toward the direction of motion.

Fig. 6. Critical care nurse faced toward the direction of motion.

As the next step, the jerk was measured and comparatively analyzed through the markers attached on the top of the SCR' and the SP's heads, for quantifying the physical stress imposed on them as they were seated on the portable toilet. The data was collected from 30 frames (0.483 s) before the SCR or the SP was seated on the portable toilet until the moment the care worker or nurse lifted their hand after making sure the patient was completely seated. When comparing the footage, it was evident that the care worker and the nurse took the different approaches. The care worker supported the SCR's upper body with her own and pulled her left leg further backward as his body leaning on her. Then, while maintaining support of the SCR's upper body and without tilting her own upper body forward, assisted the SCR to a completely seated position on the portable toilet. After checking that the SCR was fully seated, she shifted her upper body weight toward the SCR, so that they could sit up straight, and then the care worker brought her hands away. The nurse supported the SP on the both sides and helped him to stand straight. Then, she shifted her weight toward the SP and lowered her gravity center by bending her knees, and had the SP sit back on the portable toilet by slightly pressing down the SP's body.

Although the care worker and the nurse took the different approaches, both of them provided the care assistance considering the physical stress on care-receivers and patients as well as on themselves through weight shifting in accordance with body mechanics theory. Regarding the objective to maintain the safety of care-receivers and patients, if you compare Figs. 7 and 8, there is a relative difference in the largeness of the base of support. The care worker secured a wider base of support, so her approach is perhaps safer. They also supported the SCR's upper body with her upper body. This posture enables the SCR to sit on the portable toilet by just bending their knees. Whereas the nurse supported the both sides of the SP and made the SP walk backward when approaching the portable toilet, these motions increase the possibility of the SP falling down or experiencing discomfort when walking backward and not being able to see where they are going. This suggest that the care worker's approach is safer, more comfortable and effective at preventing accidents.

 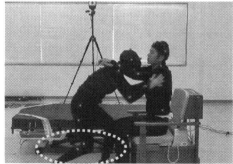

Fig. 7. Care worker's base of support.   **Fig. 8.** Critical care nurse's base of support.

In order to verify how much physical stress was imposed on the SCR and the SP during the movements described above, the head motion jerk analysis results are as shown in Figs. 9 and 10. The head movements of the care worker and the nurse are shown in the Figs. 11 and 12, along with those of their respective SCR and SP. When we compared the footage, it was clear that the nurse's movements were just to have the standing SP seated on the portable toilet. Therefore, the SP's head moved along the path shown in Fig. 12. While the care worker supported the SCR's upper body with her own, and after the SCR completely seated, the care worker shifted her weight toward the SCR, helping him sit upright. The SCR's head moved along the path shown in Fig. 11. The differences in the paths of motion between the SCR and the SP is, as expressed earlier, indicative of their comfort.

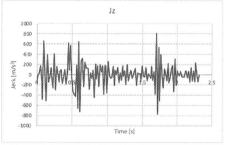

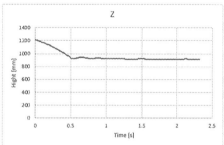

Fig. 9. SCR's head motion jerk analysis results.

Fig. 10. SP's head motion jerk analysis results.

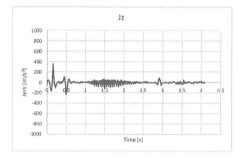

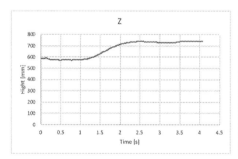

Fig. 11. SCR's head trajectory.

Fig. 12. SP's head trajectory.

When comparing the velocity (Figs. 13 and 14) and acceleration (Figs. 15 and 16) of the SCR' and the SP's head movements and jerk (Figs. 9 and 10), the SP's head was swaying a lot around 0.5 s after the sitting action started, however, hardly any sudden movements were observed in the SCR's entirely gentle trajectory.

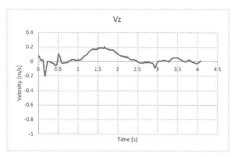

Fig. 13. SCR's head velocity.

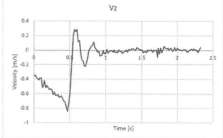

Fig. 14. SP's head velocity.

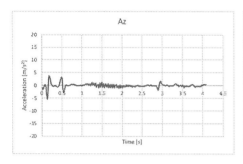

Fig. 15. SCR's head acceleration.

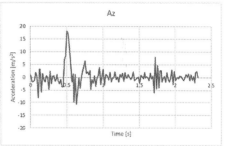

Fig. 16. SP's head acceleration.

When the nurse supported the SP to sit on the portable toilet, the nurse slightly pressed him down on the portable toilet. As his head movement track shows, the SP's head swayed considerably from the recoil of being seated suddenly. As stated earlier, when the care worker helped the SCR to sit, she supported the SCR's weight so he could sit gently by just bending their knees, so there was no recoil from being seated. The care worker took more time to finish seating the SCR, but thereby encountered less physical stress. It is perhaps the case that these differences come from their working background. While care workers usually focus on improving the remaining functions of care-receivers, critical care nurses focus on taking action as quickly as possible. Since it is generally the case that critical care nurses support patients recovered enough from critical care to use portable toilets, their focus is shifted toward completing excretion as quickly as possible, rather than towards minimizing physical stresses on the patient's body. Even so, unnecessarily moving the patient's head so much may cause instability in blood pressure and, especially since the patient is just recovered from the critical care, might solicit undue physical stress. It is important to pursue movements that minimize physical stresses on the patient from unnecessary movements, rather than focusing on reducing the time taken for a given movement.

When checking how care workers and nurses are educated to attain the proper actions required for safe transfer assistance of care-receivers and patients, they are educated mostly by the body mechanics theory that is devised to protect care workers and nurses. Even the movements of the critical care nurse seemed to be somewhat burdensome on the SP, even though their actions followed body mechanics principles. Nurses are also educated the torque principle how to move patients with less burden imposed on nurses, but through this study, we would like to return their awareness to the fact that the most important thing in transfer assistance is not to impose physical stress on patients or care-receivers. Although body mechanics principles aim to achieve both stability and efficiency, the result of this study suggests that the excessive reliance on body mechanics theory may increase the possibility of imposing physical stresses on patients or care-receivers.

4 Conclusion

This study, conducted on the premise that care workers and nurses take the different approaches in transfer assistance, attempted to verify the common elements of their movements in order to ensure the safety of their care recipients. Among the daily tasks that both care workers and nurses are engaged in, we focused on the transfer assistance motions from the bed to the portable toilet. The outcomes were evaluated in the two phases, the safety of the care-receiving side, and that of the care-providing side. In order to secure the safety of care-receivers and patients, care workers and nurses must provide stable transfer assistance, according to body mechanics theory, maintaining as wide a base of support as possible is important for stability of posture. Moreover, for securing the safety of care-providing side, body mechanics principles recommend that care-providers use weight shifting techniques when they are moving patients, being sure not to take unreasonable postures. These two outcomes have been already reported in other preceding studies, so they are not newly discovered knowledge. However, our findings throws a stone to the body mechanics supremacy myths that nursery personnel are currently relying on. By quantifying the physical burden imposed on the SCR and SP in this study, it was verified that the approach that body mechanics principles stipulate still impose physical stresses on the care-receiving side. Therefore, in further study, we aim to pursue the most ideal motions which will imposed the least physical stress on the both care-receiving and care-providing sides, while prioritizing the safety and comfort of the care-receiving side.

References

1. Kitajima, Y., Takai, Y., Yamashiro, K., Ogura, Y., Goto, A.: Comparative analysis of wheelchair transfer movements between nurse and care worker. In: Duffy, V.G. (ed.) DHM 2017, Part I. LNCS, vol. 10286, pp. 281–294. Springer, Cham (2017). https://doi.org/10.1007/978-3-319-58463-8_24
2. A website of the Ministry of Health, Labour and Welfare: Outline of Certified Care Worker. http://www.mhlw.go.jp/kouseiroudoushou/shikaku_shiken/kaigohukushishi/. Accessed 22 Feb 2018. (in Japanese)
3. Act on Public Health Nurses, Midwives and Nurses: Article 5 (Act No. 203 on July 30, 1948) final revision, Act No. 83 on June 25, 2014. (in Japanese)
4. Kitajima, Y.: op.cit., pp. 281–294

5. Ogawa, K.: Assisting Nursing and Care: Work Posture and Movement, Learning Body Mechanics Through Illustration, pp. 53–54. Tokyo Denki University Press, Tokyo (2010). (in Japanese)
6. Koshino, Y., Ohno, Y., Hashimoto, M., Yoshida, M.: Evaluation parameters for care-giving motions. J. Phys. Ther. Sci. **19**(4), 299–306 (2007)
7. Kubota, S.: The Way to Improve the Living Environment Using Assistive Devices, pp. 50–55. Japanese Nursing Association Publishing Company, Tokyo (2017). (in Japanese)

Indirect Evaluation of Nurse's Transfer Skill Through the Measurement of Patient

Chingszu Lin[1(✉)], Zhifeng Huang[2], Masako Kanai-Pak[3],
Jukai Maeda[4], Yasuko Kitajima[4], Mitsuhiro Nakamura[4], Noriaki Kuwahara[5],
Taiki Ogata[1], and Jun Ota[1]

[1] Research into Artifacts, Center for Engineering of the University of Tokyo,
Chiba 277-8568, Japan
lin@race.u-tokyo.ac.jp
[2] Department of Automation of Guangdong University of Technology,
Guangdong 510006, China
[3] Faculty of Nursing of Kanto Gakuin University,
Yokohama 236-8501, Japan
[4] Faculty of Nursing of Tokyo Ariake University of Medical and Health Sciences,
Tokyo 135-0063, Japan
[5] Department of Advanced Fibro-Science, Kyoto Institute of Technology,
Kyoto 606-8585, Japan

Abstract. Nowadays with the advancement of technology, many evaluation systems have been developed for skill learning. However, those systems are inevitable to set the sensors on trainees or environment (e.g. camera). Therefore this study aims to propose a method to indirectly evaluate the patient transfer skill through only measuring the patient, instead of the nurse. Based on the observation of the patient's movements during transfer, joint angle and acceleration of patient are determined as two parameters to evaluate the nurse's skill. Incorrect ways of transfer skill were added into a checklist, proposed in our pre-work, based on clinical experience of nursing teachers. An experiment was conducted by two nursing teachers, and they were asked to carry out the patient transfer skill through both correct and incorrect ways as proposed in the checklist. The results exhibit those two parameters enable to show the difference while the nurses carried out the incorrect way. The angles of hip and knee joints enable to reveal the difference in the steps related to standing up and sitting down; while the acceleration of patient can exhibit the difference of patient's dynamic movement. According to such results, the indirect evaluation became practical for the future works.

Keywords: Patient transfer skill · Motion measurement · Indirect evaluation

1 Introduction

According to American Association of Colleges of Nursing's report [1], an issues of faculty shortage is raised, which contributes to the ratio of students and teachers in clinical courses becomes smaller. However, many currents researches state the smaller class sizes tends to be associated with higher quality [2, 3]. In this way the students enable undergoing the supervision and evaluation of teachers and obtain the guidance and feedback of their performance. Such evaluation and feedback in clinic education have been considered an essential step in the acquisition of clinical skills [4]. Therefore, according to the background of faculty shortage, proposing the evaluation system for nursing students without the teacher's supervision becomes urgent.

Accompanying with the technological progress, many researches dedicate a great effort on developing the evaluation and motion measurement of skills in a diversity of fields. Particular in sports, the measurement of the trainees through sensors are widely utilized to enhance the motor skill learning. For example, a single 2D stationary camera was employed to analyze the user's motion in Taichi and golf swing [5]. Other research employed the 3D motion to extract the difference between expert and novice of goal player [6]. Another system used the MEMS inertial sensors attached on the goal club to evaluate the golf swing [7]. In addition, a system was proposed by using the underwater camera, wearable LED marker, and pressure sensor to analyze the skill of swimmer [8]. Furthermore, *Gray et al.* employed magnetic-field search-coil technique to measure the position, velocity, and acceleration of the arm between expert and unskilled pitcher [9]. Except from the sports, a learning system of dancing with immediate feedback by employing the 3D motion capture technology was proposed in [10]. Also a study investigated the difference of expert and novice piano player in the of upper-limb movement through both EMG and camera [11]. For the fields related to the nursing education, a research developed an evaluation system for self-training of bed-making activity [12]. And our pre-work proposed a self-help training system for learning the patient transfer skills by using the same Kinect sensor [13]. However, those previous studies had not measured what will occur if the incorrect skill was applied by trainees. Particularly in the field of nursing, it is important to realize what kind of influence will bring to the patient if the nurses employ incorrect ways. Furthermore, despite that those previous studies had proposed different methods to evaluate the learner's performance, the installations of sensor on the learner and environment are inevitable, such as markers on learner' body or the cameras around the learner.

To propose an evaluation system, we assume the nurse's correct and incorrect ways will contribute the different influence on the patients, because the transfer skill has a cooperative and mutual relation between nurse's skill and patient's movement. Accordingly, this study aims to verify if only the measurement of patent enables to exhibit the difference while the nurses carry out the correct and incorrect ways of patient transfer skill. The first challenging point is there are various parameters to measure the influence of patient (e.g. position, velocity, acceleration). Therefore, how to determine the enough parameters to observe the influence caused by the nurses is difficult. The approach is first to observe the movements of patient during the transfer, and then the joint angle and acceleration were selected as optimal parameters to exhibit the difference between the correct and incorrect ways. The other challenging point is during the whole process of transfer skill, different steps have the influence. In short, the some previous steps causes the influence on the following steps. Therefore a checklist based on the clinic experience of nursing teacher was proposed. In the checklist the following step that may causes the influence on the patient is also listed down; and measurement of the patient should also cover those following steps.

2   Proposed Method

2.1   Process of Patient Transfer Skill

With the aging society, patient transfer become more indispensable to take care of senior patients and other physical injured patient frequently in hospitals or homes [14]. Patient transfer skill can be executed in many different scenarios. Transfer skill allows the patients to be able to move from the wards to other places and conduct the daily routine, such as going to toilet or bathroom. However, this skill is one of the most complicated and difficult tasks, because it requires entire body mechanics (e.g., position, posture, method of movement), and also the knowledge related to wheelchair. Furthermore, the appropriated mutual interaction and cooperation between patient and nurses are required to ensure patient comfort and prevent incident. To move the patient from There are 6 main steps during patient transfer as shown in Fig. 1. The steps are placing the wheelchair, mutual hugging, standing up, pivot turning, sitting down on the wheelchair, and final posture adjustment.

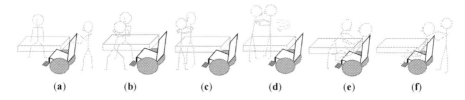

(a)   (b)   (c)   (d)   (e)   (f)

Fig. 1. Patient transfer skill of (a) placing the wheelchair, (b) mutual hugging, (c) standing up, (d) pivot turning, (e) sitting down on the wheelchair, and (f) final posture adjustment

2.2   Checklist

To observe the influence of patient while the nursing skills were carried out, the checklist were proposed by the nursing teachers with more than 10 year clinical experience. The checklist were comprised by the step No. 1 to 16 with the correct way which represent the appropriate way which extracted from the nursing material. Because there are many different incorrect ways which differs from nurses to nurses, we selected the incorrect ways as the most common mistake to nursing student base on the experience of nursing teachers. In this way the influence on the patient become more meaningful to represents the conventional situation when the incorrect were applied. In addition, the step, which may occur the difference influence on the patient while the correct and incorrect way were applied, were also listed down in the last column of the checklist. Some difference influence of the patient occurs on the present step when the incorrect skill were applied, while some occurs in following steps. Such scenario that the previous steps affect the following steps is because transfer skill has strong connection between different steps. For example, the placement of wheelchair of No. 1 and No. 3 will have the influence on patient during the pivot turning step of No. 12. The checklist contains 16 evaluation items, and 12 items were written with the common mistakes. Each referring to clinical experience and nursing material (Table 1).

Table 1. Checklist of patient transfer with correct and incorrect ways

Step No.	Correct way	Incorrect way	Step occurs different influence
1	Place the wheelchair at the bedside and adjust the angle to 20–30°	Place the wheelchair at the bedside with too large angle	No. 12
2	Place the wheelchair near the patient	Place the wheelchair too far from the bed	No. 12
3	Apply the wheelchair brakes	Did not apply the brake	No. 15
4	Place one of your feet behind you, and another foot between the feet of the patient	–	–
5	Enable the patient to sit on the edge of the bed by rocking the patient's bottom.	Did not move the patient to the edge of the bed	No. 10
6	Adjust the patient's leg posture and move ankle closed to the bed	Move the patient ankle far from the bed	No. 6 No. 11
7	Place both arms of the patient on your shoulders and hugging mutually	Did not (hug with the patient) place both arms of the patient on your shoulders	No. 7 No. 12
8	Clutch the lower back of the patient.	–	–
9	Place your right foot behind you and left foot between the feet of the patient	Place the woring position that left foot behind and right foot between the feet of the patient	No. 12
10	Squat down and lower your waist in order to prepare the patient to stand up	Did not bend your knees and lower the waist	No. 11
11	Make the patient lean down, and then assist the patient to stand up	Did not make the patient lean down first, stand up the patient vertically	No. 11
12	Use your left foot as a pivot axis to help the patient turn to the wheelchair	–	–
13	Place one of your feet behind you, and another foot between the feet of the patient	–	–
14	Lower your waist in order to prepare to assist the patient to sit down	Did not lower waist and bend the knee to assist the patient to sit down	No. 15
15	Make the patient lean down and assist the patient to sit down	Did not make the patient lead down first, before making them sit down	No. 15
16	Make the patient sit in the wheelchair through pulling with both arms	Lift the patient up vertically and move the patient sit at inner side of wheelchair	No. 16

2.3 Determination of Parameter

In this section, we determined two parameters to observe the patient, which are joint angle and acceleration. Those two parameters were selected because, firstly human posture refers to the physical configurations that comprised of the different angles of joint; and secondly, acceleration in physics enables to exhibits the dynamic movement of patient caused by the forces of the nurses.

3   Experiment

3.1 Purpose

In order to evaluate the nurse's skill through the measurement of patient, the following crucial points should be realized in this experiment.

- To approve the nurse's correct and incorrect skill cause the different influence of the joint angle and acceleration on patient.
- To observe where are the location on patient to measure the difference influence between correct and incorrect ways executed by the nurses,

3.2 Participant

The experiment invited two experienced nursing teachers as the participants. Both nursing teachers have the clinical experience in patient transfer. The nursing teaches were asked to be a skill performer and also a simulated patient during the experiment. In addition, the procedures were approved by the Ethics Committee at the University of Tokyo, and both participants provided their written informed consent prior to enrollment.

3.3 Experiment Procedure

The first step is to ask the nursing teachers conducting the correct way of patient transfer from step No. 1 to 16 for one trail. The second step is ask the nursing teacher to execute the step with the incorrect way for also one trial. An experimental picture is shown in Fig. 2.

In each step, firstly one nursing teacher carry out the transfer skill, and the other nursing teacher simulates the patient. After that they switched the role and carried the transfer skill again. The simulated patient by the nurses is determined as the patient affected by week lower limbs that required assists during transferring. And this is the reason that participant reproducing the patient should be the nursing teachers who have the clinic experience to imitate such patient.

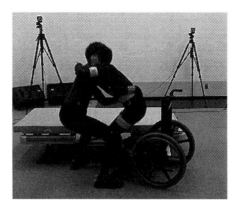

Fig. 2. Patient transfer trial conducted by nursing teachers

3.4 Experiment Setting

The basic elements of patient transfer include a bed and a wheelchair. The height of the bed was adjusted at 50 cm, and the wheelchair was placed beside the bed. In addition, 12 motion capture cameras were set around the bed to measure the joint angle. Also motion capture markers are attached on the patient. Additionally, the inertial sensors were attached on the patient's arms, thighs, chest and waist to measure the acceleration. Even though the motion capture system enable to measure the both joint angle and acceleration, but in the future we aims only use angular sensor and inertial sensors to avoid complication setting. Thus in this study, the acceleration was measured by inertial sensors to verify the feasibility our proposed method. The sensor and marker setting had described previous as shown in the Fig. 3. All the x axis of inertial sensors is facing down. And the z axis of sensor on the chest, waist and thigh is facing backward during standing pose; while the y axis of both arm is facing front side. Last, two web cameras were utilized to record the experiment.

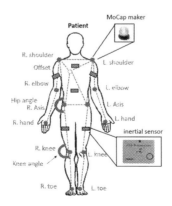

Fig. 3. Setting of motion capture marker and inertial sensor on the patient

3.5 Result

The results of all the steps in checklist are a large among of information; therefore, this paper only presents partial results.

- Posture of patient's joint

For the step No. 5, 6, and 11, the difference influence on the patient between correct and incorrect ways occurred at the step No. 11, which is to assist the patient standing up. First of all, the flexion angle of knee and hip through the correct way are presented in Fig. 4, and those Figures will be compared with other results through the incorrect ways.

For the step No. 5, the correct way is to move the patient to the edge of the bed; while the incorrect way is not carrying out this step, making the patient did not move to the edge of bed. The difference influence on patient between correct and incorrect ways occurs on the hip joint during the standing up step No. 11. If the incorrect way was executed, then the flexion angle of hip joint increased from 60 to 80° for trial of Teacher

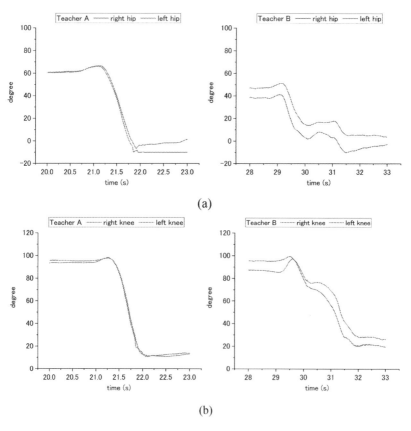

Fig. 4. Flexion angle of patient's (a) hip and (b) knee during step No. 11 (standing up) when correct way was conducted

A; while the angle increase from about 50 to 60° for the trial of Teacher B, as shown in Fig. 5.

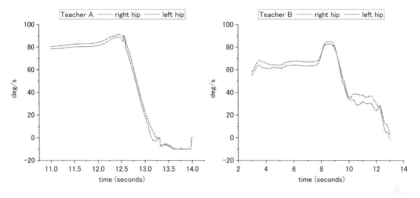

Fig. 5. Flexion angle of patient's hip during step No. 11 (standing up) when incorrect way was conducted at step No. 5

The step No. 6 is to move the patient's ankle closed to the bed; and the incorrect way is moving the patient's ankle too far from the bed. Those ways lead to the difference on the present step No. 6 and also the standing up step No. 11. As shown in the Fig. 6, when putting the heel too far away from the bed, the flexion angle of keen of the patient become smaller at the beginning, compared with Fig. 4(b). Also during the standing up at step No. 11, the hip joint will increase and form a peak cure which cannot be seen in the correct way.

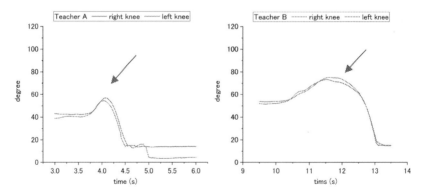

Fig. 6. Flexion angle of patient's knee during the step No. 6 and 11 when incorrect way was conducted at step No. 6

In term of the step No. 15, the appropriate way is making the patient lean down first before assisting them to sit down; while the common mistake is making the patient to sit down on the wheelchair by moving the patient's trunk vertically downward from standing condition to sitting. In Figs. 7 and 8, the result shows through the correct way the hip joint kept increasing until the patient sitting on the seat surface, and then angle started to decrease until reaching he angle which smaller than 40°. However, the results through the incorrect way did not have such obvious decreasing after the patient sit on the wheelchair.

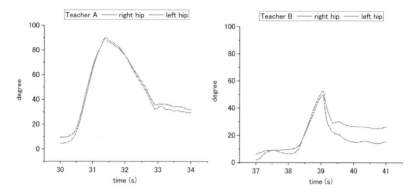

Fig. 7. Flexion angle of patient's hip during step No. 15 (sitting down) when correct way was conducted at step No. 15

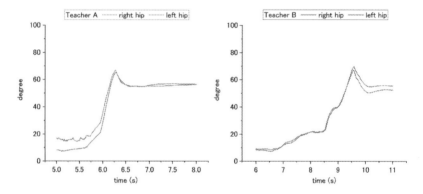

Fig. 8. Flexion angle of patient's hip during step No. 15 (sitting down) when incorrect way was conducted at step No. 15

For the last step No. 16 adjusting the final posture to make the patient sitting against to the backrest of wheelchair, the correct way is to hold the patient' both arm and make then leaning down before pulling them to the backrest. And the support the patient trunk making them to lean against on the backrest. In contrast, the incorrect way is holding the patient's armpits and lift them up, and then move them closed to the backrest. Finally release the armpits and make the patient sit on the wheelchair. The results show the flexion angle of hip joint first increased and then decreased when the correct was applied; while through the result is contrary, then angle decreased first and then increased, as shown in Figs. 9 and 10.

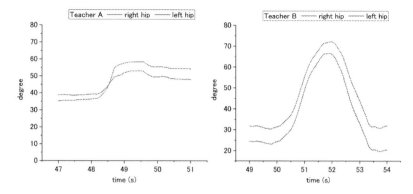

Fig. 9. Flexion angle of patient's hip during step No. 16 when correct way was conducted at step No. 16.

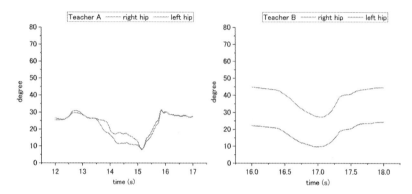

Fig. 10. Flexion angle of patient's hip during step No. 16 when incorrect way conducted at step No. 16.

- Acceleration of patient's motion

For the step No. 10, the appropriated way of nurses is to squat down and lower their waist before assisting the patient to stand up. The incorrect way is standing straightly without lower their waist when supporting the patient to stand up. The difference influence on patient happens during the standing up at step No. 11. When the nurses did not lower the waist and then holding the patient to stand up, the acceleration increase from -600 to -1000 mG during the process while standing up in the trial of teacher A. However, for the trial of teacher B, such difference in acceleration is not significant, as shown in Figs. 11 and 12. The explanation is presented in the discussion.

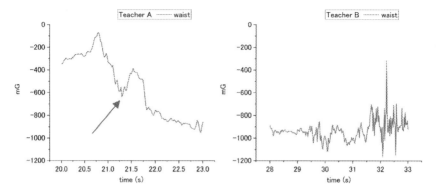

Fig. 11. Acceleration of patient's waist during step No. 11 (standing up) through correct way conducted at step No. 10.

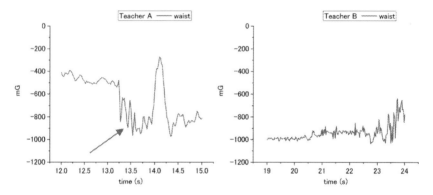

Fig. 12. Acceleration of patient's waist during step No. 15 (sitting down) through incorrect way conducted at step No. 10.

The step No. 14 is asking the nurses to lower their waist before making patient to sit down. And the incorrect way is not lower their waist. The different influence is the acceleration of the patient's waist during the sting down No. 15. The correct way has the smaller acceleration downward; while the acceleration downward became larger when the nurses do not lower their waist as shown in Figs. 13 and 14.

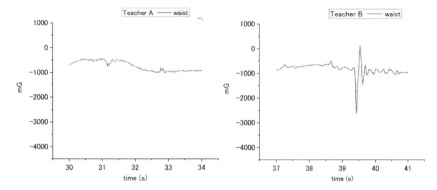

Fig. 13. Acceleration of patient's waist during step No. 15 (sitting down) through correct way conducted at step No. 14

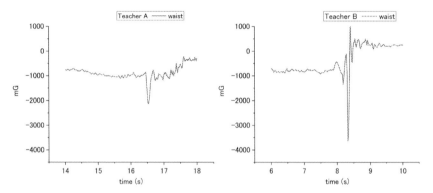

Fig. 14. Acceleration of patient's waist during step No. 15 (sitting down) through incorrect way conducted at step No. 14

3.6 Discussion

According to the results, the joint angle enables to evaluate many steps in the checklist. This reveals the joint angle is one of the crucial parameter to evaluate the nursing skill during the transfer. Those angle joints of hip and knee which are highly effected by the performance of nurse. The angle of hip and knee are capable to reflect the different influence of lower limbs when standing up, sitting down, and the movement involved leaning down.

In addition, the acceleration of waist enables to distinguish the correct and incorrect ways of nurse. Also the acceleration associates with the feeling of patient; therefore it can be a critical parameter to evaluate the skill performance of the nurses. However, in this experience, the different height of patients which simulated by different nursing teachers brings about the limitation. For example the step No. 10, as shown in Figs. 11 and 12, because Teacher B is shorter than the patient simulate by the Teacher A, making the Teacher B difficult to quickly lift up the patient when lower limbs are straight without bending. Therefore, the quality of acceleration did not become larger when Teacher B did not lower the waist on the step 10. Such condition reveals that the different height of patient also influence the skill perforce of nurses, and this issue should be solved for in the future works, such as using the same simulated patient.

4   Conclusions and Future Works

With the goal to evaluate the nurse's skill through only the measurement of patient, this study verified if the joint angle and acceleration of patient enable to show the difference while the correct and incorrect ways were applied by the nurses. The checklist comprised by 16 steps were proposed by the nursing teacher with correct and incorrect way. The incorrect was is determined by the most common mistake of nursing student. An experiment was conducted by the two nursing teachers. They are asked to carry out both correct and incorrect ways. According to the result, the joint angle exhibits the difference between correct and incorrect ways on more than five steps, revealing the joint angle is an essential parameter to evaluate the nursing skill. Especially the hip and knee joint can informatively exhibit the standing up and sitting down movement of patient with details. The acceleration of waist enables to show the difference of two steps, and the quantitative value reveals the dynamic condition of patient.

For the future works, more parameters will be found to observe the steps that are unable to exhibit the difference through the joint angle and acceleration. In addition more participants will be invited to conduct the transfer skill, so that the threshold for evaluation can be determined. Furthermore the angular sensor will be developed to attach on the patient, in order to replace the motion capture system which requires the complicated setting on both patient and camera.

References

1. American Association of Colleges of Nursing (AACN) Homepage. http://www.aacnnursing.org/News-Information/Fact-Sheets/Nursing-Faculty-Shortage
2. Burruss, N.M., et al.: Class size as related to the use of technology, educational practices, and outcomes in web-based nursing courses. J. Prof. Nurs. **25**(1), 33–41 (2009)
3. Gibbs, G., Lucas, L., Spouse, J.: The effects of class size and form of assessment on nursing students' performance, approaches to study and course perceptions. Nurse Educ. Today **17**(4), 311–318 (1997)
4. Branch Jr., W.T., Paranjape, A.: Feedback and reflection: teaching methods for clinical settings. Acad. Med. **77**(12), 1185–1188 (2002)
5. Wang, R., Leow, W.K., Leong, H.W.: 3D-2D spatiotemporal registration for sports motion analysis. In: IEEE Conference on Computer Vision and Pattern Recognition, 2008. CVPR 2008. IEEE (2008)
6. Paradisis, G., Rees, J.: Kinematic analysis of golf putting for expert and novice golfers. In: ISBS-Conference Proceedings Archive. vol. 1. No. 1 (2000)
7. Burchfield, R., Venkatesan, S.: A framework for golf training using low-cost inertial sensors. In: International Conference on Body Sensor Networks (BSN). IEEE (2010)

8. Chakravorti, N., et al.: Design and implementation of an integrated performance monitoring tool for swimming to extract stroke information at real time. IEEE Trans. Hum. Mach. Syst. **43**(2), 199–213 (2013)
9. Gray, S., et al.: Comparison of kinematics in skilled and unskilled arms of the same recreational baseball players. J. Sports Sci. **24**(11), 1183–1194 (2006)
10. Chan, J.C.P., et al.: A virtual reality dance training system using motion capture technology. IEEE Trans. Learn. Technol. **4**(2), 187–195 (2011)
11. Furuya, S., Kinoshita, H.: Organization of the upper limb movement for piano key-depression differs between expert pianists and novice players. Exp. Brain Res. **185**(4), 581–593 (2008)
12. Nagata, A., et al.: Measurement and evaluation system for self-training system of bed-making activity. Trans. Control Mech. Syst. **2**(12), 422–431 (2013)
13. Huang, Z., et al.: Self-Help Training System for Nursing Students to Learn Patient Transfer Skills. IEEE Trans. Learn. Technol. **7**(4), 319–332 (2014)

Optimization of Proton Therapy Based on Service Design Theory

Xinxiong Liu and Wanru Wang[✉]

Huazhong University of Science and Technology, No. 1037, Luoyu Road,
Wuhan, Hubei Province, China
m201570705@hust.edu.cn

Abstract. Proton therapy has been regarded the promising method for curing cancer. The proton therapy room plays an important role in the treatment procedure. With the rapidly spread of the proton therapy service, the treatment experience becomes a margin factor for improving treatment effect. In this paper, the service design theory was applied to guide the design of the proton therapy room. The prototype of proton therapy room was proposed. Based on our proposed design, the resource would be allocated more efficiently and the treatment experience would be improved in a large extent.

1 Introduction

Proton therapy [1] has been regarded as one of the most important methods for curing cancer in the future. Different to traditional radiation treatment by X-rays or gamma rays, the proton therapy utilizes the proton rays to cure the cancer by radiating at the diseased tissue. The protons energy radiation is first slow and then fast, which means the energy will not be released too much after the proton enters the body in a depth. Thus, when the position where the energy is released heavily matches the position of the diseased tissue, the diseased tissue can be killed without affecting normal cells. Proton therapy outperforms current ways of curing cancer and reaches an ideal level of treatment.

Thanks to the outstanding treatment performance of proton therapy, proton therapy center has been developing rapidly in the world. Until January 2016, over 45 proton therapy centers have been established. Most of them located in USA, Europe and Japan. Over 96537 patients have received proton therapy. However, the proton therapy is currently a new thing in China. With the developing of treatment methods and the living standard of people, proton therapy will gradually gain a more rapid speed of developing.

Nowadays, the main focus of proton therapy is improving the success rate of treatment. The demand is higher than the hospital resources. In this circumstances, patients may not be sensitive to the experience when getting treatment. However, as more and more hospitals are able to provide proton therapy, the treatment experience will become a major factor affecting the patients selection

© Springer International Publishing AG, part of Springer Nature 2018
V. G. Duffy (Ed.): DHM 2018, LNCS 10917, pp. 454–465, 2018.
https://doi.org/10.1007/978-3-319-91397-1_36

for the hospital. Whats more, with the development of technology, the basic success rate of treatment is relatively high. The treatment experience will become an essential margin factor affecting the effect of the treatment. Also, proton therapy is a complex treatment method comprising many processes and resources integration. The optimization of resources utilization is beneficial to improving the treatment effect. From these points of view, the design for a more friendly and reasonable proton therapy has been an meaningful topic.

Proton therapy has complex procedures of treatment. The proton therapy room plays an important role during all the procedures since cancer cells of patients will get irradiated by the proton rays in this room. In this paper, the service design theory [2–4] is applied to offer the patient a more reasonable and pleasant treatment experience in the proton therapy room. As far as we know, few study has studied this field. There are mainly three contributions of our work: 1. Service touchpoints of proton therapy were extracted based on theoretical analysis; 2. Insights from the questionnaires survey and field survey were obtained to find the demand of patients; 3. A prototype design based on service design theory was provided to optimize the treatment experience of proton therapy.

2   Service Design Analysis of the Proton Therapy Treatment Room

The particular treatment process from different proton therapy centers may be different from each other. The optimization conducted on a specific type of treatment process is not general enough. The aim of our work is to provide the optimization for the overall service in the proton therapy treatment room based on service design theory. So the abstraction of the process in the proton therapy room is conducted and a process model of treatment is established. Based on the obtained process model, touchpoints of the proton therapy service are extracted from the view of service design.

2.1   Process Model of Proton Therapy Treatment Room

By comparing the proton therapy in the treatment room of different centers, the process model of proton therapy treatment room is established in Fig. 1. The process model is composed of five parts: 1. Before the treatment, the patient need to make some preparations. Particular preparations include changing clothes or getting medical instructions. 2. The patient enter the treatment room, put on their specially design mold and get fixed in the specific gesture and position with the help of the doctor. 3. The machine starts to work. CT is taken on the patient to locate the targeted diseased tissue. And the machine rotates to find the angle for radiating the proton rays. 4. The proton rays are radiated on the tissue. 5. Treatment is over and the patient leaves the treatment room. The whole treatment process last around 30 to 40 min, regarding the specific disease. The process model provides the basic material for the service design of the proton therapy treatment room.

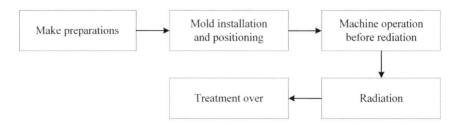

Fig. 1. Process model of proton therapy treatment room

2.2 Service Touchpoint Extraction of Proton Therapy

The process model is the generally an indication of the patient experience. The service touchpoints could be extracted from the process model. Based on the service design theory, service touchpoints interact with the patient through senses. Combining the process model and five senses, the service blueprint of the proton therapy treatment room is proposed and service touchpoints are extracted based on the service blueprint. The service blueprint of proton therapy is shown in Fig. 2.

Patient	Change clothes	Enter the treatment room	Be positioned and fixed	Be scanned	Be radiated	Leave the treatment room		
Doctors	Help with the patient		Give medical instructions	Observe or give instructions	Observe or give instructions	Help with the patient		**Patients behavior**
Treatment bed			Support the patient	Support the patient	Support the patient			**Frontstage service**
Treatment machine				Target zone confirmation	Cure the cancer			
Treatment room space		Provide atomsphere	Provide space for treatment					**Backstage service**
Maintaining team						Maintain		

Fig. 2. Service blueprint of proton therapy treatment room

Five service touchpoints are extracted from the service blueprint, including treatment room space, treatment bed, treatment machine and doctors. Treatment room space is the visual image of the patient. The space elements include the light, layout and decorations. The space could have effect on patients psychology through space elements. Treatment bed is the main service touchpoint when the patient getting treatment. The patient has to contact the with treatment bed through the whole process. Treatment machine radiates the proton rays to the patients body. Doctors help the patient fix the body and get on the treatment bed, give medical instructions when the treatment goes on and supervise the treatment procedure. The optimization of the proton therapy service is mainly conducted on the service model through service touchpoints.

3   Insights of the Proton Therapy Service

Optimization of service touchpoints should base on the insights of the service touchpoint. In order to get insights of the service touchpoint, three ways of research have been conducted, including public information collection, questionnaire survey and deep interview. Public information collection is the basis for questionnaire survey. The questions of questionnaire is extracted the public information collection. Questionnaire survey focuses on some general problems of the patient. Deep interview is conducted with both patients and the stuff in the hospital in order to dig more valuable information.

3.1   Public Information Collection

In order to design a reasonable questionnaire, the question should be carefully designed. Since the aim of the work is optimize the service touchpoint, the potential part for optimization should be found. In this section, the public information collection is conducted to find the potential part for service touchpoint optimization. Several images of the service touchpoint were found to illustrate the potential part.

In Fig. 3, the proton therapy treatment space is shown. From Fig. 3, it can found that the proton therapy treatment space service touchpoint mainly contains three part, the light, the layout and the decorations. The luminance and color of light may have effect the overall atmosphere of the proton therapy treatment room. The layout of the room represents the position of different function zone of the treatment. And the decoration mean the additional furniture not directly related the treatment. Some potential problems were also shown in Fig. The color of light may be cold, combining with the cold machine and technology, the feeling of color may be not warm enough. The space seems empty and lacks of positive visual elements.

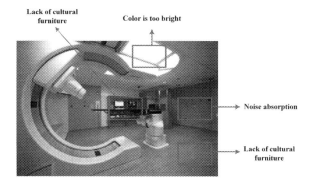

Fig. 3. Proton therapy treatment space

In Fig. 4, the treatment machine is shown. When operating, the machine brings some noise which causes tension feeling of the patient. The rotation of the machine may causes some feeling of dizzy. The distance between the treatment bed and the alarm light may be too close. The flash of the light causes tension feeling of the patient.

Fig. 4. Treatment machine

The treatment bed service touchpoint is shown in Fig. 5. Several potential problems in Fig. 5 exist. The patient may feel cold since the treatment rooms temperature is relatively low in order to maintain the operation of the machine. The height of the treatment room may cause the patient feel unsafe. The patient is not protected from falling of the treatment bed. In addition, the channel for calling doctors for help is missed from the picture.

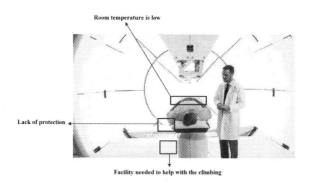

Fig. 5. Treatment bed

3.2   Questionnaire Survey

Proton therapy and the traditional radiation therapy utilize similar ways of treatment method which is radiating particles into the human body. The similar mechanism causes the similar arrangement of the treatment room and similar outlook of the treatment machine. Similar treatment room and treatment machine lead to similar experience of the patient. Since the proton therapy center has not been widely used, the questionnaire survey is conducted among the patient who have received traditional radiation therapy. 200 questionnaires have been distributed and 152 were retrieved. The analysis was conducted on the retrieved questionnaire.

The questionnaire is designed based on the service touchpoint of the service model, as shown in Table 1. For each touchpoint, several related questions were surveyed. The questions were extracted from but not directly borrowed from the public information collection. For the treatment space, the color and luminance of light were surveyed. The high level of light intensity may bring the patients pressure. Cold series of color strengths the sense of technology, leading the feeling of distanced. Alarm light is necessary for operation of the therapy, but the visibility by patients may bring additional pressure. For treatment bed, the convenience for climbing, the feeling of temperature and the height of position are surveyed. For the doctor, the privacy protection and the effect of communication are surveyed. And for the treatment machine, the noise of the machine, the procedure notation and the luminance of light are surveyed. The questionnaire is designed using the Likert scale, with the score of each question from 1 to 5. The result of the questionnaire is shown in Table 1. For the treatment room space, the average score of light intensity is 3.3, which indicates that the intensity is normal. But the average score of light color is 3.8, representing that the color is too light. The alarm clock also affects patients feeling. So the treatment room space needs optimization on the light color and alarm light. For the treatment bed, the temperature seems a little bit cold for the patient. This phenomenon is caused by the material of the treatment bed. Also, the feeling of height when

Table 1. Questionnaire about the service touchpoint

Service touchpoints	Questions	Score from 5 ro 1	Average score
Space of treatment room	Luminance of light	Too high→Too low	3.3
	Color of light	Too bright→Too dark	3.8
	Effect of alarm light	Much affected→No affected	3.9
Treatment bed	Convenient to climb	Easy→Hard	4.1
	Feeling when contacted	Cold→Warm	3.5
	Feeling of height	Too high→Too low	3.8
Doctor	Respect of privacy	Excellent→Terrible	4.2
	Communication	Effective→No effect	2.9
Treatment machine	Noise of machine	Too loud→Too low	4.0
	Familiarity of machine procedure	Well familiar→Lack of knowledge	2.1
	Luminance of light	Too high→Too low	3.5

the patient lying on the treatment bed is obvious, with the average score of 3.8. For the doctor, the communication with the patient scores low. The communication between the patient and the doctor when the patient lies on the bed may contain instructions and the current progress of treatment. For the treatment machine, the noise is relatively loud and the patient is not familiar with the current operation progress of the machine. And the light of the machine is normal.

3.3   Deep Interview

The public information collection and the questionnaire survey mainly deals with some general problems. In this section, three representatives of the proton therapy service were deeply interviewed in order to get a deep understanding of the current service. 2 oncologists, 3 radiation doctors and 5 patients were interviewed about the experience of the radiation therapy service. Based on the material collected from the interview, the character profile is established in Table 2.

From Table 2, it can be concluded that the optimization on the service model is also necessary. Some demands can not be satisfied only by the service touchpoint optimization. The optimization should be extended to the process of the proton therapy.

Table 2. Character profile of the stuff

Name	Li Wei
Occupation	Oncologist

Demand statement:
The treatment procedure is complex and time consuming. Some patients do not understand my work and treatment plan. Thus some misunderstandings are created. The way to inform patients are difficult. Sometimes the patient is difficult to reach

Name	Zhao Shi
Occupation	Radiation doctor

Demand statement:
I have to go from room to room to conduct different tasks. This is time consuming and makes people feel tired. Different people have different target zone, thus making the fixing procedure cost too much time. Although the instruction have been told to the patient, some patients still act the wrong way

Name	Zhou wu
Occupation	Patient

Demand statement:
When lying on the treatment bed, I do not know current status of the machine. Since there is no one in the treatment room when the radiation happens, I feel helpless and worried. When getting treatment, I have to stay static, which is very tired since the process lasts long

4   Service Design of Proton Therapy

The abstraction of the proton therapy service is conducted and the service model is obtained. Combining with insights obtained from the public information collection, questionnaire survey and deep interview, the new service of proton therapy service is proposed. There are mainly three aspects of innovations: static service touchpoint optimization, new service touchpoint optimization and process optimization.

4.1   Static Service Touchpoint Optimization

Based on the insight obtained from previous mentioned survey, the service touchpoint optimization is conducted. Current static touchpoint mainly contains treatment room space, treatment bed, treatment machine and doctors. Treatment room space affects patients psychology. The optimization should focus on ease psychology tension and pressure. The aspects of treatment room space optimization include light, layout and decorations. Treatment bed interacts with the patient through touching. The patient lying on the bed and the treatment bed acts as the role of supporting and fixing. Thus, the optimization of treatment bed should focus on safety, comfort and stability. The treatment machine optimization should be based on not reducing the treatment effect. On the premise of this, the psychology pressure should be reduced. The doctor provides more instructions and communicates better with the patient.

The space of the room creates the atmosphere of treatment. The atmosphere affects the patients psychology. The aim of treatment room optimization is to create positive feeling for the patient. The light in the room contain primary light, light for the machine to position the target zone and the assisting light. The primary light usually locates on the ceiling of the room. In traditional service model, the potential of primary light has not been fully exploited. In the proposed service model, the adaptive light system is applied. The color and the intensity of the light system is able be modify to meet the demand of different patients. The optimization of light system can provide different atmosphere to fit different psychology status of the patient. The illustration of the light system is shown in Fig. 6.

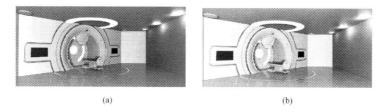

(a)   (b)

Fig. 6. Light system prototype

For the layout of the treatment room, the structure can also be optimized. The overall layout can be classified into three different zones including treatment zone, observation zone and patient zone. The design of these zones is that the patient zone and the observation zone connect to the treatment zone through different entrances, but the patient zone and the observation zone are separated. In addition, the observation zone should be hided from the public contact. From our insights, doctors suffer from heavy body work from going from room to room, the separation of patient room and separation room reduces the distance that doctors have to cover. Also, the privacy of the patient could also be protected if the doctor get in the treatment room through a different door. Since the doctor can observe some privacy of the patient in the observation room, the observation should be protected from public contact. In conclusion, the proposed layout satisfies the demand of patients and doctors. The service touchpoints are optimized and the efficiency of the operation improves. The proposed layout principle is presented in Fig. 7. For the decoration, the principle is to create the positive indication of feeling. Specifically, the wall of the treatment room should be placed with pictures and paintings. The picture and the painting should contain positive images and the treatment room should be placed with some green plant. The aim of decoration is to create the atmosphere of warmth and health.

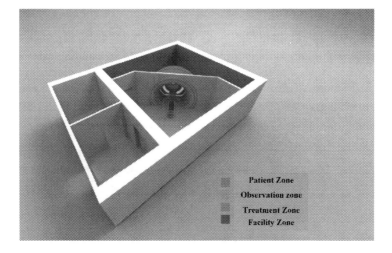

Fig. 7. Layout of the treatment room

The principle of designing the treatment bed should consider comfort, safety and stability. The main design relating to the comfort is that the treatment beds material should be carefully selected to protect the patients body temperature. And the treatment bed should be equipped with a automatic height changing facility to release the feeling of height. The safety design part is that the structure of the treatment bed should be designed as a semi surrounded one. This structure can protect the patient from falling from the bed and provide the patient with a feeling being protected. In addition, an emergency call button should be provided to the patient to call for the doctor. Whats more, the treatment bed could be designed as a mobile bed. This design can realize the customized treatment bed and prevent from cross infection. The stability part design is that the treatment bed should implements a smart control system. The control system can adjust the position of the bed more precisely compared to the artificial way. The prototype of the treatment bed in shown in Fig. 8.

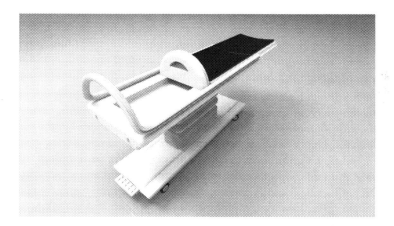

Fig. 8. Treatment bed prototype

The treatment machine surrounds the patient when the patient get treatment, thus creating an enclosure space. The principle of the treatment machine design is to reduce the pressure to the patient. The light inside the machine should be designed as relatively low. The rotation of the machine can cause the patient feel dizzy thus some protection method should be implemented. The machine should report the current status of the operation to inform the patient in order to release the pressure. In addition, the alarm light should be placed in some place invisible by the patient. The prototype of treatment machine is shown in Fig. 9.

The doctor should perform duties of instructing and conciliating the patients. The optimization contains in the aspects of informing every stage of treatment, explaining the phenomenon of current operation and answering questions of the patient. The communication between the doctor and the patient should not be negative way which the patient starts but the positive way, which is controlled by the doctor.

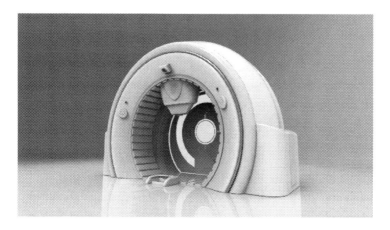

Fig. 9. Treatment machine prototype

4.2   New Service Touchpoint Application

New service touchpoint application is necessary to optimize the treatment experience and improve the treatment effect. Two potential additional service touchpoints are proposed to enhance the service model.

VR/AR system could be used in the proton therapy treatment. The system could be used in multiple ways to improve the efficiency of the treatment. First, the system could be used in the rehearsal phase of the treatment providing guidance in a vivid way. In addition, the VR device could be used when the patient is getting treatment. The dizzy feeling caused by rotation can be reduced.

Media playing system could be added in the treatment room to provide enhancement of service touchpoint through the hearing sense. The customized list of song could be played when the patient lying on the treatment bed. In this way the pressure could be reduced.

4.3   Process Optimization

Traditional service blueprint includes changing clothes, getting customized mold, entering the treatment room, fixing the position, getting treatment and ending. The traditional service blueprint has several disadvantages. First, the mold installation and position fixing take a long time for the doctor to cooperate. Also, the patient has to wait for a relatively long time to get treatment after last patients treatment is over. In addition, the doctor has to get into the room several times to operate and stays in the room for a long time. Thus the accumulated received radiation is large and impairs the doctors health. In conclusion, the doctor suffers from much frequent room entrance and long time staying, when the patient suffers from long time waiting.

We propose to moves the mold installation procedure from after entering the treatment room to before entering the room. This change is based on the layout optimization and the treatment bed optimization. One patient is installing the mold and get fixed on the movable treatment bed with the help of the doctor while the other patient is getting treatment in the treatment zone. When the other patient finishes the treatment, the patient in the patient zone can enter the treatment room. This mechanism saves the time for doctors staying in the treatment room. In addition, the doctor can be separated into two groups, with one group in the patient zone helping the mold installation and position fixing, the other group in the observation zone. The proposed process improves the operation efficiency and protects the doctors health.

5 Conclusion

The optimization of proton therapy treatment room was conducted on this paper. Based on the service design theory, the service touchpoint was extracted through viewing the proton therapy room as a service. In this way, the principle for designing the proton therapy treatment room was proposed. And the prototype of the treatment bed, treatment room and treatment machine was realized. Future direction could contain the design of the proton therapy hospital.

References

1. Smith, A.R.: Proton therapy. Phys. Med. Biol. **51**(13), R491–504 (2006)
2. Stickdorn, M., Schneider, J.: This is service design thinking: basics, tools, cases. Loan/open Shelves (2011)
3. Zomerdijk, L.G., Voss, C.A.: Service design for experience-centric services. J. Serv. Res. **13**(1), 67–82 (2010)
4. Patricio, L., Fisk, R.P., Cunha, J.F.E., Constantine, L.: Multilevel service design: from customer value constellation to service experience blueprint. J. Serv. Res. **14**(2), 180–200 (2011)

Log4Care: Unified Event Logging Service for Personalized Care

Haruhisa Maeda[1(✉)], Sachio Saiki[1], Masahide Nakamura[1], and Kiyoshi Yasuda[2]

[1] Graduate School of System Informatics, Kobe University, 1-1 Rokkodai, Nada, Kobe, Japan
haruhisa@ws.cs.kobe-u.ac.jp, sachio@carp.kobe-u.ac.jp, masa-n@cs.kobe-u.ac.jp
[2] Chiba Rosai Hospital, 2-16 Tatsumidai-higashi, Ichihara, Japan
fwkk5911@mb.infoweb.ne.jp

Abstract. Our research group has been studying person-centered care (PCC) support systems for elderly people living at home, using contextual information of individual users (called *user context*). PCC is an ideal care principle, which monitors and understands individual circumstances, and plans and executes optimized care. Since the current systems individually manage different user contexts, reusing the contexts across multiple systems is quite different. In this paper, we propose a new service that uniformly manages the user context, and allows external applications to retrieve necessary user contexts efficiently. More specifically, the proposed service gathers heterogeneous data from different systems, and standardizes the data with a common database with domain-independent attributes of when, who, whom, where, what, how, and why. Using a practical use case, we show how the proposed service efficiently manages user contexts.

Keywords: Smart health-care · Context-aware services
Person-centered care

1 Introduction

Japan is currently facing hyper-aging society, which causes many social issues. According to a report by the Government of Japan, the number of elderly people over the age of 65 is 34.59 million in 2016, which is 27.3% of the total population [2]. Due to the long average life and the low birthrate, the number of elderly over 65 is increasing in Japan and will reach 40% of the total in 2050. There are many challenges, including the lack of caregivers, the increasing cost of social security, and the decreasing labor force. In particular, the issues concerning dementia are extremely serious. Dementia is a general term for a decline in mental ability by an organic brain disease.

There are several kinds of dementia. Alzheimer's type dementia is a major disease, which comprises 60% of the total dementia. People with dementia usually

© Springer International Publishing AG, part of Springer Nature 2018
V. G. Duffy (Ed.): DHM 2018, LNCS 10917, pp. 466–477, 2018.
https://doi.org/10.1007/978-3-319-91397-1_37

have trouble in carrying out daily activities. For example, they struggle with memory loss, impair their reasoning and judgement, and wander and become lost. The number of people with dementia will reach 7 million in 2025, where one-fifth of five elderly people in Japan will suffer from dementia. It is thus important to take effective measures for people with dementia as soon as possible. However, the main cause of dementia is yet ambiguous. There is no silver bullet that can completely cure the dementia. Nowadays, the symptomatic treatment is taking a leading part for dementia care, including the music therapy. Reflecting these situations, Person-Centered Care (PCC), proposed by Tom Kitwood in the 1990s [3], is attracting a lot of attention. He said there are five psychological needs of people with dementia, inclusion, comfort, identity, attachment, and occupation. However, in order to cover these needs, a large amount of efforts is required for caregivers. Moreover, the caregivers must carefully observe people with dementia, and face every person for a long time. Therefore, it is difficult to achieve PCC at the nursing home, likewise it is almost impossible to do at home.

To achieve the principle of PCC at home, our research group has been studying PCC support systems using the virtual agent, IoT (Internet of Things), and cloud technologies. These systems include *Virtual Care Giver* [9] providing personalized communication and reminder service, the activity recognition system based on environmental sensing [6,7], and indoor positioning system using BLE beacons [4]. To achieve the PCC, these systems exploit *user contexts* [1], which refer to any situational or contextual information of individual users. For example, a user context may be where the user is, how the user is, what the user is doing, or so on.

A user context is typically derived from *event logs* collected within the system. For instance, user's current location can be obtained from the latest log of the indoor positioning system. The current condition of a user may be reasoned from dialogue records with the virtual agent. Thus, every PCC support system must collect event logs to manage the user contexts. To implement sophisticated home care, it is essential to *combine* heterogeneous user contexts. In the present PCC support systems, however, it is not easy to reuse the user contexts across different systems. This is because the event logs are separately managed within individual systems in their own data formats.

In this paper, we propose a new framework, which universally manages PCC-centric user contexts, by integrating heterogeneous event logs of heterogeneous PCC support systems. The framework also provides the user contexts in a domain-neutral way, in response to various queries from external services and applications. More specifically, we design and implement the following two components in this paper.

- **Log4Care:** Common database unifying heterogeneous event logs of PCC support systems
- **Care–API:** General-purpose API to retrieve user contexts from Log4Care.

To provide PCC for a person, it is essential to understand the detailed user contexts of the person, including their health conditions and mental states. The proposed Log4Care is carefully designed with a data schema that can store event logs essential for PCC. Specifically, we propose the data schema based on *6W1H perspectives*, where the heterogeneous event logs are standardized in what, who, whom, when, where, why, and how. On top of Log4Care, we deploy Care–APIs to allow external applications to insert the event logs in the Log4Care database, and to retrieve user contexts from the database. For this, we consider application-neutral design without assuming any specific applications, so that Care–API can be used for various purposes. A typical use-case is that a care application combines user contexts from different systems. A human caregiver checks the current status of the person under care.

In this paper, we also implement a prototype system that integrates our existing PCC support systems using Log4Care and Care–API. Through practical use cases, we show how the event logs are integrated from heterogeneous systems, and how the user contexts are retrieved across the different systems.

2   Preliminary

2.1   Elderly Care at Home

In Japan, along with the aging society, single households whose head is over 65 years old, is increasing. However, it is difficult to accept all elderly in medical facilities and carry out the care for them. On the other hand, there are a lot of elderly that prefer to receive care at their own home or their family's home rather than to receive at nursing home or care house. Against these backgrounds, in recent years, many attempts to care for elderly people at home have been made in various fields. Japanese Government is focusing on training human resources for home health care and promoting cooperation in the community. The general companies are starting to work hard on developing new services that relieve elderly of loneliness using a communication robot. These efforts aim to improve the quality of life (QoL) of the elderly.

2.2   User Context

User context refers to every information that indicates user's current situation in a certain system. The information includes "What is the user doing", "Where is the user?", and "What circumstances is the user in?". Additionally, user's preference is also a part of user context. In [1], an adaptive message notification service that utilizes user context is proposed. This service sends a context-aware and personalized message to a smartphone, based on user's current place, physical limitation, and so on. To provide useful information for the user, the service integrates various user contexts. Thus, to construct a service based on an individual person, considering the user contexts is essential.

2.3   PCC Supporting Service Using User Context

Our research group is extensively using the user contexts to implement PCC support systems at home. For example, the person-centered dialogue system with a virtual agent (VA) [9] obtains user contexts from speech communication. This system aims to provide daily counseling for elderly at home, even if human caregivers do not exist. VA asks elderly people about their body condition or whether they have taken the medicines on that day, and read their state from their reply. On the other hand, the ADL recognition system [5] manages user contexts from environmental sensor data. This system read the change of the value of sensors and BLE beacons, and detects user's activity by machine learning technology.

In this way, using the user contexts is essential for these PCC support systems. However, since these two systems manage the user contexts individually and have own formats of data, reusing the contexts across the two systems is quite difficult. More generally, each service acquires and manages the user context exclusively by itself, which is quite inefficient. Figure 1 shows the conventional architecture of PCC support systems. Each application obtains the user contexts from different data sources and utilizes them for PCC. In order to achieve more efficient development and deployment of PCC support systems, it is essential to establish a uniform framework dealing with user contexts for PCC.

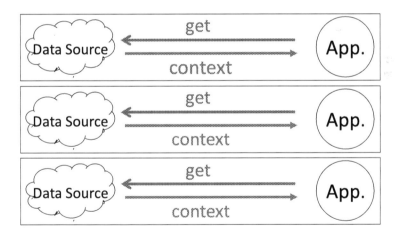

Fig. 1. The conventional architecture of PCC support systems

3   Proposed Methods

In this research, to share the information about users in PCC support systems efficiently, we propose a framework that integrates the data from other services and uniformly manages them.

3.1   Goal and Challenge

The goal of this paper is to propose and implement a framework that universally manages PCC-centric user contexts. The proposed service helps other applications to understand user's state in detail and make the care plan for individuals by analyzing the accumulated the user contexts. Figure 2 shows the system architecture of the proposed service. The challenges here are how to mediate heterogeneous data from different systems and what are specific properties for data logging in PCC. To share various user contexts from different data sources, the proposed service deploys a common database called log4care in the center of the architecture. The database manages heterogeneous types and formats of data used in PCC support service, in a standard data model. The user context dealt with in this research is not only human-centric, but also include PCC support service-centric information such as what kind of action was given to a specific user and what kind of effect was obtained as a result. In the present circumstances, each service exclusively manages such context information based on its own data format. This information is standardized to fit the data schema covering necessary items from the viewpoint of PCC, and stored in the common database. The standardized user contexts are exposed to external applications via general-purpose API, which accepts various queries. Thus, all the applications can easily query user contexts in a standard manner. The following subsections describe the two key components of the proposed service: The common database and the general-purpose API.

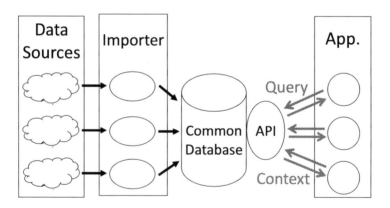

Fig. 2. The proposed system architecture

3.2   Log4Care: Common Database for Managing User Contexts for Person-Centered Care

User contexts from different data sources have their own semantics and formats. Thus, the challenge here is how to define a universal data schema that can accommodate such heterogeneous data within the common database. In this section, we decide how we to manage the user contexts from various systems.

[10] describes how to write a nursing care record in a caring field. The nursing care record describes a series of progress such as changes in the health condition of the user, contents of nursing care, living conditions and the like. By sharing the described information, there is the purpose of organizing nursing care systematically, reflecting it in future care plans, and providing better services to users. Nursing care records need to be written so that facts are accurate and understood by everyone, so it basically describes the events related to users from the 5W1H perspective (i.e., WHAT, WHO, WHERE, WHEN, WHY, and HOW). However, in this research, we handle not only the information about users' current health condition and their activities, but about what kind of care is done by the PCC support service and what happened as a result. Thus, we need a point of view to *whom* the service took care of.

In reference to the practical nursing record, we design the new data schema based on the *6W1H perspective* (i.e., WHAT, WHO, WHOM, WHERE, WHEN, WHY, and HOW). We empirically know that this perspective can cover most of the user contexts in a MECE (Mutually Exclusive and Collectively Exhaustive) fashion. Table 1 shows the 6W1H perspective that determines the data schema of the common database. From a viewpoint of PCC, the WHY and the HOW is especially important, because they construct a causal chain of activities explaining why the user is currently like that. The causal information is essential for making and reconsidering personalized care plan considering the reason. The database records time-series activities of a target user within PCC, from which various kinds of user contexts can be retrieved.

Table 1. User context from the 6W1H perspective

Perspective	The contents of information
The WHAT	An activity that a user (or a system) did within PCC
The WHO	The subject of the WHAT (a human user, or a system)
The WHOM	The object of the WHAT (a human user, or a system)
The WHERE	The location where the WHAT was done
The WHEN	The time when the WHAT was done
The WHY	The previous activities that motivated WHAT
The HOW	The description of the WHAT

3.3   Care–API: General-Purpose APIs on Top of the Data Model

We use API (Application Programming Interface) refer to the stored user contexts. We develop general-purpose APIs on top of the data model to access the database. These APIs are deployed as Web service that transmits and receives the data through HTTP protocol. There are two kinds of APIs that the proposed method provides. One is to convert the data from other PCC support services to fit the data schema of Log4Care, and insert the standardized data. The other is to accept multiple arguments from other service and search the stored contextual information using SQL. Thus, the external applications are able to obtain the user contexts using Care–APIs.

4   Prototype Development

In this paper, we develop the prototype based on the proposed method mentioned in Sect. 3. In particular, we construct the common database that handles PCC-centric user contexts from various PCC support services. Additionally, we deploy API to send and receive context information to the database from external applications and services. In the following, we discuss how to decide the data model and the details of the API.

4.1   Data Model

We construct the data model of Log4Care with 6W1H perspectives indicated in Sect. 3.2. Figure 3 shows the entity relationship diagram of Log4Care. The notation conforms to [11]. In Fig. 3, $+$——$\cdots$ means the parent-child relationships, $+$——$\in$ means reference relationships, and $+\bullet$——$\bullet+$ means derived relationships.

In this subsection, We explain about each entity. The data structure of *Log* entity which manages what happpens in PCC, is as follows.

```
    log_ID     : ID
   datetime    : The time when the event was done
    subject    : An user who was the subject of the event
    object     : An user who was the object of the event
   location    : The place where the event was done
     event     : The event name
description : The detailed explanation and user's state
   recorder    : An user who records the log
  rdatetime    : The time when the log was recorded
```

Among these, each event corresponds to the idea that *event* is "WHAT", *subject* is "WHO", *object* is "WHOM", *location* is "WHERE", *datetime* is "WHEN", *description* is "HOW". In addition, an entity of *Log* also includes the information on who recorded and when it was recorded. By doing this, when there was an error or shortage in the log and need to correct or append, the updated difference becomes easy to understand. On the other hands, an entity of *Reference* corresponds to the information included in the viewpoint of the remaining "WHY" out of 6W1H. For example, in [6], when the user replies to the question from the system, it can be said that the behavior of "answer" by the user was caused by the behavior of "question" of the system. An entity of *Reference* manages casual relation of two logs using each of *log_ID*, if the one was triggered by the other. By linking a log with its originating log, it is possible to grasp a series of actions of users when searching by API and obtain the detailed information about appearance and effectiveness of the care. An entity of *Agent* manages the users' own information. In this research, as a user, we assume two kinds, human and other system or application. If these two users are managed in the same entity, there is a lot of waste such as mutual occurrences of items that cannot be input. Therefore, we distinguish these two users as an entity of *Human* and an entity of *Systems*. An entity of *Event* and an entity of *Location* associates key id and the name and manages events and location respectively. Using relation database management system MySQL, we construct the common database Log4Care that has the above data model.

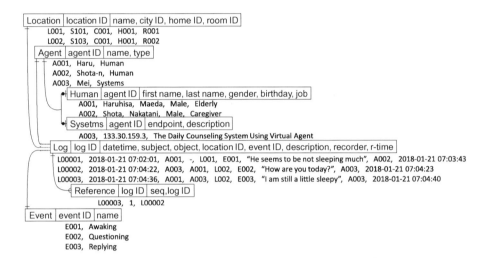

Fig. 3. The date model of log4care

4.2   The Development of API

To insert the user contents to Log4Care from external applications and to share the accumulated contexts efficiently, we develop Care–APIs indicated in Sect. 3.3 on the above data model. These APIs exchanges multiple types of data with external applications by using HTTP protocol. To develop these APIs, we utilize *MyBatis* [8] which is one of the O/RM (Object-Relational Mapper) and connects the database with the object-oriented language. Combining the object in Java and SQL statement allows to search the contexts precisely responding to various queries. The followings show examples of the proposed APIs:

- Log insertLog(id, datetime, subj, obj, location, event, description, recorder)
- Log[] getCasualLog(user, event)
- Log[] getLogByPeriod(user, since, until)
- Agent getAgent(event, location, since, until)
- Location getlocation(user, event)
- Event getEvent(user, location)
- String getDescription(user, event, since, until)

The insertlog() is to insert the data handled by each PCC support service into the common database Log4Care. This API accepts arguments and stores the data in an entity of *Log*. We here identify the *rdatetime* when the log is recorded and the time when the insertLog() is called. The getCasualLog() is to obtain the list of logs related to users using the user id (or the user name) and the event id (or the event name) as arguments. Similarly, the getLogByPeriod() is to acquire logs related to users and was done at the date and time that was sandwiched between since and until. That is, we can get information on what the users did in a certain period of time and what kind of state they were in. Additionally, we develop the getAgent(), the getLocation(), the getEvent(), and the getDescripton() to make a finer search.

Thus, Care–APIs are to insert the user contexts extracted from other systems to fit the data schema of Log4Care, and provide them It aims to facilitate the mutual use of various user contexts between different systems which were difficult under the present circumstances.

4.3   Development Environment

The development environment is as follows.

Development language : Java
Database   : MySQL 5.6.38
Web server   : Apache Tomcat 7.0.77
Web service framework : Apache Axis2 1.7.4

5   Use Case

To illustrate the effectiveness of the proposed service, we integrate the prototype into the conventional PCC support systems, and describe a practical use case scenario, showing how the user contexts from different heterogeneous systems are integrated and shared. In the scenario, we assume the following four actors as shown in Fig. 4. The description of each user is as follows.

- *Takeshi*: 78 years old man with mild dementia living alone.
- *Danny*: A home environment sensing system with sensors and beacons [7].
- *Greg*: A care execution service that triggers a PCC based on the situation.
- *Mei*: A communication chat-bot using Virtual Agent technology [9].

Danny is a service that detects the daily activities of a user based on the change of various sensor values and beacon information. Greg has the role of monitoring database log4care. When the information about is recorded by Danny, Greg gathers the related logs using Care–API and comprehends the state of Takeshi. Greg then instructs Mei to carry out the voice calling care depending on the state of Takeshi. Mei starts the care for Takeshi when triggered by Greg, and acquires what Takeshi reply using speech recognition and inserts the communication logs at that time into the common database. Through this use case,

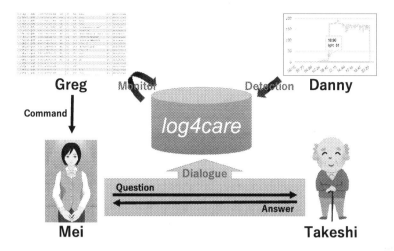

Fig. 4. Relationship diagram of the users in the use case

we confirm how these series of interactions are efficiently managed by the proposed architecture. The following table shows the timetable of the care scenario in the use case.

Table 2 describes the scenario in a timetable. In this scenario, first, Takeshi gets up on January 22. He then goes to a living room, and have breakfast. Dunny detects each activity by changing of the values of the environmental sensors and BLE beacons, and stored the information as the user contexts. Greg perceives that Takeshi's blood pressure shows comparatively high score recently, and instructs Mei to confirm whether Takeshi takes a medicine every day. Through the interaction with Takeshi, Mei asks him what he is eating for breakfast and make sure the medication of him. Mei then recognizes that there is a possibility that medication is not taking place on a daily basis based on Takeshi's reply, and encourage him to take a medicine the location of that. During the scenario, the three systems (Danny, Greg, and Mei) individually perform PCC-related events. In the proposed service, we standardize each event to adapt the data schema with 6W1H perspectives, and accumulate it in the common database.

Figure 5 shows the activities recorded in the common database. For instance, in (4) in Table 2, Danny detects the entering living room from the brightness of the living room turn on, based on the light sensor. This activity is described as data {time: "6:16", subject: "Dunny", object: "Takeshi", location: "Living room", activity: "Detecting", description: "Entering the living room"}. Similarly, the data is accumulated from the activities of Greg and Mei. For example, through the interaction between Takeshi and Mei, the contents of the conversation are also stored in the proposed database. Thus, we can see that the heterogeneous data from different systems are well accommodated within the proposed common database. Using the data, we obtain various contexts about Takeshi, which explain his physical or mental state in his daily living. For example, "Did Takeshi gets up on time on January 22?", "How much was his blood pressure on January 21?", "Where was Takeshi at 6 o'clock on January 22?" are included. Currently, we assume that basic contexts are covered by the proposed APIs, and that the application-specific contexts are defined and managed within individual applications.

Table 2. The timetable of the care scenario

Datetime	Event	Sequence
1/21 10:42	Mei: "Do you measure your blood pressure?"	(1)
1/21 10:43	Takeshi: "142 over 98"	(2)
⋮	⋮	⋮
1/22 06:15	Takeshi goes to the living room	(3)
1/22 06:16	Dunny detects Takeshi's entering to the living room	(4)
1/22 06:18	Takeshi start eating breakfast	(5)
1/22 06:19	Dunny detects Takeshi's starting breakfast	(6)
1/22 06:20	Greg instructs Mei to greet Takeshi	(7)
1/22 06:20	Mei: "Good Morning, What is your breakfast?"	(8)
1/22 06:20	Takeshi: "Some bread and coffee"	(9)
1/22 06:21	Mei: "Recently, your blood pressure is high. Do you take a medicine everyday?"	(10)
1/22 06:21	Takeshi: "Oh, I might forgot."	(11)
1/22 06:21	Mei: Don't skip your medicine. It is in the drawer of the kitchen"	(12)
1/22 06:21	Takeshi: "Thank you"	(13)

log_ID	datetime	subject	object	location	event	description	recorder	rdatetime
⋮	⋮	⋮				⋮	⋮	⋮
L0054	2018-01-18 10:42:49	Mei	Takeshi	Livingroom	Asking	"Do you meassure your blood pressure today?"	Mei	2018-1-18 10:42:55
L0055	2018-01-18 10:43:05	Takeshi	Mei	Livingroom	Replying	"142 over 98"	Mei	2018-1-18 10:43:11
⋮	⋮					⋮		⋮
L0081	2018-01-19 06:16:07	Danny	Takeshi	Livingroom	Detecting	Entering	Danny	2018-1-19 6:16:10
L0082	2018-01-19 06:19:37	Danny	Takeshi	Livingroom	Detecting	Starting to eat breakfast	Danny	2018-1-19 6:19:41
L0083	2018-01-19 06:20:04	Greg	Mei	Livingroom	Instructing	To speak	Greg	2018-1-19 6:20:08
L0084	2018-01-19 06:20:25	Mei	Takeshi	Livingroom	Asking	"Good Morning. What is your breakfast?"	Mei	2018-1-19 6:20:28
L0085	2018-01-19 06:20:45	Takeshi	Mei	Livingroom	Replying	"Some bread and coffee"	Mei	2018-1-19 6:20:49
L0086	2018-01-19 06:21:11	Mei	Takeshi	Livingroom	Asking	"Recently, your blood pressure is high. Do you take a medicine everyday?	Mei	2018-1-19 6:21:14
L0087	2018-01-19 06:21:25	Takeshi	Mei	Livingroom	Replying	"Oh, I might forgot"	Mei	2018-1-19 6:21:29
L0088	2018-01-19 06:21:38	Mei	Takeshi	Livingroom	Asking	"Don't skip your medicine. It is in the drawer of the kitchen"	Mei	2018-1-19 6:21:42
L0089	2018-01-19 06:21:50	Takeshi	Mei	Livingroom	Replying	"Thank you"	Mei	2018-1-19 6:21:55

Fig. 5. The activities recorded in the common database

6   Conclusion

To achieve efficient development of person-centered care (PCC) support systems for elderly people, we have proposed a framework that universally manages

PCC-centric user contexts. The proposed method manages heterogeneous data within a common database with 6W1H perspectives. It also provides standardized user context for external applications via general-purpose API. We also showed a practical use case to see how the proposed system efficiently shares the data among different systems. Our future work includes the implementation and evaluation of the proposed method.

Acknowledgements. This research was partially supported by the Japan Ministry of Education, Science, Sports, and Culture [Grant-in-Aid for Scientific Research (B) (16H02908, 15H02701), Grant-in-Aid for Scientific Research (A) (17H00731), Challenging Exploratory Research (15K12020)], and Tateishi Science and Technology Foundation (C) (No. 2177004).

References

1. Egami, K., Matsumoto, S., Nakamura, M.: A consideration of user context managing service for ubiquitous cloud. The Institute of Electronics: Information and Communication Engineers Technical report, vol. 111(255), pp. 85–90 (2011)
2. Government of Japan: Annual report on the aging society, June 2017. http://www.cao.go.jp/
3. Kitwood, T.: Dementia Reconsidered: the Person Comes First. Open University (1997)
4. Niu, L., Saiki, S., Nakamura, M.: Integrating environmental sensing and BLE-based location for improving ADL recognition. In: The 19th International Conference on Information Integration and Web-based Applications & Services (iiWAS 2017), December 2017
5. Niu, L., Saiki, S., Nakamura, M.: Recognizing ADLS of one person household based on non-intrusive environmental sensing. In: 18th IEEE/ACIS International Conference on Software Engineering, Artificial Intelligence, Networking and Parallel/Distributed Computing (SNPD 2017), Kanazawa, Japan, pp. 477–482. No. CFP1779A-USB. IEEE Computer Society and International Association for Computer and Information Science (ACIS), June 2017
6. Sakakibara, S., Saiki, S., Nakamura, M., Yasuda, K.: Generating personalized dialogue towards daily counseling system for home dementia care. In: Duffy, V.G. (ed.) DHM 2017. LNCS, vol. 10287, pp. 161–172. Springer, Cham (2017). https://doi.org/10.1007/978-3-319-58466-9_16
7. Tamamizu, K., Sakakibara, S., Saiki, S., Nakamura, M., Yasuda, K.: Capturing activities of daily living for elderly at home based on environment change and speech dialog. In: Duffy, V.G. (ed.) DHM 2017. LNCS, vol. 10287, pp. 183–194. Springer, Cham (2017). https://doi.org/10.1007/978-3-319-58466-9_18
8. The MyBatis team: Mybatis, December 2017. http://blog.mybatis.org/
9. Tokunaga, S., Tamamizu, K., Saiki, S., Nakamura, M., Yasuda, K.: VirtualCareGiver: personalized smart elderly care. Inter. J. Softw. Innov. **5**(1), 30–43 (2016)
10. Tomikawa, M.: How to write nursing record (in Japanese). Medical-friend Co. (2015)
11. Watanabe, K.: Introduction to data modeling for database designing (in Japanese). Nihon jitugyo (2003)

Whole-Body Robotic Simulator of the Elderly for Evaluating Robotic Devices for Nursing Care

Kunihiro Ogata, Yoshio Matsumoto$^{(\boxtimes)}$, Isamu Kajitani, Keiko Homma, and Yujin Wakita

Robot Innovation Research Center,
National Institute of Advanced Industrial Science and Technology,
Tsukuba Central 2, 1-1-1 Umezono, Tsukuba, Ibaraki 305-8568, Japan
yoshio.matsumoto@aist.go.jp

Abstract. This paper describes the development of whole-body robotic simulator of elderly person for evaluating robotics devices for nursing care. To improve the quality of life of the elderly persons, physical assistance, such as transfer assistance, movement assistance, toileting assistance is important. It is also important to reduce the workload of the care givers in the aging society. In recent years, assistive robotic devices for nursing care have been developed and commercialized for such purposes. However, such assistive robotic devices have not become popular in the care facilities yet. One of the reason is that it is still difficult to evaluate the effects of the devices on the care receivers and care givers. Especially it is necessary to quantitatively evaluate the effect of the devices on the human body in the viewpoint of safety and comfort. We have been developing a whole-body robotic system to simulate the pose and motion of elderly person. The purpose of the system is to realize quantitative physical evaluation of robotics devices for nursing care on the human body. Experimental results of preliminary evaluation of assistive robotic devices are also indicated.

Keywords: Humanoid robot · Human simulator · Evaluation
Robotic devices for nursing care

1 Introduction

1.1 Background

In Japan, more than 25% of the population is over the age of 65 [1]. The population of other advanced countries is also rapidly aging. In order to solve such a social problem by improving the QoL (Quality of Life) of the elderly persons, and reducing the workload of the care givers, the assistive robotic devices for nursing care have been intensively developed (e.g. [2,3]). However, these assistive robotic devices have not become common in the care facilities yet. One of the

V. G. Duffy (Ed.): DHM 2018, LNCS 10917, pp. 478–487, 2018.
https://doi.org/10.1007/978-3-319-91397-1_38

reasons is that the insufficient evaluation of the benefits. To clarify the benefit, it is necessary to quantify the physical load and effect on the human body, and the performance of the assistive robotic devices. However, measuring the effect of assistive robotic devices on the human body using an actual human in clinical experiments may present ethical and safety problems especially in the early stage of the development where safety issue is not guaranteed.

1.2   Related Research

Several kinds of human body models have been developed and utilized in order to evaluate the safety and performance of industrial products. Numerical human simulators in software such as OpenSim and DhaibaWorks [4] are utilized to simulate the physical interaction between a product and the human body in the area of product design and rehabilitation science. A forward dynamic simulation algorithm using a human body model with a skin model has been developed for evaluating robotic care devices [5]. However, since the human body has many DOFs with high redundancies, determining proper boundary conditions for the simulation is sometimes quite difficult. Therefore, physical human simulators or "dummy figures" were developed to evaluate some devices in the real world. The crash-test dummy with acceleration sensors embedded was commonly utilized by car manufacturers. Humanoid robots in general can be regarded as a simulator of human body, and there are also some trials to apply humanoid robots to the evaluation of assistive robotic devices. For example, the humanoid robot WABIAN-2R [6] was focused on performing human-like bipedal walking motion, and was applied to the evaluation of a walking support device. To evaluate the comfort and safety of the clothes and assistive devices, a humanoid dummy robot simulating the persons with spinal cord injury was developed [7,8]. This robot has the mechanism of the pectoral girdle, thus can realize the motion of propelling wheelchair.

There are another type of human body models which are utilized in order to promote medical education. Doll-like human figures have been commercialized and utilized in the classes for students to learn how to handle human body in the nursing care. Such human figures usually don't have high similarity to human body, and any sensors and actuators are not embedded inside the body. Moreover, a dummy humanoid robot simulating a patient have also been developed and used for medical education. A dental patient robot called "Hanako2 Showa" was developed jointly by Showa University and TMSUK [9]. This robot has a realistic appearance of a human, and it has been programmed to show certain behaviors to evaluate the clinical ability of medical students.

1.3   Purpose of This Study

As mentioned above, there is very limited types of physical human simulators that can be utilized for evaluating the assistive robotic devices, and it is still difficult to simulate the complex contacts and the deformation of shape in the computer simulation. In this study, a novel whole-body human simulator is to be developed using the robotic technologies in order to evaluate the mechanistic effects of assistive robotic devices such as transfer aids on the care receivers. It is assumed to be utilized to find the problems in the viewpoint of comfort and safety especially in the early stage of development of assistive robotic devices.

In this study, specifications regarding the function of the human simulator is determined as follows:

- It should be able to make arbitrary postures to fit various shapes of the assistive robotic devices.
- It should be able to move joints to simulate the behavior of a person.
- It does not need to have functions for the independent ambulation.

The whole-body robotic simulator is named the "Active Dummy Robot."

2   Design and Structure of Active Dummy Robot

2.1   Mechanical Design

The developed active dummy robot is shown in Fig. 1, and the mechanical specification of the active dummy robot is shown in Fig. 2. The height is 165[cm], and the total weight is approximately 50[kg], and its surface is covered with soft materials. The size, the shape and the weight of each body segment of the active dummy robot was determined based on the statistical data of Japanese males in 60s [12]. It has 28 active joints together with 22 passive joints. All active joints are driven by pneumatic cylindrical actuators and are controlled based on the position control and partially on the pressure control. Pneumatic actuators has been adopted by many robots recently allowing soft control which is compliant to environment. The compressed air of 6–7[atm] is supplied from an external air compressor.

As mentioned above, the active dummy robot was designed to make arbitrary postures to fit various shapes of the assistive robotic devices. Therefore the developed active dummy robot was tested to investigate its compliance to the assistive robotic devices. Figure 3 shows the examples of devices tested. It can be observed that the active dummy robot was able to fit assistive devices such as an electric wheelchair, a hoist sling, and a transfer assist device which supports human body from front side. However, there are other types of assistive devices which the active dummy robot is hard to fit due to the limited motion range of joint angles especially in the waist and in the shoulder. Since the pneumatic actuators together with angle sensors and air tubes are embedded inside the body, the mechanical design of some joints are simplified compared to that of the human body.

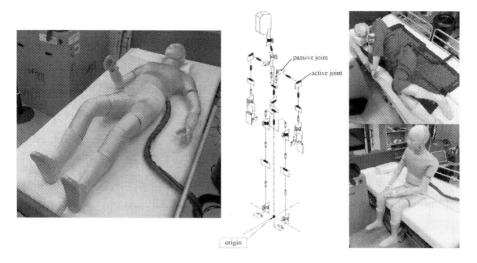

Fig. 1. Overview and schematic diagram of the active dummy robot.

Height	1650 [mm]
Weight	50 [kg]
Number of active joints	22
Number of passive joints	28

Fig. 2. Parameters of the active dummy robot.

2.2   Embedded Sensors

The active dummy robot has angle sensors (potentiometers) in all active and passive joints. Thus it has 50 potentiometers in total. By acquiring joint angle information in real time, posture of the active dummy robot can be captured. In order to measure the absolute orientation of the body origin with respect to the ground, 3-axis acceleration sensor is also utilized. Figure 4 indicates an example of measured posture when the active dummy robot is lying on a sling and sitting on assistive robotic devices. Without utilizing a real human body together with a large-sized optical motion capture system, it is possible to capture the whole-body posture easily.

3-axis force sensors to measure the perpendicular stress and 2-axis shear force are also attached to the body of the active dummy robot as shown in Fig. 5 (left). More specifically, three capacitance type force sensors are attached to the skin parts, at the sacral bone and the ischial bones of the buttock where pressure ulcers are prone to develop. Figure 5 (right) indicates the structure of the sensor. Each sensor head is 16[mm] in diameter and 1.5[mm] in thickness, and is capable of measuring 10[N] at a maximum. In order to increase the sensitivity, a small soft bulge is attached to the sensor head.

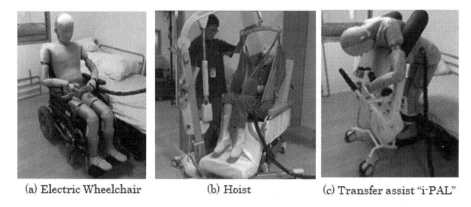

(a) Electric Wheelchair   (b) Hoist   (c) Transfer assist "i-PAL"

Fig. 3. Examples of postures to show the mechanical compliance of active dummy robot to various devices.

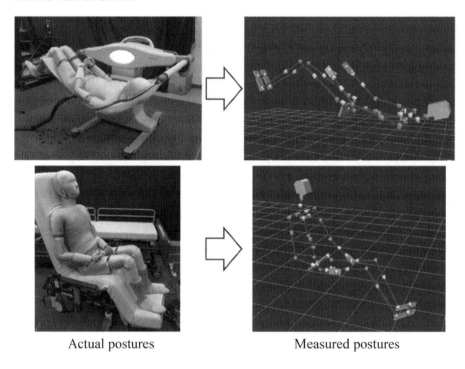

Actual postures   Measured postures

Fig. 4. Examples of pose measurement on assistive robotic devices "SASUKE" (upper) and "Resyone" (lower).

In addition to the embedded force sensors, a pressure mapping system "XSENSOR" is also utilized as shown in Fig. 1 (right). The ability of the system is to map the interface pressures between the assistive robotic device and the active dummy robot accurately in real time.

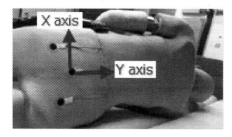

Fig. 5. Force sensors attached to the active dummy robot.

3   Experiments for Evaluating Robotic Care Device

The developed active dummy robot was utilized to show the feasibility of the concept. It was utilized to show the physical property the mechanism and the movement of devices, which are related with the comfort and safety. In this section, experimental results of preliminary evaluation of robotic care device "Resyone" by utilizing the active dummy robot are shown.

3.1   Robotic Care Device "Resyone"

The overview of the robotic care device "Resyone" utilized in the experiment is shown in Fig. 6. It is an assistive robotic device developed and commercialized by Panasonic Corporation based on a new concept which fuses an electric care bed with an electric reclining wheelchair. The half of the electric care bed detaches off to serve as the electric reclining wheelchair, thus allowing the user to easily transfer from bed to wheelchair without placing burden on the care giver or utilizing hoists.

Fig. 6. Transfer assist robot "Resyone".

3.2   Measurement of Displacement Due to Transformation

In this experiment, the active dummy robot was utilized to quantitatively show the displacement of the body which occurs on the bed during the transformation. The robotic simulator was utilized in a passive manner, i.e. no actuator was driven by air in the experiménts. Figure 7 shows the body motion of the active dummy robot on Resyone with different initial positions. After the reclining motion, the body usually moves to the lower position on the bed. This phenomena inevitably occurs due to the fact that the rotation center of the mattress and the human body do not coincide with each other. The human body is moved to the lower position by the gravity, and the displacement changes depending in the initial position. When the initial position was too low (in case (c), the leg part of the robotic simulator was fallen off the bed. After conducting the experiments multiple times, it was confirmed that the maximum displacement was 155[mm] and the minimum displacement was 65[mm]. It was also confirmed that the deviation of the measured displacement was quite small (less than 14[mm] on average) which means that it has high repeatability. This is an important factor of the active dummy robot which is difficult for human subjects to achieve.

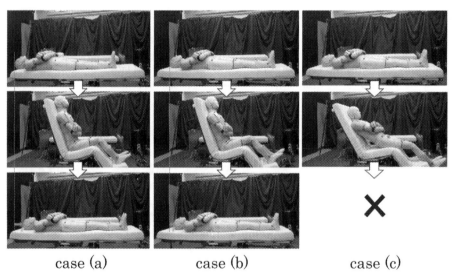

case (a)   case (b)   case (c)

Fig. 7. Displacement caused by reclining.

3.3   Measurement of Shear Force Due to Transformation

Figure 8 indicates the measured shear force while reclining mechanism was activated to adjust the angle of the bed to the upper position for approximately 10[s]. The output of the shear force changes depending on the size of the small soft bulge attached to the sensor head. It also depends on the cloth that the active dummy robot wears. Therefore it is necessary to carefully consider the measurement condition in the experiment.

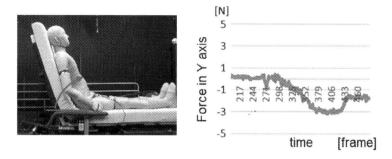

Fig. 8. Measured shear force due to reclining.

3.4   Generation of Dangerous Motions

By taking advantage of the moving function of the active dummy robot, it is possible to reproduce dangerous motion when using an assistive robotic devices. Figure 9 indicates examples of manually generated dangerous motion on Resyone. Since the active dummy robot has 22 active joints, it can generate complex whole-body motion repeatedly. It will be useful for evaluating the safety of the device by conducting the experiment multiple times with high repeatability.

3.5   Discussion

Through the preliminary experiments, the potential of the developed whole-body active dummy robot simulating the elderly was confirmed to be utilized for evaluating assistive robotic devices. The advantages of utilizing the active dummy robot are as follows:

– It has higher repeatability compared to the real human,
– It can keep arms and legs free of tension which is hard to achieve for the real human,
– There is no ethical issue in conducting experiment compared to the real human,
– There is no need to build virtual model of the assistive robotic device for computer simulation.

However the developed active dummy robot has limitations as follows:

– It is difficult to change the mechanical parameters of the body (hight, weight etc.),
– Some assistive devices requires larger and more complex motion especially in the waist and in the shoulder joints,
– Not only the forces on the surface but the internal forces are also important for safety evaluation which is hard to measure.

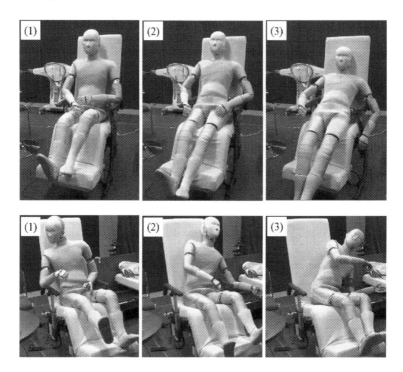

Fig. 9. Examples of dangerous motions on Resyone.

By considering these points, the potential usage of the active dummy robot would be as follows:

- To compare the performance of products from multiple manufacturers which have same or similar functions,
- To investigate the performance and safety of prototypes with mechanical modifications,
- To enhance the reality in the training of care by replaying dangerous behavior of the elderly and showing inappropriate usage.

There are actually newer version of Resyone with some modification. Due to the mechanical modification, the reclining motion pattern in the transformation is slightly changed, and the material of the mattress surface is changed to be smoother. To investigate and clarify the effects of such modification, the active dummy robot will be utilized in the near future.

4   Conclusions

We described the development of whole-body robotic simulator of elderly person for evaluating assistive robotics devices for nursing care. The developed robotic simulator was shown to be applicable to the quantitative evaluation of physical effects of the devices on the human body through preliminary experiments. As future works, we are planing to investigate the evaluation method using the active dummy robot for wider variety of assistive robotic devices for nursing care to show the feasibility of the developed system.

Acknowledgment. This research was supported by the Robotic Devices for Nursing Care Project of the Japan Agency for Medical Research and Development (AMED).

References

1. United Nations: World Population Prospects The 2012 Revision (2013). https://esa.un.org/unpd/wpp/publications/Files/WPP2012_HIGHLIGHTS.pdf
2. Panasonic. http://news.panasonic.com/global/topics/2014/26411.html
3. ROBOHELPER SASUKE, Muscle Cop. (in Japanese). http://robotcare.jp/?page_id=110
4. Mochimaru, M., Kouchi, M., Miyata, N., Tada, M., Yoshida, H., et al.: Dhaiba: Functional Human Models to Represent Variation of Shape, Motion and Subjective Assessment. SAE DHM, 2006-01-2345 (2006)
5. Yoshiyasu, Y., Ayusawa, K., Yoshida, E., Yoshio, M., Endo, Y.: Forward dynamics simulation of human figures on assistive devices using geometric skin deformation model. In: Proceedings of the Annual International Conference of the IEEE Engineering in Medicine and Biology Society (EMBC), pp. 2442–2445 (2015)
6. Omer, A.M.M., Kondo, H., Lim, H., Takanishi, A.: Development of walking support system based on dynamic simulation. In: Proceedings of the IEEE International Conference on Robotics and Biomimetics (Robio 2008), pp. 137–142 (2009)
7. Ogata, K., Kawamura, T., Ono, E., Nakayama, T., Matsuhira, N.: Upper body of dummy humanoid robot with exterior deformation mechanism for evaluation of assistive products and technologies. J. Robot. Mechatron. **28**(4), 600–608 (2016)
8. Ogata, K., Umino, T., Nakayama, T., Ono, E., Tsuji, T.: Dummy humanoid robot simulating several trunk postures and abdominal shapes-Report of element technologies. Adv. Robot. **31**(6), 303–310 (2017)
9. Official curriculum for dentistry by robot, rst in the world. More humanized Showa Hanako 2debut (2011). http://www.tmsuk.co.jp/topic/2011/06/detail15.tml
10. Niiyama, R., Nishikawa, S., Kuniyoshi, Y.: Athlete robot with applied human muscle activation patterns for bipedal running. In: IEEE-RAS International Conference on Humanoid Robots (Humanoids 2010), pp. 498–503 (2010)
11. Hosoda, K., Sakaguchi, Y., Takayama, H., Takuma, T.: Pneumatic-driven jumping robot with anthropomorphic muscular skeleton structure. Auton. Robot. **28**(3), 307–316 (2010)
12. Digital Human Laboratory, AIST. Japanese Body Dimension Data. https://www.dh.aist.go.jp/database/fbodyDB/

Definition of Strategies for the Reduction of Operational Inefficiencies in a Stroke Unit

Miguel Ortiz-Barrios[1], Dionicio Neira-Rodado[1], Genett Jiménez-Delgado[2(✉)], Sally McClean[3], and Osvaldo Lara[4]

[1] Department of Industrial Management, Agroindustry and Operations,
Universidad de La Costa CUC, Barranquilla, Colombia
{mortiz1,dneira1}@cuc.edu.co

[2] Department of Engineering in Industrial Processes, Engineering Faculty,
Institución Universitaria ITSA, Soledad, Atlántico, Colombia
gjimenez@itsa.edu.co

[3] School of Computing, University of Ulster, Coleraine,
Co. Londonderry BT52 1SA, UK
si.mcclean@ulster.ac.uk

[4] Department of Neurology, Clinica de la Costa, Barranquilla, Colombia
osvaldo.laras@gmail.com

Abstract. Stroke disease is the second common cause of death in the world and is then of particular concern to policy-makers. Additionally, it is a meaningful problem leaving a high number of people with severe disabilities, placing a heavy burden on society and incurring prolonged length of stay. In this respect, it is necessary to develop analytic models providing information on care system behavior in order to detect potential operational inefficiencies along the stroke patient journey and subsequently design improvement strategies. However, modeling stroke care is highly complex due to the multiple clinical outcomes and different pathways. Therefore, this paper presents an integrated approach between Discrete-event Simulation (DES) and Markov models so that integrated planning of healthcare services relating to stroke care and the evaluation of potential improvement scenarios can be facilitated, made more logically robust and easy to understand. First, a stroke care system from Colombia was characterized by identifying the exogenous and endogenous variables of the process. Afterward, an input analysis was conducted to define the probability distributions of the aforementioned variables. Then, both DES and Markov models were designed and validated to provide deeper analysis of the entire patient journey. Finally, the possible adoption of thrombolytic treatment on patients with stroke disease was assessed based on the proposed approaches within this paper. The results evidenced that the length of stay (LOS) decreased by 12,89% and the mortality ratio was diminished by 21,52%. Evaluation of treatment cost per patient is also carried out.

Keywords: Discrete-Event Simulation (DES) · Healthcare modelling
Markov model · Stroke

© Springer International Publishing AG, part of Springer Nature 2018
V. G. Duffy (Ed.): DHM 2018, LNCS 10917, pp. 488–501, 2018.
https://doi.org/10.1007/978-3-319-91397-1_39

1   Introduction

Stroke disease represents a heavy burden on society because it leads to high costs to the health and social care services, high costs to the economy alongside prolonged periods of stay in clinics, hospitals, and care homes. In response to this, costing models have been designed taking into account the periods of stay of patients and their journey through the clinical services required for their recovery; different patient dispositions have also been considered including, a normal return to daily routine, referral to special care at the patient's own home or a specialized nursing home and even death where the modelling tools cover the path of patients from admission to exit from the health and social care systems.

Stroke is considered the second cause of death and disability in the world [1]. According to WHO (World Health Organization), stroke causes the death of 5.7 million people per year. Of every 100 people who suffer a stroke, ten die immediately, 15 die in the first year and 8 in the second year [2]. In particular, stroke is known as the main cause of disability in the United Kingdom, becoming a huge concern for public admin- istrators, who report high costs for their treatment. In the United Kingdom alone, the total cost of cerebrovascular diseases has been estimated at around 9 billion euros per year [3], of which 50% is represented by direct costs of care, including hospitalization, external consultation, medication costs and home care. In this sense, 27% of the total costs are given by indirect costs and the rest by indirect costs to the economy due to premature death and disability. It is also estimated that 25% of post-stroke patients (patients who have suffered at least one stroke) enter a care institution [4]. Additionally, long-term nursing care adds costs to health services [5].

Colombia is also no stranger to this problem and reports stroke as the third cause of death and one of the most representative in functional disability. 28% of the deaths presented in this country is due to Stroke [6]. In addition, the mortality rate for this type of diseases is 150.2 per 1000 inhabitants. Although the scenario is quite worrisome, it should be noted that the WHO foresees that by 2030, deaths from cerebrovascular diseases will amount to 23.3 million [7].

All such considerations have led to the development of different studies aimed at determining the main causes of the cost overruns and death rates previously experienced. Among them, the London Protocol mentions that among the most common failures related to damage to health of the patient with stroke are latent failures (actions or omis- sions that occur during the process of health care by members of the processes of support or administrative) which translates to a lack of good administration of the processes and operations assigned to the care pathway of these patients [8].

The main causes of these latent failures are linked to a series of operational ineffi- ciencies such as: insufficient number of personnel compared with the user demand, inadequate shift pattern, non-availability of equipment or lack of maintenance, fatigue due to work overload of under-provisioned care personnel, poor policies or procedures for the replacement of incapacitated personnel and absence of a health care process from the beginning of the consultation until exit from the care center. For all of the above, the following research question was posed: What operational strategies can be implemented in the process of caring for stroke patients to reduce their mortality rate, latent failures, and associated operational costs.

The next step, then, is to design and evaluate strategies that reduce operational inefficiencies, to diminish the high costs involved in the care of patients with stroke. The present project proposed the construction of a phase-type simulation model of the attention process in the aforementioned pathway. For this, first a data collection of the process was carried out, then, an input analysis took place. Subsequently, the model was built and validated. Finally, improvement strategies were designed and evaluated through an output analysis, based on a phase-type model [9].

2   Strategies to Reduce Operational Inefficiencies in Stroke Units: A Brief Literature Review

Analytic models have previously been developed for stroke services [10, 11]. For example for stroke patients, a three-compartment approach (short stay, medium stay, long stay) was used in [12] to estimate the number of patients in any state and their lengths-of-stay. [9, 13–15] have generalized this to Markov models, based on the Coxian phase-type distributions, to help capacity planning within a stroke department. In addition, [9, 16] have developed analytic cost models and applied them to a stroke service to assess the cost-effectiveness of the department.

In recent years, the use of discrete event simulation (DES) to support healthcare economic evaluation has become increasingly common [17–19]. [20] modeled bowel cancer services using DES to explore costs and health outcomes resulting from changes in the service. [21] used DES to assess different treatments from a health economic perspective for osteoporosis in post-menopausal woman.

Healthcare facilities, such as stroke units, are known for their complexity and models are required for such diverse services, with different management structures and funding streams. Also, many diseases are highly complex with heterogeneous outcomes and multiple strategies for treatment, therapy, and care. Such factors contribute to the fact that most researchers choose DES as their preferred technique for health economic evaluation [22]. These models are commonly used in economic evaluation of healthcare to compare strategies and provide solutions that produce health benefits and cost-effective strategies, in a transparent way that is intuitive for the healthcare provider [23].

A phase-type modeling approach can be utilized to underpin a DES framework to facilitate better management of the specific elements of patient pathways using measures such as clinical outcomes, patient quality of life, and cost. There is a need to assess whether existing services are cost-effective across the whole system and if new interventions can increase efficiency [24–26]. As well as tracking outcomes and risks, we can predict the length-of-stay (LOS) and costs for individuals in different components of the system (e.g. accident and emergency department, hospital in-patient, patient own home or nursing home), thus providing resource managers and clinical staff with useful feedback about the decisions they make.

In this study, an analysis of the care process was carried out in an intensive care unit for patients with stroke, with the identification of the exogenous and endogenous variables of the process. Then, after gathering data from the process, a computational simulation model was designed and validated that allowed the analysis of the behavior of the system for the identification of operational inefficiencies and the design of improvement strategies.

3 Proposed Methodology

For the correct modeling of stroke care systems, it is important to consider the number and diversity of pathways along the entire patient journey as well as the multilayered dynamic influences that may affect the health outcomes. Therefore, it is highly relevant to reach a sufficient level of correspondence between the real-world and simulated systems in terms of functionality, structure, and behavior [27, 28]. Given the nature of stroke care systems and healthcare in general, it is then worth searching for global improvement strategies instead of reaching local progress [29]. In order to give accurate answers regarding the cause of process inefficiencies, assist clinical decision-making and allocate resources effectively, a 5-step methodology has been proposed (refer to Fig. 1). This approach has been developed with the foresight to be applied in practical clinical scenarios. This is even more useful upon considering the scant evidence base relating to the implementation of both DES and Markov models [29].

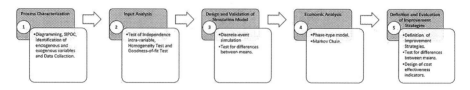

Fig. 1. Methodological approach for the stroke care modeling and the subsequent definition of improvement strategies.

- **Step 1 (Process characterization):** Here, the healthcare managers and stakeholders are asked to provide information on the different stages (e.g. Emergency Department, Hospitalization Unit) and states of the stroke care system. Afterward, the exogenous/ endogenous variables and cost parameters of the process are identified to enable us to provide a complete representation of the real system. Then, the data regarding the above-mentioned variables and parameters should be properly collected from the hospital information sources. To this regard, SIPOC (Supplier, Input, Process, Output, and Customer) and flow diagrams are widely suggested to provide a conceptual model of the system under analysis [30, 31]. The resulting model will be later considered for the suitable development of both DES and Markov models.
- **Step 2 (Input analysis):** Once the Step 1 is complete, it is important to initially investigate the presence of potential outliers for better debugging the data. Now, the next step is to carry out a test of independence (intra-variable) in order to evaluate whether the data distribution is random. This will underpin the uncertainty analysis

as extensively discussed in [32]. Then, a heterogeneity analysis should be performed in order to identify potential sub-groups of data. In this regard, statistical techniques such as box-and-whiskers plot, Kruskal-Wallis and log-rank can be implemented. If the data are concluded to be heterogeneous, each sub-group must be modeled as a separate parallel pipeline; otherwise, only one probability distribution is enough to represent the dataset. Afterwards, a goodness-of-fit test is conducted to determine whether a statistical model adequately fits the data and subsequently estimate the distribution parameters that should be incorporated into the DES model.

– **Step 3 (Design and validation of the simulation model):** A DES software (Arena 14.5 ®) is used to provide a virtual representation of the real-world system. Additionally, it facilitates user engagement by animating the resources, stages and patient flows associated with stroke care. To validate the model, it is first necessary to define the key performance indicators and simulation run length. Then, 10 runs are performed to calculate the sample size that will be used to determine whether the simulated model is statistically equivalent to the stroke care system under analysis. Herein, if the p-value is higher than alpha level (0.01), the model is concluded to be realistic and useful for predictions. Otherwise, it should be reviewed and corrected to ensure appropriateness and usability.

– **Step 4 (Economic analysis):** When analyzing the administrative and medical strategies that can be implemented for reducing the inefficiencies of stroke care systems, it is important to consider the treatment costs and potential hard savings. In this regard, phase-type models, a type of Hidden Markov Model (HMM), are decided to be here applied since their ability to predict individual behaviors, determine future resource needs and costs and provide a good representation of patient's progression [13]. In phase-type models, both absorbing $(S_1, S_2, \ldots, S_r)$/transient states $(S_1, S_2, \ldots, S_t)$ and the associated costs must be defined. On the other hand, transition and absorption probabilities should be clearly determined (based on the reported literature and information provided by the healthcare managers) and assumed to be unchanged over time so that Markovian property can be fully satisfied. Afterwards, the one-step transition matrix P is built (refer to Eq. 1) and describes the probability p_{ij} of being in a state $j(S_j)$ the next day considering an initial state $i(S_i)$ today. Then, an n-step $(k = 0, 1, \ldots, n)$ transition matrix $\{x_n, n = 0, 1, 2, \ldots\}$ containing the long-term probabilities (refer to Eq. 2) is computed. This matrix denotes the probability of reaching an absorbing state $j(S_j)$ in the long term given an initial state $i(S_i)$ today. After this, considering the *canonical form* of the transition matrix (refer to Eq. 3), the fundamental matrix N is obtained for the absorbing Markov model (refer to Eq. 4). Here, Q is an t-by-t matrix, I is an r-by-r identity matrix, 0 is an r-by-r zero matrix and R is a nonzero t-by-r matrix.

$$P = \begin{array}{c} \\ s_1 \\ s_2 \\ \vdots \\ s_r \end{array} \overset{\displaystyle s_1\ s_2\ \cdots\ s_r}{\begin{bmatrix} p_{11} & p_{12} & \cdots & p_{1r} \\ p_{21} & p_{22} & \cdots & p_{2r} \\ \vdots & \vdots & \ddots & \vdots \\ p_{r1} & p_{r2} & \cdots & p_{rr} \end{bmatrix}} \tag{1}$$

$$p_{ij}^n = P(x_{n+k} = j | x_k = i) \text{ for n } \geq 0 \text{ and states } i, j \tag{2}$$

$$P = \cfrac{TR \quad ABS}{\begin{matrix} TR \\ ABS \end{matrix} \begin{bmatrix} Q & R \\ 0 & I \end{bmatrix}} \tag{3}$$

$$N = I + Q + Q^2 + \ldots \tag{4}$$

- **Step 5 (Definition and evaluation of improvement strategies):** There is an increasing need to design and pretest potential interventions on stroke care systems so that service effectiveness across the whole system can be meaningfully augmented. For this purpose, improvement strategies are defined with the aid of clinicians and healthcare managers in order to ensure that the proposed scenarios are realistic and can be implemented without modifying existing constraints (e.g. legal restrictions and budget availability). The scenarios are then modeled and simulated in Arena 14.5 ® software. Similarly to the Step 3, 10 runs are carried out to determine the sample size that will be used to compare the current stroke care system with each scenario in terms of different performance metrics (previously defined by the stakeholders). If the p-value is lower than alpha level (0.01), the proposed strategy is cost-effective and provides a better process behavior. Otherwise, it is deemed as non-significant and should not be then implemented.

4 An Illustrative Example: Modeling the Stroke Unit

4.1 Process Characterization

Considering the above-mentioned methodology, an analytic model was created to describe the patient journey from admission to the absorbing states (discharge to home or death). Particularly, the stroke care system (refer to Fig. 2) was divided into different pathways (pipelines) providing a panoramic view of the patient flows. Our model was based on a 3-year prospective dataset extracted from the User Information System (UIS) and comprising of all the patients admitted to a local clinic located in Colombia between 1 April 2014 and 1 April 2017 with a diagnosis of stroke. UIS is a database that was designed for registering clinical records of patients, scheduling appointments and monitoring patient treatment response.

Patients are women and men between the ages of 2 and 104 years old. In the aforementioned period, there were 85.6% (n = 561) who were diagnosed with unspecified cerebrovascular disease, 11.5% (n = 75) with after-effects of cerebrovascular disease and 2.9% (n = 19) with cerebral hemorrhage. Stroke patient care in this clinic is provided by a stroke care unit where patient outcomes can be improved by diminishing preventable complications of a stroke and achieving independence in activities of daily living [33]. In order to cost the whole patient journey, administrative staff extracted information from the Financial Information System (FIS) regarding the expenses for rehabilitation, recovery and intensive care. On the other hand, the modelers identified the following

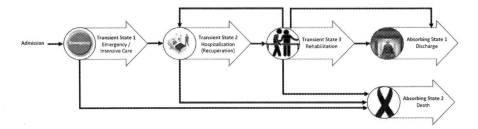

Fig. 2. Stroke patient journey from admission to absorbing states

process variables to be included in the simulation model: Time between arrivals (for each type of diagnosis), length of stay (for each type of diagnosis) and the daily number of admissions (discrete variable).

4.2 Input Analysis

After collecting data, a statistical auto-correlation test was first carried out to determine whether the identified process variables were random. A summary of these tests is described in Table 1. In this case, both variables were concluded to be independent since the p-values were higher than the alpha level (0.01).

Table 1. P-values derived from the randomness tests

Process variable	P-value
Time between arrivals	0.999074
Length of stay	0.405

Once the intra-dependence analysis was completed, a heterogeneity test was performed for each dataset in order to identify sub-groups of data (refer to Table 2). Particularly, an Analysis of Variance (ANOVA) detected that the *time between arrivals* should be modeled in accordance with the type of diagnosis since the p-value (0) is lower than the alpha level. Whilst, *length of stay* was found to be homogeneous since the observed p-value (0.914) provided evidence to accept the null hypothesis.

Table 2. ANOVA results for homogeneity assumption

Process variable	F-statistic	P-value
Time between arrivals	34.69	0
Length of stay	0.09	0.914

Given the randomness of the variables, probability distributions should be therefore identified through Goodness-of-fit tests. The chi-squared test ($\chi^2 = 11.3$, d. f. = 5, p-value = 0.0464) provided support for the exponential assumption of *time between arrivals (unspecified cerebrovascular disease)*. For *time between arrivals (after-effects of cerebrovascular disease)*, the chi-squared test ($\chi^2 = 5.01$, d. f. = 4, p-value = 0.297) provided good evidence for the lognormal assumption. Regarding *time between arrivals (cerebral hemorrhage)*, the Beta fit was concluded through the Kolmogorov-Smirnov (K-S) test (Z = 0.208, p-value > 0.15). On the other hand, the *length of stay* was confirmed to be log-normally distributed ($\chi^2 = 9.09$, d. f. = 4, p-value = 0.0617). The mathematical expressions to be used to represent the process variables in the simulation model are enlisted in Table 3.

Table 3. Probability expressions representing the process variables

Process variable	Mathematical expression
Time between arrivals (unspecified cerebrovascular disease)	0.5 + EXPO(2.03) days
Time between arrivals (after-effects of cerebrovascular disease)	0.5 + LOGN(16.8, 34) days
Time between arrivals (cerebral hemorrhage)	5 + 151 * BETA(0.467, 0.864) days
Length of stay	−0.001 + LOGN(11.5, 17.9) days

4.3 Design and Validation of the Simulation Model

A DES model was developed to provide a virtual representation of the stroke care system under analysis (refer to Fig. 3). To ensure the reliability of the simulation results, we ran the model for a time period of 1086 days with 24 h per day. In addition, 10 replications were performed to estimate the required sample size for properly describing the system variability. On the other hand, the model was programmed to be started with no patients in the system. Then, results in terms of the number of admissions per replication period, were collected and used to validate the hypothesis ($H_o: \mu = 652\ admissions |$ $H_a: \mu \neq 652\ admissions$). In this respect, a 1-sample Z test was performed with the aid of Minitab 17 ® software in order to establish whether the simulation model differs significantly from a specific value derived from the real-world system. A p-value = 0.036 proves that the simulated system is statistically comparable to the stroke care system under analysis. Thus, it can be used for further analysis, diagnosis, and prediction (pretest improvement scenarios).

With these considerations in mind, we assessed the resulting mortality rate in the current system (20.8%) which is represented by $\mu = 45$ dead patients and $\sigma = 3.97$. These values are considered as very high compared to the world death rate (0.42%) [34]. Furthermore, the average length of stay for stroke patients is 10.86 days with a $\sigma = 0.52$ days. These results suggested that we should proceed to design and pretest improvement scenarios addressing the aforementioned problems.

4.4 Economic Analysis

It is clearly functional to model the stroke care system as a Markov chain where treatment costs and length of stay can be deemed for patients with stroke. Particularly, the proposed model has two absorbing states and three transitory stages (refer to Fig. 2). In addition,

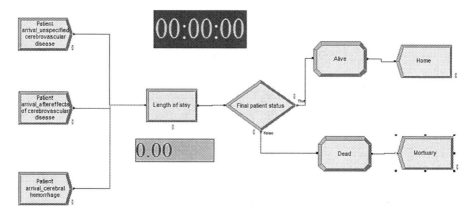

Fig. 3. Simulation model for the stroke care system

it will be assumed that these probabilities do not change over time so that the Markovian property can be fully satisfied.

The states will be named and numbered as shown below:

0: ER-Intensive Care
1: Recovery
2: Rehabilitation
3: Discharge
4: Death

Once the process states were defined and numbered, the one-step transition matrix was then built by using Eq. 1. All the possible values of p_{ij} are described in Fig. 4.

$$\begin{bmatrix} 0.40 & 0.55 & 0.00 & 0.00 & 0.05 \\ 0.05 & 0.85 & 0.05 & 0.04 & 0.01 \\ 0.00 & 0.00 & 0.97 & 0.03 & 0.00 \\ 0.00 & 0.00 & 0.00 & 1.00 & 0.00 \\ 0.00 & 0.00 & 0.00 & 0.00 & 1.00 \end{bmatrix}$$

Fig. 4. One-step transition matrix for a stroke care system under analysis

Figure 4 shows that $p_{10} = 0.05$, denoting the probability of being today in state 1 (hospitalization) and the next day in state 0 (Urgency/Intensive care). Similarly, it can be found that $p_{23} = 0.03$ is the probability of reaching the state 3 (discharge) after an initial state 2 (rehabilitation) today. These data were extracted from interviews with medical personnel and existing data in the literature [9, 35].

Considering the aforementioned facts, this model can be categorized as an absorbing Markov chain where it is possible to estimate the long-term probability of both discharge and death. On the other hand, if the associated costs of each stage are known, it is possible to estimate the average value-added cost per patient. The associated costs of each transitory state can be observed in Table 4. On the other hand, the matrix containing the long-term probabilities was created (refer to Fig. 5).

Table 4. Daily costs for transitory states

Transitory state	Daily cost (US$)
Emergency room/Intensive care	289.65
Recovery	770.26
Rehabilitation	14.53

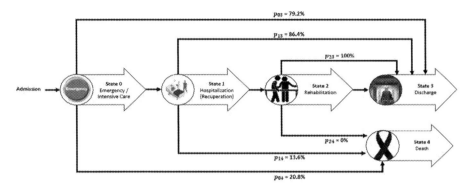

Fig. 5. Long-term absorption probabilities from state i to state j

In accordance with Fig. 4, it can be concluded that a person who is in the Emergency room due to stroke (status 0) has 79.2% of probabilities to survive (discharge-state 3) and die with 20.8%. Afterwards, the fundamental matrix is obtained (refer to Table 5).

Table 5. Fundamental matrix for the stroke care system under analysis

State i	State j		
	0	1	2
0	2.40	8.80	14.67
1	0.80	9.60	16.0
2	0	0	33.33

The N matrix shows the number of transitions (days) that a patient spends in each transitory state of the system. If a patient is in the Emergency room, the average stay will be 2.4 days in this area and 8.8 days in hospitalization. The total average length of stay is then 11.2 days. Additionally, the patient will spend 14.67 days (on average) in rehabilitation. Taking into account the daily costs of each state (refer to Table 4), it can be concluded that the average cost per patient is US$7656.82.

4.5   Definition and Evaluation of Improvement Strategies

Despite DES models provide a means to pre-test changes in healthcare systems before implementation in an effective manner, little work has been done to assess improvement strategies [36]. In this respect, the present study focuses on validating the cost-effectiveness of administering thrombolysis to stroke patients. Thrombolysis is the standard of care for patients with acute ischemic stroke within 4.5 h after symptom start [37]. Since their potential to reduce mortality rates and treatment costs, it has been proposed by healthcare managers to be proved in both DES and Markov models.

From an HMM perspective, a one-step transition matrix (refer to Fig. 6) was built by considering that all patients receive rt-PA treatment (thrombolysis).

$$
\begin{bmatrix}
0.30 & 0.67 & 0.00 & 0.00 & 0.02 \\
0.03 & 0.85 & 0.05 & 0.05 & 0.01 \\
0.00 & 0.00 & 0.97 & 0.03 & 0.00 \\
0.00 & 0.00 & 0.00 & 1.00 & 0.00 \\
0.00 & 0.00 & 0.00 & 0.00 & 1.00
\end{bmatrix}
$$

Fig. 6.   One-step transition matrix for stroke care system with the implementation of rt-PA

It can be observed, that one-step transition probabilities changed as a result of applying the rt-PA. Additionally, the absorption probabilities were subsequently modified (refer to Table 6) as well as the fundamental matrix of the process (refer to Table 7).

Table 6.   Long-term absorption probabilities for a stroke care process with thrombolysis

State i	State j	
	3	4
0	0.836	0.164
1	0.867	0.133
2	1	0

Table 7.   Fundamental matrix considering rt-PA treatment

State i	State j		
	0	1	2
0	1.76	7.90	12.51
1	0.35	8.25	12.97
2	0	0	28.57

According to the information described in Tables 6 and 7, it can be concluded that the average length of stay in the hospital can be reduced to 9.66 days and the rehabilitation can be diminished to 12.51 days. Similarly, the probability to survive the stroke (discharge) would be 83.6%, which is higher compared to the performance obtained without rt-PA treatment (79.2%). This is also reflected by the fact that patients are exposed to minor sequels, which provides a better life expectancy. Therefore, the treatment cost per patient receiving the rt-PA will be US$6776.57. However, this value does not include the cost of the rt-PA vials (US$2625). The mean total cost per patient is then US$9401.57. This denotes that the total cost when considering thrombolysis is greater compared to the current system. A similar finding was illustrated in [38]. However, the authors conclude that life expectancy is higher in patients receiving rt-PA.

On the other hand, when analyzing the effects of thrombolysis from a DES perspective, the simulation evidenced that the process performance derived from the proposed scenario would be significantly better compared to the current behavior as evidenced above. Specifically, it was found that the *number of dead patients* would be meaningfully reduced by 21.52% ($t = 6.24$; d.f. $= 23$; p-value $= 0$). Besides, the *average length of stay* would be significantly diminished by 12.89% ($t = 4.91$; d.f. $= 17$; p-value $= 0$).

5   Conclusions and Future Work

Stroke care systems are difficult to model due to the wide variety of pathways and tasks that may derive from the patient health status. Hence, it is highly required that the modelers work closely with the healthcare managers and medical staff aiming at to ensuring that the designed models are statistically equivalent to the real system so that improvement strategies can be effectively deployed from theory to practice.

An aspect of concern is the availability of high-quality data. Both Markov and DES models will be as detailed as possible depending on the available information. Of course, this affects the robustness of the decisions. Therefore, it is necessary to count on the engagement of the healthcare institutions (e.g. hospitals and clinics) involved in the study with the foresight to developing complete healthcare models.

The proposed approach facilitates the creation of integrated models representing the required processes for appropriate stroke care. However, it can be extended to deploy more detailed models providing further analysis on the process stages. For future work, it is intended to include specific data on ER, hospitalization and intensive care units with the goal of designing and assessing more detailed improvement strategies.

The intervention here described evidenced the use of Markov and DES models in a stroke care unit. Based on the results, it can be concluded that thrombolysis provides a reduced mortality rate (21.52%) and length of stay (12.89%). This is reflected in better life expectancy and diminished after-effects for patients which would alleviate the burden faced when addressing this kind of disease.

References

1. Hernández, B.J., Benjumea, P., Tuso, L.: Indicadores del desempeño clínico fisioterapéutico en el manejo hospitalario temprano del accidente cerebrovascular (ACV). Revista Ciencias de la Salud **11**(1), 7–34 (2013)
2. Rosamond, W., Flegal, K., Friday, G., Furie, K., Go, A., Greenlund, K., Haase, N., Ho, M., Howard, V., Kissela, B., Kittner, S.: Heart disease and stroke statistics—2007 update. Circulation **115**(5), e69–e171 (2007)
3. Saka, Ö., McGuire, A., Wolfe, C.: Cost of stroke in the United Kingdom. Age Age. **38**(1), 27 32 (2009)

4. Sackley, C., Pound, K.: Setting priorities for a discharge plan for stroke patients entering nursing home care. Clin. Rehabil. **16**(8), 859–866 (2002)
5. Sundberg, G., Bagust, A., Terént, A.: A model for costs of stroke services. Health Policy **63**(1), 81–94 (2003)
6. Hoffmann, A., Chockalingam, P., Balint, O.H., Dadashev, A., Dimopoulos, K., Engel, R., Schmid, M., Schwerzmann, M., Gatzoulis, M.A., Mulder, B., Oechslin, E.: Cerebrovascular accidents in adult patients with congenital heart disease. Heart **96**(15), 1223–1226 (2010)
7. Santulli, G.: Epidemiology of cardiovascular disease in the 21st century: updated numbers and updated facts. J. Cardiovasc. Dis. **1**(1), 1–2 (2013)
8. Verlaan, P.: London convention and London protocol. Int. J. Mar. Coast. L. **26**, 185 (2011)
9. McClean, S., Gillespie, J., Garg, L., Barton, M., Scotney, B., Kullerton, K.: Using phase-type models to cost stroke patient care across health, social and community services. Eur. J. Oper. Res. **236**(1), 190–199 (2014)
10. Fackrell, M.: Modelling healthcare systems with phase-type distributions. Health Care Manag. Sci. **12**(1), 11–26 (2009)
11. Gunal, M.M., Pidd, M.: Discrete event simulation for performance modelling in health care: a review of the literature. J. Simul. **4**(1), 42–51 (2010)
12. Vasilakis, C., Marshall, A.H.: Modelling nationwide hospital length of stay: opening the black box. J. Oper. Res. Soc. **56**, 862–869 (2005)
13. McClean, S.I., Barton, M., Garg, L., Fullerton, K.: Combining Markov models and discrete event simulation to plan stroke patient care. Trans. Model. Comput. Sci. **21**(4) (2011). Article 25
14. Garg, L., McClean, S., Barton, M., Meenan, B.J., Fullerton, K.: Intelligent patient management and resource planning for complex, heterogeneous, and stochastic healthcare systems. IEEE Trans. Syst. Man Cybern. A Syst. Hum. **42**(6), 1332–1345 (2012)
15. Barton, M., McClean, S., Gillespie, J., Garg, L., Wilson, D., Fullerton, K.: Is it beneficial to increase the provision of thrombolysis- a discrete event simulation model. QJM Int. J. Med. **105**(7), 665–673 (2012)
16. Gillespie, J., McClean, S., Scotney, B., Garg, L., Barton, M., Fullerton, K.: Costing hospital resources for stroke patients using phase-type models. Health Care Manag. Sci. **14**(3), 279–291 (2011)
17. Caro, J.J., Briggs, A.H., Siebert, U., Kuntz, K.M.: Modeling good research practices-overview: a report of the ISPOR-SMDM modeling good research practices task force-1. Value Health **15**(4), 796–803 (2012)
18. Pari, A.A., Simon, J., Wolstenholme, J., Geddes, J.R., Goodwin, G.M.: Economic evaluations in bipolar disorder: a systematic review and critical appraisal. Bipolar Disord. **16**(6), 557–582 (2014)
19. van Karnebeek, C.D.M., Mohammadi, T., Tsao, N., Sinclair, G., Sirrs, S., Stockler, S., Marra, C.: Health economic evaluation of plasma oxysterol screening in the diagnosis of Niemann-Pick Type C disease among intellectually disabled using discrete event simulation. Mol. Genet. Metab. **114**(2), 226–232 (2015)
20. Pilgrim, H., et al.: The costs and benefits of bowel cancer service developments using discrete event simulation. J. Oper. Res. Soc. **60**(10), 1305–1314 (2009)
21. Stevenson, M.D., Brazier, J.E., Calvert, N.W., Lloyd-Jones, M., Oakley, J.E., Kanis, J.E.: Description of an individual patient methodology for calculating the cost-effectiveness of treatments for osteoporosis in woman. J. Oper. Res. Soc. **56**(2), 214–221 (2005)
22. Caro, J., Moller, J., Getsios, D.: Discrete event simulation: the preferred technique for health economic evaluations? Value Health **13**(8), 1056–1060 (2010)
23. Neil, N.: Transparently, with validation. Med. Decis. Mak. **32**(5), 660–662 (2012)

24. Ortiz Barrios, M.A., Escorcia Caballero, J., Sánchez Sánchez, F.: A methodology for the creation of integrated service networks in outpatient internal medicine. In: Bravo, J., Hervás, R., Villarreal, V. (eds.) AmIHEALTH 2015. LNCS, vol. 9456, pp. 247–257. Springer, Cham (2015). https://doi.org/10.1007/978-3-319-26508-7_24

25. Ortiz Barrios, M., Felizzola Jiménez, H.: Reduction of average lead time in outpatient service of obstetrics through six sigma methodology. In: Bravo, J., Hervás, R., Villarreal, V. (eds.) AmIHEALTH 2015. LNCS, vol. 9456, pp. 293–302. Springer, Cham (2015). https://doi.org/10.1007/978-3-319-26508-7_29

26. Barrios, M.A.O., Jiménez, H.F.: Use of six sigma methodology to reduce appointment lead-time in obstetrics outpatient department. J. Med. Syst. **40**(10), 220 (2016)

27. Martischnig, A.: Modeling Healthcare Systems (2009)

28. Coronado Hernandez, J.R., Viloria, A., Gaitán Angulo, M., Mercado Caruso, N.N., Arias Perez, J.E.: Analysis of Probability of Dropout, Continuation and Graduation through Markovian Chains of University Students in Bolivar, Colombia (2016)

29. Eldabi, T., Paul, R.J., Young, T.: Simulation modelling in healthcare: reviewing legacies and investigating futures. J. Oper. Res. Soc. **58**(2), 262–270 (2007)

30. Shankar, R.: Process Improvement Using Six Sigma: A DMAIC Guide. ASQ Quality Press, Milwaukee (2009)

31. Hamza, S.E.A.: Design process improvement through the DMAIC Six Sigma approach: a case study from the Middle East. Int. J. Six Sigma Competitive Adv. **4**(1), 35–47 (2008)

32. Briggs, A.H., Weinstein, M.C., Fenwick, E.A., Karnon, J., Sculpher, M.J., Paltiel, A.D.: Model parameter estimation and uncertainty: a report of the ISPOR-SMDM modeling good research practices task force-6. Value Health **15**(6), 835–842 (2012)

33. Langhorne, P., Pollock, A.: What are the components of effective stroke unit care? Age Age. **31**(5), 365–371 (2002)

34. Feigin, V.L., Krishnamurthi, R.V., Parmar, P., Norrving, B., Mensah, G.A., Bennett, D.A., Barker-Collo, S., Moran, A.E., Sacco, R.L., Truelsen, T., Davis, S.: Update on the global burden of ischemic and hemorrhagic stroke in 1990-2013: the GBD 2013 study. Neuroepidemiology **45**(3), 161–176 (2015)

35. Gordon, A.S., Marshall, A.H., Zenga, M.: Predicting elderly patient length of stay in hospital and community care using a series of conditional Coxian phase-type distributions, further conditioned on a survival tree. Health Care Manag. Sci., 1–12 (2017)

36. Mohiuddin, S., Busby, J., Savović, J., Richards, A., Northstone, K., Hollingworth, W., Donovan, J.L., Vasilakis, C.: Patient flow within UK emergency departments: a systematic review of the use of computer simulation modelling methods. BMJ Open **7**(5), e015007 (2017)

37. Dorn, F., Prothmann, S., Patzig, M., Lockau, H., Kabbasch, C., Nikoubashman, O., Liebig, T., Zimmer, C., Brückmann, H., Wiesmann, M., Stetefeld, H.: Stent retriever thrombectomy in patients who are ineligible for intravenous thrombolysis: a multicenter retrospective observational study. Am. J. Neuroradiol. **37**(2), 305–310 (2016)

38. Collazos, M.M., Gutiérrez, Á.M., Londoño, D., Bayona, H., Herrán, S., Enrique, G.: Stroke in Colombia: a cost-effectiveness study Artículo original. Acta Neurol. Colomb. **24**(4), 158–173 (2008)

A Proposal for Combining Ultrasound, Magnetic Resonance Imaging and Force Feedback Technology, During the Pregnancy, to Physically Feel the Fetus

Jorge Roberto Lopes dos Santos[1,2(✉)], Heron Werner[3],
Alberto Raposo[1], Jan Hurtado[1], Vinicius Arcoverde[1], and Gerson Ribeiro[1]

[1] Pontifícia Universidade Católica do Rio de Janeiro, Rio de Janeiro, Brazil
jorge.lopes@puc-rio.br, {abraposo,hurtado}@tecgraf.puc-rio.br,
vinicius.p.arcoverde@gmail.com,
gerson.ribeiro.md@gmail.com
[2] Instituto Nacional de Tecnologia - INT, Rio de Janeiro, Brazil
jorge.lopes@int.gov.br
[3] Clínica de Diagnóstico por Imagem - CDPI, Rio de Janeiro, Brazil
heronwerner@hotmail.com

Abstract. Evolutions in image-scanning technology have led to vast improvements in the fetal assessment. Ultrasound (US) is the main technology for fetal evaluation. Magnetic resonance imaging (MRI) is generally used when US cannot provide high-quality images. This paper presents an interactive bidirectional actuated human-machine interface proposal developed by the combination of a haptic device system (force-feedback technology) and a non-invasive medical image technology.

Keywords: Fetus · Ultrasound · MRI · Haptics · Interaction

1 Introduction

Advances in image-scanning technology have led to vast improvements in the fetal evaluation. The use of magnetic resonance imaging (MRI) as an adjunct to ultrasound (US) in fetal imaging is becoming widespread in clinical practice.

This paper presents an interactive bidirectional actuated human-machine interface proposal developed by the combination of a haptic device system (force-feedback technology) and a non-invasive medical image technology as the MRI and/or US employed by a pregnant patient actively interacting with a virtual 3D model of her own fetus during the pregnancy.

This proposal is part of the fetus 3D, a project being developed in Brazil, by the collaboration of radiological sector of a private clinic with research university laboratories, where several technologies as virtual reality – VR, 3D printers, and more recently haptic 3D devices are combined with non-invasive image technologies for diagnostic purposes in fetal medicine as ultrasound, MRI and in some special cases, computerized tomography scanners.

For this proposal, the haptic device adopted was the touch 3D stylus system from the American company 3D Systems. In order to include the virtual human reference, a simple cursor was included on the interface screen. The 3D models of the fetuses tested on the experiment were modeled through the superimposition of the several slices obtained from the US and MRI equipment where the patient was scanned.

Once the 3D model was obtained, the virtual characteristics and the womb ambience were then created (coloring, shades, positioning, and other characteristics). Some physical responses were also developed using Open Haptics library and Unity 3D. These responses include the heart beating, skin pressure, textures and the collision of the cursor with the fetus.

Some tests with US and MRI exams were done using our proposal. We developed the cases considering the pathologies as our areas of interest to have a better visualization and interaction within it.

The structure of this document is described as follows. In Sect. 2, we describe some related work relevant for our proposal. Since our proposal consists of two main steps (reconstruction and environment set up), in Sect. 3 we describe in detail how the 3D model is obtained, and in Sect. 4 how to set up the environment considering the visualization and the haptic device interaction. Our test cases are presented and described in Sect. 5, considering a medical point of view and the processing of the data. In Sect. 6, we present our conclusions and possible future works.

2   Related Work

There are many applications of three-dimensional imaging techniques in fetal medicine. In general, two types of examinations are used in order to obtain images of the uterine cavity during pregnancy: US and MRI. For example, Werner et al. proposed in [1], the generation of 3D printed models for medical analysis. In the case of Virtual Reality (VR) there exists a large amount of methods which include different types of interaction [2]. In [3], dos Santos proposed an immersive fetal 3D visualization using the mentioned acquisition techniques. Combining these techniques is helpful to have a more accurate morphological analysis of the fetus. Werner et al. uses in [4] a correlation between them to detect typical lesions in the fetal nervous system, and in [5], the authors proposed a 3D model reconstruction using the same acquisition techniques to detect a malformation.

Haptics is a relatively new research field which is growing rapidly. The involved brain processes are partially understood and new sensory illusions were discovered recently [6]. In the field of medicine, several applications using this kind of technology were proposed such as clinical skill acquisition [7, 8]. Haptics technology was also used in fetal medicine to allow mothers to interact with the virtual representation of the fetus. Prattichizzo et al. proposed in [9] an application to allow this interaction using ultrasound imaging. They process the ultrasound exam, reconstruct a 3D surface (mesh) and then interact with the fetus using the haptic device. Severi et al. proposed the usage of this proposal to decrease maternal anxiety and salivary cortisol [10]. In fact, the last two works are the main references for our proposal.

3 Fetus 3D Model Reconstruction

Our proposal allows the user to interact with the surface of a virtual fetus generated from medical image acquisition, i.e. US and MRI. Generating a surface from this kind of data involves several topics of image processing and geometry processing, which are areas of computer science. The fidelity of the generated surface regarding the real fetus surface will define a better interaction with the user. For this reason, we opted to combine the mentioned acquisition techniques and obtain a more robust representation. In this section we will explain how we generate the fetus surface, represented by a polygon mesh (triangular mesh), following a semiautomatic process.

We receive as input two volumes (a set of continuous slices) with intensity values generated by US and MRI imaging. These values represent a physical response depending on the acquisition technique. In our case, we obtained these volumes in DICOM or NRRD file formats, which are file formats supported by most of MRI and US machines. We read these types of files using the loader and DICOM module of 3D Slicer [11], which is an open source software for medical image processing and visualization. In fact, we use this software for the entire model reconstruction pipeline. It is important to say that 3D Slicer was developed using the Insight Segmentation and Registration Toolkit (ITK) [12], a library used in several works of the medical area. Both platforms are part of the Kitware company.

Images generated using MRI are usually well defined without the presence of undesired noise. In counterpart, US images present speckle noise which is a challenging problem for the segmentation. In our proposal, we can perform an anisotropic volume denoising algorithm included in the filtering module of 3D Slicer (e.g. curvature anisotropic diffusion) to preserve details while removing noise.

To reduce the domain of the segmentation, obtaining a less complex input, we can define a region of interest delimited by a 3D bounding box, such that the final result is also restricted to it.

In the case of MRI images, it is possible to recognize different structures defined by the voxel intensity values. For example, the skin and the bones of the fetus have different values. So, it is important to segment all components that form the fetus body and differentiate them from external structures like the placenta, due that the image comes with mother's body components.

In the case of US images, it is harder to recognize internal structures but it is possible to recognize the external shape of the fetus. We are interested in binarizing the volume, such that the shape is preserved and non-fetus components are excluded.

In both cases, to perform the segmentation, we use thresholding tools/removal and manual/assisted selections. This task is usually addressed by a designer with experience in medical imaging because this expertise is helpful to obtain a segmentation with high fidelity.

Once we have a segmented image (binarized image), where we can recognize the surface of the fetus, we reconstruct a polygon mesh (triangular mesh) using it. In specific, we use the marching cubes algorithm [13] to generate the mesh, and the λ-μ Taubin smoothing algorithm [14] to remove the noise of the reconstruction avoiding mesh shrinkage. These algorithms are implemented in the model maker module of 3D Slicer.

Then, for each image acquisition technique, we have a rough mesh that needs to be processed. Using mesh processing algorithms, we can obtain a better one which is closer to the ideal fetus surface. For these tasks we used MeshLab [15], which is an open source software for processing and editing 3D triangular meshes. As a first step of this subprocess, we perform a remeshing over the initial mesh, preserving the shape and generating a new regular mesh (regular triangles) which will be helpful to avoid distortion in the subsequent algorithms. Since in the reconstruction step we generate a rough mesh with probably millions of vertices, we perform a mesh decimation to reduce the complexity and avoid heavy processes in the next steps. It is important to take care in the decimation criteria because we do not want to remove important details for the later analysis. As the last step, we can smooth the mesh again in an interactive manner to obtain a better representation for visualization.

Finally, we have to align the clean meshes (one from US and other from MRI) and merge them to obtain the final result. We use the align tool of MeshLab which supports

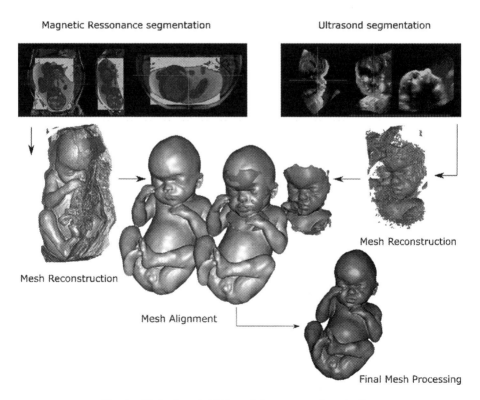

Fig. 1. 3D fetal model (28 weeks) reconstruction pipeline.

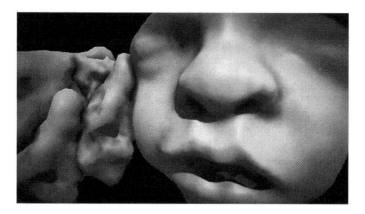

Fig. 2. Example of normal fetal face visualization using the proposed rendering features (27 weeks of gestation).

manual and automatic alignment using reference points. Both alignment techniques allow us to find the linear transformation that better fits one mesh to other. Once we have the two meshes aligned, we manually remove regions without coherence and merge close vertices generating a point cloud formed by the set of vertices of both meshes. Then we compute a mesh based on the point cloud and start a mesh processing pipeline similar to the previous one. This resulting mesh is then used in the virtual environment.

In the case that we have only one type of image acquisition we can avoid the alignment step and just use a single reconstructed mesh.

Figure 1 summarizes the 3D model reconstruction pipeline of a fetus.

4   Virtual Environment and Interaction

In this section we will explain how we set up the environment and how the user will interact with the virtual fetus representation, visualizing and touching it.

Once we have a 3D polygon mesh representation of the fetus surface, we preprocess it before including it in the environment. The first thing we do, is an adaptive decimation, such that we highly reduce the number of polygons while maintaining a high number of them in the regions of interest. Otherwise, the visualization and collision detection for haptic device, will require higher computational time that can disrupt the interaction (user's comfort with the application). These regions of interest that have a higher number of polygons are, for example, surface areas with a fetus pathology which need a more accurate and soft interaction than others (higher sensibility and likelihood possible in the touch). We perform this adaptive decimation using Blender [16].

After this, we have a model with less number of triangles which is easy to handle but has a really bad resolution for visualization. For this reason, using the original model, we generate a normal map (represented as a texture) for the decimated mesh. This normal map results from the projection of the normals of the original mesh onto the decimated mesh (normal baking). So, using this map, we can calculate the normals for each fragment in the rendering pipeline (normal mapping or bump mapping). With this technique, it is possible to visualize a low resolution mesh with high level of detail.

We set up the virtual environment using Unity 3D [17] due to its large amount of tools for visualization and interaction. We were aiming to generate empathy to the user through the connection with the virtual fetus. In this way, it is important to make the experience as realistic as possible. We know that the user maybe has no idea of how the fetus looks like inside the womb, and the nearest experience to this one, is the visualization of the volume implemented in ultrasound machines. So, the latter is a good reference for us to replicate it. We use a lighting scheme composed by three fill lights such that their positions and intensities simulates the mentioned volume rendering effect. Also, we added some rendering features such as: antialiasing to smooth the edges, ambient occlusion to give notion of ambient light, shadowing projection to help the user to identify where is the haptic cursor, and color grading to reach the same color as in the mentioned volume renderings (Fig. 2).

In addition to a static visualization, modern US machines are able to generate 4D images that give sense of movement. Trying to simulate this movement we introduced animations that are similar to the movements showed when using US machines. With this feature, the visualization is closer to the mentioned experience.

Another important thing that we need to set up, is the haptic device interaction. We use the Touch 3D Stylus as haptic device and a Unity plugin [18] that allows us to have access to the Open Haptics library [19]. This library allows us to manipulate some information and functionalities of the device. The main feature that we have to manage is the detection of collisions. When the fetus is virtually touched, the device must produce a force that gives touching sensation to the user in the real world. In addition to the collision, it is possible to define different materials and textures that give to the user different sensations generated by the vibration of the device. The surface should be smooth with a certain level of friction, avoiding a slippery sensation, and sufficiently soft to simulate the skin. Also, when the fetus skin is pressed the haptic device should generate a little damping.

Different areas of the fetal body can have different stiffness properties. For example, the forehead or other areas with prominent bones should be more rigid than other ones like the cheeks or the lips. So, we implemented a stiffness mapping to allow us to define the stiffness value of a point in the surface. We use this map to dynamically update the global properties of the object and simulate the definition of local properties (for each vertex of the mesh). This mapping is introduced as a texture, in a similar way to the normal mapping.

Another important feature is that the touching sensation should be synchronized with the visualization. So, if we press a soft region of the fetus and we feel that we are deforming it, the mesh used in the visualization should be deformed too. To obtain this effect, we developed a simple mesh deformation algorithm that reads the same local stiffness values used by the haptic device.

In addition to the mentioned features, we implemented an effect to simulate the fetus heart beating, such that when the user is touching an area near to the heart, the device starts the beating effect.

Figures 3 and 4 show examples of interactions with a fetus using the haptic device.

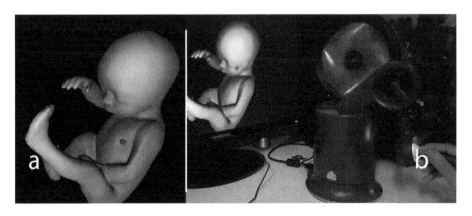

Fig. 3. Example of an interaction using a complete fetus model (28 weeks). (a) Screen visualization. (b) User interaction.

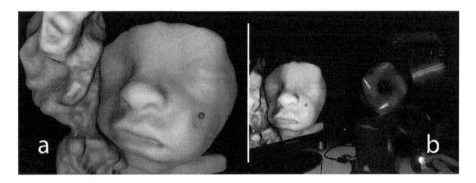

Fig. 4. Example of an interaction using a fetal face model (27 weeks). (a) Screen visualization. (b) User interaction.

5   Test Cases

We performed tests with real data acquired from exams done to patients. The test cases contain exams with healthy fetuses and fetuses presenting pathology. For all cases, in Fig. 5 we show the visualization of each one and the user cursor virtually touching it. Each of these cases will be explained in this section with a medical point of view and the respective data processing using our proposal.

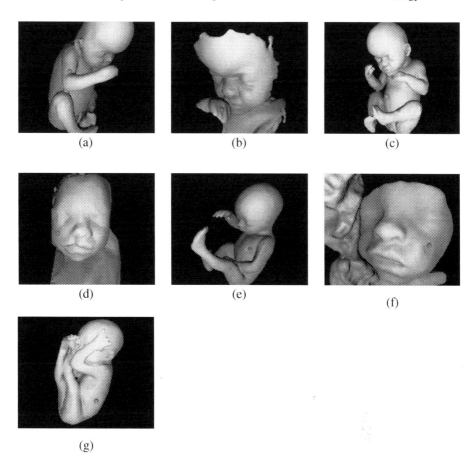

Fig. 5. Visualization of all test cases. (a) Apert syndrome – MRI. (b) Apert syndrome – US. (c) Apert syndrome – MRI + US. (d) Cleft lip – US. (e) Normal fetus – MRI. (f) Normal fetal face – US. (g) Normal fetal body – MRI.

5.1   MRI (Apert Syndrome)

Prenatal US and MRI at 28 weeks of gestation allowed the identification of all phenotype of Apert syndrome. The 3D visualization allowed better understanding of fetal abnormalities by parents and medical team.

For this case, it was generated a MRI volume which has a good quality and the fetal shape is well defined. The main challenging problem in this case is that we have to preserve the details of the region containing the pathology. For this reason, we take special care when segmenting and processing the hands and feet. We performed the segmentation using two different layers, one for the region that contains the pathology and the other for the rest of the body. So, the segmentation process is executed independently over each differentiated region. The mesh processing steps are treated as in most cases considering the adaptive decimation for the interest regions (See Fig. 5a).

5.2 US (Apert Syndrome)

Three-dimensional (3D) US allows better assessment of face and extremities surface abnormalities and can be a useful adjunct to 2D US for parental counseling in Apert syndrome cases.

In this case we received as input an US volume with less speckle noise that allows us to use thresholding algorithms without too much of manual processing. As in much of ultrasound volumes, applying a simple thresholding produces floating fragments and holes. To address this problem, we use small component removal and hole filling. Then the rest of the process is executed normally (See Fig. 5b).

5.3 US Combined with MRI (Apert Syndrome)

3D virtual models from US and MRI scan data allows better understanding of fetal malformations.

Here we used the final result of the previous two cases, executing an automatic mesh alignment algorithm two match the corresponding shapes. Then we refine manually this alignment such that the meshes are as close as possible. MRI gives us the shape of the fetus body and ultrasound gives us a better approximation of the fetus face shape. With the point cloud generated by both meshes we reconstruct a new mesh which is processed like the others, removing non-aligned regions (See Fig. 5c).

5.4 US (Cleft Lip)

3D reconstruction of the fetal face from US allows an immersive real environment, improving the understanding of fetal congenital anomalies such as cleft lip by the parents and the medical team.

Here we received as input an US volume. As in a previous case the volume does not have too much speckle noise and the face of the fetus is relatively clear. Using a thresholding scheme gives us a good initial result with detailed enhancing of the region containing the pathology (See Fig. 5e).

5.5 MRI (Normal Fetal Body)

MRI provides additional information about fetal anatomy and conditions in situations where US cannot provide high-quality images.

In this case we received as input a MRI volume with high quality. The main difficulty is that the fetus is too close to the pouch, due that external structures can disrupt the segmentation. Several manual crops were done to define our target volume. We decided to segment it in independent parts and then merge all of them to generate the final model. The mesh processing steps are executed normally (See Fig. 5f).

5.6   US (Fetal Face)

US is currently the primary method for fetal assessment during pregnancy because it is patient friendly, useful and considered to be safe.

The input in this case was an US volume with more speckle noise than the other US cases. For this reason, we previously filtered the volume to have a better definition of the fetus shape without too much noise. Then we treated it as in the other ultrasound cases, with the difference that the fetus does not have a region of interest (See Fig. 5g).

5.7   MRI (Blind Pregnant Patient)

Maternal–fetal attachment (MFA) is defined as the extension in which women engage in behaviors that represent an affiliation and interaction with their unborn child. The ability to view a fetus as an independent being at an earlier point in pregnancy likely contributes to the MFA developing at a much earlier point in fetal development. Force-feedback technology would be very important to the assessment of MFA in blind pregnant women.

In this case the input was a MRI volume without too much artefacts. Due that the fetus was static during the exam, the borders of the volume are well defined but the contrast of the voxel values turns more difficult the segmentation. The other processes are executed normally (See Fig. 5h).

6   Conclusion and Future Work

As we can see in Figs. 5a, b and c, the model that was reconstructed using US and MRI, gives us a more detailed shape description which results in a better morphological analysis and a more faithful interaction.

The invited patients and physicians who tested the device, described that the overall level of engagement and realism was satisfactory, as an interesting experience to physically feel features such as the skin pressure and texture combined with the heartbeat of the fetus. The team aims to improve the proposal by testing different haptic devices, such as a haptic glove in order to provide as result a more realistic and friendly experience of touching the fetuses for parents to be and physicians.

References

1. Werner Júnior, H., Santos, J.L.D., Belmonte, S., Ribeiro, G., Daltro, P., Gasparetto, E.L., Marchiori, E.: Applicability of three-dimensional imaging techniques in fetal medicine. Radiologia Brasileira 49(5), 281–287 (2016)
2. Yoshida, E.A., Castro, M.L., Martins, V.F.: Virtual Reality and Fetal Medicine – A Systematic Review (2017)
3. dos Santos, J.R.L., Werner, H., Ribeiro, G., Belmonte, S.L.: Combination of non invasive medical imaging technologies and virtual reality systems to generate immersive fetal 3D visualizations. In: Duffy, V.G.G. (ed.) DHM 2016. LNCS, vol. 9745, pp. 92–99. Springer, Cham (2016). https://doi.org/10.1007/978-3-319-40247-5_10

4. Werner, H., Gasparetto, T.D., Daltro, P., Leandro, E.G., Araujo, E.J.: Typical lesions in the fetal nervous system: correlations between fetal magnetic resonance imaging and obstetric ultrasonography findings. Ultrasonography (2017)

5. Werner, H., Lopes, J., Tonni, G., Júnior, E.A.: Physical model from 3D ultrasound and magnetic resonance imaging scan data reconstruction of lumbosacral myelomeningocele in a fetus with Chiari II malformation. Child's Nervous Syst. **31**(4), 511–513 (2015)

6. Kajimoto, H., Saga, S., Konyo, M.: Pervasive Haptics. Springer, Sendei (2016)

7. Okamura, A.M., Basdogan, C., Baillie, S., Harwin, W.S.: Haptics in medicine and clinical skill acquisition [special section intro.]. IEEE Trans. Haptics **4**(3), 153–154 (2011)

8. Kapoor, S., Arora, P., Kapoor, V., Jayachandran, M., Tiwari, M.: Haptics-Touchfeedback technology widening the horizon of medicine. J. Clin. Diagn. Res. (JCDR) **8**(3), 294 (2014)

9. Prattichizzo, D., La Torre, B., Barbagli, F., Vicino, A., Severi, F.M., Petraglia, F.: The FeTouch Project: an application of haptic technologies to obstetrics and gynaecology. Int. J. Med. Robot. Comput. Assist. Surg. **1**(1), 83–87 (2004)

10. Sevenri, F.M., Prattichizzo, D., Casarosa, E., Barbagli, F., Ferretti, C., Altomare, A., Vicino, A., Petraglia, F.: Virtual fetal touch through a haptic interface decreases maternal anxiety and salivary cortisol. J. Soc. Gynecol. Investig. **12**(1), 37–40 (2005)

11. Fedorov, A., Beichel, R., Kalpathy-Cramer, J., Finet, J., Fillion-Robin, J.C., Pujol, S., Bauer, C., Jennings, D., Fennessy, F., Sonka, M., Buatti, J.: 3D Slicer as an image computing platform for the Quantitative Imaging Network. Magn. Reson. Imaging **30**(9), 1323–1341 (2012)

12. Yoo, T.S., Ackerman, M.J., Lorensen, W.E., Schroeder, W., Chalana, V., Aylward, S., Metaxas, D., Whitaker, R.: Engineering and algorithm design for an image processing API: a technical report on ITK-the insight toolkit. Stud. Health Technol. Inform. **85**, 586–592 (2002)

13. Lorensen, W.E., Cline, H.E.: Marching cubes: a high resolution 3D surface construction algorithm. ACM SIGGRAPH Comp. Graph. **21**(4), 163–169 (1987)

14. Taubin, G.: A signal processing approach to fair surface design. In: Proceedings of the 22nd Annual Conference on Computer Graphics and Interactive Techniques, pp. 351–358. ACM (1995)

15. Cignoni, P., Callieri, M., Corsini, M., Dellepiane, M., Ganovelli, F., Ranzuglia, G.: Meshlab: an open-source mesh processing tool. In: Eurographics Italian Chapter Conference, vol. 2008, pp. 129–136 (2008)

16. Blender Homepage. https://www.blender.org/. Accessed 07 Feb 2018

17. Unity 3D Homepage. https://unity3d.com/. Accessed 07 Feb 2018

18. Poyade, M., Kargas, M., Portela, V.: Haptic Plug-In For Unity3D (2014)

19. Itkowitz, B., Handley, J., Zhu, W.: The OpenHaptics™ toolkit: a library for adding 3D Touch™ navigation and haptics to graphics applications, pp. 590–591 (2005). https://doi.org/10.1109/WHC.2005.133

Developing Face Emotion Tracker for Quantitative Evaluation of Care Effects

Arashi Sako[1(✉)], Sachio Saiki[1], Masahide Nakamura[1], and Kiyoshi Yasuda[2]

[1] Graduate School of System Informatics Kobe University,
1-1 Rokkodai, Nada, Kobe, Japan
kosa-a@ws.cs.kobe-u.ac.jp, sachio@carp.kobe-u.ac.jp, masa-n@cs.kobe-u.ac.jp
[2] Chiba Rosai Hospital, 2-16 Tatsumidai-higashi, Ichihara, Japan
fwkk5911@mb.infoweb.ne.jp

Abstract. In 2017, the Japanese government declared to start "scientific long-term care" as a national policy. In the practice of scientific long-term care, it is essential to assess the quality and effect of care services, since the caregivers must know if the care was effective for the target person. Currently, however, the effect of the long-term care has been evaluated by subjective observation and/or the questionnaire. Hence, it is difficult to justify the quality and effect as such the evidence encouraged in the scientific long-term care. To cope with the challenge, this paper proposes a novel system Face Emotion Tracker (FET) that evaluates the effect of care as a transition of emotions of a person under care. The proposed system can produce real-time data quantifying emotions of the target person under care, which is more objective and fine-grained clinical data compared to the conventional manual assessment sheets. We also implement a prototype and conduct experiments using the prototype.

Keywords: Cognitive computing · Face recognition · Scientific care

1 Introduction

Currently, Japan has been facing a hyper-aging society. In 2025, 30.0% of the total people will be older than 65 years old [5]. As the increasing of elderly people, social problems are expected. The long-term care facilities are suffering from the chronical lack of caregivers and resources. There is also a big pressure for the cost of social security from the government. Therefore, it becomes more important to assign the limited care resources efficiently to appropriate targets.

In 2017, the Japanese government declared to start "scientific long-term care" as a national policy [6]. The scientific long-term care is a long-term nursing care whose effect must be justified by scientific evidence. It assumes to use quantitative and objective big data. By doing this, the scientific long-term care aims to provide cares optimized for individuals to support independent living. In the

V. G. Duffy (Ed.): DHM 2018, LNCS 10917, pp. 513–526, 2018.
https://doi.org/10.1007/978-3-319-91397-1_41

practice of the scientific care, it is essential to assess the quality and effect of long-term care services, since the caregivers must know if the care was effective for the target person.

Currently, however, the effect of the long-term care has been evaluated by subjective observation and/or the questionnaire. Both methods heavily rely on human subjective decisions based on an experience of caregivers. Furthermore, it takes caregivers and/or subjects a lot of time and effort to evaluate the effect of care. Hence, it is difficult to justify the quality and effect as such the evidence encouraged in the scientific long-term care.

To cope with the challenge, this paper proposes a novel system *Face Emotion Tracker* (FET, for short). FET evaluates the effect of care as a transition of emotions of a person under care. The emotions are captured from facial expressions using the latest cognitive computing technology. FET is comprised of four key features: (A1) face recognition, (A2) recording data, (A3) visualization of data, and (A4) quantification of effects.

In (A1), we periodically capture a face image of the target person under care, and send the image to Face Emotion API, which is one of cognitive cloud services. For a given face image, the API returns emotional values calculated from the facial expressions. For this, the emotion is characterized by the confidence of eight emotional attributes: (1) neutral, (2) happiness, (3) surprise, (4) sadness, (5) fear, (6) anger, (7) contempt, and (8) disgust. In (A2), a system operator records every treatment that a caregiver performs during the care. As a result, the system can record real-time data, describing what kind of emotion appeared by which care treatment, at when of the care session. In (A3), we visualize the measured emotions to see in real time or to look back afterwards. In (A4), We then propose metrics that quantify the quality of care, using the emotional values of happiness in care session.

In this paper, we implemented a prototype system of FET using Microsoft Azure Emotion API based on four key features. In practice, we conduct long-term care using the prototype for various people such as an elderly person and person with dementia, and examine the practical feasibility of FET.

2   Preliminaries

2.1   Long-Term Care in Practice

The long-term care refers to a nursing care for elderly people in a broader sense. It includes not only physical supports for daily living, but also activities to maintain healthy mental conditions and good quality of life. There are typical activities such as therapy, recreation, ensemble, and conversation. The purpose of these activities is to stabilize the emotion, to improve cooperativeness, and to encourage recollections.

Currently, the effect of the long-term care has been evaluated by subjective observation and/or the questionnaire. In the observation-based evaluation, a caregiver observes behaviors of the target person, and reads the emotions of the target person. For example, a caregiver evaluates the effect by observing,

"Mr. Tanaka is smiling a lot when talking about movies" or "Mr. Sako seems to be sad when talking about old tales". In the questionnaire-based evaluation, a caregiver conducts a survey that asks the target person what were good and bad treatments, and what to be improved after care.

However, both methods heavily rely on human subjective decisions. Furthermore, it takes caregivers and/or subjects a lot of time and effort to evaluate the effect of care. It is therefore difficult to justify the quality of the care, as such the evidence encouraged in the scientific long-term care. In reality, the care programs at care facilities are often planned by subjective judgment and intuition, based on experience of caregivers.

2.2 Cognitive Computing

Cognitive computing is a computing paradigm where a system imitates the human brain and learns itself to derive answers [1]. It often refers to a smart system or algorithm that recognizes moods and emotions from non-numerical data, such as natural language, images, and sounds, and derives the values. Enabling technologies include natural language processing, emotion analysis, face analysis, and speech recognition. These can be used to implement a machine that supports human decision-making.

IBM Watson [3] is a famous platform of cognitive computing and has been used as a system to support clinicians such as discovering cancer and proposing medicine. In recent years, more and more companies have published cognitive computing APIs, which allows people and external applications to use the cognitive technology, easily and efficiently. Famous cognitive computing APIs include Google Cloud Vision API [2] and Microsoft Azure Emotion API [4].

3 Evaluation of Care Effect Using Face Emotion Tracker

3.1 Goal and Approach

The purpose of this research is to record objective fine-grained clinical data and quantitatively evaluate care for the practice of scientific long-term care. In order to objectively and quantitatively evaluate the quality and effect of care, we select what kind of data we need to acquire. For example, as care clinical data, there are data such as facial expression of caregivers and subjects, body movements, voices. There are also data on the environment that carries out care such as temperature and humidity. Since the influence on evaluation of the quality and effect of care depends on data, it is necessary to select data considering ease of acquired and handling, a noise of data.

In this research, we develop a system that evaluates the effect of care as a transition of emotions of a person under care. The reason why we use facial expression is that human facial expressions are universal in the world and it expresses most emotions. In addition, facial expression has abundant amount of information, and in the case of elderly care, facial expressions of the subjects can are easily acquired with a camera because the subjects see the caregivers. Also, in terms of system evaluation of care, it is easy to judge whether the evaluation performed by the system is correct by human observation. For these reasons, we use facial expressions in this research.

3.2   Face Emotion Tracker (FET)

In order to achieve objective assessment required by the scientific long-term care, we develop a novel system, *Face Emotion Tracker (FET)* in this paper.

FET evaluates the effect of care as a transition of emotions of a person under care. The emotions are captured from facial expressions using the latest cognitive computing technology. Figure 1 shows the main screen of FET. Before a caregiver initiates a care session, the caregiver inputs a title of session, a name of a target person, remarks in Session setting. For example, the title is "1st Dementia Counseling at Kobe Center Hospital", the target person is "Sako", the remarks are time, treatments, and target person"s characters.

Next, when the caregiver presses the Start button, FET periodically captures a face image of the target person with the web camera (as shown in lower left of Fig. 1), and sends the image to Face Emotion API. For a given face image, the API returns emotional values calculated from the facial features within the given image. In Recognition image (shown in lower right of Fig. 1), the recognized face

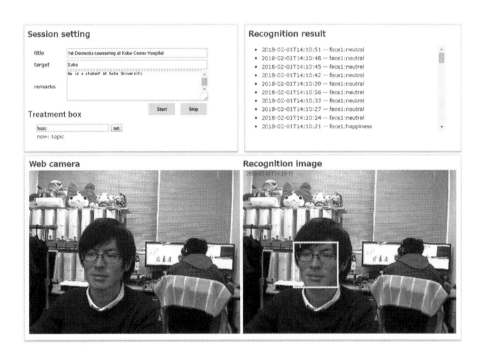

Fig. 1. Main screen of FET

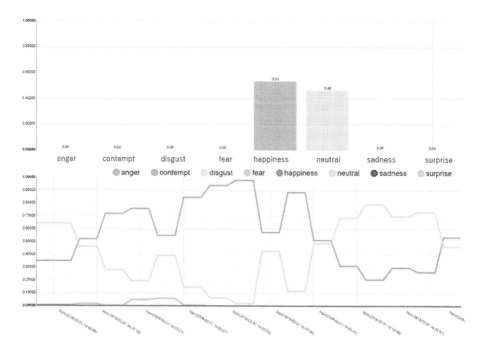

Fig. 2. Visualization of data

is surrounded by a rectangle. In Recognition result (shown in upper right of Fig. 1), the attribute with the highest emotional value is displayed.

During the care, a system operator registers every treatment that the caregiver performs in the Treatment box. As a result, the system can record real-time data, describing what kind of emotion appeared in the target person, by which care treatment, at when of the care session.

Figure 2 shows the visualization feature of FET, visualizing the measured emotions using two graphs to see in real time or to look back afterwards. Furthermore, using the emotional values of happiness acquired during care, FET quantitatively evaluates care. We describe the details in the following subsections.

3.3   Face Recognition

In order to implement the face recognition feature of FET, we use Microsoft Azure Emotion API [4]. Figure 3 shows an example usage of Emotion API. For a given face image, the API returns coordinates of the recognized face, and emotional values calculated from the facial features. Emotion API tries to classify the given face image into eight emotion categories: (1) neutral, (2) happiness, (3) surprise, (4) sadness, (5) fear, (6) anger, (7) contempt, and (8) disgust. For each category, Emotion API returns a confidence representing how the given

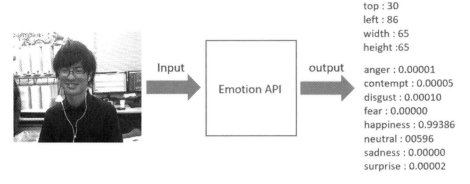

top : 30
left : 86
width : 65
height :65

anger : 0.00001
contempt : 0.00005
disgust : 0.00010
fear : 0.00000
happiness : 0.99386
neutral : 00596
sadness : 0.00000
surprise : 0.00002

Fig. 3. Emotion API

face is likely to belong to the category. Therefore, we use the confidence as the quantitative indicator of the emotion.

Based on the coordinates, FET draws a rectangle indicating the recognized face. FET also displays an emotional attribute with the highest confidence in Recognition result. During the care session, FET executes the Face Recognition feature every 3 s.

3.4 Recording Data

As FET automatically measures the emotion values every 3 s, a system operator manually registers every treatment that the caregiver performs in Treatment box. For example, the system operator inputs like "singing", "ensemble", "conversation with Mr. Sako". As a result, FET can record real-time data, describing what kind of emotion appeared in the target person, in response to which care treatment, at when of the care session. FET stores the captured image, the attribute name, and emotional values, the treatment name, and the time in a relational database (RDB). Thus, it is possible to record more objective and fine-grained care clinical data, as compared with conventional manual evaluation.

3.5 Visualization of Data

As shown in Fig. 2, FET has a feature that visualizes the measured emotion data with two graphs. The explanation of each graph is as follows.

- G1: A bar chart visualizing the emotional values. The horizontal axis represents the eight emotion categories, while the vertical axis represents their confidence.
- G2: A line chart visualizing the time-series value of emotion. The horizontal axis presents time with treatment names, and the vertical axis plots the emotional values.

The visualization feature can be used in both during care and after care. In the case of during care, the two graphs change in real time. In G1, one can check what kind of emotion appeared in the target person immediately during care. In G2, one can check how the emotion is changing as the care session progresses. Thus, using two graphs, the caregiver can improve the treatment dynamically on the spot. In the case of after care, G1 displays the average value of each emotion throughout care or each treatment. In G2, a caregiver can see the transition of emotion throughout care or each treatment. Using two graphs, the caregiver can review the whole care and each treatment, and improve the treatments for the future care sessions.

3.6   Quantification of Effects

Using the emotion data captured by FET, we propose quantitative metrics, which evaluate the quality of care by the emotional value of happiness. The reason why we use happiness is that the long-term care aims to make elderly happy. On the other hand, a situation where the target person is always laughing is problematic, since there is a suspect of euphoria. Therefore, we assume that an ideal care session produces many happy emotions, where happiness and other expressions are alternatingly observed. Based on the assumption, we define the following two metrics:

$$E = \frac{1}{n} \sum_{i=1}^{n} P_i \tag{1}$$

$$V = \frac{1}{n} \sum_{i=1}^{n} (P_i - E)^2 \tag{2}$$

In the definition, n represents the number of facial images captured during a care session, and P_i represents the emotion value of happiness appeared in i-th image. Equation (1) represents the average value of happiness. Intuitively, E characterizes the degree of how the target person was happy throughout the session. Equation (2) represents the variance. Intuitively, V characterizes how dynamically the happiness appeared, distinguishing the happiness from the euphoria.

We can say that a care session A was better than B when the values of E and V for A are better than those of B. By using E and V, it is possible to quantitatively and objectively understand what treatment is suitable for the target person, what treatment is not suitable. As a result, a caregiver can find better treatment such as "Mr. Sako was very pleased when talking about Mr. Tanaka". The caregiver may also find a symptom euphoria such as "Ms. Suzuki was always laughing at the time of the ensemble ".

4   Implementation of Prototype

We have implemented a prototype system of FET based on the proposed method described in Sect. 3. Considering the portability of the system, the FET system

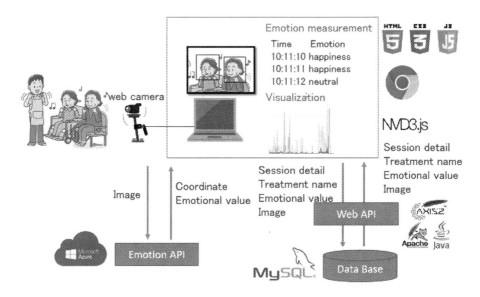

Fig. 4. System architecture of FET

was implemented as a Web application working on a Web browser. The user interface was implemented by HTML5, CSS3 and JavaScript. Just using a PC with a Web camera, the user can use FET from anywhere without installing any software.

The system architecture is shown in Fig. 4. During the care session, FET captures the face image and sends to the Emotion API of Microsoft Azure. When the Emotion API receives the image, it returns the coordinates of the face detected from the image, and eight values of the emotional attributes.

We also implemented Web API to record and retrieve care clinical data in the database, which was deployed on a server. By using the Web API, it is possible to record session detailed information, emotional value, face image data received from the Web service of the system in the database. In addition, these data are acquired using the Web API and used for visualization of data, evaluation of care.

Technologies used for the implementation are summarized as follows:

– Development language: Java1.7, HTML5, CSS3, JavaScript
– JavaScript library: JQuery 2.1.4, NVD3 1.8.1
– Web server: Apache Tomcat 7.0.69
– Web service framework: Apache Axis2 1.6.3
– Database: MySQL 5.7.18
– API: Microsoft Azure Emotion API

5   Experimental Evaluation

In this section, we conduct an experiment to evaluate the practical feasibility of the proposed system. The objective of the experiment is to see if the system can actually obtain quantitative emotion data from individual person under care. We also see whether or not the effect and quality of the care can be quantitatively evaluated by visualizing and analyzing the data.

All procedures used in the experiment were approved by the Ethical Committee of Graduate School of System Informatics, Kobe University (No. 29-04).

5.1   Experiment with Virtual Care Giver [7]

This experiment was performed together with another experiment of our project, where elderly people communicate with *Virtual Care Giver (VCG)* [7]. VCG is a system that supports elderly people at home by using the virtual agent (VA) technology. The VA is an animated chat-bot software with speech recognition and synthesis technologies. Through a PC screen, a user can talk to the VA who behaves like a human being.

VCG implements various sessions of communication care, using available Web resources including text, pictures, and movies. Each care session is extensively personalized to a person under care, considering his/her life history and circumstances [7]. The main goal of the experiment was to see how elderly people accept and communicate with the VCG.

Cooperated with the VCG project, our interest here is to evaluate the quality and effect of the care sessions provided by VCG, by using the developed FET system. In addition, we compare the results of different subjects, and see how the individual differences on communications and symptoms appear on the quantitative data. By doing this, we consider the validity and effectiveness of the evaluation method of the proposed system.

5.2   Method of Experiment

For the experiment, we asked an elderly day-care center to recruit elderly volunteers. As a result, five elderly people in the center kindly participated in the experiment. Let A, B, C, D, E denote the five subjects. Subject A was a man of 81 years old, and B, C, D, E were women of 99, 74, 84, 86 years old, respectively. Subject E was a person with heavy dementia.

Before the experiment, we asked the manager of the day-care center to collect questionnaire from five subjects, asking their personal information, including life history, circumstances, hobby, favorite music, and so on. The questionnaire was used to create personalized care scenarios of VCG.

VCG provides personalized communication care for each person. A session consists of multiple dialogue scenes, each of which talks about a certain topic personalized to the person under care. The dialogue scenes used in the experiments were: (1) self-introduction, (2) health check, (3) feature description

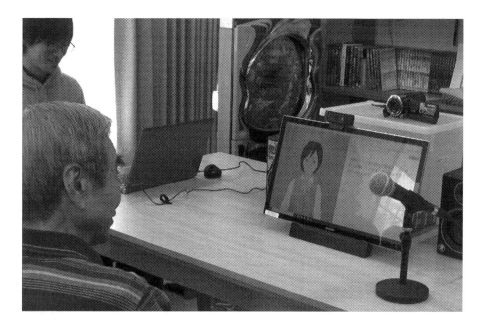

Fig. 5. Elderly communicating with Virtual Care Giver

(of the robot), (4) origin, (5) age of birth, (6) childhood, (7) work, (8) hobby, (9) favorite music, and (10) ending. Each session lasts about 20 min.

Figure 5 shows a scene in the experiment, where an elderly person is talking to VCG via a microphone. As seen in the picture, an operator of FET sits besides the subject. When a new dialogue scene starts, the operator manually inputs the scene name as a care treatment in FET. A Web camera placed on the display of VCG captures face images of the subject. It is connected to FET deployed in the laptop PC of the operator.

During each session, FET records the emotion values as clinical data, which is derived from the face image of the subject. FET also visualizes the values with charts, associated with the ten dialogue scenes.

5.3 Result of Experiment

Figure 6 shows a time-series graph of emotion values of Subject A, captured throughout the session. In the session, we observed that Subject A was moved to tears while he was singing his favorite music (i.e., the last part of the session). It appeared that the song might remind him of something nostalgic. It can be seen in Fig. 6 that the emotion value of sadness increased significantly in the scene of favorite music. Thus, FET captured well his transition of emotion from his face image.

Figure 7 shows the emotion values of Subject E. In the session, we observed that Subject E was gently smiling all the time during the session. This can be

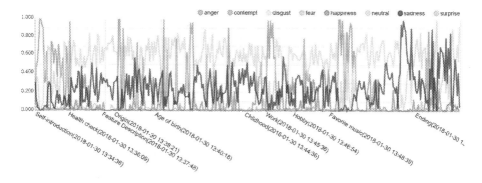

Fig. 6. Time-series graph of Subject A

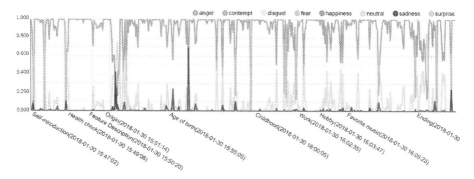

Fig. 7. Time-series graph of Subject E

seen in Fig. 7, where the emotion of happiness sticks to 1.0 most of the time. Thus, the proposed system was able to properly recognize the face, and record the care clinical data for the elderly people.

Figure 8 shows the average values of happiness, i.e. the metric E proposed in Sect. 3.6, for each dialogue scene. On the other hand, Fig. 9 shows the variance values of happiness i.e. the metric V proposed in Sect. 3.6, for each dialogue scene. These metrics give us interesting observation.

For example, as for Subject A, both metrics E and V take large values in the scene of Childhood significantly, compared to other scenes. This is justified by the fact that subject A talked about his childhood very cheerfully. Thus, talking about the childhood can be an effective communication care for Subject A.

5.4   Discussion

In addition to Subject A, the emotions of Subjects B and C dynamically changed in singing or listening to a song, which was observed in their time-series data (like the one in Fig. 6). In the interview after the experiments, they did not tell especially how the songs moved their minds. However, FET surely captured their emotions.

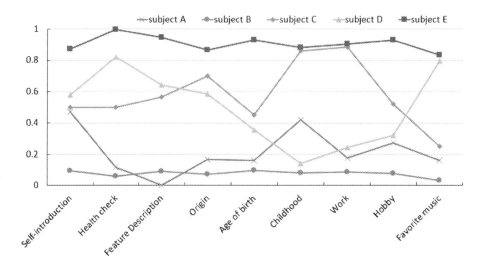

Fig. 8. Average of happiness (metric E)

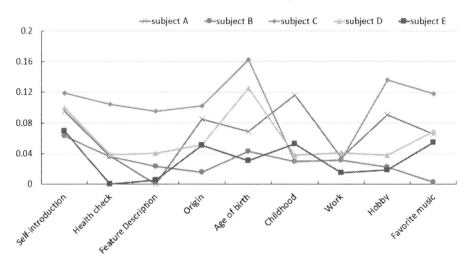

Fig. 9. Variance of happiness (metric V)

Indeed, in singing the song, emotions other than happiness were well observed, which could not quantified by the metrics E and V. Therefore, further investigation of effective metrics should be investigated. However, the clinical data acquired by the system can be used to provide evidence-based care considering emotional status of individuals.

As seen in Figs. 8 and 9, the empirical data shows that the happiness of Subject B was always low, and that her emotional ups and downs were very small, compared to other subjects. On the contrary, the care manager says that she enjoyed the communication with VCG well, which contradicted with the data. The reason is that Subject B is 99 years old, and her facial muscle has been weakened. Indeed, it is difficult even for general people to read her emotion from her facial expression only. Thus, this is the limitation of FET. In order to capture emotions from elderly people like her, we need to combine other features such as voice and postures.

Also, the empirical data shows that Subject E was always happy, and her emotional ups and downs were very small. As mentioned before, Subject E suffers from heavy dementia. Hence, the symptom of euphoria might be captured in the data. Since we have not yet consulted any doctors or medical professionals for this observation, this is yet an observation. However, the empirical data captured by FET would be used to characterize the euphoria and other disease. Further investigation will be left for our future work.

6   Conclusion

In this paper, we proposed a novel system, called Face Emotion Tracker (FET), to support the quantitative assessment of the quality of long-term care. Exploiting the latest cognitive computing technology, FET computes emotion values of a target person from facial images, and uses the values to define metrics characterizing the quality of care. We implemented a prototype system based on proposed methods and conducted experiments, and examined the practical feasibility of FET. Utilizing FET, we can contribute to the practice of scientific long-term care.

In our future work, we plan to combine other features related to emotions such as voice and postures. Introducing environmental data such as temperature and humidity is also interesting. Furthermore, we will propose other effective metrics quantifying the quality of care with other facial emotions.

Acknowledgements. This research was partially supported by the Japan Ministry of Education, Science, Sports, and Culture [Grant-in-Aid for Scientific Research (B) (16H02908, 15H02701), Grant-in-Aid for Scientific Research (A) (17H00731), Challenging Exploratory Research(15K12020)].

References

1. Cognitive Computing. https://en.wikipedia.org/wiki/Cognitive_computing
2. Google Cloud Vision API. https://cloud.google.com/vision/
3. IBM Watson. https://www.ibm.com/watson/
4. Microsoft Azure Emotion API. https://azure.microsoft.com/ja-jp/services/cognitive-services/emotion/

5. Cabinet Office, Government of Japan: Annual report on the aging society in 2017 (full version). http://www8.cao.go.jp/kourei/whitepaper/w-2017/html/zenbun/index.html
6. Headquarters for Japan's Economic Revitalization (No.26): Future investment strategy (2017). http://www.kantei.go.jp/jp/singi/keizaisaisei/dai26/siryou.pdf
7. Sakakibara, S., Saiki, S., Nakamura, M., Yasuda, K.: Generating personalized dialogue towards daily counseling system for home dementia care. In: Duffy, V.G. (ed.) DHM 2017. LNCS, vol. 10287, pp. 161–172. Springer, Cham (2017). https://doi.org/10.1007/978-3-319-58466-9_16

Strategies to Reduce Uncertainty on the Diagnosis Quality in the Context of Virtual Consultation: Reviews of Virtual Consultation Systems

Vania Yuxi Shi[✉], Sherrie Komiak[✉], and Paul Komiak[✉]

Memorial University of Newfoundland, St. John's, NL, Canada
{Ys8378,skomiak,pkomiak}@mun.ca

Abstract. The research literature on virtual consultation is sparse while video consultation between clinician and patient are technically possible and increasingly acceptable. With virtual consultation, people can remotely visit doctors anytime anywhere and access many options of doctors. However, it's surprising that not so many patients in real life as expected are willing to use such virtual consultation systems in spite of all the above theoretical conveniences. Based on uncertainty reduction theory, this paper investigates the strategies to reduce patients' uncertainties about the diagnosis quality. The research question is how to reveal doctors' consultation information to reduce patients' uncertainty on diagnosis quality in the context of virtual consultation.

A review of existing 12 famous virtual consultation systems will be conducted. A following survey and content analysis of patients' reviews on these systems will also be conducted regarding doctors' diagnosis quality. We propose that demonstration of consultation process, review availability and communication naturalness can reduce patients' uncertainty level of diagnosis quality in the context of virtual consultation.

This paper explores how to design virtual consultation systems to enhance patients' trust and certainty on diagnosis quality before actual consultation, which shed a light on future research of online consultation quality. The results can practically facilitate healthcare providers to understand patients' concerns on diagnosis quality of virtual consultation. They can also guide the design of virtual consultation systems industrially to reduce patients' uncertainties on online consultation, and consequently to attract more people using these systems.

Keywords: Uncertainty · Communication · Healthcare · Virtual consultation

1 Introduction

Online consultations between clinician and patient are technically possible and increasingly acceptable in healthcare area. The most recent Health Information National Trends Survey (HINTS) data of US shows that in 2013, 29.6% of U.S. citizens have communicated with doctors or a doctor's office via the internet (National Cancer Institute, 2014; Jiang and Street 2017). Similar trends have been observed in Europe where the estimated percentage of patients who have approached family doctors or other healthcare providers

© Springer International Publishing AG, part of Springer Nature 2018
V. G. Duffy (Ed.): DHM 2018, LNCS 10917, pp. 527–536, 2018.
https://doi.org/10.1007/978-3-319-91397-1_42

on the internet is 12.3% in 2007 (Jiang and Street 2017; Kummervold et al. 2008). Online virtual consultation enables patients to access multi-options of doctors anywhere and anytime. However, despite many benefits virtual consultation brings to people especially rural patients, there is a gap between the numbers of patients who are receptive to communicate with doctors via virtual consultation from those who are actually doing so. For many laypersons, all the things that happen 'inside' a telemedicine service or online consultation are indistinguishable from magic (Fischer et al. 2014; Van Velsen et al. 2017), which may explain why many people have a trust issue on virtual consultation, especially on diagnosis quality of the consultation. People are uncertain about the quality of online diagnosis, thus they hesitate to use virtual consultation systems in spite of all the theoretical benefits. This paper aims to answer the question of how to reduce people's uncertainty level on diagnosis quality of virtual consultation.

Virtual consultation refers to a telemedicine service that enable patients to receive treatment in their daily living environment. This paper focuses on the remote video consultation whereby patients remotely select doctors and consult with them via video conferencing, and explores strategies to reduce patients' uncertainty on virtual online consultation quality based on uncertainty reduction theory. In human communication, uncertainty refers to an interactant's subjective sense of the number of alternative predictions available when thinking about a partner's future behavior, for example, or the number of alternative explanations available when thinking about a partner's past behavior (Bradac 2001). In the context of virtual consultation, we define patients' uncertainty on consultation quality as people's feeling unsure on doctors' past and future consultation behavior.

The uncertainty reduction theory suggests three strategies to reduce uncertainty level: passive, active and interactive. Passive strategies are those in which an informant unobtrusively observe the target person, for instance, by observing videos of the doctor's previous consultation for patients in virtual consultation. Active strategies pertain to proactive efforts to get to know the target person, without confronting the person, for example, by reading other people's review about the doctor before virtual consultation, and interactive strategies require a direct interaction between the communication partners, for example, by asking questions or through reciprocal self-disclosure. We propose that patients are more certain about the diagnosis quality if they are provided the demonstration of doctors' consultation process and other people's reviews on doctors, according to the three strategies.

To explore strategies to reduce patients' uncertainty level on diagnosis quality during virtual consultation, we review 12 existing famous virtual consultation systems on how they present doctors' information, how they demonstrate doctors' consultation process, and how they enable people to review on doctors. A following content analysis of patients' reviews on these systems is conducted regarding doctors' diagnosis quality, and a survey to test our results are conducted. We have the following propositions: (a) Demonstration of doctors' consultation process can reduce patients' uncertainty on diagnosis quality. (b) Other people's reviews especially other doctors' reviews on doctors can reduce patients' uncertainty of diagnosis quality. (c) The more natural the consultation is, the less uncertainty people have on diagnosis quality. (d) The number of these strategies is negatively related patients' uncertainty on diagnosis quality.

This paper focuses solely on conceptual developing process on how to reduce patients' uncertainty of diagnosis quality on remote video consultation due to time limitation. This paper understands the status of system design to reduce patients' uncertainty level on diagnosis quality, which can be basis to further research on patients' physiological and cognitive processes when they visit doctors online, and how these processes are influenced by the revealing of doctors. It explores how to design virtual consultation systems to enhance patients' trust and certainty on diagnosis quality before actual consultation, which shed a light on future research of online consultation quality. The results can practically facilitate healthcare providers to understand patients' concerns on diagnosis quality of virtual consultation. They can also guide the design of virtual consultation systems industrially to reduce patients' uncertainties on online consultation, and consequently to attract more people using these systems. One future direction can be exploring other strategies and design features to reduce patients' uncertainty not only on diagnosis quality, but also on consultation experiences and so on before actual consultation. The other direction can be investigating how to reduce patients' uncertainty level in the actual interaction with doctors for better communication, which can promote diagnosis quality as a result. Multi-methodologies can also be applied to test our results.

2   Literature Review

2.1   Virtual Consultation

Technology-supported consultation in healthcare area is viewed by many as at least a partial solution to the complex challenges of delivering healthcare to diverse population especially rural people (Greenhalgh et al. 2016). Telemedicine (or telehealth), as one of these technologies to travel video and audio as a high-definition digital signal from one computer to another for the purpose of direct patient care, can add an additional dimension to patient care by providing a logical extension of existing face-to-face physical doctor-patient consultation (Brooks 2016; Jue et al. 2017; Klaassen et al. 2016; Segato and Masella 2017). Virtual consultation specifically refers to creating a virtual online doctor-patient consultation environment similar as physical consultation with the use of video-conferencing telemedicine technology.

To many, doctor-patient consultation in the context of virtual consultation may be very similar with how they communicate to each other in a physical doctor's room. Thus, virtual consultation is often overestimated and may be deemed so important that it can very likely replace physical face-to-face consultation at some point in the future. However, the desire to have a face-to-face interaction and not trusting on virtual consultation quality are cited by many patients as reasons not to use virtual consultation services despite the added time and cost to travel to appointments (Gardner et al. 2015; Greenhalgh et al. 2016).

Benefits of Virtual Consultation. It's widely accepted that virtual consultation has many benefits delivering healthcare to diverse patients. One of the most well-known and freely available internet video applications to conduct virtual consultation is skype. Previous review of the clinical use of skype provide evidence to support the clinical use of skype (Armfield et al. 2015, Armfield et al. 2012). Armfield et al. (2015) review twenty-seven articles and conclude that skype is reported to be feasible and to have benefits, especially in the management of chronic diseases such as cardiovascular diseases and diabetes. Their results show that skype allows good communication between individuals and health professionals, and is mostly used in developed countries. While not many studies consider the economic effects associated with using skype and similar free or inexpensive tools to do virtual consultation, those that did agree that skype is more economical than face-to-face appointments with savings from avoided travel and waiting (Armfield et al. 2015; Daniel et al. 2012; Travers and Murphy 2014).

The feasibility of clinical use of these tools motives the development of different virtual consultation systems. One famous commercial type is the systems which enable patients to select certified doctors from a sea of options, no matter whether they are familiar with or not, to do virtual consultations online (Greenhalgh et al. 2016; Segura and Bustabad 2016; Zilliacus et al. 2010). With these systems, patients can access professional healthcare anytime and anywhere, without the risk of getting infected by other patients in hospital (Ellenby and Marcin 2015; Greenhalgh et al. 2016; Klaassen et al. 2016).

Besides the benefits above virtual consultation brings to patients, other parties including physicians, nurses, healthcare institutes also receive massive convenience and benefits. Virtual consultation improves the efficiency of physicians, and largely reduces the rate of no-show appointments (Hanna et al. 2012). virtual consultation can complement nursing in cost-effective ways and increase the intimacy between patients and nurses (Reed 2005, Stern 2017). Virtual consultation can also benefit hospitals and other healthcare providers with easier doctor-physicians-specialists-hospitals connection. For example, Patterson and Wootton (2013) carry out a survey by questionnaire of referrers and specialists over a six months period, and find that the patient management and diagnosis efficiency are improved due to the use of telemedicine technology (Patterson and Wootton 2013).

Concerns of Virtual Consultation. Not all the people use virtual consultation system as they claimed despite all the benefits. One important reason for this probably is the people's not trusting on the diagnosis quality of virtual consultation as on face-to-face consultation (Gardner et al. 2015; Van Velsen et al. 2017; Wald et al. 2007). Wilson et al. (2006) examine the development of trust in computer-mediated and face-to-face teams by having fifty-two, three-person groups work on a mixed-motive task over a 3-week period using computer-mediated or face-to-face interaction. The results suggest that electronical group doesn't develop comparable level of trust to face-to-face one (Wilson et al. 2006). In 2015, Gardner et al. conduct a phone survey of a random sample of patients and find that there are significant hurdles to effectively implement telehealth care as part of mainstream practice though many patients are likely to accept telehealth care (Gardner et al. 2015). Besides the trust issue of patients on telemedicine or virtual consultation, many literature also brings the concern of care quality in the remote consultation environments including telephone, email, video, and internet consultation (Daniel et al. 2012; Hewitt et al. 2010; McKinstry et al. 2010; Roter et al. 2008).

2.2 Uncertainty

In the uncertainty reduction theory, uncertainty refers to "an interactant's subjective sense of the number of alternative predictions available when thinking about a partner's future behavior, or the number of alternative explanations available when thinking about a partner's past behavior" (Bradac 2001). There are two types of uncertainty including cognitive uncertainty and behavioral uncertainty (Berger and Bradac 1982). Cognitive uncertainty refers to the level of uncertainty associated with the beliefs and attitudes of each other in the communication, while behavioral uncertainty refers to the extent to which behavior is predictable in a given situation (Berger 1986; Berger and Bradac 1982). In the context of doctor-patient communication in virtual consultation, patients have uncertainties on many things including doctors they selected, the system, the diagnosis, and the uncertainties can exist along with the entire consultation (Andreassen et al. 2006). Nonetheless, very few studies are conducted on increasing people's willingness to do virtual consultation from an angle of reducing uncertainty (Greenhalgh et al. 2016).

3 Conceptual Development

3.1 Theoretical Foundation

The Uncertainty Reduction Theory

The uncertainty reduction theory (Berger and Calabrese 1975) was first developed to deal with the initial stage of interpersonal interaction. Berger and Calabrese (1975) label three stages of a communication including entry phase, personal phase and exit stage. By assuming the persons involved in the communication transactions are strangers, they define the entry stage as the beginning of communication during which communication content is somewhat structured. That is, the information received and given by the interactants tends to be symmetric (Berger and Calabrese 1975). For example, the message content tends to be demographic information about the interactants. By the end of this phase, the interactants have a fairly confident estimate of whether or not they will develop the relationship to a more intimate level. The personal phase refers to the second stage of the communication transaction which begins when the interactants engage in communication about central attitudinal issues, personal problems, and basic values (Berger and Calabrese 1975). The exit phase is the final stage during which decisions are made concerning the desirability of future interaction.

According to Berger and Calabrese (1975), when strangers meet, their primary concern is one of uncertainty reduction or increasing predictability about the behavior of both themselves of others in the interaction. Uncertainty involves both prediction and explanation components. Prediction components refers to a proactive process of creating predictions. That is, an individual aim to predict how the other interactants will act during the communication. Explanation components refers to the retroactive process of explaining the other's behavior (Berger and Calabrese 1975). High level of uncertainty in a relationship cause decreases in the intimacy level of communication content. Low levels of uncertainty produce high level of intimacy.

The degree of one's perceived uncertainty can be lowered by three different uncertainty reduction strategies: (1) passive, (2) active, and (3) interactive (Antheunis et al. 2012; Shin et al. 2017). Passive strategies are those in which an informant unobtrusively observes the target person, for instance, by observing videos of the doctor's previous consultation for patients in virtual consultation. Active strategies pertain to proactive efforts to get to know the target person, without confronting the person, for example, by reading other people's review about the doctor before virtual consultation, and interactive strategies require a direct interaction between the communication partners, for example, by asking questions or through reciprocal self-disclosure (Antheunis et al. 2012; Berger and Calabrese 1975), which means actual video consultation with the doctor. Due to the ability of this theory to explain people's strategies to reduce uncertainties about other parties in a communication, we believe this theory can provide a theoretical perspective on how to better design virtual consultation system to help patients reduce uncertainties during communication with doctor and computer, and consequently improve their satisfaction about the experience.

3.2   Propositions

According to the uncertainty reduction theory, we develop our framework as shown in Fig. 1 and use it as the basis of our propositions.

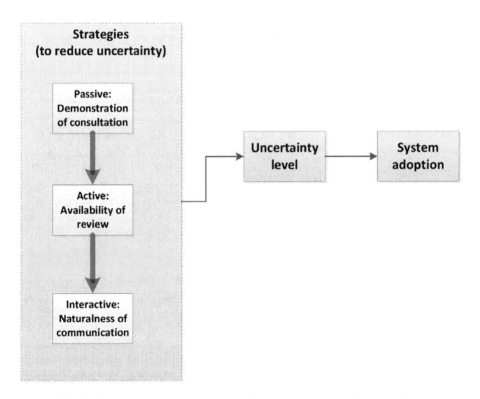

Fig. 1. Strategies to reduce uncertainty in the context of virtual consultation

The strategy reduction theory suggests three strategies to reduce uncertainty during communication. In the context of virtual consultation interaction, the preliminary strategy is passive strategy which enable patients to get an initial sense of the consultation. For patients who are not familiar with the consultation or the consultation system, this step could arise many uncertainties to patients without providing necessary information. People tend to understand the process better by watching vivid video demonstration than solely rigid text description. Therefore, we have the following proposition:

Proposition 1. Demonstration of doctors' consultation process can reduce patients' uncertainty on diagnosis quality.

The second strategy is active strategy which involves patients' actively collecting information from different sources, important one of which is reviews. People can get better product information before actual purchase by browsing other purchasers' reviews in electronical commerce (e-commerce) (Shen and Ulmer 2015). And similarly, patients can better understand virtual consultation and consultation system by retrieving information from other patients' reviews as well. therefore, we have the following propositions:

Proposition 2. Other people's reviews especially other doctors' reviews can reduce people's uncertainty on diagnosis quality.

The final strategy requires patients interacts with doctors by asking questions and self-disclosure. Patients tend to trust what they are used to. Since people are used to use a natural face-to-face way to do consultation, they would be more acceptable of the virtual consultation which can be so natural that both verbal and non-verbal information are delivered, just as in face-to-face communication. Therefore, we have the following propositions:

Proposition 3. The more natural the consultation is, the less uncertainty people have on diagnosis quality.

Some patients may make decision on adoption of virtual consultation system relying on one strategy, while careful patients may use different strategies to ensure themselves as possible before actual usage of the system. Therefore, we have the following propositions:

Proposition 4. The number of these strategies is negatively related patients' uncertainty on diagnosis quality.

4   Methodology

We plan to conduct a systematic review of 12 famous virtual consultation systems including Teladoc, American Well, Carena, Zipnosis, Ringadoc, PlushCare, MeVisit, Stat Health, MDLive, iSelectMD, Virtuwell, MeMD, and Doctor on Demand, on their demonstration of consultation process, review availability and communication naturalness. All of the 12 systems allow people to self-select doctors and do video-consultation online. This study helps us to understand the status of system design to reduce patients' uncertainty level on diagnosis quality.

We also plan to analyze people's attitudes towards and satisfaction on the systems by conducting a survey and content analysis of patients' reviews. These analyses can help us better understand how the strategies influence patients' usage of the systems.

5 Conclusion

This paper focuses on a strategy developing process to boost people's willingness to use virtual consultation systems from an angle of reducing uncertainty on diagnosis quality, based on uncertainty reduction theory. No such study is conducted to our knowledge. We propose that the virtual consultation system should provide patients consultation process demonstration to reduce their uncertainty on the consultation, enable people leave reviews, and make consultation as natural as possible by delivering both verbal and non-verbal information as face-to-face consultation. With strategies combined, the uncertainty of patients can be greatly reduced.

Our method to explore how to increase people's trust on virtual consultation can broaden the academic body of virtual consultation and doctor-patient relationships. The perspective of reducing patients' uncertainty shed a light on future research of system adoption, not only in healthcare area. The propositions can practically facilitate healthcare providers to understand patients' concerns on diagnosis quality of virtual consultation. They can also guide the design of virtual consultation systems industrially to reduce patients' uncertainties on online consultation, and consequently to attract more people using these systems.

One limitation of this paper is the lack of data support due to the time limitation. We plan to publish the results of our review and content analysis in a near future. We expect our propositions being empirically supported. One future direction can be exploring other strategies and design features to reduce patients' uncertainty not only on diagnosis quality, but also on consultation experiences and so on before actual consultation. The other direction can be investigating how to reduce patients' uncertainty level in the actual interaction with doctors for better communication, which can promote diagnosis quality as a result.

References

Andreassen, H.K., Trondsen, M., Kummervold, E., Gammon, D., Hjortdahl, P.: Patients who use e-mediated communication with their doctor: new constructions of trust in the patient-doctor relationship. Qual. Health Res. 16(2), 238–248 (2006). https://doi.org/10.1177/1049732305284667

Antheunis, M.L., Schouten, A.P., Valkenburg, P.M., Peter, J.: Interactive uncertainty reduction strategies and verbal affection in computer-mediated communication. Commun. Res. 39(6), 757–780 (2012). https://doi.org/10.1177/0093650211410420

Armfield, N.R., Bradford, M., Bradford, N.K.: The clinical use of Skype—for which patients, with which problems and in which settings? a snapshot review of the literature. Int. J. Med. Inform. 84, 737–742 (2015). https://doi.org/10.1016/j.ijmedinf.2015.06.006

Armfield, N.R., Gray, L.C., Smith, A.C.: Clinical use of Skype: a review of the evidence base. J. Telemed. Telecare 18(3), 125–127 (2012). https://doi.org/10.1258/jtt.2012.SFT101

Berger, C.R.: Uncertain outcome values in predicted relationships uncertainty reduction theory then and now. Hum. Commun. Res. **13**(1), 34–38 (1986). https://doi.org/10.1111/j.1468-2958.1986.tb00093.x

Berger, C.R., Bradac, J.J.: Language and social knowledge: uncertainty in interpersonal relations. E. Arnold. (1982). http://mun-primo.hosted.exlibrisgroup.com/primo_library/libweb/action/display.do?tabs = detailsTab&ct = display&fn = search&doc = Alma-MUN2131106924000 2511&indx = 1&recIds = Alma-MUN21311069240002511&recIdxs = 0&elementId = 0& renderMode = poppedOut&displayMode = full&frbrVer

Berger, C.R., Calabrese, R.J.: Some explorations in initial interaction and beyond: toward a developmental theory of interpersonal communication. Hum. Commun. Res. **1**(2), 99–112 (1975). https://doi.org/10.1111/j.1468-2958.1975.tb00258.x

Bradac, J.J.: Theory comparison: uncertainty reduction, problematic integration, uncertainty management, and other curious constructs. J. Commun. **51**(3), 456–476 (2001)

Brooks, N.P.: Telemedicine is here. World neurosurg. **95**, 603–604 (2016). https://doi.org/10.1016/j.wneu.2016.02.113

Daniel, W.G., Darren, F.L., Michael, L., Seamus, M., John, P.M.: Skype: A tool for functional assessment in orthopaedic research. J. Telemed. Telecare **18**(2), 94–98 (2012). https://doi.org/10.1258/jtt.2011.110814

Ellenby, M.S., Marcin, J.P.: The role of telemedicine in pediatric critical care. Crit. Care Clin. **31**(2), 275–290 (2015). https://doi.org/10.1016/j.ccc.2014.12.006

Fischer, S.H., David, D., Crotty, B.H., Dierks, M., Safran, C.: Acceptance and use of health information technology by community-dwelling elders. Int. J. Med. Informatics **83**, 624–635 (2014). https://doi.org/10.1016/j.ijmedinf.2014.06.005

Gardner, M.R., Jenkins, S.M., O'Neil, D.A., Wood, D.L., Spurrier, B.R., Pruthi, S.: Perceptions of video-based appointments from the patient's home: a patient survey. Telemed. e-health **21**(4), 281–285 (2015). https://doi.org/10.1089/tmj.2014.0037

Greenhalgh, T., Vijayaraghavan, S., Wherton, J., Shaw, S., Byrne, E., Campbell-Richards, D., Morris, J.: Virtual online consultations: advantages and limitations (VOCAL) study. BMJ Open **6**(1), e009388 (2016). https://doi.org/10.1136/bmjopen-2015-009388

Hanna, L., May, C., Fairhurst, K.: The place of information and communication technology-mediated consultations in primary care: GPs' perspectives. Fam. Pract. **29**(3), 361–366 (2012). https://doi.org/10.1093/fampra/cmr087

Hewitt, H., Gafaranga, J., McKinstry, B.: Comparison of face-to-face and telephone consultations in primary care: qualitative analysis. Br. J. Gen. Pract. **60**(574), e201–e212 (2010). https://doi.org/10.3399/bjgp10X501831

Jiang, S., Street, R.L.: Factors Influencing Communication with Doctors via the Internet: A Cross-Sectional Analysis of 2014 HINTS Survey. Health Commun. **32**(2), 180–188 (2017). https://doi.org/10.1080/10410236.2015.1110867

Jue, J.S., Spector, S.A., Spector, S.A.: Telemedicine broadening access to care for complex cases. J. Surg. Res. **220**, 164–170 (2017). https://doi.org/10.1016/j.jss.2017.06.085

Klaassen, B., Van Beijnum, B.J.F., Hermens, H.J.: Usability in telemedicine systems—A literature survey. Int. J. Med. Inform. **93**, 57–69 (2016). https://doi.org/10.1016/j.ijmedinf.2016.06.004

Kummervold, P.E., Chronaki, C.E., Lausen, B., Prokosch, H.U., Rasmussen, J., Santana, S., Wangberg, S.C.: eHealth trends in Europe 2005–2007: a population-based survey. J. Med. Internet Res. **10**(4), e42 (2008). https://doi.org/10.2196/jmir.1023

McKinstry, B., Hammersley, V., Burton, C., Pinnock, H., Elton, R., Dowell, J., Sheikh, A.: The quality, safety and content of telephone and face-to-face consultations: a comparative study. Qual. Saf. Health Care **19**(4), 298–303 (2010)

Patterson, V., Wootton, R.: A web-based telemedicine system for low-resource settings 13 years on: insights from referrers and specialists. Glob. Health Action **6**(1), 21465 (2013). https://doi.org/10.3402/gha.v6i0.21465

Reed, K.: Telemedicine: benefits to advanced practice nursing and the communities they serve. J. Am. Acad. Nurse Pract. **17**(5), 176–180 (2005). https://doi.org/10.1111/j.1745-7599.2005.0029.x

Roter, D.L., Larson, S., Sands, D.Z., Ford, D.E., Houston, T.: Can e-mail messages between patients and physicians be patient-centered? Health Commun. **23**(1), 80–86 (2008). https://doi.org/10.1080/10410230701807295

Segato, F., Masella, C.: Telemedicine services: how to make them last over time. Health Policy Technol. **6**, 268–278 (2017). https://doi.org/10.1016/j.hlpt.2017.07.003

Shen, W., Hu, Y.J., Ulmer, J.R.: Competing for attention: an empirical study of online reviewers' strategic behavior. MIS Q. **39**(3), 683–696 (2015). https://doi.org/10.1111/j.1468-2486.2005.00546.x

Shin, S.I., Lee, K.Y., Yang, S.B.: How do uncertainty reduction strategies influence social networking site fan page visiting? examining the role of uncertainty reduction strategies, loyalty and satisfaction in continuous visiting behavior. Telematics Inform. **34**, 449–462 (2017). https://doi.org/10.1016/j.tele.2016.09.005

Stern, A.: Exploring the Benefits of telehealth. Trustee **70**(10), 4 (2017)

Segura, B.T., Bustabad, S.: A new form of communication between rheumatology and primary care: the virtual consultation. Reumatología Clínica (English Edition) **12**(1), 11–14 (2016). https://doi.org/10.1016/j.reumae.2015.03.001

Travers, C.P., Murphy, J.F.: Neonatal telephone consultations in the National Maternity Hospital. Ir. Med. J. (2014)

Van Velsen, L., Tabak, M., Hermens, H.: Measuring patient trust in telemedicine services: Development of a survey instrument and its validation for an anticoagulation web-service. Int. J. Med. Inform. **97**, 52–58 (2017). https://doi.org/10.1016/j.ijmedinf.2016.09.009

Wald, H.S., Dube, C.E., Anthony, D.C.: Untangling the web—the impact of Internet use on health care and the physician–patient relationship. Patient Educ. Couns. **68**, 218–224 (2007). https://doi.org/10.1016/j.pec.2007.05.016

Wilson, J.M., Straus, S.G., McEvily, B.: All in due time: the development of trust in computer-mediated and face-to-face teams. Organ. Behav. Hum. Decis. Process. **99**(1), 16–33 (2006). https://doi.org/10.1016/j.obhdp.2005.08.001

Zilliacus, E., Meiser, B., Lobb, E., Dudding, T.E., Barlow-Stewart, K., Tucker, K.: The virtual consultation: practitioners' experiences of genetic counseling by videoconferencing in Australia. Telemed. e-Health **16**(3), 350–357 (2010). http://online.liebertpub.com/doi/pdf/10.1089/tmj.2009.0108

Improving Computerized Charting in an Intensive Care Unit

Ben Smith[1]([✉]), Sivamanoj Sreeramakavacham[1], Jung Hyup Kim[1],
and Laurel Despins[2]

[1] Industrial and Manufacturing Systems Engineering Department, University of Missouri,
Columbia, MO 65211, USA
{blsg48,ssxx9}@mail.missouri.edu, kijung@missouri.edu
[2] Sinclair School of Nursing University of Missouri, Columbia, MO 65211, USA
DespinsL@health.missouri.edu

Abstract. The purpose of this study is to look deeper into an electronic medical record (EMR) system to find inefficiencies within the overall charting process. Along with collecting observation data on nurses within the University of Missouri Hospital Intensive Care Unit, EMR activity log data was gathered from the EMR system through a real time measurement system (RTMS). By using the RTMS data, the average time for several designated charting activities were analyzed based on different levels of patient sickness and nurse experience. The results showed that there were several significant differences on EMR documentation time in an ICU. The comprehensive findings of this study will help point to areas where improvements can be made in order to optimize efficiency within the EMR charting process and increase time nurses spend in direct patient care, which should in turn increase patient safety as well.

Keywords: Intensive Care Unit · Electronic medical record · Charting

1 Introduction

The University of Missouri Hospital Intensive Care Unit implemented electronic medical records in 1999 with the goal of increasing overall efficiency in the ICU [1]. Although these electronic medical records have seemed to increase documentation efficiency within the intensive care unit compared to the conventional paper method, there is still room for improvement. The first question that needs to be answered is why EMR charting has such a high percent time distribution for nurses and what factors may or may not affect it. Although past research has looked at the implementation of EMR systems and compared it to the paper charting system, this study looks deeper within the processes in the EMR system to discover how different factors affect the time spent of using the EMR system. By doing so, the charting activities that are causing the inefficiency can be optimized to maximize the overall efficiency within the entire EMR charting process and increase time nurses spend in direct patient care.

© Springer International Publishing AG, part of Springer Nature 2018
V. G. Duffy (Ed.): DHM 2018, LNCS 10917, pp. 537–546, 2018.
https://doi.org/10.1007/978-3-319-91397-1_43

1.1 Significance to Efficiency and Patient Safety

Efficient use of EMR charting in the ICU is significantly related to the improvement of healthcare service and patient safety. With an overall goal of improving safety and efficiency in the ICU, even one or two main issues within the EMR system can cause inefficiency or create more significant problems that can take away from overall patient experience and well-being. In an article by Richard Holden when talking about the implementation of EMR systems in hospitals, he stated, "The primary goal should not be to reduce error or harm. The goal should be to design work systems that support and enhance work process performance. Error reduction and harm prevention will follow in turn" [2]. To elaborate on Holden's words, before these systems are implemented the developers have to account for the human factor to help improve performance and cut down on EMR charting time. In another article, K.E. Bradshaw discusses the time efficiency of EMR charting and goes on to say, "Contrary to our expectation, our studies showed a decrease in the proportion of time that nurses spent in direct patient care (from 49.1% to 43.2%) and an increase in the proportion they spent entering clinical data (from 18.2% to 24.2%) after computerization" [3]. Although that was during the early stages of EMR implementation, this study shows that without an easy-to-use program, the EMR system can cause a nurse to spend less time with the patient, increasing the risk of missing signs of worsening patient conditions. A nurse who has little experience with not only the technology but also medical records has to be able to understand the system. After several years of EMR systems being used, new advances in technology can allow researchers to analyze the computerized charting system to account for human factors that were not relevant in years past. By doing so, EMR charting time can be reduced and, in turn, time spent in direct patient care can be optimized.

1.2 Risk Factors That Affect Patient Safety

One of the primary goals of implementing a computerized charting system in hospitals is to increase patient safety and well-being. In a study conducted by Parente and McCullough [4], they concluded that "EMRs are the only health IT application to have a clear and statistically significant effect on patient safety. EMR use is associated with reduced infections attributable to medical care. EMRs became more effective with each passing year, which suggests that hospitals were either improving their EMR implementation or that EMR technology itself was improving." While EMR systems themselves can affect different aspects of patient safety, the nurses who chart within the EMR system can also be affected by different factors. These factors can then in turn affect the efficiency of EMR charting, which will also heavily impact patient safety. As shown in Fig. 1, a Fishbone Diagram was created to represent all of the factors that affect how nurses chart within the EMR system. Some of the important risk factors that are used in the data analysis portion of this paper are nurse experience, patient sickness, patient medication demands, type of input task, and amount of data to input into the EMR system. Overall, increasing patient safety should be one of the primary goals in healthcare environments. By identifying the risk factors that may negatively affect how nurses chart in the EMR system, those factors can be examined and improved upon in order to optimize the EMR charting process and increase patient safety.

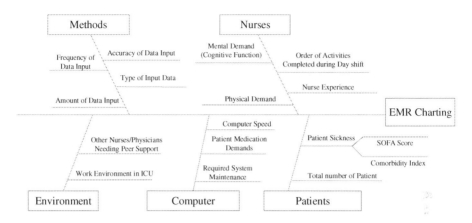

Fig. 1. Fishbone diagram for the EMR charting process

1.3   Literature Review

By looking at previous research conducted for analyzing the implementation and use of hospital EMR systems, the methods and results from their studies can be helpful when examining the gaps between the literature and this experiment. In a study conducted by Pierpont and Thilgen [5], they explored the differences in time distribution for ICU nurses' activities both before and after computerized charting had been implemented in the hospital. The study was conducted in a six-bed coronary care unit and an eight-bed medical ICU unit. An experienced study technician observed two ICU nurses per eight-hour shift. Before the installation of the computerized charting system, a total of 58 nurses were observed for 390.5 h [5]. After installation, a total of 60 nurses were observed for 417 h. The study technician recorded each activity to the nearest minute and conducted the time study as continuous throughout the eight-hour shift. Instead of creating a list of nurses' activities to mark down the observed time, this study technician just denoted each activity by location. If a nurse was in a patient room, he/she was either gathering patient information, providing direct patient care, or charting. Activities in the central nurse station were considered either charting or monitoring, which included all non-charting activities. After the observations were completed, statistical analysis on the data was conducted using the chi-square test statistic. There were three main results from the statistical analysis. First, the percentage of time spent in the patient room and central nurse station did not change once the computerized charting system was implemented. Second, the time spent on charting within the central nurse station decreased from 40% to 22% after the computer was installed. Third, in the patient room the percent time spent on patient care decreased from 78.3% to 65.7%, the time spent gathering data decreased from 15.6% to 9.6%, and time spent on the computer was calculated to be 20.3% after the computer was installed [5]. This last finding is significant to the hypothesis of this project as it suggests that the implementation of computerized charting actually decreased the amount of time spent in direct patient care. The gaps between Pierpont's study and this research project are two-fold. First, the research done by Pierpont's team only measured the differences before and after computerized charting implementation. Instead, this research project focuses on ICU nurses, who have already had an electronic medical records system for a few years, in an attempt to optimize the efficiency of the system, whereas Pierpont's study mainly compares the performance of the computerized and paper charting systems. Second, Pierpont's research only covers the surface to show differences in the percent of time spent charting before and after computer installation, whereas this research project is looking to find the specific reasons why EMR charting has such a high percent time distribution and what factors may or may not affect it. That being said, Pierpont's research has found significant results with regard to the effect of computerized charting on many ICU nurses' activities, including its effect on time spent in direct patient care.

Another research project conducted by Wong et al. [6] looked at the EMR usage of nurses using extensive time study software and third-generation intensive care unit information systems. They investigated the percentage of time nurses spent on documentation and other nursing activities before and after the installation of an advanced EMR system in the ICU. Their focus was to show, with the implementation of this new technology, a decrease in documentation activities and an increase in activities that were related to direct patient care. To do so, they closely observed the nurses during their shift and used a custom software that separated the nurses' activities into 70 tasks. Those 70 tasks were then separated into five different nursing activity categories: direct patient care, indirect patient care, documentation, administration, and housekeeping. One important thing to note about the research is that the nurses were also given up to six months of training and experience with the new third-generation EMR systems before the experiment. That being said, the results showed a decrease in documentation time from 35% to 24% and an increase in direct patient care time from 31.3% to 40.1%. About half of the time cut from documentation time was reallocated to patient care and patient assessments [6]. This is contrary to what has been hypothesized in this paper and ultimately can be used to show how superior training and differing ICU tasks and procedures can make EMR implementation a much smoother and efficient process. As previously mentioned, each nurse had greater than six months of training with the new EMR system in a live ICU environment. This minimized the learning curve of the nurses and caused the documentation time to decrease once the study was conducted. In addition, the study goes on to say, "It is possible that ICU information systems may affect ICU nurse task activity differently in different ICU's simply because of differences in workflow, task requirements, training, or culture" [6]. Each ICU has its own set of unique tasks and rules which may or may not affect the EMR documentation time of nurses. Therefore, the differences in training and procedures between intensive care units may affect the impact of the implementation of an electronic medical records system on the documentation and direct patient care time of nurses. Even though in this study the computerized charting system outperformed the paper charting system, the efficiency of charting within EMR systems still needs to be vastly improved.

2   Methods

2.1   Data Collection

For five months, we collected log data for twenty-eight observation days (7 am to 7 pm) from ICU nurses at the University of Missouri Hospital Intensive Care Unit. A Real-Time Measurement System (RTMS) marked the time duration for every completed EMR activity during the nurses' shifts. In conjunction, RTMS also provided all of the log data from the nurses' EMR charting. The RTMS data was used to create sequence diagrams that contained the location, duration, and time of each EMR activity that the ICU nurse performed. The time duration for all of the EMR activities was used as a basis for the preliminary data analysis. In addition, we collected the Sequential Organ Failure Assessment (SOFA) scores, Charlson Comorbidity Index (CI) scores, and each nurse's work experience in ICU during the data collection. The Charlson Comorbidity Index predicts the ten-year mortality rate for a patient who may have comorbid conditions [7]. The Sequential Organ Failure Assessment is a measure "to objectively quantify the degree of dysfunction/failure of each organ daily in critically ill patients" [8]. Years of nurse work experience, CI score, and SOFA score were all used as factors for defining different levels of patient sickness and nurse experience.

2.2   Hierarchical Task Analysis

Although there are many studies related to the effects of EMR implementation and its efficiency in hospitals, few studies have looked into the detailed workflow of EMR systems to determine their inefficient processes and how to improve them. To understand the ICU nurse's EMR documentation workflow, the EMR data was split into several categories by using the hierarchical task analysis (HTA) method. HTA helped us create diagrams of all tasks and subtasks that were completed by nurses during EMR charting processes. As Annett [9] states, "The process of HTA is to decompose tasks into subtasks to any desired level of detail…. The overall aim of the analysis is to identify actual or possible sources of performance failure and to propose suitable remedies, which may include modifying the task design and/or providing appropriate training."

By using the HTA chart, it is possible to conduct the process analysis for intensive care nursing [10]. Figure 2 shows one of the plans related to the four main areas of EMR charting input based on RTMS data: (1) update assessment results, (2) review documents, (3) check and updating medical requests, and (4) check lab specimen orders.

2.3   Procedure for Analysis

By using the HTA and RTMS data, the ICU nurses' EMR activities were classified into five main EMR categories: in-room assessment, out-of-room assessment, medication, lab specimen, and others. The in-room assessment category includes every activity charted inside the patient room that is related to patient assessment, and the out-of-room assessment category is the same with the lone exception of the charting being conducted outside of the patient room. The medication category is comprised of all charting

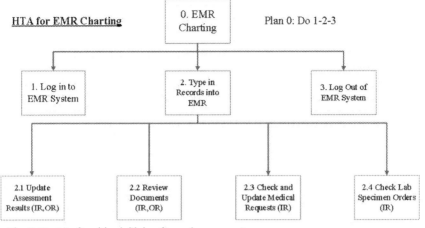

Fig. 2. HTA chart for EMR charting process

activities related to scanning and administering medication to patients. Similarly, the lab specimen category contains every charting activity related to scanning and transporting bloodwork and other lab specimens. This includes the nurse scanning the barcode on the patient's tag, scanning the specimen container's barcode, and then scanning the container's barcode again once the lab specimen has been collected. Lastly, 'others' category includes every EMR charting activity that is not related to the other four RTMS categories, which mainly consists of nurses reviewing documents or previous orders within the EMR system.

During the data analysis, the times for each occurrence of EMR usage were marked and distributed into the five categories. After that, an average process time of each category was calculated. In this study, SOFA, CI, and nurse experience were used as independent variables to understand the effects of the levels of patient sickness and nurse experience on these five main EMR activities. Nurse experience is based on how many years nurses have worked in an intensive care unit. The levels of patient sickness are given by the SOFA and CI scores that each represent different levels of risk of death for each patient. Those scores were then separated into "high" and "low" categories based on the mean value for both metrics. A Charlson Comorbidity Index score of less than or equal to four was categorized as "low," and a SOFA score of less than or equal to seven was categorized as "low." For the nurse experience, if a nurse has more than two years of working experience in an ICU, then we considered that he or she was an experienced nurse. After categorizing the factors and data for the RTMS analysis, a one-way ANOVA test was conducted. The results show how patient sickness and nurse experience contributed to the total time spent on EMR documentation.

3   Results

After creating the ANOVA tables for the average EMR documentation time, several significant differences for each factor were found. Table 1 shows the ANOVA results for the in-room assessment total time, where the CI score has $p = 0.057$, and the nurse experience has $p < 0.001$. The EMR documentation time difference caused by the CI is close to being significant. The mean time for nurses whose patients had low CI scores is higher than those who had high CI scores. Also, the mean time for nurses with high experience is longer than those with low experience.

Table 1. ANOVA results for average time for in-room assessment charting

Factor	Level	N	Mean	StDev	F	P
CI	Low	19	36.00	18.64	3.97	0.057
	High	9	21.39	16.90		
SOFA	Low	17	27.94	17.59	1.36	0.254
	High	11	36.50	20.98		
Nurse experience	Low	19	23.21	16.80	16.85	**<0.001**
	High	9	48.39	10.56		

Table 2 shows the ANOVA results of the out-of-room assessment total EMR documentation time, in which the difference in the average times between the nurse experience levels is significant with a $p = 0.047$. Contrary to the in-room assessment total time, the ICU nurses who had less experience level in an ICU used the EMR system longer when charting an assessment outside the patient room. Table 4 shows the average time for documenting the data related to lab specimens. The nurses with low CI score patients spent significantly longer time to record lab specimen data than those with patients who had high CI scores. Table 5 shows the ANOVA results of charting 'others' category EMR data. The results show that there is a significant difference on EMR documentation time between low experienced nurses and high experienced nurses. The nurses with high experience spent more time reviewing documents or previous orders in the EMR system than nurses with low experience.

Table 2. ANOVA results for average time for out-of-room assessment charting

Factor	Level	N	Mean	StDev	F	P
CI	Low	19	42.47	23.95	1.29	0.266
	High	9	54.00	27.45		
SOFA	Low	17	44.71	16.02	0.14	0.708
	High	11	48.50	36.00		
Nurse experience	Low	19	52.63	15.36	4.35	**0.047**
	High	9	32.60	36.10		

Table 3. ANOVA results for average time for medication charting

Factor	Level	N	Mean	StDev	F	P
CI	Low	19	14.21	5.05	2.15	0.155
	High	9	11.22	5.02		
SOFA	Low	17	12.03	5.37	2.58	0.120
	High	11	15.14	4.34		
Nurse experience	Low	19	12.79	5.79	0.46	0.502
	High	9	14.22	3.50		

Table 4. ANOVA results for average time for lab specimen charting

Factor	Level	N	Mean	StDev	F	P
CI	Low	19	3.697	3.763	4.36	**0.047**
	High	9	1.000	1.118		
SOFA	Low	17	2.662	4.055	0.10	0.750
	High	11	3.091	2.119		
Nurse experience	Low	19	2.750	3.836	0.03	0.859
	High	9	3.000	2.345		

Table 5. ANOVA results for average time for other charting

Factor	Level	N	Mean	StDev	F	P
CI	Low	19	29.50	14.17	0.02	0.885
	High	9	28.56	19.37		
SOFA	Low	17	26.21	15.34	1.61	0.215
	High	11	33.82	15.71		
Nurse experience	Low	19	24.34	14.44	6.93	**0.014**
	High	9	39.44	13.58		

4   Discussion and Conclusion

In summary, this study showed that the RTMS data could be used as an important tool to improve the EMR charting process in ICU. Several takeaways can be made from the results of the RTMS analysis. First, nurses with higher experience spend more time in the EMR system for in-room assessment charting, but spend less time in the EMR system for out-of-room assessment charting. This means that nurses with high experience prefer to chart patient assessments inside the patient room, likely because they are trying to chart immediately after an assessment is performed instead of waiting until a later time. Consequently, nurses with low experience prefer to wait to chart assessments until they are outside the patient room. Second, nurses with high experience charted inputs within the "other" category for a much longer time than nurses with low experience. A survey of responses on the amount of computer training for each nurse conducted by Eley et al. [11] concluded that 70.6% of nurses who have worked as a nurse for five years or less have had formal computer training, whereas only 23.7% of nurses who have worked as a nurse for five years or longer have had formal computer training. This can cause non-direct care-related tasks to appear in the RTMS data, which would explain the large total time that highly experienced nurses spend charting for the designated "other" category. Third, for charting related to lab specimens, nurses with patients who have low CI scores chart much longer than those with high CI scores. In a study conducted by Rusanov et al. [12], they looked at the American Society for Anesthesiologists Physical Status Classification (ASA class) for patients to determine if the health of patients affected the number of days where laboratory results were taken and medications were ordered. ASA Class 4 patients, who are designated as the sickest, had 5.05 times the number of days with laboratory results as ASA Class 1 patients, who are designated as the least sick. This contradicts the corresponding result from the RTMS analysis relating CI scores to charting about lab specimens, so further tests should be done to verify these results and find the cause for that significant difference.

Although significant results were found that help to fill previous research gaps, there will always be more that can be done in terms of improving the electronic medical record system in the ICU. One test that would prove to be useful would be to determine the average time for each task within the EMR system to see which tasks are taking up the most amount of the ICU nurses' time. The averages then could then be tested with nurse experience and patient sickness to see if such factors are affecting EMR usage. From there, the EMR programming or ICU procedures could be improved to help cut down EMR usage time. Another component of the research that could be developed is a simulation model of the ICU. A simulation of the ICU would directly show how different tasks in the EMR system affect a nurse's EMR usage over a long period of time. It would also show the value that would be gained from improving the tasks that are causing inefficiencies within the EMR system. Another aspect of the experiment that could be expanded is the control variable of where to test for EMR usage time. Instead of just looking at the ICU, the entire hospital or even multiple hospitals could be tested for EMR usage time. Although much more equipment and time would have to be invested, it would supply a much larger set of data to test, which would give better insight into inefficiencies within the EMR system in different environments. This would also help to improve EMR usage times not only in the University of Missouri Hospital but hospitals everywhere.

Another way that the research could be expanded is by looking at the limitations that were faced with this research project. One limitation was the data set that was used for the experiment since the data was collected from a previous experiment. To improve the data set, an independent study could be done with a larger sample size that focuses primarily on the tasks within the EMR system. This would allow the results to be drawn from a better data set that has different factors as independent variables. Another minor limitation was the RTMS data that was collected. Although the RTMS data was collected for every task that was charted within the EMR system, the data was difficult to interpret at times and there were several gaps in the log data that could not be explained. These gaps heavily affected the sample size for our experiment, so better consistency within the RTMS system would allow for a larger and more accurate data sample.

References

1. Kauffman, A.: Doctors disagree on efficiency of electronic medical records. In: KOMU 2014 (2014)
2. Holden, R.J.: Cognitive performance-altering effects of electronic medical records: an application of the human factors paradigm for patient safety. Cogn. Technol. Work **13**(1), 11–29 (2011)
3. Bradshaw, K.E., et al.: Computer-based data entry for nurses in the ICU. MD Comput. Comput. Med. Pract. **6**(5), 274–280 (1989)
4. Parente, S.T., McCullough, J.S.: Health information technology and patient safety: evidence from panel data. Health Aff. **28**(2), 357–360 (2009)
5. Pierpont, G.L., Thilgen, D.: Effect of computerized charting on nursing activity in intensive care. Crit. Care Med. **23**(6), 1067–1073 (1995)
6. Wong, D.H., et al.: Changes in intensive care unit nurse task activity after installation of a third-generation intensive care unit information system. Crit. Care Med. **31**(10), 2488–2494 (2003)
7. Charlson, M.E., et al.: A new method of classifying prognostic comorbidity in longitudinal studies: development and validation. J. Chronic Dis. **40**(5), 373–383 (1987)
8. Ceriani, R., et al.: Application of the sequential organ failure assessment score to cardiac surgical patients. Chest **123**(4), 1229–1239 (2003)
9. Annett, J.: Hierarchical task analysis. Handb. Cogn. Task Des. **2**, 17–35 (2003)
10. Song, X., Kim, J.H., Despins, L.: A time-motion study in an intensive care unit using the near field electromagnetic ranging system. In: Proceedings of the 2017 Institute of Industrial and Systems Engineers (IISE). IIE Annual Conference (2017)
11. Eley, R., et al.: The status of training and education in information and computer technology of Australian nurses: a national survey. J. Clin. Nurs. **17**(20), 2758–2767 (2008)
12. Rusanov, A., et al.: Hidden in plain sight: bias towards sick patients when sampling patients with sufficient electronic health record data for research. BMC Med. Inform. Decis. Making **14**(1), 51 (2014)

Effect of Patient Acuity of Illness and Nurse Experience on EMR Works in Intensive Care Unit

Sivamanoj Sreeramakavacham[1(✉)], Jung Hyup Kim[1], Laurel Despins[2], Megan Sommerfeldt[1], and Natalie Bessette[1]

[1] Industrial and Manufacturing Systems Engineering Department, University of Missouri, Columbia, MO 65211, USA
{ssxx9,mlsyv3,njbvyc}@mail.missouri.edu, kijung@missouri.edu
[2] Sinclair School of Nursing University of Missouri, Columbia, MO 65211, USA
DespinsL@health.missouri.edu

Abstract. The objective of this study is to analyze the impact on the nurse's process time during the electronic medical record (EMR) charting task in an intensive care unit (ICU). The dynamic uncertainty of clinical tasks in the ICU can make it difficult for nurses to take care of critically ill patients. According to the literature, EMR documentation is one of the tasks on which nurses spend most of their time during the shift. To understand and improve the EMR documenting process, a time & motion study was conducted in a medical ICU at the University of Missouri Hospital. Data was collected on processes and standard times of every EMR activity performed by ICU nurses. Based on the results of this study, hierarchical task analysis (HTA) charts were developed and analyzed nurse's workflow during EMR documentation. After that, a simulation model was developed for documenting in the EMR in an ICU.

Keywords: Electronic medical record systems · Simulation · Patient acuity level
Nurse experience

1 Introduction

An intensive care unit (ICU) is one of the most complex and dynamic places in a hospital. Healthcare providers must perform various clinical tasks while managing patient health records. Moreover, they must spend time to understand how to use IT technologies in their work areas. IT technologies have been increasingly influencing the healthcare sector [1]. IT systems such as the electronic medical records (EMR) were introduced to improve the safety and quality of care, in part by helping the healthcare professionals' carry out their tasks more efficiently. However, most studies have noted a substantial increase in the time spent documenting when using an EMR due to the high demand of documenting patient-related data [2]. Overall healthcare professionals are confronted with an increasing need for high quality and timely patient-oriented documentation [3]. This study considers the documentation done by nurses as the implementation of the EMR system was found to have a higher influence on nurses' documentation time than

© Springer International Publishing AG, part of Springer Nature 2018
V. G. Duffy (Ed.): DHM 2018, LNCS 10917, pp. 547–557, 2018.
https://doi.org/10.1007/978-3-319-91397-1_44

the physicians' [2]. It is important to understand how nurses perform documentation in the ICU to guide improvements in the quality of healthcare delivery processes as nurses perform multiple tasks associated with the daily monitoring of patients. To improve the process of EMR documentation, the factors that increase process time and decrease throughput should be identified and eliminated from the existing process. Various studies in the past identified multiple factors. In this study, we considered patient acuity level and nurse experience as two primary factors impacting the nurse's process times on EMR documentation. To further understand and improve the EMR documentation process, a time and motion study was conducted in a medical ICU at the University of Missouri Hospital. Through the study, we identified the detailed steps of the documentation process conducted by ICU nurses. Multiple hierarchical task analysis (HTA) charts were developed using the data from the time and motion study. According to the research done by Parameshaewara, Kim [4], an HTA chart can provide detailed information regarding the various decisions and steps of the nurse's workflow in an emergency department. A simulation model was then developed using the HTA charts from the time and motion study. The simulation model was used as a tool to understand the workflow and measure the process time during EMR documentation in an ICU.

2   Literature Review

Nursing documentation has been viewed as a vital part of the nurse's work since the time of Florence Nightingale [5]. Studies carried out by Hendrich [6] and Hefter [7] have shown that nursing documentation consumes a tremendous amount of time during a shift. In a paper documentation system, illegible handwriting, manual data entry, and searching for lab results, orders, or patient records are some of the issues that can result in inefficient workflow and poor productivity [8]. Hence, the documentation task has transitioned from traditional paper-based systems to electronic medical record (EMR) systems. EMR systems can increase the quality and efficiency of patient care, and support healthcare professionals in their daily task [3].

Despite the benefits, EMR systems still have several drawbacks (e.g., spending longer time for EMR documentation) [9]. The study done by Hripcsak, Vawdrey [10] found that the nurses spent a significant amount of time documenting in EMRs. The time and motion study carried out by Bosman [11], Bian, Wade [12], also showed that the documentation time was significantly increased due to the EMR system. Researchers have tried to identify the factors impacting documentation time in EMR systems. According to Bradshaw [13], access to the EMR system from a patient's room could be one of the influential factors of EMR documentation. The study identified that using the EMR system present in the patient's room by the bedside had increased the documentation time. Bosman, Rood [14] found that the type of content documented also had an impact on the documentation time. The study of complexities in nursing documentation done by Cheevakasemsook, Chapman [15] had identified three direct and three indirect factors affecting the documentation time using multiple methods such as in-depth interviewing; participant observation; nominal group processing; focus group meetings; time and motion study of nursing activities; and auditing of completeness of nursing documentation. The three direct factors were interruptions in documentation, incomplete charting, and inappropriate charting while the three indirect factors identified were limited nurses' competence, ineffective nursing procedures and inadequate nursing staff development. The factors identified by these studies are directly related to EMR systems or nurses. Among all the factors identified in previous studies, our study focusses on the patient's morbid conditions and the nurse's competence, which is associated with the nurse's experience level.

2.1 Patient Severity

Analyzing and predicting the mortality and morbidity of the patients is of rising importance in the healthcare system [16]. The systems that analyze and predict the mortality and morbidity rates provide information to healthcare personnel about the condition of the patient. These systems can be used as a comparative approach for assessment of performance in an ICU [16]. There are many scoring systems to predict the mortality and morbidity rates. Among them, we used Sequential Organ Failure Assessment (SOFA) score and Charlson Comorbidity Index (CI) in this study. The combination of both scoring systems can accurately evaluate the seriousness of patient's conditions.

SOFA describes the time course of multiple organ dysfunctions using a limited number of routinely measured variables [17] and considers the organ dysfunction into account while calculating the prediction rates. The SOFA score is primarily used to assess critically ill patients in ICU [18]. The SOFA score is composed of scores from six organ systems (respiratory, cardiovascular, hepatic, coagulation, renal, and neurological), graded from 0 to 4 according to the degree of dysfunction/failure [19]. The reliability of the SOFA score to predict mortality is complicated by different derivatives of the SOFA score such as the Fixed Day SOFA and Delta Sofa Score. The Fixed Day SOFA score can help in comparing mean organ dysfunction in the trials while Delta SOFA allows comparing the trajectory of organ dysfunction from the baseline in the trial arms. Other SOFA derivatives contain the score at the day of death or discharge, or the mean or maximum score during the ICU stay.

The Charlson Comorbidity index is designed to classify prognostic comorbidity in longitudinal studies [20]. It is used in various studies to classify patients based on the influence that the comorbid conditions have on the overall survival of the patient. The CI scores provide a readily applicable, valid and straightforward method for evaluating the risk of death from the comorbid disease. This index also includes the consideration of the seriousness and the number of comorbid diseases.

2.2 Nurse Experience

The other factor in this study, nurses' competence, can be associated with the nurse's experience. Cheevakasemsook, Chapman [15] by the interviewing process found out that some nurses were unable to create a nursing plan while some nurses felt their charting was dubious due to lack of confidence. These factors are a result of lack of proper training and experience for the nurses. Benner [21] interpreted skill acquisition and clinical judgment between the high experience and low experience nurses. The study showed that the high experience nurses were able to change their perception of the nature of the situation and act accordingly in response to the new situation. Thus, this study considers nurses' experience as one of the important factors for increasing in the documentation time as we assume that the highly experienced nurse may perceive more details in an unfolding situation which they document in the EMR.

3   Methodology

3.1   Time and Motion Study

The time and motion study was conducted in the Medical intensive care unit (MICU) at the University Hospital, University of Missouri, Columbia [22]. The MICU had 18 single patient rooms and a reception area located at the center. Eleven nurses participated in the study voluntarily, and three to four nurses were observed on each observation day during the day shift hours (7:00 am to 7:30 pm). The volunteer nurses were all registered nurses and had at least 1-year experience of working in an ICU. The nurses were well informed about the time and motion study and the information collected about the nurses and the patients were kept confidential. Two observers observed the volunteer nurses on the observation day. The observation was conducted one day per week for thirteen weeks. The observers recorded the start time and end time of each task done by the nurses in an observation form and made notes for any special events that took place. To minimize the Hawthorne effect, the observer maintained a considerable distance from the participants and did not initiate any conversation with the nurses. To ensure patient privacy, the observers did not enter the patient room.

From the data collected using the time and motion study, the nurses were aggregated into four groups. The groups were created based on the illness severity level of the patients assigned to the nurse and the nurse's experience level. A HIGH patient severity level indicates that the patients assigned to the nurse had high SOFA score. The SOFA score is considered to be high if the value is larger than the threshold value of 8.6 and the CI score is considered to be high if the value is greater than the threshold value of 7.3. The threshold values are the mean values of the SOFA and CI scores for the collected data set. Based on regression analysis, it was identified that the SOFA score was more significantly influential than the CI score. Thus, the SOFA score was considered as patient's illness severity level. The nurse experience is considered to be HIGH if the nurse had experience working in an ICU for more than 2 years. Based on the threshold values, the four groups are shown in Table 1.

Table 1.   Four groups based on patient severity level and nurse experience

Group number	Patient severity level	Nurse experience level
1	HIGH	HIGH
2	HIGH	LOW
3	LOW	HIGH
4	LOW	LOW

3.2 Data Analysis

The time and motion study data was combined with the EMR system logs called the Real-Time Measurement Systems (RTMS) data to obtain a more detailed view of nurses' documentation workflow. The RTMS data provides detailed information of the usage of the EMR system. From the RTMS data, it is possible to identify the section of the EMR system that was accessed to carry out charting and the time taken for each charting. The RTMS data also gives information related to which computer was used, a number of clicks that the nurse made during the charting and the moving distance of a mouse pointer. By combining the RTMS data and the observation data, we were able to analyze the accurate view of how the nurses used EMR systems.

3.3 Hierarchical Task Analysis (HTA)

The hierarchical task analysis (HTA) technique was used to create a view of the EMR charting process in the MICU. The HTA chart revealed the ICU nurses' EMR charting pattern by systematically breaking down the nurse's charting procedure into different task levels and goals. The HTA chart consists of high-level tasks and subtasks, and each level of tasks has its own goals and sub-goals. Once the goals and sub-goals were identified, a plan was created for each level of tasks. The plan helps in identifying the order in which each subtask needs to be carried out to achieve the goal of the high-level task. The plan also states the conditions that need to be satisfied to perform the subtasks. Figure 1 shows the HTA for the EMR charting process up to level 2. The top-level goal of the HTA chart is to complete documenting in the EMR system. The multiple subgoals must be completed to achieve the goal shown in level 1, and the subtasks in level 2 need to be achieved based on the given conditions to meet each subgoal. Here, the plan 0 shows how the tasks in level 1 need to be carried out to achieve the top-level goal. Plans 1, 2, 4, 5 shows how the subtasks in level 2 need to be carried out to achieve the goals of level 1. This way, the HTA chart helps us identify the different requirements of each task associated with the EMR process. Based on the description of the HTA chart, a simulation model using discrete event simulation was developed to analyze the impact on the nurse's process time during EMR documentation in ICU.

3.4 Simulation Model

The simulation model was developed using the HTA chart and further breaks down a high-level goal into a chain of tasks. The simulation model helped us to improve our understanding of the EMR charting process that is currently being followed by the nurses in the ICU. The simulation model was developed using the Micro Saint Sharp software. The simulation model is similar to HTA chart wherein, all the goals of a particular level are to be completed to move to lower level goals in the model. The simulation model shows the step by step procedure that the nurses follow to chart on the EMR system. The timing information used in the simulation model was obtained from the RTMS data in the form of mean time and standard deviation. The main purpose of modeling was to determine the different factors that influence the time taken by the nurses to document

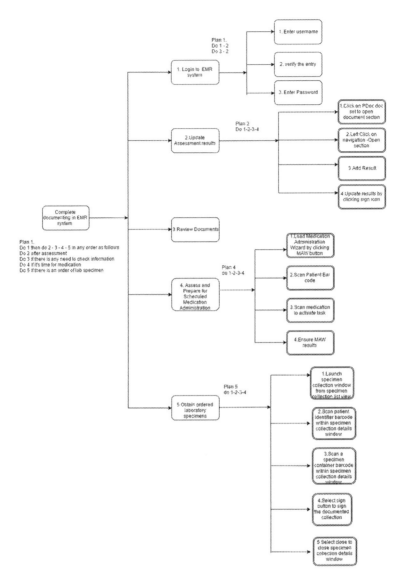

Fig. 1. HTA chart for EMR process

on the EMR system. Figure 2 shows a screenshot of the ICU nurse's discrete event simulation model for EMR documentation.

The simulation model shown in Fig. 2 consists of networks and tasks that represent the charting process. Each method in the model represents a human task and is considered as a node. In the model, the nodes are connected by arrows to denote the sequence in which the tasks were performed. The simulation model allowed us to create a real-time scenario of the nurse's documentation process on the EMR system and conduct experiments to determine the factors influencing the documentation time.

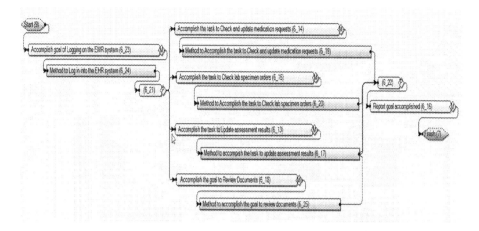

Fig. 2. ICU Nurse's discrete event simulation model to document on EMR system

4   Results

The simulation model was executed to collect the EMR documentation time per a task. According to the RTMS data, the ICU nurses used the EMR system 49.2 times during the 12-h day shift. Based on this, we assumed that average frequency of accessing the EMR system was 1,476 times per month. Hence, the simulation was run 1,476 times, and the simulation results were collected. After that, a one-way ANOVA was conducted to compare the effect of patient severity level and nurse experience on EMR documentation time between the groups. The interval plot from the ANOVA analysis is shown in Fig. 3.

The ANOVA analysis showed that there was the significant effect of patient severity level and nurse experience on EMR documentation time at $p < .05$ [F(44.12), $P < 0.001$]. The mean process time of EMR documentation was significantly longer for Group 1 and Group 3 followed by Group 4 and Group 2 (Group 1 and Group 3 $\gg$ Groups 4 $\gg$ 2). To identify the impact of patient severity level and nurse experience on the content charted, Fischer test was conducted for each type of charting and the four groups. The interval plots for the analysis is shown in Fig. 4.

The analysis showed that the patient severity level and nurse experience had a significant impact on the content being charted. For assessment, the mean process time for EMR documentation was significantly longer Group 1 followed by Group 3, Group 2 and Group 4 (Group 1 $\gg$ Group 3 $\gg$ Group 2 $\gg$ Group 4). For review documents, the high experience nurses took significantly longer time than the low experience nurses (Group 1 and Group 3 $\gg$ Group 4 $\gg$ Group 2). For medication, Group 3 nurses took longer time than Group 1, Group 4, Group 2 (Group 3 $\gg$ Group 4 and Group 1 and Group 2). The next section discusses more in-depth about the impact of patient severity level and nurses experience on each type of charting carried out by the nurses.

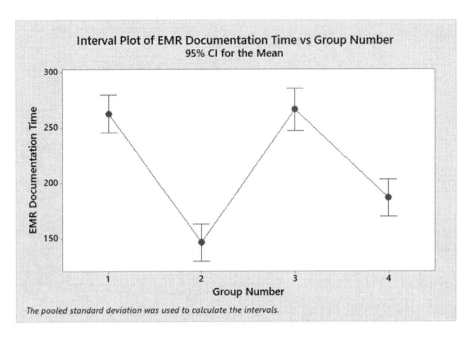

Fig. 3. Interval plot for the time taken to document on EMR system (secs).

5   Discussion and Conclusion

The ANOVA results from Fig. 2 showed that the high experienced nurses charted for a significantly longer time on the EMR system than the low experienced nurses. The more experienced nurses used the EMR system after they conducted multiple assessments whereas the less experienced nurses documented after each assessment. When the more experienced nurses recorded multiple assessment results together, they must handle more information during the EMR documentation compared to the low experienced nurses. It resulted in spending longer time for the EMR charting. On the other hand, the low experienced nurses documented a small amount of data based on the specific prede-fined charting steps because they were not fully adopted in the EMR environment. According to the previous study [23], the user's clinical experience can significantly influence the pattern of the EMR usage. Also, Moody and Slocumb [24] found that the user's experience level related to an EMR system played a significant role in the EMR documentation. Although the EMR system is designed to fit its intended purpose, nurses must take time to learn the system [25]. For that reason, the nurses showed the different patterns of EMR documentation based on their experience level.

According to the group comparisons (see Fig. 4), for the groups 1 and 3, the average time of documenting medication request, reviewing documents and lab specimen infor-mation were significantly different from the time taken by the nurses in groups 2 and 4. However, for the assessment charting, both the nurse experience level and the patient severity level significantly influenced the documentation time. It means that the patient

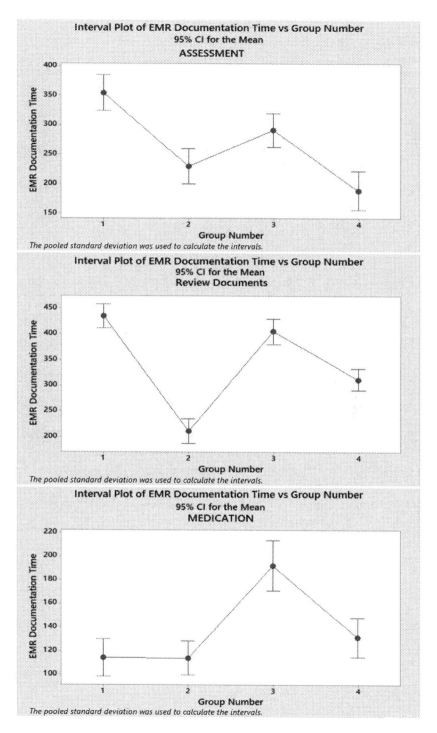

Fig. 4. Interval plots for the different content charted on the EMR system.

severity level had an impact on the assessment charting while all other charting were influenced only by the nurse experience level.

The assessment charting section in the EMR system is where the nurses chart all the results of the assessment conducted during the shift. The nurses performed "initial assessment" at the beginning of the shift. After that, "focused assessment" was performed every hour until the end of the shift. The nurses in group 1 spent longer time to documenting the assessment results because of more results to be charted in the EMR system.

For documenting administered medication in the EMR system, the nurses of groups 3 and 4 took longer time than the nurses of groups 1 and 2. We presume that, when a patient was very sick, the medications that the patient usually took at home were discontinued as they were too sick to take them and were restarted when they became less sick. Thus, the nurses assigned to less severe patients spent longer time in medication administration section. This documentation time is also related to medication requests, and that is the reason why the nurses who assigned in the group 4 showed a significantly longer overall EMR documentation time than the group 2 (see Fig. 3).

6   Limitations and Future Research

There are some limitations in this study. First, nurse's interruption was not considered in our simulation model. Although the ICU nurses experience multiple interruptions during their shift, we did not include the EMR process deviations caused by interruptions in the model. Another limitation is that the model did not consider the workflow variations caused by nurse's workload and emergency situations. The nurse's workload and urgent situations can significantly impact the process time and nurse's care flows in ICU. Hence, for future study, we will expand our simulation model to include the components related to interruptions, nurse's workload, and emergency situations to identify the impact on EMR works in ICU.

Acknowledgments. The Interdisciplinary Innovations Fund and Mizzou Advantage supported this research. We also thank nurses at the University Hospital, University of Missouri Health Care in Columbia, Missouri.

References

1. Haux, R., et al.: Healthcare in the information society. A prognosis for the year 2013. Int. J. Med. Inform. **66**(1), 3–21 (2002)
2. Poissant, L., et al.: The impact of electronic health records on time efficiency of physicians and nurses: a systematic review. J. Am. Med. Inform. Assoc. **12**(5), 505–516 (2005)
3. Ammenwerth, E., Spötl, H.: The time needed for clinical documentation versus direct patient care. Methods Inf. Med. **48**(1), 84–91 (2009)
4. Parameshwara, N., et al.: NGOMSL simulation model in an emergency department. In: Proceedings of the 2016 Winter Simulation Conference. IEEE Press (2016)
5. Iyer, P.W., Camp, N.H.: Nursing Documentation: A Nursing Process Approach. Mosby Inc., St. Louis (1999)

6. Hendrich, A., et al.: A 36-hospital time and motion study: how do medical-surgical nurses spend their time? Perm. J. **12**(3), 25 (2008)

7. Hefter, Y., et al.: A time-motion study of ICU workflow and the impact of strain. Crit. Care Med. **44**(8), 1482–1489 (2016)

8. Mador, R.L., Shaw, N.T.: The impact of a Critical Care Information System (CCIS) on time spent charting and in direct patient care by staff in the ICU: a review of the literature. Int. J. Med. Inform. **78**(7), 435–445 (2009)

9. Saarinen, K., Aho, M.: Does the implementation of a clinical information system decrease the time intensive care nurses spend on documentation of care? Acta Anaesthesiol. Scand. **49**(1), 62–65 (2005)

10. Hripcsak, G., et al.: Use of electronic clinical documentation: time spent and team interactions. J. Am. Med. Inform. Assoc. **18**(2), 112–117 (2011)

11. Bosman, R.J.: Impact of computerized information systems on workload in operating room and intensive care unit. Best Pract. Res. Clin. Anaesthesiol. **23**(1), 15–26 (2009)

12. Bian, D., et al.: A novel virtual reality driving environment for autism intervention. In: Stephanidis, C., Antona, M. (eds.) UAHCI 2013. LNCS, vol. 8010, pp. 474–483. Springer, Heidelberg (2013). https://doi.org/10.1007/978-3-642-39191-0_52

13. Bradshaw, K.E., et al.: Computer-based data entry for nurses in the ICU. MD Comput. Comput. Med. Pract. **6**(5), 274–280 (1989)

14. Bosman, R., et al.: Intensive care information system reduces documentation time of the nurses after cardiothoracic surgery. Intensive Care Med. **29**(1), 83–90 (2003)

15. Cheevakasemsook, A., et al.: The study of nursing documentation complexities. Int. J. Nurs. Pract. **12**(6), 366–374 (2006)

16. Juneja, D., et al.: Comparison of newer scoring systems with the conventional scoring systems in general intensive care population. Minerva Anestesiol. **78**(2), 194–200 (2012)

17. Vincent, J., et al.: The SOFA score to describe organ dysfunction/failure. On behalf of the Working Group on Sepsis-Related Problems of the European Society of Intensive Care Medicine. Intensive Care Med. **22**(7), 707–710 (1996)

18. Frohlich, M., et al.: Which score should be used for posttraumatic multiple organ failure? - Comparison of the MODS, Denver- and SOFA- Scores. Scand. J. Trauma Resusc. Emerg. Med. **24**(1), 130 (2016)

19. Vincent, J.-L., et al.: Use of the SOFA score to assess the incidence of organ dysfunction/ failure in intensive care units: results of a multicenter, prospective study. Crit. Care Med. **26**(11), 1793–1800 (1998)

20. Charlson, M.E., et al.: A new method of classifying prognostic comorbidity in longitudinal studies: development and validation. J. Chronic Dis. **40**(5), 373–383 (1987)

21. Benner, P.: Using the Dreyfus model of skill acquisition to describe and interpret skill acquisition and clinical judgment in nursing practice and education. Bull. Sci. Technol. Soc. **24**(3), 188–199 (2004)

22. Song, X., Kim, J.H., Despins, L.: A Time-Motion Study in an Intensive Care Unit using the Near Field Electromagnetic Ranging System. In: Proceedings of the IIE Annual Conference. Institute of Industrial and Systems Engineers (IISE) (2017)

23. Miller, L., et al.: Novice nurse preparedness to effectively use electronic health records in acute care settings: critical informatics knowledge and skill gaps. Online J. Nurs. Inform. (OJNI) **18**(2) (2014)

24. Moody, L.E., et al.: Electronic health records documentation in nursing: nurses' perceptions, attitudes, and preferences. Comput. Inform. Nurs. (CIN) **22**(6), 337–344 (2004)

25. Leonard-Barton, D.: Implementation as mutual adaptation of technology and organization. Res. Policy **17**(5), 251–267 (1988)

Construct of Learning Model
for Laparoscopic Surgery

Kazuaki Yamashiro[1]([✉]), Akihiko Goto[2], Hisanori Shiomi[3],
and Koichiro Murakami[4]

[1] Kyoto Institute of Technology,
Goshokaido-cho Matsugasaki Sakyo-ku, Kyoto, Japan
k.yamashiro546@gmail.com
[2] Osaka Sangyo University, Daito-shi, Osaka, Japan
[3] Nagahama Red Cross Hospital,
14-7 Miyamae-cho, Nagahama-shi, Shiga, Japan
[4] Tesseikai Neurosurgical Hospital,
28-1 Nakanohomma-chi, Shijonawate, Osaka, Japan

Abstract. Laparoscopic surgery is one of surgery method. It requires many experiences to acquire the techniques and time to educate others because, for example, it has little information that the operator can acquire through field of view and sense of touch, and need to get used to through the operation of forceps. Laparoscopic surgery have four learning method (Dry box, Wet lab, Simulator, animal lab). With the simulator, learnings are that immersed in the most realistic skills, training environment, gave the opportunity to develop proficiency in laparoscopic surgical techniques, provided accurate tactile, feel of need procedures and complications and gave risk–free learning before touching their first patient. However, it is impossible to train according to personal skills only simulator. Previous studies have shown that the surgeon' gaze point revealed when using the surgery simulator, thereby indicating that the result of the eye movement is useful for learning. The goal of this study is construction of learning system that to feedback the evaluation result to the learner. We analyzed the medical students' eye movements, there were individual differences in the medical students' gazing points, and there was a pattern in the medical students' gazing points. We were able to cluster them and divide them into groups.

Keywords: Eye movement · Laparoscopic surgery · Guidance

1 Introduction

Laparoscopic surgery is modern surgical technique in which operations are performed far from their location through small incisions (usually 5–15 mm) elsewhere in the body using laparoscope. It has some Characteristics compared the open procedure.

1. Specific surgical instruments are used include laparoscope forceps, scissors, probes, dissectors, hooks, retractors, and more.
2. Pain and hemorrhaging are reduced due to smaller incisions.
3. Recovery times are shorter than open procedure.

© Springer International Publishing AG, part of Springer Nature 2018
V. G. Duffy (Ed.): DHM 2018, LNCS 10917, pp. 558–566, 2018.
https://doi.org/10.1007/978-3-319-91397-1_45

In this way, Laparoscopic surgery will reduces the Patient's burden. However, this surgery demand some hard work on surgeon. For example, the restricted vision, the difficulty in handling of the instruments, the limited working area are the factors which add to the technical complexity of this surgical approach and additional training is necessary after completing their basic surgical skill. Therefore, Laparoscopic surgery has problems that require long time to get skills.

Learning method of Laparoscopic surgery are Dry box, Wet lab, Simulator and Animal lab. With the simulator, learnings are that immersed in the most realistic skills, training environment, gave the opportunity to develop proficiency in laparoscopic surgical techniques, provided accurate tactile, feel of need procedures and compli-cations and gave risk–free learning before touching their first patient. However, it is impossible to train according to personal skills only simulator.

In previous studies, we analyzed surgeons' eye movement in simulator of laparo-scopic surgery and clarified that gaze point under surgery is stabilized as experience becomes longer. We thought that elucidation of eye movement in Laparoscopic surgery was useful to get skills. The goal of study is to construct system that feeds back the evaluation results to learners. This time, we do experiments for medical students and show the relationship between the medical students' eye movement and the contents of teaching done to medical students and the evaluation of simulator.

2   Experiment

2.1   Participants

Participants was 36 medical students who used the simulator for the first time, and the advising doctors was 2 surgeons with similar experience. Medical student divide into 7 groups. Table 1 indicates the number of medical students in each group and their advising doctors.

Table 1.   Group breakdown

Group Number	Advising doctors	Medical student
G1	A	5
G2	B	6
G3	A	6
G4	B	4
G5	A	5
G6	B	4
G7	A	6

2.2   Measuring Device

Measuring device were employed a surgery training simulator LapVR (Gadelius Medical K.K.) and Calibration free gaze measurement EMR ACTUS (nac Image Technology Inc.). The detection rate was 60 Hz.

2.3   Experiment Method

In the experiment, we measured eye movements during practical training of laparo-scopic cholecystectomy using a simulator. The experiment was done twice. The 1st experiment was the surgeon performed laparoscopic cholecystectomy in front of medical students as an experiment, and then medical students conduct the same surgery with guidance by him. The 2nd experiment was medical students perform the same case without any guidance. Figure 1 indicates how medical students are practicing.

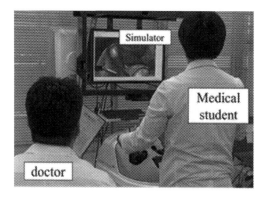

Fig. 1. Appearance of training

3   Analysis Method

3.1   Eye Movement

The eye movement data measured by the experiment was analyzed by Area of Interest (AOI). Figure 2 indicates examples of AOI range. This time, we clarified the gaze time ratio of the gallbladder to be worked.

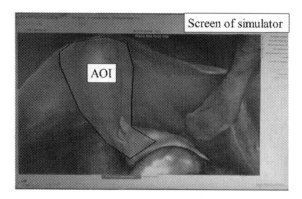

Fig. 2. Examples of AOI range

3.2   Evaluation of Simulation

It is evaluated that the work is completed by LapVR. We focused on the evaluation items "Actual result for Left. Path. Length" and "Actual result for Right. Path. Length". They are items directly related to the operation of the forceps and are easy to evaluate as numerical data.

3.3   Guidance Content

In the 1st experiment the advising doctors instructed medical students. The guide content was analyzed by SPSS Text Analytics for Surveys. We extracted specific words and counted those words into categories. Table 2 indicates category content. We revealed the guidance received by medical students by category.

Table 2. Category content

Category	Notation
Organ	A
Organ + Operation	B
Organ + Direction	C
Organ + Operation + Direction	D
Forceps	E
Forceps + Operation	F
Forceps + Direction	G
Forceps + Operation + Direction	H
Operation	I
Operation + Direction	J
Operation + Organ + Forceps	K

4   Result

4.1   Result of Eye Movement

It is important to keep watching the gallbladder during work. We calculated the ratio from the gaze ratio of the 1stexperiment and the 2nd experiment gall bladders and clarified the trend. Figure 3 indicates the increase or decrease of gaze ratios of each group. A positive value indicates that medical students are gazing at the gallbladder more than the 1st experiment, and a negative value indicates that medical students are gazing at the gallbladder less than the 1st experiment. For that reason, a positive value is said to be improving. In G1, the gaze ratio increased by 2 medical students. In G2, the gaze ratio increased by 4 medical students. Here was no medical student whose gaze ratio increased in G3. In G4, the gaze ratio increased by 3 medical students. In G5,

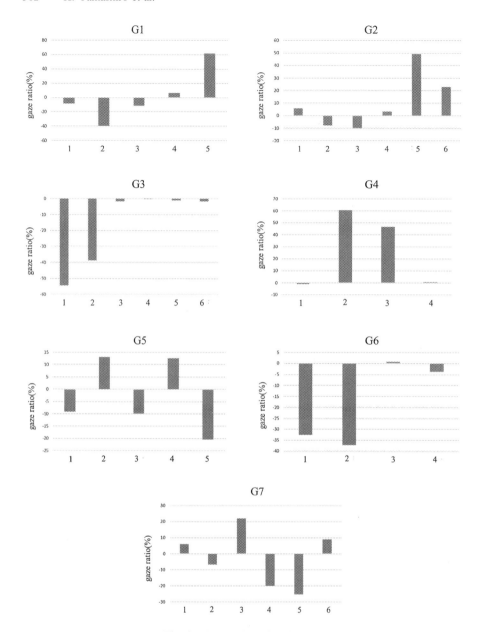

Fig. 3. Gaze ratios of each group

the gaze ratio increased by 2 medical students. In G6, the gaze ratio increased by 1 people. In G7, the gaze ratio increased by 3 medical students. 15 medical students as a whole had an improvement trend. There was also a medical student with an improvement tendency in each group except G3, and there was no group with all medical students tending to improve.

4.2 Evaluation of Simulator

The shorter the moving distance of the forceps, the more unnecessary work is being done. As with eye movements, we clarify the increase or decrease from the 1st experiment and the 2nd experiment results. Figure 4 indicates the increase or decrease

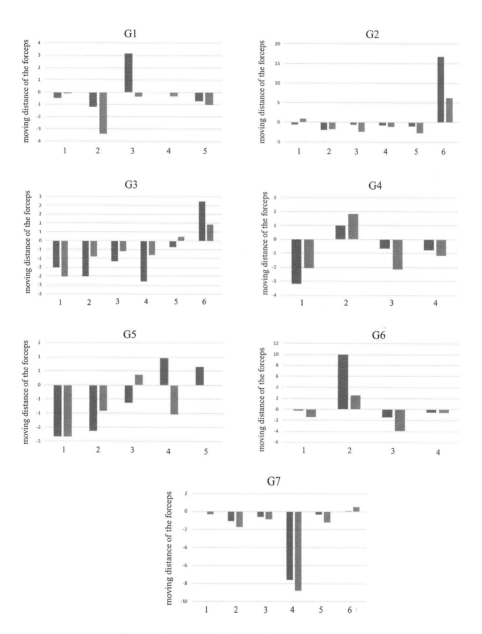

Fig. 4. Movement distance of forceps in each group

of the moving distance of the forceps of each group. A positive value indicates that the moving distance of the 2nd experiment is longer than that of the 1st experiment. A negative value indicates that the 2nd experiment moving distance is shorter than the 1st experiment. Therefore, a negative values can be said to be improving. In G1 as a whole there was an improvement trend, with only one left trending upward. In G 2, G 3 and G 4, only 1 medical student was not improving. In G5, there was an improvement trend in 2 medical student, there was 1 medical student with improvement tendency only on the left hand, and 1 medical student with improvement tendency only on the right hand. In the G6, there was a tendency for improvement to 3 medical student. In G 7, there was a tendency to improve in 4 medical student.

4.3   Guidance Content

Figure 5 indicates the proportion of remarks when teaching at the time of demonstration and guidance to medical students. In G1, G2, G3, G4, G5, the most "I" remark was made both for demonstration and guidance to medical students. In the G6, "E" was given at the time of demonstration and "I" was guided most guidance to medical students. In the G7, "A" and "E" was given at the time of demonstration and "I" was guided most guidance to medical students. Overall "I" remarks were made well. Also, there was a remark that became instructed after guidance to medical students.

5   Discussion

From the results of the eye movements and the results of the evaluation of the simulator, we thought that it is easy to get used to the operation of the forceps than to gaze the gallbladder. Because the number of medical students accustomed to operation of the forceps was larger than the number of medical students who can gaze at the gall bladder. From this, medical students can be divided into categories for each proficiency level. From the results of the guidance contents, the explanation of the operation has been increased, and as guidance to medical students guides the operation in more detail. We think that there are many medical students who improved the operation of forceps by guidance. It is necessary to investigate whether gaze improvement is further made by teaching gaze points as guidance.

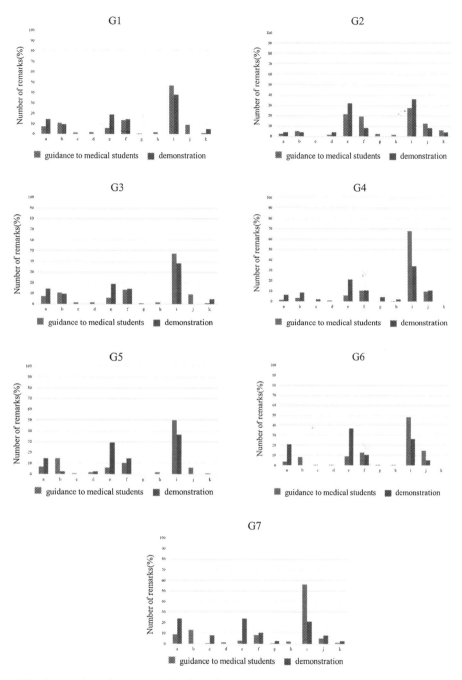

Fig. 5. Number of remarks at the time of demonstration and guidance to medical students

6 Conclusion

This study revealed the characteristics of medical students. We propose feedback method by evaluation given to learners. For example, we give scores on the result of eye movements and evaluation of the simulator, and make it possible to confirm our own skill level by score. The learners can receives the necessary training according to the score. This will allow learning more suitable for individuals.

Transportation Human Factors

Monitors vs. Smart Glasses: A Study on Cognitive Workload of Digital Information Systems on Forklift Trucks

Benno Gross[✉], Michael Bretschneider-Hagemes, Andreas Stefan, and Jörg Rissler

Institute for Occupational Safety and Health, Alte Heerstraße 111, 53757 Sankt Augustin, Germany
benno.gross@dguv.de

Abstract. New digital work equipment is increasingly affecting the approach to work. They enable more efficient, mobile and flexible operation, at the same time, however, new potential hazards and risks may arise for employees. A number of digital devices and their corresponding application context have not yet been comprehensively researched in the field of occupational sciences. In order to be able to recognize potential hazards in a preventive approach, this study examines the impact of the use of such devices in the context of forklift trucks on the safety and health of employees. In particular, the use of two types of smart glasses and of a monitor has been investigated. For the assessment of cognitive workload, the study made use of a standardized reaction test procedure, the Detection Response Task (DRT) according to ISO 17488 as well as subjective assessment using the NASA Task Load Index (NASA-TLX). This research will provide valuable information about possible work related hazards regarding the use of smart glasses on forklift trucks with respect to cognitive workload.

Keywords: Smart glasses · Augmented reality · Logistics · Cognitive workload Detection Response Task (DRT) · Occupational Safety and Health (OSH)

1 Introduction

1.1 Smart Glasses

Smart glasses are head-mounted micro-computers (wearables) that have optical displays in the user's field of vision. Therefore, these devices are classified as head-mounted displays (HMD). Similar to smartphones, they have an operating system, usually Bluetooth- and WLAN-sensors as well as a camera, with which videos and photos can be recorded and displayed. By using smart glasses, reality is enriched by additional virtual overlays of information or objects in real time. Therefore, in the context of smart glasses we are referring to assisted reality or augmented reality.

Potential use cases can be found in all areas of work: Tasks that require guidance, information recording, collaboration or external control, but where visual obstruction or interaction with an external display is impeding. Advantages include, for example, the

© Springer International Publishing AG, part of Springer Nature 2018
V. G. Duffy (Ed.): DHM 2018, LNCS 10917, pp. 569–578, 2018.
https://doi.org/10.1007/978-3-319-91397-1_46

reduction of training requirements through context-related work instructions that are displayed in the employee's visual field with smart glasses (training on the job). Or for other applications, assistance and support (remote expert) can also be consulted for specific operations, or the work quality can be checked via video stream and documentation [1].

1.2 Smart Glasses in Warehouse Logistics

In recent years, the potential of smart glasses and augmented reality has met with great interest in different areas of the working world, especially in warehouse logistics. This service sector with its complex work processes, high demands on mobility and flexibility is particularly affected by technological transformation. Today, order picking scenarios can already be implemented by using smart glasses in the form of pick-by-vision systems: Hands-free operation, integrated barcode scanners, and the reduction of glances on external information devices when working with smart glasses provide significant advantages over conventional picking systems. Therefore, the US market research company Gartner expects that 20% of large enterprise businesses companies will start implementing virtual or augmented reality solutions by 2019 [2].

Although recent operational scenarios of smart glasses have mostly been limited to picking activities, it is also conceivable that such devices can be used as digital information systems for operations forklift trucks. In general, forklift truck drivers receive work related information via monitor display systems in the passenger compartment. In 2016 alone, the German Social Accident Insurance (DGUV) reported 218 213 industrial accidents in internal transport, the most frequent of which were accidents involving industrial trucks (forklifts, hand trucks) and 12 671 of which with forklifts [3]. The most common cause of accidents is the driver's misconduct or inadequate operational safety precautions. And while there are no exact figures on distraction related accidents, corresponding studies on information and communication technology in road traffic show that reducing the number of non-driving activities can make a fundamental contribution to accident prevention [4]. In this respect, the driver's workplace should be designed in such a way that the cognitive workload is minimized [5]. In addition, long-term effects in the musculoskeletal system due to the use of conventional and head-mounted displays are also conceivable.

With smart glasses, information is presented to the user in the ego-perspective, which may lead to a reduction of glance related distraction from the driving activity. Therefore, it is essential to examine whether this positive aspect corresponds with a reduction of cognitive workload.

2 Leading Question

The study examines whether the use of display systems while driving forklifts is related to an increase in cognitive workload, and to what extent the use of smart glasses on forklifts differs from conventional monitoring systems.

3 Methods and Materials

3.1 Forklift Truck Simulator

For the study, the forklift truck simulator of the Institute for Occupational Health and Safety (IFA) was used, which simulates the original working environment and a vehicle with a fully haptic passenger compartment (see Fig. 1). Standardized mounts for mobile devices have been attached to the center console to enable display-driven interaction with external control panels.

Fig. 1. Forklift truck simulator in the experimental setup.

The simulation software (Unity Engine) was presented on three 55-inch flat screen full HD monitors. Depending on the settings of the position-adjustable driver's seat, the eye to display distance varied from 85–100 cm.

Both, the technical structures and their arrangements were based on a maximum achievable level of realism regarding operational practice.

3.2 Digital Information Systems

Three different digital information systems were used: As a representation of a monitor system, a 10.1-inch tablet (tablet) was used, which was attached to the center console with a bracket for the duration of the respective runs. For the runs with head-mounted displays, two different smart glasses were used: A smart glass (head-mounted display 1: HMD1) with a monocular display and touchpad on the side frame. The second smart glass (head-mounted display 2: HMD2) has a binocular display system and an external touchpad connected to the frame with a wire and mounted in the center console.

3.3   Participants

Only persons with a valid forklift license were included as test persons in the study collective. In addition, the drivers were not allowed to wear glasses or at least had to be able to drive a forklift truck without glasses. This restriction was necessary because the head-mounted display devices could not be fully used with glasses. Prior to the test, the participants were informed about the general conditions of the study. All persons participated on a voluntary basis after giving informed consent in written form. It has been possible to terminate the test at any point without negative consequences for the participants.

A total of 32 male participants of the IFA and the cooperating partner, a company for warehousing and logistics, were invited to take part in the study. Data from nine participants were not evaluated because there were cases of simulator sickness or incomplete data sets. The remaining 23 participants had an age between 23 and 53 years with a mean value of 40 years. One of the subjects had glasses, but took part in the experiment without glasses. The other 22 subjects were not wearing glasses.

According to the participants, the driving experience with forklifts was between 0.3 h and 40.0 h per month with a mean value of 6.5 h and a median of 3.0 h.

3.4   Tasks

The three tasks according to ISO 17488 [6] were implemented as follows:

The primary task was to operate in the driving simulator, which displayed a virtual warehouse without other road users with numbered shelf paths. In this warehouse, shelves with certain numbers had to be approached, and driving errors were also recorded in every run. A driving error occurred when objects (walls, shelves) were touched by the vehicle in the simulation.

The secondary task consisted of reading information from three different types of outlined digital information systems. The participants were instructed to read a randomly selected shelf number and approach the corresponding target (see Fig. 2). This task was repeated until the end of the respective run. In addition, the task load has been held on the same level by constantly reading out numbers (1–10) appearing on the respective display. Each participant completed a total of four runs in random order, each lasting two minutes: One run each with one of the two smart glasses, the tablet and a run without additional tasks. This baseline run consisted of driving without display units, whereby the shelf numbers to be approached were read aloud by the test supervisor.

The reaction test was carried out according to the standard with an optical stimulus using the Detection Response Task (DRT). The light emitting diode was located in the participants' field of view. For each run, participants had to react to about 30 stimuli by pressing a button mounted to their index finger. A hit was counted and stored with the corresponding response time if a reaction took place between 100 ms and 2500 ms. In addition to the response time, the hit rate was also recorded.

Fig. 2. Secondary task performed with smart glasses (HMD1).

3.5 Questionnaires

Before each session, participants were asked to complete a questionnaire with demographic information. It included questions on the following aspects:

age (in years)
gender
wearer of glasses (yes/no)
driving experience (in hours per month)

In addition, the subjective load for the respective devices was reported by the participants after each run by means of a standardized questionnaire (NASA-TLX) [7]. It consisted of six individual questions on different aspects of the load, which were answered by placing a cross on a scale. Since the scale contained 20 tick marks between "low/good" and "high/bad", the crosses were evaluated as numbers between 0 and 20. The individual answers were not weighted.

After the sessions, general questions were asked about which system was suited best, which one was least distracting, and whether a certain device obstructed the view.

3.6 Procedure

Before each session, participants were asked to carry out training runs without any secondary tasks until they felt comfortable with the handling of the simulation. Thereafter the secondary task, the reaction task as well as the respective display units were introduced to the participants. Subsequently, a further practice phase was carried out, the procedure of which corresponded to the real test without a reaction test and questionnaire. This was followed by 4 runs, during which the test persons had to perform the DRT additionally:

run without display unit (baseline)
run with monocular display unit (HMD1)
run with binocular display (HMD2)
run with an external monitor (tablet)

The order of the runs was determined randomly. Overall, one session lasted approximately 30 min.

4   Results

Three performance parameters from the objective measurements are used in the experimental setup: the driving errors, the response times of the hits and the hit rates. The results of the objective measurement are accompanied by a standardized questionnaire, the NASA-TLX. The general questionnaire can only provide supporting information.

4.1   Driving Errors

The analysis of driving errors for entirety of the runs by the 23 participants shows a small number of driving errors: only in 21 out of 92 complete runs driving errors occurred. When adding up the errors during the runs regarding the corresponding digital information systems, four driving errors were recorded for the baseline run and 12 driving errors each for HMD2 and tablet. However, there were only five driving errors when using HMD1. It has not been possible to infer with statistical methods a dependence of the driving errors on the participants and their cognitive task load. The driving errors appear to happen randomly on a low level.

4.2   Response Times and Hit Rates

The study examined, whether the cognitive workload increases when using digital information systems compared to baseline runs and whether the workload of the evaluated devices differ from one another. The results show that mean response times per participant with digital information systems were lower compared to runs without additional tasks (see Fig. 3): For runs with HMD1, the differences in response times per participant were on aver-age 147 ms lower, with HMD2 130 ms and with the tablet 103 ms. This effect is statistically significant.

In addition, the hit rate decreases on average per participant when digital information systems are used in the runs.

However, this effect cannot be observed among the devices examined: There was no significant distinction in response times or hit rates for the use of one device compared to another. It should, therefore, be noted that the cognitive workload during runs was lower if no additional tasks had to be carried out on digital information

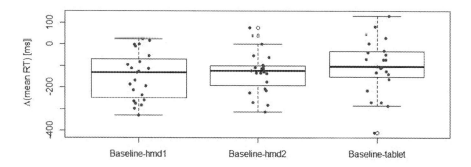

Fig. 3. Distribution of the differences of mean reaction times per participant as box plots and scatters plots. Mean reaction times while using a device is subtracted from runs without device, i.e., negative values indicate an increase in cognitive load.

systems. But none of the examined devices produced a higher or lower cognitive workload in direct comparison of the devices.

4.3 Questionnaires

The results of the NASA-TLX support the findings of the objective measurement: If comparing the results of the NASA-TLX for runs without devices and runs with digital information systems, the analysis shows that the subjective workload when using the devices increases. In addition, if one compares the differences between different devices, the analysis does not show any significant difference in the workload.

When it comes to the results of the general questionnaire, most of the respondents liked the tablet best, HMD1 came in second, and only two respondents preferred the HMD2 display. This was also the case when referring to the least distracting device: only two respondents gave a different answer to the question of the preferred device in this regard. The issue of visual obstruction implied the same understanding as the question of least distracting device: Overall, the tablet was associated with the least distraction and least general obstruction, the HMD2 display with the largest.

5 Discussion

5.1 Participants

Participants in the study were selected in advance according to specific criteria: they had to be employed either by the partner company or at the IFA, and they were not allowed to wear glasses.

They also had to hold a valid forklift truck license. However, it can be assumed that forklift truck drivers generally have a higher monthly driving experience than the ones reported by the participants of this study. Therefore, the study collective is not representative and the results of the study can only be applied to the group of all forklift truck drivers with limitations.

5.2   Driving Errors

Since the driving errors occur in this test at a low rate, that appears to be independent from the participants and their workload, the primary task of driving in the simulator has been successfully accomplished regardless of the comparatively low reported driving experience.

On the other hand, one cannot infer from this that driving errors are generally independent from personal training level and/or workload. However, this has to be investigated in a different test design.

5.3   Response Times and Hit Rates

The results of the objective measurement show that the cognitive workload on the participants has increased significantly due to the use of display devices (HMD1, HMD2, and tablet).

Furthermore, it was not possible to clarify whether there is a difference between the digital information systems regarding cognitive workload. Neither the response times nor the hit rates had conclusive or significant effects that allow a specific device to be prioritized. Therefore, the question of the differences between the devices must be clarified in subsequent studies.

5.4   Questionnaires

The analysis of the exposure aspects in the NASA-TLX questionnaire has been inconclusive. Thus, a weighting of these aspects in the analysis is not possible, and only a mean value of all six questions has been analyzed. This quantity is more related to a general, subjectively felt workload than a measurable cognitive workload.

However, it is plausible that the results of the NASA-TLX strongly correlate with the cognitive workload of the outcome of the objective measurements.

Despite the NASA-TLX's lower validity compared to the objective measurements, the analysis delivers the same qualitative results: Generally, workload increases significantly with the use of devices, but no difference in workload between the devices can be determined.

The results of the general survey were the least reliable. The preference for a certain device can be influenced by various factors and therefore indicates only a partial connection to the issue of cognitive workload. Nevertheless, it is not unlikely that the preference for the tablet is due to the fact that the participants felt least distracted by this device. Although no objective difference in workload has been observed in this study, it can be assumed that the acceptance of the tablet is higher than for the head-mounted display devices.

6   Conclusion

The study investigated cognitive workload caused by the use of digital information systems on forklift trucks during driving. The results provide information on the cognitive workload potential of the investigated devices types: monitor monocular and binocular smart glasses.

Regarding the key study issue, it has been found that the cognitive workload on drivers when using display information devices increases significantly. This was verified both by the results of the objective measurements according to ISO 17488 and by the subjectively perceived workload according to the NAS-TLX questionnaire. However, the results of the study do not reveal any significant differences in cognitive workload between the three digital information systems. Therefore, the question of the differences between the devices must be clarified in subsequent studies. However, the use of a monitor as a digital information system has the distinct advantage over smart glasses that it can also be used by spectacle wearers. In addition, the study has shown that the acceptance of this device is probably higher than with head-mounted display systems.

In addition, it is unclear whether the workload determined in the study is associated with physical strain. The use of smart glasses in this work scenario may, for example, cause musculoskeletal problems that could become chronic if exposed for a longer period of time. It is also possible that the use of smart glasses will increase the risk of accidents caused by distraction. This would have to be clarified in further studies.

The impact of using smart glasses on forklift trucks in a real-world working environment cannot be fully covered by the study. It would be substantially influenced by factors that have to be assessed in the context of the respective risk assessment: type and complexity of tasks to be performed, duration of use, and the software employed. Before using Smart glasses on forklift trucks, companies should therefore consider whether an additional workload is acceptable.

References

1. Terhoeven, J., Wischniewski, S.: Datenbrillen im Einsatz. Gute Arbeit 05/2017, pp. 24–26 (2017)
2. Hompage. https://www.gartner.com/smarterwithgartner/transform-business-outcomes-with-immersive-technology. Accessed 06 Feb 2018
3. Deutsche Gesetzliche Unfallversicherung (eds). Statistik Arbeitsunfallgeschehen 2016, Berlin (2017)
4. Schömig, N., Schoch, S., Neukum, N., Schumacher, Wandtner, B.: Simulatorstudien zur Ablenkungswirkung fahrfremder Tätigkeiten. Berichte der Bundesanstalt für Straßenwesen, M253, Bremen (2015)
5. Kirchhoff, B., Wischniewski, S., Adolph, L.: Head Mounted Displays - Arbeitshilfen der Zukunft. BAuA. Dortmund, Bedingungen für den sicheren und ergonomischen Einsatz monokularer Systeme (2016)

6. ISO 17488:2016 -Road vehicles – Transport information and control systems – Detection-response task (DRT) for assessing attentional effects of cognitive load in driving (2016)
7. Hart, S.G., Staveland, L.E.: Development of NASA-TLX (Task Load Index): results of empirical and theoretical research. In: Meshkati, N., Hancock, P.A. (eds.) Human Mental Workload, Amsterdam, pp. 139–183 (1988)

An International Survey on Automated and Electric Vehicles: Austria, Germany, South Korea, and USA

Myounghoon Jeon[1(✉)], Andreas Riener[2], Jason Sterkenburg[1], Ju-Hwan Lee[3],
Bruce N. Walker[4], and Ignacio Alvarez[5]

[1] Michigan Tech, Houghton, USA
{mjeon,jtsterke}@mtu.edu
[2] Technische Hochschule Ingolstadt (THI), Ingolstadt, Germany
andreas.riener@thi.de
[3] Seoul Media Institute of Technology, Seoul, South Korea
jhlee@smit.ac.kr
[4] Georgia Tech, Atlanta, USA
bruce.walker@psych.gatech.edu
[5] Intel Corporation, Hillsboro, USA
ignacio.j.alvarez@intel.com

Abstract. As development of automated vehicles and adoption of electric vehicles continue to grow, there is an increasing interest in the public opinions on these technologies. We conducted an international online survey to gather information about people's hopes and concerns for automated and electric vehicles from a total of 866 people from four countries – Austria, Germany, South Korea, and USA. Results revealed some differences across countries in the perceptions of automated and electric vehicles. However, differences between the same countries have shrunk compared to our previous survey completed in 2012. Results are discussed with limitations and future work.

Keywords: Automated vehicles · Electric vehicles · Cultural differences
Survey

1   Introduction

The landscape of the automobile market is currently undergoing a dramatic evolution. A number of researchers have predicted autonomous vehicles [1–3] and electric vehicles [4] to be increasingly adopted in the future. It is likely, we will soon witness the rapid introduction and development of autonomous vehicles as well as the further adoption of electric vehicles. Along with these technology-driven changes come many questions about how the public will receive these technologies, such as: What are the barriers to widespread adoption of autonomous and electric vehicles? What features do drivers want in their future vehicles? Are opinions consistent across countries and cultures? To answer these questions we conducted an international survey, collecting data from six countries: Austria, China, Germany, South Korea, Taiwan, and USA.

© Springer International Publishing AG, part of Springer Nature 2018
V. G. Duffy (Ed.): DHM 2018, LNCS 10917, pp. 579–587, 2018.
https://doi.org/10.1007/978-3-319-91397-1_47

2   Methods

Following up on a 2012 international survey on vehicle area network services in three countries [5], we have updated and expanded the survey questions, and repeated the data collection in 2016 in the original participating countries (Austria, Korea, and USA) plus Germany, China, and Taiwan. The English version was first created and reviewed by the consortium members. Then, the survey was translated by researchers in each country. The survey containing 72 questions was distributed online (http://www.pervasive.jku.at/VANSurvey2015/). This paper will focus only on preliminary results pertaining to autonomous and electric vehicles from four countries: Austria, Germany, South Korea, and USA.

2.1   Recruitment

Volunteer participants were recruited either by word of mouth or the university partic-ipation recruitment system. Data collection is ongoing as of the time of this writing. Our preliminary results include 866 participants from four countries between February 2016 and May 2016: Austria (383), Germany (78), South Korea (81), and USA (324).

3   Results

3.1   Demographics

Age. The mean age for all respondents was 27.9 years (SD = 10.2). There were large differences among countries. Korea (M = 38.4; SD = 9.3), Germany (M = 35.0; SD = 11.4), and Austria (M = 30.7; SD = 9.7), had older respondents than USA (M = 20.3; SD = 3.4).

Gender. The overall gender split was 510 males (59.6%) and 345 females (40.3%). The gender distribution was similar for each country: Austria (M: 60.7%; F: 39.3%), Germany (M: 54.5%; F: 45.5%), Korea (M: 70.4%; F: 29.6%), and USA (M: 57%; F: 43%).

Driving Experience. Average years of driving was 9.7 years (SD = 9.0). Given the age differences, there were large differences in experience. Germany (M = 17.3; SD = 11.2), Korea (M = 12.5; SD = 9.5), and Austria (M = 12.3; SD = 9.1) had more experience than USA (M = 4.1; SD = 3.31).

Driving Environment. Overall, respondents drive in a broad range of environments: Urban (252), Suburban (229), Rural (212), Highway (125), Other (36). However, the distribution of driving environments was unbalanced across countries (Fig. 1). It appears that Austria and Germany are very similar. USA shows a somewhat similar distributions to the European countries, but less rural and more suburban driving environments. Korea has a distinctly high percentage of urban driving (81%). This may be a result of the geographic distribution of the recruited samples, but we cautiously infer that this distribution reflects the country population

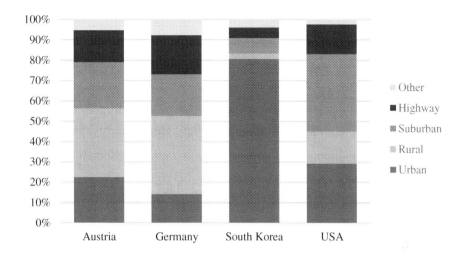

Fig. 1. Distribution of driving environments per country.

Transmission Type. There were large differences in the transmission type among countries, with USA and Korea being dominated by automatic transmissions (84% and 93%, respectively), and with Austria and Germany (82% and 78%, respectively) by primarily manual transmissions. Interestingly, populations of using automatic transmission increased across countries, compared to 2012 (USA 76%, Korea 83%, and Austria 4%).

3.2   Autonomous Vehicles (AVs)

We asked participants about familiarity of AVs, perceived benefits, preferred activities, critical issues, and best approaches.

Familiarity with Autonomous Vehicles. Most participants stated that they had either heard of autonomous vehicles (29%), or were familiar (59%) with the concept. A Chi-squared test of homogeneity showed that familiarity with AVs differed by country $\chi^2(12, 865) = 47.24$, p < .001. Respondents from Korea (56% never heard of AVs or are unfamiliar) appear to be relatively less familiar with AVs compared to other countries, especially Germany (20% never heard of AVs or are unfamiliar).

Perceived Benefits of Autonomous Vehicles. Responses from all countries revealed that the biggest perceived benefit of AVs was safety, followed by increased free-time, and assistance for people who are unable to drive (Fig. 2).

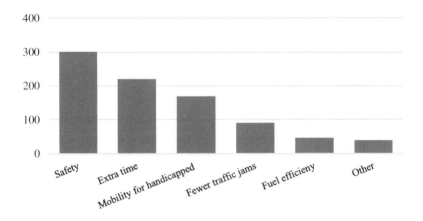

Fig. 2. Frequencies of benefits of AVs across countries.

There were some differences among countries in what they perceived to be the biggest benefits of AVs, $\chi^2(15, 866) = 71.20$, p < .001. Responses suggest that Koreans may perceive fewer benefits in safety (12%), or seem to be less interested in safety, compared to other countries (Austria 37%, USA 39%, Germany 28%). Instead, they perceive relatively more benefits in increasing free time (44%) compared to other countries (Germany 31%, Austria 23%, and USA 22%).

Preferred Activities in Autonomous Vehicles. Respondents showed that they would prefer to sleep, eat, do office work, and monitor in-vehicle operations above other things with their free time in an autonomous vehicle (Table 1).

Table 1. Percentage of preferred activities in AVs.

Activity	N	Percent
Sleep	424	50%
Eat	424	50%
Office work	423	50%
Monitoring vehicle operation	415	49%
Phone call	354	41%
Watch TV	238	28%
Social networking	227	27%
Other	71	8%

Critical Issues with Autonomous Vehicles. Overall, respondents answered that decreased situation awareness is their biggest concern with autonomous vehicles (Fig. 3). These data resonated with responses from the participants who assume that driver takeover will be necessary in some driving environments. Responses also showed strong differences among countries $\chi^2(27, 866) = 226.46$, p < .001. Koreans showed more concern about abrupt system errors (49%) than other countries (Austria 13%, USA 13%, and Germany 8%). Americans showed greater concern over decreased situation awareness (38%) than other countries (Germany 17%, Korea 16%, and Austria 14%).

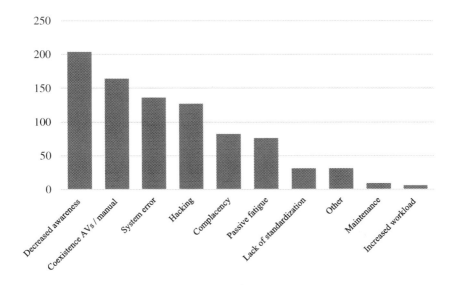

Fig. 3. Frequencies of critical issues in AVs across countries.

Responses from all countries suggest that earning drivers' trust is the biggest obstacle facing AVs, as indicated by 47% of all respondents selecting it as the biggest barrier followed by legal issues at 24% of respondents. The collected data show that country did influence perceptions of which barriers are biggest for autonomous vehicles $\chi^2(15, 866) = 75.07$, p < .001. Americans generally thought driver trust is a bigger barrier (60% selected as biggest barrier) to AVs than other countries (Germany 41%, Austria 39%, and Korea 37%).

Best Approach to Autonomous Vehicles. We asked respondents for their opinions on the best approaches to future autonomous vehicles. The most popular response across all countries was to develop a fully autonomous, self-driving car, but allow the driver to takeover whenever he/she wants (83%) (Table 2). Results also showed that 41% of participants were afraid of the potential for others "hacking" and taking control over the self-driving vehicle.

There were small differences across countries, $\chi^2(15, 866) = 32.49$, p = .001, especially between Austria and Korea with regard to the use of limited self-driving in vehicles. In Austria, a much higher percentage (25%) prefers to have automated vehicles with limited self-driving ability, such as automated on highway only, compared to Korea (7%). This difference may reflect the difference in driving environments, which shows that Korean respondents overwhelmingly drive in urban environments, whereas

Austrian respondents drive more in rural and highway environments, for which limited automation may be sufficient.

Table 2. Percentages of preferences for design of AVs.

Statement	N (agree)	Percent (agree)
Takeover whenever I want	710	83%
Afraid of others being able to control	350	41%
Want car to autonomously drive in critical situations	206	24%
Could own a car without driving controls	151	18%
Want to prohibit manual driving on public roads	118	14%
Other	25	3%

3.3   Electric Vehicles (EVs)

Similar to AVs, we asked participants about familiarity and barriers of EVs, and other EVs-specific questions, such as acceptable ranges and battery recharge times.

Familiarity with Electric Vehicles. A high portion of respondents (62%) stated that they were familiar with EVs or heard of EVs (15%). Chi-square analysis showed that the distribution of responses was different among countries $\chi^2(12, 865) = 75.51$, p < . 001. Koreans reported much less familiarity with EVs (38%) compared to Germans (19%), Austrians (14%), and Americans (8%).

Benefits of Electric Vehicles. The most frequently cited benefit of electric vehicles was their ecological "friendliness" (59%), followed by the fuel economy benefits (26%). We also saw country differences $\chi^2(15, 865) = 108.44$, p < .001 (Fig. 4). Further analysis suggests that Germans were more likely to consider the reduced noise of electric vehicles as the primary benefit (21%) compared to Austrians (8%), Americans (3%), and Koreans (3%). Germans also reported the economic benefits of EVs to be less (8%) than other countries (Korea 35%, USA 30%, and Austria 24%). Further research will consider electricity prices in each country.

Barriers to Electric Vehicles. The most frequently selected concern was limited vehicle range, followed by recharge time (Table 3). Given that the biggest issues of respondents across all countries were vehicle range and battery recharging time, we will focus on what respondents consider acceptable ranges, and recharge times.

Acceptable Vehicle Ranges. Overall responses suggest that participants find ranges between 151–240 miles (37%) acceptable, and another 36% desire a range over 241 miles. Chi-square analysis showed a significant difference among countries, $\chi^2(30, 866) = 78.49$, p < .001. A closer look shows respondents from Korea were much less tolerant of vehicles with low ranges (6%) compared to Germans (31%), Austrians (25%), and Americans (20%) (Fig. 5).

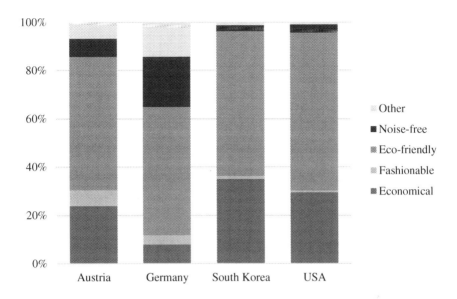

Fig. 4. Distribution of benefits of EVs by country.

Table 3. Barriers to EVs.

Issues with electric vehicles	N	Percent
Range	591	69%
Recharging time	498	58%
Availability of an electric plug	406	47%
Vehicle cost	350	41%
Dead battery	301	35%
Need to plan recharging	272	32%
Battery cost	242	28%
Cost of service for battery runout	153	18%
Uncertainty of possible savings	104	12%
Performance	89	10%

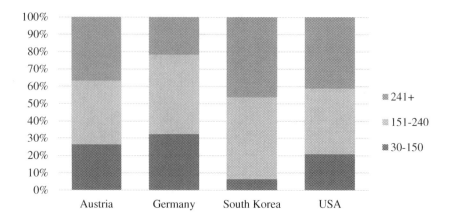

Fig. 5. Distribution of preferred ranges for EVs by country.

Acceptable Battery Recharge Times. Responses across all countries suggest that drivers want their EV batteries to recharge within two hours (45%), or four hours (29%) (Fig. 6). Analysis by country reveals significant differences, $\chi^2(12, N = 865) = 240.12$, $p < .001$, and suggests Koreans were more likely to tolerate long recharge times – 54% accept recharge times of over eight hours - which other countries were less likely to accept (USA 8%, Germany 6%, and Austria 3%). This is in line with results showing Koreans are less tolerant of low EV ranges. Although we need further investigation, it seems that Koreans want to recharge their EVs at one time (e.g., at night) for long distance, perhaps, due to lack of battery charging stations.

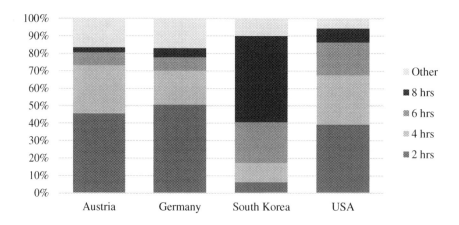

Fig. 6. Recharge rates for EV batteries by country.

4   Discussion and Future Work

Advances in the development of autonomous and electric vehicles leave us with many questions about public perception and acceptance of these technologies and what they hope future autonomous and electric vehicles will look like. We conducted a global survey to answer some of those outstanding questions. We found that people are excited for the safety improvements through autonomous vehicles and for gaining free time to do other activities, such as sleeping, eating, and working. Respondents also think that earning drivers' trust and sorting out legal issues will be essential to the widespread adoption of autonomous vehicles. Electric vehicles are desired for their eco-friendliness and cost savings, but respondents find low vehicle ranges and long battery recharge times as inhibitors for adoption. They generally prefer vehicle ranges over 150 miles and recharge times under 4 h.

These results suggest that vehicle manufacturers should focus on the design of in-vehicle information systems with the intention of earning driver trust in the performance of autonomous vehicles; the survey also highlights range and recharge milestones for developers of electric vehicles. In our previous survey [5], Austrians seemed to be more conservative compared to Americans and Koreans. However, those differences are disappearing. While a one-time survey presents limitations, this cross-cultural study triggers discussions on how to design systems. Should they be culturally adapted, standardized, or customizable? Moreover, industry might get some hint where to test their novel vehicles. While these results are not yet generalizable, we will continue to collect data from more representative and heterogeneous populations with the evenly distributed number of participants across countries, age and gender. Furthermore, we propose to discuss ways to identify the underlying mechanisms of the cultural differences in the AutomotiveUI community.

Acknowledgements. Authors would like to thank Dr. Shao-wen Yang, Dr. Nyuk Kin Koo, Dr. Linxiao Geng, Jonathan Schuett, Thomas Gable, and Brittany Noah for their help.

References

1. Begg, D.: A 2050 vision for London: what are the implications of driverless transport? (2014). https://www.transporttimes.co.uk/Admin/uploads/64165-transport-times_a-2050-vision-for-london_aw-web-ready.pdf
2. Underwood, S.E., Marshall, S., Niles, J.: Automated, connected, and electric vehicles. A report for the Graham Environmental Sustainability Institute (2014)
3. Hancock, P.A.: Automobility: the coming use of fully-automated on-road vehicles. In: Proceedings of IEEE International Inter-Disciplinary Conference on CogSIMA 2015. IEEE (2015)
4. Mohseni, P., Stevie, R.G.: Electric vehicles: holy grail or fool's gold. In: Power and Energy Society General Meeting, PES 2009. IEEE (2009)
5. Jeon, M., Riener, A., Lee, J-H., Schuett, J., Walker, B.N.: Cross-cultural differences in the use of in-vehicle technologies and vehicle area network services: Austria, USA, and South Korea. In: Proceedings of AutomotiveUI 2012 (2012)

Modelling the Process of Controlling
an Automated Steering Maneuver

Luis Kalb[(✉)] and Klaus Bengler

Chair of Ergonomics, Technical University of Munich, 85748 Garching, Germany
{luis.kalb,bengler}@tum.com

Abstract. Automated steering maneuvers have the potential to further reduce collisions in automobile traffic. High torques on the steering wheel and steer-by-wire are two concepts to prevent unwanted interference by the human driver during such maneuvers. Yet both methods lack controllability required by regulations in case of a false alarm, which is required by regulations. This paper tackles the problem of controllability by structuring the process of overriding a maneuver. Six chronological elements are presented which open up new specific research areas each. Research so far is sorted into this process and possible future research is evaluated for each element.

Keywords: Controllability · Automated driving
Automated steering maneuvers

1 Introduction

Driver assistance systems are continuously improved and implemented in cars today. The ultimate goal is to reach a fully automated vehicle control system in which the driver becomes a mere passenger. The standard SAE J3016 [1] specifies to what extent an automated control system takes over the driving task from the human driver in a structure of levels. Up to level 3 – conditional automation, the human driver is still required as at least a fallback option if the system reaches certain system boundaries. With the introduction of level 4 – high automation and level 5 – full automation the system is able to overcome any critical scenario the vehicle might encounter.

Systems capable of solving any given scenario require use of nearly the full range of vehicle dynamics in a precise and fast manner. Studies report up to approx. 6 m/s^2 in lateral acceleration [2]. Development of these systems permits to transfer parts of the functionality on SAE levels below 4.

Collision avoidance systems benefit most from fast longitudinal or lateral movements of the vehicle. Two concepts are established for collision avoidance: Emergency braking and emergency steering. Automated braking systems are already on the market today while automated steering systems that fully control the vehicles lateral motion are still under investigation. Automated evasive maneuvers can improve collision safety better than braking especially at higher speeds [3]. Research on automated steering first concentrated on technical feasibility and then moved on to inspect the human machine interface. Studies shifted towards the role of the driver in the event of an automated

© Springer International Publishing AG, part of Springer Nature 2018
V. G. Duffy (Ed.): DHM 2018, LNCS 10917, pp. 588–598, 2018.
https://doi.org/10.1007/978-3-319-91397-1_48

steering maneuver since regulations like [4, 5] still require the driver to be in charge of his vehicle at all times.

Early results for automated steering maneuvers are stated by [6] from the project "Proreta". The authors successfully implemented an automated steering maneuver but report first signs of disrupting human interference. [7] also determine any human torque applied on the steering wheel as disturbance for the planned maneuver. [8] observed a reflex like behavior by human drivers at the onset of an automated steering maneuver which led the participants of their study to hold the steering wheel or even counter-steer. Similar results were found by [9] who measured 200–600 ms of initial damping of the steering wheel movement.

In the effort to improve automated steering systems, two methods to prevent any human interference were investigated in published studies: The first method proposes to apply a torque on the steering wheel that is too high for a human driver to control, i.e. [8–10]. The second method uses the concept of steer-by-wire, meaning the steering wheel is decoupled from the actual movement of the wheels on the street, rendering any human input ineffective, i.e. [10].

Despite the success of both methods in justified emergency cases, controllability remains a problem with both in case of a false activation [8–11]. ISO 17287 defines controllability at the "manner and degree to which drivers can influence TICS function and pace of interaction" [12]. No compromise has been found yet on how to prevent human interference for true positive cases while allowing the driver to overrule in a false positive case.

The described results in the literature expect the human interference, positive or negative, to execute and communicate different parts of an overruling intervention all with one single action, i.e. counter-steering. On the one hand reducing the required actions to a single one may reduce the workload and save valuable reaction time. Plus, choosing a steering input as overruling action may seem subjectively intuitive because it is the natural way of interacting with a vehicle. Yet on the other hand, results so far show that one single action combining all necessary information hasn't been found yet. Consequently, this paper aims at unraveling the different parts of an overruling intervention by chronically structuring the process of controllability of an automated steering maneuver.

2   Process of Controlling an Automated Steering Maneuver

Figure 1 shows an approach of structuring the process of controlling an automated steering maneuver with six chronological elements. Relevant actions and points for communication are isolated as single elements in contrast to one combined action as used in the literature.

Time

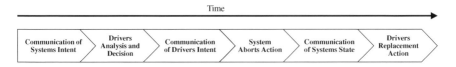

Fig. 1. Proposed process of a human driver controlling an automated steering maneuver in case of a false alarm

1. Communication of Systems Intent

An automated Steering Maneuver is initiated, once the automated control system deems it necessary based on the available information. At this moment the evasive maneuver is defined by aspects of time, i.e. time until maneuver starts, and aspects of space, i.e. direction of maneuver. All aspects which sufficiently describe the planned maneuver are summarized as intent of the automated system. Without any knowledge about an upcoming maneuver a human driver can't react to or control the automated steering input. So the systems intent should be communicated to the human driver in the first step (Fig. 2).

Time

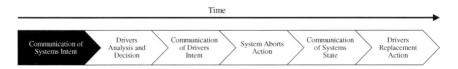

Fig. 2. Proposed process of a human driver controlling an automated steering maneuver in case of a false alarm with emphasis on the first element "Communication of Systems Intent"

Possibilities to inform the driver ahead of an automated steering maneuver are often labeled as warnings and divided into visual and acoustic warnings as well as haptic in the form of directional steering torques [13].

Acoustic signals used by [7] as well as [11] show tendencies to improve the overall success of automated steering maneuvers, yet no significant influence was found. [10, 11] used directional haptic tics to infer the following steering maneuver but also fall short of significant results. [14] argue for applying torque on the steering wheel as a form of warning, but add the possible danger of injury for the driver with this modality.

For future research [8] recommend to use improved acoustic warnings in the form of spoken word. The haptic modality could be preserved yet moved away from applying possibly dangerous torque by adding functionalities to a standard steering wheel. [15] present a version of haptic communication by installing a thin stretch of silicone on the front of the steering wheel which can be moved independently from the steering wheel rotation. Thereby [15] show that haptic communication of the systems intent can be realized on more detailed levels than steering wheel torque in future research.

[16] introduce a new modality that could hold potential for the communication of the systems intent. They present a system through which a roll motion of the vehicle can achieved independent from the vehicle dynamics. The method could make use of the vestibular sensory system by rolling the car in the direction of the intended maneuver.

[16] also recommend future research for higher dynamics as is the case with emergency steering maneuvers.

Overall the communicated information should be expanded. Warnings used in studies so far only carry binary information whether a maneuver is imminent or not. Information about direction, duration or justification of the maneuver have not been communicated yet. Relevant aspects of the maneuver for the driver should be identified and the design of warnings adapted with respect to the required information to fully inform the driver about the systems intent.

2. Drivers Analysis and Decision

The support of the human information processing is not exclusive to the topic of controllability and not the main concern of this paper. Appropriate information reception is accounted for with the mentioned modalities for communicating the intent of the system. The ways in which the human driver can express his reaction after processing the information is considered in the next element, communication of the drivers intent (Fig. 3).

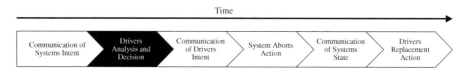

Fig. 3. Proposed process of a human driver controlling an automated steering maneuver in case of a false alarm with emphasis on the second element "Drivers Analysis and Decision"

3. Communication of Drivers Intent

The drivers intent contains all relevant aspects about where and when the driver wants the vehicle to move. The driver can agree or disagree with the systems intent, yet research has shown that both options should be communicated to the system to improve its performance: The initial damping of the steering wheel movement costs valuable time since it is unclear whether a reflex or an intentional counter-steering occurred [8, 9]. This influences the systems ongoing behavior (Fig. 4).

Fig. 4. Proposed process of a human driver controlling an automated steering maneuver in case of a false alarm with emphasis on the third element "Communication of Drivers Intent"

Most of the presented studies handled a steering input by the driver as a communication of his intent. Only [11] argue that counter-steering might not necessarily represent the drivers intent to overrule because some participants in their study steered even while unaware that an automated system took over control of the steering wheel and that they were no longer in a purely manual drive.

A different approach could be to introduce a new control element for the driver to explicitly communicate his intent without steering. A new control element has to meet certain requirements fitting the scenario, i.e. the short period of time available in a critical scenario. An example, which will be presented in a future publication, is installing a third pedal left to the brake pedal. This resembles the former clutch pedal from vehicles with manual transmission. Training for driving vehicles with manual transmission included stepping on the clutch pedal simultaneous to the brake pedal in case of an emergency. Whether drivers still automatically press both pedals if a third one is present or whether stepping on the left pedal requires a conscious decision will be investigated in future research.

4. Systems Aborts Action

The automated system has to seize its actions and return to a state in which the human driver can safely access the pedals and the steering wheel, once the driver communicated his intent to overrule the system (Fig. 5).

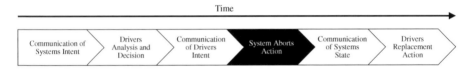

Fig. 5. Proposed process of a human driver controlling an automated steering maneuver in case of a false alarm with emphasis on the fourth element "Abort Systems Action"

The design of the systems retreat is only mentioned by [9] in the literature so far. The authors reduced the applied torque over a period of 250 ms to 0 Nm. The decline was fixed and applied for all participants in all scenarios.

We suggest two research questions that could benefit the abort of an automated steering maneuver:

1. How should the decrease of torque be designed regarding duration until the torque is zero and shape or gradient of the decrease curve?
2. What final state concerning the guidance of the vehicle should the abort of the automated maneuver lead to?

At a functional level the automated system should decrease the torque with respect to the actuators capabilities. The first proposed research question on the other hand considers the expected latter replacement action by the driver. A steep decrease potentially maximizes the drivers timeframe to execute his later replacement action because it shuts down the systems input the fastest (Fig. 6). Yet a following slower fade out of the automated torque might prevent the driver from accidentally overshooting his own replacing steering input due to the suddenly missing counter-torque (Fig. 7). Another option could be to insert a short break in the decrease, meaning the automated torque stops its decrease and remains at a certain level and continues to decrease after a short time. This could serve as a safety net in case there is a change in the drivers intent. If the drivers intent to abort the maneuver persists, the decrease could continue – in case the drivers intent changes and the automated maneuver should continue, the automated torque can rise to its original level faster than it would starting at zero (Fig. 8).

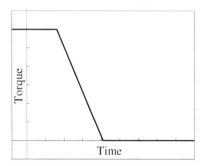

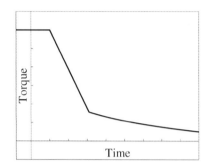

Fig. 6. Linear decrease of torque (after [9])   **Fig. 7.** Linear decrease of torque with a fade out

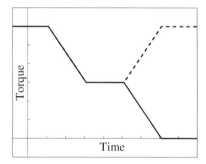

Fig. 8. Linear decrease with intermediate level and possible increase as dashed line

The second suggested research question aims at not at the torque but at the steering wheel movement the driver is confronted with.

Three options could be possible:

1. The automated torque is reduced to zero and without human interference the vehicle would continue to follow the path determined by the current steering wheel angle until the self-aligning torque sets the steering wheel angle back to approx. zero (Fig. 9).

Fig. 9. Digressive self-aligning torque on the steering wheel causing the steering wheel angle to slowly turn back to zero in case of an aborted automated steering input to the left

2. The automated torque is changed in a way to return the steering wheel angle back to zero before it is shut off. This results in the vehicle continuing in a straight line if the driver doesn't interfere (Fig. 10).

Fig. 10. Constant counter-torque applied by the automated system to quickly turn the steering wheel angle to zero after an aborted automated steering input to the left

3. The automated torque is changed in a way that leads the vehicle back to its original path (Fig. 11).

Fig. 11. Constant counter-torque applied through the zero position to compensate the false steering maneuver and bring the vehicle back to the original trajectory after an aborted automated steering input to the left

The first option offers the least support for the driver, yet hands back control the fastest. The second option offers the driver a neutral starting position, yet probably has to apply automated torque longer to bring the steering wheel angle to zero. The third option might comply with the drivers intention to not swerve at all in case of a false alarm the most, yet it takes the longest before the automated torque is completely shut off. In conclusion the third option might lead to better results concerning the overruling in case of a false alarm since it already supports the drivers intention to not change the trajectory and should be tested in future research.

4. Communication of Systems State

None of the published studies about automated steering maneuvers mention the communication of the state of the emergency steering system. [11] even report that some drivers were not aware of an ongoing automated maneuver. Clear communication of a successful shutdown of the automated maneuver might further decrease the risk of injuries as mentioned by [14]. A driver would only then put his hands back on the steering wheel when he has been informed that no further torque will be applied by the automated system. The same modalities as in the communication of the systems intent at the beginning of the process could be used to ensure consistency throughout the system (Fig. 12).

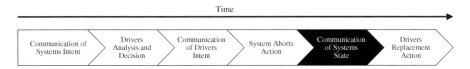

Fig. 12. Proposed process a human driver controlling an automated steering maneuver in case of a false alarm with emphasis on the fifth element "Communication of Systems State"

Also not investigated yet is the potential of the decreasing torque from element four to serve as a modality to inform about the systems state. The reduction of the torque to zero mainly serves to guarantee an uninterrupted replacement action later. Adding torque to explicitly inform about the systems state might collide with the design of the torque on the functional level. It is also still subject to further research whether a driver perceives and understands the applied torque as implicit information about the systems state.

5. Drivers Replacement Action

We suggest that a drivers intentional steering action is most effective when neither steer by wire nor high torques on the steering wheel are applied. This requires the system to be turned off completely by the time the driver starts his steering input. With respect to element four "Abort Systems Action", the drivers replacement action can start with different preconditions in form of the current steering wheel angle or current position and orientation of the vehicle on the road (Fig. 13).

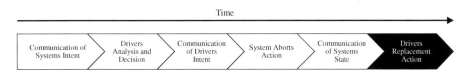

Fig. 13. Proposed process of a human driver controlling an automated steering maneuver in case of a false alarm with emphasis on the sixth element "Drivers Replacement Action"

To summarize: The published studies about controllability of an automated steering maneuver don't completely or at least partly fit the presented process above. [7, 10, 11] evaluate warnings ahead of a maneuver with limited content about the full intention of the system. The communication of the drivers intent and the replacement action of the driver are combined in one single step in all presented studies. Only [11] mentions that steering input not necessarily reflects the drivers intent. The design of the actual shut down of the automated maneuver has not been investigated in nearly all studies, with the exception of [9]. No study reported a feedback by the system regarding its state – still active or turned off.

In addition to the process modelled above, further research areas can be identified by crossing the different possible roles of the human driver and the automated system in case of an emergency steering maneuver. Table 1 shows the possible cases for the process of overruling with respect to the possible correct and incorrect actions by the human driver and the automated system. Three boxes are crossed out. These boxes represent cases that have an inconsistent logic, i.e. if a system already steers correctly by definition there can't be a human intervention to make the maneuver even more correct. The remaining boxes are filled with a description of the expected outcome as well as references to studies where the corresponding case was investigated.

Table 1. System actions and driver reactions: Possible cases to investigate controllability.

Driver	System	
	Steers correctly	Steers not correctly
Intervenes correctly	–	Driver overrules unjustified steering maneuver [7, 8, 10, 11]
Withholds correctly	System successfully executes maneuver [10]	–
Intervenes not correctly	Driver overrules justified steering maneuver [6–11]	Driver overrules system and steers into collision
Withholds not correctly	–	System steers into collision [10]

A driver intervention describes an action by the driver with consequences. A withheld driver intervention describes either a passive driver or an action by the driver with no consequences by design, i.e. steer by wire.

Table 1 shows where most experiments have been conducted yet and what other areas lack research so far. To the authors best knowledge, no study has been published yet reporting cases where the overruling of an automated maneuver caused an even more critical scenario. The two cases with steer correctly/withholds correctly and steers not correctly/withholds not correctly are represented by the studies by [10] where the method steer by wire was used.

3   Limitations and Conclusions

The presented process for controlling an automated steering maneuver offers six separated elements. Their appearance was structured in a chronical and linear way. Each element offers different research questions concerning its specific function in the process. Yet two important aspects have to be taken into consideration when experiments are underway to answer the proposed research questions:

1. The interaction between two consecutive elements. As mentioned before the design of the communication of the systems intent influences the following analysis and decision of the driver. The communication of the drivers intent in return is dependent on the drivers decision. A longer information processing could lead to certain

communication strategies to be eliminated since there is no more time to safely execute them. In the next step the chosen method to communicate the drivers intent might narrow down the possible strategies to abort the systems action. Lastly the driver has to adapt his replacement action depending on the process so far. A combination of steering and braking or even accelerating could be possible.

2. The proposed process is modelled as linear. It doesn't yet account for iterations that could occur after certain steps. If the system reverses its maneuver according to Fig. 11 it might communicate the original trajectory as new intent and the driver once again decides whether this fits his own intention.

In the beginning we pointed at the current development of automated steering systems in the context of automated vehicles. Yet the studies presented in this paper all investigated steering interventions during manual drives. Both driving modes come with at least one significantly different precondition: In automated driving the driver is allowed to take his hands off the steering wheel per definition [1]. The driver of i.e. a partly automated vehicle may not have his hands on the steering wheel at the beginning of a falsely initiated automated steering maneuver. This supports the development of alternative methods to communicate the drivers intent apart from counter-steering as discussed in element three.

Time is rare in critical scenarios in which automated steering maneuvers are initiated. [10] argued that the long reaction time of drivers was a major reason for the unsuccessful overruling of false automated maneuvers. In automated driving the driver has to put his hands back on the steering wheel in time for his replacing action. This time could be used to execute to abort of the systems action as discussed in element four if the driver communicated his intent to overrule before. In conclusion further research should use the reaction time, calculated by adding the individual times each element of the proposed process takes, as a metric to determine the efficiency of an investigated design.

References

1. SAE J3016: Taxonomy and Definitions for Terms Related to Driving Automation Systems for On-Road Motor Vehicles. http://standards.sae.org/j3016_201609/
2. Keller, C.G., Dang, T., Fritz, H., Joos, A., Rabe, C., Gavrila, D.M.: Active pedestrian safety by automatic braking and evasive steering. Trans. Intell. Transport. Sys. **12**(4), 1292–1304 (2011). https://doi.org/10.1109/TITS.2011.2158424
3. Winner, H.: Grundlagen von Frontkollisionsschutzsystemen. In: Winner, H., Hakuli, S., Lotz, F., Singer, C. (eds.) Handbuch Fahrerassistenzsysteme. A, pp. 893–912. Springer, Wiesbaden (2015). https://doi.org/10.1007/978-3-658-05734-3_47
4. United Nations Economic Commission for Europe: Convention on Road Traffic, Version 1993 with Amendments in 2006. http://www.unece.org/fileadmin/DAM/trans/conventn/Conv_road_traffic_EN.pdf
5. Brockmann, M.: Code of Practice for the Design and Evaluation of ADAS (2009). http://www.acea.be/uploads/publications/20090831_Code_of_Practice_ADAS.pdf
6. Bender, E., Landau, K., Bruder, R.: Driver reactions in response to automatic obstacle avoiding manoeuvres. In: 16th World Congress on Ergonomics (IEA) (2006). http://tubiblio.ulb.tu-darmstadt.de/43003/

7. Sieber, M., Siedersberger, K.H., Siegel, A., Färber, B.: Automatic emergency steering with distracted drivers: effects of intervention design. In: IEEE 18th International Conference on Intelligent Transportation Systems, pp. 2040–2045 (2015). https://doi.org/10.1109/ITSC.2015.330

8. Fricke, N., Griesche, S., Schieben, A., Hesse, T., Baumann, M.: Driver behavior following an automatic steering intervention. Accid. Anal. Prev. **83**(Supplement C), 190–196 (2015). https://doi.org/10.1016/j.aap.2015.07.018

9. Schneider, N., Purucker, C., Neukum, A.: Comparison of steering interventions in time-critical scenarios. Procedia Manuf. **3**(Supplement C), 3107–3114 (2015). https://doi.org/10.1016/j.promfg.2015.07.858

10. Hesse, T., Schieben, A., Heesen, M., Dziennus, M., Griesche, S., Köster, F.: Interaction design for automation initiated steering manoeuvres for collision avoidance. In: 6. Tagung Fahrerassistenzsysteme, München (2013)

11. Schieben, A., Griesche, S., Hesse, T., Fricke, N., Baumann, M.: Evaluation of three different interaction designs for an automatic steering intervention. Transp. Res. Part F Traffic Psychol. Behav. **27**, 238–251 (2014). https://doi.org/10.1016/j.trf.2014.06.002

12. ISO 17287: Road vehicles – Ergonomic aspects of transport information and control systems – procedure for assessing suitability for use while driving (2003)

13. Schneider, N., Berg, G., Paradies, S., Zahn, P., Huesmann, A., Neukum, A.: Designing emergency steering and evasion assist to enhance safety in use and controllability. In: Bengler, K., Drüke, J., Hoffmann, S., Manstetten, D., Neukum, A. (eds.) UR:BAN Human Factors in Traffic. A, pp. 479–494. Springer, Wiesbaden (2018). https://doi.org/10.1007/978-3-658-15418-9_28

14. Dang, T., Desens, J., Franke, U., Gavrila, D., Schäfers, L., Ziegler, W.: Steering and evasion assist. In: Eskandarian, A. (ed.) Handbook of Intelligent Vehicles, pp. 759–782. Springer, London (2012). https://doi.org/10.1007/978-0-85729-085-4_29

15. Ploch, C.J., Bae, J.H., Ju, W., Cutkosky, M.: Haptic skin stretch on a steering wheel for displaying preview information in autonomous cars. In: IEEE/RSJ International Conference on Intelligent Robots and Systems (IROS), pp. 60–65 (2016). https://doi.org/10.1109/IROS.2016.7759035

16. Müller, C., Siedersberger, K.-H., Färber, B., Popp, M.: Aktive Aufbauneigung als Rückmeldekanal bei Querführungsassistenz über entkoppelte Lenkaktorik. Forschung im Ingenieurwesen **81**(1), 41–55 (2017)

Driver Behavior at Simulated Railroad Crossings

Steven Landry$^{(\boxtimes)}$, Yuguang Wang, Pasi Lautala,
David Nelson, and Myounghoon Jeon

Michigan Technological University, 1400 Townsend Dr,
Houghton, MI 49931, USA
{sglandry,yugwang,ptlautal,dannelso,mjeon}@mtu.edu

Abstract. Highway-rail grade crossing collisions and fatalities have been in decline for several decades, but a recent 'plateau' has spurred additional interest in novel safety research methods. With the support of Federal Railroad Administration (FRA), Michigan Tech researchers have performed a large-scale study that utilizes the SHRP2 Naturalistic Driving Study (NDS) data to analyze how various crossing warning devices affect driver behavior and to validate the driving simulation data. To this end, representative crossings from the NDS dataset were recreated in a driving simulator. This paper describes driver behavior at simulated rail crossings modeled after real world crossings included in the NDS dataset. Results suggest that drivers may not react properly to crossbucks and active warnings in the off position. Participants performed the safest behaviors in reaction to STOP signs. The majority of participants also reported an increase in vigilance and compliant behaviors after repeated exposure to RR crossings, which was supported by the results of a linear regression analysis. Participants used the presence of active RR warnings (in the off position) as a cue that there is no oncoming train and it is safe to cross without preparing to yield (operationalized as visually scanning for a train and active speed reduction). Drivers react the most appropriately to STOP signs, but it is unclear whether or not these behaviors would lead to a decrease in train-vehicle collisions.

Keywords: Driving simulation · Rail crossings · Driver behavior

1 Introduction

1.1 Literature Review

Historically, safety at highway-rail grade crossings (crossings) has been an area of special attention due to the gravity of accidents that occur at those locations. Crossing collisions and fatalities have been in decline for several decades, but a recent 'plateau' has spurred additional interest in novel safety research methods [1]. With support from the Federal Railroad Administration (FRA) we have conducted a large-scale study that utilizes the SHRP2 Naturalistic Driving Study (NDS) data to analyze how various crossing warning devices affect driver behavior and to validate the driving simulation data. To this end, representative crossings from the NDS dataset were recreated in a

© Springer International Publishing AG, part of Springer Nature 2018
V. G. Duffy (Ed.): DHM 2018, LNCS 10917, pp. 599–609, 2018.
https://doi.org/10.1007/978-3-319-91397-1_49

driving simulator using the National Advanced Driving Simulator (NADS) MiniSim simulation software and hardware. This paper describes driver behavior at simulated rail crossings modeled after real world crossings included in the NDS dataset.

The Naturalistic Driving Study (NDS) data with its five million trips provided an unprecedented opportunity to collect direct observations of drivers' negotiating crossings, and to see how they react to the crossing environment, including the traffic control devices (warnings) currently used to warn drivers as they approach railway tracks [2]. The NDS data set includes trip data that can be used to observe driver behavior, and relate it to vehicle position during a traversal of a given crossing. Analysis of that behavior is complicated by the facts that traversals occur at different speeds, crossings are located in varying environments, and actions taken by drivers may occur in a different order at any given crossing.

Sign Types. Most rail-related safety analyses start by categorizing crossings by warning sign type. Passive warnings such as crossbucks are the minimal level of warning at a crossing, are cheaper to install and require less maintenance than their active counterparts [3]. Of course, the downside of passive warnings is that they provide no information on the presence or absence of a train, only the presence of a crossing. Time-to-arrival judgment errors may cause incidents at passive crossings, but there are many more "failure to notice crossing/train" errors than at active crossings. Intervention methods such as increasing the saliency of the crossing and providing train-present information are expected to be as effective at passive crossings as active warnings with no physical barrier (flashing lights and bells) [4].

Non-compliant behavior such as gate-running is the biggest cause of accidents at crossings protected by active gates, while failure to detect the crossing or train, or at least, a poor time-to-arrival judgment is the largest cause of accidents at crossings protected by passive warning signs [4]. Because the nature of the breakdown in safety is due to different issues depending on the type of crossing, multiple countermeasures to increase safety must be developed to specifically target each issue independently and to promote respect for RR warnings in general.

Previous studies have shown that driver behavior varies even within types of passive crossings. For example, historical analyses of incident reports suggest that controlling for amount of traffic, STOP signs are associated with the highest rate of incidents [5]. However, previous simulation studies have shown that drivers are more likely to properly comply at STOP signs than at RR crossings with crossbucks only [6]. Drivers may not understand how to properly comply with crossbucks while STOP signs are much more common and explicit about behavior than crossbucks. The past inconsistent findings between real world and laboratory simulation driver behavior studies open up questions on "how should safety engineers use these conflicting findings to make better decisions about which type of warning to place at new or problematic RR crossings"? To answer these questions, we designed this line of research.

Naturalistic and Simulated Driving Studies. Incident records in the FRA database often lack details, making interpretation of the data difficult. Each record includes quantitative and qualitative data that describe each incident, including a narrative section.

Unfortunately, most of the narratives fail to describe the behavior of the driver and sometimes even conflict with the other information provided in the quantitative descriptions [4]. In addition to the lack of consistency and accurate or descriptive narratives, records of the signage type at crossings are often out of date. This suggests that some crossings are upgraded from passive to active warnings without the FRA crossing inventory being updated. However, the accident reports of incidents should show the existing traffic control devices at the time of the accident.

For the reasons listed above, it is worthwhile to search for more reliable datasets for rail safety analyses. We have approached the issue of unreliable or incomplete FRA incident records with two lines of research. The first line of research involves aggregating data from the SHRP2 NDS (naturalistic driving study) related to highway-rail grade crossings. This dataset includes camera, GPS, and vehicle sensor data describing how drivers actually behave in the real world.

Unfortunately, observational studies lack the control of laboratory simulations to allow for systematic manipulation of variables of interest. In short, the naturalistic driving data may not have the predictive validity to infer how driver behavior would change in response to novel warnings. To this end, the second line of research includes a high fidelity driving simulator to recreate and manipulate real-world crossing scenarios. The following sections will outline a study where participants are exposed to simulated crossings, modeled after real world crossings from the NDS data set. Behavioral data collected from the driving simulator is presented and preliminarily compared to the observed behaviors from the NDS.

Driving simulators have been increasing in fidelity over the previous decades. However, questions remain open about the predictive validity of laboratory simulations. Can the NDS dataset be used to validate the use of driving simulators to predict driver behavior to novel RR warnings? Can driving simulators be used to help understand and put into context the driving behaviors collected in observational studies such as the NDS? Can the combination of both laboratory simulation and naturalistic observation reveal new explainable patterns in driver behavior? Answers to these questions and more are the motivation for the following study.

2   Methods

2.1   Participants

Seventeen ($M_{age} = 19.4$, $SD_{age} = 2.1$, 11 male, 6 female) undergraduate participants were recruited from the local university participant pool in exchange for course credit. All participants had at least three years of driving experience. Fifteen (88%) of the participants reported encountering a railroad crossing at least once per month on average. None of the participants reported any simulator induced motion sickness.

2.2   Apparatus (Driving Simulator)

For this study, we used the NADS simulator running the MiniSim version 2.2 software. The simulation software runs on a single computer, running Microsoft Windows 10 Pro on an Intel Core i7 processor, 3.07 GHz and 12 GB of RAM, and relays sound through a 2.1 audio system. Three Panasonic TH- 42PH2014 42″ plasma displays with a 1280 × 800 resolution each allow for a 130° field of view in front of the seated participant. The center monitor is 28 in. from the center of the steering wheel and the left and right monitors are 37 in. from the center of the steering wheel. The MiniSim also includes a real steering wheel, adjustable car seat, gear-shift, and gas and brake pedals, as well as a Toshiba Ltd. WXGA TFT LCD monitor with a 1280 × 800 resolution to display the speedometer, etc. Environmental sound effects are also played through two embedded speakers. These sounds included engine noise, brake screech, turn indicators, collisions, auditory alerts, etc.

A single webcam was positioned to capture the visual scanning behavior of the participant's face while in the simulator. This video feed was recorded and integrated with screen capture recordings of the driving simulator's visuals and instrument panel. Open Broadcast Software (OBS) was used to capture and integrate the visuals from the driving simulator and webcam into one video file.

2.3   Stimuli (Scenario Description)

The simulated scenarios were developed using the Tile Mosaic Tool (TMT) and Inter-active Scenario Authoring Tool (ISAT), and presented to the participant using the NADS MiniSim version 2.2 software and hardware. Three scenarios were created, which will be referred to henceforth as scenarios "A", "B", or "C".

All scenarios included moderate amounts of automated traffic driving in the other lane. All scenarios were comprised of three laps, and each lap had two identical crossings as far away from each other as possible (Figs. 1 and 2). Each lap took about 5 min for the participant to drive, resulting in around 15 min of drive time and 6 crossing events per condition. All scenarios could be described as "rural", featuring very few intersections and buildings. All additional signage (Pre-warning signs and pavement markings) were included and placed at the appropriate locations for all simulated crossings.

All scenarios included one train present event on the 5th of the six crossing events. The train event was triggered by the participant crossing over the pre-warning pavement markings, and the train would arrive at the crossing approximately 17 s after warning activation. We acknowledge that the Manual of Uniform Traffic Control Devices (MUTCD) recommends a minimum of 20 s between the activation of the traffic control device and the arrival of the train. However, based on pilot testing the 17 s warning time helped ensured that drivers were forced to make a decision whether or not to stop at the appropriate time on approach to the crossing.

Scenario A attempts to model crossing 505650D, a location in Sardinia, NY. This crossing includes active warning devices in the form of gates and blinking lights and was selected as a representative of one of the most common types of crossings represented in the NDS dataset. The crossing is perpendicular to the road and has an almost unobstructed view down the tracks except for a few trees. The entire scenario is a loop that takes about 5 min for the participants to drive one lap. Each lap includes two identical crossings modeled after the crossing described above. A yield intersection was included approximately 1/8th miles before the first crossing warning in an attempt to control for the driver's speed on approach. The lights, bell sounds, and gate arm are activated

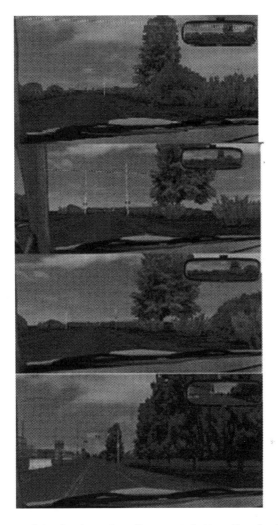

Fig. 1. The four types of simulated crossings (from top to bottom: Crossbuck, Gate, STOP, and Cantilever) featured in the scenarios.

approximately 17 s before the arrival of the train at the intersection. The fifth crossing event of this scenario includes a train present event. All other crossing events contain no trains.

Scenario B is identical to scenario A, except for the type of warnings present at the highway-rail crossings. In scenario B the first crossing was changed to a passive crossbuck, and the other crossing was changed to a STOP sign and crossbuck. Scenario B is the only condition to incorporate two different types of crossings. The train present event (crossing event #5) in scenario B occurred at the crossbuck-guarded crossing.

Scenario C is modeled after crossing 621549W in Plant City, FL. This crossing has an overhead cantilever with flashing light warning, but no gate arm. Roughly, ½ a mile

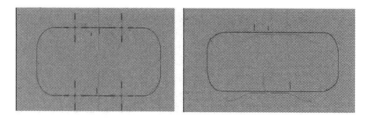

Fig. 2. Maps of scenario loops (left is condition A and B, right is condition C). RR crossings are located at the 12 and 6 o'clock positions of each loop.

of road was recreated before and after the crossing to model the real world environment using Google Maps' street view as a reference. This was necessary to reflect the uniqueness of this intersection. The view down one direction of the track is completely obstructed by buildings, and the track curves behind trees obstructing the view down the other direction of the track. On the 5th crossing event, the train approaches from behind the building. The lights and bell sounds are activated approximately 17 s before the arrival of the train at the intersection.

2.4   Design and Procedure

Each participant drove through all three conditions to set up a within-subjects comparison. The order of presentation was fully counterbalanced to wash out its' effect over the whole group of participants. Participants were allowed to practice driving for 1 min to adjust to the idiosyncrasies of the driving simulator. After all three conditions, participants completed an online survey before being released. The survey questions included:

- "How many times do you encounter a train crossing per month on average?"
- "How realistic were the scenarios/your driving behavior?"
- "How did your behavior at railroad crossings change over the course of this experiment?", and
- "What should/would you do when approaching this sign?" (presented with pictures of the different types of railroad warnings depicted in the simulation).

Driver Behavior Coding Scheme. Driver behavior was operationalized as a score ranging from 0–4 using a novel coding scheme developed in a previous study (Table 1) [6]. The coding scheme awards 1 point (max of 2) for each direction looked at the appropriate time. This visual scanning behavior was only counted if the behavior was performed after passing the pre-warning traffic sign, but early enough to allow for appropriate braking time if an oncoming train was spotted. The driving simulator also recorded pedal depression and vehicle speed. One point was awarded if the participant completely removed their foot off the accelerator pedal (an indication of coasting), and another point was awarded if the participant placed any pressure on the brake pedal (an indication of active speed reduction). Again, points were only awarded if the behavior occurred at the appropriate time (after passing the pre-warning sign, but early enough to react appropriately to an oncoming train).

Table 1. Behavior score coding scheme

Behavior	Score (max 4)
Visual scan in either direction	+1 for each direction (max 2)
Foot off accelerator	+1
Press on brake pedal	+1

It is necessary to modify the behavior score coding scheme to accommodate for the intended behaviors at STOP protected crossings. For STOP protected railroad crossings, one point is given for active speed reduction (no force on the accelerator pedal), and another is given for coming to a complete stop (when vehicle speed is virtually 0 mph). Visual glances down either side of the track are only awarded points if they occur while the vehicle is completely stopped. Theoretically, more behaviors are required to achieve the same 4 point score at STOP protected rail crossings than for all other warning types. There was no modification to the driver behavior coding scheme for train present events (event #5 in each condition). The presence of the train (or activation of active RR warnings) results in inflated scores compared to train-absent events, but its effect is washed out in within-subject comparisons. One researcher applied the coding scheme on the collected videos to create the visual scanning portion of the behavior score. "If" statements for pedal depression by event were coded in Rstudio to create the other half the behavior score. These two data sets were then combined (summed together) to create the total 0–4 behavior score.

3   Results

Due to experimenter and software errors the data for four participants was dropped because it was incomplete. As a reminder the behavior score combines visual scanning behavior (coded from the videos) and vehicle data (pedal depression and vehicle speed) collected by the simulator. A score of 0 indicates that the driver virtually ignored the crossing, and a score of 4 indicates that the driver responded appropriately in relation to the crossing.

A repeated measures ANOVA was conducted to observe the effect condition (warning type) has on behavior scores. Results suggest condition (warning type) has no significant effect on participant's behavior scores ($F(1.1.37, 9.096) = 4.654, p = .056$) (Table 2).

However, given that the results are approaching significance, post hoc pairwise comparisons with a Least Significance Difference (LSD) adjustment were conducted to compare individual conditions against each other. The post hoc pairwise comparisons suggest condition B (passive STOP and crossbuck) behavior scores are significantly higher than condition C (active cantilever) scores ($p = .027$) (Table 3).

Table 2. Tests of within-subjects effects ANOVA.

Measure: Score

Source		Type III Sum of Squares	df	Mean square	F	Sig.	Partial eta squared	Noncent parameter	Observed power[a]
Condition	Sphericity assumed	4.570	2	2.285	4.654	.026	.368	9.307	.699
	Greenhouse-Geisser	4.570	1.137	4.020	4.654	.056	.368	5.291	.512
	Huynh-Feldt	4.570	1.200	3.810	4.654	.053	.368	5.582	.528
	Lower-bound	4.570	1.000	4.570	4.654	.063	.368	4.654	.475
Error (condition)	Sphericity assumed	7.856	16	.491					
	Greenhouse-Geisser	7.856	9.096	.864					
	Huynh-Feldt	7.856	9.596	.819					
	Lower-bound	7.856	8.000	.982					

[a]Computed using alpha = .05

Table 3. Post hoc pairwise comparisons between all conditions.

Pairwise comparisons

Measure: Score

(I) Condition	(J) Condition	Mean difference (I-J)	Std. error	Sig.[b]	95% confidence interval for difference[b]	
					Lower bound	Upper bound
1	2	−.907	.445	.076	−1.933	.118
	3	−.074	.187	.702	−.504	.356
2	1	.907	.445	.076	−.118	1.933
	3	.833[*]	.308	.027	.123	1.544
3	1	.074	.187	.702	−.356	.504
	2	−.833[*]	.308	.027	−1.544	−.123

Based on estimated marginal means

[*]The mean difference is significant at the .05 level.

[b]Adjustment for multiple comparisons: Least Significant Difference (equivalent to adjustments).

Analyzing participant's behavioral data chronologically also allows for extrapolating how driver behavior can change after repeated exposure. Note how behavior scores increase at the train present event 5 in both active warning conditions A and C. In condition B (green line in Fig. 3), all of the even numbered events (2, 4, & 6) have STOP protected rail crossings, while all odd events (1, 3 & 5) have crossbuck protected rail crossings.

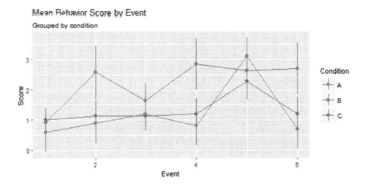

Fig. 3. Mean behavior score by event, grouped by condition (warning type). Error bars represent standard error. (Color figure online)

Figure 4 depicts mean compliance scores by event experienced chronologically in the experimental session. This is the truest representation of how behaviors change after repeated exposures to railroad crossings, regardless of warning type. A simple linear regression was calculated to predict behavior score based on event number. A significant regression equation was found ($F(1,229) = 10.22$, $p = .0016$, with an R^2 of .042. The model predicts that behavior scores increase on average .05 points for each additional exposure to a RR crossing.

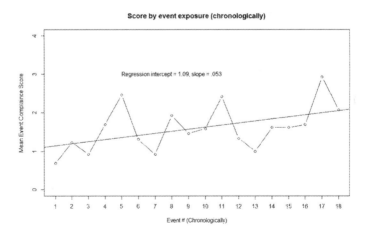

Fig. 4. Behavior scores over the entire course of the experiment (chronologically).

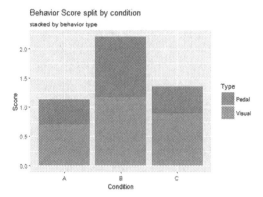

Fig. 5. Stacked behavior score by condition, split by visual scanning and pedal depression behavior. Scores are averaged across all participants by condition.

Additionally, the very slight increase in behavior score over time is backed up by the responses in the post experiment survey. Thirteen (75%) of the participants reported becoming more cautious at following events after experiencing a train present event. Alternatively, one of the participants reported becoming less cautious over time because they "trusted the signs".

From the stacked bar chart (Fig. 5), we can see the majority of points awarded in conditions A and C are from visual scanning behaviors. This suggests that participants are more likely to visually scan for a train than actively reduce vehicle speed on approach to active (but OFF) rail warnings. Figure 5 also shows how participants are more likely to perform "yield behaviors" such as coasting or actively reducing speed for passive warnings than for active (but OFF) warnings.

4   Discussion

Overall, results have followed patterns seen in previous driving simulator experiments. Behaviors scores are at their highest at STOP protected rail crossings, and the lowest for active (but OFF) warnings. It is promising that behavior scores associated with train present crossing (event #5) are consistently high across all warning types. This is partic- ularly interesting in condition B, where the train present event occurred at a passive crossbuck protected crossing. In the simulation, the train was completely silent due to software limitations. Participants were able to identify an oncoming train during their visual scans on approach even without the aid of an active warning.

Visualizing the data chronologically does provide some evidence that participants become slightly more vigilant over time after repeated exposures to railroad crossings (Fig. 4). Perhaps the consistent presence of a train on event 5 in each condition was the main driver of this trend. Similar chronological analysis will be performed with the NDS data which may shed light on how behavior changes over time in naturalistic settings.

5   Conclusion and Future Works

It is useful to mention that our behavior score coding scheme cannot predict likelihood of an incident. It is possible to score low while completely avoiding the train. It is also possible to score high and still collide with the oncoming train. The fact that the train is technically in the driver's field of view does not guarantee the driver will notice the train, and understand how to behave in order to safely avoid an incident.

In conclusion, the data from this study suggest that participants in a driving simulator generally understand that the burden of safety is on the driver for passive crossings, but not for active crossings. Participants trust active warnings to warn drivers of approaching trains, and the OFF status of the warning device is used as a cue that there is no hazard. Unfortunately, active warnings are not immune to malfunctions, which could lead to deadly consequences if drivers are of this mindset in the real world.

Future works include comparisons between the driving simulator data and NDS data. If similar patterns are observed in both data sets, more effort could be spent conducting simulator studies as a valid representation of real world driving behaviors.

Acknowledgments. This project is partly supported by the Federal Railroad Administration (FRA) and the National University Rail (NURail) Center, a US DOT-OST Tier 1 University Transportation Center.

References

1. Operation Lifesaver: Federal Railroad Administration Safety Statistics. https://oli.org/about-us/news/statistics/frasite. Accessed 21 Nov 2016
2. Dean, A., Lautala, P., Nelson, D.: Effectiveness of using SHRP2 naturalistic driving study data to analyze driver behavior at highway rail grade crossings. In: IEEE/ASME Joint Rail Conference, Philadelphia, Pennsylvania (2017)
3. Abraham, J., Datta, T., Datta, S.: Driver behavior at rail-highway crossings. Transp. Res. Rec. J. Transp. Res. Board **1648**, 28–34 (1998)
4. Yeh, M., Multer, J.: Driver behavior at highway-railroad grade crossings: a literature review from 1990–2006. DOT/FRA/ORD-08/03 (2008)
5. Raub, R.: Examination of highway-rail grade crossing collisions nationally from 1998 to 2007. Transp. Res. Rec. J. Transp. Res. Board **2122**, 63–71 (2009)
6. Landry, S.: Getting Active with passive crossings: investigating the efficacy of in-vehicle auditory alerts for rail road crossings. Master's thesis, Michigan Technological University (2016)

Evaluation of an Intelligent Collision Warning System for Forklift Truck Drivers in Industry

Armin Lang[✉]

Chair of Materials Handling, Material Flow, Logistics, Technical University of Munich, Munich, Germany
lang@fml.mw.tum.de

Abstract. The number of collisions caused by lift trucks in the area of intralogistics is still increasing despite the availability of collision avoidance systems. Commercially available products for collision avoidance mounted on forklifts often issue false alarms activated by minimum distances during daily work. Consequently, the drivers sooner or later turn those systems off. A collision warning system based on computer-vision methods combined with a time-of-flight camera delivering 2D and 3D data can overcome inflationary warnings in warehouse situations. The 3D data delivered is used to identify objects by clustering as well as to get information about the movement of objects in forklift's path. Machine-learning algorithms use the 2D data mainly to detect people in the path. Distinguishing people from non-human objects makes it possible to establish a two-level warning system able to warn earlier if humans are endangered than in collision situations in which no humans are in sight. This system's general functionality has already been proven in lab tests. To transfer the academic results to application in an industrial environment, the same test procedure has been executed during daily work in a warehouse at a company in the production sector. In this paper, the authors aim to list the differences and commonalities between the academic and industrial runs.

Keywords: Forklift safety · Warning system · Computer vision
People detection · Machine learning · Evaluation

1 Introduction

Occupational health and safety are especially important in those fields where employees cross paths with mobile machines. This is happens often in the warehouses of small and medium-sized enterprises, where industrial trucks or similar vehicles follow the same routes as walking employees do. Since forklifts are repeatedly involved in accidents, products have been developed to try to prevent accidents with humans as well as with storage equipment. They all share distance as the criterion for deciding whether or not a collision is impending. That leads to many warnings in a lift-truck driver's day-to-day routine, because forklifts often travel within small distances of storage equipment such as racks. Due to this problem, methods of computer vision will be investigated in the "PräVISION" project for use in a collision

© Springer International Publishing AG, part of Springer Nature 2018
V. G. Duffy (Ed.): DHM 2018, LNCS 10917, pp. 610–622, 2018.
https://doi.org/10.1007/978-3-319-91397-1_50

warning system for industrial trucks. The main aim is to simultaneously reduce the incidence of false warnings and retain warnings of true collisions. To accomplish this, distance will no longer be the sole indicator of an impending collision but also the movement of objects in the forklift's path. This makes it possible for the collision warning to be issued as soon as a collision is inevitable by calculating the time-to-collision for each object. In addition, a distinction between human and non-human objects enables a two-level warning system. If a non-human object is endangered, a minimum-time-to-collision threshold is used. The threshold is increased by a security factor if a human is involved. Further information about the system and computer-vision methods employed can be found in the paper by *Lang* and *Günthner* [1]. This paper also reveals the reliability of person detection in academic test scenarios.

The system's general functionality has already been proven, but its industrial application has not yet been examined. That's why we wanted to record the daily routine of forklift trucks in a warehouse at a production company in Germany. By evaluating these recordings, we analyze the ability to transfer the results of previous academic tests into industrial application.

2   State of the Art

Several assistant systems are available that try to prevent accidents caused by forklifts. Those systems use technologies such as radar, ultrasonic waves, radio, or laser to capture the environment [2–5]. They all decide whether or not a collision is impending based on a minimum distance being fallen below. When that happens, a sound alerts the driver to stop. Because lift trucks work in tight areas, those systems issue warns very often, resulting in their being turned off. New technologies in the sector of depth cameras and computer vision allow the development of more intelligent warning systems. The most important methods required for such a computer-vision-based collision warning system will be introduced below.

2.1   3D Cameras

The combination of ordinary color images with depth information is no novelty. This has be done for years, but the color-image data always had to be calibrated onto the depth data. The calibration can be very complex and expensive if special calibration patterns are required. Newer 3D cameras such as stereo or time-of-flight cameras no longer require this. They're already calibrated at delivery. Stereo cameras supply an RGB image and a matching depth image. Sometimes, the camera doesn't calculate the depth image itself, but it can be done easily with a suitable framework. For time-of-flight cameras, the depth image can always be obtained directly from the camera. Depth information is calculated by measuring the time between the emission and the reception of infrared light waves. Obviously, the camera also takes infrared images through the infrared sensor, which is almost independent from environmental illumination. This type of image always matches the depth image. In addition, some cameras such as the "Microsoft Kinect One®" also supply color images, but unlike the infrared ones these have to be calibrated when using the Kinect. Color-image calibration is unnecessary for industrial time-of-flight cameras.

2.2   Movement Calculation with Computer Vision

An important part of predicting impending collisions is predicting the movement of objects in a forklift's path. That can be done either by clustering objects within the 3D camera's field of view and tracing their movements or by using the methods of optical flow. The latter exploit distinctive features in a 2D picture to calculate the movement of pixels in consecutive images [6]. By adding the depth data, the so-called scene flow can be calculated. Scene flow represents the real movement of all pixels within the camera's field of view in world coordinates [7].

2.3   Object Classification and Localization with Computer Vision

There are a few methods for classifying objects in 2D or 3D data. The past was shaped by defining the geometrical patterns of different kinds of objects to be able to detect those objects. More recent approaches use machine learning algorithms, which are able to identify objects without given geometrical patterns. Those algorithms can be trained by feeding them suitable training data. In regard to computer vision, this data contains pictures with and without the objects to be classified.

The theory of machine learning had already been postulated in the early 20th century. One of the first algorithms, the support vector machine (SVM) postulated in 1963, first became applicable in 1992 [8, 9]. This algorithm belongs to the category of deformable-part models and is able to classify data with predefined features. In combination with the sliding-windows method, localization of objects is also possible. The most common feature used to detect people is the "histogram of oriented gradients [10]."

The latest developments in hardware have also made neural networks suitable for object classification and localization. Those also have to be trained first, but the features don't have to be defined. Neural networks find the important features by themselves.

In their paper "Pedestrian Detection: An Evaluation of the State of the Art," *Dollar et al.* introduced a method for evaluating people-detection algorithms. This became a standard reference in the field of person detection. The "miss rate" (mr) and "false positives per image" (fppi) are the target values. The miss rate is the percentage of unrecognized persons; the fppi indicator describes how many false detections are made per image [11]. Those two indicators depend on the threshold used to accept a detection proposal as a human or not. By using various thresholds, a chart as seen in Fig. 1 can be created.

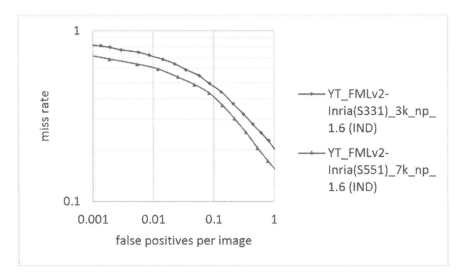

Fig. 1. Example chart of the evaluation of two people detectors according to Dollar et al.

Each marker on a line represents the miss rate and the false positives per image at a specific threshold. The nearer the line is to the origin of coordinates, the better the detector used. Consequently, detector 'YT_FMLv2-Inria(S551)_8k_np_1.6 (IND) is better than the other one, because the former's line is nearer to the origin of coordinates.

3   Software Framework

The developed system uses only open source libraries and its own methods. The main library is OpenCV 3. This library contains a huge number of image processing methods and, among other things, implementations of various machine learning algorithms, too [12].

Figure 2 shows an overview about the developed methodology. The first step is to fetch 2D and 3D images from a camera. Those images will be preprocessed and segmented. Preprocessing includes all of the methods that are necessary to prepare the images for the following collision and person detection. These include, for example, scaling, color conversion, or filling empty pixels. The last is needed mainly for the depth image, because due to the sensor technology there's no depth value for all pixels.

After some preprocessing has been done, irrelevant parts of the images will be removed in the "segmentation" module. The most important part for clustering reasons is removal of the ground floor in the depth image, because otherwise all pixels would be connected through the ground floor. The sequences of preprocessing and segmentation methods vary depending on the following algorithm and performance.

Collision detection uses a scene-flow method [7] to calculate the relative movement of objects in the forklift's path. This data is used to get each pixel's time-to-collision with a virtual box surrounding the forklift.

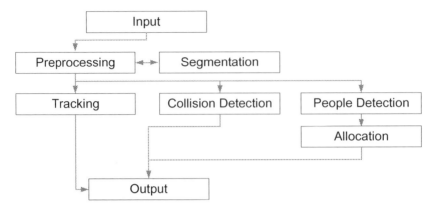

Fig. 2. Methodology of the collision warning system

Machine learning algorithms are used for person detection. The intent is to use both shallow learning methods like the support vector machine and deep learning networks. The SVM is implemented because it needs very little computing power, so it can be used in real-time. Deep learning is better at detection, but execution can't be done in real-time on a mid-sized computer. So detection based on deep learning is being reviewed for future application when graphic-card performance has increased.

When a person is found, a history is created or updated in the "allocation" module. If at least one person has been found before, various tracking methods [13–16] are provided to relocate him or her in the current frame. Tracking should increase detection performance, because no person detector can detect everyone.

The last step is output to the driver. The information from the tracking, collision, and person detection modules is collected and evaluated. The number of pixels falling below either the maximum time-to-collision for humans or the maximum time-to-collision for objects will be counted. The pixel count will be normalized according to the pixels' real distance in meters. A warning will be issued if a certain amount is exceeded, whereby different sounds are used for endangered humans or objects.

4 Approach and Frame Conditions of the Industrial Evaluation

The developed system can in principal be used on most kinds of forklifts, but some up-front work has to be done before making the recordings. Frame conditions in the industrial test area, such as the types of lift trucks available, first have to be determined. Data recording should be prepared based on previous recordings in the laboratory. Having done the preparation, the system is started-up on-site and run over several days. Afterwards, we extracted interesting video scenes from the dataset, because evaluating the whole dataset entails considerable difficulty. Persons have to be tagged manually on each frame to control the results of person detection.

The following evaluation focuses on person-detection performance. General collision detection has already been validated, so it's not repeated.

The same components are used in the industrial evaluation as were in the academic one. The only difference is the forklift used and some mechanical additions for mounting the system on the lift truck.

4.1 System Setting

The following equipment was used for the demonstrator:

- Forklift: STILL FMX-14 (type: high-reach truck)
- Notebook: Tuxedo XC1707 (i7-6820HK, 16 GB RAM, NVIDIA GTX 1070)
- Camera: Microsoft Kinect One (mount height: 3.4 m to bottom)
- Power converter: DC/AC 400 W 48 V/220 V

The developed demonstration system is generally applicable on just about every kind of industrial truck or other vehicle, but the required equipment (camera, notebook) has to be mounted and powered. A converter was needed to power the notebook and the camera. A box containing notebook, power converter, and camera was constructed for mounting the system on the forklift (see Fig. 3).

Fig. 3. Mounting the system on the forklift

4.2 Test Area

The records for the industrial trial were taken over three days during the daily routine of a lift-truck driver in the warehouse of a white goods manufacturer. The forklift on which the system was mounted operated within two areas (see Fig. 4). The lift truck loads its goods in the first area (1), where all incoming goods are temporarily stored on pallets. Different kinds of vehicles such as hand pallet trucks, roll containers, electric stacker trucks, and reach trucks as well as pedestrians cross ways there. The destination is the mobile pallet racks (mpr) (2). The other mobile pallet racks shown in Fig. 4 are supplied only rarely. The maximum speed allowed is at 8 km/h for every kind of vehicle.

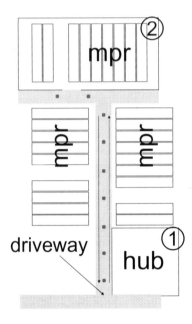

Fig. 4. Schema of the storage area

5   Statistical Aspects of the Data

The recorded data is analyzed below to enable the results to be compared with other person-detection evaluations.

Three shifts were recorded representing over 2 million frames per image type. Forty-four sequences containing persons totaling 17,385 frames overall in the whole set were chosen for evaluation. In these scenes, all of the persons standing or walking were tagged manually (see Table 1). 14,933 tags arose this way for the infrared images. In 84% of the selected frames, the camera angle was at 30°, in 7% at 35°, and in 9% at 40°, whereby the number of degrees is for the angle between the horizon and the camera axis. The reason for the difference in the distribution is that the bigger the angle the less area, and so the fewer persons are within the camera's field of view.

Table 1. Summary of tag data recorded in the industrial environment

Image type	Frames	Frames with tags	Frames with multiple tags	Tags	30% occluded tags	50% occluded tags	70% occluded tags
Color	17,385	10,763	2,671	14,349	2,761	1,823	1,014
IR	17,385	11,186	2,805	14,933	2,798	1,830	1,027

There are fewer tags for the calibrated color images because the depth sensor only captures pixels of objects that are at most 8 m away, so some persons are visible in the infrared images but not in the depth image. That's also true for the calibrated color image, because it's generated from the color and depth image. About 64% of the infrared frames contain at least one person, 16% of all infrared frames contain more than one tag. In nearly 19% of the tags, about 30% of the person is occluded, for example by boxes or shelves. 12% of the tags are almost half occluded and 7% are occluded more than 70%. Persons are consequently fully visible in only about 60% of the tags.

The position distribution of the tags can be seen in Table 2. The tags are divided into the maximum distance from the top respectively from the left of the image. A tag whose center is 40% of the image width (512 pixels) to the left and 40% of the image height (424 pixels) to the top of the image, counts as "Left 50% | Top 50%". The horizontal distribution is quite normal, but the vertical one is very imbalanced to the top. The reason for this is that humans are most likely far away from the forklift during daily work. They are thus found more often in the images' upper regions.

Table 2. Distribution of tag positions

	Left 0–30%	Left 30–50%	Left 50–70%	Left 70–100%	Σ
Top 0–30%	18.15%	15.15%	14.14%	12.03%	59.47%
Top 30–50%	8.49%	7.09%	6.62%	5.63%	27.83%
Top 50–70%	2.94%	2.45%	2.29%	1.95%	9.63%
Top 70–100%	0.93%	0.78%	0.73%	0.62%	3.06%
Σ	30.52%	25.47%	23.78%	20.23%	200%

The size distribution of the tags in the images can be obtained from Table 3. The real dimensions of the tagged persons were also analyzed (see Fig. 5). The sizes were determined automatically by creating clusters of tags in the depth image and transforming the data into the world coordinate system. Some false clusters caused the data show not just the dimensions of whole persons, but also the dimensions of some parts of them. That's especially important for the height, because some clusters only reach from the ground to the hip. In addition, the floor was removed for clustering purposes. This is done by removing all pixels which are closer than 0.2 m to the ground floor. Consequently, 0.2 m has to be added to all height values. The highest peaks can be found at widths from 0.4 m to 0.6 m and at heights from 1.4 m to 1.6 m (raw data, 0.2 m has to be added).

Table 3. Tag size distribution in pixels

	Minimum	Maximum	Average	Median	Deviation
Width [px]	8.00	266.00	65.84	57.00	34.21
Height [px]	16.00	306.00	127.87	117.00	57.93

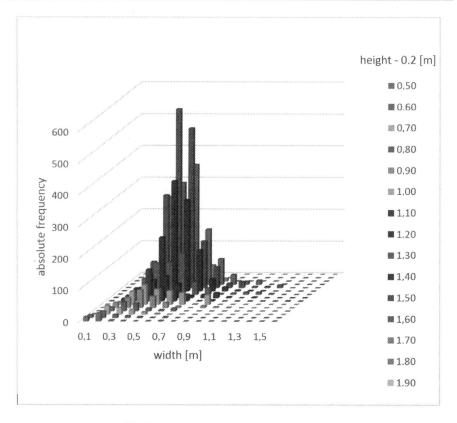

Fig. 5. Real-person dimensions of the tags

6   Evaluation of Person Detection

The industrial run was intended to validate the hypothesis that person detection trained with data from an academic environment and with reference to pedestrian databases also works in an industrial environment. 114 different support machines have already been trained and evaluated on test data that was recorded in the experimental laboratory of the Chair for Materials Handling, Material Flow, Logistics. The different SVMs' training data varied. Videos from the laboratory or warehouse videos from Youtube were taken as negative data—meaning pictures lacking humans. For positive data containing only humans, we used pictures from reference pedestrian databases such as INRIA [10] or the 'Monocular Pedestrian Detection' database [17] as well as artificially generated pictures of humans. The evaluation was done according to *Dollar et al.* as described in Sect. 2.3.

For better presentation, only the results of the three best-detecting support vector machines evaluated in the academic test data are shown in Fig. 6.

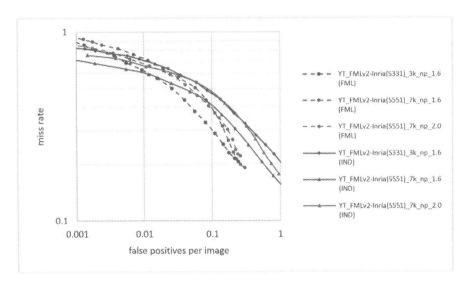

Fig. 6. Evaluation results for academic (FML) and industrial (IND) test data, whereby calibrated color images were used for person detection

Table 4. Comparison of the best (academic environment) three support vector machines

Image type	SVM	Avg. miss rate (FML)	Avg. miss rate (IND)	Relative change
Color	YT_FMLv2-Inria(S551)_7k_np_1.4	0.286194	0.521047	+82.06%
Color	YT_FMLv2-Inria_7k_np_1.8	0.306845	0.487052	+58.73%
Color	YT_FMLv2-Inria_3k_np_2.0	0.335521	0.525198	+56.53%
Infrared	YT_FMLv2-Inria(S551)_7k_np_1.8	0.187238	0.295612	+57.88%
Infrared	YT_FMLv2-Inria_7k_np_2.0	0.189408	0.341561	+80.33%
Infrared	YT_FMLv2-Inria_3k_np_1.4	0.191005	0.303023	+58.65%

The figure shows – in this case for calibrated color images – that detection is worse when the trained support vector machines have to detect people in an industrial environment (solid lines). There is also a discrepancy in the infrared image with regard to detection performance. It is not always worse, but the miss rate's variance is significantly high.

The two scenarios' average miss rates are compared in Table 4. The average miss rate is calculated by integrating the miss rate over the range of 0.01 to 0.1 false positives per image. The miss rate approaches 1 (100%) at fppi less than 0.01, so that no one will be detected any longer. At fppi greater than 0.1, classification generally ceases to come under discussion, because there are too many wrong detections [11].

Some SVMs performed better in the industrial evaluation than in application at the laboratory. The maximum increase is 11.71% more detections when using color images and 23.32% when infrared images are used (see Table 5). On average, the miss rate was about a quarter higher in the industrial test data than in the academic test data, hence about 25% fewer people were detected.

Table 5. Evaluation over all SVMs

Image type	Average miss-rate change	Standard deviation	Minimum MR change	Maximum MR change
Color	24.25%	22.33%	−11.71%	129.78%
Infrared	26.18%	18.42%	−23.32%	98.94%

As shown in Table 6, the best SVM in the industrial evaluation is still 59% (respectively 54%) worse than the best SVM in the academic evaluation.

Table 6. Comparison of the absolute best (lowest) average miss rates

Image type	Best avg. academic miss rate	Best avg. industrial miss rate	MR(IND)/MR(FML)
Color	0.286194	0.455677	159%
IR	0.187238	0.288959	154%

7   Discussion

The resulting assumption is that training is very application sensitive and thus has to be adapted to the use case. The SVM has never been trained with positive data from the videos taken in the laboratory so as not to complicate the results. Unlike the positives, the negative data was always trained with videos from the laboratory due to the lack of negative data from the warehouses. Only some SVMs were trained with a mix of the previously mentioned Youtube videos and videos from the laboratory. An example of this is the "YT_FMLv2-Inria_7k_np_2.0" SVM, which was trained with a mix of both negative data sources and positives from the INRIA data set.

So not adding negative data from the application area to the training set could be one reason for the decrease in the detection rate. Another reason could probably be the different quota of occluded tags. In the industrial data set, at least 30% of the person was occluded in about 38% of the tags as against 17% in academic recordings. In addition, there are many more people in non-upright postures such as bowing in the industrial set.

Person detection with the SVM applied works best if persons are standing and are fully visible, because those positions were trained before. The combination of more occluded and non-upright persons therefore could be the reason for the decrease in the detection rate. The tag types were not differentiated enough during evaluation at this point, so this can't be validated as a reason yet.

8 Summary

A new collision-warning system for lift trucks is currently being developed in the "PräVISION" project. The system uses a time-of-flight camera to capture information about the environment. Computer-vision algorithms use this data to predict impending collisions, whereby collisions with humans and objects are distinguished. The distinction is made using machine learning algorithms for detecting people in different image types. This system has already been evaluated in academic settings. Industrial evaluation of the support vector machine used for people detection showed that the results of academic tests cannot be transferred to industrial application. The detection rate decreased about 25% on average. Either the lack of training data from the application area or the divergent distribution of the tags is responsible for the decrease. Consequently, the next step will be to find out why detection is significantly worse when trained SVMs are applied in an industrial environment.

Acknowledgement. The "PräVISION" project is funded by the German Social Accident Insurance (DGUV). The project partners involved are:
- BIBA Bremen
- SICK AG
- STILL GmbH
- Berufsgenossenschaft Handel und Warendistribution (BGHW)

References

1. Lang, A., Günthner, W.A.: Evaluation of the usage of support vector machines for people detection for a collision warning system on a forklift. In: Nah, F.F.-H., Tan, C.-H. (eds.) HCIBGO 2017. LNCS, vol. 10293, pp. 322–337. Springer, Cham (2017). https://doi.org/10.1007/978-3-319-58481-2_25
2. Acure: Blaxtair. https://blaxtair.com. Accessed 20 Feb 2018
3. ELOKON GmbH: ELOprotect; ELOshield; ELOback^2. http://www.elokon.com. Accessed 20 Feb 2018
4. tbm hightech control GmbH: RRW-207/3D; RAM-107; RRW-107plus. http://www.tbm.biz. Accessed 20 Feb 2018
5. U-Tech GmbH: U-Tech. http://www.u-tech-gmbh.de. Accessed 20 Feb 2018
6. Horn, B.K.P., Schunck, B.G.: Determining optical flow. Artif. Intell. **17**(1–3), 185–203 (1981)

7. Jaimez, M., Souiai, M., Gonzalez-Jimenez, J., Cremers, D.: A primal-dual framework for real-time dense RGB-D scene flow. In: Proceedings of the IEEE International Conference on Robotics and Automation (ICRA) (2015)
8. Vapnik, V., Lerner, A.: Pattern recognition using generalized portrait method. Autom. Remote Control **24**, 774–780 (1963)
9. Boser, B.E., Guyon, I.M., Vapnik, V.N.: A training algorithm for optimal margin classifiers. In: Haussler, D. (ed.) Proceedings of the Fifth Annual Workshop on Computational Learning Theory, COLT 1992, New York, NY, USA, pp. 144–152 (1992)
10. Dalal, N., Triggs, B., Schmid, C.: Human detection using oriented histograms of flow and appearance. In: Leonardis, A., Bischof, H., Pinz, A. (eds.) ECCV 2006, Part II. LNCS, vol. 3952, pp. 428–441. Springer, Heidelberg (2006). https://doi.org/10.1007/11744047_33
11. Dollar, P., Wojek, C., Schiele, B., Perona, P.: Pedestrian detection: an evaluation of the state of the art. IEEE Trans. Pattern Anal. Mach. Intell. **34**(4), 743–761 (2012)
12. OpenCV. https://opencv.org/. Accessed 20 Feb 2018
13. Danelljan, M., Khan, F.S., Felsberg, M., van de Weijer, J.: Adaptive color attributes for real-time visual tracking. In: IEEE Conference on Computer Vision and Pattern Recognition, pp. 1090–1097 (2014)
14. Kalal, Z., Mikolajczyk, K., Matas, J.: Forward-backward error: automatic detection of tracking failures. In: 2010 20th International Conference on Pattern Recognition (ICPR), pp. 2756–2759. IEEE (2010)
15. Kalal, Z., Mikolajczyk, K., Matas, J.: Tracking-learning-detection. IEEE Trans. Pattern Anal. Mach. Intell. **34**(7), 1409–1422 (2012)
16. Pérez, J.S., Meinhardt-Llopis, E., Facciolo, G.: TV-L1 optical flow estimation. Image Proc. On Line **3**, 137–150 (2013)
17. Enzweiler, M., Gavrila, D.M.: Monocular pedestrian detection: survey and experiments. IEEE Trans. Pattern Anal. Mach. Intell. **31**(12), 2179–2195 (2009)

Auditory Displays for Take-Over
in Semi-automated Vehicles

Erin Richie[✉], Thomas Offer-Westort,
Raghavendran Shankar, and Myounghoon Jeon

Michigan Technological University, Houghton, MI 49931, USA
{enrichie,tofferwe,rshanka1,mjeon}@mtu.edu

Abstract. With the field of automated vehicles rapidly growing comes the question of how we communicate to a driver that they need to take over in emergency or other urgent situations. Auditory displays can enhance communications between the driver and the automated vehicle. After a review of related literature, guidelines for audio displays were determined and a preliminary pilot experiment was conducted to further understand how drivers' reaction time to urgent situations would vary based on the type of sound they were alerted with. Results suggest that speech may give the quickest response time and a word choice may matter if using a spearcon. This paper is expected to contribute to designing further research studies for take-over displays in the automated vehicle.

Keywords: Auditory displays · Automated vehicles · Take-over

1 Introduction

As automated vehicles become more popular, scientists and engineers alike have begun to imagine ways to integrate them into our world. Vehicles with degrees of autonomy are already on the road. As technology grows, the ability for a vehicle to perform tasks without user input grows. As technology moves rapidly towards automated vehicles, the need for guidelines as to when it is acceptable for machines to be in control and when the user needs to take over increases. This paper seeks to provide a review of some of the current research on the best uses of auditory displays in take-over between semi-automated vehicles and their operators. Specifically, we try to use this review to provide a set of guidelines of what auditory cues can be used to alert drivers to when they should be completing a task and at what instance the auditory cues alert the drivers. In addition, we have conducted a pilot experiment to further understand the areas where research has yet to reach.

© Springer International Publishing AG, part of Springer Nature 2018
V. G. Duffy (Ed.): DHM 2018, LNCS 10917, pp. 623–634, 2018.
https://doi.org/10.1007/978-3-319-91397-1_51

2   Related Work

2.1   Why Auditory Displays?

Given that vision is heavily taxed while driving, an auditory channel can be used for additional communication between a driver and a vehicle. Audio is a separate modality from vision and allows for concurrent information processing while limiting the impact on visual processing capacity (Multiple Resources Theory, [1]). In a simple RT task, audio cues elicit a faster response time than visual cues [2] (Woodworth and Schlossberg). Further, directional audio can be utilized to indicate the direction of important events, such as vehicle accidents. This provides a similarity to the real-world events (sounds coming from the accident or crash). However, when working with auditory displays, there are a few important considerations. Vehicles have many other auditory warnings and alerts, including collision warnings, seatbelt warnings, and lane departure warnings, and thus, new auditory displays need to be integrated with these in a distinguishable manner. Moreover, while visual cues alone are generally inferior to auditory cues regarding their ability to grab attention and elicit quick responses [3], it may be beneficial to have multimodal displays.

2.2   Types of Auditory Displays

Obviously, speech can be used for clear communications between the operator and the vehicle. Research has typically shown that human speech is better than text-to-speech (TTS), but nowadays, synthesized speech is also of high quality (e.g., voice assistants such as Alexa or Google Home). In addition to speech, auditory researchers have designed and developed a number of non-speech sounds for better communications between people and technologies. Auditory icons [4] are designed by adopting the representative sound of the object or event. For example, the engine sound of the motor cycle can be used to represent the approaching motor cycle for a driver. Earcons [5] are short musical sounds. Repeated sound patterns usually represent a warning. Auditory icons use an inherent analogy between sounds and referents, whereas earcons use arbitrary mappings, which require user training. Spearcons [6] are made by algorithmically compressing speech without pitch change. Thus, when there are many items to speak out, spearcons can make it faster than speech while maintaining the relationship with the original speech. These auditory displays have been designed and tested with computer systems, mobile devices, and in-vehicle technologies.

2.3   General Display Design Guidelines

Wogalter et al. [7] suggested six guidelines for the design of warnings in displays - salience, wording, layout and placement, pictorial symbols, auditory warnings, and personal factors. While these guidelines may have been created with primarily visual display in mind, a number of the concepts lend themselves well to auditory displays. Salience, for instance, is a concept related to noticeability or conspicuity. Nees and Walker [8] note that maximal sensitivity to sound falls between 2000 Hz and 5000 Hz, which overlaps with the range of human speech. This range may not be perfectly appropriate in a motor vehicle, where competing sounds and noise can be numerous and varied. In addition, older adults tend to lose their sensitivity to sounds above 4,000 Hz. Thus, more adjustment should be followed. Wording may impact performance for speech systems. Wogalter et al. [7] found that "Danger" instills a greater sense of urgency than either "Warning" or "Caution", all of which communicate greater urgency than "Notice." They also noted a need to be specific, complete, and brief. Completeness and brevity particularly may come into competition. They suggested that ideal wording would also include consequences, but this may not be feasible if danger is imminent. In their discussion specifically regarding auditory components, they noted that frequency and pulse rate can all affect response times. Generally, the greater pulse rates are interpreted as communicating the greater urgency. Their sixth guideline relates to personal factors. To a large extent personal variation cannot be accounted for, but there may be trends within a demographic. Some aspects may be uniform across a specific market. At the very least, it suggests that there may be some benefit to testing auditory warnings within regions where the product will be released. Sounds may communicate slightly different messages in different cultures.

One additional concept explored by Wogalter et al. [7] is the benefit of repetition in recall. Sounds that are heard more frequently are more likely to be understood. Since ideally, the sounds requiring the most immediate response and having the direst consequences should come up very infrequently, there may be benefits to finding other situations in which drivers can be exposed to those sounds. For example, purchase of a semi-automated vehicle requires would-be owners to take a short training course in which they are exposed to various auditory warnings that their vehicle might produce.

Possible guidelines from this line of reasoning include:

1. Placement. The direction that a sound comes from may impact performance.
2. Clear and simple wording. Fewer concise words should lead to quicker responses.
3. Good at attracting attention. Words should convey an appropriate level of urgency.
4. Sonic parameters. The sonic parameters, such as intensity, frequency, repetition of sound, duration, timbre and harmonicity must differ significantly to create awareness to the drivers during the change in manual and automatic mode.

2.4   Comparison of Auditory Warning Types

A study [9] compared several types of auditory cues in a simulated driving environment and then judged their relative effectiveness. These findings were then used to make recommendations on how sounds could and should be used when a driver is approaching a hazard. When comparing speech, auditory icons, environmental sounds, and abstract warning sounds, the author found that auditory icons and speech performed best in both accuracy and response time and that abstract sounds performed poorest in both categories. However, it should be noted that speech was noted as pleasant, but not ideal at communicating urgency, where this was less of an issue for auditory icons. It is also noted that since sounds for high emergency situations will (hopefully) not be heard often, they need to be more intuitive than normal, day-to-day alerts so that drivers know what to do quickly in an emergency. Hellier and Edworthy [10] have expanded on the well-established research that urgency is needed when implementing a warning. This finding and continued research in the subject area suggest that an urgent warning may be effective and/or necessary in an automated vehicle.

Hester et al. [11] compared different types of alert (sound alert, task-irrelevant voice alert, and task-relevant voice alert) on drivers' trust and their reaction when the automation was failed. Results showed that different audio feedback did not make a difference on participants' trust, their eyes down time, and collision avoidance. However, they discussed that the trend in the collision avoidance should be considered due to the limited number of participants. Results showed that in the task relevant voice condition such as "the car in front of us seems to be slowing down" caused more drivers to avoid collisions.

We can take away several guidelines from these findings:

1. As unpleasant sounds are associated with more urgent situations, it would be useful to use an unpleasant sound to express that a driver needs to take immediate action. For purposes of this paper, an unpleasant sound indicates a sound that is perhaps dissonant, repetitive, loud, or a combination of the latter that a user does not enjoy listening to. However, using extremely unpleasant sounds may have the user turn off the system [10].
2. Pleasantness and urgency are inversely correlated, suggesting that some balance may need to be found to create a system that is both safe and acceptable to the user [10].
3. Speech and auditory icons receive more immediate and accurate responses and should be considered to use to inform drivers of tasks to be completed. However, another study [12] showed while the auditory icons produced significantly faster reaction times than the conventional warnings, they suffered from more inappropriate responses, where drivers reacted with a brake press to a non-collision situation. Therefore, more research is required.
4. It is difficult to associate speech with an urgency level, so sounds and speech may need to be explored as a combination for best results.

2.5   Auditory Displays When Multitasking

Research has shown that spearcons (compressed snippets of speech) may be particularly useful for multitasking. Moskovitch et al. [13] used a dual task in which their participants navigated a mobile phone contact list for a target name (secondary task) while playing a perceptual-motor, ball-catching game, representative of driving (primary task). The phone menu was enhanced with two audio navigation cues: traditional text-to-speech (TTS, where a phrase is spoken for each menu item) and spearcons. These cues were tested with and without visual display of the contact list. Spearcons in conjunction with TTS enhanced performance on the primary task while having no negative effect on the secondary task. Auditory menus reduced perceived workload and increased subjective ratings. In another study, Jeon et al. [14] conducted a study where their participants did a similar menu navigation task on the telematics system while playing the same ball-catching game. They found that when auditory assistance was given, users were more likely to perform better on their primary task. Participants were tested using just the visual interface, TTS cues, TTS and spearcons, TTS and spindex (speech index), and all three forms together. Secondary task performance was best when sound assistance was given. In driving applications, the primary task (driving) would be the higher priority, suggesting that any auditory displays are beneficial.

Guidelines that can be taken from this study include:

1. Auditory cues can be useful tools to help grab drivers' attention.
2. Multimodal presentation is effective to help alert drivers to a task.
3. Adding advanced auditory cues (e.g., spearcon, spindex) to speech improves performance even more.

2.6 Research Gap

For non-speech sounds, research shows either contradictory results (e.g., performance of auditory icons) or the different range of numerical values for each sonic parameter (e.g., earcons). Therefore, further work needs to be done to determine the best auditory display systems in vehicles and make them a standardized set of values. A more detailed, comprehensive experimental study will help to determine sound qualities, such as frequency, timbre, and their ability to elicit faster response time from operators.

For speech sounds, it is obvious that speech can satisfy completeness, but it is still questionable, how speech can obtain brevity at the same time. As a form of shrunken speech, spearcons have been tested by adding them to speech, but not as an independent auditory cues. Also, little research has been conducted on how much this compressed speech can deliver urgency in the vehicle context. If spearcons can provide higher urgency than speech, while conveying the similar level of meaning, it will potentially contribute to the road safety. We also hypothesize that the task-relevant spearcons ("Take Over" or "Drive Now") will be more capable of achieving quicker response times than the task-irrelevant spearcons ("Warning"). To this end, we conducted a pilot study comparing various spearcons with speech (both male and female) and a simple earcon (a beep) during a driving simulation.

3   Methods

3.1   Participants

Of the 15 undergraduate students who registered for the study, 14 participants (12 male, 2 female) completed the experiment for partial credit in psychology courses and one failed to show. They reported normal or corrected-to-normal vision and hearing, and provided informed consent. No participants reported simulation sickness. Recruitment was done using the Sona System – University subject recruitment system.

3.2 Apparatus

Figure 1 shows a mid-fidelity National Advanced Driving Simulator (NADS) MiniSim. The simulation software runs on a single computer, running Microsoft Windows 7 Pro on an Intel Core i7 processor, 3.07 GHz and 12 GB of RAM, and relays sound through a 2.1 audio system. Three Panasonic TH-42PH2014 42″ plasma displays, each with a 1280 × 800 pixel resolution, allow for a total of 130° field of view in front of the seated participant. The center monitor is 28 in. from the center of the steering wheel and the left and right monitors are 37 in. from the center of the steering wheel. The MiniSim also includes a steering wheel, adjustable car seat, gas and brake pedals, buttons for shifting gears (a substitute for a gear shift, in more conventional vehicles), as well as a Toshiba Ltd. WXGA TFT LCD monitor with a 1280 × 800 resolution to display the speedometer, etc. Environmental sound effects are also played through two embedded speakers. These sounds included engine noise, brake screech, turn indicators, collisions, etc. The graphic display replicates a fairly rural loop of road, with few cars and only intermittent signs of business. The simulator is designed to support both manual and automated vehicle modes. A MacBook Air laptop was also provided to for the secondary task, 2048. The laptop was placed to the lower right of the steering wheel, approximately where a central display might be in a vehicle.

Fig. 1. NADS minisim driving simulator in use

3.3 Stimuli

Our project required the use of sounds within a vehicle and would be tested using a driving simulator in a hand-over, take-over situation. Although the literature suggests that "Danger" is the most urgent wording, we thought that it might not be as universally applicable as "Warning." For instance, in a situation where an automated vehicle is stuck behind a slower vehicle, the driver is not in "Danger." We compared the urgency of "Warning" with two task-specific spearcons, "Take Over" and "Drive Now." We also compared the urgency of spearcons to speech ("Take control of vehicle now" said in both male and female voices) and an earcon (a beep) (Table 1).

Table 1. Sounds chosen

Sound type	Word spoken or sound played
Spearcon	Drive Now
Spearcon	Warning
Spearcon	Take Over
Speech - male voice	Take control of vehicle now
Speech - female voice	Take control of vehicle now
Earcon	Beep Tone

As a secondary task, the game 2048 was provided and participants were asked to play the game while the simulator was in the automated mode. The game consists of a board that starts with 2 squares featuring the number two. The participant used the arrow keys to shift all numbers in one direction. When they are moved in this direction, matching numbers add together and mold into one square that is now worth twice the value. After each move, more tiles are added to the board. The goal is to move the squares around the board in such a way that they continue to add numbers together and keep the number of tiles on the board low. If the board fills and the player is unable to make another move, the game ends (Fig. 2).

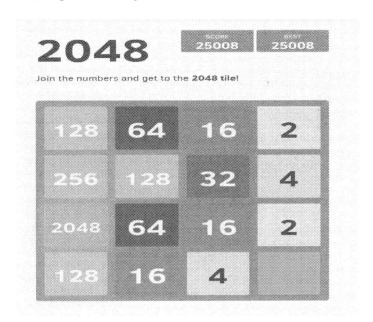

Fig. 2. Secondary Task, 2048 Game

3.4   Design and Procedure

Each participant completed two runs, paired into three different sets, as shown in Table 2. All participants completed either set A, B, or C. In other words, participants who drove run A1 also drove run A2. This allowed each driver to test each warning sound once, as shown. Participants were instructed that an initial beep would let them know to let go of the controls and allow the simulator to drive on its own. They were told then any other sound was intended to alert them that a hazard had appeared in the road and that they should take control of the vehicle. Another beep, after each obstacle, informed them they could once again let go of the controls, as in the beginning of the experiment.

Table 2. Possible simulation combinations

Run number	Sounds used in order
A1	Beep, Male Voice, Drive Now
A2	Warning, Take Over, Female Voice
B1	Take Over, Warning, Beep
B2	Female Voice, Drive Now, Male Voice
C1	Drive Now, Female Voice, Take Over
C2	Male Voice, Beep, Warning

When not driving, participants were asked to play 2048 to achieve the highest score they could. They were informed that their highest scores would be recorded.

The researcher present recorded how long it took for each participant to respond to each warning sound. Response time was measured from when the sound occurred to whenever the participant took control of the simulator, either by stepping on the brake or touching the steering wheel.

Each participant was instructed as follows:
To begin operation of the simulator:

1. Apply pressure the brake pedal.
2. Use the buttons to the right of the steering column to navigate the simulator to "D."
3. Release pressure from the brake pedal.
4. Apply pressure to the gas pedal.

The simulator will give you audio notification when it has taken control of driving. Until a warning sound is given, do not press either pedal or touch the steering wheel. Doing either will return control of driving to you and terminate automation.

4   Results

Table 3 shows the raw data from our experiment. Response times are averaged for each sound at the bottom and for each participant at the right (before secondary task scores). Individual response times ranged from less than a quarter of a second to almost seven seconds. The data show that the fastest average reaction time was given by male speech, followed by the beep, female speech, and then the spearcons "Take Over", "Warning", and "Drive Now" in that order.

Table 3. Response times by sound and participant

	Set	Beep	SpeechF	SpeechM	DriveNow	Takeover	Warning	Average	Secondary task
1	A	2.03	–	1.52	1.67	–	–	1.74	2452
2	B	2.19	1.34	1.40	0.53	1.42	0.94	1.30	4984
3	C	1.05	1.43	1.14	4.03	1.56	1.03	1.71	15696
4	B	1.54	0.90	–	–	2.34	1.17	1.49	17612
5	C	–	1.12	1.05	6.80	0.88	–	2.46	11084
6	A	0.95	0.84	0.23	1.30	0.53	0.88	0.79	3100
7	B	1.14	0.87	1.27	1.68	1.54	1.02	1.25	4680
8	C	1.57	1.43	0.59	3.54	1.93	1.15	1.70	2960
9	A	1.65	3.11	1.58	2.86	3.33	4.00	2.76	1904
10	B	1.26	1.67	1.24	5.89	1.16	3.50	2.45	11220
11	C	1.01	1.14	1.32	0.97	1.02	1.49	1.16	9072
12	A	1.20	1.50	1.13	1.02	1.46	1.30	1.27	8232
13	B	1.14	2.15	1.35	2.43	1.81	1.88	1.79	8096
14	C	1.41	1.30	1.26	0.97	1.01	1.52	1.25	1256
Average		1.40	1.45	1.16	2.59	1.54	1.66	1.63	7311

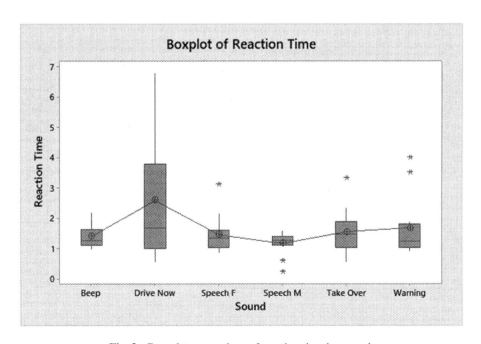

Fig. 3. Box plot comparison of reaction time in seconds

The dashes represent instances in which we were unable to collect a response time. For participant 1, this was caused by accidentally touching the controls (which caused premature surrender of control of the simulator). For participants 4 and 5, this was due to a system crash part way through the experiment.

Figure 3 presents the data from Table 3 as a boxplot, to more easily show the range of response times. The outliers for the spearcons "Take Over" and "Warning" are occurrences in which participants heard the spearcon but seemed momentarily unsure if it was intended to be the sign to take control of the simulator. These occurrences happened frequently enough with "Drive Now" to not be outliers. The longest response time, 6.80 s, was due to a driver not registering the spearcon at all, only avoiding the obstacle when they saw it out of their peripheral vision.

5   Discussion

To explore the effects of various auditory displays for the take-over situation in the automated vehicle, we conducted a pilot study. We were particularly interested in testing the potential of spearcons. Because of the small number of participants, it was hard to apply inferential statistics to our results. However, we could get some guidelines for future research. Speech (especially, male voice) and a beep were faster than spearcons. Among the spearcons, the task-specific spearcon, "Take Over", performed better than the more general "Warning," but "Drive Now" performed much worse. We hypothesized that spearcons would increase perceptual urgency than speech, but they did not induce an urgent response as either speech or earcons that we tested. We observed several cases, in which participants did not recognize the spearcons as intended warning signals. Future studies can assess the effects of spearcons after brief training or at least, exposure to spearcons before the experiment.

Interestingly, the male voice performed best while the female voice seemed less urgent than the simple beep (i.e., an earcon). We can consider a few possible explanations. First, the male voice might sound more authoritative than the female voice. Literature [15] shows that the authoritative style message promoted greater compliance than the notification style message. Although the difference was not initially obvious, the recording for male speech may be slightly louder than the recording for female speech. Alternatively, our participants may have responded more quickly to the male voice because they were themselves predominantly male. The other possibility is that participants responded to the male voice more quickly because it was a recording of the lead facilitator, who also instructed them on how to use the simulator and play the game, 2048. Because the participants were already following his instructions, they may have been more apt to respond to his voice when used as a warning. This could be seen as aligning with a finding from Wogalter et al. [7] suggesting that repetition helps with recall. They found that participants responded more quickly after having heard a cue multiple times. Perhaps, similarly, they also respond to the voices that they have heard before.

While we will continue to explore auditory displays, we will also consider multimodal displays. In the next iteration, we will compare visual displays (warning icons and/or text displays) and tactile displays. Mohebbi et al. [16] found that the participants responded to brake to avoid the accident more quickly when tactile warnings were used, rather than auditory warnings when there was an auditory distraction (i.e., conversation via a headset). We hope that this continuous effort can contribute to the design and implementation of advanced warnings for urgent situations in the automated vehicle.

Acknowledgments. This research was supported by a grant (code 17TLRP-B131486-01) from Transportation and Logistics R&D Program funded by Ministry of Land, Infrastructure and Transport of Korean government.

References

1. Wickens, C.D.: Multiple resources and performance prediction. Theor. Issues Ergon. Sci. **3**(2), 159–177 (2002)
2. Woodworth, R.S., Schlosberg, H.: Experimental Psychology. Holt, Rinehart & Winston, New York (1965)
3. Colavita, F.B.: Human sensory dominance. Atten. Percept. Psychophys. **16**(2), 409–412 (1974)
4. Gaver, W.W.: Auditory icons: using sound in computer interfaces. Hum. Comput. Interact. **2**, 167–177 (1986)
5. Blattner, M.M., Sumikawa, D.A., Greenberg, R.M.: Earcons and icons: their structure and common design principles. Hum. Comput. Interact. **4**, 11–44 (1989)
6. Walker, B.N., Lindsay, J., Nance, A., Nakano, Y., Palladino, D.K., Dingler, T., Jeon, M.: Spearcons (speech-based earcons) improve navigation performance in advanced auditory menus. Hum. Factors **55**(1), 157–182 (2012)
7. Wogalter, M.S., Conzola, V.C., Smith-Jackson, T.L.: Based guidelines for warning design and evaluation. Appl. Ergon. **33**(3), 219–230 (2002)
8. Nees, M.A., Walker, B.N.: Auditory displays for in-vehicle technologies. Rev. Hum. Factors Ergon. **7**(1), 58–99 (2011)
9. McKeown, D.: Candidates for within-vehicle auditory displays. Georgia Institute of Technology (2005)
10. Hellier, E., Edworthy, J.: On using psychophysical techniques to achieve urgency mapping in auditory warnings. Appl. Ergon. **30**(2), 167–171 (1999)
11. Hester, M., Lee, K., Dyre, B.P.: "Driver Take Over": a preliminary exploration of driver trust and performance in autonomous vehicles. In: Proceedings of the International Annual Meeting of Human Factors and Ergonomics Society (2017)
12. Graham, R.: Use of auditory icons as emergency warnings: evaluation within a vehicle collision avoidance application. Ergonomics **42**(9), 1233–1248 (1999)
13. Moskovitch, Y., Jeon, M., Walker, B.N.: Enhanced auditory menu cues on a mobile phone improve time-shared performance of a driving-like dual task. In: Proceedings of the Annual Meeting of the Human Factors and Ergonomics Society (HFES 2010), San Francisco, 27 September–1 October 2010, pp. 1321–1325 (2010)
14. Jeon, M., Davison, B., Wilson, J., Nees, M., Walker, B.N.: Enhanced auditory menu cues improve dual task performance and are preferred with in-vehicle technologies. In: The 1st International Conference on Automotive User Interfaces and Vehicular Applications (AutomotiveUI 2009), pp. 91–98. ACM Press, Essen, September 2009

15. Lee, J.D., Gore, B.F., Campbell, J.L.: Display alternatives for in-vehicle warning and sign information: message style, location, and modality. Transp. Hum. Factors **1**(4), 347–375 (1999)
16. Mohebbi, R., Gray, R., Tan, H.Z.: Driver reaction time to tactile and auditory rear-end collision warnings while talking on a cell phone. Hum. Factors **51**(1), 102–110 (2009)

Safety Performance Evaluation for Civil Aviation Maintenance Department

Yijie Sun[(⊠)], Yuan Zhang, Rong Zhao, and Yanqiu Chen

China Academy of Civil Aviation Science and Technology, Beijing, China
{sunyj,zhangy,zhaor,chenyq}@mail.castc.org.cn

Abstract. The MMEM model and the core risk analysis method are applied to construct the safety performance index system of the civil aviation maintenance department, and four categories of the safety performance indicators are set up, including maintenance error, aircraft condition, safety foundation and safety management. In order to take into account the different effects of subjective and objective weights, the comprehensive evaluation model based on the subjective and objective combination weight method for the safety performance of the airline maintenance department is established. The analytic hierarchy process and entropy method are used to calculate the subjective weight and objective weight of the index respectively, and the optimization theory is used to calculate the combination weight of the index. The data from 2011 to 2016 in a maintenance department of an airline is used as an example of application, and the results of the evaluation are analyzed. The results show that the proposed safety performance evaluation model can quantitatively reflect the safety state of the maintenance department and the evaluation results are reasonable.

Keywords: Maintenance department · Safety performance
Combination weight · Evaluation model

1 Introduction

Aircraft maintenance is one of the important guarantees for the safe operation of the aircraft. According to the statistics of the International Air Transport Association, the proportion of aviation accidents caused by aviation maintenance errors has risen from 20% in the early twentieth Century to 80% in 1990s [1]. The maintenance department in the airline undertakes most of the maintenance work and activities in Chinese aviation transportation, and it is the basic unit of airline safety management. By evaluating safety performance of maintenance department, the airline can understand the maintenance department's overall safety situation, and discover the safety problems in time, so as to take corresponding countermeasures. Besides, the evaluation results can be used as the basis of incentive system, and are conducive to the safety performance oriented safety culture, thus improving the airline safety level.

Based on MMEM model and core risk analysis, a comprehensive safety performance index system of maintenance department is developed in this paper. And based on the subjective and objective combination weight method, a comprehensive evaluation model of safety performance is established. The subjective weights and objective

© Springer International Publishing AG, part of Springer Nature 2018
V. G. Duffy (Ed.): DHM 2018, LNCS 10917, pp. 635–646, 2018.
https://doi.org/10.1007/978-3-319-91397-1_52

weights of the indexes are calculated by means of analytic hierarchy process and entropy method respectively, and the combination weights of the indexes are calculated by the optimization theory. The data of maintenance department of an airline from 2014 to 2016 is used as an example of application to verify the feasibility and applicability of the evaluation model.

2   Safety Performance Index System Based on MMEM Model and Core Risk Analysis

To evaluate the level of safety performance accurately, we need to establish a comprehensive and scientific index system. With the development of safety management theory, it is difficult to fully reflect the safety status only by accident, incident of this kind of high consequence indexes. A systematic and scientific index system needs to be set up to assess the safety of the organization, and to expose problems in the process of operation and management while reflecting the safety results. Therefore, the safety performance indicators established in this paper are not only limited to high consequence indicators, but also include low consequence indicators including aircraft condition, safety foundation and safety management.

2.1   The Principle for Setting Safety Performance Indexes

MMEM model is a relatively independent and closely related system composed of four components of Man, Machine, Environment and Management, and is expressed as the mutual influence and association between the four principal components of " Man - Machine - Environment - Management " [2]. The theory of MMEM is developed on the basis of the traditional theory of Man, Machine and Environment. It compensates for the shortcomings of traditional analysis methods, and puts forward a "management" factor that people once ignored. Modern safety management emphasizes the role of management especially. Excellent management can not only make up for the safety defects in the process, but also can effectively control the cost [3].

As a safety system, civil aircraft maintenance system is also composed of four subsystems: human, machine, environment and management. Essentially, it is also a MMEM system. According to the MMEM system theory, we establish various elements that involve safety performance from four aspects, and we can more comprehensively analyze all the factors that affect the safety status and avoid omissions. In order to accurately reflect the maintenance department's safety status, it is necessary to take full account of its relevant historical data. Through the analysis of historical data, we find the core risk of maintenance department, and derive the safety performance indicators that affect core risk from four aspects of people, machine, environment and management.

According to this idea, index types can be divided into four categories. As shown in Fig. 1.

The first category is the maintenance error. These indicators correspond to the subsystem of man, and are the indicators of high consequences. They are used to assess the risk of human error in the maintenance department.

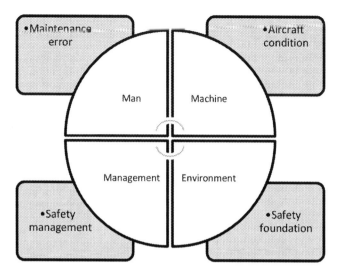

Fig. 1. The idea of establishing safety performance indexes

The second category is the aircraft condition. This kind of index is corresponding to the subsystem of machine, and is a low consequence index, which is used to evaluate the technical fault status of the flying fleet.

The third category is safety foundation. This type of index corresponds to the subsystem of environment to evaluate the personnel composition and maintenance quality of the maintenance department.

The fourth category is safety management. This type of index corresponds to the subsystem of management to assess the development of safety management.

2.2   Methods for Setting Safety Performance Indexes

Setting of maintenance error indexes. According to the standards of the unsafe events of the CAAC and the airlines, combined with the results of historical data analysis, it is possible to select the type of events related to the maintenance department as maintenance error indexes. In accordance with the event rank, it can be divided into accidents, accidents, errors, and other unsafe event etc. Table 1 is an example of part of the maintenance error indexes.

Table 1. Maintenance error indexes samples

Occurrence rank	Indexes samples
Accident	Ground collision
Serious incident	In flight shutdown
Serious error	System failure
General error	Discovery of foreign objects

Setting of aircraft condition indexes. According to the historical data of the airline, the core risks associated with the maintenance department can be combed. Then the Reason model and the SHEL model are used to analyze the unsafe status that may lead to the occurrence of core risks, as shown in Fig. 2. The unsafe status related to the aircraft can be set as aircraft condition indexes, and Table 2 is an example.

Fig. 2. Methods for setting aircraft condition indexes

Table 2. Aircraft station indexes samples

Core risk	Indexes samples
System malfunction	Windshield shedding
	Flap failure
	Landing gear failure
	APU failure

Setting of safety foundation and safety management indexes. These indicators are used to assess the personnel composition, maintenance quality and safety management of the maintenance department. For these indicators, the brainstorming method can be used in combination with the safety management system element method. Table 3 is a part of the example of these two types of indicators.

Table 3. Safety foundation and safety management indexes samples

Index category	Indexes samples
Safety foundation	Qualification rate of maintenance personnel
	Safety management personnel ratio
Safety management	The rate of risk management in time
	Execution rate of unsafe incident investigation
	Safety inspection discovery rate

3   Safety Performance Evaluation Model Based on the Subjective and Objective Combination Weight Method

The determination of weights plays a very important role in the comprehensive evaluation. And the difference in the method of comprehensive evaluation is also mainly reflected in the difference of the method of weight calculation. There are various kinds of weight calculation methods at present [4, 5], but in general, it can be divided into two categories: subjective method and objective method.

These two kinds of methods have their own advantages and disadvantages. Subjective weight calculation method is greatly influenced by the subjective impression of the evaluator, and the result often cannot reflect the real situation objectively. Objective method, though more objectivity in most cases, is sometimes contrary to the actual importance of each index.

Combination weight method is used to determine index weight, that is to say, the weights calculated by two or more than two weighting methods are combined, and the optimal theory is applied to build the model to get the combination weight. This method can take into account the influence of subjective and objective, and the result is in good agreement with the actual situation, so it has good practicability.

In this paper, a comprehensive evaluation model of maintenance department safety performance is established. The weight is determined by the combination weight calculation model of AHP and entropy method, considering the influence of subjective and objective factors.

3.1   Establishment Scheme of Safety Performance Evaluation Model

This paper establishes four kinds of safety performance indicators, which are different in data characteristics and attributes. Different safety performance indicators calculation models are needed. The overall scheme of safety performance evaluation model is shown in Fig. 3.

According to the principle of risk evaluation and the Hayne rule, the risk value calculation model is set up for the indexes of maintenance error and aircraft condition. For the indexes of safety foundation and safety management, the scores of various performance indicators are calculated according to the airlines' assessment methods and sorting methods.

After obtaining these four kinds of performance indicators, we use AHP and entropy method to calculate the subjective weight and objective weight respectively, and then use the optimization theory to establish the model and get the combined weight of indicators. Finally, the weight vector is linearly weighted with the value vector of the evaluation index, and the comprehensive evaluation results can be obtained.

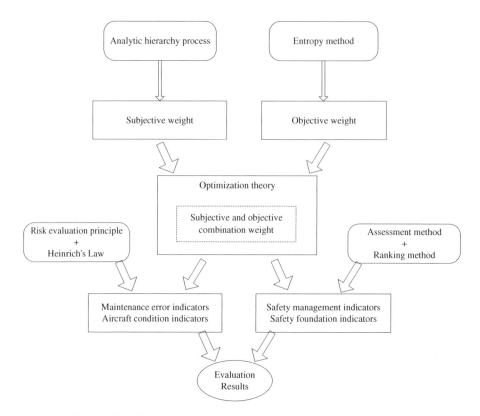

Fig. 3. Establishment scheme of safety performance evaluation model

3.2 Calculation Models for Different Types of Indexes

Risk value calculation for maintenance error and aircraft condition indexes.
According to the risk assessment theory, the risk value calculation model needs to be integrated with the possibility and severity of the unsafe events. For the risk of maintenance error and aircraft condition indicators, probability is the frequency of unsafe events corresponding to the index. Severity requires a unified quantitative standard, and the severity of the unsafe events of different levels is assigned according to the Hayne rule.

On the basis of calculating methods of the possibility and the severity of each index, it can be obtained the risk value of the maintenance error index of the airline maintenance department R in a given period of evaluation.

$$\text{R} = \frac{\sum (\text{severity of each index corrending to unsafe event})}{\text{flight movements}} \tag{1}$$

Calculation for safety foundation and safety management indexes. These two types of indicators are process indicators related to management. Take the safety management index as an example, in the internal assessment of the airline, there is a clear definition of the score for each index. The weight of different indexes can be calculated by the sorting method, then the index value of the safety management is obtained by the weighted arithmetic average method.

3.3 Comprehensive Evaluation Model

In this paper, a comprehensive evaluation model of maintenance department safety performance is established. The weight of indicators is determined by the combined weight calculation model of AHP and entropy method, considering the influence of subjective and objective factors.

For the convenience of expression, it is assumed that there are m evaluation objects ($i = 1,2,...m$) and n evaluation indicators ($j = 1,2,...n$), x_{ij} represents the value of the ith evaluation object on the jth index. w_j^1 represents the subjective weight of the jth index, w_j^2 represents the objective weight of the jth index, and w_j^o represents the combination weight of the jth index.

Determination of subjective weight by AHP [6–8]. On the basis of determining the indicators, pairwise comparisons are made by experts to the importance of each indicator based on their years of experience. Then the weight of each evaluation index is calculated by using the comparison judgment matrix and the hierarchy order. And the random consistency ratio is used to calculate the consistency of comparison judgment matrix.

Determination of objective weight by entropy method [9]. Entropy is the measure of the degree of disorder of the system, and the information is interpreted as the expression of the degree of disorder of the system, which is expressed as the variability of a certain index of the system.

That is, the smaller the variation degree of a certain index of a system is, the smaller the information content it contains, the greater its entropy value, the smaller the corresponding weight of the index in the multi index comprehensive evaluation system. Conversely, the greater the variability of a certain index of a system is, the larger the amount of information it contains and the smaller its entropy, the greater the weight of the index in multi index comprehensive evaluation system.

According to the above principle, the steps of determining the coefficient of evaluation index by entropy method are as follows.

- To deal with the indicators so that they are in the same trend.
- Using the normalization method, the proportion of the index value of the ith evaluation object under the jth index is calculated.

$$p_{ij} = \frac{x_{ij}}{\sum_{i=1}^{m} x_{ij}} \quad j = 1,2,...n \tag{2}$$

It is assumed that $x_{ij} > 0$, if the hypothesis is not satisfied, a suitable method can be used to transform the data.
- Calculating the entropy of the jth index.

$$h_j = -\frac{1}{\ln m} \sum_{i=1}^{m} p_{ij} \ln p_{ij}, \ 0 \le h_j \le 1 \tag{3}$$

For a given jth index, the smaller the difference between x_{ij}, the greater the h_j.
- Calculating the difference coefficient of the jth index.

$$g_j = 1 - h_j \tag{4}$$

The greater the difference coefficient, the more important the index is.
- Calculating the objective weight of each index.

$$w_j^2 = \frac{g_j}{\sum_{j=1}^{n} g_j} \tag{5}$$

Combination weight method for calculating subjective and objective combination weight [10]. In order to make the results of comprehensive evaluation more scientific, a reasonable approach is to combine the weight coefficients obtained by different weighting methods according to certain methods. Through combination weighting, the results can not only embody subjective information, but also embody objective information.

It is assumed that there are n items and s weighting methods for a multi index comprehensive evaluation problem, then the weight vector obtained by the kth method is expressed as $W^k = \left(w_1^k, w_2^k, \ldots w_n^k\right)$, k = 1,2,...s, and $\sum_{j=1}^{n} w_j^k = 1$. The combined weight vector is expressed as $W^o = \left(w_1^o, w_2^o, \ldots w_n^o\right)$, and $\sum_{j=1}^{n} w_j^o = 1$.

The combined weight of the jth index can be expressed as a linear combination of the known s weights, that is, $w_j^o = \sum_{k=1}^{s} \theta_k w_j^k$ j = 1,2,...n.

w_j^k is known, and the combination vector can be obtained by finding the coefficient vector of the weight.

The optimization model is set up, the goal is to minimize the square sum of the deviation of the combination weight and the known s weight. According to the differential property of the matrix, the first derivative condition of its optimization can be obtained, which corresponds to the linear equation set below.

$$\begin{vmatrix} W^1 \cdot \left(W^1\right)^T & W^1 \cdot \left(W^2\right)^T & \cdots & W^1 \cdot \left(W^s\right)^T \\ W^2 \cdot \left(W^1\right)^T & W^2 \cdot \left(W^2\right)^T & \cdots & W^2 \cdot \left(W^s\right)^T \\ \cdots & \cdots & \cdots & \cdots \\ W^s \cdot \left(W^1\right)^T & W^s \cdot \left(W^2\right)^T & \cdots & W^s \cdot \left(W^s\right)^T \end{vmatrix} \begin{vmatrix} \theta_1 \\ \theta_2 \\ \cdots \\ \theta_s \end{vmatrix} = \begin{vmatrix} W^1 \cdot \left(W^1\right)^T \\ W^2 \cdot \left(W^2\right)^T \\ \cdots \\ W^s \cdot \left(W^s\right)^T \end{vmatrix} \tag{6}$$

To solve the above formula, we can get the solution of $(\theta_1, \theta_2, \ldots \theta_s)$, and then the combined weight is obtained.

Calculation of comprehensive evaluation results. The weighted sum of the weight vector and the index value vector can be calculated, and the comprehensive evaluation result Y_i can be obtained.

$$Y_i = \sum_{j=1}^{n} w_j^o x_{ij} \quad (i = 1, 2, \ldots m) \tag{7}$$

4 Application Example

Taking 2011–2016 years' data of an airline's maintenance department as an example, the safety performance evaluation model established is applied to evaluate the performance for 6 years.

4.1 Calculation of Subjective Weight by AHP

Using the AHP described in Sect. 3.3, the judgment matrix and weight value of the index are calculated, and the consistency judgment is carried out. The consistency ratio of judgment matrix is less than 0.1, which satisfies the requirement of consistency.

Table 4. Judgment matrix and weights of second grade indexes

	Maintenance error	Aircraft condition	Safety foundation	Safety management	w_j^1
Maintenance error	1.0000	0.3333	0.5000	0.3333	0.1059
Aircraft condition	3.0000	1.0000	2.0000	0.5000	0.2829
Safety foundation	2.0000	0.5000	1.0000	0.3333	0.1636
Safety management	3.0000	2.0000	3.0000	1.0000	0.4476

4.2 Calculation of Objective Weight by Entropy Method

According to the method described in Sect. 3.2, the evaluation results of four categories of indexes of the maintenance department from 2011 to 2016 are obtained (see Table 5).

Table 5. Evaluation results of four types of indexes

	2011	2012	2013	2014	2015	2016
Maintenance error	6.9561	6.7453	6.3666	6.6008	7.5429	7.2864
Aircraft condition	7.4306	6.7574	8.0000	6.1880	7.8120	5.4306
Safety foundation	6.8138	6.8986	5.7654	7.575	6.4572	5.9679
Safety management	7.0327	7.4691	6.8918	7.0517	7.3282	7.0137

Table 6. Proportion of evaluation object index value

	2011	2012	2013	2014	2015	2016
Maintenance error	0.1676	0.1625	0.1534	0.1591	0.1818	0.1756
Aircraft condition	0.1785	0.1624	0.1922	0.1487	0.1877	0.1305
Safety foundation	0.1726	0.1747	0.1460	0.1919	0.1636	0.1512
Safety management	0.1644	0.1746	0.1611	0.1648	0.1713	0.1639

According to the formula (2), the proportion of the index value of the evaluation object is calculated, as shown in Table 6.

According to the formula (3) and the formula (4), the entropy value and the difference coefficient of each index are calculated, and the objective weight of the index is calculated according to the formula (5), as listed in Table 7.

Table 7. Entropy, difference coefficient and objective weights

	Maintenance error	Aircraft condition	Safety foundation	Safety management
Entropy value	0.9991	0.9951	0.9976	0.9998
Difference coefficient	0.0009	0.0049	0.0024	0.0002
w_j^2	0.1103	0.5853	0.2786	0.0258

4.3 Calculation of Combination Weight

According to the algorithm described in the formula (6), for this example, there is:

$$\begin{cases} W^1 \cdot \left(W^1\right)^T \cdot \theta_1 + W^1 \cdot \left(W^2\right)^T \cdot \theta_2 = W^1 \cdot \left(W^1\right)^T \\ W^2 \cdot \left(W^1\right)^T \cdot \theta_1 + W^2 \cdot \left(W^2\right)^T \cdot \theta_2 = W^2 \cdot \left(W^2\right)^T \end{cases} \tag{8}$$

The W^1 represents the subjective weight, and the W^2 represents the objective weight. The subjective weight and objective weight calculated in Sects 4.1 and 4.2 are replaced by the formula (8), and the equations can be obtained.

$$\begin{cases} 0.3184\theta_1 + 0.2344\theta_2 = 0.3184 \\ 0.2344\theta_1 + 0.4330\theta_2 = 0.4330 \end{cases}$$

The solutions are $\theta_1 = 0.4386, \theta_2 = 0.7626$.

Because θ_1 and θ_2 are also weighted vectors, we require that $\theta_1 + \theta_2 = 1$. The normalization of θ_1 and θ_2 can be obtained.

$$\theta_1' = 0.3652, \theta_2' = 0.6348$$

The optimal combination weight vector can be calculated by the linear weighted sum of the subjective weight and the objective weight, as listed in Table 8.

Table 8. Combination weights

	Maintenance error	Aircraft condition	Safety foundation	Safety management
w_j^O	0.1087	0.4749	0.2366	0.1798

4.4 Results and Analysis of Comprehensive Evaluation

According to the combination weights, the weighted sum of the index is calculated, and the comprehensive evaluation results of the maintenance department from 2011 to 2016 can be obtained, as shown in Fig. 4.

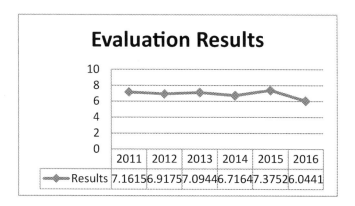

Fig. 4. Results of safety performance evaluation

From the comprehensive evaluation results of combination weight method, we can see that safety performance level is related to maintenance error, aircraft condition, safety foundation and safety management, and these factors affect and restrict each other. Safety foundation and aircraft condition are the basis and guarantee of high level safety performance, and the level of safety performance depends on the effective development of safety management.

The safety performance not only depends on the maintenance error, but also depends on the aircraft condition, the safety foundation and the safety management. For example, in 2016, although the evaluation of the maintenance error category is higher, the aircraft condition and safety foundation are poor, and the final results of the safety performance evaluation are lower than that of other years.

Compared with Tables 4, 7 and 8, the weight of the index obtained by the combination weight method is between the weights obtained by the AHP process and the entropy method. The proportion of the two in the comprehensive evaluation is determined, and their functions and effects are coordinated and balanced, and the best combination is achieved, which overcomes the one-sidedness of the single weight and makes the comprehensive evaluation more reasonable and scientific.

5   Conclusion

Safety performance evaluation index system of maintenance department of airlines was established, and the comprehensive evaluation model based on the combination of the subjective and objective weights is set up. With the historical data of 6 years, the comprehensive evaluation of the safety performance level of the airline maintenance department has been carried out.

The safety performance index system based on MMEM and core risk analysis can reflect the safety status of maintenance department from four dimensions of maintenance error, aircraft condition, safety foundation and safety management, and the index system is more comprehensive.

The established safety performance evaluation model can not only compare the performance level of each year from four dimensions, but also draw the overall level of safety performance every year, which is conducive to further analysis of safety performance level and reasons.

From the result of the evaluation, the level of safety performance should not only pay attention to the results, but also should pay more attention to process management. Process management affects the overall evaluation of safety performance.

References

1. Li, Z., Sun, Z., Gong, E., et al.: Research on the relationship between aviation maintenance error modes and error causes based on correspondence analysis method. Saf. Environ. Eng. **20**(4), 106–108 (2013)
2. Zhang, J.: System Safety Engineering. Aviation Industry Press, Beijing (1990)
3. Xu, J.: Formal Safety Assessment for Shipping Company Safety Management. Shanghai Maritime University, Shanghai (2004)
4. Liu, T., Zhang, X., Liu, G.: The Method of Safety Evaluation and Application Guide. Chemical Industry Press, Beijing (2005)
5. Tong, R., Li, G., Yu, C.: Commonly used Safety Evaluation Method and Its Application. China Labor and Social Security Publishing House, Beijing (2011)
6. Han, L., Mei, Q.: Analysis and study on AHP-fuzzy comprehensive evaluation. China Saf. Sci. J. **14**(7), 86–89 (2004)
7. Du, H., Wang, X.: Multi-index safety comprehensive evaluation of air traffic control based on principal element analysis method. China Saf. Sci. J. **9**(7), 124–128 (2009)
8. Chen, D., Cao, Y., Xia, H., et al.: Weight fusion of dam monitoring indexes based on entropy and G1 methods. Water Resour. Power **30**(6), 92–95 (2012)
9. Sun, T.: Multi-objective Synthesis Optimization of Construction Projects Based on Entropy Method and the Improved Topsis Method. Chongqing University, Chongqing (2010)
10. Huang, X., Wang, R., Zhou, Y., et al.: Application of method of combined weights in comprehensive evaluation on inhabitants' health status. J. Math. Med. **19**(4), 402–405 (2006)

Indicating Severity of Vehicle Accidents Using Pupil Diameter in a Driving Simulator Environment

Rui Tang[1(✉)], Jung Hyup Kim[1], Rebecca Parker[1], and Yoo Joo Jeong[2]

[1] Department of Industrial and Manufacturing Systems Engineering,
University of Missouri, Columbia, USA
{rtgv4,rp522}@mail.missouri.edu, kijung@missouri.edu
[2] Ulsan National Institute of Science and Technology, Ulsan, Korea
dbwn0930@unist.ac.kr

Abstract. This study investigated the driver's pupil diameter involved in car accidents within a driving simulation environment. The purpose of this research is to understand the relationship between the vehicle accidents and the changes in pupil diameter. We hypothesized that the patterns of pupil diameter could indicate the occurrence of a collision and the severity of car accidents. To investigate the relationship between the drivers' pupil diameter and the levels of a car accident, multiple hazard events were tested in a driving simulation environment. The eye-tracking technology was used to analyze the changes of pupil diameter and the vehicle accident events. We compared the patterns of pupil diameter trace among various levels of car accidents. The result showed that there was a significant difference on the patterns between minor crashes and severe crashes.

Keywords: Pupil diameter · Driving simulator · Eye tracking · Driving safety

1 Introduction

Emergency medical service (EMS) for a vehicle accident is a type of emergency service which is designed for responding automobile injuries that require out-of-hospital acute medical care. The goal of the EMS for the vehicle accident is to provide urgent medical care and to move patients to an emergency department at a hospital as fast as possible. The EMS response times often predict the likelihood of a patient's survival. According to the previous study [1], a minute increase in response time can result in up to a 17% increase in mortality 90 days after an incident involving EMS response. However, it is hard to notice the need for EMS until someone made an emergency call. Also, it is difficult to predict patient conditions until medical crews arrive at the scene. Hence, in this study, we investigated the new way to predict the severity of vehicle accident by analyzing the pattern of pupil dilations. So that, the need for EMS will be automatically sent to 911 operators immediately.

Many researchers have proposed various methods to reduce the EMS response time for car accidents. One study has focused on using geographic information system (GIS) capabilities to determine the optimal placement of emergency response vehicles based on differences in accident density across a city [2]. Another study developed a

© Springer International Publishing AG, part of Springer Nature 2018
V. G. Duffy (Ed.): DHM 2018, LNCS 10917, pp. 647–656, 2018.
https://doi.org/10.1007/978-3-319-91397-1_53

smartphone app that records collision data and provides approximate values of the external forces caused by accident. The app could then send this information to EMS operators. Also, new technologies, such as OnStar, have already been created to provide an automatic rapid crash response. OnStar, created by General Motors, uses built-in sensors on the car that provides data such as the change in velocity and the directions of the force of the crash. After a collision is detected, an OnStar advisor will contact a driver and emergency responders [3]. However, these technologies rely on data from the vehicle itself. Also, the sensors in a car could be destroyed during the accident. For that reason, it is necessary to develop the method for the driver-centered monitoring rather than the vehicle-centered monitoring to reduce the EMS response time for vehicle accidents.

In this study, we investigated the relationship between driver's pupil dilations and severity of vehicle crash. According to the previous study [4], the diameter of the pupil changes not only reflexively, as a function of the intensity of light reaching the retina, but also in response to other cognitive functions, such as arousal level, emotion, and attention. Therefore, we hypothesized the changes in pupil diameter could indicate the occurrence of a collision and predict the severity of an accident. In our experiment, we examined pupil diameter changes during vehicle collisions to determine how pupil diameter changes in response to vehicle collisions in a driving simulator environment. We concluded that pupil diameter would increase before rear-ended collisions, and the rate of pupil diameter change was significantly greater for severe crashes compared to minor crashes.

2 Method

2.1 Apparatus

In this study, we used OpenDS (see Fig. 1), which is a cross-platform, open-source driving simulation software [5]. The Logitech G27 driving device (see Fig. 2a) was used as a steering wheel, a break, and an accelerator [6]. OpenDS consists of two major components: the simulator and the drive analyzer. The simulation component can load the driving task which is available in XML formats. The simulation provides multiple modules to redesign scenarios and create complex driving environments.

An eye tracker, which is a device for measuring eye positions and eye movement, was used to examine the data of the driver's eye movements. This study used the Tobii Pro Glasses 2 eye-tracking device (see Fig. 2b). It is a wearable eye-tracking device which is designed to capture the natural viewing behaviors in a real-world environment. There are three cameras in this device (frame rate 100 Hz). One is a full HD wide-angle scene camera to capture all the details of the surrounding environment. Other two cameras record the gaze movement of both eyes. Tobii Pro Glasses 2 has been used for a wide range of applications, such as measuring cognitive load, performance assessment, and usability studies.

Fig. 1. Screenshot of OpenDS driving simulation

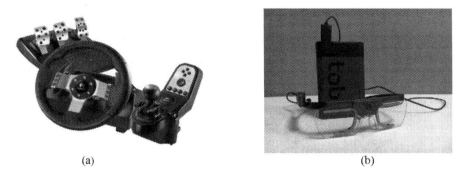

(a)   (b)

Fig. 2. (a) Logitech G27electronic steering wheel and pedal and (b) Tobii Pro Glasses 2 eye tracking device

2.2 Participants

A total of twenty college students (Age: 20–22, 18 males and 2 females) participated in this experiment. Their average driving experience was 4 years.

2.3 Experimental Setup

Vehicle accidents data was collected through the driving simulator experiment with two scenarios of different weather conditions. The traffic condition of each scenario was designed based on the previous research [7]. Each scenario was designed to include the event that had the potential cause of car accidents. This event occurred when participants drove onto the ramp and tried to merge onto the highway. As the participants had attempted to merge, the car in front of the participants was decelerated immediately. The speed of the leading vehicle abruptly decreased from 43 miles per hour to 3 miles per hour (see Fig. 3 from position A to position B). Then, the leading vehicle accelerated to merge onto the highway along the dashed line with an arrow. As merging required short-term visual searching, this event significantly increases the risk of vehicle crash.

Specifically, when the participants drove into the orange areas shown in Fig. 3, the participants must utilize their divided attention, which is an ability to process two or more responses or react to two or more different demands simultaneously. In this situation, the driver must check a side view mirror to prepare for merging and reacting to the deceleration of the front vehicle. The events were randomly occurred to prevent any driving behaviors caused by effects on the learning of those events.

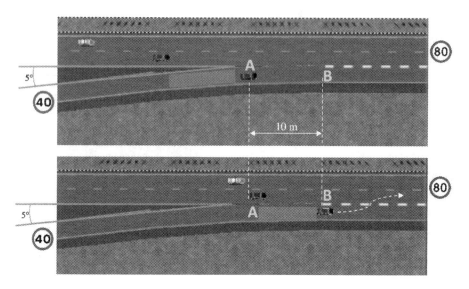

Fig. 3. The event occurs when participants drive onto the ramp and try to merge onto the highway

According to Wu, Abdel-Aty [8], the crash risk was prone to increase at ramp vicinities in fog weather conditions. Therefore, we developed two scenarios for this study: (1) sunny weather and (2) foggy weather. In both scenarios, the participants drove along a local road and drove to the entrance to the highway. After that, they merged onto the highway and drove along the highway itself. Finally, they exited the highway and returned to the local road (see Fig. 4). The participants drove each scenario for 30 min. After that, NASA-TLX questionnaires were asked to the participant in order to measure their workload during the driving simulation. The experiment was conducted in the laboratory (see Fig. 5), where indoor lighting would be turned off once the simulation began. The illumination during the experiment was 24 lx for the sunny scenario and 38 lx for the foggy scenario.

2.4 Procedure

Before the experiment, the participants completed a questionnaire to collect demographic information about each participant such as age, gender, driving experience (in years), level of video game experience from novice to expert, and whether the participant had ever been in a car accident and if yes, the severity on a scale of 1 to 10. When finished with the questionnaire, the task for the experiment was given. To further explain

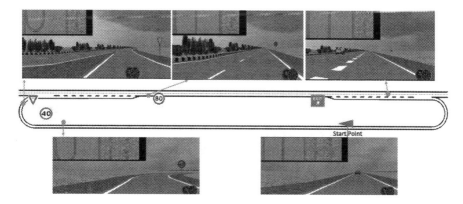

Fig. 4. Route of driving scenario

Fig. 5. Setup of experiment

and clarify the task, each participant completed a training scenario using a training simulation on the OpenDS simulator. Then, the participants put on the eye tracking glasses. The glasses were calibrated while the participants looked at the center of the calibration card while the card was held up in the center of the middle monitor at a distance of 2.3 feet ahead. The participants were given two scenarios with different weather conditions: a scenario with sunny weather and a scenario with foggy weather. They drove each scenario for 30 min using the driving simulator. Ten minutes of break were given between each scenario. After completing each scenario, they were asked to fill out the NASA-TLX form. After the second scenario and the NASA-TLX survey were completed, the participants were free to leave. The whole experiment took about 90 min (see Fig. 6).

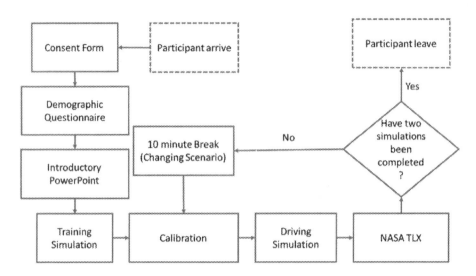

Fig. 6. Procedure of driving simulator experiment

3 Results

After the experiment, twenty-six accident data points were collected. They were cate-gorized into two levels based on the severity level of the accident (minor and major level). The minor level indicates a minor car accident, which is a near crash. The major level represents a severe crash, which means that the cars collide and at least one of vehicles is knocked entirely off of the road and possibly flipped over. Figures 7(a) and (b) show the scatterplots of participants' pupil diameter changes in these two cases (minor and major) data.

According to the result of the pupil diameter scatterplots, we found that the pupil began to dilate when the subjects indicated that the car in front reduced speed rapidly. The size of the pupil diameter reached to the largest point at the moment of the collision. In addition, the slopes of the linear lines in Fig. 7 were significantly different between the minor level and the major level. The slope of the pupil trace was measured by fitting a line (using linear regression analysis). The trace of pupil diameter size change was highlighted as a function of time. The line started with a driver's first fixation point of the accident vehicle. The moment of the collision was the end point of the line (see the solid lines in Fig. 7). The results showed that the slope was steeper for more severe accidents. According to the slope comparison between the minor level and the major level, there was a significant difference in pupil size slope for both eyes [left: $F (1, 24) = 6.85, P = 0.015$; right: $F (1, 24) = 6.35, P = 0.019$].

Figure 8 shows the result of interval plot of pupil size slope between minor and major vehicle accidents. The result indicated that the mean score of pupil size slope of the major accident (left eye: $M = 0.814, SD = 0.305$; right eye: $M = 0.873, SD = 0.414$) was significantly higher than the minor accident (left eye: $M = 0.497, SD = 0.247$; right eye: $M = 0.523, SD = 0.258$).

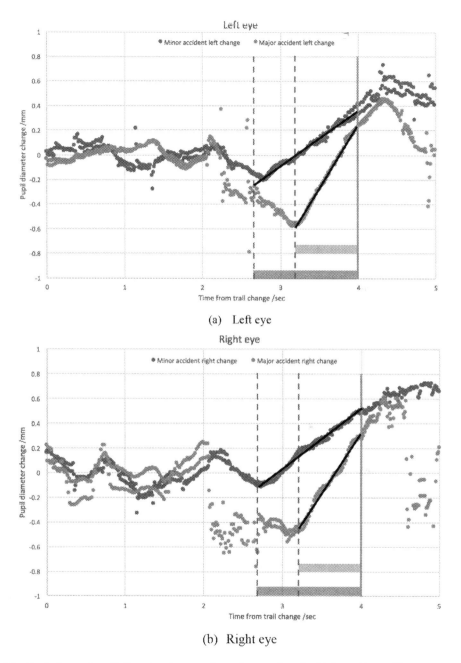

(a)   Left eye

(b)   Right eye

Fig. 7. A slope of pupil diameter change reflects the severity of vehicle accidents. Time courses of pupil diameter modulation around the occurrence of car accidents in minor and major severity. The vertical grey line indicates the beginning of the collision moment. Vertical dash lines indicate the driver's first fixation point of the accident vehicle before the crash accident. Shaded areas, intervals used for estimation of response amplitude. Blue represents minor accidents; orange represents major accidents. Black lines are the linear model lines. (Color figure online)

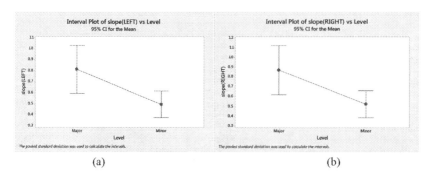

Fig. 8. Interval plot of slope vs accident level

4 Discussion and Conclusion

This study compared the driver's pupil diameter in car accidents with different severity levels in a driving simulation environment. The objective of this research is to understand the relationship between changes in pupil diameter and a vehicle accident. The results indicate the rapid increment in pupil diameter is associated with a more severe vehicle accident. In the experiment, the participants recognized the collision events by noticing the brake lights and the shortened distance to the car in front. Therefore, we used the participants' first fixation point on the illuminated brake lights of the leading vehicle as the start point for the data analysis. When the participants noticed the brake lights (aware of the possible collision), the pupil diameter started to increase and it stopped at the moment of the vehicle collision. According to the results of the pupil diameter trace, we found the different patterns of pupil dilation caused by different severity levels of vehicle crash. There was a significant difference in the slope of pupil diameter between the major and minor car collisions. When the participants experienced severe accidents, their increment speed of pupil diameter was much faster compared to the minor accidents. Since the hazard events were designed as unexpected decelerating of a leading vehicle (the details in Sect. 2.3), all accident events were all rear-ended accidents. The rear-end collision is a traffic accident wherein vehicle crashes into a leading vehicle. In contrast to other traffic accidents, such as being hit by the following car, the driver can witness the whole process of the vehicle accident. Based on the scene in front of the driver, drivers will have mental accounts for the prediction of the severity level of car accidents.

According to the previous studies, the pupil response is a direct reflection of neurological activities and is associated with specific areas of the brain and nervous system [9]. Fong [10] found that the stimulation of the autonomic nervous system, known for triggering "fight or flight" responses, induces pupil dilation. The fight-or-flight response is defined as a physiological reaction that occurs in response to a perceived harmful event, attack, or threat to survival. Hence, the participants' pupils could be dilated as the consequence of the "fight or flight" response when the participants were aware of the dangers of driving during the experiment. When the driver first fixated on the car in front, the pupil initially dilated. Then, as the drivers recognized the car in front as a threat due to the imminent collision, the pupil rapidly dilated. In the major accidents, the increment of the pupil size was faster compared to the minor accidents, because the driver recognized the danger of a collision earlier. With the faster response time, the "fight or flight" response started sooner, causing the faster pupil dilation. Therefore, the fast speed of the pupil size increment indicates more severe crashes and result in shorter available response time.

In conclusion, the result showed that the pupil diameter pattern could indicate the level of accident severity. The slope of pupil diameter change in the major vehicle accidents is steeper than in the minor vehicle accidents. The finding of this study provides a new direction of the human-centered monitoring system for automatic crash response and improves the speed of the roadside rescue. This study will contribute to developing an algorithm to detect the accident severity and inform Emergency Medical Personnel to respond car accidents quickly and efficiently.

There are several limitations of the current study. Since the experiment was conducted in a driving simulator environment, we have no real crash data to measure the injury to drivers due to the collisions. Secondly, we did not consider other factors (e.g., fatigue, heavy traffic conditions, age, and others) that might influence the severity of vehicle accidents.

5   Future Work

For the future work, we will increase the number of the participants to collect more severe accident data. Since the severe accidents have the lowest survival rate, it is crucial to collect various car accident data. Also, the different levels of driving experience might contribute different patterns of the pupil diameter [11]. Hence, it is essential to investigate the relationship between the changes in pupil diameter and driving experience. Furthermore, our study only investigated the changes in pupil diameter for the rear-end collision. Other types of accidents might result in different patterns of pupil dilation. So that, it would be necessary to develop scenarios that simulate different types of road accidents. Finally, other factors that affect pupil dilation, such as changes in light intensity, workload, and fatigue, should be considered in a future study. These factors must be incorporated into any prediction of accident severity using pupil diameter.

References

1. Wilde, E.T.: Do emergency medical system response times matter for health outcomes? Health Econ. **22**(7), 790–806 (2013)
2. Estochen, B.M., Strauss, T., Souleyrette, R.R.: An assessment of emergency response vehicle pre-deployment using GIS identification of high-accident density locations (1998)
3. Mimar, T.: Vehicle security with accident notification and embedded driver analytics (2016). Google Patents
4. Suzuki, Y., et al.: Changes in pupil diameter are correlated with the occurrence of pareidolias in patients with dementia with Lewy bodies. NeuroReport **28**(4), 187 (2017)
5. Math, R., et al.: OpenDS: a new open-source driving simulator for research. In: GMM-Fachbericht-AmE 2013 (2013)

6. Bian, D., et al.: A novel virtual reality driving environment for autism intervention. In: Stephanidis, C., Antona, M. (eds.) UAHCI 2013. LNCS, vol. 8010, pp. 474–483. Springer, Heidelberg (2013). https://doi.org/10.1007/978-3-642-39191-0_52

7. Yang, X., Kim, J.H.: The effect of visual stimulus on advanced driver assistance systems in a real driving. In: IIE Annual Conference. Proceedings. Institute of Industrial and Systems Engineers (IISE) (2017)

8. Wu, Y., Abdel-Aty, M., Lee, J.: Crash risk analysis during fog conditions using real-time traffic data. Accid. Anal. Prev. **114**, 4–11 (2018)

9. Hess, E.H., Polt, J.M.: Pupil size in relation to mental activity during simple problem-solving. Science **143**(3611), 1190–1192 (1964)

10. Fong, J., Eye-Opener: Why Do Pupils Dilate in Response to Emotional States. Scientific American (2012). https://www.scientificamerican.com/article/eye-opener-why-do-pupils-dialate/

11. Underwood, G., et al.: Visual attention while driving: sequences of eye fixations made by experienced and novice drivers. Ergonomics **46**(6), 629–646 (2003)

Author Index

Printed in the United States
By Bookmasters